The Rising Generation

EARLY AMERICAN STUDIES

Series editors: Kathleen M. Brown, Roquinaldo Ferreira, Emma Hart, and Daniel K. Richter

Exploring neglected aspects of our colonial, revolutionary, and early national history and culture, Early American Studies reinterprets familiar themes and events in fresh ways. Interdisciplinary in character, and with a special emphasis on the period from about 1600 to 1850, the series is published in partnership with the McNeil Center for Early American Studies.

A complete list of books in the series is available from the publisher.

The Rising Generation

Gradual Abolition, Black Legal Culture, and the Making of National Freedom

Sarah L. H. Gronningsater

PENN

UNIVERSITY OF PENNSYLVANIA PRESS

PHILADELPHIA

Published by
University of Pennsylvania Press
Philadelphia, Pennsylvania 19104-4112
www.pennpress.org

Printed in the United States of America on acid-free paper
10 9 8 7 6 5 4 3 2 1

Hardcover ISBN: 978-1-5128-2631-9
eBook ISBN: 978-1-5128-2632-6

A Cataloging-in-Publication record is
available from the Library of Congress

For my family

A careful attention to the moral and literary improvement of the rising generation is justly considered by all as essential to the civil and religious welfare of society.

—New York Manumission Society, *To the Convention of Delegates, from the Several Abolition Societies of the United States*, 1805

Whereas complaint has been made . . . by Darby a negro servant . . . that [he has not had] four quarters schooling (he being eighteen years of age) and that his name age and sex hath not been delivered to the Clerk of the Town of Southold. . . . We therefore by these presents do discharge him the said Darby of and from his servitude.

—Order of Justices for the Discharge of Darby, Southold, February 3, 1819

I would address myself to all mothers. . . . It is their bounden duty to store their daughters' minds with useful learning. They should be made to devote their leisure time to reading books.

—Matilda, *Freedom's Journal* (New York), August 10, 1827

The rising generation is advancing under more favorable auspices that we were permitted to enjoy, soon to fill the place we now occupy. . . . They are advancing, not to fill the place of slaves, but of freemen.

—Nathaniel Paul, *An Address, Delivered on the Celebration of the Abolition of Slavery, in the State of New York* (1827)

"I am an American: yes, a black American! The son of a father who fought in the Revolution!—a black citizen of New York—a black American am I." . . . Mr. Ward then went on to show that there was nothing in the Constitution prohibiting the Committee from assisting fugitive slaves. Besides, they were acting with perfect legality in the matter.

—"New York State Vigilance Committee,"
North Star (Rochester), May 16, 1850

Miss Maud D. Molson of Addison, New York gave her lectures on the "Issues of the Hour." It was a tremendous effort for woman suffrage.

—*Republican* (Goshen), April 14, 1870

Cut out the Petition printed in the right hand upper corner. . . . We will see that it goes before Congress. Let every man, woman, and child be active.

—Lewis H. Douglass, *New National Era*
(Washington, D.C.), October 23, 1873

CONTENTS

Introduction. "Emancipate, Enfranchise, Educate" 1

Chapter 1. Poor Law, Slave Law, and the Golden Rule: Quaker Antislavery and the Early Modern Origins of Gradual Abolition Policy 22

Chapter 2. "To Be Born Free" . . . and Bound: The 1799 Gradual Abolition Law and Its Consequences 55

Chapter 3. Educating the "Rising Generation": Associational Culture and the Politics of Black Schools 95

Chapter 4. Citizenship National: Slavery, Democracy, and Black Citizenship in the 1820s 128

Chapter 5. Male and Female "Citizens of the State": Rights, Politics, Petitions, and Parties 165

Chapter 6. Antislavery Legal Culture: The *Lemmon* Slave Case and the Coming of the Civil War 205

Chapter 7. The Great Question of Equality Before the Law: The Civil War and Reconstruction 239

Epilogue. The Two Charlottes 289

List of Abbreviations 293

Notes 297

Index 381

Acknowledgments 395

INTRODUCTION

"Emancipate, Enfranchise, Educate"

In 1811, a young black servant girl named Charlotte told a grand jury in New York City that, despite living under the roof of a master, she was "free." The district attorney, seeking clarification, prodded: "What do you understand by being free?" She explained that she was bound for "a certain number of years only" and would serve "untill I was a big woman." She had landed in court after being accused of trying to set her master's house on fire. Charlotte had a habit of running away and her master had a habit of whipping her. The attorney, in his final question, asked if she could write. "No sir," she said.[1]

Charlotte was a member of a generation of black New Yorkers who were born during the era of gradual abolition in the early republican North and, assuming they reached old age, died after the transformative events of the Civil War. As her court testimony suggests, Charlotte's childhood was infused with slavery's routine cruelties. But Charlotte and her generation also encountered possibilities their parents had not. A 1799 state law declared that children born to enslaved mothers would be born free, categorized as servants, and released from service when "big," to use her word. Although Charlotte could not write, a substantial number of her peers could. This unique generation, born between an enslaved past and a murky but promising future, fought both individually and collectively to determine the contours of freedom in their daily lives. By midcentury, they had fused their local efforts with national campaigns to destroy slavery and rewrite the laws of civic belonging. For this generation of children, many of whom became actively antislavery adults, life was one long, mercurial, and contingent emancipation struggle.[2]

This remarkable generation of New Yorkers—the children of gradual abolition—played an outsized role in the development of American freedom and citizenship. They came of age in a northern state where slavery had been

P.
Filed 7th day of June 1811
Pleads Nonful
The People vs Ind for a
Charlotte a black Girl Misdemeanor

Figure 1. Charlotte's Grand Jury Testimony, 1811. Charlotte, "a black girl," explains that she knows she has to serve Mr. Ward until she is "a big woman." District Attorney Indictment Papers, Courtesy of the Municipal Archives, City of New York.

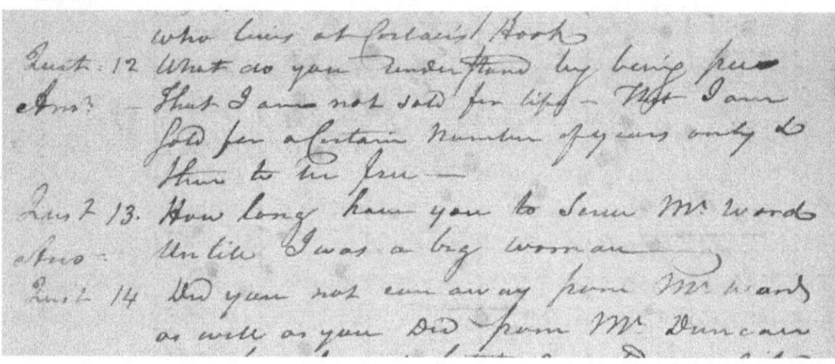
who lives at Corlaer's Hook
Quest: 12 What do you understand by being free
Ans: That I am not sold for life — but I am sold for a certain Number of years only & then to be free —
Quest 13. How long have you to serve Mr Ward
Ans: Untill I was a big woman
Quest 14 Did you not run away from Mr Ward as well as you did from Mr Duncan

especially embraced and widespread. For decades, the everyday mechanics of gradual abolition produced ways of thinking, acting, and collaborating that subsequently affected how various influential cohorts of New Yorkers approached the problems of slavery in their state and in the United States. Black New Yorkers' and their white supporters' engagement with antislavery laws, hazy versions of citizenship, shifting ideologies of abolition, party politics, and interstate legal conflicts prepared them to blaze particular paths toward freedom, even though no one at the time could know precisely what the outcomes would be. It is impossible to fully grasp the evolving politics of nineteenth-century antislavery, the coming of the Civil War, and the statutory and constitutional freedoms defined during Reconstruction without accounting for the people, ideas, and movements that northern emancipation produced. *The Rising Generation* offers a detailed exploration of the children of gradual abolition both to uncover the particularities of their experience and to provide new vantage points on the political and legal roots and results of the Civil War and Reconstruction.[3]

Understanding this generation's particular capacities and objectives requires exploring how gradual abolition was designed, regulated, and negotiated. Emancipation in New York was a halting, piecemeal process. Quakers began to manumit their slaves in the mid-1700s and state legislators further weakened slavery's foundations after the Revolution, but as late as 1841 visitors could hold slaves in New York for up to nine months. The two most important acts designed to undo slavery were the 1799 "Act for the gradual abolition of slavery" and the 1817 "Act relative to slaves and servants." The 1799 act, drawing on early modern poor law, decreed that children born to enslaved mothers after July 4 of that year would be "born free," with the major caveat that they labor as servants for their mothers' masters until 25 (if female) and 28 (if male), or be bound out by local overseers of the poor "under the same terms and conditions" as the "children of paupers." The 1817 act issued a different promise: all of the state's slaves would be free on July 4, 1827. Children born to enslaved mothers up until that date would be born free but labor as servants until age 21; masters who did not educate children as required by a supplementary 1810 act would release them at 18. When the district attorney asked Charlotte in 1811 if she could write, the question acknowledged demonstrable changes in black children's literacy. For nearly half a century, gradual abolition comprised a labor regime that left black children somewhere between complete enslavement and incomplete freedom.[4]

Gradual abolition was no instant solution to slavery, but it nonetheless produced significant shifts in black socialization and the politics of everyday life. Mothers and fathers, many still enslaved themselves in the early 1800s, encountered laws, political parties, educational opportunities, and philanthropic associations that helped them protect and nurture their children in new ways. Black teachers, ministers, and mentors called the boys and girls in their midst "the rising generation" and spoke explicitly about their special responsibilities and opportunities. This older generation of black New Yorkers, born before the Revolution, raised sons, daughters, students, wards, and congregants to envision free adulthoods in which they would use laws, politics, associations, and literacy to serve "the interests of the people of color."[5]

As the children of gradual abolition grew up, they witnessed both the fragility and the importance of what many understood to be the legal opposite of slavery: equal citizenship. All Americans, including black New Yorkers, experienced shifting and liminal definitions of citizenship and its attendant rights in the decades after the Revolution as states and the nation deliberated what being a citizen in a republic entailed. Between 1777 and 1821, for example, black men in New York voted according to the same state constitutional rules as white men. The state curtailed this right, however, when it adopted a new constitution in 1822 that included a race-based property qualification. Provoked by the added sting of fighting for a right they had once enjoyed, black men spent years petitioning the state government for redress. By the 1850s, they had managed to convince the legislature, but not enough of the state's voters, to support an equal suffrage referendum. Black men and women also employed and safeguarded nonelectoral aspects of their citizenship, including the right to personal liberty, to petition, to due process, to free movement, and to common school education—rights that were particularly important in a nation where enslaved and free black people frequently crossed state borders, kidnapping was a constant threat, and literacy was a legal weapon. In 1865, when one of the most famous children of gradual abolition, the minister Henry Highland Garnet, became the first black man to speak in the National Capitol, he argued that federal emancipation must include "every right of American citizenship" and insisted that legislators "*Emancipate, Enfranchise, Educate*."[6] Given the history of black citizenship to date, Garnet and his peers had every reason to worry that the national government might enact an incomplete, northern-style emancipation.

Garnet was a particularly well-known and prolific member of his generation, but he was as representative as he was exceptional. A wide range of black New Yorkers engaged with questions and manifestations of formal law and politics. The experience of gradual abolition prompted thousands of slaves, servants, and free black citizens across time and space to nurture and maintain a shrewd grasp of law, politics, and interracial cooperation. Ordinary laborers, middling shopkeepers, striving farmers, tenacious domestics, and obscure schoolteachers were crucial to the culture, relationships, and collaborative work of this generation.[7]

An expansive view of this generation reveals that black women and girls were as vital to the long attack on slavery as their male counterparts. That said, their experiences were distinct from boys' and men's, which makes teasing out their particular encounters with bondage and citizenship all the more important. This book features the views of servant children, like Charlotte, whom we will encounter again in Chapter 2; the middle-aged laundress-turned-education-advocate Phebe Ray, whom we will meet in Chapter 5; and Ellen Anderson, a civil rights litigant and war widow who appears in

Chapter 7. A robust and chronologically long history of gradual abolition likewise helps contextualize the activities of better-known women such as Sojourner Truth, Harriet Tubman, Julia A. J. Foote, and Elizabeth Jennings. The rising generation of black New Yorkers at the heart of this book was a generation of men and women who shared the common experience of residing in the most politically important northern state of the nineteenth century while nonetheless approaching questions of emancipation and equality from specific social, civic, geographic, and gendered vantage points.[8]

A long history of American emancipation told through the eyes and experiences of the children of gradual abolition also requires understanding how the sites of antislavery legal activity and politicking moved and changed. This book starts in early modern and late colonial households, crucial loci of governance in the Anglo-American imperial world. Gradual abolition was in many ways, for real people, experienced at the level of the household and in local communities of households within towns and wards. As the nineteenth century progressed, black New Yorkers moved into schools, courts, polling sites, and public political spaces in growing numbers. This was not only because they were becoming more free as a population, but also because political norms, associational life, and the state's role in education were changing more broadly. By the 1830s and '40s, black men and women who as children had eavesdropped on their masters in kitchens and stables were subscribing to homegrown black newspapers and attending sessions of the legislature as recognized citizens of their state. This now-adult generation also began organizing colored conventions, manifestations of both a growing regional free black northern reform energy and concurrent transformations in transportation and communication. Meanwhile, they increasingly became instigators of major legal cases involving slavery that drew nationwide scrutiny as sectionalism intensified in the 1840s and '50s. By the Civil War, black New Yorkers were moving back and forth, in writing and in person, among their hometowns, the state legislature in Albany, and the national government in Washington, D.C. In short, the children of gradual abolition were always after better, safer lives, but where and how they pursued these efforts changed as the legal and political practices of American democracy and federalism writ large changed.

* * *

Gradual abolition took place within a constitutional order that left tremendous power over people's lives in the hands of the individual states. When state governments began either shoring up or disassembling slavery in the 1770s and '80s, lawmakers may not have liked what they saw happening elsewhere, but few politicians argued that the disparate approaches were surprising or unconstitutional. The mainland English colonies had operated differently from each other, under distinct charters, for hundreds of years. The architects of the independent United States national government did not wipe away longstanding jurisdictional borders and local prerogatives, at least not in any wholesale fashion. When the electorates of the thirteen states ratified the 1787 federal constitution, they approved a document that included a fugitive slave clause that implicitly acknowledged that the rules of slavery were different in various states. When these same voters ratified the Tenth Amendment (1791), they affirmed that the "powers not delegated to the United States by the Constitution, nor prohibited by it to the States, are reserved to the States respectively, or to the people." Neither the Constitution nor the Bill of Rights spelled out precisely who could be a citizen of the United States, what that citizenship fully entailed, or the relationship between state and national citizenship. State constitutions were similarly vague, if they even used the word "citizen" at all. Definitions of citizenship and its attendant rights were clarified, often at the state level, through much debate and with frequent confusion. On a practical level, federalism meant that many aspects of black people's lives in the United States were shaped by the state in which they lived.[9]

Within this larger constitutional picture, gradual abolition operated as a state and local regime. The rules and procedures were developed by legislators at the state level and most often enforced at the level of towns, cities, and wards. Both jurisdictional layers were important in shaping the fates and legal consciousness of black New Yorkers. Ordinary people engaged with local officials (town clerks, overseers of the poor, aldermen, justices of the peace, election inspectors); at the same time, black leaders and their white partners regularly turned to the state government in Albany in search of remedies for problems that could not be solved at the local level and for problems that arose, often unforeseen, during the course of a drawn-out emancipation process. These political dynamics prompted legislators to pay attention to what was happening on the ground and prompted those on the ground to stay attuned to the ways that the legislature affected the everyday lives of slaves, servants, and free black people. Questions arose in New York City and Albany, but also in agricultural towns and the wider countryside. In 1790, when 21,000 enslaved people lived in the state, the vast majority of New

Yorkers overall—300,000 out of 340,000—lived in rural areas. In the first decade of the nineteenth century, 80 percent of the state's black population lived outside of New York City.[10]

Because so much of the day-to-day process of gradual abolition occurred locally, the full diversity of the state's black population, rural and urban, was exposed to the workings of law and politics in varied ways. Masters often ignored antislavery statutes or tried to cheat the rules. Enslaved mothers across New York made efforts to ensure that their freeborn children's status was certified by town clerks. Servant children spread information among peers and drew attention to laws that might force the white men and women who held them in bondage to release them early from their terms of labor. Free black men from outer Long Island to the Great Lakes met in political meetings to determine which party best promoted their interests and to organize campaigns to regain equal voting rights. Women and children joined men in freedom suits, civic gatherings, and petition campaigns concerning the laws of slavery, personal liberty, education, and civil rights. Gradual abolition, in short, was a spur to black legal knowledge statewide.

As black New Yorkers went about the daily business of protecting their freedom, they worked with antislavery white New Yorkers, particularly those with influence, expertise, and money. These collaborations rarely embodied equal partnerships between black and white, but the relationships were nonetheless fundamental to the course of emancipation and to the development of black citizenship in New York and eventually the nation. Colonial Quakers and founding fathers were the original designers of gradual abolition policy; their white antislavery sons and daughters grew up observing the politics and mores of their parents. Like their black counterparts, white children raised in antislavery households took lessons from emancipation in the early republic. There was a crucial and consistent interracial tenor to antislavery reform in New York from the Revolution through Reconstruction.[11]

As their willingness to work alongside white abolitionists and politicians suggests, a strong streak of pragmatism marked the antislavery strategies of black New Yorkers. Their goals, at times, were as radical as those of any reformers operating in the early 1800s, but their methods were often rooted in the daily need to get things done: a child needed a birth certificate, a servant needed a lawyer to prove her master had failed to educate her, a man needed manumission papers copied in order to vote, an Underground Railroad operative needed a writ of habeas corpus to free an imprisoned slave, a political committee needed an assemblyman to support a bill. The children of gradual abolition were taught by parents, mentors, benefactors, and each other how to practice this politics of access. Although the routines of American democracy changed over the course of the century, black New Yorkers' interest in locating the most useful white official or lawmaker in any given situation in order to obtain a result was near constant.[12]

Both the achievements and the limitations of gradual abolition steered the rising generation toward an embrace of legislative immediatism: the idea that elected lawmakers could end slavery at once, rather than in staggered fashion with lingering forms of servitude. The growing strength and viability of immediatism in New York in the 1810s, decades before William Lloyd Garrison of Massachusetts famously took up the banner in the 1830s, resulted from a potent combination of local factors. Black New Yorkers enacted individual forms of immediatism by negotiating, litigating, and fleeing their way out of bondage in unprecedented numbers, Quaker meetings and elite founding fathers in the New York Manumission Society began calling for the "immediate relief" of slaves as early as 1811, and black and white antislavery voters backed immediatist efforts in the legislature. The persistent work of these early immediatists eventually resulted in the 1817 state law, flawed though it was, that freed thousands of adult slaves in one day on July 4, 1827. It was, in truth, a peculiar act, bold for its time in freeing healthy adult slaves without compensation to owners, conservative for its delayed emancipation date and for keeping children of slaves born during the ten-year lag time in service until age 21. It was the only law of its kind ever passed in the United States. It shaped the lives of black New Yorkers in its moment as well as antislavery citizens' conceptions of what was possible thereafter. It was also yet one more piece of consequential legislation that ordinary people had to get their heads around.[13]

As black New Yorkers pushed to broaden and protect their own freedom under the evolving rules and realities of gradual abolition, they simultaneously and increasingly worked to broaden and protect the freedom of enslaved and free black people who entered their state's borders. Runaways as well as enslaved people traveling with masters were stark evidence of bondage's presence elsewhere. As long as slavery existed nationally, there was the chance a black northerner might be kidnapped and sold. For reasons practical and moral, the children of gradual abolition became invested in affirming the "free soil" of their state and in denying opportunities for slave states to expand the reach of slavery. As part of these efforts, they absorbed newcomers into their communities. Enslaved and free black southerners who settled in New York joined schools, neighborhoods, churches, and associations with the children of gradual abolition, becoming part and parcel of their generation with varying degrees of intensity.[14]

Some of these adopted New Yorkers became famous. Most were regular people. They all taught each other. In 1848, the abolitionist doctor James McCune Smith, born and raised in New York, expressed delight that Frederick Douglass had caught up with him and his peers once he moved to Rochester. Douglass had finally become "a colored man!" Smith wrote in private. On the "church question, the school question, separate institutions," Douglass now argued in his newspaper, the *North Star*, the same way "active young men" like Smith did "years ago." Similarly, the black lobbyist and barber William H. Johnson recalled how, after moving to Albany from Virginia, he "trained with" local black and white abolitionists. Harriet Tubman, who settled on land in northwest New York sold to her by one of New York's most prominent antislavery politicians, William H. Seward, was an especially electrifying reminder, given her exploits on the Underground Railroad and military feats during the Civil War, that freeing human beings in bondage—people who did not have enough food and clothing, who routinely had their children stolen from them—was worth risking one's life. The history of emancipation in New York shows how the state was home to long-standing, multigenerational relationships and institutions at the same time that new people and ideas were constantly moving in and out.[15]

One trend newcomers discovered when they arrived in New York was that many ordinary people could talk about and explain relevant laws. Black locals may not have had formal legal training, but they possessed and shared basic legal literacy. In their relentless pursuit of complete citizenship, black New Yorkers developed a shrewd awareness of court decisions, statutes, petitions, and constitutions. They wanted the law on their side, because when it was enforced, it had proved to be of great use during gradual abolition. That said, they were rarely naïve about the uses of law and politics, nor were they naïve about the power of constitutions. Jurists and lawyers enlisted and interpreted law in order to restrain black freedom and citizenship just as often as—if not more often than—they used law as an instrument of liberty. One of the reasons black New Yorkers became so adept at political and legal maneuvering was precisely because they had to make certain that useful laws were followed and unfair ones were erased from statute books, constitutions, law reports, and legal treatises. Laws were not silver bullets, but they and the politics surrounding them could not be ignored.[16]

Of course, not all black New Yorkers were in agreement on strategies, goals, politics, and relationships. Not all black New Yorkers devoted their spare hours to thinking about politics and legal protest. Not all black New Yorkers liked each other just because they happened to live in the same state, nor did black New Yorkers always think highly of or work smoothly with white partners. The point, however, is that perceptible shared patterns of thought and action existed among the generation of black New Yorkers who experienced gradual abolition during the late 1700s and early 1800s. This book highlights a particularly significant and visible form of antislavery politics, but it does not suggest that no other forms of antislavery politics existed.[17]

A fine-grained legal, political, social, and constitutional history of gradual abolition in New York offers both a deeper understanding of northern emancipation itself and a fresh perspective on the causes and results of the more well-known emancipations and rights revolutions that took place during the Civil War and Reconstruction. The children of gradual abolition may not have created the Civil War by themselves, but their tireless and multiple campaigns to enlarge black freedom drove influential southerners and proslavery northerners to extreme frustration. They also forced white northerners to take stands on questions regarding slavery, even when those white northerners might have preferred to ignore the issue. There are multiple reasons why the Civil War came when it did and why constitutional Reconstruction looked the way it did, but in searching for influences, we should look to free black northerners, particularly if not exclusively the New Yorkers that gradual abolition produced. White and black New Yorkers who fought for the principles inscribed in the Thirteenth, Fourteenth, and Fifteenth Amendments did so because of their experiences of gradual abolition. For them, immediate emancipation, national birthright citizenship, and federally backed guarantees of equal access to the vote for men and of civil rights for men, women, and children were as much prescriptions for the present as they were solutions for the ongoing problems of the past.

* * *

New York was not the only state to undergo an emancipation process in the young nation. Although this book focuses on New York, the story it tells occurred within a wider regional experience. Eight states abolished slavery in the early national era. The five states to do so using gradual abolition laws were those with the highest rates of slaveholding. Pennsylvania passed a gradual abolition act first, in 1780. Connecticut and Rhode Island followed in 1784. New York passed its law in 1799. New Jersey was last, in 1804. Vermont, home to a few hundred slaves, abolished slavery in its 1777 constitution (the document freed adults, but allowed masters to keep a female "servant, slave or apprentice" until 18, a male until 21). New Hampshire's 1783 constitution was interpreted as prohibiting slavery. In the wake of earlier emancipations occurring in individual households, wills, and local courts, Massachusetts formally freed its slaves in a state court decision in 1783.[18] Meanwhile, in 1787, the national government approved an ordinance governing the Northwest territories with a clause declaring "there shall be neither slavery nor involuntary servitude" except "in the punishment of crimes." As these territories became the states of Ohio, Indiana, Illinois, Michigan, and Wisconsin between 1803 and 1848, a critical mass of citizens in the original northeastern states found that they shared enough politics, relationships, and priorities with their counterparts in the Midwest that they began to think of themselves as part of a wider trans-Appalachian region called the "free North."[19]

New York was thus hardly alone in confronting the problems of slavery and freedom in the late eighteenth and early nineteenth centuries. Inhabitants throughout the region were well aware of antislavery laws, decisions, and organizations in other free states. The politics and realities of early republican emancipation, in other words, sowed the seeds of nineteenth-century sectionalism. New York, which bordered New England, the mid-Atlantic, and the Great Lakes, was at the crossroads of this larger region physically and in many ways politically.

There are several reasons for concentrating specifically on the Empire State. First, New York oversaw the largest emancipation on U.S. soil before the Civil War. Of the eight states to abolish slavery in the early republic, New York was the colony and subsequently the state where slavery had most consistently thrived. Slaves comprised roughly 15 percent of the colony's population in 1749, and the proportion in New York City was even higher, at 20 percent. The Revolution ideologically and materially disrupted chattel bondage to some extent, but neither the war nor the state's new government managed to destroy the institution. By the 1780s, New York counted the same number of slaves as Georgia (over 20,000), and nearly three times as many as Pennsylvania. New York's 1799 gradual abolition act was not a symbolic gesture involving just a few people or resources, nor was its passage an easy political feat.[20]

Second, New York was home to an especially large, active, vibrant, and vocal population of free black northerners. The state included the early republic's largest black school system, the nation's first black newspaper (*Freedom's Journal*, founded in 1827), and myriad religious, literary, and mutual aid organizations. To be sure, black populations in other northern states—especially Pennsylvania, Massachusetts, and Ohio—were also busy. New York was not unique in having dynamic free black citizens, but its population contributed heavily to northern black abolitionism and promoted a notable form of antislavery politics stemming from the precise history of emancipation, citizenship, and partisanship in the state. Moreover, given the timing of emancipation in New York—the 1799 act was comparatively late—many of the state's children of gradual abolition lived through and shaped two emancipations, one state and one national.[21]

Last, New York deserves focus because it was the most politically powerful state in the North. In the words of a contemporary proverb, "As New York goes, so goes the Union." After 1808, the state consistently claimed the country's highest number of electoral college votes—besting most other states by significant degrees. In 1812, New York claimed 29 votes next to Virginia's 25 and Pennsylvania's 24. By 1852, New York's count was up to 35, compared to Pennsylvania's 27, Ohio's 25, and Virginia's 15. National parties had every reason to pay attention to New York's voters, and New York's voters continually elected and supported politicians who could maintain the state's influence. This truth was not lost on black New Yorkers. In 1848, the black editor Samuel Ringgold Ward reminded "four thousand colored voters" that "we are citizens of the largest, most populous, and therefore, in a political point of view, the most important State in the Union, and that therefore our action will exert a much more certain and potent influence upon that nation, than it would from any other point." In addition to New York's importance to the major parties, the state nurtured antislavery third parties and politically oriented abolitionist organizations. Entire books have been written on New York's role as a competitive, innovative, fractious swing state in nineteenth-century American politics.[22]

All told, New York provides a particularly compelling example of how a powerful free state was influenced by its own history of slavery and emancipation. The argument of this book is not that New York had an exemplary antislavery past that the state's citizens could then apply to the nation. To the contrary: the fact that slavery had been so important to New York's political economy is part of what makes the state's emergence as a powerful free state in the 1830s and '40s worthy of analysis. Its "slavery past" remained as resonant as its "antislavery past." Race remained a vital social construct dividing black from white. Many white New Yorkers, to the extent that they were antislavery at all, cared more about slavery's effect on national politics and on white freedoms than they did about the actual people the institution harmed. Nothing in New York's history of slavery and antislavery between the 1770s and 1870s was simple, linear, or unchanging. What is certain, however, is that as white and black New Yorkers confronted the politics of race, slavery, and citizenship over and over in the nineteenth century, internal state concerns and external national concerns became ever more deeply intertwined.

When the Civil War and Reconstruction cracked open questions and possibilities regarding the legalities of slavery, citizenship, and federalism, black New Yorkers rushed into the conversation. It was an extraordinary stretch of moments—national ruptures and reconfigurings—in which longstanding northern free black claims for equality combined with calls for southern emancipation. The children of gradual abolition had overlapping objectives during this second founding of the United States. Their desire to secure their own just rights at home converged with their advocacy for enslaved people in the South, whom they hoped would gain the version of citizenship that they had been promoting for themselves in the North for years. For this generation, the goal of emancipation and the quest for equal rights, citizenship, and voting could not be separated. By virtue of their multifaceted efforts, the children of gradual abolition were among the founders of the Thirteenth, Fourteenth, and Fifteenth Amendments (1865–1870), federal election legislation, and the Civil Rights Acts of 1866 and 1875. Their legal and political work was crucial to the making of national freedom and its attendant rights.

* * *

Animating the role of law in black New Yorkers' lives, as well as explaining how they shaped and changed the law, requires examining a deep and diverse archival base. Town and county officials kept voluminous records, many of which still exist, sitting on dusty shelves, in those same extant offices across New York State. The court records in the New York City Municipal Archives are a trove of social and legal history. It is possible to stitch together the movements and political efforts of otherwise ordinary laboring families through census records, local directories and newspapers, state legislative journals, black associational records, town and city council minutes, and school district exhibitions and reports. Due to the rising generation's relatively high rates of literacy, it is also possible to uncover first-person accounts in letters and autobiographies, including self-published ones. This generation also read and created over half a dozen newspapers, which featured the opinions not only of black editors but of active citizens in towns, churches, and schools statewide. The well trod papers of the New York Manumission Society remain an invaluable source of white abolitionist activity, but so too are the less-mined minutes of Quaker meetings in rural counties. Black voices, actions, and petitions are cited in state and national legislative session journals. The personal papers of white politicians, who had to address slavery and black citizenship publicly, are likewise revealing. Many of these white lawmaking men had personal relationships with enslaved and free black people, reminding us that public-facing legal postures were often informed as much by the personal and the private as by what was said in courtrooms and capitols. No archive is perfect—historians have been especially cognizant of all that written sources do not tell us about enslaved and free black people, of the pain and secrets that sources obscure, and of the power dynamics involved in who wrote sources and for what reasons in the first place. That said, there is abundant black presence in the archive of New York. Fastened together, the records generate a mosaic-like picture of how thousands and thousands of black men, women, and children shaped the history of their state and their country.[23]

Employing this wealth of statewide sources, *The Rising Generation* proceeds in seven chapters. It moves forward both chronologically and thematically, at moments moving briefly back in time in order to contextualize the main themes of a given chapter. As the book unfolds, readers will discern braided narratives and notice familiar names in new places. Black New Yorkers who appear as boys and girls in early chapters emerge as adults later in the book.

Chapter 1 examines early modern proposals for gradual abolition in the Anglo-Atlantic world, particularly among Quakers, as well as contemporary legal conceptions of poverty and child labor; it concludes with the legislative history of the 1799 gradual abolition act. The second chapter explores emancipation as it occurred in everyday life, paying close attention to the ways that the actions of slaves, servants, and free people affected the recurrent legislation directing New York's long abolition process. Chapter 3 studies the formal education of the children of gradual abolition in the famous New York African Free School while also uncovering school politics, educational associationalism, and classroom experiences from across the state. The fourth chapter outlines the multiple fates of black citizenship in New York and the nation in the early 1800s, connecting struggles over citizenship to the history of black voting, party politics, the Missouri Crisis (1819–1821), and the state's 1827 general abolition. Chapter 5 considers how the children of gradual abolition, now adults, emerged as political actors in both local and state contexts in the second quarter of the nineteenth century; this chapter shows how their earlier engagement with schools, as well as their knowledge of legislative politics, informed several consequential and partially successful state petition campaigns in the 1830s and '40s. Chapter 6 highlights the antislavery legal work of black laborer Louis Napoleon and his peers; it narrates the dramatic events of the Lemmon Slave Case (1852–1860), a protracted legal battle between New York and Virginia that captured the anxious attention of the nation and provided proslavery southerners evidence of increasing northern intransigence. Chapter 7 treats the Civil War and Reconstruction, demonstrating how antislavery New Yorkers influenced the course of national abolition and the federal constitutional transformation of black citizenship; their advocacy for national emancipation policy was informed by their earlier histories in their home state.

Because these chapters span more than two hundred years of emancipation, cross the colonial-to-national divide, and explore dozens of locations in the province and then state of New York, a brief sketch of the area's geography, colonial development, and territorial growth might be useful. Among the key claims of this book is that the laws, politics, and experiences of gradual abolition are best understood within a statewide study that takes local, national, and imperial contexts seriously. Interpreting what the children of gradual abolition did in the nineteenth century requires some grounding in the literal and figurative landscapes into which they were born.

Founded in 1664, the colonial province of New York looked the way it did for several reasons. To begin with, Native nations had lived in what eventually became New York for centuries before European colonization. The Haudenosaunee (whom the French called the Iroquois and the English called the Six Nations) controlled vast swaths of land around the lower Great Lakes and the Saint Lawrence River Valley, including the area where New Yorkers later built the Erie Canal. Skilled traders and warriors, the Haudenosaunee commanded the area northwest of the Hudson River into the late 1700s. On the eastern side of the Hudson lived various smaller Algonquian-speaking nations, whose control over their homelands eroded more quickly as Dutch and English colonizers seized their territory in the 1600s and early 1700s.

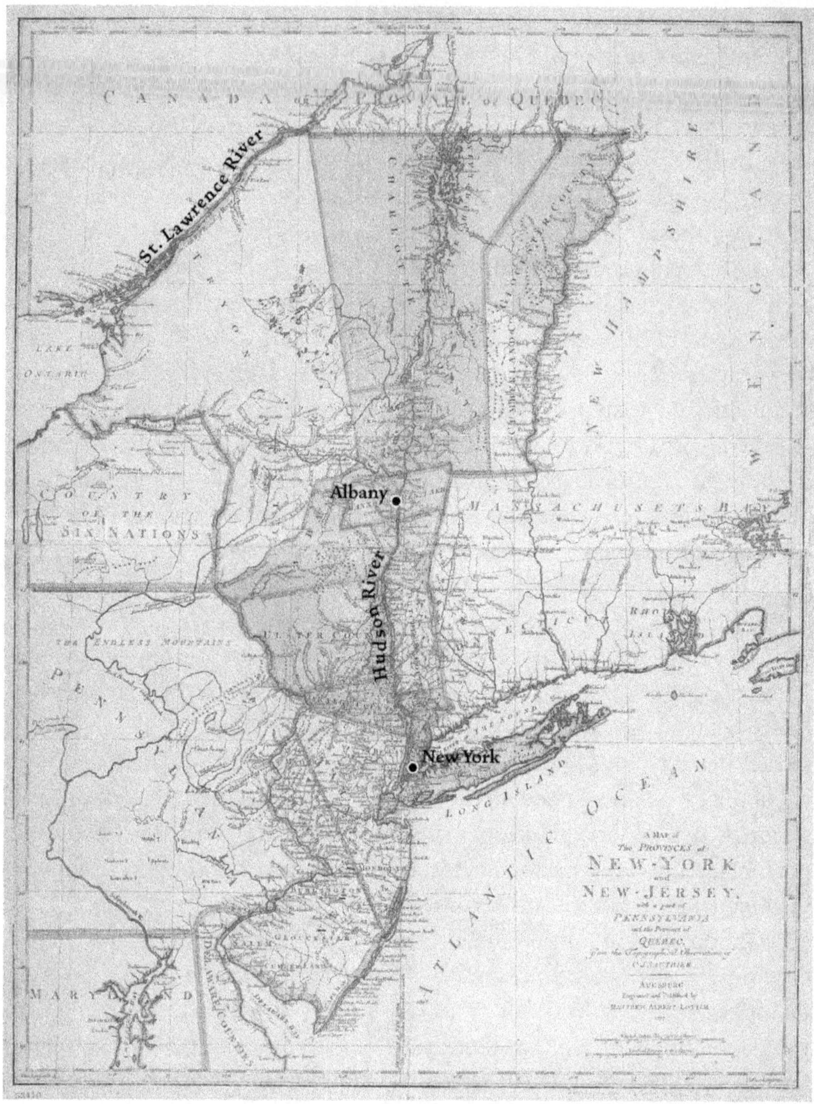

Figure 2. A Map of the Provinces of New-York and New-Jersey: with a part of Pennsylvania and the Province of Quebec, from the Topographical Observations of C. J. Sauthier (1777), with additional text by Dan Miller. This map of late colonial New York suggests the *L* pattern of European settlement, north and south along the Hudson River and east along Long Island. The Haudenosaunee, or Six Nations, possessed what later became northwestern New York State.

In the 1620s, Dutch traders established their first permanent settlement at a trading fort they named Fort Oranj (now Albany)—in a colony they called New Netherland—near the northern source of the Hudson River. Their second major settlement was New Amsterdam (now New York City), where the Hudson River meets the Atlantic Ocean and a skinny stretch of land, Long Island, juts east for 118 miles into the sea toward Europe. The Dutch used these sites for trade with Native nations; meanwhile, Dutch farmers grew crops in the rich soil of the Hudson Valley between Fort Oranj and New Amsterdam. The Dutch also created six towns on western Long Island (now the borough of Brooklyn) in the 1640s. During this same period, English farmers, fishermen, and merchants colonized eastern Long Island, where they maintained ties with nearby settlements in Connecticut and Rhode Island. In sum, New York's early European settlement comprised an *L* shape—the colonists planted up and down the Hudson and east along Long Island. In the 1660s, during the Second Anglo-Dutch War, the English took control of New Netherland and renamed it New York. English settlers continued to develop the extant forts, towns, and farmlands. Many Dutch settlers stayed and made lives under the English crown.

African slavery was vital to both the Dutch and the English. The Dutch brought several hundred enslaved people to New Netherland in the early 1600s, relying on their labor to protect and cultivate the colony. In 1644, the director-general of New Netherland, Willem Kieft, explained the colony's desire for more slaves: "Negroes would accomplish more work for their masters, and at a less expense, than [European] farm servants, who must be bribed to go thither by a great deal of money and promises."[24] In the 1650s, Nathaniel Sylvester, an English merchant, brought his family and slaves from Barbados to Shelter Island, between the forks of eastern Long Island. The resulting Sylvester manor became one of the largest plantations in the Northeast. In 1664, when the English took over, there were approximately 75 free black people and 300 enslaved people in New Netherland out of a total population of 1,500.[25]

The enslaved population of New York grew under the English. Some of this growth derived from children born to enslaved mothers, but traders also imported people from Africa, the West Indies, and other mainland colonies. Between 1712 and 1731, the number of slaves in New York City grew from roughly 1,000 to 1,600. Rural areas witnessed similar trends, as farmers in the Hudson Valley, Long Island, and northern New Jersey, whose economy was deeply tied to New York, encouraged slave labor. In 1755, the province compiled a census, the results of which demonstrated the prevalence of slaveholding in all counties and local economies. In urban areas, enslaved men worked for artisans, merchants, shipbuilders, and tavern keepers. Women worked as domestics, laundresses, cooks, and nurses. Children worked as well, although their presence was often less desirable; some city masters believed that infants took up too much space and time. In rural areas, black family life was similarly constrained, for although slaveholding was widespread, masters on northern farms rarely owned more than a few slaves at a time. These trends continued through the American Revolution. In absolute numbers, slavery grew in the wake of the war. By 1790, almost 40 percent of the households in the three rural counties surrounding New York City owned slaves. In the city itself, one in five households used slave labor.[26]

The black generations who feature in this book were born into a society where the laws of slavery, freedom, and poverty stretched back centuries and shaped their present. There were variations in experience depending on where people lived across New York's physical and cultural geography, but all of the main characters were affected by the state's capacity to regulate their daily lives, their avenues for freedom, and their rights as citizens.

A Note on Language

In referring to the era of gradual abolition or emancipation, I mean the period spanning the 1780s to 1840s. Chapters 1 and 2 will explore the myriad laws New York passed during these decades to constrict slavery bit by bit. The state passed its most consequential acts in 1799 and 1817; both included rules about freeborn children's required terms of service. I use "gradual abolition" and "gradual emancipation" interchangeably. "Gradual abolition" was the more popular term at the time. Abolitionists, lawmakers, slaveholders, servants, and enslaved people all understood that gradualist laws were meant to abolish slavery slowly, even if they did not agree on much else about the policy.

When I refer to "gradual abolition New Yorkers" or "black New Yorkers," I mean to include all black people who lived in the state during that given moment. When I refer to the "children of gradual abolition" or the "rising generation," I mean specifically those children born after the 1799 law. This generation—children who were young in the first three decades of the nineteenth century—are the historical protagonists of this study. At times, I also include children who were born several years before the 1799 act who nonetheless experienced similar gradual transitions into free adulthood, or who were born elsewhere but moved to New York at a young age. In the early 1800s, the "children of gradual abolition" were actual children. (More generally speaking, "childhood" in the early republic ended, legally, at 18 for girls and 21 for boys, with less reference to our modern conception of teenagerhood.) When I use "children of gradual abolition" as I follow this generation into adulthood, it is to emphasize their common experiences as children, not to suggest they remained "childlike." There is a long history in the United States of referring to grown black men and women as "boys" or "girls" as a means of diminishing their dignity and justifying their civic exclusion. The way I narrate the history of this generation over time makes clear they are adults when they are adults.

I use black people's names and otherwise highlight their chosen self-identities as much as possible. When referring to groups of people, such as "black New Yorkers," I have kept "black" lowercase because many of the main historical actors in the book used lowercase designations, referring to themselves as "men of color," "colored ladies," "citizens of color," "colored children," "black editors," and "black citizens." Their use of the lowercase, especially in the early to mid-1800s, was deliberate. (Their parents' generation often used "African," which readers will see in institutional names and quotations in the earlier chapters of the book.) In the face of the colonization movement, black leaders in the 1820s and beyond insisted that they were "colored citizens of the State of New York" or "black citizens." They emphasized their native New Yorkerness and Americanness as primary categories of identity. In 1837, the *Weekly Advocate*'s editors explained: "We are *Americans,*—colored Americans, brethren." *The Rising Generation* is more a story of conscious politics and contingent moments than it is an analytic account of racialization, which is another reason I follow historical black New Yorkers' lead. My hope is to honor their preferences, while never ignoring what they were up against.[27]

I sometimes use the word "master," especially in the early modern portions of the book, for carefully considered reasons. In Anglo-American law, a "master" of a household was a property-owning man who controlled, to varying degrees, the wife, children, servants, slaves, wards, apprentices, and paupers living with him. The law gave him different rights over people of each status. *Gradual abolition specifically* becomes more legible if we recognize the multiple legal and social meanings and powers accorded to masters in early America. While "enslaver" works for analyzing the relationship between an owner and enslaved person, it does not work as well for thinking through the various other forms of patriarchal, racialized power attached to the multifaceted but unifying legal status of "master," or the specific ways that servants, slaves, paupers, apprentices, and other dependents all lived in a master's domain but with distinct legal rights and life opportunities. I use "owner" at times as well, to stress the fact that men and women possessed other people as chattel property; this relationship was sanctioned by law and state violence. Masters who owned slaves also commanded the work and bodies of servants, paupers, children, and wives, but the property relationship was less absolute. These details mattered in real people's lives during gradual abolition. To use "masters" and "owners" does not require uncritically adopting their perspectives. On the contrary, the point is to examine the legal and ideological systems that propped up their power, and to understand how black people continually fought back and changed the legal and ideological terrain in which they all lived.[28] Following the logic of historians Tiya Miles and Leslie M. Harris, I use both "enslaved people" and "slaves" alongside a persistent effort to personalize and identify individuals and families.[29]

The main characters of this book are the many different black people in New York—young and old, male and female, free and quasi-free and unfree, optimistic and doubtful, alone and attached, formally and informally educated—who understood the various ways in which the law and the political system upheld the power of masters and also how those same laws and political systems might be tactically applied to undoing masters' power. Their resistance and their language choices were specific to the time and place in which they lived; their resistance and language choices were not uniform, but there were clear patterns.

Finally, a note on the adjectives "antislavery" and "abolitionist." As David Brion Davis pointed out long ago, eighteenth- and nineteenth-century reformers often used these words interchangeably. It is difficult to assign the words any sort of unchanging definition across time and space. In general, I aim to make clear what historical actors' contemporary objectives were. I will also adhere to Davis's observation that "'abolitionism' is a more specific term than 'antislavery,' and is associated with the doctrine that slavery or the slave trade must be abolished. 'Abolitionism' . . . is the most activist expression of 'antislavery.'"[30]

With the main characters, arguments, sources, geography, and language of this book now sketched, let us turn to Chapter 1. There, we will meet a proslavery lawmaker and an enslaved woman, living in the same rural household, both existing within a wider county, state, and Atlantic world where the tensions between slavery and freedom had been simmering for centuries. The lawmaker and his wealthy neighbors did not want change, at least not in terms of their right to hold people in bondage. The county's slaves, however, had other ideas.

CHAPTER 1

Poor Law, Slave Law, and the Golden Rule

Quaker Antislavery and the Early Modern Origins of Gradual Abolition Policy

In the spring of 1796, slaves in the Hudson River Valley were making local masters nervous. Rumors circulated that state lawmakers in Albany were once again deliberating an abolition bill. Some black New Yorkers seized the moment as an opportunity to destabilize slavery on the ground, practically willing the potential law into being where circumstance allowed. In Shawangunk, an agricultural town in Ulster County on the west side of the river, fifteen anxious masters responded by forming a Society for Apprehending Slaves, explaining: "Whereas a suspicion seems to prevail among many of the Negro Slaves that the Legislature of the State has liberated them and that they are now held in servitude by the arbitrary power of their masters contrary to law, and their uneasiness [is] increased by some mischievous whites who secretly encourage them to Run away," it was necessary to thwart runaways and to punish the "whites or free negroes" who helped them.[1]

With historically minded care, we can imagine the ways Shawangunk's slaves learned about the legislative possibilities. We might peer inside the house of John Addison, a member of the assembly from Ulster County who wrote a steely speech against the antislavery bill that spring. Addison, a lawyer with substantial land, owned six people in the 1790s. Perhaps an enslaved woman sweeping his floors eavesdropped as he railed to a neighbor that the bill was "illegal and unjust." Were she pregnant, she might have wondered whether the child growing inside her would be free, since emancipating those "yet to be born" was the bill's primary aim. Addison, so confident in his speech that he wanted to publish it, defined property in slaves as "a Right to their labour and services for life founded on a bona fide consideration

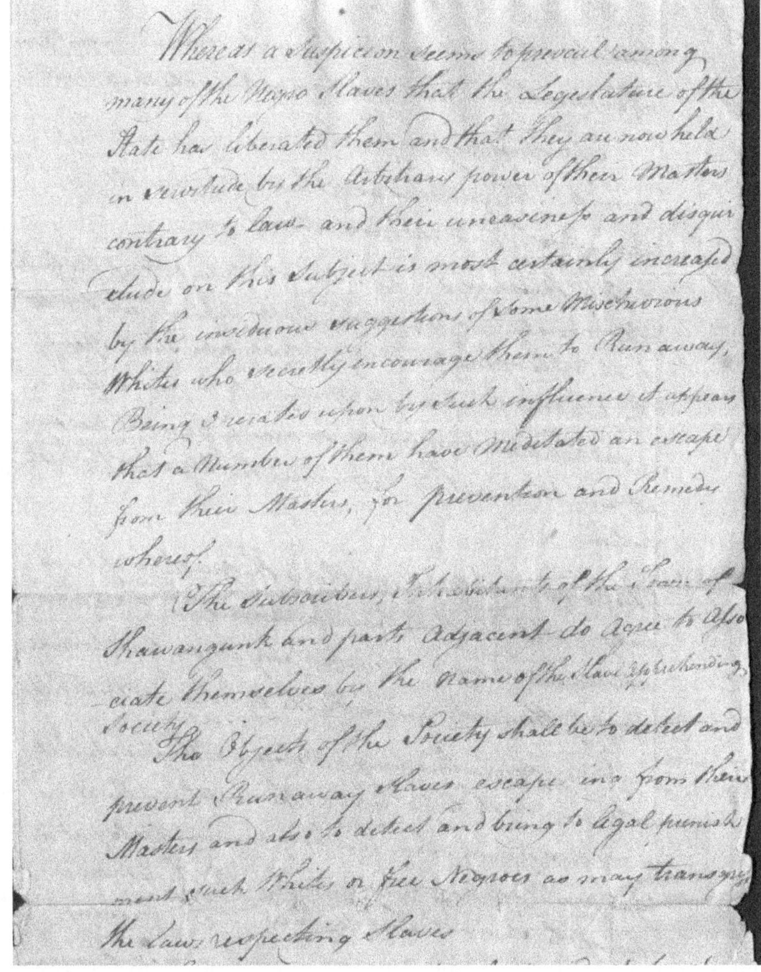

Whereas a Suspicion seems to prevail among many of the Negro Slaves that the Legislature of the State has liberated them and that they are now held in servitude by the Arbitrary power of their Masters contrary to law and their uneasiness and disquietude on this Subject is most certainly increased by the insiduous suggestions of some Mischievous Whites who secretly encourage them to Run away, Being Operated upon by such influence it appears that a Number of them have Meditated an escape from their Masters, for prevention and Remedy whereof

The Subscribers, Inhabitants of the Town of Shawangunk and parts Adjacent do Agree to Associate themselves by the Name of the Slave Apprehending Society

The Object of the Society shall be to detect and prevent Runaway Slaves escaping from their Masters and also to detect and bring to legal punishment such Whites or free Negroes as may transgress the Laws respecting Slaves

Figure 3. Society for Apprehending of Slaves, Shawangunk, Ulster County, May 1796, from the collection of the New York State Library, Manuscripts and Special Collections, Albany, New York.

paid for them and the Masters' clothing, supporting and maintaining them through all the vicissitudes of Life, of Infancy, manhood, sickness, and old age." He disagreed that masters should pay for rearing future freeborn children; that expense should be divided among the state's taxpayers. The intensity with which Addison dissected the bill, the woman may have thought, was revealing of its viability.[2]

Perhaps she told other black laborers what she heard. And perhaps an enslaved man sent on an errand to the county seat in Kingston shared her intelligence with a friend, who in turn reported overhearing similar discussions at a local tavern. There was, after all, a simultaneous debate unfolding in the press. An anti-abolitionist, writing under the pseudonym "Justice," blamed growing antislavery sentiment on the state's Quakers, who had long since implemented abolition plans among themselves: "They will not stop short of enforcing their opinions as the *rule for others*, continually harassing government with their petitions." A writer named "Humanitas" issued a rebuttal, defending Quaker conduct.[3] Quakers were among the antislavery "whites" who had galvanized the reactionary owners in the Society for Apprehending Slaves.

The 1796 gradual abolition bill failed that spring, but the fervor around it in Ulster County suggests the range of New Yorkers who took interest in its fate. Proslavery advocates fought hard against abolition. It turns out that ending slavery in the state was not easy, natural, or the inevitable result of the American Revolution. This was not because antislavery forces, including enslaved and free black people, did not try; it was because proslavery forces pushed back. It took years of effort by Quakers and their slower-to-act founding father allies to achieve legislative abolition. Reformers in the formal political sphere were assisted by black New Yorkers, whose challenges to slavery in homes and neighborhoods weakened the institution's solidity.

In 1799, three years after Addison's grandstanding speech, New York finally passed "An Act for the gradual abolition of slavery." The law decreed that children born to enslaved mothers after July 4 of that year would be free at birth, with the caveat that they serve as servants to their mother's masters until adulthood or be bound out by local overseers of the poor should masters "abandon" them. Girls would serve until age 25, boys until 28. The children would be subject to "the same terms and conditions [as] the children of paupers."[4] What lawmakers did, in essence, was replace slave law with long-existing poor law, with a focus on children. Both pro- and antislavery advocates worried constantly, albeit with differing motives, about what Addison called "the vicissitudes of life"—moments when slaves or freed slaves were dependent because they were young, sick, disabled, or old. Who would shoulder the costs?

For all the rich work that has examined abolition in the Atlantic world and in the northern United States in particular, the origins and processes of gradual abolition policy and law have been given short shrift. Historians tend to begin their accounts during the Age of Revolution. The common narrative explains that the ideology of the American rebellion, combined with the arming of slaves during the war and the opportunity to craft republican state governments, resulted in an antislavery moment. We then learn in broad terms of the methods by which northern states abolished slavery.[5] Most historians argue that gradual abolition laws were designed to protect individual owners' property rights in existing slaves and force children to compensate their lost property value through their labor.[6] Many of these accounts briefly acknowledge the earlier antislavery proclivities of Quakers and other scattered objectors, but it remains hard to discern in any detail how early modern reformers conceived, in ideological and practical terms, of abolishing slavery. To the real people involved—masters, state and local officials, black children and their families—the specifics of the policy mattered enormously.

If our eyes are closed to colonial legacies, it becomes tempting to view gradual abolition as a product of "Revolutionary fervor" without acknowledging its gestation in the social, legal, religious, and economic context of the early modern Atlantic world. The Revolution was, as the scholarship rightly suggests, a moment of widening antislavery sentiment and constitutional innovation crucial to northern abolition. The new nation's federal structure allowed states to make individual decisions about slavery. Had the colonies remained British, it is unlikely the imperial Privy Council or Board of Trade would have allowed abolition in the 1700s. As pivotal as the Revolution was, however, it does not tell us much about why the laws looked the way they did. Their substance and logic were rooted in colonial labor laws and antislavery activity.[7]

Emancipation plans had been in circulation, primarily among Quakers, for a century by the time of the Revolution. New York's Quakers began executing self-imposed abolition programs in the 1750s, and these same Quakers were instrumental to the passage of the 1799 law.[8] Ultimately, the law owed its design to a combination of Quaker-inflected religious principles (especially the Golden Rule), early modern notions of patriarchal household governance, and coercive poor laws that long predated the Revolution. Of key concern was who would pay for the "poor relief" of former slaves. Debates over abolition were as much about tax avoidance and jurisdictional fiscal responsibilities as they were about property rights or the virtues of liberty. The 1799 law's final shape was an amalgam of clashing ideas and priorities.

New York's 1799 law incorporated early modern assumptions about work, age, and poverty. It bolstered a hierarchical social and legal world that considered a child's labor either the property of independent fathers or, absent parents' economic independence, the property of a designated household in the local jurisdiction. The 1799 law turned black children who would themselves have been property into children whose labor was the property of a master or local officials. Because enslaved parents were dependent, the law presupposed black children would be legally "poor." Masters, in this view, were being compensated—in the form of the infant's future adolescent labor—for the cost of raising the dependent child.[9] An extended history of gradual abolition shows that the Revolution was a catalyst for rather than an originator of important strands of emancipationist thought. It reveals the fundamental relationships not only among poor law, labor law, and slave law, but among poor law, labor law, and emancipation law. Gradual abolition may have conferred freedom on children, but it was premised on continued rights to control the work and mobility of dependent people. In 1799, freedom and personal autonomy were neither legally nor conceptually synonymous.[10]

To understand what shaped the politics, legal consciousness, and everyday lives of the parents and the children of gradual abolition—people like the enslaved laborers living in John Addison's household and their immediate descendants—we first have to look back in time. The laws and labor practices undergirding gradual abolition were as old as they were new.

* * *

"In most early American societies," one historian has observed, "slaves were the poor." They lived from hand to mouth, toiled manually for survival, and led a precarious and tenuous existence. In early modern governmental logic, slavery "solved" the problem of the poor by employing the able-bodied and by transferring "the responsibility for the aged, the disabled, and the young from parish to the individual plantation owner." Slavery and poverty were connected, conceptually and practically, in the minds of early American lawmakers and officials. Slaves frequently suffered from being poor, and the poor frequently suffered from labor coercion.[11]

In colonial New York, slaves, free black people, white servants, child apprentices, and paupers were at once distinct entities at law while also frequently grouped together as problematic sources of vice, destitution, and disease. In crafting their legal regulations, provincial leaders preferred that both dependent black people and dependent white people live in private households run by patriarchal masters. Crucial to the functioning of this colonial political economy was the idea that neither enslaved nor impoverished parents had a legal right to their children or their children's labor.[12]

Officials began to enact local statutes regulating poverty and slavery soon after the English claimed New York from the Dutch. In 1683, the colonial assembly, borrowing from English poor law, passed a statute charging each local jurisdiction with the care of its own poor. Any poor stranger attempting to reside in New York could do so only after providing "sufficient Security that he shall nott bee a burthen." Ship captains who brought paupers were required to transport them back "from whence they came," and local constables could return "vagabonds" who entered their counties. A 1695 law began by observing "the Poor in great distress." A 1703 law noted that pauper care was causing "disputes" and "Mistakes."[13]

Anxiety about the poor was related to the regulation of slaves. In a 1712 law that built on the colony's extant slave code, lawmakers explained that since "free Negroes of this colony are an Idle slothfull people and prove very often a charge on the place where they are," masters would have to post a two-hundred-pound bond when manumitting slaves. Masters would also be required to give former slaves twenty pounds a year to prevent them from becoming public burdens. Freedom for slaves, in other words, was associated with poverty and public expense. Officials did not seem to care about why the formerly enslaved were poor in the first place.[14]

Poverty was a widespread problem. The records of the mayor's court in New York City suggest the demographic patterns: most of the poor were women, children, the old, and the sick. The court bound children to local families, even at extremely young ages. In 1728, for example, the court noted that "a female child aged about two or three months was lately left in this city" and ordered "the Church Wardens do provide for the maintenance of said child til such time as they can put [her] out for the Term of one and twenty years." This practice was common. In a typical example, the son of a sick chimney sweep was "to be apprenticed and in the meantime the sum of 2s. per week is to be allowed to such person as it thought fit toward the maintenance of the child." As these records suggest, households that received children collected fees for their care. While older children paid the cost of their room, board, and education with their labor, young children were not expected to pay for themselves. A 1754 act affirmed that overseers of the poor should raise funds "for putting poor Children apprentices." Poor relief was consistently the most expensive item in the city's budget.[15]

Many of the children whose labor was claimed by local officials were orphans, half-orphans, or illegitimate. But poor and middling parents who maintained nominal control over their children's labor often indentured their children on their own accord, signing agreements stipulating their children would live with and work for a given master for a term of years. As owners of their children's labor, parents had the right to assign it to others. Fathers had first rights over children's labor; mothers had control if the father were dead or gone. An economically independent father could place his children in better apprenticeships than a desperate, widowed mother. Completely dependent parents lost rights to their children all together. At law, children were analogous to servants and vice versa. As the famed seventeenth-century English jurist William Blackstone wrote: "[A father] may indeed have the benefit of his children's labour while they live with him, and are maintained by him: but this is no more than he is entitled to from his apprentices or servants." Both children and servants were customarily released from patriarchal labor coercion at 18 if female and 21 if male. Young women often found themselves transitioning from working under the authority of fathers and masters to working under the authority of husbands or, if single and poor, the authority of local poor law officials.[16]

When parents, whether reluctantly or not, bound out their own children, they tried to have some say in choosing the household where their child would be raised. The majority of parent-negotiated agreements in New York City's indenture records from 1718 to 1727 bound children to masters for five to eighteen years. Some children were bound to artisans who agreed to educate them in a lucrative craft; others were bound as menial servants. Often, the children were to be taught to read and write. In 1726, eight-year-old Mary, with her uncle's consent, was apprenticed to a yeoman for eighteen years—until she was twenty-six years old—during which time he would provide room and board and "learn the said apprentice to read."[17]

Rural New Yorkers were vulnerable to poverty, as well. In Huntington, Long Island, the overseers of the poor seemed particularly preoccupied with so-called illegitimate children. When they could find the father, they required the man to save "Huntington from all trouble" that "shall acrew on account of a bastard child." The overseers also regulated children's shelter and labor. In 1767, they paid nine pounds to a resident "for Keeping a poor Child." They later bound a five-year-old as a non-descript "apprentice" for eleven years.[18]

What all of these records—the involuntary and the voluntary indentures, the urban and the rural—indicate is that long terms of bound labor were common for poor children. Although pauper adults were occasionally placed in the workhouse or bound out for one-year terms, it was children who were routinely bound to strangers for years, even decades, at a time. In the eyes of the town official, child indenture addressed several problems: it delivered cheap labor to masters, ostensibly provided vocational training for children, and limited public expenses. What it did not do was keep children with their parents. In fact, poor children's labor was sometimes sold at auction to the households willing to accept the lowest fees for the pauper's care. Pauper apprenticeship was not racialized, hereditary slavery, but its logic and laws found nourishment in the same ideological soil.[19]

During these same decades, it was a slave master's duty to provide the equivalent of "poor relief" for his own sick or old slaves and to care for children whose labor output did not, in the early years of their lives, meet the costs of their upkeep. Put in the crude terms of poor law, a master was to provide for the "unmarried mothers" and "bastard children" of his own household. That said, many masters did not embrace their role as privatized overseers of the poor. Some masters tried to sell infirm slaves rather than care for them.[20] Likewise, masters tried to avoid the expense of enslaved children. Unlike in plantation regions, where an enslaved woman's pregnancy was usually welcomed, northern masters often disliked infants in the household. Few masters in New York held many slaves, which meant there were fewer people to nurse or mind children. A female slave with a small child was a preoccupied and weakened worker. Moreover, masters in urban settings had little space to house laborers and their families.[21]

Newspaper advertisements show that masters often attempted to avoid the costs of supporting fertile women and their babies. They tried to sell women with newborns and boasted when a woman was "barren" or "gets no children." New York's tax code likewise reflected young children's lack of productive value. A 1734 law raised one shilling a head on all slaves between ages 14 and 50. Slaves under 14 and over 50 were not taxed. In 1772, when an abolitionist impersonated a master objecting to emancipation, he wrote: "I have a woman bought when young, who having had children fast, hath earned very little of her purchase money."[22]

It was in this particular mid-Atlantic context of slavery, poverty, and regulatory lawmaking that Quakers began their attacks on chattel bondage and issued the first sustained English calls for gradual abolition in colonial America.

* * *

The world's first Quakers were not officially opposed to slavery, but lifelong bondage disturbed some members from the earliest years of the sect's existence. George Fox, the Quakers' principal founder, expressed his reservations after confronting slavery in person for the first time. In 1671, Fox sailed to the West Indies to minister to local Quakers. Arriving in the sugar-producing, slave-labor colony of Barbados, Fox recuperated for a month before delivering his first sermon. Addressing the "government of Families according to the Law of Jesus," Fox called for well-ordered hierarchical households governed by paternalistic masters. He affirmed slaves' spiritual equality, suggested slaves marry legally, and urged masters to manumit slaves after a "term of years." His inspiration was the Bible. He cited the Jews who freed their servants and counseled masters not to let their slaves "go away empty-handed." He urged empathy inspired by the Golden Rule: "[Do] to them, as you would willingly have them or any other do unto you." In Quaker thought, all humans were capable of and deserving of "the light"—of Christ's light in their hearts, of the Grace of God—a theological notion that did not necessarily topple all worldly hierarchies, but did infuse Quaker practice and rhetoric with a degree of egalitarianism distinct from that of their Anglo-Christian peers. In 1676, Fox published the Barbados sermon as *Gospel Family-Order: Being a Short Discourse Concerning the Ordering of Families, Both Whites, Blacks, and Indians.* It was reprinted by Philadelphia Quakers in 1701 and cited by advocates in both the colonies and metropole.[23]

Quakers' familiarity with Fox's proposal that masters release slaves after a term did not result in spontaneous mass emancipation in the English Atlantic. But a few Friends may have taken his advice seriously. In 1685 and 1708, for example, two Quaker women from different families in Oyster Bay, Long Island manumitted their slaves.[24] Quakers throughout the colonies, however, continued to own people, including in Pennsylvania, New York, and New England, the sites of the continent's three largest yearly meetings.[25] Ministers, elders, and overseers did not condemn chattel bondage, nor lead by antislavery example. William Penn, the Quaker proprietor of Pennsylvania, owned slaves. Nevertheless, in the years following Fox's plea for benevolent treatment toward black people in "your Families," a string of laymen Quakers asked nagging questions about the morality of slaveholding. These antislavery Friends were outliers even within their own outlier sect, but their ideas remained in circulation.[26]

Almost all Quaker antislavery treatises combined Christian-inspired arguments for freedom with practical suggestions for effecting gradual abolition. Like Fox's 1671 sermon, these texts emphasized the potentially "free" place of black servants within a white household. Neither civic egalitarianism nor liberalism guided early modern plans for emancipation. While radical in objecting to slavery, Quaker emancipation schemes hewed to contemporary norms about work, family, and the right of local leaders to supervise households in their midst.[27]

In 1693, Pennsylvania schismatic George Keith and his Delaware Valley allies published the colonies' first homegrown antislavery text. Printed in New York, the *Exhortation and Caution to Friends Concerning buying or keeping of Negroes* recommended: "Not to buy any Negroes, unless it were on purpose to set them free, and that . . . Negroes' Children born in their House, or taken into their House, when under Age, that after a reasonable time of service to answer that Charge, they may set them at Liberty, and during the time they have them, to teach them to read, and give them a Christian Education."[28] Not much would change in Quaker abolition proposals over the next one hundred years.

Although Keith was a polarizing figure among Quakers, his influence endured. Several decades after Keith's death, the eccentric Pennsylvanian Benjamin Lay reported that New England Friends continued to speak of Keith's example. Lay and the New Englanders' familiarity with Keith's work is not surprising. Quakers—known for their epistolary habits, their literacy, and their travels among each other—were an ideal community in which to sustain even unpopular ideas. Their commitment was to the sect and to its laws, their "holy nation," not to the colony in which they lived. Friends in Pennsylvania, New Jersey, New York, and New England were often in better touch with each other than with their non-Quaker next-door neighbors.[29]

Quakers' reading materials were not limited to published sources. Lay, for example, knew of a speech that Long Island Quaker William Burling had delivered in 1718. Burling's topic was the sin of "compelling certain Persons, and their Posterity, to serve them continually and arbitrarily" without compensating them "as their labour deserveth." Horsman Mullinex, another Long Islander, expressed reservations to the yearly meeting about "buying Negroes for slaves" and a fellow congregant proposed a paper on the subject. The yearly meeting "tenderly" discussed the matter, reporting that several Friends "wore fully sattisfide in their consionce" that slavery "was not Rite." The New York meeting wrote to the London meeting for guidance on "whether friends might Buy, sell or keep negroes slaves for Term of Life." London's reply is absent from the records, but in 1719, the New York meeting adopted the Philadelphia meeting's "Book of Discipline." The regulations mandated that none "be concerned in the fetching or importing of Negro

Slaves from their own Country, or elsewhere." This stipulation was an internal ban on the slave trade, a precursor to laws that various states would adopt much later in the century.[30]

Quaker leaders—so-called weighty Friends—brooked a certain level of antislavery questioning, but there were no emancipation orders in the early 1700s, nor was there much antislavery proselytizing by Quakers to the wider public. An exception to this rule is instructive for its engagement with poor law. In 1733, Elihu Coleman published a tract in Boston in which he confessed he had heard men say that if they let slaves "go free after some Time, if any Mishap befel them, their Estates were obliged to maintain them."[31] Coleman knew that masters would use expenses tied to poor law as an excuse not to free people.

In the 1750s, as American Quakers enacted a religious "Reformation" among themselves, abolitionism became a core feature of Quaker practice and identity rather than a sidelined concern. Younger generations of Friends were increasingly troubled by their coreligionists' tendency to separate church and religion from economic and political life. One way that Quaker reformers implemented their project of purification—a perceived return to original values—was by endorsing emancipation. Slavery, they noted, was marked by avarice, violence, and corruption.[32] During this era of Quaker introspection, Pennsylvania abolitionist John Woolman was especially prolific. In a 1754 tract urging emancipation, he addressed poor law with vague advice that masters do the right thing, arguing they were "justly chargeable" with "whatever difficulties" came with freeing slaves. In a 1762 update, he was more specific, and perhaps more politically realistic: masters should release slaves who had "paid for their Education and given reasonable Security to those who owned them, in case of their becoming chargeable."[33]

One of Woolman's careful readers was Anthony Benezet of Philadelphia, a weighty Friend and increasingly ardent abolitionist. Significantly, Benezet began to argue that colonial authorities, not just Quakers, should adopt abolition plans: "The government . . . might bring [slaves] under such Regulations, as would enable them to become profitable Members of Society. . . . After [they] serve so long as shall be adequate to the Money paid, or the Charge of bringing them up . . . let them by Law be declared free . . . [but remain] under the inspection of the Overseers of the Poor. Thus . . . children have an opportunity of such Instruction . . . under the Tuition of proper Instructors."[34] Benezet thus supported a government-led, poor-law-structured program in which age was a prime factor in determining the mechanics of acquiring freedom. Quakers were not simply reforming themselves; they would now work to reform the wider world around them. Benezet was aware, however, that the British Board of Trade and Privy Council might not permit local antislavery lawmaking in Pennsylvania.[35]

As mid-Atlantic Quakers began to reach their own tipping point in favor of community-wide emancipation, poverty exploded. Facing a depression in the wake of the Seven Years' War, the colonies' poor relief expenses skyrocketed in the 1760s. New York City's population increased by about half, while rates of poverty jumped fourfold.[36] To combat these trends, lawmakers enacted new regulations. A 1766 act in New York stipulated that children could be bound until "twenty one years," except for children brought "from beyond the Sea," who could be bound for even longer. A 1772 law declared that when fathers left their families, overseers of the poor could seize their "Goods and Chattels" for "providing for such Wife Child or Children." Enslaved people, too, were affected. An act "to prevent aged and decrepit slaves from becoming burthensome" explained that some masters forced them "to go about begging for the common Necessaries of Life." The colonial assembly also penalized tavernkeepers who sold "Liquor to any Apprentice, Servant, or Negro or other Slave."[37] These laws illustrate a culture in which it remained acceptable to compel poor people, especially the young, to live with masters not of their choosing; demand masters keep slaves off the poor rolls; regulate which slaves could be sold; and seize the property of men who did not provide for their dependents. When New York wrote its first constitution in 1777, it received these acts into its body of republican law.[38]

In the midst of the depression, Quakers in the Northeast began to put their antislavery ideas into practice. The Quakers of Oblong, in the town of Pawling in the eastern Hudson Valley, were particularly committed. In 1759, without direction from a larger Quaker meeting, Oblong Friends began insisting that local members who bought, held, and sold slaves make plans to free them. Through cajoling and threats of discipline, visiting committees forced stubborn masters to act.[39] In 1764, for example, Stephen Haight was accused of "buying a Negro." After repeated visits and threats of disownment, Haight acknowledged buying the man and proposed to free him in ten years and pay freedom dues. The Oblong meeting approved the plan, but the story did not end well. Despite his promises, Haight sold the man in 1766 and was disowned.[40]

In 1767, the Oblong Quakers wrote the New York Yearly Meeting to push for more measures against slaveholding region-wide. The yearly meeting equivocated: "Negroes as Rational Creatures are by Nature born free. . . . But to turn them out at large indiscriminately—which Seems to be the tendency of the Query, will we apprehend be attended with great Inconveniency as some are too young and some too old to procure a livelihood."[41] Constraints on individual liberty were in order when balanced against a person's age, dependency, and the public expense.

In 1774, the New York Yearly Meeting finally acted, declaring that Friends could not keep slaves past 18 or 21, "according to their Sex."[42] At monthly meetings, Friends would assess whether "care is taken to learn Negro Children to read and qualify them for Business."[43] It was the household's duty to educate children not only spiritually, but in a trade or marketable skills.

The records of the Westbury meeting on Long Island demonstrate how the commands were put into practice. A committee was charged to ensure that "no Friend hire any negro that is held in bondage," nor "take any negro as slave that is not set free when of age."[44] The supervisors collected manumission documents. Between 1775 and 1790, Westbury owners freed over 150 slaves. They freed adults unconditionally, while promising future liberty to children when they reached adulthood. For example, Thomas Pearsall "set free my Negro boys Jacob and Tony and Negro girl Named Judith when . . . the boys age of twenty one years & the girl at eighteen years." Charles Doughty freed ten people; owning this many slaves made him among the wealthiest masters in the state. Masters were to compensate former slaves for their past labor, an echo of Fox's recommendations. The Flushing meeting appointed a committee to oversee "such monies as may be necessary to hand out to the blacks so set free."[45] The meetings were also charged with caring for the sick or elderly. Overall, these practices were on the generous side of eighteenth-century emancipation efforts.

As Quakers put their values into practice, they continued to circulate their policy ideas in the wider public sphere, emphasizing what they thought the Golden Rule required in the context of black children's labor and emancipation. New Jersey Quaker David Cooper explained the situation in a published tract: "'Do unto others, as ye would they should do to you.' This will oblige you to set your negroes free at the same age your own children are, without unjustly coveting their labour till they are 25 or 30 years of age. . . . Should one of your own sons be kept an apprentice by force, a year longer than his master had a right, satisfaction must be made."[46] Cooper believed masters should release black children at 18 and 21, the same ages when white apprentices, paupers, and children were released from their masters and parents. He urged masters to fulfill "a father's duty" toward black children. Cooper was right, however, to be worried that once gradual abolition plans were enacted, masters would try to keep black children longer than white children. He was prescient about the fights over length of service that would soon occur in state legislatures.[47]

Quaker emancipations started well before the American Revolution. When the republican founders of the various new states looked for possible ways to end slavery in the late 1770s, they could turn to examples in their midst, examples whose origins and execution had little to do with the colonies' fight for independence or the politics and disruptions of the war. The Quaker holy nation—a "state" unto itself—had been the first to require and enforce abolition, providing subsequent American states with an example. The Revolution was indeed crucial for opening legislative opportunities to end slavery, for propagating Enlightenment ideals, and for providing enslaved people new routes to escape bondage, but Quakers had already demonstrated that gradual abolition was feasible.

* * *

As Quakers throughout the northern colonies manumitted their slaves in the late 1760s and early 1770s, a number of non-Quaker religious leaders and political figures, including black men, amplified their own calls for abolition. These various antislavery advocates seized on Quaker models, combining both new and old Christian arguments against slavery with the ideology of the burgeoning Revolution. In their capacities as patriot leaders, clergymen, and intellectuals, they roused antislavery sentiment in public spaces and encouraged each other in private. Simultaneously, black women found new space to speak or maneuver on behalf of antislavery. Female efforts may have, on the whole, appeared less overtly and formally political, but their exertions nonetheless tested the strength of chattel bondage on the ground in local areas.[48]

From his perch in Philadelphia, Anthony Benezet was particularly adept at enlisting non-Quaker allies to the cause. In 1773, he inspired one of his protégés, the prominent physician and patriot Benjamin Rush, to publish *An Address to the Inhabitants of the British Settlements in America, upon Slave-Keeping*. Rush urged the same form of abolition that his Quaker mentor promoted: "let the young Negroes be educated in the principles of virtue and religion" and "let them be taught to read, and write—and afterwards be instructed in some business, whereby they may be able to maintain themselves. Let laws be made to limit the time of servitude."[49]

Rush was an effective diplomat for Benezet, distributing antislavery ideas to a broader, non-Quaker audience. Together, Benezet and Rush kept pressure on Benjamin Franklin to assume a stronger antislavery position. In 1774, Franklin wrote letters of introduction for the Quaker-descended Thomas Paine when Paine moved to Philadelphia and became a successful pamphleteer. Paine wrote an essay proposing that, should the colonies gain independence, the patriots should pass "continental legislation, which shall put a stop to the importation of Negroes for sale, soften the hard fate of those already here, and in time procure their freedom."[50]

During these same months, a black woman named Dinah Nevil, who had arrived in Philadelphia in 1773, began insisting to Quakers and local authorities that "she and her children were Free people." Inspired by Nevil's freedom suit, a Quaker tailor named Thomas Harrison, along with a handful of coreligionists, founded the Society for the Relief of Free Negroes Unlawfully Held in Bondage. The society, renamed the Pennsylvania Abolition Society after the Revolution, was the colonies' first antislavery association. Nevil was one in a long line of black mothers who would advocate for her children and, in the process, spur wider antislavery action.[51]

The heightened antislavery activity in Pennsylvania helped antislavery reformers elsewhere promote their cause. In 1773, a writer using the pseudonym Eleutheros published a letter in the *New York Journal*. Quoting Benezet and pointing to Rush, Eleutheros called for antislavery legislation. He worried, however, about slaves' "capacity of maintaining themselves" and noted that current laws "provided against the evils resulting from a manumission, obliging the masters to secure the publick from any expense in supporting their freed slaves."[52] Almost all abolition plans circulating in print in the 1770s, like this one, emphasized gradual emancipation for the young, continued enslavement for the old, and the problem of dependent former slaves who would tax local poor relief resources.

Protestant clergy also became increasingly vocal, particularly the Calvinists at the helm of New England's New Divinity movement. Ministers such as Jonathan Edwards Jr. (son of the famous Great Awakening theologian), Lemuel Haynes (a black Revolutionary War veteran in Vermont), Levi Hart (a Connecticut minister), and Samuel Hopkins (the founder of Hopkinsian theology) viewed slaveholding as a sin. The theological framework for their beliefs derived from their notion of "disinterested benevolence" and the conviction that the New Testament trumped the Old Testament, which sanctioned slaveholding, as a guide for behavior.[53]

These divines had their particular theological justifications for emancipation, but they found the Quaker model of *how* to emancipate useful. Hopkins, the most influential of the New Lights, wrote from Newport, Rhode Island, where he was alarmed by the city's thriving slave trade. In 1776, he published *A Dialogue Concerning the Slavery of the Africans,* noting that "Quakers have been for a number of years bearing testimony against this oppression" and "striving to purge themselves."[54] Batting away concern about property rights and denying the state's obligation to compensate masters, Hopkins was more concerned with postemancipation poverty. He assumed extant poor relief systems could structure the lives of former slaves and urged readers to "assist those who want discretion" as "if they were your own children." Hopkins urged colonial assemblies and the incipient national government to adopt "general manumission."[55]

Writing early in 1776, Hopkins was typical of the era's non-Quaker abolitionists in linking the cause of antislavery with the cause of American independence. The *Dialogue* was addressed to the Continental Congress, whom he urged to "act a consistent part, who have been such mighty advocates of *our own liberty.*" The colonists' success against the British depended on addressing the "very great and public sin" of slavery. Paine, Franklin, and Rush likewise connected the Revolution to antislavery ideals, both with and without recourse to religious reasoning.[56]

Black Americans also seized on the hypocrisy of white Americans fighting for liberty while enslaving others. In Massachusetts, black men petitioned their government throughout the 1770s, employing Revolutionary rhetoric about the natural rights of man. While these petitions are well-known among historians, their inclusion of gradual abolition proposals centered on children is seldom noted. In 1774, for example, "A Grate Number of Blackes" petitioned Governor Thomas Gage and the General Court for a law "to be pessed that we may obtain our Natural right our freedoms and our children be set at lebety at the yeare of twenty one." In 1777, a similar black petition, spearheaded by the Freemason and patriot Prince Hall, asked for a law whereby "Children who wher Born in this Land of Liberty may not be held as Slaves after they arrive at the age of twenty one."[57]

In New York, several years later, a Long Island slave named Jupiter Hammon, known for publishing Christian-inspired poetry, wrote a speech for a black civic organization claiming that he was too old to want his own freedom, but that he supported gradual emancipation for the young. "I should be glad," he wrote, "if others, especially the young negroes, were to be free.... That liberty is a great thing we know from our own feelings."[58]

The fact that the black Massachusetts petitioners and Hammon hoped that legislatures would free children after terms of service does not mean they were tepidly antislavery. It is possible, rather, to read their concerns in light of the very real struggles faced by poor people in early America. For adults to establish independent households immediately upon emancipation would be difficult; they had, after all, been robbed of a lifetime of wages and the chance to accumulate capital. Poor parents, black and white, routinely had to turn to households other than their own to raise children. Older slaves, like Hammon, felt that their masters owed them "comfort" in their twilight years.[59] Hammon argued that the enslaved should be good servants to the masters, but he also insisted that masters fulfill their obligations in return—a point that is trenchantly political when recalling how cruelly some northern masters treated old and sick slaves.

While Hammon and the petitioners put pen to paper, most American slaves searching for freedom during the Revolution did so not by writing but by exploiting the tumult and possibilities of war and displacement. Most famously, hundreds of runaways fled to British forces in the Chesapeake after Lord Dunmore, the royal governor of Virginia, offered freedom to "indented servants, Negroes, or others" who were "willing to bear arms" against the rebel patriots in late 1775. Enslaved New Yorkers were quick to follow suit. In early 1776, a man named Will packed clothes, shoes, and two hats before fleeing from Rye in Westchester County. His owner noted that since Will was "an ingenious fellow, it's thought he will . . . go to the King's forces."[60] When the British occupied New York City a few months later, the stream of freedom seekers continued. Although men fled in greater numbers than women and children, at times families and kin took their chances together. A merchant named Samuel Sackett reported, for example, that a man and a woman had fled to the army with a five-month-old.[61]

Masters watched with anxiety as enslaved people gleaned the dangerous but real opportunities for freedom that the war presented. In Orange County, the local patriot committee (the ad hoc revolutionary government in the area) noted that "negroe slaves" were making "menacing speeches," "gathering themselves into companies," "procuring arms," and issuing "calls for redress." The committee moved to restrict black assembly and mobility in the area. Meanwhile, a New York City master noted that a runaway named Caesar was "pleased and elevated when any one speaks with him about the war." In 1779, British general Henry Clinton provided a further opening by issuing a proclamation from his headquarters in Philipsburg, in the lower Hudson Valley, promising "full security" to slaves who deserted rebel masters. In some households, the instability created by the British presence provided black people more leverage to assert their will, even when they stayed with owners. A patriot in the Hudson Valley complained that he could not easily move houses because "our wench Sarah" wanted to remain where she was. The patriot's adult son lamented that "the stubborn will of a slave" thwarted his parents' plans. At the close of the war, three thousand freed black people left New York City on British ships; 21 percent were from New York and New Jersey.[62]

Black people also cast their lot with the patriots, for reasons of pragmatism, principle, or both. Just as slaves owned by patriots might run to the British, some slaves of Loyalists hoped to find liberty among the American forces, even though the Continental Congress never enacted the same broad emancipatory policies that Lord Dunmore and General Clinton embraced. In some cases, patriot masters permitted slaves to enlist. New York's provincial government accepted black men into its forces, passing an act to raise two regiments that included a clause promising freedom to any male slave whose master consented that he join.[63]

In one of the most consequential moments of the war, a black patriot veteran from Westchester County named John Peterson, who had been honorably discharged after the Battle of Saratoga, played a crucial role in the capture of Major John André, the head of the British spy service. Peterson, along with his master's cousin, Moses Sherwood, fired on the British sloop *Vulture* as it carried André up the Hudson River to meet patriot traitor Benedict Arnold at West Point. In the resulting chaos, André was discovered by three patriot militiamen. The foiling of André and Arnold's meeting led to the unmasking of Arnold as a turncoat and to the patriots' rescue of West Point, a turn of events that changed the course of the entire war. While it is unclear precisely what motivated Peterson to fight, we know that he survived the war, raised his family in Westchester as a free man at the head of his own household, was feted as a hero of the Revolution, and died at the age of 103.[64]

But just because hundreds of black New Yorkers gained freedom during the Revolution does not mean that the majority of slaves had the capacity or the opportunity to self-emancipate. Three years after the Declaration of Independence, slavery remained legal in all thirteen colonies. Those who risked running away often died of disease, met death in battle, or faced recapture and brutal punishment. Wars have historically created conditions conducive to individual emancipations and the politics of antislavery, but wars do not by themselves topple the laws, dismantle the household violence, or strangle the state powers that uphold slave regimes. In the case of the American Revolution, it was the winners of the war—white American patriots—who got to decide whether their various new governments would sanction race-based hereditary slavery or not. Enslaved people certainly made plain what their own position was, but their efforts played out differently, both individually and collectively, from state to state.[65]

* * *

By the late 1770s, the antislavery proposals that had been swirling in public arrived in the lawmaking bodies of the northern states as white antislavery patriots began thinking about how their revolutionary governments might take steps to end lifelong chattel bondage. Over the winter of 1776–1777, the leading patriots of New York, seeking to avoid the invading British, darted from town to town along the Hudson while trying to govern the newly independent state. The Convention of the People, as the nascent government was called, assigned Gouverneur Morris, John Jay, James Duane, and Robert R. Livingston the task of drafting a republican constitution. During the final days of debate on the document, Jay left to visit his dying mother. Morris attempted to include a clause that "future Legislatures" take "measures consistent with the public safety, and the private property of individuals, for abolishing domestic slavery." Procedural stonewalling prevented the clause from appearing in the final version, which was adopted hastily and before Jay could return. Jay, on learning of the fait accompli, wrote Morris and Livingston that the constitution was "like a harvest cut before it was ripe"; he had wanted "a clause against the continuation of domestic slavery." That same year, the breakaway republic of Vermont, to New York's east, managed to do what New York had not. Its 1777 constitution included an abolition plan that looked similar to Quaker practice: it freed adult men and women, while permitting masters to hold boys in service until 21 and girls until 18.[66]

Unsurprisingly, the first major legislative breakthrough occurred in Pennsylvania. In 1779, assemblyman George Bryan introduced a bill for gradual abolition. The text itself had been drafted, or at least heavily influenced, by a Quaker lawyer named William Lewis. As lawmakers considered the proposal, Benezet visited every member of the legislature to urge its adoption.[67] In 1780, Pennsylvania became the first state in the nation whose elected officials passed a gradual abolition act. It decreed that any child born of a slave would work as a servant for his mother's master until age 28 in the same manner as "servants [are] bound by indenture" and receive "like freedom dues." Any master wishing to abandon a child could place him or her with the overseers of the poor to be bound like other pauper children.[68]

The rule that children serve until 28 in Pennsylvania would not have pleased those who believed the Golden Rule dictated that black servant children not serve longer than white counterparts. All the state legislatures that passed gradual abolition acts confronted this problem. In 1784 in Connecticut, lawmakers ruled that "no Negro or Molatto Child" shall "be held in servitude, longer than until they arrive to the Age of twenty-five Years." Rhode Island's 1784 act came closer to the Quaker model. It stipulated that the "children declared free" should "remain with their mothers a convenient time" after birth; the mothers' masters would receive funds from their towns to "support such children," provided, however, that "town councils may bind out such children as apprentices" until 18 and 21. A year later, lawmakers repealed the clause requiring that towns support freeborn children and ruled instead that children be "maintained by the owner of the mother" until 21. All of these laws bear evidence of clashes among legislators, masters, local governments, and state governments.[69]

There is no question that these acts were designed to be slow in effect. They were also the first successful abolition laws passed in the hemisphere. Elected legislatures agreed to strip citizens of what had long been considered private property in an effort to address a moral wrong. In so doing, they drew on long and established traditions of child servitude.[70]

Both pro- and antislavery Americans took notice. Among the impressed was Jay. On a diplomatic mission to Spain when the Pennsylvania law passed, Jay wrote to Egbert Benson, the New York attorney general: "An excellent law may be made out of the Pennsylvania one for the gradual abolition of slavery. . . . I would prepare a bill for the purpose with great care."[71]

Jay's views on abolition are worth contemplating not only because of his role as a significant political figure, but because of his choices and self-conception as an antislavery slave owner. He was one of a recognizable type: an elite, well-educated master who embraced conservative abolition policy. A critical mass of New York slaveholders like Jay eventually made gradual abolition in the state possible. Their votes secured legislative enactment. Just as crucial, their efforts in their local jurisdictions ensured that the legislative plan worked, albeit imperfectly, on the ground. From Jay's perspective, gradual abolition balanced "justice due to the [slaves], with the justice due to their masters, and with the regard due to the actual state of society."[72]

Jay and his ilk's personal relationships with slavery informed their policy preferences.

Jay implemented emancipation schemes in his household before state laws required him to do so. In 1784, he manumitted an adolescent named Benoit, whom he had purchased en route to Europe in 1779, explaining that after "Benoit shall have served me until the value of his services amount to a moderate compensation of the money expended for him, he shall be manumitted." He executed a similar plan for a mother named Dinah and her child, Mary. Jay sold Dinah's labor to a rope maker for nine years, after which she would be free, and required Dinah's master to raise Mary in a "Christian-like" manner, teaching her to read and write.[73]

As he supervised his own household's gradual abolition program, Jay worried about elderly slaves. In a letter to his nephew and protégé, Peter Jay Munro, Jay insisted that the family care for a woman called Old Mary, who had been enslaved by the family since Jay was a boy: "I requested your particular attention to Old Mary, and desired you to make her comfortable (in case those who ought to do it, should not) at my expense. . . . If she should suffer I should be hurt and mortified."[74] Jay's acknowledgement that those "who ought" to take care of elderly slaves did not always do so squares with evidence that masters sometimes abandoned "decrepit" slaves.[75] Jay's paternalistic sense of mutual duties and obligations—Mary provided service, Jay would give her care—is telling. He maintained his right to make decisions for his dependents.

Jay's views on race are likewise revealing. While he did not believe that all men should occupy equal social positions, Jay did not embrace an ideology of black inferiority or racial exclusion from civic life. In 1785, he wrote Benjamin Rush: "I wish to see all unjust and all unnecessary discriminations everywhere abolished, and that the time may soon come when all our inhabitants of every colour and denomination shall be free and equal partakers of our political liberty." Views like Jay's would inform a variety of consequential legal and political debates over race and citizenship in New York well into the nineteenth century.[76]

Jay's personal experiences help explain why he embraced laws that centered on children and failed to free adult or elderly slaves. He and his peers were intent on forcing owners to do something minimally morally imperative while at the same time saving taxpayers from assuming the care of old or sick slaves. These legalistic men could insist that they were not interfering with existing private property (children not yet born were not yet property, the antislavery side of the argument went), and, more to the material point, they could pass laws that allowed masters to maintain ownership over healthy adults whose labor and market value was most lucrative.[77]

In sum, even for those reformers who thought slavery was counter to the Golden Rule or to the spirit of the Revolution, regulating the labor of dependents or the poor was not, in itself, objectionable. Lawmakers and abolitionists who promoted abolition schemes built around the service and training of black children understood "freedom" as a variegated category allowing for different privileges to be ascribed to different ranks. This was not a strange concept in the eighteenth century. "Free" did not mean "equal" in the early nation. "Free" could encompass rather stringent limitations, and being free did not mean one was due the full complement of existing liberties. In a world where dependents—women, children, paupers, indentured servants, hirelings—were simultaneously "free" and bereft of many social and political rights, men like Jay could define freedom for slaves in constricted terms and still call it "freedom" without having to wrestle with wider conceptual inconsistencies or dismantle other existing hierarchies.[78]

The question was not, therefore, whether it was illogical or anomalous, in the late eighteenth century, to suggest that freedom for black children born to enslaved mothers would look very different from the freedom enjoyed by a property-owning white adult male. Instead, the question was whether these black children, who were born free, poor, and naturally incapacitated by their age, would be allowed to strive for equal, independent, and autonomous adulthood. Would they be permanently dependent? Would race factor into their social and legal status? Could they become equal citizens? These were the vexing and ongoing questions.

* * *

Despite the fact that several northern states abolished slavery during the Revolutionary era, New York lagged behind. Slavery continued to grow both in the absolute number of slaves and in prevalence across white social classes in the years after the war. Between 1790 and 1800, the enslaved population of New York City rose by 22 percent, and the number of slaveholders increased by 33 percent. In Kings, Queens, and Richmond Counties, 39.5 percent of households owned human beings. The average number of slaves in a household, however, was smaller than in the southern colonies.[79]

In consequence of the state's slaveholding diversity, New York's legislators represented various constituencies for whom slavery was important.

Dutch-descended New Yorkers, many of whom lived in the Hudson Valley and Long Island, were known for their adherence to slavery—although they were hardly alone. There were also emerging party differences. Federalists (Jay's party) were more associated with antislavery than their rival Republicans, but lawmakers crossed the party divide in both directions. Given slavery's prevalence in many parts of the state, there were few calls in the eighteenth century for immediate emancipation. Every abolition bill drafted in the legislature between 1784 and 1799 assumed the program would proceed gradually, that it would focus on children, and that the overseers of the poor would play a role.[80]

As the legislature spent years debating abolition, some black New Yorkers continued to find their own routes to freedom. Men, especially, negotiated conditional manumissions and self-purchase agreements, in which they promised to "work faithfully" for a term of years in exchange for eventual manumission or earn wages in what spare time they had in order to buy themselves. Some parents purchased family members this way. Black patriot veterans—dozens? hundreds?—established independent free households. The free population also included slaves whose owners who had manumitted them in their wills. Some masters declared themselves so genuinely moved by the revolutionary rhetoric of liberty that they freed slaves voluntarily.[81]

Each individual antislavery success could destabilize the institution just a bit more on that street, in that neighborhood, on that farm. That said, only a minority of the state's slaves could wrest freedom for themselves. Options differed dramatically depending on age, gender, and residence. In some rural areas, slavery looked as grim and ubiquitous in the 1780s as it had for decades. Enslaved people always looked for ways to improve their lives and their family's lives—always looked for freedom or security on their own terms—but it would be easier, if not easy, to pursue such goals as the state began to pass increasingly substantial antislavery laws.

The legislative fight for gradual abolition began in February 1784, when state senator Ephraim Paine introduced a bill "Declaring the freedom of the persons therein mentioned." Paine was a doctor from Oblong, the section of Dutchess County where Quakers had enacted abolition among themselves in the 1760s and '70s. After learning of Paine's effort, Quaker leaders petitioned the legislature to support the bill. They were disappointed when lawmakers postponed the bill until the next session. A year later, in February 1785, Paine made his second attempt. The senate and the assembly both received a petition from Edmond Prior, the clerk of the New York Yearly Meeting, "complaining that Africans are continued in a state of bondage."[82]

The 1785 Quaker petition explained their "ardent concern for the general good of our fellow creatures," who deserved "their natural and inalienable rights without distinction." The petitioners objected to manumission laws held over from the colonial era that operated "to the discouragement" of "conscientious" New Yorkers who wanted to free their slaves. They believed "the entire abolition of Slavery to be a matter worthy of most serious attention." The Quakers reminded lawmakers of the Golden Rule. The legislature also received a proslavery petition from constituents in Kings County, "praying the bill for manumitting negroes may not pass into law." Another proslavery petition, from Ulster County, included detailed arithmetic about how expensive it was for masters to raise the children of enslaved women because children could not pay for their own upkeep through their labor until around age 8. Abolition, even of the gradual sort, was not going to come easily.[83]

An assembly committee charged with addressing the Quaker petition recommended a bill that would free all slaves born since July 4, 1776, as well as "all that may hereafter be born within this State." The committee also recommended allowing masters to free slaves "without giving the security now required" unless the slave "be maimed or a cripple." In essence, the proposed law would free children age 9 and younger as well as future children born to enslaved mothers; presumably, all affected children would be bound until adulthood. The assembly subsequently dropped the 1776 idea, but kept the rest. Meanwhile, the senate passed its own "act for the gradual abolition of slavery" and sent it to the assembly for consideration.[84]

The ensuing legislative debate revealed the competing goals of various stakeholders. The assembly consented to parts of the senate bill, approving the clause declaring that future children of enslaved mothers would "be free born" and agreeing that the children would remain in the "capacity of a servant" and be "entitled to the remedies provided for indented servants" by state law until the girls reached 22 and the boys 25. Masters would teach both sexes how to read and boys how to write, as well as provide a Bible and clothes on release.[85]

Members of the assembly then proposed amendments. The first came from Comfort Sands, a slave owner from New York City whose wealth derived from the West Indian trade. Sands proposed that masters be permitted to give freed children (because children were expensive to support) to the overseers of the poor, who "shall bind and put out such." The proposal did not pass. The assembly agreed, however, to three amendments curtailing black citizenship rights. First, Albany slave owner Peter W. Yates added a provision forbidding any black person from holding public office. Second, he added a clause denying free black men the vote. Third, the assembly agreed to an unnamed lawmaker's proposal that "if any negro, mulatto, or mustee, shall marry any white person," he or she would be fined one hundred pounds. The senate rejected all three amendments. After negotiation, the assembly prevailed on disfranchisement but relinquished the clauses against office holding and interracial marriage. In arguing over the rights of freed children, legislators combined longstanding concerns about poverty with newer concerns about who was eligible for republican citizenship.[86]

With the senate and assembly in agreement, the bill seemed likely to become law. The final hurdle was approval by the Council of Revision. Comprising the governor, the chancellor, and varying justices of the state supreme court, the council's duty was to vet and revise proposed legislation. In this instance, Governor George Clinton, Chancellor Robert R. Livingston, and Justice John Sloss Hobart considered the bill "improper." Livingston wrote:

> The last clause of the bill enacts that no negro, mulatto or mustee shall have a legal vote in any case whatsoever, which implicatively excludes persons of this description from all share in the Legislature, and those offices in which a vote may be necessary, as well as from the important privilege of electing those by whom they are to be governed. The bill having in other instances placed the children that shall be born of slaves in the rank of citizens, agreeable both to the spirit and letter of the Constitution, they are as such entitled to all the privileges of citizens, nor can they be deprived of these essential rights without shocking those principles of equal liberty which every page in that Constitution labors to enforce.[87]

The council's belief that the state constitution did not recognize racial difference comported with the views of figures like Jay. Such views were by no means universal—there were plenty of flagrantly racist New Yorkers—but they were sustained in enough quarters to make a lasting difference, especially as black people themselves, in subsequent years, insisted that New York honor the better parts of the state's earlier legal and political history.

The council sent the abolition bill back to the legislature for reconsideration. The senate succeeded in mustering a two-thirds majority to override the council's negative, many of them likely assuming that the best chance of passing the bill relied on allowing the assembly to keep their disfranchisement clause. The assembly, however, did not muster two thirds. The bill failed.

At the end of the session, perhaps as a form of consolation, the legislature passed a law that addressed other aspects of the Quaker petition. The act forbade anyone from bringing slaves into the state for sale. The penalty for breaking the law was the slave's freedom. It also liberalized manumission rules, permitting masters to free any enslaved person under age 50 as long as the person was of "sufficient Ability to provide for themselves" according to the overseers of the poor. Although this act did not have the sweeping consequences of a gradual abolition law, these were early moves by the state to limit the property rights of slaveholders and to provide some enslaved people new routes to freedom.[88]

* * *

During the same winter weeks that state lawmakers argued over the abolition bill, a group of well-heeled Quakers and prominent patriots founded the New York Manumission Society in New York City. Of the nineteen men gathered at the first meeting in January 1785, twelve were Quaker. Their mission, "as free Citizens and Christians," was "to endeavor by lawful ways and means, to enable" slaves "to Share, equally with us, in civil and religious Liberty." At the second meeting—which happened to be the same day that Ephraim Paine reintroduced his abolition bill in the senate—a larger group of thirty-two created a constitution. At the third meeting, John Jay was elected president of the society. The early membership included well-known politicians, jurists, and patriots, including Alexander Hamilton, Egbert Benson, James Duane, Robert Troup, Alexander McDougall, Hercules Mulligan, Melancton Smith, James Kent, and Peter Jay Munro. The Quakers, however, did much of the day-to-day work: Samuel Franklin was vice president, John Murray Jr. was treasurer, John Keese was secretary, and William Shotwell was standing committee secretary. During the Society's first forty years, 251 of its 454 members were Quaker.[89]

Historians tend to see the Society, with its famous founding fathers in leadership, as the first driving force in antislavery politicking and lawmaking in New York. This tendency obscures the significance of earlier and ongoing Quaker activities. In fact, one reason the new society was able to get to business so quickly was precisely because of the work that had been done before the organization existed. As the black abolitionist William Hamilton explained, the state's Quakers "were the first to enter their protest against the deadly sin of slaveholding." Quakers had "passed [their own] laws; first forbidding its members from holding slaves for life, next forbidding the use of slaves altogether."[90]

That said, once the Manumission Society formed, there is no question that it played a vital role in the progress and trajectory of antislavery lawmaking and legal administration. In the early republic, associations like the Society inhabited an energetic civic space between the public and the private, inserting themselves regularly into state lawmaking and at times even serving as arms of the government. Indeed, public authorities often relied on private entities for information, infrastructure, and enforcement. Precisely because the Society included some of the most elite lawyers, judges, and politicians in New York, as well as Quakers who donated reams of time operating subcommittees that performed work that would later be assumed by the state, we should see the Society as more than just a private charitable organization (although it was that, too).[91]

The Society embarked on three major projects in its early months. First, the standing committee petitioned the legislature for "an Act for the gradual abolition of Slavery." It is unclear whether the petition reached the legislature before or after the Council of Revision's negative on the existing bill.[92] Second, the Society distributed two thousand copies of Samuel Hopkins's updated *Dialogue on Slavery* to state and national lawmakers.[93] Third, it founded the African Free School, an institution to prepare black children for citizenship and nonmenial labor. The school's mission echoed some of the logic of gradual abolition, for it supposed that paternalist white men would train black children for freedom. What made its mission distinct, however, was the notion that the students' freedom would be defined by access to intellectual and civic equality. By this logic, gradual abolition could be fashioned as an apprenticeship for republican citizenship, designed for the very group of freedpeople who were the right age to be apprentices and young enough, and thus malleable enough, to be trained in good civic habits.[94]

The Manumission Society was two years into its work when several dozen prominent patriot leaders met in Philadelphia in the summer of 1787 to draft a new constitution for the United States. The existing Articles of Confederation, in their view, were not working. The delegates at the 1787 constitutional convention had many, and often conflicting, priorities and agendas. Some of their debates concerned the present and future status of slavery in the nation. Most salient for black New Yorkers, the delegates' final draft, ratified by the states in 1788, implicitly left the legality of slavery and abolition in any given state up to the state itself. The new constitution permitted Congress to abolish the international slave trade if it wanted to, but not until 1807. It also declared that representatives in the lower house of Congress, as well as direct taxes, would be apportioned among the states according to the whole-number free people, including those bound to service for a term of years (i.e., servants), and "three fifths of all other persons" (i.e., slaves). In recognition of the growing number of antislavery laws in northern states, the constitution included a fugitive slave and servant clause ruling that: "No person held to service or labour in one state, under the laws thereof, escaping into another, shall, in consequence of any law or regulation therein, be discharged from such service or labor."[95]

During the final weeks of the convention, the Manumission Society decided to compose a petition to the Philadelphia delegates that would "promote the attainment of objects of this Society." A committee, including Jay, prepared a petition, but the Society "being informed that it was probable the Convention would not take up the Business resolved not to send the same."[96] The Society was likely correct that its pleas would have fallen on deaf ears.

The Society's lackluster attempt to influence the federal convention is telling, especially during a year when members were otherwise so deeply committed to pursuing antislavery projects. Indeed, these reformers tried much harder at the state level. It is not that antislavery actors never tried to push the national government to take action on slavery—they did—but in a young nation where many were skeptical of centralized federal power, where southern states made very clear they were committed to protecting slavery, where proslavery northern interests persisted, and where the states retained enormous control over their populations' everyday lives, abolitionists spent most of their energy in their local arenas. In the very early republic, the state was where the most intense antislavery action occurred.[97]

For the Manumission Society, petitioning the state legislature, distributing literature, enforcing antislavery laws already on the books, and building the African Free School were interlocking endeavors aimed at bolstering support for gradual abolition. In 1788, after two years of lobbying, the Society successfully pushed for a state law prohibiting the export of slaves for sale, thus adding to the existing anti-import law.[98] With this goal accomplished, they tried again for a gradual abolition law. In 1790, assemblyman Matthew Clarkson, a member of the Society, introduced a bill, but it was easily defeated.[99] The Society's hopes were raised, however, when Jay ran for governor as a Federalist in 1792.

Jay's antislavery views were a factor in his campaign against the popular incumbent George Clinton, a Republican from the western Hudson Valley. Clinton, a prosperous land speculator, lawyer, and slave owner, was married to Cornelia Tappen, whose father was a Dutch-descended slave owner with substantial land in Ulster County. Clinton was on record as vaguely antislavery, but he was far less committed than Jay. He did next to nothing in his long career to promote abolition, nor did he join the Manumission Society.[100] As the race progressed, Jay's friends fretted over whether his position would hurt or help. Egbert Benson wrote Peter Van Schaack that Jay's abolitionism "will in some parts of the state operate against him, but I have hope that this will be counterbalanced by the interest and influence of the Quakers." One warned Jay directly: "It is said that it is your desire to rob every Dutchman of the property he possesses more dear to his heart, his slaves; that you . . . wish further to oblige their masters to educate the children of those slaves in the best manner."[101] Jay narrowly and controversially lost the election.

In 1795, Jay ran again and won, a victory that put necessary political power behind the fight for a successful abolition law. When the new legislature gathered in the winter of 1795–1796, Jay's Federalist ally James Watson introduced a bill in the assembly. This was the same session in which John Addison of Ulster County made his lengthy proslavery speech. Although the 1796 bill failed, the debates surrounding it exposed just how important the details were to the various factions. These details are crucial to understand, for they mattered deeply to the black children and families whose lives would be affected by the bill that eventually passed in 1799.

During the 1796 session, proslavery assemblymen succeeded in attaching amendments to Watson's bill stipulating that children born of slaves would not be born free but rather remain as slaves until young adulthood. Further, the assembly suggested that the state remunerate masters when these children were released because it was "unconstitutional" to deprive "citizens" of "their property." Thus, the only time the state seriously considered compensating masters at the end of a child's term of service coincided with the only time an abolition bill stipulated that these children would not be free at birth. The bill tacitly acknowledged that were children born free, masters would not be eligible for such compensation. Both the 1785 bill and the eventual 1799 law made clear that children born to enslaved mothers would not be slaves at birth. As he tracked the wrangling over the 1796 bill, Charles Adams wrote his father, Vice President John Adams, that "people [in this case, masters] do not like to be forced to be generous."[102]

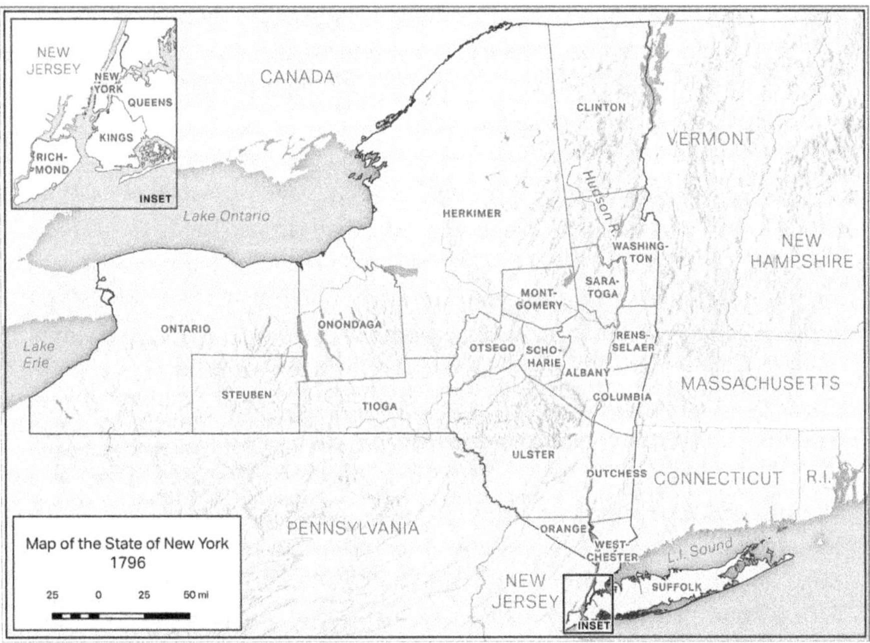

Figure 4. County Map of the State of New York, 1796. Map by Dan Miller. In 1796, when John Addison of Ulster County and his fellow proslavery assemblymen defeated the gradual abolition bill in the state legislature, there were twenty-two counties in New York State. The legislature created Steuben County that year. In 1798, Oneida, Rockland, and Chenango were added, west of the Hudson. The newer counties sent representatives to the state legislature who helped form the antislavery majority that passed the gradual abolition bill in 1799.

As we know from the Shawangunk Society for Apprehending Slaves, some black New Yorkers were keenly aware of what was happening in the 1796 legislature and how new laws might affect them. Their determined belief that the legislature was on their side made life more difficult for their owners and gave lie to any notion that they were not interested in freedom. The aforementioned William Hamilton, who worked as a free carpenter in New York City, wrote Governor Jay to express these sentiments explicitly. Explaining he was "a native of New York," Hamilton lamented that New York was not a "free state with respect to the negroes." He asked Jay to support antislavery measures. He also summoned the Golden Rule. Although Shawangunk's tenacious slaves and Hamilton's claims for liberty could not on their own achieve an abolition law, their actions nonetheless discredited slavery at a time when lawmakers were trying to do the same in the formal political sphere. This dynamic, which would grow increasingly powerful in the years ahead, put slave owners on the defensive.[103]

In 1798, several freshman assemblymen were elected from newly formed counties in western New York with substantial antislavery constituencies. With Jay still in office, the prospects for abolition were strong. The 1798 assembly agreed to a bill declaring that children would be born free but remain as servants until adulthood. Masters who did not want to support freeborn servant children could abandon them with the overseers of the poor as pauper children were. No master would be compensated directly for property loss.[104]

With this framework settled, the assembly discussed poor law and its associated taxes. The legislators added a clause clarifying that black children's settlement would be determined by where the mother's master lived. This rule followed the logic of the state's 1788 poor law, which declared that "every bastard child" inherited the settlement of "his or her mother" (in common law,[105] by contrast, children's settlement followed the father). They rejected a suggestion that free black people "in each town" annually pay "one dollar towards" the "support of the free black poor." They also rejected a clause making the state financially responsible for dependents freed by the act.[106] In sum, lawmakers preoccupied themselves with the question of who would bear responsibility for the economic disruptions of emancipation—the local government, the state government, masters, or black New Yorkers themselves. In this regard, New York lawmakers joined a larger conversation occurring throughout the emancipating Northeast.[107]

Proslavery assemblyman Samuel Ten Broeck, a member of the subcommittee working on the bill, was among those worried about paying higher taxes. Like many of his Columbia County constituents in the eastern Hudson Valley, Ten Broeck was a Dutch-descended slaveholder.[108] He voted consistently against the bill, but as various portions of it passed, he maintained that the state, and not local towns, should pay for supporting young black servant children. After the session ended with the bill stalled in the senate, Ten Broeck wrote a private letter demonstrating resignation over the bill's eventual passage and his unease over who would bear the costs of raising black children. "The greatest objection I have to the bill," he explained, "is that the expences arising on such as are to [be] liberated by this bill is to be defrayed by a partial tax whereas I think it ought to be equally born by all taxable inhabitants of the state."[109] He wanted to ensure that localities with high slaveholding, like his home district, would be spared higher poor rates by requiring low-slaveholding areas to subsidize the cost.

When the next session convened in 1799, an antislavery slaveholder from New York City, assemblyman John Swartwout, introduced the bill anew. The press covered the ensuing debates closely.[110] The senate decided that the state would be responsible for "any person who shall become free by virtue of this act [who] shall become chargeable"—a departure from traditional poor law funding. Ten Broeck got his wish.[111]

In March 1799, Jay and the Council of Revision approved an "Act for the gradual abolition of slavery." In the end, the law was an amalgam of eighteenth-century poor laws, slave laws, and servant laws—it looked very much like what Quakers had been proposing for children for over a hundred years, except that Quakers would not have approved that girls had to serve until 25 and boys until 28. Local overseers of the poor were put in charge of managing black children's indentureships. Local clerks would file birth certificates for each freeborn child; any master who neglected to file a certificate would be fined, with the proceeds funneled to poor maintenance. Should masters wish to abandon freeborn children, the overseers would bind out the child "on the same terms and conditions that the children of paupers were subject to." Masters were required to support any newborn child for a year before abandonment. After this year, the overseers would pay the assigned master a monthly fee (reimbursable by the state) for supporting the pauper child, as was long traditional for white children. The law placed no restrictions on black office holding, marriage, or voting. Without expressly addressing the issue, the law seemed to allow free black children the equal privileges of state citizenship.[112]

* * *

In August 1799, one month after New York's gradual abolition law went into effect, Janet Montgomery, the widow of Revolutionary War hero General Richard Montgomery, corresponded with the town clerk of Rhinebeck in Dutchess County. She registered the birth of a child named John, born to an enslaved mother named Margaret. Across the river in Ulster, Joseph Hasbrouck registered Jane; two months later, he registered another child named Frans. In Hempstead, on Long Island, John Hendrickson Jr. reported that "a female black child named Beck" was born "of a Negro Woman my Slave." In New York City, one of the first children registered was Betty, born July 19. Betty's mother was owned by Isaac L. Kip, a well-connected lawyer serving as a clerk for the Court of Chancery. A slave owner of more modest status, a ship chandler, certified that "a male negro child," Thomas, "was born of a slave of mine."[113]

In 1802 and 1804, John Swartwout, the assemblyman who introduced the abolition bill in 1799, followed the requirements of his own law. He registered a "Female Child named Susan" and a "Female Child named Harriot."[114] As Swartwout's example suggests, a critical minority of New York slave owners helped dismantle slavery in their own state. Gradual abolition was in part made possible because of their legislative and public support, but their involvement in the process also meant that their concerns—financial and moral, selfish and selfless—were incorporated into the plans. As with many laws, the 1799 law was the result of compromises, arguments, and concessions made by a range of propertied men with a range of motives.

The 1799 law placed black children on a bridge between bondage and freedom, between poverty and independence, with the assumption that, on reaching adulthood, they would step off on the side of personal liberty. The law was, at heart, an early modern, Quaker-promoted labor law whose design and logic appealed to New York's early republican antislavery politicians. Black work and mobility would continue to be heavily regulated; simultaneously, black children would be granted the most minimal rights a free child might have under the law, with the promise of adult autonomy at an older age than what white children were promised. The antislavery architects of the law, and their reformer allies, saw children as both coercible *and* improvable. There was thus a tension in gradual abolition: forms of servitude would remain, but there was a simultaneous belief among some white antislavery New Yorkers that black children could be educated into independent adults with equal access to the prerogatives of citizens. Black parents, mentors, ministers, and teachers would seize the openings presented by the gradual abolition law to create better lives for the children in their care.

Black New Yorkers whose lives were changed by the 1799 law were largely unimpressed by its gradualist, conservative features. They tugged on every possible string to make slavery unravel faster than the law intended. Gradual abolition thus proceeded more quickly than the original law suggested it would. There was only so much an abolition act could do to implant an early modern regulatory structure on a population who had so little invested in preserving a colonial past defined by their enslavement.

CHAPTER 2

"To Be Born Free" . . . and Bound

The 1799 Gradual Abolition Law and Its Consequences

In March of 1825, an eighteen-year-old black servant girl named Betsey Meserole reported to the New York Manumission Society that she "is held by Isaac Jacques who lives at no. 29 Pearl Street" and "has had but one month schooling." Later that spring, Charles Hamilton, another black servant, told the Society that he "is claimed by Paul VanDuser of Staten Island," "was born free," and "had been deprived of schooling until 21." Within weeks, Betsey and Charles were, in the words of the Society, "enjoying freedom."[1] Aware of their freeborn servant status, cognizant of the attendant rights, and intent on legal remedy, Betsey and Charles had enlisted the Manumission Society's lawyers to secure their release from service in accordance with New York's 1799 gradual abolition law and its subsequent amendments.[2]

Betsey and Charles were members of the generation of young New Yorkers whose legal status was regulated by the state's gradual abolition laws and corresponding antislavery legislation. The 1799 act granted freedom to children born to enslaved mothers after July 4 of that year with the significant caveat that they serve as bound servants until age 25 if female or 28 if male. A child born under this law was obligated to work and live in the household of his or her mother's master; should this master choose to "abandon" the child, the child would be reassigned to a master chosen by the local overseers of the poor. Between 1801 and 1817, the legislature passed nearly a dozen laws amending, clarifying, or expanding the original set of restrictions and rights set forth in the 1799 act. These new laws were responses to unexpected and transforming conditions on the ground. In most cases, their content was first suggested to legislators by white abolitionists, who themselves were informed and persuaded by the testimony and political organizing of black

New Yorkers. By virtue of this dynamic, black children and their parents took part in shaping gradual abolition law at the same time that gradual abolition law was shaping them.[3]

At first, the daily life of a black child born before July 4, 1799 and a black child born after July 4, 1799 did not look materially different. Both slave and servant were born into service, tied to a master, relegated to menial labor, and vulnerable to violence and family separation. And yet, as the examples of Betsey and Charles demonstrate, there were crucial ways, over time, in which being born a servant was different from being born a slave. A slave could not induce a court to release her from servitude because her master had not taught her to read. A slave could not describe himself, in positive law terms, as "born free." But what did it actually mean to be "born free" *and* bound? What were the broader ramifications of a rolling, law-oriented, age-based emancipation process on the development of free black life and legal definitions of freedom? Gradual abolition laws both did and did not change the lives of black New Yorkers.

Historians sometimes describe black children's status under northern gradual abolition schemes as a form of slavery, emphasizing its indistinguishability from chattel bondage and employing terms such as "statutory slaves" or "slaves for a term" to categorize the status. These scholars have not overstated the brutal conditions these children endured, and this terminology may be especially useful for describing children's experiences in New Jersey and Pennsylvania. But it mattered significantly, if not always immediately, that black children in New York occupied a legal status as freeborn servants. To ignore the distinction is to risk missing how exactly it was that people crafted, used, and transformed the law to unravel slavery. The legal details mattered, and the precise content and application differed from state to state.[4] In New York, the combination of an effective Manumission Society, an influential statewide black voting population, the relevance of antislavery to partisan politics, persistent Quaker activity, and robust black institutional life resulted in a gradual abolition era that was at times more conducive to black freedom and citizenship than in other northern states. The most obvious legislative manifestations of this distinct state culture were the 1810 gradual abolition law, which among other significant clauses reenforced the requirement that servant children be educated by adding a penalty in the form of the child's early release from service, and the 1817 general abolition law, which both lowered the age at which servants left service (21 for both sexes, 18 if not educated) and promised all of New York's slaves their freedom on July

4, 1827. This 1817 act—"general" in the sense that it freed all enslaved New Yorkers on one day—was the only state law of its kind in American history.

The specific legal category applied to black children born during gradual abolition in New York was a status different from slavery, even if it was by no means freedom. The 1799 law altered the traditional relationship between masters and children born to enslaved mothers. Almost everyone concerned knew this—masters, slaves, local officials, judges, politicians, abolitionists, and even many children themselves. Black New Yorkers and their allies sought to make the laws work faster in favor of emancipation and masters sought to cling to their old prerogatives. White New Yorkers exercised considerable control over these developments, but black New Yorkers urged those with greater political power to respond. Indeed, black New Yorkers engaged with the legal system and the ballot box in ways that were hardly intended by lawmakers who had hoped for a slow and contained emancipation process. Despite claims that gradual abolition laws would leave slavery intact where it lay and alter only the status of the newly born, it became impossible to separate the fates of freeborn children from those of their families or to sustain older ways of selling labor and people. The 1799 law ultimately affected the manner in which all black New Yorkers, not just children, approached the meaning of freedom, foiled kidnappings and illegal sales, publicized masters' physical cruelty, negotiated opportunities to protect family and kin, forged relationships among peers, sought formal education, and conceived the rights of citizenship.[5]

Although New York's laws generally applied across the state, there were variations in local operation. A black child's specific experience was affected not only by the particular household into which he or she was born, but by the predilections of local officials, white neighbors, and lower court judges. It was easier for a master to hide awful behavior in a remote and conservative agricultural area than in a waterfront town or city. The New York Manumission Society operated most effectively in New York City, where it was based. At the same time, some rural regions were home to helpful Quakers, small antislavery societies, and sympathetic officials. Moreover, black people sometimes managed to leverage relationships across town and county lines to protect themselves and loved ones. Parents were critical to making gradual abolition's emancipatory potential real for their children.

Individual and collective experiences of freedom were also affected by the fact that the state itself was growing. Between 1790 and 1810, the legislature created twenty-eight new counties and incorporated the cities of Hudson and Schenectady. In 1825, Governor DeWitt Clinton opened the Erie

Canal, an east-west engineering marvel signaling New York's ascendency as the "Empire State." Thus, at the same time New York was emerging as one of the most politically powerful, wealthy, and commercial states in the union, its polity was wrestling with questions of race, freedom, and belonging. For multiple reasons, New York was becoming a place to watch, a state whose history, people, and example would increasingly matter on the national stage.

* * *

The 1799 gradual abolition law had the strange effect of freeing the very human beings who were least able to exercise freedom: newborn children. Their parents, enslaved and poor, found themselves inhabiting two legal categories that gave them no rights over their sons and daughters. Masters would remain in charge. Nevertheless, the state assumed a more intrusive role in the master's world. The hierarchical household retained daily command over black labor and bodies, but not its right to claim babies as chattel property. Every time a black child was born, rule-abiding masters encountered a new role of the law in their households when they certified these free births with town clerks. The three states that had already enacted gradual abolition—Pennsylvania, Rhode Island, and Connecticut—had not initially required this documentation. Details of New York's 1799 law that were less advantageous to slave owners were thus reactions to problems on the ground elsewhere. Pennsylvania's 1780 law, for example, required masters to register slaves, but not servant children born to slaves, which meant that people's lifelong bondage was inscribed on official paper while a new generation's freeborn status was not. Abolitionists wrote each other across state lines sharing information about what was not working, a practice that informed their legislative lobbying.[6]

The birth certificates created a relationship between the child and the state that recognized children's nonslave status. In this guise, the documents precipitated the very slow demise of masters' authority, tipping the balance of power away from the absolute patriarchy of the private white household and signaling to masters and black families that children were now defined differently. At the same time, they legitimated the service relationship, emphasizing how slowly ties would be severed between white masters and coerced black workers.

Town clerk records from over fifty towns across the state suggest that, at least on paper, white New Yorkers understood these children were not slaves.

Almost universally, masters and clerks used different language to describe enslaved parents as opposed to their freeborn offspring. Black parents were called "slaves" or "property"; the word "slave" was almost never used for their children. Masters and clerks often noted a right to the "service" of the child, echoing the familiar legal language characteristic of binding out poor white children.[7]

For example, in 1799, the town clerk of Castleton created what he called "A Town Book Made for Castleton for Entering all the Black Children that are Born of a Slave after the first day of July." A few months later, John Mercereau informed him that "a male negro child named Nicholas" was born, requesting that "the birth of that said child may be entered." In 1800, Thomas Valentine of Yonkers wrote to his clerk "that a certain negro wench slave belonging to me" was "on the first day of May instant, delivered of a male child called William. I do therefore, request, that agreeable to a law of the State of New York, you register the same." In New York City, John Bailey, an ironmonger, wrote that "a certain female child named Till" was born of his "Negro Woman Slave named Luce." In Albany, William Staats declared that, "Jude my negro woman slave was delivered of a male child named Simon to whose services I am entitled." Beekman's clerk recorded that "Tom, a male child of a wench the property of Zachariah Haight was born the 14th of June 1803." In Flatbush, an owner certified, "a free male child named Jack was born on the first day of June."[8]

Another feature of the 1799 law altering the relationship among black children, masters, and the state was the clause providing for abandonment of the child. Masters had long operated under strict laws regulating which slaves they could manumit and which slaves they were financially responsible for should a formerly enslaved person require local resources. Children, of course, would never meet the requirements of self-sufficiency and were therefore rarely if ever legally freed on their own. Officials were already troubled by the expense of pauper white children and had little desire to allow masters to release poor black children into their hands. But now masters could. When the 1799 law declared that freeborn children would be "considered as paupers," black children became, at law, like the most disadvantaged of free white children. This change left black children exposed to family separation within the town where they were born.

Masters took advantage of the clause that allowed them to abandon infants. There were at least two reasons they did so. First, masters often considered black children to be a burden; not until adolescence would their

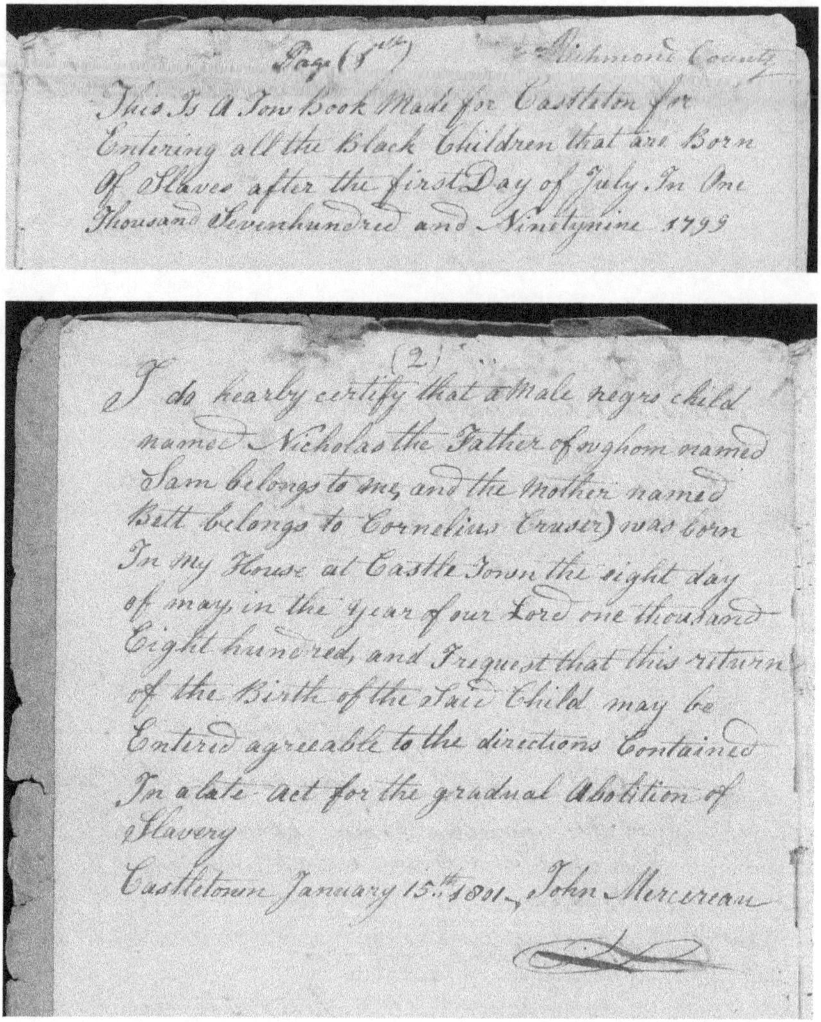

Page (5th) Richmond County

This Is A Town Book Made for Castleton for Entiring all the Black Children that are Born Of Slaves after the first Day of July. In One Thousand Sevenhundred and Ninetynine 1799

(2)

I do hearby certify that a Male negro child named Nicholas the Father of whom named Sam belongs to me, and the Mother named Bett belongs to Cornelius Cruser) was born In my House at Castle Town the eight day of may in the year of our Lord one thousand Eight hundred, and I request that this return of the Birth of the said Child may be Entered agreeable to the directions Contained In a late act for the gradual Abolition of Slavery

Castletown January 15th 1801, John Mercereau

Figure 5. Town Book for Castleton for the Entry of Black Children, 1799–1827. In this book, the town clerk of Castleton, Richmond County, recorded the births of children born to enslaved mothers according to the rules of the 1799 gradual abolition law. The example on page 2, certifying the birth of Nicholas, is a rare instance in which a master included both the mother's and the father's names (Sam and Bett). Courtesy of the New-York Historical Society.

labor be productive enough to balance the cost of their maintenance. Knowing this, legislators allowed masters to give away dependent black children. Second, cunning masters used the provision to "abandon" children and then immediately bind those same children back from the overseers of the poor at the state's expense, receiving the government's monthly allowance until the child reached the age of 4. In some towns, therefore, taxpayers found themselves paying both local taxes to support poor white children in their town as well as state taxes to fund masters binding back black children. The legislature grew weary of the subterfuge, reducing state funding in 1802 and ending the program all together in 1804.[9]

Masters who released black children from service used different language to describe this act than they did to manumit a slave. Masters abandoning children "abandoned rights to the service of said child"; masters manumitting slaves released "rights, title, and property of said slave." Thus, there was an on-paper distinction made between owning labor and owning a body. This language was echoed across the state, despite minor variations in local practice. For example, Jacob Bleeker of Albany abandoned his "right to the service of a female child of a Negro Woman Slave."[10] Thomas Storm of New York wrote "that I abandon all my claim of service from the said female child and request a registry of my abandonment agreeably to law."[11] By contrast, slaves in manumission documents were legally construed as chattel. In 1802, Simon Van Antwerp recorded that he did "manumit set free and release from slavery my female slave Sara . . . and absolutely relinquish and release all my right title and property."[12] These abstract distinctions in language might seem trivial, but the words reflected a contemporary understanding that while a servant and a slave were both dependent laborers, there were distinct rights and processes attached to each status that could at times matter deeply to that individual.

In order for town officials to receive state support for abandoned black children, local overseers of the poor, justices of the peace, supervisors, or town clerks were required to present audited accounts to the state treasurer. These records provide further evidence of how children's legal identity was understood—indeed, created—in practice. For example, the overseers of the poor in North Hempstead submitted a receipt for the "Board and maintenance of Betty a female black child (free born) the daughter of Suke a female slave of the said Daniel Whitehead Kissam (she being four years old) . . . 2 dollars per month." In Newburgh, the clerk certified "the maintenance of a pauper named Jacob abandoned by John McAulay." In New Rochelle, Theodosious

Bartow acknowledged that he received from the overseers "Forty Five dollars in full for the support and maintenance of a Negro Male Child born of my woman slave." In some towns, local officials devised accounting worksheets. Overseers in Orange listed children's names, birthdays, and sexes, as well as "the Names of the Masters of the Mothers of the Children who are also their present keepers." In Northfield, the overseers submitted their list under the heading: "For Boarding and Cloathing the under mentioned Negro Children which are now Living and were Born of Slaves and Abandoned."[13]

The acknowledgment of black children's specific legal status was also reflected in instances when children were assigned to new masters. The 1799 act explained that a master along with "heirs or assigns" was "entitled to the services of such child" in "the same manner as if such child had been bound by the overseers of the poor." Legally, this was a rather confusing statement, for it blended two sets of labor law. Slaves could be sold by one master to another within the state. Traditionally, at common law, apprentices could not be assigned from one master to another, for an apprenticeship was meant to bind a child to one specific master.[14] And yet, white pauper children, occupying the bottom rung on the ladder of white bound labor, were assigned from master to master with some regularity, and sometimes even sold at auction—features of their servitude that made them "saleable."[15] Regardless of whether it was formally legal or simply everyday custom that white paupers were sold back and forth, it is clear that masters could and did sell the labor of black servant children. The documents orchestrating these exchanges generally employed the language of child pauper contracts, not slave sales.

In 1803, for example, Tobias Ten Eyck of Montgomery County sold as an "apprentice" a girl named Bet to Jacob Tise. The person writing the indenture first called two-year-old Bet a "negro wench slave," but was then instructed to cross out the word "slave." (A margin note explains that the word was "erazed before executed.") The document was otherwise written similarly to indenture contracts exchanged between white parents or town officials and a master when white children were apprenticed. Tise would instruct Bet in "housework becoming a negro wench apprentice so as to be as competent hand at Housework as women in general are" and "shall for the space of six months in the said term put the said apprentice to some good English school." Bet would work until 25, the age black female servants were to be released under the 1799 act. Bet's indenture is an example of the ways that black servant children inhabited a legal position removed from slavery, similar to white apprenticeship, but different in key details. Bet's race was inscribed on her labor—"housework becoming a negro wench"—and she would work for more years than a white female apprentice usually would. And yet, like white apprentices, she would be educated at school and in a (so-called) trade, as well as guaranteed "meat, drink, washing, lodging, mending." In similar situations elsewhere in the state, assigned black servant children were bound until 18 and 21, as white children were. The text of the 1799 law was unclear about the age requirements in such circumstances.[16]

That same year, the New York City common council concluded that black servant children were akin to white apprentices and denied that apprentices of *any* color could be assigned. The case involved the attempt by a man named Benjamin Ferris to abandon a black servant child to the overseers of the poor. The problem was that Ferris was not the original master; he did not own the child's mother. Ferris could not, according to the common council's lawyer, abandon the child, because "Children born of slaves after 4th July 1799, are servants to the owner of the mother" as "if bound by the overseers of the poor, and as in case of such binding the trust upon the master is personal, and cannot be legally assigned." Ferris was not "entitled to the Services of the Child."[17] The ruling was in the interest of the city, which was now relieved from assuming care of the child. Motive aside, the common council decided there were limitations on the assignment of child servants.

Across this range of town records—in birth certificates, declarations of abandonment, manumissions, and assignments—children entered local records as "servants," "paupers," "apprentices," or "negro [or "black"] children," but almost never as "slaves." At law, these were distinct labor statuses that stood apart from slavery.[18] While these distinctions may, at first, have been a legal nicety from the perspective of daily life, they demonstrate how the everyday uses of law slowly moved children from one status category into another. As these children grew older, the potential consequences of these legal details could be dramatic. These were the distinctions that allowed Betsey and Charles to legally leave masters who failed to provide schooling. Proof of their freeborn status lay in birth records. Their right to an education was mandated by the state, as was their right to leave service early when their masters faltered.[19]

Masters themselves understood that the 1799 law and its successors weakened their authority—which is why some tried to ignore it. In eastern Long Island, the editors of the *Suffolk Gazette* urged that "the penalties" of not registering children "be enforced," implying that some local masters were cheating. Records from Warwick, Newburgh, and Oppenheim—to cite a few examples from western New York—indicate that some masters did not register children born in the early 1800s until the 1810s, well past the time they were required to.[20] In New York City, masters also neglected to register black newborns with the local clerks. Alerted to the extent of this problem, the Manumission Society explained, "The situation of children born of slaves since the year 1799 loudly calls for the intervention of the Society [for] but a small part of the births are duly registered. They therefore cannot but look forward with deep concern to the many disputes that must arrive when these children arrive at legal age."[21] The Society wrote to the county clerk, who advised the members take on the "delicate" task of "making every suitable enquiry, with hearing complaints and representing them to me." The clerk's directive was common practice in early republican governance: a state official would entrust a private organization to help enforce public laws. These sorts of partnerships between the state and civil society not only affected the course of gradual abolition in areas where civic society was most robust, but also oriented incipient black organizations toward their own quest for recognition by and communication with the state.[22]

In order to catch noncompliant masters, the Society solicited the help of those New Yorkers most aware of devious masters: slaves and servants. The committee "attended several meetings of the Coloured People on the subject and have placed it now on such ground as to render the liberty of such children more secure." A few months later, the county clerk received the names of fifty unregistered children.[23]

Even though some masters tried to keep slaves and servants in the dark about antislavery laws, black New Yorkers found ways to educate themselves. They made use of communication networks across kitchens, alleyways, ship holds, churches, and taverns to foster common knowledge about the evolving rights and remedies available under the state's myriad antislavery statutes. Sojourner Truth, from Ulster County, later reported that she learned of changes in state law by eavesdropping on "the white folks." One of the most intangible but important effects of gradual abolition acts, in both the short and long run, was the tendency they had to increase black consciousness about the uses and malleability of law and of the political and judicial authorities who controlled law's implementation. What black New Yorkers realized in the early republic was that a legal system that for years had worked to ensure their bondage was slowly providing some avenues for authorized escape and civic recognition.[24]

The consequences of black legal acumen could mean a great deal in practical terms. Black adults, often enslaved themselves, used their knowledge to protect children. For example, in 1800, a slave on Staten Island named Jack Parkinson got word to the Manumission Society that his fourteen-year-old daughter, Teeny, and a woman named Hagar were eligible for freedom because their former master had violated state law. The master had taken Teeny and Hagar to New Jersey, where they lived for six years. Subsequently, two New York masters bought Teeny and Hagar, violating the 1788 anti-import law. Teeny died before the Society intervened, but Hagar was freed and reunited with "her child and cloathes." In a similar example, a black mother reported "that her son James who was born since 1799" was in danger of being sold across state lines. James's master, "hearing a representation of the case," agreed to release the boy from the sale. "Representing" the case to a master was a frequent strategy. The Society at times pursued cases in court, but their successes often stemmed from convincing masters they had broken a law and would be better off obeying it. The Society also proved useful in providing personal connections and financial resources. When a father named Caesar Lee reported that his son Daniel was illegally held in New Jersey, Society members contacted a lawyer they knew in Newark who could "issue a writ for his relief." Lee's son was freed.[25]

Parents who were able to reach the Manumission Society were not always successful in rescuing their children, however. Failure was particularly likely when masters had acted cruelly, but not necessarily outside of the law. In 1801, a woman named Matty Pierpoint managed to have someone write a letter to the Society for her, which she signed with her mark. Enslaved in Albany, Pierpoint had given birth to a "sickly" child named Tom well before 1799. She was sold to a new master, but Tom was given to her "to bring up as free" and "although a slave herself," she had "to provide for said male child by procuring a place for his board." Pierpoint was sold again to a master in New York City named Delves, who refused to shelter Tom. Now Delves was trying to claim Tom as a slave, presumably because he was now a healthy older child. The Society wrote Pierpont's former master in Albany to investigate Tom's status. Soon thereafter, the committee reported they could not find sufficient proof of Tom's freedom and had to drop the case. Pierpont, after caring for her sick son during a time no master cared to support him, lost him once the boy had survived long enough to become profitable property.[26]

As Pierpont's story suggests, mothers played an outsized role in advocating for children. During both slavery and gradual abolition, black children's status depended on mothers' status; mothers' masters therefore had legal control over black children, not children's fathers. Black children were thus far more likely to live in their mothers' households, unless both parents labored for the same master. As children grew, they were often employed in domestic labor, which likewise kept them close to women—whose domestic labor was also especially coveted in the commercial North—in intimate household settings. For these reasons, mothers and other women often had information about children's well-being or their whereabouts. These dynamics shed light on why, for example, when the Manumission Society's standing committee reported success on a slew of cases in March 1800, all of the cases involved women and children. This is not to say that men—such as Teeny's father, Jack Parkinson—did not also intervene, but rather that the specific configurations of bondage in New York put women in particularly vital roles.[27]

Children themselves, especially as they grew older, also understood what was at stake and developed language for explaining their status. Consider, for example, the case of Charlotte, the black servant girl who was brought before New York City's court of general sessions when she tried to set her master Samuel Ward's barn on fire in 1811. During initial questioning, Charlotte insisted to the district attorney that despite having a master, she was not a slave. After stating, "I am free" to the grand jury, Charlotte explained that she had been sold to Ward by a Mr. Duncan because she had tried to run away. The district attorney asked her "what right had Mr. Duncan to sell you to Mr. Ward if you [were] free." Charlotte replied, "I am not sold for life. I am sold for a certain number of years only and then to be free."[28] She would serve Ward until she was "a big woman." Charlotte did not deny she set the barn on fire. She had recently absconded from Ward, who had whipped her in punishment. She had also been beaten for another reason: "I did something naughty—I pulled up my petticoats before a little white boy which my mistress had forbidden." The district attorney asked if the beatings prompted the fire. After replying, "I don't know," Charlotte made clear that "I intended to burn it all down." Charlotte was indicted, tried for arson, found guilty, and sentenced to prison for twelve months.[29]

Several months later, a young girl named Rose told a similar story before the same court. Rose, bound to a Mr. Haines, explained that she was nine years old and "a free girl." She had parents living "somewhere in the country" and had not seen her mother since her recent move to the city. Mr. Haines's wife had "struck her with a twig or whip. . . . She took a stump of fire out of the kitchen and carried it into Mr. Haines' stable."[30] Rose's testimony, like Charlotte's, demonstrates the ways in which being a black servant could be as brutal as being a slave. Separated from parents and subject to physical abuse,

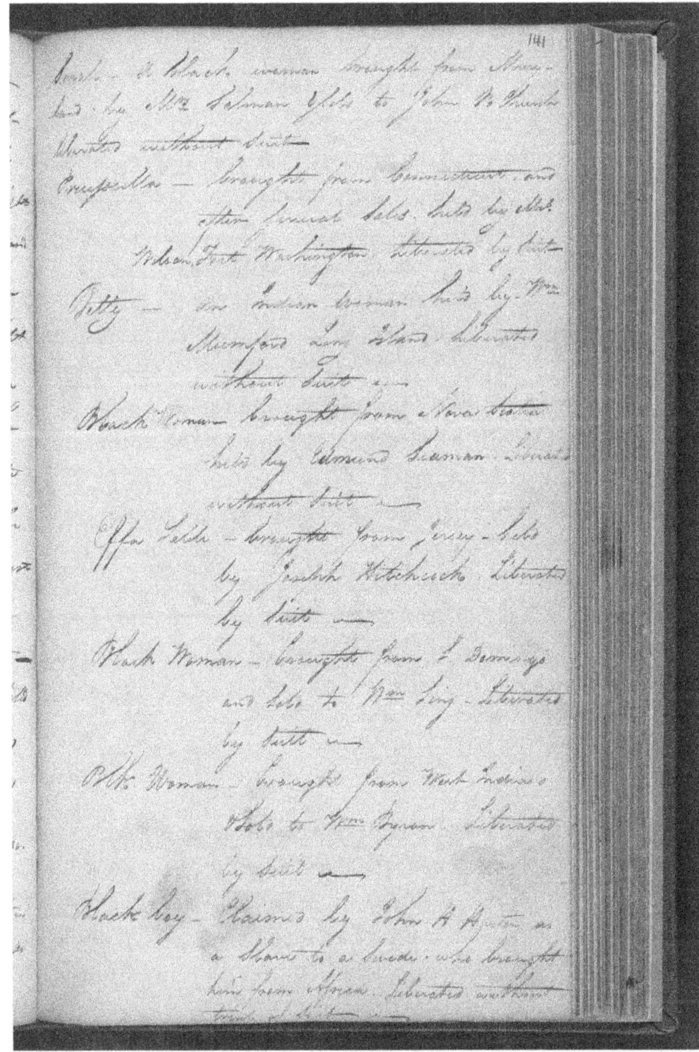

Figure 6. New-York Manumission Society, Volume 7, Standing Committee Minutes, 1791–1807, New-York Historical Society. On this typical page of the Standing Committee minutes, the committee records its work on seven cases involving women and one case involving a child. The Manumission Society interacted with enslaved and free black women and children regularly. Note that the abolitionists resolved some cases "without suit" and some "by suit." Effa Sable and her infant, whose case is noted here, spent years in state courts trying to affirm their freedom. *Sable v. Hitchcock,* 2 Johns. (1800), 79; *Hitchcock v. Sable,* 2 Johns. (1802), 487.

these girls' lives must not have felt particularly "free." But their testimony also indicates that gradual abolition wrought changes in the social and legal experiences of black children. Both girls knew they were born into a status different from slavery. Their awareness was a small form of power, even if it was a weak form compared to the power of the men in the courtroom. Their awareness of the changed rules of their status signaled that the contours of bondage were slowly changing.[31]

In neither Charlotte's nor Rose's case did the outcome of her trial hinge on legal status or knowledge. In other instances, however, this type of generational legal consciousness could alter the course of a life. Young slaves learned how to use import and export laws to free themselves. In 1807, eighteen-year-old Nancy Blake from Philadelphia told the Manumission Society that she was entitled to freedom: "she was born in the family of Elizabeth Cullup in Georgetown, Pennsylvania," was sold to another master in Philadelphia, and then sold once more to a master in New York City. Sold in violation of New York's anti-import laws, Nancy was set free.[32] Of course, these sorts of cases relied on masters breaking the technicalities of state law. The Society's minutes are filled with cases similar to Nancy's in which the hoped-for legal transgression on the part of the master turned out to have been painfully wishful thinking.

* * *

Despite the fact that gradual abolition resulted in some forms of freedom for young black New Yorkers, black people of all statuses remained vulnerable to the worst aspects of chattel bondage. The threat of kidnapping or illegal sale and the perils of violence were particularly acute. What made this time period different from the slave society that preceded it, however, were the growing restrictions around these practices.

Aware of the changing circumstances, antislavery New Yorkers probed the possibilities. Laws on the books since the 1780s forbade the import and export of slaves for sale. The 1799 law turned slave infants into pauper infants. Using these acts as a foundation, black New Yorkers and their white allies not only worked to enforce them, but pressed for additional laws to further circumscribe masters' control. Servants and slaves in and near New York City in particular had a direct effect on the passage of new legislation due to their proximity to the Manumission Society, whose members maintained longstanding connections to the state's political, financial, and legal elite. As black men, women, and children presented their complaints, the Society's members noted patterns of abuse and formed committees to draft and petition for new laws in Albany. They were often successful. In 1807, 1808, 1810, 1813, and 1817, the legislature—comprising men elected, in part, by a growing number of black male voters in New York State—issued new acts at the Society's behest or with its help. In this manner, black protest on the ground and choices at the polls affected statewide law.

Kidnapping and illegal slave trading were among the most glaring problems. As New York became an increasingly free state, resistant masters and fortune hunters tried to turn a profit while they still could. The consequence of this impulse was a rise in the illegal transport of black New Yorkers. Buyers and sellers had particular incentive to trade young (but not infant) servants. Prices for servant children, when assigned as apprentices, were not as high as for young slaves who could be sold elsewhere. Furthermore, whether young or old, free people were easier to transport out of state, because no local master would lose out. If a trader managed to smuggle a child servant, a young slave, or a free black person into the southern or Atlantic slave market, he could fetch a high price for the worker whom he had bought cheaply or stolen in New York.[33]

Masters, ship captains, slave traders, and their agents routinely sneaked black workers out of New York to sell in ports such as Norfolk, Wilmington, Savannah, and New Orleans. In the spring of 1800, the Manumission Society reported that a schooner hiding over twenty black people had recently slipped out of the city without official clearance. A few days later, an "informant" reported an illegal vessel docked at Corlear's Hook. Four Society members, along with Alderman Jotham Post, found three adolescents and a woman locked in the hull. They brought the captives to shore and called an emergency meeting. Following the advice of attorney Peter Jay Munro (John Jay's nephew), the Society sued the two owners of the vessel, the captain, and a fourth man who had enticed two of the victims on board. The penalty for exporting a slave was one hundred pounds and the slave's liberty. Despite the threat of such punishment, white fortune seekers continued to smuggle black victims. As a result, black New Yorkers, particularly children and women, remained at risk of kidnapping and dishonest employment offers.[34]

The Society, with the assistance of the many black dockworkers who labored in the city's port, tried to prevent this smuggling before it happened.

In 1802, they learned that John McCullen from Georgia had purchased a black man named Cato, his wife, and four children and concealed them on a schooner. The Society "brought writs of replevin for the slaves" and the family was "set at liberty." The committee recorded their evidence against McCullen: member Preserved Fish had seen the family brought to the vessel, a sheriff saw McCullen bring them down the dock, the captain knew their passage was engaged, and someone knew the porter (likely a black man) who carried the baggage. The committee decided to reward the sheriff fifteen dollars for his help. The Society may have been composed of elite gentlemen, but they were street-oriented enough to spend time scouting the city's port, developing contacts among laborers, and encouraging and renumerating the antislavery loyalties of the police.[35]

There was also the problem of coerced laborers brought into the state illegally. Slavery was thriving in much of the United States, including in neighboring New Jersey. New Yorkers who wanted slaves tried various tricks to circumvent importation laws. In the prosecution of one such case, Munro represented a New Jerseyan named Fish in the Albany term of the state supreme court. Fish had run away to New York City, where his master caught him and sold his labor for twenty-five years to a new master named Fisher. Was selling a grown man's labor for twenty-five years the same as selling him as a slave? The court thought so. Justice James Kent, the renowned common law jurist—and member of the Manumission Society—reasoned that the sale fell within the purview of New York's anti-import act, noting "no annual or periodical render is reserved, which is the usual incident of letting to hire." In 1805, Munro's cocounsel from *Fish v. Fisher* represented a man named Bartley in a similar case. Bartley had fled his master, "claiming to be free." Relying on *Fish v. Fisher,* the court ruled in Bartley's favor.[36]

Besieged with cases of kidnapping, smuggling, and illegal sales, the Society—not to mention New York's black population—wanted stronger laws. In 1807, the Society consulted its lawyers, a group including future New York City mayor and congressman Cadwallader D. Colden, and drafted model legislation. They proposed no master be allowed to leave the state with a slave without first obtaining proof that the slave was his or hers. Addressing the tendency to smuggle slaves who were conditionally manumitted, the Society suggested "prohibiting the carrying away" of "any person who shall be a slave for a term only." A committee was appointed to accomplish these changes, as well as an act of incorporation for the Society.[37]

The committee had some success. In March 1807, the legislature passed "An Act to amend the Act, entitled 'An Act concerning Slaves and Servants.'" The law made it more difficult for masters to leave the state permanently with their slaves. They could take slaves they had owned for over ten years, and only after licensing this fact with a local official. The act also stipulated that it was illegal for a master "entitled to any slave or servant for a time only" to take such person out of the state permanently; in other words, conditionally manumitted slaves and freeborn servant children had to remain in New York. Captains who transported black people out of the state without a removal license would be fined $250 for each person smuggled.[38]

Motivated by the progress, the Society persisted in its lobbying. Anxious that "the illegal Transportation of slaves is now carried on to an alarming extent from North to South and particularly to New Orleans" and still eager to incorporate the organization, the Society dispatched two members to the 1808 legislative session in Albany. That winter, lawmakers passed "An Act to incorporate the Society" and "An Act to prevent the Kidnapping of Free People of Color," which stipulated that the first offense for kidnapping would be punishable by up to fourteen years in prison, the second offense by a lifetime sentence.[39]

The Society turned next to closing other legal loopholes that perpetuated slavery and to improving conditions for children bound by the 1799 law. The Society's 1810 petition to the legislature proposed measures to curtail the ability of visiting masters to bring their slaves into the state, to outlaw tricky indenture contracts like the one in *Fish v. Fisher,* and to better ensure at least minimal educational opportunities for black servants. In pursuing this last goal, the Society was informed and inspired by the ongoing success of their African Free School. Armed with suggestions, a committee was "instructed to consult those of this Society who are members of the Legislature and others friendly to the cause of Emancipation."[40]

In their push for an updated gradual abolition law, the Society was joined by New York's Quakers. In late 1809, the Yearly Meeting for Sufferings discussed problems in state laws affecting black people. Vowing to advocate the cause of this "oppressed part of the human family," the Friends drafted a petition asking for "legislative interposition" to promote "school learning" among children regulated by the 1799 law. A committee traveled to Albany to meet with lawmakers in person.[41]

The result was a substantial legislative victory in 1810. Passed on March 30, the new gradual abolition law (1) made it illegal for any visiting master to bring his or her slaves into the state for more than nine months without freeing the slaves; (2) declared free any slave speciously "manumitted" in another state and then brought into New York under an "indenture, contract or bond, conditioned for personal service"; and (3) included the education clause stipulating that any servant child not taught to read would be released at age 21.[42]

As essential as the Manumission Society and Quakers were to these improvements, the state's black voters also played a crucial and historiographically underappreciated role in encouraging antislavery legislation.[43] Indeed, black men's participation in elections contributed directly to the passage of laws, such as the 1810 act, that black children and adults used to their advantage. By this means, black voters in New York influenced formal politics to a degree unmatched in other states. Black men did vote elsewhere in the union. But the combination of New York's relatively large free black population and the fact that voters within this population faced comparatively minor challenges at the polls in the early 1800s resulted in especially consequential electoral participation during the height of gradual abolition.[44]

Although black men had voted sporadically in the eighteenth century, their numbers expanded dramatically after the 1799 gradual abolition act. Between 1800 and 1810, the number of free black citizens in the state grew from 10,417 to 25,333. In New York City, the population jumped from 3,499 to 8,137. In Albany, it increased from 157 to 501. In Hudson, there were 194 free black citizens by 1810. Black New Yorkers made up roughly 5 percent of the state population; in some cities and towns, the proportion hovered near 10 percent. Of course, not every black man could vote. The $250 property requirement to participate in gubernatorial and state senate elections was a high bar. But the property requirement for voting in municipal, assembly, and congressional elections—$50—was achievable for many.[45]

Because New York was a state where party politics resulted in tight elections, even a handful of black votes could decide a contest. The Federalists remained the party more closely tied to antislavery, although there were exceptions to this rule of which black voters themselves were well aware. In the cities of New York and Hudson, editors commented on the power of black voters as well as their preference for candidates who promoted antislavery policies. In the process, these editors also recognized the formal citizenship of the growing free population. In 1810, for example, Federalist state senator Jonas Platt from Oneida, a new county west of Albany, earned black voters' loyalty due to his championing of their political rights and his support of that year's updated abolition law. An opponent of Platt's sarcastically noted that "almost every negro" in Hudson "had the honor of voting for" Platt when he ran for statewide office later that year.[46]

Even after April 1811, when the Republican-majority legislature passed a heavily debated race-based "certificate of freedom" law aimed at thwarting black access to the polls, a wide range of black men continued to cast ballots. In other words, despite being forced to bring cumbersome identification to the polls starting that spring, black men continued to turn out. Their Federalist defenders in government and the press encouraged their persistence.[47]

With the stakes so high, it is not surprising that black men made efforts to vote across the state, from remote fishing villages on eastern Long Island, to rocky-soiled mountain towns in far upstate New York, to growing western farmland counties that would soon host the Erie Canal. It is telling, for example, that the small city of Schenectady recorded at least fifty black voters on the rolls; that a father and his young adult son in Castleton, Staten Island, registered to vote the year after the local assembly race had been decided by a single ballot; and that elderly men, stolen from Africa in the early 1700s, let neither worn bodies nor bureaucratic fees stop them from acquiring the necessary certificates. Free black men thus supported black children not only by advocating for boys and girls in their families or neighborhoods, but by choosing the officials who made and enforced the laws. Black electoral might was at its strongest during the precise decade—roughly 1809 to 1819—when antislavery lawmaking was most potent.[48]

In New York City, black men who organized at the polls were the same men supporting black children's education, collaborating with white abolitionists, and running new black civic organizations and churches. The cooper Joseph Sidney, for example, helped voters navigate the certificate rules, stumped for the Federalists, served in the African Society for Mutual Relief and Wilberforce Philanthropic Association, and facilitated relationships with the Manumission Society. John Teasman—an avid Republican despite most black men's preference for Federalists—was former headmaster of the African Free School. In an 1811 speech, Teasman thanked DeWitt Clinton, mayor of New York and former state legislator, for helping the African Society for Mutual Relief receive its charter from the state government. Thomas Sipkins, an established business owner who ran a granary, was a founding trustee of the city's African Methodist Episcopal Zion Church; he was also the father of Henry Sipkins, an emerging abolitionist leader. The elder Sipkins helped

Henry acquire his voting paperwork. All of these men knew that their votes mattered to the course of abolition in their state.[49]

It is easiest to trace black men's multipronged abolitionist efforts in New York City, home to the state's largest free black population, but black voters in quieter rural districts also created space for black children to pursue freer lives than they did. Reuben Reeve, a tenacious father on the North Fork of eastern Long Island, is one example. Born enslaved in 1757 in Southold, Reeve labored in a long-colonized agricultural and fishing area more culturally and commercially associated with coastal Connecticut and Rhode Island than with the rest of New York. He was passed back and forth among local members of the white Reeve family until 1794. In 1807, Reuben published an advertisement in the *Suffolk Gazette* explaining that he was "a stout able-bodied black man" who had been "set free from slavery by Mr. Joseph Reeve" and "would be glad to be hired for six or eight months, at any kind of farming business." He had "never had a settlement" of his own. By 1810, however, he had acquired property and began to vote. Nicknamed "Reuben the Lawyer," he held on to his hard-won gains. In 1825, he transferred his land to his son, Elymas, who had also been enslaved by the Reeve family. Elymas, who could read and write, was a devoted member of the local Presbyterian Church. With his equally pious wife Hagar, he raised a free family of eight children on the property his father had acquired. One of Elymas and Hagar's sons, John B. Reeve, graduated from Columbia University and Union Theological Seminary; he later founded the theological department at Howard University. One of their granddaughters, Josephine Silone Yates, became president of the National Association of Colored Women's Clubs and a college professor. Reuben, the Reeve paterfamilias, may have been utterly unknown outside of Southold, but his work, persistence, smarts, and voting lay a foundation that permitted his descendants to go places and do things that he never could.[50]

When men like Reuben Reeve insisted on voting, they had both current and future generations of children in mind. The laws they saw passed by their legislature in the early 1800s may not have been perfect, but they nonetheless mattered to ordinary people's lives, especially when black people could make use of the half-measures available. On March 20, 1811, for example, the Manumission Society reported that a woman named Mary and her three children had been living in New York with their New Jersey owner, Captain Robert Dunn, since May 11, 1810. Dunn stood in violation of the new "nine months rule." A few weeks after Mary got word to the Society, she and her children were "free, according to the 1st section of law of this state, passed March 30, 1810." There is almost no chance that Reeve knew of Mary, but a man nicknamed "the Lawyer" would likely have felt a degree of satisfaction that the three assemblymen from his county had voted in favor of the 1810 law that freed her family.[51]

Small, piecemeal victories for people like Mary Dunn and her children, however, stood alongside cases where abolitionists had to record that they could provide "no relief." In particular, black workers continued to face "cruel and inhuman conduct." Flooded with tales of abuse, the Manumission Society began during this decade of ameliorative lawmaking to "collect all cases of inhuman treatment" in order to send them to the "Legislature for their interposition by passing an act punishing the offender in some exemplary manner." Despite some success in punishing masters via individual court cases, legislation on the subject proved elusive and violence remained rife. Women and children were particularly vulnerable, not only because of their comparative physical defenselessness, but because they often worked as domestics. Enclosed in tight urban spaces or laboring in farmhouses, they faced the wrath of master and mistress. Black men, by contrast, often worked at sea or on the docks, along the rivers or in fields, or in occupations that took them outside as tubmen, cartmen, or chimney sweeps.[52]

For all the cases of cruelty that the Society encountered, the brutality of evangelical minister Amos Broad and his wife Demis stood out to its members and the public at large. The usually phlegmatic Standing Committee called the Broads "monsters" in their account.[53] After learning that Broad "abuses his black woman and her child very much," four Society members were dispatched to investigate the case, rather than the usual two. At the Society's behest, the district attorney filed two indictments for assault, one each against husband and wife.[54]

The records in the grand jury testimony are harrowing. White neighbors and servants testified that Broad whipped Betty with "birch rods, after having forced her to strip herself entirely naked" and "turned her out" in "very cold weather." He rubbed her child Sarah's "face on the carpet until it bled" and kicked her "in the stomach." In another instance, he "took the child by the ear and carried it a considerable distance." Sarah's "feet were frosted" and "her ankles so sore that she was hardly able to crawl." Hannah, another woman, was beaten until she "shriek[ed] in a heart-moving manner." One witness "heard Broad direct the family not to give Betty any food." Broad's wife threw a knife at Sarah's head that left a gash so large that a doctor was called.[55]

When the trial reached the court of special sessions three days later, the Broads' lawyer tried to remove a man named Nehemiah Allen from the jury because he was a member of the Manumission Society. The court overruled the challenge. Witness after witness testified to the Broads' crimes. Sensing he was losing his case, the Broads' lawyer proposed that they "manumit the mother and her child and also a third slave named Hannah." Sarah, Betty, and Hannah were delivered to the Manumission Society for care. The foreman of the jury recommended further punishment. Ultimately, the court sentenced Amos to sixty days in prison and fined him $1,000; Demis was fined $250. The case, which was publicized locally, stimulated antislavery commentary in the press.[56]

That same year, the Society tried to convince the legislature to pass a statute explicitly addressing the cruel physical treatment of slaves. As the Broad case demonstrates, masters could be tried for the common law offence of assault and battery, but the Society wanted slaves and servants to have access to a specific remedial statute. That way, both the crime and the remedy would be spelled out, and masters could not fall back on the common law privilege that allowed them to "correct" servants. The legislature did not oblige. Despite this failure, notorious events like the Broad case seem to have affirmed to black New Yorkers that masters' abuse *might* be punished in court. They continued to appeal to the Standing Committee, as did concerned white New Yorkers. These white sympathizers were often crucial witnesses in courtrooms, as were free black people, who were allowed to testify in New York's courts.[57]

Without a clear law punishing physical cruelty, however, the Society's successes and failures seemed arbitrary. For example, when one master abused his ten-year-old servant girl by "whipping, starving" and by leaving her outside until "her feet were frozen," the Society managed to free the girl. They achieved the same outcome for a two-year-old who could rely on the fact that "many of the neighbors can prove the truth of this charge." But when "Grace a colour'd woman" stated that "she found a child about 10 years old in an open cellar" and "the neighbors can prove her being beat cruelly," the child found no relief.[58]

Cruelty cases both spurred the Society to continue advocating for better laws and inspired the members' decision to embrace immediate, not gradual, abolitionism. In 1811, they drafted a petition to the legislature asking that something be done about the "barbarous and inhuman treatment" of slaves. The Society praised the courts for "inflicting exemplary punishment" when they could, but asked for a law that would permit judges to "withdraw the injured slave from the power of his irritated master" and provide "for his future security." As a committee slowly gathered signatures on this petition, a more ambitious legislative plan was conceived: at a "special meeting" of the Society in November, members announced that this might be "the proper time to make an application to the legislature" for "an Act of General Abolition of Slavery." In other words, forget anticruelty measures—the Society wanted the all-out, immediate emancipation of all enslaved New Yorkers.[59]

A Quaker voice on Long Island agreed. That same year, Elias Hicks, an increasingly influential minister, published a pamphlet calling on the legislature "to declare freedom to every slave in the state." He also suggested that black children be released from service at 18 and 21, which would make them equal to "children born of white women in this state" and allow them to enjoy the same freedom "as other citizens." Hicks's Golden Rule-style recommendations were essentially the program that Quakers had been promoting among themselves for over one hundred years and that black petitioners in Massachusetts had proposed during the Revolution.[60]

The reformers' campaign to end slavery outright had an ally in the popular Republican governor, Daniel D. Tompkins, a former lawyer for the Manumission Society. In early 1812, five of his abolitionist colleagues attended the legislative session with a new petition. Optimistic, they looked forward to welcoming "many fellow beings to the enjoyment of numerous civil and religious privileges" and removing "wretchedness, cruelty, and evil."[61]

The 1812 legislative session opened on a somewhat promising note. Tompkins issued a call for "the gradual and ultimate extermination" of slavery, and the assembly appointed a committee to consider "the abolition of slavery." Tompkins did not embrace the more unqualified immediatism the petitioners wanted, but he agreed to push for a faster end to slavery than was currently on the books. The Manumission Society's petition was placed in the committee's hands. But momentum faltered. The committee reported, "A just and liberal policy requires that the offspring of those persons who are held in bondage should be placed, as far as practicable, on an equal footing with other children. But your committee are not of the opinion, that either the peace of society, or the happiness of the slaves themselves, would be promoted by enacting a law for entire emancipation."[62] Rejecting the memorialists' main objective, the committee nevertheless regretted that the state's "borders are stained and contaminated with slavery" and opined that slaves' "condition, and especially the condition of their children, ought to be further ameliorated." But the legislature sat on its hands that year. During the next session, as part of a broad revision of the state's laws, there were changes made on behalf of children, including a new rule that slave owners moving to New York had to treat children born after 1799 as though they were born in-state and a clause clarifying that black servant children's complaints against abusive masters would be tried "with like effect as complaints by and between masters and apprentices under the laws of this state." In other words, the latter rule put statutory force behind children's quests to escape cruel masters, providing another route to early release from service.[63]

The Manumission Society persisted in advocating for a faster end to slavery. In 1813, they sent delegates to the American Convention of Abolition Societies in Philadelphia, where they promised to pursue "the total abolition of slavery" in New York. The Society's mission had changed in a substantial way: whereas "gradual" had once been the key modifier to abolition, now "immediate" was. The Society sent a committee to the legislature asking for the "immediate relief of those held in slavery"—a general emancipation. They prayed for a "law fixing a day and that at a short date, when there should not be any slaves in this state under a given age."[64]

Black voters kept simultaneous pressure on lawmakers. During the April 1813 state election, for example, the *New York Post* reported that a large flag depicting a white man and a black man "cordially shaking hands" was flying "at the place of rendezvous for the Tompkintonian people of color" in the Fifth Ward. The men on the flag were Tompkins, the incumbent Republican governor, and John Teasman. The two knew each other—Tompkins had been a lawyer for the Manumission Society during the same time that Teasman ran the Society's schools. The Fifth Ward black Republicans believed that Tompkins would be a crucial source of antislavery legislative brokering on their behalf.

The majority of black voters, however, stuck with the Federalists. The *Columbian* reported that "black voters, amounting to several hundreds" preferred "the federal ticket." That same spring, a "Free Man of Color" published a letter citing the Republican-backed 1811 voting certificate law as a reason to maintain Federalist loyalty. Objecting to the claim that Governor Tompkins was a "friend" to the people of color, he alleged that during the debate over the 1811 certificate bill, Tompkins had said, "*I have heretofore been a friend to the rights of those people*" but "*if my vote shall be necessary to carry this law into operation, I shall vote for it.*" If the Republicans were so antislavery, the writer concluded, why had they not yet passed "an act for general emancipation of all the slaves"?[65]

Tompkins won reelection in April 1813, but the Federalists achieved a majority in the assembly. Although white voters were obviously necessary to precipitate this upset, New York City's black voters were credited with and criticized for the Federalist victory. Republican newspapers in Albany, Utica, and Cooperstown asserted that this was "perhaps the first instance on record in this country, of the complexion of a house of assembly being decided" by "*negro votes.*" The votes "exceeded 500, and were almost exclusively given to our opponents."[66]

When the Republicans regained the majority in 1815, they endeavored anew to stem black influence. Assemblyman Peter Sharpe introduced a bill aimed specifically at thwarting black voters in New York City, his home district. The bill required that the city's black men file proof of their property qualifications before voting, that they acquire new certificates, and that the City Register provide election inspectors with a book listing which black men could vote. Federalist assemblymen, including Peter Jay Munro, tried to amend or kill the bill, but they failed. In the Senate, Federalist Peter Radcliff likewise tried and failed to stop the bill.[67] As frustrating as the Republican-sponsored certificate laws were, a minority of black men stuck with the Republicans. In 1816, a group of black Republicans explained that they esteemed Tompkins "not only for his exemplary military services," but "also for his steady, humane, and uniform conduct towards many of us, while a member of the Manumission Society."[68]

The black Republicans were not wrong about the influence of both Tompkins and the Society. In 1816 and 1817, the Society made a series of breakthroughs. In early 1816, Peter A. Jay, one of their longtime lawyers, began his tenure as president of the Society *and* as a Federalist member of the assembly. Son of John Jay, Peter had followed in his father's antislavery and political footsteps. Jay introduced "an act concerning slaves and servants," which was printed for the legislature's consideration. Much of this bill reorganized and clarified existing laws, while proposing two major changes related to the punishment of slaves accused of crimes. During debate on Jay's bill, some members attempted to remove the existing 1813 abuse clause that promised "all complaints by any servant born of a slave" against a master would be tried in the same manner "as complaints by and between master and apprentice under the laws of this state." Initially, the proslavery side won and the clause was removed. Jay drew large *X*s through this section of his personal draft.[69] But he scribbled too soon, for a member from Columbia County begged the men to reconsider. The substance of the ensuing debate was left unrecorded, but the abuse clause was reinserted. It is likely that Jay and his allies, drawing on their firsthand experience with violent masters and an inconsistent court system, convinced their colleagues to reconsider. The assembly passed the bill, but it foundered in the senate.[70]

Later that fall, a new Committee of Five was formed to press again for general abolition. This group included John Murray Jr. and Willet Seaman, two elderly Quakers who had been among the handful of founding members of the Society in 1785 and who had served in the organization with Jay's father.[71] Using Jay's 1816 bill as a template, the Society inserted a key additional clause: that at a future date, slavery would cease to exist in New York. On January 2, before the 1817 legislative session began, the Society's new president—and soon-to-be Mayor of New York City—the Federalist Cadwallader Colden, wrote an editorial in favor of general abolition. Addressing "the great question of *emancipating slaves*," Colden explained: "More than fifteen years ago, the 'hand writing' of *slave*, as to all who are born after the 4th of July, 1799, was blotted from our statute book. Who then are slaves? None that are under seventeen years of age. . . . It is for those unfortunates, above the age of seventeen, most of whom have brothers and sisters, or children, or grand-children, that are free . . . that we appeal to the justice of the legislature. . . . Fix the period of emancipation."[72] Colden's entreaty, with its explicit reference to the children freed by the 1799 law and the family members it left enslaved, demonstrates both how potent and how limited gradual abolition had been thus far. Running three pages long, the appeal was loaded with evidence and logic stemming from what black New Yorkers repeatedly told the men in the Society.

The state's Quakers also crafted a petition, which was hand delivered to lawmakers by two members sent to Albany. They noted that enslaved people born before 1799 were justified in feeling that the law operated "unequally as relates to them." It was time "to take that step for which the public mind has been gradually preparing—to declare by the law the Extermination of Slavery within this state." Gradual abolition had both demonstrated that emancipation was salutary and led to the conclusion that immediatism was necessary and just.[73]

Tompkins, recently elected vice president of the United States, made a final plea to lawmakers. In March, the new "Act relative to slaves and servants" passed. The law declared that every slave born *before* July 4, 1799, "shall, from and after the fourth of July, one thousand eight hundred and twenty-seven, be free." Children born to slaves before that 1827 date would be bound until the age of 21. Children not properly educated would be released at 18. The contentious abuse clause was included; child servants retained explicit access to existing apprenticeship laws regulating masters' conduct. This was yet another instance when a clear line was drawn between slaves and children born to slaves.[74]

Somewhat strangely, then, the party that tried to disfranchise black voters also passed one of the most significant emancipation laws in the early republic. Republicans' desire to thwart black voting was at least partially motivated by partisan concerns and did not preclude a genuine distaste of slavery. This is not to deny that Republicans, like many white northerners, disdained both slavery and black people. But the practical politics of race, slavery, and citizenship were hardly neat, unchanging, or determined. In the context of 1817, perhaps some Republicans even hoped that the new abolition law would increase the number of black Republicans.[75]

The 1817 law, significant though it was, did not end slavery overnight. A decade was a painfully long time for those forced to wait. Sojourner Truth later recalled, through a heartbreaking dialogue in her autobiography, what it felt like in 1817 to know that freedom was still ten years away. Truth told her father, an enslaved man who did not live with her, "that all the slaves in the State would be freed in ten years and that then she would come and take care of him." Her father replied, "I cannot live that long." His daughter begged, "Oh do, daddy, do live, and I will take such good care of you." Truth's father did not live for long after this conversation; he died enslaved.[76]

The state's most committed abolitionists—not to mention the state's slaves—had not achieved as fast-acting a law as they wanted. But the law nonetheless made it easier for servants, slaves, and white allies to broker conditional manumissions and to demand specific protections. Like the gradual abolition laws that came before it, the 1817 general abolition law did not simply change the rules: it changed the atmosphere around the everyday practices of bondage and negotiation. There were 15,017 slaves in New York in 1810 and 10,088 in 1820. Even though no slaves were immediately freed by the 1817 act, the law further weakened the short- and long-term viability of holding people as property.[77]

The 1817 law was the result of Manumission Society and Quaker lobbying, black and white antislavery men voting, and lawmakers' delayed but nonetheless necessary action. But the law's existence should also be credited to the wider group of people it sought to benefit. Black New Yorkers played a role in their own emancipations by forcing lawyers, judges, and politicians to respond both to their desire to be free and to their resistance to kidnapping, illegal sales, physical violence, and unequal apprenticeship rights. By exploiting the possibilities inherent in the state's initially modest antislavery statutes, New York's enslaved, servant, and free black population forced the passage of more substantial laws.

* * *

As the decade of the 1810s came to a close, antislavery forces could see that they had made gains as recent laws began to bear fruit. More and more older children who either knew or wanted to know whether their masters had broken age-based gradual abolition laws took their cases to the Manumission Society. For example, Phillis Jackson said "she belongs to Sylvanus Miller, was born in 8 mo. 1799" and was "desirous of being released from slavery." John Francis believed he was entitled to his freedom because he had not been registered with a birth certificate or properly educated. Rosanna Johnson, the minutes recorded simply, "thinks she is entitled to her freedom." All three of these servants won release.[78]

This rising generation of young black New Yorkers also helped each other. Ann Ingerson, for example, explained that her master "has been in the habit of hiring her out to the highest bidder and taking her wages until lately, when she left by the advice of friends. She is now engaged at Martin Thompson's, where her master has found her and demands her wages—she had not had the necessary schooling." Whatever it was precisely that her friends told her, Ingerson was confident enough to leave. When her master questioned this decision, she found lawyers to defend her actions. A few months later, William Jarvis, living across the East River from New York City in northern Kings County, reported that his brother Jeffrey, age 18 or 19, "has had no schooling." Jeffrey was released from service.[79] As the story of the Jarvis brothers suggests, black servants living outside of New York City found ways to share information among peers and sometimes even managed to employ the services of the city-based Manumission Society. In this sense, they followed in the footsteps of resourceful—and at times, plain lucky—rural parents who operated successfully on behalf of the youngest children of gradual abolition.

In other cases, servants living well beyond the usual borders of the Manumission Society's influence managed to wrest freedom for themselves on their own. In February 1819, "a negro servant" named Darby in Southold, Suffolk County, told three justices of the peace that he had not learned to read, nor "received four quarters of schooling." Darby also produced a certificate from the town clerk "certifying that [Darby's] name age nor sex" had "been recorded in his office according to law." Knowing that his master had broken multiple gradual abolition laws, Darby successfully persuaded the justices that he was owed immediate freedom. The document he received—a "discharge from servitude" (not a "manumission")—did not explain how Darby learned about state law, but the fact that he did suggests that legal knowledge could travel far and wide across New York State. Perhaps Reuben "the Lawyer" Reeve, the aforementioned black voter in Southold, had whispered the necessary and powerful information in Darby's ear.[80]

Darby was fortunate in his quest, but maneuvering out of servitude was often harder in the more remote and conservative areas of the state. Surviving records are less abundant for agrarian areas and small towns, but there is enough evidence to provide windows into broader geographical experiences. Records of birth certificates, for example, exist from every pocket of the state, suggesting that laws were at least partially followed everywhere. This does not mean that all areas were antislavery, or that white officials or masters were universally eager to adopt the moderately antislavery spirit of various state acts. What emerges from non–New York City records, unsurprisingly, is that gradual abolition operated according to plan in some towns and counties more than others. For example, it was helpful to have Quakers or newer Protestant denominations (Methodists, Baptists) living in the area; it also helped if Federalists held local office, although there were certainly non-Federalists with antislavery sentiments or willingness to follow the rules. Experience also varied depending on how old a given American settlement was and therefore how long slavery had been countenanced. The ethnic or cultural background of an owner could also shape household practice. Yankee migrants to New York, for example, remained more likely to be antislavery than long-settled Dutch-descended New Yorkers.[81]

One of the more intriguing accounts of gradual abolition in a rural, conservative region of the state comes from William H. Seward's recollections of his childhood in the southwestern Hudson Valley. Seward—future antislavery governor, U.S. senator, and secretary of state under Abraham Lincoln—grew up in Warwick, Orange County. His father, Samuel S. Seward, had moved to New York from a slavery-friendly area of northern New Jersey. His mother, Mary Jennings, was an Orange County native, the daughter of a well-to-do farmer. During William's childhood, his father made a living as a doctor, landowner, Republican politician, and judge. The family worshipped in the local Presbyterian church. The Presbyterians, in general, were known for being neither as radical as Quakers on slavery nor as conservative as the Dutch Reformed. Between 1811 and 1819, the elder Seward registered the births of seven servant children—Neal Galighen, Charles, Mary Cesar, June Cesar, Cathrine Cesar, Sally Cesar, and Mary Coe—born to two enslaved mothers, Cloe Sulware and Dina, living under his roof.[82]

As an old man, William recalled what it had been like as a boy in this rural household of slaves, servants, and white family members ruled over by a stern father. The "two black women"—presumably Cloe and Dina—were "exclusive tenants of the kitchen and the garret over it." They were "vivacious" and "affectionate"; he found "their conversation a relief from the severe decorum" elsewhere in the house. He remembered that he did not at first "have any distinct idea of any difference between children and slaves"—a testament to how persistent early modern notions of a commanding father at the head of a household of dependents shaped William's first understandings of who was in charge in the domestic domain.

William's parents took slavery for granted, but at the same time "never uttered an expression that" made him "think that the negro was inferior to the white person." His father, following the 1810 state law, sent some of his household's black servant children to school with William, where they sat next to him. William was aware that the town's black population suffered a range of abuses and poor treatment. His neighborhood playmate, a boy named Zeno, ran away after a whipping and returned with "an iron yoke around his neck." Zeno eventually "fled forever." Another nearby family owned an elderly woman who had been born in Africa; she was certain she would return home to her birthplace after she died. As he matured, William learned about "gradual emancipation laws" and determined that he would "be an abolitionist."[83]

Seward wrote these memories in the 1870s, after a successful political career and the conclusion of a national war that ended slavery—a war in which he played a major role for the winning side. His grasp of the details of his early life may have been imperfect, and his post hoc narrative self-serving, but his stories nonetheless comport with contemporary evidence.[84]

During the same years that Seward was awakening to the realities of rural slavery as a white adolescent, the future abolitionist Austin Steward was discovering the possibilities and pitfalls of gradual abolition from a black perspective. Born enslaved in Prince William County, Virginia, in 1793, Steward worked on a large plantation as a young boy. Around 1800, his owner,

Captain William Helm, moved the household to Bath, a village in the Finger Lakes region of western New York. This resettlement was legal. In fact, Helm was part of a substantial migration of slave-owning Marylanders and Virginians who bought inexpensive land in New York recently wrested from the Haudenosaunee. These southern transplants brought so many slaves into the Genesee Country, as this area was called, that it was one the few regions of the state where the enslaved population actually grew in the nineteenth century.[85]

Steward found bondage no less brutal in the North than it had been in the South. As he later quipped, "I found it just as hard to be beaten over the head with a piece of iron in New York as it was in Virginia." That said, slavery in New York was changing, both in practice and at law. Steward watched his uncle leave Helm's household and live out his days in self-proclaimed freedom. Soon thereafter, Helm began hiring Steward out for short terms of service. Steward kept his ears open as he went from place to place. He bought a spelling book and taught himself to read. In his late teens, Steward identified a potential route to freedom: "I had listened to the conversation of others, and determined to ask legal counsel on the subject the first opportunity I could find. Very soon after, as I was drawing wood, I met on the river bridge, Mr. D. Cruger, the eminent lawyer before mentioned, and I asked him to tell me if I was not free, by the laws of New York."[86] Cruger told Steward to visit Darius Comstock and James Moore, members of a local Quaker-heavy antislavery society. Steward learned that his master had violated the 1810 law that forbade masters from outside the state from hiring out slaves in New York; were a master caught, the slave would be free. Convinced he stood on firm legal ground, Steward left Helm. He earned wages working for Comstock for several years, attended school, and eventually moved to Rochester, where, with Comstock's backing, he embarked on a grocery business.[87]

Although Steward never had to pursue his claims in court, some of his generational peers in upstate New York did. A number of these cases made it far enough up the appellate ladder to appear in published case reports. These reported cases were another means by which young black New Yorkers, including those who lived in rural areas, shaped the development of state law and forced legal figures to wrestle with the problems of an abolition regime in which the lines between freedom and slavery were shifting and precarious.[88]

Ultimately, knowing the law mattered both to individual lives as well as to collective politics. Knowing whom to turn to—whether it be the right local official, the nearest manumission society, or a sympathetic country lawyer willing to dole out advice—also mattered. Black legal knowledge and local wisdom were not necessarily put down in books, but they clearly existed.

The story of an unnamed girl, rescued in 1825, is an illustrative case. That summer, the Manumission Society reported that a man named "Stoutenbergh laid violent hands on a coloured girl early this morning and bound her in a cart." Before the Society had time to intervene, black New Yorkers took the case into their own hands. Stoutenbergh was interrupted "when his horse was led to the Police Office by some blacks. No doubt is entertained that she is entitled to her freedom." What is striking in this account—and it is not the only example—is the rescuers' decision to bring her to the Police Office. They likely knew she was entitled to legal relief. As a servant, she would have been eligible for release due to cruel treatment under the clause that Jay had fought to maintain in the 1817 general abolition law. It is also possible the rescuers learned she had not been properly educated. There was no guarantee of a favorable result, but appealing to the law and its official agents was worth a try. The girl in question was freed.[89]

* * *

Although children were the targeted beneficiaries of gradual abolition laws, they did not live, work, survive, or fight alone. Black children's rights and status were bound up in the rights and status of others. They were born into households and families whose structures and relationships were confirmed and mediated by domestic law. The 1799 act and its successors opened a Pandora's box of legal conundrums and unintended consequences for black families; these statutes raised questions about the contradictory implications of various old and new laws about marriage, property, and inherited status. Hardly a year went by after 1799 that jurists did not enact legislation or preside over court cases that clarified or redetermined not only the rights of black New Yorkers, but also the nature of their relationships to each other.

One of the most striking examples of gradual abolition's legal effect on families was an 1809 statute that legalized slave marriage and allowed enslaved parents to bequeath property. It also stipulated that manumitted slaves could inherit property and also turn to the state's courts for "the recovery of such estates, or for injuries done to the same," as if they "had been free born citizens of this state." The statute was particularly unusual given that slaves' status had long been defined by their inability to make contracts, including the contract of marriage, and their inability to *be* and *own* property simultaneously. But the reason for this anomalous statute becomes more evident when one considers that the 1799 law had freed the newborn children of slaves while at the same time making them all legal "bastards." Only legally married parents could bear legitimate children to whom they could bestow property. By 1809, lawmakers apparently realized that it was problematic to refuse marriage and the property prerogatives of citizens to the state's rapidly growing number of partially free black families. On the most pragmatic level, denying free children legitimacy and inheritance rights increased the potential that they would burden state resources as pauper adults and fail to become independent adults.

Indeed, a close examination of the 1809 act reveals that this law was less about marriage, per se, than about black children's property rights and financial independence. The title of the act did not even mention "marriage"; it was, rather, an act "to enable certain persons to take and hold estates." The law declared that slave marriages previously or thereafter contracted would be "considered equally valid" and "children of any such marriage" deemed "legitimate." The act made very clear, however, that the ability to marry would not, in fact, make spouses free, despite longstanding assumptions that legal marriage was an emblem or enactment of freedom.[90]

Crucially, the 1809 law also allowed masters to abandon a servant child to his or her parents, rather than with the overseers of the poor, as long as local authorities certified the parents were "able and willing to maintain and provide." Previously, a master technically could not do this—he or she could either raise the child himself or abandon the child to the overseers of the poor. Even if a master wanted to use the state's manumission law, meant for slaves, to release a child servant, the master would have to prove the child was sufficiently able to take care of him- or herself—which was unlikely, for a child. The new law, therefore, allowed a master to release a child directly to the parents, placing the burden of responsibility on mothers and fathers. Explained another way, the law gave parents a chance to raise their own sons and daughters.

Masters and parents made use of this law in practice. In 1818, for example, the mayor and recorder of Albany registered the decision of John Doun to free Sarah Banker along with her two young children and certified that "Sarah Banker the mother of the children Helen Hensen and Eliza Edwards" declared "herself willing to support and maintain said children."[91] Mary Francis's master manumitted her along "with her female negro child of four weeks old whose services I hereto had retained." Francis consented to "support the said child."[92] These examples not only are revealing of the 1809 law's potential to ease restrictions on black families' freedom, but provide clues to masters' own thinking about the course of gradual emancipation. Perhaps the manumissions were genuine acts of benevolence, but they also suggest that some masters continued to consider child servants to be burdens rather than useful sources of labor.

Black children's servant status likewise made it easier for parents to buy their sons' and daughters' terms of service from their masters. It was less expensive to purchase "the labor of a servant" than "the body of a slave." Consider the following 1815 bill of sale issued by Albany master Stephen Lush to a free black husband named Thomas Allison:

> For the consideration of one hundred and fifty dollars . . . thirty dollars whereof is now paid to me by Thomas Allison of the same city a freed-man and the remainder secured to be paid to me by named Thomas—[I] have granted and bargained . . . to the said Thomas a certain female slave named Catherine the wife of the said Thomas and all my right to the services of the following children of the said Catherine to wit of Lewis a male child born on the twenty-sixth day of February one thousand eight hundred and nine—of Catherine a female born on the nineteenth day of February one thousand eight hundred and twelve and of Samuel a male born on the twenty-seventh day of July last.[93]

From Allison's perspective, he was neither buying a piece of property in his wife nor purchasing his children's labor for the sake of capital investment—he was freeing, protecting, and uniting his family. But, in legal terms, Allison had purchased the right to be master of his own household, a role that, according to domestic law, included ownership of his children's labor.[94] And the price here is noteworthy. Lush practically gave the children away—a healthy enslaved boy, by contrast, could be sold for $250.[95] It is likely that, from Lush's perspective, Allison's freeborn children were not "worth" much to him—he could not sell them as slaves once they got older, nor could he keep *their* children, if they had any, to work for him. Allison had been able to buy his family more easily because laws had changed the status of his children.[96]

Parents like Allison had earned enough in wages to take control over their families, but many fathers and mothers were not so fortunate. Parents who were enslaved, living alone or at sea, or scraping by on low wages had to search for alternate ways to care for their children. Often, this meant finding suitable masters to support and educate their sons and daughters. Like poor parents had done for generations, black parents tried to place children in households where they would be treated well and learn a lucrative trade. This was better than allowing them to be bound out by the overseers of the poor, who had less incentive to find the best possible placements.

In New York City, the Manumission Society brokered such arrangements. After Robert Brown's fourteen-year-old daughter had been almost kidnapped twice, he asked a Society member named Richard Lawrence to take her in for "instruction and protection."[97] In 1814, a man named Titus asked for help saving his wife and three children from being sold at auction. Titus had the money to purchase them and requested "that some person will have the bill of sale made out in his name and manumit them." The Society purchased the family, and at Titus's instruction "endorsed the bill of sale to the Reverend James Thompson a colored man," who "would make [the wife] free and take the necessary care of the children."[98]

It became easier for parents to keep families together during the later years of gradual abolition even though it remained difficult to escape poverty in a post-slavery labor landscape that offered limited access to independent livelihoods. In 1820, the overseers of the poor in Huntington, Long Island, examined two black fathers, Joseph Potter and David Helmes, who had recently settled in the town with their wives and young children. Neither was in immediate need of assistance, but the state's 1788 poor law, drawing on colonial norms, required newcomers to a town to explain their circumstances to officials. If the new arrivals lived peacefully and independently in the town for twelve months thereafter, they were then deemed legal residents.[99] Potter explained that his mother had bound him out when he was eight and that he had recently completed his indenture term. Helmes had lived with his "Father until he was eight years old and at that period was put out." Since turning 21, Helmes had been renting "Sundry Tenaments but has never paid more than thirteen dollars in any one year." Potter's mother and Helmes's father, who had likely been enslaved, had not been able to keep their sons with them. By contrast, Potter and Helmes were living as free men with their wives and children. They did so, nevertheless, on the margins of poverty.[100]

Young parents like Potter and Helmes were part of a transitional generation who obtained for the first time many of the parental prerogatives that slavery had denied their own parents. Some of these prerogatives were legally protected. But knowing the law, not to mention making it function, remained difficult.[101] Sojourner Truth's wrenching struggle to regain her kidnapped son Peter suggests the obstacles involved in making legal claims against white masters and the particular difficulties of maintaining freedom in a conservative agricultural area. Truth, like many black parents, lived with a different master than her son, and she learned only after the fact that he had been illegally transported out of state. During a cold upstate winter, Truth trekked for miles around Ulster County, in and out of conversations with white citizens (including helpful Quakers), back and forth to various courtrooms, all in efforts to make Peter's master bring him back. She eventually succeeded in restoring Peter to her care, but the boy was traumatized. Truth's story is a reminder that even when the law "worked," the emotional and psychological costs of slavery and gradual abolition remained high.[102]

Truth was not alone in waging a custody battle over a child. In fact, a handful of such cases made it to the state supreme court, where judges had to consider where to draw lines between masters' rights and black parents' rights. In 1815, for example, a master named Waring sued a free black man named Oatfield before a justice of the peace in Albany. Oatfield had, for years, taken care of his grandchild, a boy legally bound to Waring. Waring tried to recover damages from Oatfield, accusing Oatfield of "harboring" the boy. The justice decided in favor of the grandfather, for it was clear Oatfield had raised his grandson with Waring's consent. Oatfield was irritated by Waring's dishonest meddling. He sued Waring back, in the Albany circuit court, claiming that Waring owed him funds for supporting the child. Oatfield won again; a jury awarded him $143. Waring then appealed to the New York term of the supreme court, arguing that Oatfield was not really free, and therefore had no standing to sue. Oatfield's lawyer replied that there was sufficient evidence to infer a *parol* manumission. The judges agreed, citing the common law principle that "all presumptions in favour of personal liberty and freedom ought to be made." All told, Oatfield had won three cases, affirmed his own freedom, and maintained custody of his grandchild.[103]

Oatfield's success stemmed in part from his clear ability to provide for his grandson. Poor black parents—operating within a legal system that had long assumed not only the right to take enslaved children away from parents, but also the right to take poor children away from parents—did not fare as well. In *Marbleton v. Overseers of the Poor* (1822), two towns argued over the care of a poor black child. Francisca, a free black woman from Marbleton in Ulster County, had moved to Kingston and married a slave referred to as *H*. The marriage was, per the 1809 act, legal. Francisca and *H* had a daughter named

Dinah. When Francisca died, Dinah was not allowed to stay with her father, who was living in his master's house. Dinah was taken to Marbleton, her mother's birthplace, and placed in the almshouse. Marbleton officials argued, however, that the child should be the responsibility of the living father's town. But what if the father were enslaved? The court ruled that a child of a half-free, half-slave marriage would follow the birthplace of the free parent, in this case the mother. Thus, even though a white child in this situation might have been placed in the father's town, the court ruled that Dinah would stay in her mother's town. Justice Jonah Platt, despite his antislavery reputation, reasoned that even though the marriage itself was legitimate, "[The free mother] shall have exclusive custody and control of [the child], as though their father were dead; and in reference to the settlement of paupers, I think the most consistent rule will be, to consider the children of such marriages as belonging to the town in which the mother had her last legal settlement, without any regard to her *slave husband.*" [104] In this strange case, the status differential between the parents trumped all, with devastating implications for the child. Rather than staying in Kingston, where Dinah would have access to her surviving parent, she was sent to live elsewhere because her free mother had been born there.

Masters' wills are yet another source that illuminate changing and variegated experiences of slavery and emancipation during gradual abolition. They help explain, in part, why some families had better odds of staying together than others. In rural Rockland County, for example, eighteenth-century masters almost uniformly bequeathed their slaves as chattel property to their heirs or instructed executors to sell them. Beginning in the late 1700s, however, some began using their wills to effect private emancipations. In 1799, for instance, shortly after the state's gradual abolition law passed, Johannis Blauvelt willed that "my negro wench named Hen and the two children named Mary and Silas" be freed six years after his death. A handful of masters also provided such beneficiaries of testamentary manumission with forms of material security. In 1808, Jacobus Van Orden freed Will, Suck, and their children Pet, Saur, Gin, and Ton; he left Will one hundred pounds, the "kitchen furniture," and "wearing apperls." In 1824, Samuel Brewster left "old black woman Pillis the house and ground she now occupies." In 1827, Elias Gurnee gave "Benjamin Jackson, the coloured boy that has for some time worked for me" the option to earn the annual interest on $500 should he stay working in the family.[105]

Just north of Rockland, David Rumsey of Orange County wrote a will acknowledging that the children of gradual abolition needed more than bodily freedom to navigate their postservice adulthoods with independence. His ideas for providing such independence were decidedly gendered. Rumsey, who had registered the births of three black siblings (born 1815, 1817, and 1820) with the town clerk, felt some obligation to them as he approached his death.[106] He left "Joseph L Brown a colored boy now living with me" two acres of land and shortened his term of service from 25 to 21. He instructed his heirs to build Brown a house and keep him "harmless from all charges for taxes on the same." Rumsey also left Brown a cow, a bed, and bedding. Sally Jane Brown, Joseph's sister, was to be released at 18, or earlier if she married. Rumsey encouraged her to learn "the weaving business" and promised to provide the necessary tools. Hanna Maria Brown, the youngest sibling, would be released at 18 with "bed bedding and bedstead." And James Marvin, a fourth boy in Rumsey's household, would be released at 21 and "paid the sum of fifty dollars and furnished with good clothes."[107]

There is even evidence that some black New Yorkers negotiated with the families that had once owned them after their masters' deaths. In 1819, Bella, a woman manumitted by Chancellor Robert R. Livingston, managed to extract the promise of postemancipation support from his heirs. Bella and her young son, a child of gradual abolition, had been released together in the chancellor's will in 1813, but the Livingstons never obtained a certificate from the overseers of the poor consenting to their manumission. A combination of state law and Bella's own stated preferences convinced Livingston's son-in-law, Edward P. Livingston, that the family would have to make routine payments to the mother and child. After Edward agreed to give Bella three dollars a week in New York City during the winter of 1818, he reported that "of course one of the first persons who called on us [this fall] was Bella. . . . It now appears that payment for winter and summer is expected and I have no Doubt if the account be disputed that almost any thing [she demanded] would be allowed by a jury." Edward suggested that "enquiry be made for some place in the country and the rate of boarding them be fixed or else we shall have bill upon bill coming in." The story is intriguing for a number of reasons, including the implication that Bella was aware that her former master's family was legally (and perhaps morally, from her perspective) responsible for supporting her and her son. Chancellor Livingston had been one of the most important officials in the state (and the nation, for that matter) during his lifetime. In death, laws that he had approved as chancellor now governed his heirs' obligations.[108]

Bella's maneuverings, alongside the Rockland County and Orange County wills, suggest a few of the limited if nonetheless critical ways that some black individuals and families received support as they began to navigate lives outside of slavery. They are also a reminder that many, many others were freed with nothing to help them build their new lives, all but ensuring continued forms of dependence. After all, gradual abolition laws did not require what a master like David Rumsey decided to do on his own. The laws conferred a form of freedom, and the laws also encouraged private practices of delayed and immediate manumission, but they did little to ensure that black New Yorkers would leave servitude with the resources necessary to provide for life's daily needs, or the time and space required to make optimal decisions about work, shelter, and family togetherness.

Gradual abolition did not restore all family members to each other or guarantee independence to black households. But it was nonetheless a legal and social regime that altered the landscape of rights and in certain circumstances encouraged black New Yorkers to engage with local officials, legal documents, and courts. As the era unfolded, parents, children, siblings, and fictive kin continued to advocate for and support each other, at times managing forms of autonomy and material accumulation that had been impossible during the era of slavery. In some instances, they also discovered that white judges, politicians, and abolitionists were willing to support black families. The importance of familial relationships would continue to inform definitions of freedom in postemancipation New York as well as in the nation at large.

* * *

By 1820, 64 percent of the state's black population was listed as free on the federal census—some 29,297 people. In Suffolk, Queens, and Westchester counties, it was 80 percent; more than 95 percent were free in New York City. In fact, the city's 10,368 free black people made them the largest single free black community in the country.[109] Despite gradual abolition's original intent, the process proceeded more quickly than planned. Slaves, servants, and free black citizens, in cooperation with white allies, spurred abolition forward. After the passage of the 1799 law, they used both traditional and novel methods to loosen slavery's remaining grip. They negotiated with masters to buy freedom, orchestrated their own sales, ran away, exploited new laws, litigated in court, and became increasingly defiant toward white authority figures.

The New York experience of emancipation was one particularly rooted in the everyday workings of the law and in the ability of ordinary people, even some of the most vulnerable, to employ the legal system in search of protection and rights. Over the course of the gradual abolition era, from the 1780s to the 1830s, abolitionists, local officials, state legislators, jurists, enslaved and free parents, and black children themselves all used law and the legal arena to shape both individual and collective definitions of freedom. They failed as often as they succeeded, but the overall result was a honing and refining of traditions and strategies that would inform New Yorkers' antislavery efforts in the ensuing decades. The generations of black children who grew up within the legal and social structures of gradual abolition would become particularly vital figures in the longer story of nineteenth-century American freedom.

CHAPTER 3

Educating the "Rising Generation"

Associational Culture and the Politics of Black Schools

Julia A. J. Foote was born to parents who grew up enslaved in the Hudson River Valley in the years after the American Revolution. Her mother, who was once whipped for refusing her master's sexual advances, was eventually sold to the "comparatively kind" owners of a tavern in rural Schenectady County. Her father, who carted goods around the bustling valley, managed to earn enough money to buy himself, Julia's mother, and their first child. Once emancipated, the family began to worship at the Methodist Episcopal Church, where black congregants were permitted but treated like "poor lepers." Julia, the fourth of eight children, was born free in the early 1820s, before New York's 1827 general abolition took effect.[1]

When she was ten, Julia's parents bound her out to a childless white couple named the Primes in the Schenectady countryside. The decision was an ordinary one. White and black parents of limited means often placed their children in more prosperous households as a means of ensuring shelter, food, and training. The Primes, Julia later reported, were "fond" of her, even "loved" her. Relying on their status as "an old and influential family," they sent her to "a country school" where she was "well treated." Julia was an eager student with religious inclinations.[2]

As an adolescent, Julia returned home and moved with her family across the river to Albany. The Footes joined the Albany African Methodist Church, an independent black denomination incorporated by the city in 1828. Her minister gave her a Bible of her own. With her father's encouragement, she had one more brush with formal schooling when the Quaker-turned-Baptist teacher Prudence Crandell moved briefly to Albany after being chased from Connecticut for operating a school for black girls. Eventually, Foote was ordained as the first female deacon in the African Methodist Episcopal Zion Church. In 1879, having lived through both a state and a national emancipation, she published her autobiography.[3]

Foote was an exceptional woman of her generation, but much of her experience of family, work, schooling, and church was typical. Many children of gradual abolition had access to schooling in ways their parents had not, but these encounters were often truncated or inconsistent. Some towns admitted black students in their common schools; most did not. Antislavery teachers, black and white, operated privately funded day, evening, and Sabbath schools. Children often had to work rather than attend school. Curriculum and occupational expectations were gendered. Black parents did their best for their children's educations, whether this meant developing relationships with influential white figures or marshalling resources to build their own schools. Even so, some children reached adulthood without formal education.[4]

The most famous school for black children in the state, and arguably the country, was the New York Manumission Society's African Free School, which by the 1820s comprised a constellation of six buildings for educating thousands of boys and girls in Manhattan. The school graduated some of the most influential black leaders of the century, including Peter Williams Jr., Alexander Crummell, Isaiah DeGrasse, Henry Highland Garnet, James McCune Smith, George T. Downing, Samuel Ringgold Ward, Ira Aldridge, and brothers Charles, Elver, and Patrick Reason. For these abolitionists and intellectuals, as well as their less prominent peers, school was not only a place where they read, wrote, and ciphered, but where they practiced intragenerational politics and learned from adults pursuing legal goals that benefited all of their lives.[5]

Remarkable as it was on its own, the African Free School comes into fresh light when considered alongside the wider state story. It becomes easier to see the commonalities and differences experienced by the rising generation as they and their kin made education part of free life. Schools in many places became sites where black New Yorkers further developed their identities as taxpayers and citizens. Their grievances and objectives were often locally specific. A child's education was shaped by whether or not a school was urban or rural, what religious denominations predominated in the area, the politics of local white elites, and the evolving economy and corporate structure of a given town or city. Piecing together local experiences reveals that the connections families and students made in and because of schools helped them to pursue political priorities that both included and went beyond education.[6]

In schools, as within gradual abolition law itself, children were central. This fact mattered in several ways. Visions of improvement for young people had been inherent in emancipation policy for decades. Black children, parents, and teachers seized on this notion, at times making the content of curriculum and definitions of adult freedom more robust than what white authors of emancipation policy or builders of schools had imagined possible. In addition, formal schooling meant that black children spent time with people their age in settings that enslaved generations before them had not. In forming horizontal ties in novel spaces, they engaged in a modern process of age- and race-based identification. Moreover, their very presence in school had broad political resonance. Black children's literal and symbolic connections to slavery and freedom, as well as the manner in which evolving ideologies of race set them apart, made their coming of age a public story. They stood as proof of what was achievable in a nation that would, they hoped, one day be rid of slavery. They also faced violence and scrutiny that their white peers did not. All of these dynamics proved generationally formative.[7]

Viewing schools as sites where students made bonds with each other and where parents and leaders developed relationships to and within civil society ultimately demonstrates that black New Yorkers took part in constructing the terrain between "the people" and "the government" in ways we have yet to fully appreciate. Scholars have long been interested in the blossoming of associational life and transformation of the public sphere in the nation's first decades, tracking how Americans became a "nation of joiners" en route to becoming the distinctive republic that Alexis de Tocqueville famously described in *Democracy in America* (1835–1840).[8] Recognizing that associations were often formally sanctioned by lawmakers helps us understand why black New Yorkers sought incorporation for their educational organizations, under what auspices they asked for public funds, and the prevalence of constitutionalism in daily life. A vital aspect of being free was building legal ties to local and state government, as well as among fellow citizens. Schools were crucial to ground-up constructions of black citizenship.[9]

Classrooms for black children were thus important not only because of how they shaped children, but because schools were fundamental to new forms of civic and political life. The growth of black literacy, associationalism, and government interaction stoked by schools influenced subsequent developments. The hard-won successes of black education help explain why the first black newspaper in the United States was founded in New York in 1827 with eager agents and readers across the state, why the state colored convention movement of the 1830s and '40s flourished, why it was difficult to deny that black New Yorkers were state citizens and taxpayers, and why political antislavery was appealing to many black New Yorkers by midcentury. Advocates of schools viewed accessible education as crucial for preparing students for democratic citizenship and vital for sustaining the health of the young republic. New York's black school children were among the best examples of these ideals.[10]

* * *

In May 1786, members of the New York Manumission Society suggested the organization establish "a free School in the City for the Education of Negro Children." As was their wont, the Society matched their idealism with a pragmatic grasp of the pecuniary and legislative means necessary. They would petition the legislature for "a charter of Incorporation which will remove every difficulty respecting the Security to such as may be disposed to Contribute to these charitable purposes." Incorporation would give the school legal advantages—the ability to own property and to protect the institution's financial interests—as well as its own binding constitution and state recognition of the school's constituent place in civil society. A committee began raising funds and drafting the school's pedagogical design.[11]

From the start, the school's mission reached beyond educating individual children. The institution would prepare the children of slaves for the responsibilities of freedom and demonstrate to skeptical white Americans that black New Yorkers could be "useful members" of free society. In a letter to fellow abolitionists, the New Yorkers explained that educating black children was vital so that all Americans would "receive the advantages which ought to be derived from the Manumission of Slaves." The school would ensure that "the rising Generation" did not inherit "the Vices their parents acquired in Slavery." Given that one of the Society's concurrent goals was a gradual abolition law—New York had not yet passed one when the school was founded—the school's mission reflected both the optimism and anxieties of white abolitionists as they promoted child-focused emancipation.[12]

At this point in the city's history, there were few educational options available to any children. For the previous century, Anglican missionaries had operated small, segregated catechism schools for black children, but these institutions did not survive the Revolution. Some poor white children attended church-run charity schools, which offered rudimentary curricula and emphasized religious exercises. Serious education remained a perquisite of the wealthy. Rich parents hired tutors for their children and sent older boys to private academies. In the educational landscape of the early republic, the African Free School was a conspicuous undertaking. While the Society's interest in education as a social good was unremarkable in Revolutionary political culture—a healthy republic, many elites thought, required the intellectual and moral cultivation of the polity—the assumption that black children would be members of the new republic was notable. However hierarchically structured the school's vision of emancipation was, the endeavor was premised on black belonging and citizenship.[13]

The school opened quickly. In 1787, the Society raised eight hundred pounds, roughly $35,000 today. The trustees hired Cornelius Davis, a white Quaker teacher who "dismissed a School of White Children that he may devote his time to the descendants of Africans." In November, the school enrolled its first twelve scholars. The number grew to thirty in 1788. Both free and enslaved children, the latter with the permission of their masters, were permitted to attend. There was no tuition for free children, but masters paid ten shillings a quarter to send enslaved children. Were a master willing to free the child, tuition was waived.[14]

In the first years of the school, students were instructed in reading, writing, and arithmetic. The girls learned needlework and knitting and the boys studied navigation and astronomy. The curriculum was calculated to prepare the former for occupations as wives, domestics, and seamstresses and the latter for jobs in the maritime industry, a popular and relatively lucrative form of employment for black men. Few poor children of any color in the early republic would have been expected to attend college or pursue the most exclusive professions. The trustees planned for their students to work in the skilled and more respectable of trades. The best and the brightest would aim to become ministers, teachers, or small proprietors. The Manumission Society men, liberal in their racial egalitarianism, did not relinquish their gentleman's view of the world. They were not particularly interested in using their school to break down, in any radical way, status norms and class structures.

Academic skills were only one part of the curriculum. The school trustees were also keen to teach "regular behavior." Before the school opened, Davis was handed a list of rules for the pupils. The "scholars" were to come to school "decently washed and combed." They would not "injure their own or their schoolfellows books," nor "quarrel, call ill names, nor purposefully anger one another." This preoccupation with behavior extended to the parents. If there were competition for a seat in the school, "children of the most regular and orderly shall be preferred." The school was a carrot by which the Society sought to shape parents as well as children.[15]

According to the trustees, the rules were important because "Prejudice is not yet eradicated in this State, and hence the Blacks have few Associates among the Whites, except among the lowest Classes, whose morals are too generally debased." If black New Yorkers absorbed the manners prized by white philanthropists, they argued, prejudice would dissipate. The Society's environmentalist suggestion that slavery, not race, was the problem was a double-edged sword. The Society insisted repeatedly that black children were no different intellectually than white children, which meant that black children could inhabit equal adult citizenship. "Genius," they insisted, "is not confined to Colour, nor rectitude of Conduct to Symetry of Features." However, the belief that slavery had degraded black adults meant (to the trustees) that children needed figures other than their parents—white philanthropists, benevolent masters—to help instruct them. In hindsight, it is clear the Society was wrong about the easy eradication of prejudice, but their early hopefulness helps us reconstruct what they thought they were doing.[16]

For their part, black parents and adults supported the school, but they also had their own ways of advocating for themselves, protecting what was theirs, and understanding how prejudice functioned. There was an ongoing tension, both productive and fraught, between what white philanthropists wanted black freedom to look like and what black people knew they needed to do to get by on the ground. It was easy for white philanthropists to espouse respectability without understanding that sometimes "unruliness" was what it took for people to survive, or that freedom was inhabited and expressed in multiple ways.

Black men, women, and children pursued autonomy—and even revenge—in ways that fit the immediate circumstances of their enslaved or otherwise circumscribed lives. Sources outside of the neat, buttoned-up records of the Manumission Society make this clear. Cases brought before the city's justices of the peace, for example, illustrate that "regular and orderly" life was difficult for black workers trying to get by.[17] In the midsummer of 1799 alone, for example, a warrant was issued for a female slave for "running away from her mistress," a black woman was "committed for throwing a stone at a black man," a black boy was "taken up for attempting to persuade the complainant to rob his mistress," a female slave left "her master's service," a recaptured male runaway explained that "the work in this country is not easy enough [which was his] Reason of his Disobeying his master," a thirteen-year-old boy was "taken up by the watch" for "not giving a good account of" why his master was in another state while he was in the city, and a black woman was in trouble "for disorderly housekeeping" (she was likely keeping a brothel).[18] In a population-dense island city, there is little doubt that black families who utilized the Manumission Society's schools were aware of and even involved with the activities that captured legal officials' attention. Sometimes, what the courts saw as disturbing the peace or the Society saw as vice, black people saw as self-defense, making a living, maintaining family, or seeking pleasure. Running away could mean fleeing abuse, seizing liberty, or looking for better employment. Being in the wrong place at the wrong time could mean spending time with loved ones. White abolitionists and black New Yorkers may have agreed that black freedom was a good thing, but they did not always agree on how one got there or how one lived it.[19]

The Society's understanding of why people did what they did was often limited. Yet leaving the analysis there means missing the long-term effects of their approach. By inserting themselves—and their wealth and power—into black families' lives, the Society laid the groundwork for lasting relationships to form among black and white antislavery New Yorkers. By the early 1790s, there were 349 black adults and children under the Society's "patronage." The Society had visited these families' homes, approved of what they saw, admitted the children to school, and shared their advice (wanted or not). This was an early version of interracial abolitionism—it was not egalitarian, but it was interracial. On a practical level, these New Yorkers needed each other. And the Society's message to children—that they were intellectual equals and avatars of black freedom—influenced students who took the lessons into adulthood.[20]

By 1795, 223 children had attended the school and the number kept growing. The trustees regularly organized exhibitions to flaunt the students' erudition. After one event in 1796, *Greenleaf's New Daily Advertiser* argued that "the most prejudiced advocate of African slavery, if present, could have felt his favorite argument weakened; he must have acknowledged that the powers of the mind do not depend on the complexion." The *Herald* added that the students were "capable of discharging the duties of citizens and of being useful to themselves and to society." Given the repeated attempts to pass a gradual abolition law in the 1790s and the worry that John Jay might not be elected governor because of his Manumission Society membership, such articles were directly relevant to electoral politics and developing definitions of citizenship.[21]

In the second decade of the school, children began to witness the growing participation of black adults in institutional life. In January 1797, Davis left his position. The trustees hired a white man named William Pirsson and the institution's first black teacher, John Teasman. A white woman, Abigail Nicolls, stayed on to teach the girls. Soon after they were hired, Pirsson and Teasman opened an evening program for adults and children who worked during the day. That same winter, the trustees invited parents and guardians to attend the school's quarterly examination, where the children performed "their various exercises in a correct and pleasing manner." In 1799, Teasman was promoted to headmaster of the school.[22]

This was a different state of affairs from when the school first opened. In a report to the American Convention of Abolition Societies, the Society noted that one thousand black New Yorkers were under their patronage and over half were free. "Many" were freeholders, and therefore voters. Moreover, "associations among the free blacks for mutual support" ensured that the population was "in a state of progressive improvement." Between 1784 and 1812, black New Yorkers founded three churches (Methodist, Episcopal, Baptist), two incarnations of the African Society for Mutual Relief, the African Marine Fund for the Relief of Distressed Orphans, the Wilberforce Philanthropic Association, and the Boyer Masonic Lodge.[23]

Teasman was a crucial figure in this flowering of black associational activity. Born enslaved in New Jersey in 1754, he was an indefatigable educational, political, and philanthropic leader. He transformed the African Free School into a black town square. In 1807, for example, Teasman, William Hamilton, and Peter Williams Jr., an African Free School graduate and pioneering Episcopalian leader, announced that a dozen men at the schoolhouse had formed a committee to celebrate the American abolition of the international slave trade on January 1, 1808 with a parade. The group expressed gratitude to God and to the "Government," which "cooperated with them in this Cause." To ensure the parade's success, Williams petitioned the common council for "peace officers" to "prevent any tumult." After the council obliged, Williams provided the white lawmakers tickets so that they could hear "the Oration which is to be delivered by an African descendent at the African Church in Church Street."[24]

Williams was the chosen speaker. His speech credited the Quakers for their eighteenth-century antislavery efforts and applauded Anthony Benezet in particular for opening schools for black children, a venture that acknowledged "African genius." Williams emphasized the importance of law and politics for the abolition of slavery. The successful movement to end the slave trade left "no legal means . . . untried . . . books were disseminated, and discourses delivered . . . applications were constantly made to different bodies of legislature."[25]

A year later, Teasman, Williams, and other former students made their commemorative committee permanent by founding the African Society for Mutual Relief, a self-help society and sponsor of political events. Over one hundred men joined. Hamilton explained that their object was "to improve the mind, soften the couch of the sick, to administer an elixir to the afflicted, to befriend the widow, and become the orphan's guardian." Men like these ensured that the younger generation learned more than basic academics. In their hands, the school became a physical and intellectual resource that promoted autonomous black community life.[26]

The same year that the African Society prepared its inaugural January 1 celebration, Teasman introduced the Lancaster method to the school. Developed by English Quaker Joseph Lancaster, the pedagogical system was an inexpensive way to teach large numbers of children. Under the direction of a teacher, older student "monitors" taught younger students in subjects they had mastered. The method was implemented in both the African Free School and in the schools of the more recently founded Public School Society for white children.[27] School reformers would later criticize Lancasterianism as hierarchical, rigid, and superficial, but it is nonetheless intriguing to consider how the method shaped participants. It relied on more advanced students taking responsibility for newer pupils, under the guidance of a black teacher.

Just shy of his fourteenth birthday, for example, James McCune Smith, the "Monitor General of Order," took over a schoolhouse of 140 children when the regular teacher was severely ill. The visiting trustees noted that Smith, with deputy monitors helping, was "managing very well." But Smith pushed back, commenting that the students were better behaved when trustees visited than when the monitors were on their own. He asked the trustees to come more often. A week later, the trustees reported that they were visiting regularly and Smith was doing "his duty to our entire satisfaction." Impressed, the trustees called Smith a "lad of promise."[28] Smith later became the country's first black citizen to earn a medical degree. He was also a writer, philosopher, and politician. His experience as a monitor in his youth suggests that he learned early how to challenge white reformers who saw given situations differently than he did. Throughout his life, he excelled at both working with and enlightening white collaborators.[29]

Smith also learned from the career of Headmaster Teasman. Despite Teasman's loyalty to the school, the Manumission Society fired him in the spring of 1809. The Society cited lack of student progress and declining attendance. But it is also clear that Teasman and the trustees did not always see eye to eye. A few months after his dismissal, Teasman and the African Society argued with the Manumission Society over acceptable public political expression. The African Society was intent on staging their annual parade; the trustees thought the idea "improper" and hoped the group would discontinue "their processions, and Politicks in their Orations." The African Society politely said no and marched anyway. The story of the 1810 parade left so much of an impression that, years later, the tale of the defiant celebration still circulated. Indeed, Smith was still telling the story of the African Society's "bold action" in the 1860s.[30]

The African Society's determination to commemorate January 1 in the manner they saw fit marked an independent steak, but to end the story here would obscure the nuances of black politics in the early republic. Teasman continued to support the school after he left. He was no fool; the white abolitionists he knew there remained useful. Mere weeks after the African Society's contentious march, Manumission Society sympathizer DeWitt Clinton, who was both the mayor and a state senator, helped the African Society receive a charter of incorporation from the state. In an 1811 speech at the African Episcopal Church, Teasman spoke of "the happy success of the African Free School in the illumination of our minds" and thanked Clinton and the Manumission Society. In 1813, Teasman rallied fellow black voters to support Manumission Society lawyer Daniel D. Tompkins in his third successful run for governor.[31]

What Teasman knew—and what his generation passed on to the children of gradual abolition —was that black independence, perhaps somewhat ironically, at times had to rely on the ability to take advantage of white benevolent institutions and legislative resources. Indeed, successive generations remained adept at pursuing their political goals by utilizing relationships with white partners and appealing to local and state government for legal and financial support. This was an instrumental politics of access.

The Manumission Society, for its part, continued to make strides on behalf of black education, which suggests why black families continued to attend the schools. In 1810, the Society not only convinced the city to grant them lots to build a new schoolhouse, but persuaded the legislature, while Tompkins was governor, to grant them $1,500 to construct the building. This was the same year the Society successfully lobbied the legislature to pass a law mandating black children statewide receive at least some education. In 1813, the African Free School was included in an act allocating state funds to burgeoning common schools in the city. Each school would receive funds "in proportion to the average number of children between the ages of four and fifteen years, taught therein the year preceding such distribution, free of expense."[32]

Teasman and others may have harbored private dislike for the Society's highhanded ways, but it made little sense to alienate the white abolitionists. It also made little sense to disavow the workings of law and politics. For African Free School students growing up during gradual abolition, coming of age meant watching black and white adults collaborating, sometimes testily, and allying with local and state governments to achieve their objectives. This is not to say that formal law and politics were perfect mechanisms that always worked in black people's favor—laws upheld the very institution of slavery, after all—or that there was never disagreement about how to engage state systems, but it is to say that black New Yorkers pursued education and crafted free life in a manner that brought them into formal contact, as free citizens, with legislatures, councils, and governmental officials. Black New Yorkers were the democratic foot soldiers and founders of the Empire State's most visible common schools.

* * *

Although New York City was home to the largest single community of black people in the state in the early 1800s, the vast majority of New York's black population—roughly 80 percent, or 30,000 people—lived outside of Manhattan.[33] These black New Yorkers sometimes had the support of white partners, but there was no equivalent of the New York Manumission Society, in terms of size and resources, outside of New York City. Black adults nevertheless managed to piece together schooling for their children, relying on a combination of private resources, relationships with local elites, and proactive connections with lawmakers. In building schools, they bolstered the academic lives of children and claimed a space for free black people in the growing associational space that linked private and governmental spheres.

Between 1812 and 1822, the legislature created a framework for school funding and governance, an early series of steps in creating what became the modern public school system. Every county received money from the state, which was distributed to towns according to the number of resident children. Each town was responsible for raising matching funds and electing commissioners. Within the towns, taxpayers in individual school districts elected trustees. In some cities, common councils appointed trustees. A state superintendent of common schools was empowered to settle local controversies. Because common schools were built and controlled locally, experiences varied wildly across the state. Some jurisdictions moved quickly to open and centralize common school operations. Others took decades.[34]

Free black New Yorkers, as taxable citizens of their towns, fell under the purview of state school laws. The larger question was whether they would be treated equally under these laws—or what "equal" even meant. In some places, black parents wanted access to white schools. Elsewhere, parents cared more about equitable funding, curricular rigor, and hiring black teachers. Given both the diversity of local needs and the details of state law, black citizens found themselves moving between local and state arenas as they advocated for their children. In the process, they not only improved black schools, but also strengthened face-to-face ties with each other. Agitating for school rights on a local level facilitated, in the long run, black citizens' capacity to mobilize for larger campaigns on statewide issues.

In Brooklyn, where black residents made up 20 percent of the population, black families proved adept at marshaling their own private assets in combination with public resources to educate their children. In 1815, a year before Brooklyn established its first state-funded common school, a free black whitewasher named Peter Croger, a founding member of the local African Woolman Society, opened a "Day and Evening School" in his house for those wanting to be "taught the common branches of education." Croger was among a number of local leaders who worked on behalf of Brooklyn's well-rooted black community for decades.[35]

The communitarian ethos that made it possible for the Croger school to operate without public funding remained crucial in the common school era. In 1818, Brooklyn's school commissioners established the village's first district building, which included a separate floor for black children. Local officials denied the black classrooms adequate funding. In response, black families raised their own funds while also advocating for a larger share of public money. In the early 1820s, the local African Church hosted exhibitions of "Speaking and Singing" by the "coloured children attached to the district school" to meet a "debt due to a former school-master." In the course of an event like this, young performers acquired experience in public-facing racial uplift work, witnessed their educations being treasured by parents and teachers, and learned that governments needed to be pressed to provide equal resources. In 1827, after the colored school was kicked out of the district building, the Woolman

Society constructed their own schoolhouse. Meanwhile, black Brooklynites refused to let local officials off the hook. "A Colored Man Who Pays School Taxes," for example, wrote a letter to the *Long-Island Star* railing against the stingy funding: "Our school," he insisted, "needs a further proportional allowance of the school fund, that our destitute children may be properly taught."[36]

In Albany, as in Brooklyn, it was black men rather than white abolitionists who spearheaded the first black schools. At the forefront were veterans of the Revolutionary War and religious leaders, including Benjamin Lattimore Sr. and Francis Jacobs. Both men were exceptionally skilled at navigating the military, civic, political, and religious transformations and possibilities of the early republic.

Jacobs, born in 1758 in Brooklyn and likely enslaved, had served as a waiter and pioneer for George Washington in his "military family" from 1777 to roughly 1783. After a postwar stint in New York City, he moved to Albany, where by 1809 he was "licensed by the Hon. Corporation of the city" to "keep a Chimney Office." Jacobs lived a short walk from Lattimore, who was licensed by the city as a cartman. Born free in Connecticut in 1762, Lattimore had lived in the Hudson Valley for decades. In 1777, he enlisted in New York's (apparently integrated) Fifth Regiment as a private, was taken prisoner in the British capture of Fort Montgomery, and, after being rescued, rejoined his regiment. In the 1790s, he settled in Albany with an infant son named Benjamin Jr., whose mother had probably died, and bought land for one hundred pounds. He was baptized in the Presbyterian Church in 1799 and married Dina, a "servant maid of Dr. Mancius," in 1804. Lattimore, and likely Jacobs, voted in local and state elections.[37]

In 1811, Lattimore purchased a slice of land on Malcom Street from Elizabeth Schuyler Hamilton, widow of Alexander Hamilton—also a member of Washington's military family—and daughter of General Philip Schuyler. The following year, under the auspices of an association called the African Society, Lattimore, Jacobs, "& others" announced they had raised $915 from "the citizens of Albany and its vicinity" to build a church and school on the lot. In 1813, the men advertised for a teacher. Three years later, using the name "Albany School for educating People of Color," they petitioned the legislature for an act of incorporation for "the better management of their property, and regulation of their school." Federalist politician Abraham Van Vechten, who had married into the Schuyler family, shepherded the incorporation bill through committee. The resulting act granted the corporation ownership of the land and school, to be managed by seven trustees, including Lattimore and Jacobs. That summer, the Society announced that their church and school "near the mansion house of the late Gen. Schuyler" would hold a celebration, during which the law of incorporation would be read aloud.[38]

Records about the African School on Malcolm Street, as it was called, are sparse, but it is nonetheless possible to imagine some of what the students would have experienced and absorbed. Benjamin and Dina's young children—William, Betsy, and Mary—likely attended the school. There, they would have learned alongside roughly sixty students, which, given the relatively small size of Albany and its black population, meant that they would have encountered half of their local generational peers at school. For a few years, their teacher was William Levington, who would soon become the third black American to be ordained as a priest by the Episcopal Church. He was succeeded, in 1823, by a black man "remarkably well qualified" according to local white supporters. All things considered, the fact that black families—families who had been unable to accumulate much generational wealth—managed to create a successful school from scratch before a full-fledged, tax-supported common school system emerged in the city is extraordinary. The students saw adults around them employ relationships with white and black donors, state government, private landowners, and the press to build their institution. In so doing, these adults signaled their faith in the younger generation's potential to "rise."[39]

Given how difficult it was to maintain a school without public funding, it took persistence to keep the Malcolm Street school running. The trustees found themselves in constant financial precarity. In 1820, the white Albany Lancaster School Society donated $50 to keep the school afloat. The following year, they gave $125, with the stipulation that the school's mortgage be transferred to the Society in trust—a loss of black autonomy. In 1823, the Lancaster trustees agreed to superintend the school.[40] That same year, the black Baptist minister Nathaniel Paul, a Boston transplant who had recently moved to Albany, wrote to John Van Ness Yates, the state superintendent of common schools, to request the legislature appropriate funds for Albany's black children. Yates agreed, but the legislature failed to act. The school closed for a spell but then reemerged when the Lancaster Society moved its operations to the basement of Paul's new church, the First African Baptist Church on Hamilton Street. Seventy students received instruction from same black teacher who had taught them on Malcolm Street, as well as from a white teacher named Andrew McKaig. The latter commented that "the children in general seem to love learning, and in the endowment of their mental faculties, to be like others."[41]

We can glean some of the politics, values, and capacities of the generation of Albany's children who grew up in the early 1800s by tracing the adult paths of Susan Douge, an Albany-born woman who was likely educated at the African School, Michael Douge, her New York City–born husband, Benjamin Lattimore Jr., and Lattimore Jr.'s wife, Maria Coe Lattimore, a literate woman who appears to have been born a black servant child in the Hudson Valley. The Douges and Lattimores were all involved in the African Methodist Episcopal Church. There, they must have crossed paths with Julia Foote, whose story opened this chapter. In 1833, Susan was a charter member of the Female Lundy Society, an antislavery organization supporting black schoolchildren. At least one of the Douges' sons attended the African School on Hamilton Street, where he won plaudits in the press for his declaiming abilities. In 1841, the common council began funding the African School, which had moved from the Baptist to the Methodist church, as part of District 2 of the citywide school system. That same year, the Lattimores and Douges began sending their children to the white common school in District 8, presumably because it was closer to home and because they valued integrated schooling. The Douges' oldest child, Catherine Mary, became a teacher at the black common school. Meanwhile, Benjamin and Michael, along with an increasingly wealthy local tailor named William H. Topp, were active in the growing colored convention movement, in which free black men from across the state gathered to discuss their political rights and antislavery strategies.[42]

The Lattimores' and Douges' adult lives are evidence of what was made possible for children by the educational efforts of their parents. There is source material enough to show us that a critical number of mothers and fathers in the early republic ensured their sons and daughters learned to read, write, and think among peers and teachers who believed in civic obligation and antislavery politics. These efforts resulted in a generation of children who, as active adults in the 1830s, '40s, and '50s, maintained and expanded the work their parents had started.

* * *

It is worth highlighting a few more representative examples of black schooling in early New York State. These brief sketches expose the sheer range of student experiences and help explain why, as these children became adults, they were able to organize across county lines due to their literacy, associational skills, and belief that there was a place for them in New York's civic future. At the same time, it is evident that many children never received formal schooling, which does not mean that they failed to interact with lawmakers or engage in civic pursuits alongside more educated peers. On the contrary, people without school learning routinely shaped politics. The point, nonetheless, is to show how a critical mass of black New Yorkers encountered education in ways that served them both individually and as a generation.

Unsurprisingly, one of the earliest efforts in the state to create a black school originated with rural Quakers. In 1794, Elias Hicks and fellow Friends in western Long Island created the Jericho Charitable Society. Hoping the time would come when black people would "enjoy the equal priviledges of their fellow men," the charity raised money for "the Education of their Children." The Jericho school was never large—it taught one to twenty-seven children at a given time—but it lasted, fueled by Quaker donations, for decades. Given that the Yearly Meeting had, since 1775, required that Friends teach black children to "read and qualify them for business," it is certain that at least some Quakers elsewhere in the state provided rudimentary education to black children, even if the efforts were not as formalized as those in Jericho.[43]

Meanwhile, the growing ecumenical Sunday School movement provided black children and adults with elementary but meaningful opportunities to learn in some places. For example, in Troy, on the west side of the Hudson, black residents encountered formal schooling in 1816, when local Presbyterians opened four Sunday schools, including one dedicated to children of color, who had otherwise been "excluded from our ordinary schools." Concerned that "their ignorance was our fault—they were treated as an inferior race," the Presbyterians found "powerful motives" as Christians to reverse white neglect. Ninety black students, ages 5 to 60, attended school on the first day. The pupils "expressed an earnest desire to learn to read"; the majority were female.[44]

Several years later, an association called the Troy African Society convinced the common council to assume the debts they had accrued for building their own school, which had operated since at least 1820. In a turn of events similar to what occurred in Albany, the local Lancaster Society took over the school, hiring two black female teachers in the process. The press asked white citizens to contribute, arguing that they owed black children financial support: "There are some who have owned the flesh and blood of their parents, and such will not, cannot refuse to extend a little aid to those who cannot attend the school without charitable assistance." It was vital to give "colored children" an education that would "enable them to become useful citizens." This white editor thus linked the obligation to provide white funds for black children—who were explicitly "citizens"—to the wealth that had been stolen by enslaving their parents.[45]

In 1830, frustrated by the lack of public support, black Trojans decided to rededicate themselves to supporting their own independent school. A black woman, Elizabeth Wicks, was hired for ten dollars a month to run the institution. The children's families paid some of her salary, while a successful black barber named William Rich made up the difference. Alexander Thuey, another "prominent colored citizen," gave Wicks room and board, while a white politician's wife supplied the school with fuel and paper. The school survived for thirty years before the Board of Education agreed to invest seriously in it.[46]

Black schools in the Hudson Valley, like Troy's, benefited from the longstanding community roots that existed among local families. It is not hard to imagine that some of the parents sending their children to school in Troy had once been enslaved in neighboring households. But across the state, and especially in the newer settlements of western New York, schools could also be places where residents of an area met for the first time.

One of the most influential teachers in the Finger Lakes region, for example, was Jermain W. Loguen, a runaway from Tennessee. Loguen, who became one of New York's most prominent ministers and abolitionists, moved to Rochester after his escape in the 1830s. At a fancy hotel where he worked, he met generous patrons and eavesdropped on political conversations, including "boisterous discussions about slavery in the bar room." Loguen also encountered Elymus P. Rogers, a black student studying at the nearby Oneida Institute, an integrated abolitionist college in Whitesboro where African Free School graduates such as Garnet and Crummell also studied. With Rogers' help, Loguen was admitted to Oneida. In his third year, during the long winter break, Loguen started a black school in the burgeoning city of Utica. On the first day, "but three scholars came to school—but the number soon increased to forty." At term's end, "the people were desirous of a public school examination." The children "presented themselves in all the pride of juvenile humanity on the stage, to a large and mixed audience. It was the first exhibition of colored children, it is presumed, in central or western New York." Over the next decade, Loguen taught school in Bath, Syracuse, and Ithaca. It was in his role as a teacher that Loguen "began to feel the delight of living for use."[47]

Children in places like Brooklyn, Albany, Troy, and the fast-growing western municipalities where Loguen taught had the benefit of tight-knit free black communities that scraped together educational opportunities, but boys and girls in very rural areas were more often on their own when it came to schooling. Thomas James, who grew up in the sparsely settled Mohawk River Valley in central New York, received no education while in servitude. Born in 1804 in farmer Asa Kimball's household, James later recounted how his siblings and parents were sold away when he was eight years old.[48] After Kimball died, James ran away to Canada, but returned to New York several months later. In Rochester, he found employment and made friends. Zenas Freeman, a white teacher, taught a "Sunday school of his own for colored youths." The clerks in the warehouse where James worked assisted him "whenever I needed help in my studies." In 1823, he joined the African Methodist Episcopal Society, where he crossed paths with the abolitionist grocer Austin Steward, the former slave from Virginia who, like James, received an education late in childhood from white teachers. The black Methodists soon joined forces with white religious and civic leaders, including Nathaniel Rochester himself, to erect a new church and school. James ran a school for black children in the meanwhile. He was an older child of gradual abolition who taught the youngest cohort of this distinctive generation.[49]

James's story is instructive not only for what it tells us about how some children managed to find education in gradual abolition New York, but for thinking about how their youthful experiences as social beings at work, at church, and at school affected the course of antislavery history in the second quarter of the nineteenth century. In his late 20s, after reading antislavery literature by the white abolitionist Arthur Tappan loaned to him by a local judge, James committed himself to ensuring that "the colored man became the equal of the white in the eye of the law." James and white reformers began holding antislavery meetings and founded an abolitionist paper, *The Rights of Man*. He traveled to nearby communities to solicit subscriptions and conducted a survey of Rochester's 360 black residents. From there, James moved to Syracuse, then Ithaca, then Sag Harbor, all in New York State, where he opened or grew black churches. His next stop was New Bedford, Massachusetts, where he mentored the person who became the most famous black male abolitionist in the United States: the Maryland-born Frederick Douglass. In 1847, Douglass moved his family to Rochester, where he began printing the *North Star* in the basement of the church that James and his friends had founded years earlier. Harriet Tubman, the most famous black female abolitionist of the century, also originally enslaved in Maryland, likewise made Rochester Zion Church a spiritual and antislavery home. Under her guidance, the site was crucial stop on the Underground Railroad for fugitive slaves.[50]

Children of gradual abolition like Thomas James helped create the literacy, community, and material structures that helped southern-born luminaries like Douglass and Tubman execute their better-known work. In this sense, the giants of midcentury black abolitionism stood on the shoulders of the children of gradual abolition.

* * *

During the same years that black schools were sprouting—sometimes flourishing, sometimes failing—across the state, the African Free School entered an era of significant growth. Between 1809, the year Teasman left, and 1834, the year the institution was transferred to the Public School Society's common school system, the institution grew from one building into six schools dotted throughout lower Manhattan. In the 1820s and '30s, the school employed over a dozen teachers of both races who taught roughly a third of the city's black children. Enrollment hovered around six hundred to seven hundred students in the 1820s, spiking almost twice as high in the 1830s. The school's growth correlated with the course of gradual emancipation. As slavery shrank, more parents were able to choose to send their children to school.[51]

The school maintained core ideals and practices from its founding era. This institutional inertia had both conservative and radical implications. The school continued to employ the Lancaster method, trustees continued to fret over codes of behavior, and girls and boys continued to learn different skills. In these respects, the school was little different from other common and charity schools. What continued to distinguish the African Free School was its unapologetic antislavery politics. Black education remained explicitly tied to abolitionist goals. This continuity was all the more significant in a racial, labor, and political climate that was becoming increasingly hostile to black people. Indeed, the school's heyday coincided with the advent of "white man's democracy" and the growing popularity of the colonization movement, which imagined a future where black people would be free but living outside of United States borders. In many respects, the school seemed like a throwback to a more hopeful, inclusive moment.[52]

The headmaster during these tumultuous years was a white British-born teacher named Charles A. Andrews. Like Teasman before him, Andrews earned praise in some corners and ruffled feathers in others, but there is no doubt he left an imprint on his students. When Samuel Ringgold Ward published his autobiography in 1855, he recalled Andrews's "great kindness" to him at a time when the city's other white citizens harbored "ever-crushing Negro-hate."[53]

During Andrews's tenure, the students' studies remained intertwined with the campaign to free black people from bondage, not only in the nation but in the wider Atlantic world. At one public examination in 1816, for example, a student named Joseph Anthony recited verses from "Slavery," a 1788 poem by British abolitionist Hannah More. Anthony began with lines describing the horrors of kidnappings in Africa. He continued through a passage that read, "Perish the illiberal thought which would debase/The native genius of the sable race!/Perish the proud philosophy which sought/To rob them of their powers of equal thought." That Anthony lived in a country where the vast majority of his racial peers were forbidden to read and write made the poem all the more poignant. Slavery was a national and international problem. African Free School students stood as arguments against assumptions used to justify the evil.[54]

During these public exhibitions, girls and boys received equal time to demonstrate their knowledge. For example, in 1817, the nine-year-old daughter of Peter Williams Jr., Matilda, was allotted a speaking part. She likely recited an antislavery piece, or perhaps a chapter from the Bible. The trustees reported "particular" satisfaction with the "progress of the girls" under their teacher, a white woman named Lucy Turpin. Matilda won a prize for her speaking portion: a "tin toy." The following year, Matilda spoke again, this time on the slave trade.[55]

Surviving records of the African Free School's daily functioning are frustratingly thin, but the very few pages that list students' names—including Matilda's—offer tantalizing clues about the lifelong female friendships that were nurtured by the school. (The girls' parents also moved in similar social circles, so there is no question that they also encountered each other outside of school, as well.) For example, the same year Matilda won her prize, several other girls won books and trinkets for "good behavior and attention." One was Emeline Varick, the daughter of African Methodist Episcopal minister James Varick. Another was named Hannah Francis. All three girls grew up to be antislavery reformers. Matilda, who married a successful Philadelphia barber named Joseph Cassey, was a member of the Philadelphia Female Antislavery Society. Emeline married a "very worthy husband" of Haitian descent named John Bastien and raised money for the *North Star* and for runaway slaves. Hannah's adult trajectory is less clear, but she moved in the same antislavery circles as Emeline. Because many girls eventually married and changed

After the Exercises of the Scholars where completed following Rewards & Prizes were distributed viz'

To William Green -	Best Reader -	Book "London"
Caty Anderson .	2nd Best . -	Tin Toy . No
Maria Jackson	Best Writer -	Morrocco Needle
Richard Johnson -	2nd Best -	Pencill Case & Lake
Lucy Harris	Best Speller -	Wax Work
Edward Harris .	2nd Best .	Pencill Case & Lake
Charles Read .	Best Arithmetician -	Map S. Ame
James Anthony .	2nd Best -	do N. Ame
John Loane .	Best Behaved Scholar -	Knife +
Betsey Prior .	2nd Best -	Pewter Cup
James Fields .	Best Piece Ori. Composition -	Franklin on
William Hill .	Best Public Speaker .	Book
Matilda Williams .	2nd Best -	Tin Toy
Jane Dean .	Excelled in Needle Work .	Print of a

Figure 7. In 1817, Matilda Williams won second place for Best Public Speaker at an African Free School exhibition. Matilda was the daughter of Peter Williams Jr., an abolitionist and Episcopal priest. New-York African Free School Records, 1817–1832, Volume 1, New-York Historical Society.

their names, and because all of the girls faced more limited public and professional opportunities than their male classmates, it is not as easy to trace female graduates with specificity. That said, we know for certain that Matilda Williams Cassey, Eveline Bastien, and Hannah Francis performed antislavery labor alongside their more famous male contemporaries. And they were not alone: there were hundreds of other unnamed girls at the school who, as adults, took part in political campaigns, packed courtrooms during relevant trials, supported the Underground Railroad, and devoted time to churches, schools, and associations.[56]

Part of what these women, as well as their male classmates, learned at the school was that local politics mattered. They knew that city and state government affected their educational fortunes. In 1824, for example, the boys and girls gave a well-received performance to three aldermen visiting on behalf of the common council. Papers throughout the Northeast picked up the story, reporting that "several of the clergy," "a few strangers," and "a goodly number" of Quakers brought the total number present to 600, 350 of whom were students. Of particular interest was a speech delivered by a seven-year-old boy. "I have learned considerable since the last examination," he explained. "I was then entirely ignorant of writing; I now present you with these humble specimens of my attainments." The aldermen reported that the students were skilled in "Spelling, Reading, Writing, Arithmetic, Grammar, and Elocution, and Needlework" and gave good answers when peppered with questions. The aldermen recommended and received the council's continued financial support of the school.[57]

These public events were heavily scripted. Many, though not all, of the student performances were written or edited by the teachers.[58] But there is evidence that children took their own lessons from these exhibitions. The same year the seven-year-old spoke to the aldermen, eleven-year-old James McCune Smith delivered an oration at a reception held in honor of General Lafayette, French hero of the American Revolution and an abolitionist himself. In front of hundreds of students, teachers, officials, and journalists, Smith declared to Lafayette: "Here, sir, you behold hundreds of the poor children of Africa sharing with those of a lighter hue in the blessings of education." He explained that he and his friends "cherish the memory of General La Fayette as a friend of African Emancipation." Soon thereafter, Smith recited the speech to passengers on a steamship while traveling to Philadelphia. He reported receiving "a pocket full of small change, twenty-five cents of which, carefully wrapped up in a piece of cloth, I enclosed in a letter to my dear mother as my first earnings." Few American eleven-year-olds, white or black, addressed international figures or large audiences composed of different classes and races. Smith seized on his experiences for his own purposes. His pleasure at making money suggests an early recognition that he could use his intellect to make a living.[59]

For all the moments of success and celebration, students at the school also found themselves in an era of political whiplash. In 1821, New York's new constitution extended the franchise to virtually all white men while establishing a property requirement of $250 for black men, disfranchising the majority. Black families faced increasing threats to their livelihoods. White laborers, many of them immigrants, battled with black workers over access to neighborhoods and jobs. Black artisans and purveyors, who had gained ground in the early 1800s, found themselves more vulnerable. Many could get work only as domestics or unskilled laborers. On the street level, rioters struck black communities throughout the Northeast. Mobs went after black bodies, homes, churches, and businesses, as well as the property of white abolitionists.[60]

At least one African Free School family decided, in this context, that leaving the United States was a good option. In 1824, twelve-year-old Serena Baldwin sat in the African Zion Church listening to Peter Williams Jr. address 120 black New Yorkers, including her family, who had decided to emigrate to Haiti at the invitation of President Jean-Pierre Boyer. As Williams explained, "you are going to a good country, governed by good laws, where a dark complexion will be no disadvantage." He exhorted the group to be respectable, temperate, industrious, independent, and pious. Baldwin's father, a successful oysterman living on Leonard Street, fit the profile. He was listed in the county jury census as owning personal real estate of at least $150. (Next door lived Boston Crummell, also an oysterman, whose infant son Alexander eventually became one of the African Free School's most eminent graduates.) Baldwin was financially stable enough that his daughter and son could attend school rather than work, but the family nonetheless felt that New York was no longer the place for them. Black emigrants like the Baldwins—unlike many white colonizationists—thought black people should leave the country not because they were not suited to life in the United States, but because the United States had made things so unfair and difficult that it was easier to prosper elsewhere.[61]

Serena's letters from Haiti to her white African Free School teacher, Elizabeth Cox, provide a rare chance to hear the unscripted words of a young female scholar from the school. After arriving safely in Santo Domingo, Serena spoke with pride at how a "number of ladies and gentlemen" whom she met on arrival admired the needlepoint samplers and bench covers she made. She asked Cox to send her sewing supplies and closed by sending her "love" and "respect" to Cox, headmaster Charles Andrews, and her "schoolmates." After Cox sent back cloth and books, Serena wrote again to express the wonder at living in a black republic: "if ever there was a county where Liberty dwells, it is here." Serena knew her politics, too.[62]

Despite this promising beginning, within a few years, Serena's family, along with hundreds of other black emigrants, of those who had not died, made the voyage back to the United States. A combination of drought, poor food supply, a smallpox epidemic, complicated diplomatic relationships, and the inability to access promised political rights caused black Americans to rethink whether settling in Haiti was best for their families. In June 1828, Serena, her brother, and her parents arrived back in lower Manhattan.[63]

The Baldwins came home at a somewhat optimistic moment in the state. On July 4, 1827, as the legislature had promised, state slavery in New York ceased to exist. The day was marked by widespread public celebration. That same year, black Americans gained a new advocate in the form of the nation's first black newspaper, New York City's *Freedom's Journal*. In its first issue, editors Samuel Cornish and John Russwurm explained that they would devote their energies to "the dissemination of useful knowledge among our brethren, and to their moral and religious improvement." They would argue against colonization, report on nationwide antislavery activities, and facilitate the social and economic endeavors of their readers. Education was a favorite topic. Black minds had been "contracted by slavery, deprived of early education," and it was therefore vital to make children "useful members of society." Much of this language echoed the Manumission Society's. This did not mean, however, that the editors wanted white abolitionists in charge: "We wish to plead our own cause. Too long have others spoken for us."[64]

Indeed, the editors of *Freedom's Journal* were perfectly willing to criticize the African Free School. Although Cornish and Russwurm routinely emphasized the importance of education, they were skeptical of black schools throughout the Northeast. Critiquing the Lancaster method, they lamented, "The few who study Grammar, Geography, Arithmetic, advance so little that after leaving school they can derive no advantage from them. Parrot-like they have acquired them, and parrot-like they forget them." The editors also decried the low expectations placed on children. While it is difficult to prove a correlation, attendance at the African Free School dropped in the months Cornish and Russwurm wrote these articles. Advertisements in the paper show the availability of black private schools for parents who wanted to send children elsewhere.[65]

Andrews worked to reverse the tide of dissatisfaction. When the editors donated copies of the journal to the school library, the headmaster took the opportunity to prove that his students had been learning advanced topics outside of the Lancaster curriculum. He shared an anecdote: "One of our little scholars, aged about ten years, was questioned on some astronomical and other scientific subjects a few months ago, by a celebrated and learned doctor of this city; the boy answered so readily and so accurately to the queries, was at last asked, how was it he was so well acquainted with such subjects? His reply was, that he remembered to have read them in the books of the school library."[66] Cornish and Russwurm were among those responsible for ensuring Andrews's continued and perhaps deepened commitment to academic rigor.

Soon after publishing Andrews's letter, *Freedom's Journal* reported that the Manumission Society invited twelve black leaders to formulate strategies to boost attendance. The black men "expressed themselves freely" and devised a plan by which a black agent would visit families throughout the city to encourage enrollment. The editors suggested that school committees throughout the nation follow the New York example by including black men in administration. The trustees appointed Cornish to serve as the general visiting agent. Cornish, in turn, divided the city into seventeen districts and appointed thirty-four black men—including Peter Williams, Thomas L. Jinnings, and Benjamin Paul (brother of Nathaniel Paul of Albany)—to visit families. The Society ran advertisements encouraging enrollment, noting that children who could not afford the quarterly tuition of twenty-five cents to a dollar would be admitted without charge.[67]

Black women had their own parallel intensification of engagement with the school. Within a month of Cornish's appointment, a group of mothers formed the African Dorcas Association, whose purpose was to collect and make clothes for poor students. They founded the association in February, a time when attendance dropped because of cold temperatures. The group held meetings in the school and welcomed any black woman to join. Andrews crafted a constitution so the women would have their own charter of fundamental laws just as men's associations did. (The women were apparently agents enough to have their own charitable society, but not so equal as to write their own constitution, as black men routinely did.) A woman named Margaret Francis was the first president—perhaps Hannah Francis's mother? Maria DeGrasse, mother of students Isaiah and Serena DeGrasse, was also a board member.[68] *Freedom's Journal* encouraged women in "other cities" to create similar societies "for the benefit of the rising generation." The Manumission Society boasted to peers that these "benevolent colored females" were "productive of much good."[69] The school continued to be a place that both prompted black associationalism and benefited from it.

Cornish and Russwurm were now firmly behind the school. When the Society opened a new female branch, the editors urged enrollment. They praised the school for educating across class lines: "children of our colour have opportunities for gaining useful knowledge without respect to the condition of their parents, whether rich or poor, in an institution in this city, which is believed to be equal at least, to any establishment of the kind among whites in this country." Andrews earned laurels: he "has laboured indefatigably for its improvement . . . it would indeed be fruitless to search for a Teacher better qualified to teach and govern the school."[70]

Freedom's Journal also showcased student work. In 1828, the Manumission Society employed Smith's 1824 speech and other student writing at the Convention of Abolition Societies meeting in Baltimore to argue for the importance of black education as a means of achieving abolition throughout the nation. The newspaper reported that eight students contributed poetry, drawings, navigation exercises, and math problems. Fifteen-year-old George Moore, referring to the general abolition of 1827, explained to his audience that "since the last Convention, New York has been freed from slavery." Isaiah DeGrasse wrote, "It makes my heart burn within me, when I think of the poor Africans who are torn from their homes and relatives" and "forced to a distance from the means of proving and defending their rights." Elver Reason lamented, "there are so many in the southern States chained in slavery for no other crime, than the color of their skin!"[71]

George Allen demonstrated a particular interest in law, politics, and regional distinctions between free and slave states. The twelve-year-old queried, "What sound can be more delightful to the ear of a slave than the expression, 'The Laws have made you free?' This is the happy case with us in the state of New York." Cognizant that New York's "happy case" was by no means universal, Allen noted that "our brethren in the South" are "groaning under the chains of bondage." He hoped for the day when the nation would be able to give the egalitarian passages of the Declaration of Independence "their full weight." Allen knew that his daily efforts might contribute to this future moment; he understood that his own progress in school was connected to the broader project of national freedom, especially since, as he noted, visitors came "from the South and other parts of the country."[72]

DeGrasse, Reason, Moore, and Allen all grew up to be black leaders and abolitionists. Smith, describing yet another prominent fellow classmate, Peter Guignon, explained that it was the day that a student entered the African Free School that "public life began."[73]

When it came to "public life," the students learned from lessons both inside and outside of school. On the one hand, there was Andrews, who imparted the Manumission Society's "respectable" version of antislavery among pupils. A member of the Society himself, he was proud of the school's achievements. He urged students to be ambitious. Smith gave Andrews credit for boosting students' intellectual confidence: he "taught his boys and girls to look upward; to believe themselves capable of accomplishing as much as any other could, and to regard the higher walks of life as within their reach." For his advanced students, Andrews organized a "Class of Merit, which was a literary and deliberative assembly." The students elected officers, kept minutes, and held debates. This was student government—youth associationalism—for adolescents who would grow up to be deeply immersed in American politics. Andrews emphasized the importance of black citizenship, hoping for the day when "the well educated and respectable man of color shall be viewed and treated as such by his white brethren, and when character, not color, shall decide" one's reputation.[74]

And yet academic rigor and student government alone were not and would not be enough to keep slavery at bay. Both teachers and students alike knew that the world was violent, unjust, and rife with prejudice. In 1830, for example, the *Commercial Gazette* reported that local butcher boys were in the habit of setting their dogs on black students walking home from the African Free School. Andrews's son was also attacked. On one occasion, the butcher boys seized a "colored girl and held her fast, until the dogs had almost torn her clothes off."[75] It was impossible to ignore that being black, or being associated with antislavery politics if white, could be dangerous for a person who was simply trying to walk down the street.

This daily reality helps explain why one of the stories that made a lasting imprint on the students during the Andrews years was a story about fighting slavery on the streets, not in an exhibition or a Class of Merit. In 1829, recent graduate Henry Highland Garnet, fourteen years old, found himself facing the nightmarish possibility of the reenslavement of his family. The Garnets, originally enslaved in Maryland, had escaped to New York City in 1825. Henry's father worked as a shoemaker and settled his household next door to Alexander Crummell's family on Leonard Street. Henry became friends with Crummell, Smith, and a number of the brightest students in the African Free School. In late 1828, he was working at sea as a cabin boy when his family's former owner came in search of the runaways. Garnet's father, mother, and sister tried to escape out of the second floor of their home, jumping into the Crummells' yard next door, but his sister, Eliza, was caught. She was arrested as a fugitive slave and a trial was scheduled before the City Recorder, Richard Riker. The Garnets' home was destroyed and ransacked.[76]

In the midst of this turmoil, Henry returned from sea and was met on the wharf by friends who told him what happened. Henry, Smith later recalled, "purchased a large-clasp knife, openly carried it in his hand and sturdily marched up Broadway, waiting and hoping for the assault of the men-hunters." Crummell remembered that his classmate was "crazed" at the news of his family's misfortune, "prepared for an attack." His friends, worried that he would be recaptured himself or arrested for wandering the streets brandishing a knife, arranged for Henry to hide with Quakers on Long Island. Eliza, meanwhile, waited for court.[77]

Henry recalled later that his sister's case was "one of the most exciting fugitive slave cases" in the city and "the best legal aid" was secured. Manumission Society lawyers worked on the case, which appeared in their records as "E Garnet vs. C Knight." On the day of the trial, three thousand black men and women—no doubt African Free School families among them—assembled at City Hall, where Riker presided over the mayor's court. While this sympathetic crowd hoped for a favorable verdict, Henry knew that "if that failed then a rescue was to be attempted at the hazard of imprisonment or death." During the trial, a black minister and his wife who knew the Garnets swore that Eliza had been living as free. Riker, in Henry's retelling of the case, prompted a "triumphant shout" from the spectators when he declared "*Eliza Garnet you are free to go where you please.*" In April 1829, the Society affirmed that Eliza Garnet was "Free."[78]

The children of the African Free School were thus students of multiple forms of abolitionism. They learned from both their legalistic benefactors in the Manumission Society and from the "unruly" black laborers who fought slavery with more physical means. It is telling that Garnet celebrated the court's verdict while nevertheless insisting that his knife was an option. For the children of gradual abolition, law and material self-defense could be equally valid means of fighting slavery. As an adult, Garnet participated in political campaigns for black enfranchisement at the same time that he controversially urged slaves to rise up against their masters. This was "by all means necessary" not "either, or" antislavery.[79]

That said, one strand of antislavery ideology that the majority of black families in the school did not embrace was colonization, which was becoming more and more popular among antislavery white Americans, including some associated with the Manumission Society. Implicit (and sometimes explicit) for many white advocates of colonization was the notion that black people as a race were biologically distinct and not welcome in the United

States. The earlier environmentalist beliefs of sympathetic white reformers thus gave way to louder and louder statements of inherent black racial inferiority. In some respects, the Manumission Society's old-fashioned abolitionism, with its emphasis on equal access to citizenship and black intellectual capacity, looked more liberal compared to newer developments.

Andrews himself embraced colonizationist thinking, which led to his ouster as principal. In 1830, frustrated that his students faced difficulties finding employment, he made comments supporting plans for black Americans to move elsewhere. Andrews was troubled that young black men and women were being shut out of trades and respectable occupations because of their color. In his published history of the African Free School, he wrote of a student named Isaac, who, armed with his education and good character, was thwarted again and again in his search for employment: "Every place that appeared suitable to his object, was closed against him, *because he was black!* . . . he resolved to leave the country and go to the Colony of Liberia."[80]

Black families revolted against Andrews's support for colonization. They were more aware than anyone that political and occupational opportunities were closed to them, but they felt betrayed by the idea that the solution was to leave the land of their birth. Andrews had associated himself with a movement that most black people found insidious and insulting. To make matters worse, Andrews appears to have angered parents when he caned a student. Corporal punishment was common and legal in all schools in this time period, but this particular incident seems to have struck black parents as outside the acceptable norm. Elizabeth Jennings, the daughter of school agent Thomas L. Jinnings, reported in 1890 that "parents became indignant, and withdrew their children" in consequence of the physical "punishment and insult," which took place "in or about 1832." Between 1830 and 1832, enrollment at the school dropped from 716 to 467 students. The Society attempted to stem the exodus by inviting a black teacher named Benjamin Hughes, who had run his own institution for years, to teach in the African Free School. Hughes agreed, and Elizabeth's older siblings, among others, attended Hughes's African Free School branch. But the Andrews problem persisted.[81]

In the winter of 1831–1832, Andrews resigned. The Manumission Society reasoned "it would be more satisfactory to those who send their children to our schools if a person of their own color could be obtained." By this time, it was clear to the trustees that the reason Andrews left was "the prejudice now existing against him among the colored people." The Society hired a black teacher named James Adams to replace Andrews as headmaster. By summer, five of the six schools were staffed by at least one black teacher. Attendance rebounded and the total enrollment climbed to 1,068 students. The committee noted happily in the summer of 1832 that the "present quarterly attendance is more than any previous time." The Society credited this reversal in fortunes to the hiring of black teachers and "the exertion of many of the colored people to open the eyes of parents to the advantages held out to their children."[82]

In 1833, the African Free School's faculty included black female teachers Eliza Richards (a graduate of the school), Fanny Tompkins and Sarah Ennalls (who taught in the city's black schools for decades), and Sarah Mapps Douglass (on her way to becoming one of the most prominent black female abolitionists of the era). Hughes and John Peterson, both longtime educators, and Charles Reason and John Mills, both recent graduates, were their male colleagues. In a telling comment, the Manumission Society noted that these teachers "have the confidence of the colored people."[83]

In later years, James McCune Smith, who was fiercely opposed to colonization, would nonetheless lament that Andrews's "decided colonization views" had prompted "leading colored men" to ask the trustees to dismiss their headmaster, a teacher to whom the students' attachment was "ardent." It is unclear if all students felt this way, but regardless of their opinion of Andrews, the students had witnessed a revealing moment in the city's history of interracial politics. Smith and his cohort would find themselves in similar situations during their adult lives as they pushed white abolitionists in antislavery movements to respect black perspectives, or when they disagreed among themselves about how to characterize a white antislavery figure or politician.[84]

In 1834, the Manumission Society handed the African Free School over to the Public School Society, a state-chartered corporation that controlled the city's common schools. This move was part of a transformation in public education that was happening everywhere—a move toward more bureaucratic and centralized modern school systems. The change was difficult for the 1,600 black students who lost their longtime abolitionist benefactors. The school had never been perfect, but the institution and its politics had nonetheless been influential, productive, and even cherished. As Smith explained, the school had been a place where slaves escaping from the "Southern States collided with the sturdy New Yorkers" to "rejoice and press forward the young in the priceless advantages of free schools." No other black school in the nation had educated so many students and produced so many recognized and underrecognized civic leaders.[85]

By the mid-1830s, the Manumission Society's early republican educational experiment, with its interracial leadership, was over. But the students' careers were not. It was time, Smith said, to take up "the burden of their fathers."[86]

* * *

In the summer of 1838, African Free School graduates Charles Reason, Philip A. Bell, Thomas S. Sidney, and Patrick Reason, along with school parent Thomas L. Jinnings and several others, founded the New York Association for the Political Elevation and Improvement of the People of Color. The group would be governed by a constitution, which was printed in the *Colored American,* a new black newspaper run by Bell, Charles B. Ray, and Samuel Cornish. As the association gained momentum, members issued a call for "colored young men" to join them and referenced the spirit of African Free School agent and abolitionist William Hamilton, "speaking from the tomb," urging them to get busy. The call was signed by "Shade of Teasman," a reference to the beloved black headmaster. There is no question that the school—including its parent body and its black boosters—had succeeded in one of its missions: preparing a generation of black children to enlarge and champion freedom and equality using a variety of civic and associational tools.[87]

But the African Free School graduates in New York City were hardly alone. Two years later, these same men—Bell, Sidney, Charles Reason, Patrick Reason, as well as fellow schoolmates Peter Guignon and Albro Lyons, and teacher John Peterson—took part in a call for the first New York State Colored Convention. They were joined by a teacher named Augustus Washington from Brooklyn; Thomas James and Austin Steward from Rochester; Benjamin Paul and Benjamin Lattimore Jr. from Albany; William Rich, Alexander Thuey, and Henry High Garnet in Troy; Elymus P. Rogers and Jermain W. Loguen from Whitesboro; Samuel Ringgold Ward in Peterborough; and dozens of other black men from fifty towns and cities across the state. Many on the list had fought to educate themselves and supported local schools. Their "primary object" in 1840 was "to adopt such measures as can be simultaneously carried out by our brethren in every section of the State, to obtain a relief from those political disabilities under which we labor."

These were local men gearing up for a *state* fight. They would "come together to take some decisive measures to lay before the next Legislature." In seeking to engage the legislature, they followed in the footsteps of their parents, mentors, and benefactors. What made this call distinct was the cross-state emphasis. Local men would join "from Suffolk to Erie, from Clinton to Steuben" to "engage together in a common interest."[88] Observing the list of organizers, it is clear that local schools ultimately fostered statewide black political action.

The women were busy, too. While less prominent in state political circles, they were active in their local communities. In 1834, the black teacher Elizabeth Wicks spoke before the African Female Benevolent Society of Troy, whose board members included Phebe Thuey and Hannah Rich, wives of Alexander and William. She reminded the "rising generation" that they would soon "fill the places we now occupy." She believed the new generation's "advantages are greater and their prospects fairer" than what her own generation had encountered.[89] In Troy and elsewhere, the schoolchildren whom Wicks referenced in her address did indeed fill the places that their teachers and parents had occupied. In 1850, for example, Emeline Bastien, Fanny Tompkins, Elizabeth Jinnings, Mary Crummell, Serena Downing, Hannah Francis, Maria DeGrasse, and Sarah Aldridge—all of whom attended, taught in, or had family ties to the African Free School—organized a fair to support Frederick Douglass's *North Star* so that the "crime and horrors of Slavery" would be exposed in "every corner." The following year, they turned their group into the "North Star Fair Association." Black women of this generation were not allowed the same public and professional opportunities as their male peers, but they, too, employed their childhood schooling on behalf of their adult political and legal activities.[90]

Schools in the early republic were thus important to free black New Yorkers for myriad reasons. They were sites where children were asked to use their time and their minds in ways that slavery had forbidden. They were sites where children met as peers and formed friendships within a unique generation in the history of American emancipation. They were sites where black families thought about themselves and made claims for themselves as taxpayers and citizens of local and state governments. They were sites where explicit antislavery conversations took place, where black northerners thought about how their educations connected directly to the fate of enslaved people throughout the world. They were sites where associations grew and flourished, providing black men, women, and children the opportunity to form their own organizations amidst the wider flowering of civil society in the early republic. They were sites where they learned that they would not always agree with each other, much less with white reformers and officials. The nature, the details, and the richness of free black political and legal activity in the mid-nineteenth century took root in the many classrooms of gradual abolition.

CHAPTER 4

Citizenship National

Slavery, Democracy, and Black Citizenship in the 1820s

In 1793, Austin Steward was born into slavery in Prince William County, Virginia. As a young boy, he moved with his master's household to the frontier of western New York, where he and hundreds of other Chesapeake slaves remained the legal property of their southern migrant owners. As he neared the end of adolescence, Steward calculated how best to leave his master. He located a new state law that could, and did, secure his emancipation.[1]

Steward remained in western New York and thrived. With the aid of white patrons, he earned wages and attended school. In 1817, he opened a grocery in Rochester, the boomtown on Lake Ontario. The next year, he purchased a $500 lot on Main Street. According to the 1777 state constitution, which made no mention of race, Steward's property made him eligible to vote. In April 1821, a few days before the annual election, he filed a certificate of freedom—the voting document required of black men per the 1811 election law—with the county clerk. That summer, a constitutional convention disfranchised nearly all of the state's male "citizens of colour" by erecting a race-based property requirement that most could not meet. Despite this reversal, Steward stayed in New York, becoming an influential political leader.[2]

On July 5, 1827, Steward woke in Rochester and prepared to celebrate the end of slavery in his adopted home state. That morning, he and his friends visited a local politician and on "behalf of the citizens of Monroe County" thanked him for his efforts in passing the 1817 general abolition law that had, the day before, freed New York's several thousand remaining slaves.[3] A band led a parade into the public square, where a colleague of Steward's recited the Declaration of Independence and the 1817 statute. Steward gave a speech to the black and white audience.[4]

Published in *Freedom's Journal,* Steward's speech was both celebratory and cautionary. He was glad that New York's black citizens enjoyed "many of the dearest rights of freemen" and urged them to embrace "the freedom, privileges, and immunities which wise and equal laws have awarded us." He condemned the 1821 state constitution's prejudicial voting rules and also asked the audience to "remember, in joy and exultation, the thousands of our countrymen" who remained enslaved. He recommended a classic diet of uplift politics: reading the Bible, refraining from alcohol, pursuing financial independence, and sending children to common schools. Steward argued that if black New Yorkers took full advantage of freedom, their emancipation had the potential to help those still "trampled under foot by the accursed traffic in human flesh."[5]

By the time Steward gave this speech, he had witnessed a number of significant and contradictory events in the development of American slavery since his own forced migration to New York. Freedom was on the rise in the Northeast and Northwest. At the same time, slavery was expanding in the nation's ever-growing territory. Between 1800 and 1830, the enslaved population grew from 900,000 to 2,000,000, and four slave states—Louisiana, Mississippi, Alabama, and Missouri—joined the Union.[6] Across the country, debates over slavery, citizenship, and territorial growth were connected to local struggles for political power and partisan allegiance. Steward's 1827 speech emphasized that New York's politics were connected to the nation's politics. The fate of black citizenship in the state was important to the fate of slavery everywhere.

Steward's perspective not only provides insight into state-based gradual abolition but also inspires a reframing of four critical events in the history of the early republic: the Missouri Crisis of 1819–1821, the most alarming sectional controversy of the era; the New York Constitutional Convention of 1821, the last in a series of state conventions nationwide that restricted black suffrage during the First Party System; the failure of the 1822 fugitive slave bill in Congress, an outcome precipitated by a New York representative who insisted that black citizens deserved state protection and national rights; and New York's 1827 general abolition, the first time a state used a legislative act to free slaves immediately on one day. In both obvious and hidden ways, black New Yorkers influenced all four events. The attempt by Hudson Valley congressman James Tallmadge Jr. to prohibit slavery in Missouri was a testament to how deeply antislavery principles—principles shaped by black voting, associationalism, petitioning, and everyday advocacy—had entered the politics of his home state. So too were his and other delegates' efforts to prevent disfranchisement at the 1821 state convention. But Tallmadge and his allies won neither fight, at least not outright. The following year, in a last gasp of successful First Party System antislavery politicking, Congressman Cadwallader D. Colden, former president of the New York Manumission Society, squashed the congressional fugitive bill by appealing to the experiences of black citizens he knew. As black New Yorkers fêted the general abolition of 1827, they emphasized both the promises and the disappointments of recent antislavery politics.[7]

Steward's generation—the children of gradual abolition—came of age during this period of political upheaval. By the time they reached adulthood, many of them had watched their fathers, mentors, and teachers enjoy and then lose the right to vote. Some of them experienced this loss firsthand. But this generation also observed a number of white legislators, municipal officials, judges, and abolitionists work effectively to stem slavery's power and impact. They learned from black elders who persuaded white lawmakers to protect various aspects of black citizenship and bodily safety. In July 1827, the rising generation praised what the state and its citizens had accomplished in hastening slavery's local downfall. It was, at the same time, a precarious moment and an occasion to set strategies for the work remaining. Constitutional disfranchisement, while devastating, did not spell the end of black men, women, and children's engagement in formal politics or their successful claims to state citizenship.

While New York was not the only site of contestation over black citizenship in the 1820s, its politicians, reformers, and ordinary citizens played outsized roles in decisions and conversations about citizenship in the early republic. Although "citizen" had been a visible word in the founding era of the United States, "inhabitant," "free man," "person," and "resident" appeared in places where more modern eyes might expect to see "citizen." Americans had not settled how state citizenship related to federal citizenship within the national constitutional order, nor what precise catalogue of rights, privileges, immunities, and protections belonged to various state and national citizens. Was a citizen of New York automatically a citizen of the United States? Was voting, as one example, a right or a privilege? How did sex, age, race, and wealth affect claims to the prerogatives of citizenship?[8] Due to New York's particularly intense history of gradual abolition as well as its role as a powerful state within the union, the state was fertile ground for the development of ideas about what citizenship was. By the end of the 1820s, state citizenship was a widely recognized status for black people in New York at the same time that it was racialized and unequal. From birth to adulthood, the children of gradual abolition took part in the history of contested and coalescing notions of what citizenship was and who had access to it.[9]

Although in the short term New York's antislavery advocates failed to score many national victories and succeeded only moderately at the state level, in the long view, the work they did bore tremendous significance. The debates that black adults and children provoked over rights, citizenship, and democracy prompted diverse New Yorkers to stake out legal and ideological positions about the importance of racial equality and constitutional fairness. Some of the most potent strands of antislavery policy in the nineteenth century took early root in gradual emancipation New York. Examining the failures and the accomplishments of antislavery New Yorkers not only exposes these roots, but also reveals how the children of gradual abolition formulated their own political and legal priorities as they entered adulthood.

* * *

In the early 1800s, New York was still a developing republic in which crucial answers about the civic rights of former slaves had not been explicitly, legislatively determined. Manumission documents in both urban and rural areas often stipulated that the freed person in question "hereafter exercise, hold, and enjoy all and singular the liberties, rights, privileges, and immunities of a free woman [or man] as fully to all intents and purposes as if she [or he] had been born free."[10] The era's various abolition acts neither explicitly protected nor denied political privileges. The 1777 state constitution's implicit bestowal of one of the most hallowed markers of political belonging—access to the vote—on black men created the possibility of an inchoate interracial democracy among male adults. As we saw in Chapter 2, for the first two decades of the century, black men voted regularly in annual elections. Their activities were often communal, interpersonal, and public. The oldest male members of the rising generation, such as Austin Steward, voted under the 1777 constitution's rules. Younger members of the generation absorbed the importance that adults attached to voting and, dishearteningly, witnessed the power of lawmakers and voters to rob black men of this privilege of citizenship when the 1821 constitution was ratified in 1822.

Precisely because black men voted visibly and often, and because the state's fiercely competitive parties were aware of their voting, discussion of black access to the franchise occurred regularly. These debates were part of how New Yorkers began to determine what citizenship was. Simultaneously, the vote became more associated with what it meant to be a free man. Whereas in the colonial era not all free men could vote, even if white, male enfranchisement expanded throughout the nation in the early nineteenth century. Some observers began calling male access to the vote a "right" of and not simply a "privilege" of citizenship. Since slavery was slowly ending in New York during this exact period, free black voters took an especially active part in these changing ideas about American democracy.

New York's 1777 constitution mentioned the word "citizen" only once, in reference to grievances against King George. Otherwise, the document described people living in New York as "electors" (meaning voters), "inhabitants," and "freemen." In almost all cases, the premise was that such electors, inhabitants, and freemen were male. In the sections on voting, this was made explicit: the clauses referred to "male inhabitants" and "freemen." "Freemen," in this context, referred to a legally defined class of residents of New York and Albany, usually artisans, who were granted political privileges in colonial charters.[11]

By 1800, roughly two thirds of New York men were eligible to vote for assembly and a third could vote for governor and state senators. Turnout in elections was high, and more men voted over time as more met property requirements. Federalists, though less enthusiastic about unfettered male access to the vote than Republicans, were in general more committed to antislavery policy. For this reason, they were the party favored by most black New Yorkers and the party that more often protected the black franchise.[12]

When the press reported on black voters in this competitive environment, editors connected being a free man and taxpaying with the right to vote. For example, in 1809, the Federalist *Commercial Advertiser* reported that a Republican election inspector in New York City "rejected the vote of a free man of color" after deeming it "*convenient to suspect*" that he was a slave. This was an "attempt to destroy the most valuable principle of Freemen—the elective franchise." Problems surfaced up the river in Hudson, as well. The Federalist *Whig* told the story of Robin, a black Federalist who swore that "he had been sued as a freeman, that he had been taxed," but was told by dishonest officials that he had "*no right to vote.*"[13]

Black political leaders crafted the emerging language and norms of citizenship while tying black voters' role in New York's elections to the future of emancipation nationwide. Joseph Sidney, for example, counseled his fellow electors to vote Federalist. In 1809, he reminded the Wilberforce Philanthropic

Association that the vote was among "the most valuable of our newly acquired rights" and that Republican members of Congress and their supporters in "the southern section" kept "our African brethren in bondage." He praised Federalist commercial and foreign policy. He also gave his "warmest gratitude" to the Manumission Society, with its Federalist-heavy membership, for their "kind interference" closer to home.[14] For the city's black voters, all politics was local—and regional, and national.

By 1811, when the legislature debated and ultimately passed the controversial election bill (first cited in Chapter 2) mandating black voters acquire certificates of freedom, the language of citizenship and constitutional rights appeared alongside the more traditional language of freedom, residency, privileges, and economic independence. Assemblyman Robert Bogardus, a Federalist from New York City, accused Republicans of an "invasion of the rights secured by the constitution" to "persons of color." A Republican shot back that Bogardus was just afraid of losing his seat because of all the "Negro Slaves" who had voted for him.[15] Members of the bipartisan council of the revision, uncomfortable with the bill, criticized it for "imposing on many citizens whose ancestors have uninterruptedly enjoyed the elective franchise under the colonial as well as State government" the "degradation of being challenged" on account of "complexion." Black men deserved to vote "in common with their fellow citizens."[16]

In its final form, the 1811 law allowed election inspectors to ask "any person," white or black, to confirm by oath his citizenship, residency, and property. In addition, any "black or mulatto person" had to produce a "certificate of his freedom" signed by "one of the justices of the supreme court, mayor, recorder, or judge of any court of common pleas" and sealed by a town or county clerk. All of this cost money: 35½ cents for the certificate, plus clerk fees.[17]

When the unhappy Albany *Balance* printed the act, the editor included a speech by Federalist assemblyman Thomas Mercein, who insisted that "we have no power vested in us, whereby we can *constitutionally* deprive" a free man of his "privileges" whether he "be black, or white, or yellow." As "citizens of this state," black men were "entitled" to vote. The *Post* hoped black men would "exercise their right of suffrage." Republicans had violated the "constitution, [and] that principle and rule of law, settled and established in our courts, that every man whether black or white, shall be presumed equally free, and equally competent as a witness."[18]

In the wake of the 1811 election law, black men routinely sought out officials for certificates. The documents comprised, somewhat paradoxically given their purpose, a form of state-issued paper evidence that black people were formally recognized as New York citizens. In Albany, justices of the state supreme court—legal luminaries including William W. Van Ness, Ambrose Spencer, and James Kent—signed certificates in April 1811. All three later served as delegates to the 1821 constitutional convention, where Kent and Van Ness defended equal male suffrage across race.[19] On April 17, 1811, the first judge of the Court of Common Pleas in Ulster County certified that "male black person" Philip Smedes had been free since 1804. In Coxsackie, further up the Hudson, fifty-year-old Thomas Miller acquired a certificate from a county judge. In Schenectady, Cato Sherli's certificate noted he was "entitled to all the rights and privileges of a free citizen of the State." Hundreds of miles east, the East Hampton Town Clerk recorded the certificate of Isaac Plato, a "free man, according to the laws of this State." Hundreds of miles west, in the Finger Lakes, James Fletcher, a "black man about six feet high twenty five years old" filed a copy of his certificate with the Ontario County clerk in Canandaigua on April 25, 1812. Fifty-five-year-old Archelaus Fletcher—likely James's father or relative—registered his on the same day. The following year, the new clerk, Myron Holley, entered the certificates of Cato Shields from Massachusetts and Charles Hooker from New York City. Holley would later found the Liberty Party, the first antislavery party in the United States.[20]

In 1815, when Republican assemblyman Peter Sharpe's new certificate bill imposing additional requirements on New York City's black voters reached the council of revision, Federalists Jonas Platt and James Kent, long on record as antislavery in their politics and jurisprudence, withheld approval. Kent argued the bill was "inconsistent with the spirit of the Constitution and the public good," both because it made the city's black voters unequal to white voters and because it made the city's black voters unequal to black voters elsewhere in the state. The legislature mustered the votes to override the council's veto. Aware of what had happened, black Federalists praised Kent and Platt in the *Post* and criticized the legislature for passing laws that were in "flagrant violation of the rights and immunities of a portion of native citizens."[21]

The late 1810s were thus dangerous years for the black electorate. Not only had Republicans passed two laws making it more difficult to vote, but the Federalist Party as a whole was beginning to implode, giving way to a confused and enlarged Republican party with warring factions. In New York, backers of Governor DeWitt Clinton, a Republican more appealing to Federalists for policy and personal reasons, were called "Clintonians." His intraparty rivals

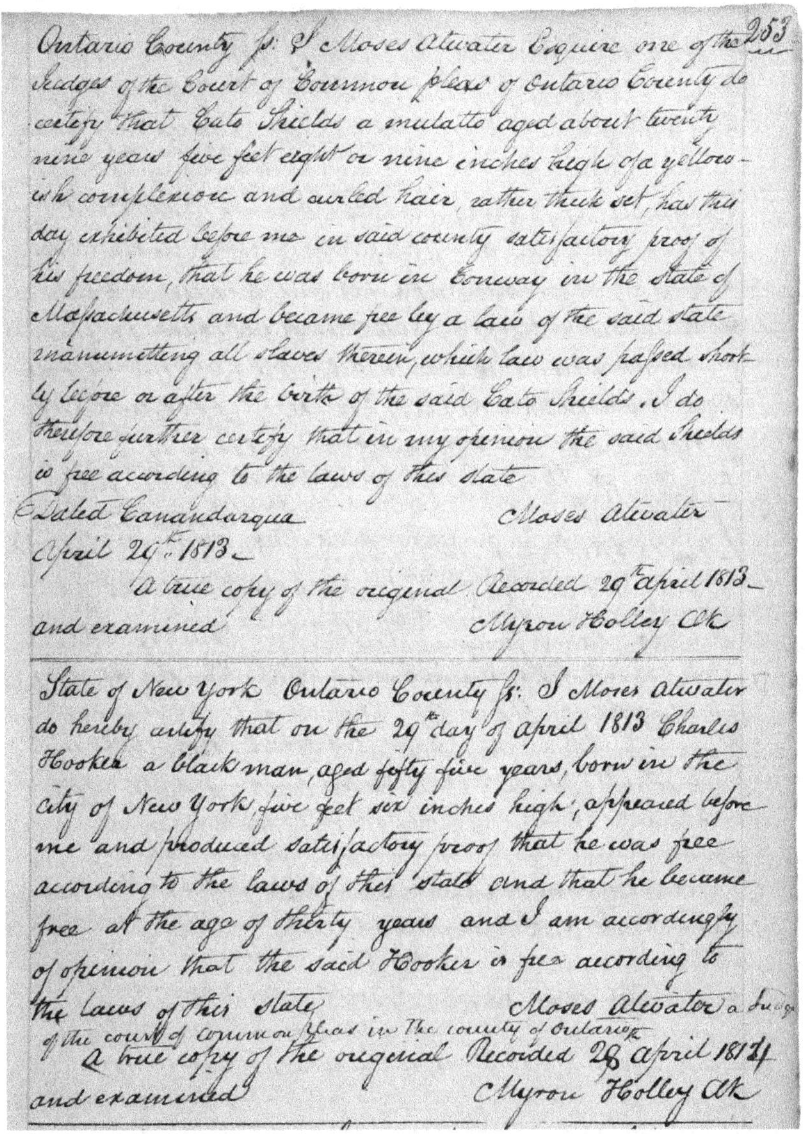

Ontario County ss: I Moses Atwater Esquire one of the 253
Judges of the Court of Common pleas of Ontario County do
certify that Cato Shields a mulatto aged about twenty
nine years five feet eight or nine inches high of a yellow-
ish complexion and curled hair, rather thick set, has this
day exhibited before me in said county satisfactory proof of
his freedom, that he was born in Conway in the State of
Massachusetts and became free by a law of the said State
manumitting all slaves therein, which law was passed shortly before or after the birth of the said Cato Shields. I do
therefore further certify that in my opinion the said Shields
is free according to the laws of this State
Dated Canandarqua Moses Atwater
April 29th 1813

A true copy of the original Recorded 29th April 1813
and examined Myron Holley Clk

State of New York Ontario County ss: I Moses Atwater
do hereby certify that on the 29th day of April 1813 Charles
Hooker a black man, aged fifty five years, born in the
city of New York, five feet six inches high; appeared before
me and produced satisfactory proof that he was free
according to the laws of this state and that he became
free at the age of thirty years and I am accordingly
of opinion that the said Hooker is free according to
the laws of this state Moses Atwater a Judge
of the court of common pleas in the county of Ontario

A true copy of the original Recorded 28 April 1814
and examined Myron Holley Clk

Figure 8. Cato Shields's and Charles Hooker's certificates of freedom, copied into Ontario County clerk Myron Holley's record book in 1813 and 1814. Shields and Hooker needed certificates of freedom in order to vote, per the state's 1811 election law. Myron Holley was an eventual founder of the antislavery Liberty Party. Miscellaneous Records, Volume B, 1804–1814, Ontario County Records and Archives, Canandaigua, New York.

were "Bucktails." It was unclear at first whether either Republican faction would support black voters.

At this very moment of party flux, a New Jersey Presbyterian pastor named Robert Finley founded the American Colonization Society, whose aim was to encourage "free people of color" to colonize "Africa, or such other place as Congress may deem most expedient." Popular among a geographically wide swath of white nominally antislavery politicians, the Society fueled the notion that free black people should be transported elsewhere, where they certainly were not going to be American citizens, voting or otherwise. Even members of the Manumission Society flirted with colonization when Finley's society emerged, although the policy never became a primary goal of the organization. In 1818, longtime Manumission Society lawyer Peter A. Jay joined a committee at the American Convention for Promoting the Abolition of Slavery in Philadelphia that reported flatly that they did not "discern, in the constitution and proceedings of the American Colonization Society" anything "friendly to the abolition of slavery in the United States." Citing "numerous meetings of the people of colour" in Philadelphia led by the prominent black sailmaker James Forten, the white abolitionists amplified black Americans' objections to colonization. The convention published their "decided opinion that" colonization "ought not to receive the support of friends of universal emancipation." But the very fact that colonization had "excited" so much public attention was an acknowledgment of how popular the idea was.[22]

Making matters even more precarious for black citizens in New York, specifically, was the fact that Bucktails craved a constitutional convention. These reforming Republicans hoped to create a more democratic state constitution that would expand (white) suffrage and abolish the autocratic councils of appointment and revision. They also wanted to blunt Governor Clinton's various powers under the 1777 constitution. A convention, everyone knew, would also mean an opportunity to reconsider the terms of black suffrage.

* * *

Before the New York electorate could agree to a constitutional convention, however, the nation faced a massive political upheaval over the expansion of slavery. In its moment, the tumult was called the Missouri Question. New Yorkers played outsized roles in the two-year controversy.

The traditional narrative explains that the crisis began in February 1819, when Congressman James Tallmadge Jr. of Dutchess County tried to insert a clause in the Missouri Territory's statehood bill that would gradually abolish slavery in the state once it entered the Union. But it is possible to start the story much earlier, with fruitful analytical consequences, by tracing Tallmadge's coming-of-age in gradual abolition New York.

Tallmadge knew about slavery and political abolitionism firsthand. Born in 1778, he grew up in rural Dutchess County, the son of a slave-owning Revolutionary War officer and a devout Baptist mother. As a boy, he saw enslaved people working at his home, on the Hudson River, and in the county's rich farmland. He was an adolescent during the state's lengthy debates over gradual emancipation. Dutchess County, long home to energetic abolitionist Quakers, sent a number of vocal antislavery lawmakers to Albany. In 1785, James's own father was elected to the assembly, where he voted on the antislavery side of various bills. In the late 1790s, as New York was crafting its 1799 gradual abolition law, Tallmadge enrolled at the College of Rhode Island in Providence, where gradual abolition had been unfolding since 1784.[23]

At his commencement in 1798, Tallmadge delivered an antislavery speech. With a youthful idealist's ardor, he attacked slave owners and defended black equality. The Declaration of Independence proclaimed that "all were blessed with equal rights and privileges and that *liberty* was the birth right" of "every individual." The "opinion that one man is inferior to another upon account of his colour" was false. Men who defended the slave trade were "viperous animals." Let a "universal emancipation take place," Tallmadge urged, so that "slaves will have a country to love and defend" and stand united alongside "all true Americans."[24]

After graduating, Tallmadge returned to New York to study law. Like many of the well-to-do antislavery New Yorkers of his generation, Tallmadge owned people at the same time that he held abolitionist beliefs. By 1810, Tallmadge was a successful lawyer living in Poughkeepsie with two enslaved adults, Sam Harris and Hannah, whom he likely inherited from his father. He served as a Poughkeepsie village councilman, county surrogate, and lieutenant colonel in the state militia. In 1817, he decided to run for Congress as a Clintonian candidate for the Fourth District (Putnam and Dutchess counties). He won handily.[25]

Just before departing for Washington in December 1817, Tallmadge freed Sam Harris and Hannah. It is unclear what prompted him to put his antislavery ideals into practice at this exact moment, but it is clear that Tallmadge went off to Congress considering himself, at a personal level, a liberator of slaves. He was also representing New York at the moment it had just passed its 1817 general abolition law.[26]

Tallmadge cast a series of antislavery votes while in Congress, but it was not until February 1819—once he had decided not to run for reelection—that he made his major stand. As his colleagues debated the admission of Missouri, Tallmadge proposed an amendment to the statehood bill that would "limit the existence of slavery in the new State by declaring all free who should be born in the Territory after its admission into the Union, and for providing for the gradual emancipation of those now held in bondage." In its final language, the amendment read like a combination of the 1787 Northwest Ordinance ("the further introduction of slavery or involuntary servitude be prohibited, except for the punishment of crimes") and a gradual abolition law ("children born within the said State . . . shall be free at the age of twenty-five"). Lawmakers from the Northeast and the Northwest knew that these earlier plans, while imperfect, had nearly ended chattel bondage in their regions. Southern lawmakers and their acquiescent northern allies (now called "doughfaces") knew this just as well, which is why they objected.[27]

To northerners familiar with gradual abolition, Tallmadge's plan seemed feasible. There were roughly 10,000 slaves in Missouri in 1819, half the number living in New York when the state had passed its 1799 abolition law. Southern members, however, argued that Congress had no right to interfere with Missourians' property and that slavery's "diffusion" into the West was desirable. Among Tallmadge's most vocal allies was a fellow Hudson Valley Clintonian named John W. Taylor, a more seasoned congressman. Taylor, professing no doubt that it was within Congress's rights to require Missouri to include antislavery provisions in its constitution, stated he "would never consent to declare the whole country west of the Mississippi a market overt for human flesh." Tallmadge himself thundered, "if a dissolution of the Union must take place, let it be so! If civil war; which gentlemen so much threaten, much come, I can only say, let it come! . . . I know the will of my constituents. . . . I will proclaim their hatred of slavery in every shape."[28]

Tallmadge was right about at least some of his constituents. When antislavery New Yorkers read the widespread coverage of his efforts, they anointed him a hero. The Manumission Society, under president Cadwallader D. Colden's direction, published Tallmadge's speech, including a letter from Tallmadge and Taylor promising their "best exertions" toward "the cause of freedom." Clintonian newspapers advertised the pamphlet, agreeing that the "further introduction of slavery into any of our states or territories is revolting."[29]

Black voters also supported Tallmadge, who had decided he would run for state senate in the Southern District. As the spring 1819 election approached, the *Columbian* reported that the "People of Colour" were pleased with "their distinguished advocate and friend, *James Tallmadge, Jun.*" and eager to exercise "their *civil rights*" in support of his candidacy. The problem was, by backing Tallmadge, black voters had "drawn upon them the squibs of the buck-tail faction."[30] From the Bucktails' perspective, the prospect of a new political alliance—one between Clintonians and black voters, based on the emergent politics of slavery's extension in the West—was not welcome news.

The Bucktail press attack on black voters during the Missouri Crisis was merciless. The powerful *National Advocate* editor Mordecai Noah, who was semi-sympathetic to the South during the crisis as well as an energetic proponent of state constitutional reforms, repeatedly condemned Clintonian efforts to embrace black voters. On April 23, 1819, shortly before the state election, Noah recalled the days when Federalists and Republicans ran in close races and the black vote often decided narrow contests. He feared that the Clintonians were reviving older practices. In black hands, he slandered, the vote was "a serious evil."[31]

Tallmadge himself knew that he had the support of black voters. On the first day of the election, a friend of the Tallmadge family wrote to James's brother Matthias: "There is a prospect of [James's] success—He will get the Quaker votes—the Manumission Society and the People of Color will generally support him—and he will get a number of Federalist Votes." Contrary to his friend's optimistic predictions, Tallmadge ended up losing. Two Bucktails, Peter Livingston and John Townsend, won the district's two empty seats.[32]

When Congress reconvened in the winter of 1819–1820, Taylor reintroduced his now absent friend's amendment to the Missouri statehood bill. Despite the restrictionist sentiments of most northern congressmen, the likelihood of emancipation in Missouri began to diminish as Kentuckian Henry Clay, the Speaker of the House, made efforts to broker a compromise. Clay quietly put together a plan to admit Missouri as a slave state, to admit Maine as a free state, and to forbid slavery in future states carved out of the Louisiana Purchase lands north of the 36°30' parallel. In March 1820, the Senate approved the compromise. Then, in a remarkably quick turnaround—Clay orchestrated the plan artfully—the House immediately passed the bill and President Monroe signed it into law. To the fury and embarrassment of antislavery New Yorkers, a small but determinative number of Bucktails supported the compromise. Two voted yes, two absented themselves. None of the four traitors won reelection to the Seventeenth Congress.[33]

The compromise in the spring of 1820 ended the first phase of the crisis but set the stage for the second. That summer, the territory approved a state constitution with two provocative clauses. One declared that the legislature was forbidden from ever abolishing slavery without owners' consent and "without paying them." Another stipulated that the legislature pass a law to "prevent free negroes and mulattoes from coming to, and settling in, this state." Both of these provisions maddened antislavery northerners, but it was the second that raised the most obvious constitutional problems. Article IV, Section 2 of the federal constitution guaranteed that "the free citizens of each state . . . shall be entitled to all privileges and immunities of citizens in the several states." Since northern states, including New York, considered black people citizens, it would be a violation of the U.S. Constitution for Missouri to bar their entry. Antislavery northerners argued that the right to move from place to place was a fundamental right of national citizenship that could not be denied to the country's various state citizens.[34]

New York's politicians and editors were explicit on this point. As the New York *American* explained, "[The U.S. Constitution] provides, that 'the citizens of each state shall be entitled to all the privileges and immunities of citizens in several states.' [When the negro] was raised to the rank of freeman or citizen of any one state, he became entitled to all the privileges and immunities of the citizens of the several states. The moment that he became a citizen of New-York, made him a citizen of the United States. He became one of us; and without regarding his nation, age or complexion, we are bound to protect him and his rights as we would our own."[35] The New York legislature agreed. In November 1820, Clintonian assemblyman John C. Spencer introduced resolutions that instructed New York's representatives in Congress to reject Missouri's constitution and to insist on the "prohibition of slavery" as a "condition of admission." New York's "first duty" as a government was "the protection of their citizens in their legitimate rights," whatever "their colour." If black New Yorkers wanted to settle in Missouri, it was their constitutional right. As Spencer noted, "in this and many other states of the union, there were free blacks and mulattoes who were citizens"; in New York, black men were "expressly recognized by our election laws."[36]

In emphasizing the state's election laws, Spencer revealed just how effective black New Yorkers had been in asserting the legitimacy of their citizenship. Ordinary black men across the state—otherwise obscure men who filed election certificates—had helped forge a consensus about black civic status. When it came time for New York politicians to declare nationally their stance on black citizenship in 1820, they were not thinking about these subjects for the first time.

With the exception of a handful of vocal Bucktails, state lawmakers gave Spencer's ideas overwhelming support. In November 1820, the assembly passed a set of resolutions echoing Spencer's suggestions by a vote of 117 to 4. The senate agreed to the assembly's resolutions, which resolved that New York politicians in Washington should "prevent the acceptance" of a Missouri constitution that denied "to any citizens of the existing states" the "privileges and immunities of citizens of such new state."[37]

New York's resolutions arrived in Congress later that month, as the second phase of the Missouri Crisis was underway. Clay once again worked to forge a compromise, assembling a committee that proposed Missouri "shall never pass any law preventing any descriptions of persons from coming to or settling in the said state, who are now or may hereafter become a citizen of any of the states in the union." South Carolina Congressman Charles Pinckney, meanwhile, argued that, as a signer of the U.S. Constitution, he "perfectly knew that there did not then exist in the Union such a thing as a black or colored citizen."[38] (Pinckney was either willfully or ignorantly a poor historian.) Clay lost a vote on his compromise after Pinckney's speech, and went back to work. In February 1821, Congress agreed by a slim margin to approve the Missouri constitution if the Missouri legislature agreed to ignore the state constitution's instructions to deny black citizens' entry and promised not to pass any law that violated the federal constitution. The Missouri territorial legislature acquiesced, passing an act declaring that the new state would not "authorize the passage of any law" by "which any citizen of either of the United States shall be excluded from the enjoyment of any of the privileges and immunities to which such citizens are entitled under the constitution of the United States."[39]

In the short term, the question of whether black state citizens were to be considered, by virtue of their acknowledged state citizenship, citizens of the United States, was left unresolved. The second Missouri compromise was not exactly an antislavery victory. ("The constitution of Missouri ought to have been sent back," the *Spectator* lamented.[40]) But it was not a proslavery triumph, either. The second compromise acknowledged most northerners' view that black people were citizens of their states and that they had certain rights under the federal Constitution. New York's representatives had been especially strong in making this point in Congress, and would continue to advocate for New York's black citizens, as "citizens," in national contexts. Several years later, Massachusetts officials proved similarly committed to state-recognized black citizenship, especially when it came to the protection of their state's black sailors abroad in the union. Black citizenship, in other words, remained variously affirmed and contested in the wake of the Missouri Crisis. Like many of the nation's compromises over slavery and race in the early republic, Congress's decisions about Missouri calmed political conflict in the moment while failing to settle sectional, constitutional, and moral issues that did not go away.[41]

* * *

That same spring of 1821, New York entered its own moment of constitution making. In March, the Bucktails passed a law to submit the possibility of a constitutional convention to the state's voters. The enthusiastic electorate, eager for democratizing reforms, approved the ballot measure by wide margins at the April election. According to the convention enabling act, each county was eligible to elect, in June, the same number of delegates to the convention as it did to the assembly. These delegates would be chosen by male voters who met lenient, nonracialized property and taxpaying requirements.[42]

Black voters were aware that the constitutional convention had the potential to impact their rights and that doughface Bucktails had voted with proslavery interests during the Missouri Crisis. In Albany, Benjamin Lattimore Jr. objected when the local Bucktail organ, the *Albany Argus*, erroneously listed him as a Bucktail supporter in the April election. Several papers printed his notice that he would not "countenance a party, who are in favour of the EXTENSION OF SLAVERY" and that he refused to "mingle in the strife of the bucktail faction."[43]

That same month, there was an uptick in men filing for certificates in order to vote both on the April ballot measure and for delegates to the convention. Austin Steward obtained his certificate from the Monroe County first judge on April 21, 1821. In Dutchess County, Sam Harris—the same man once owned by James Tallmadge Jr.—acquired a certificate with the help of Tallmadge's cousin. In Ontario County, seven black voters registered new certificates with the county clerk (compared to two in 1819 and one in 1820). John C. Spencer himself helped one of the eight, Richard Williams, acquire his certificate from a county judge. On the other side of the state, the recorder of Troy, William L. Marcy (future doughface governor, and secretary of war and secretary of state under Presidents Polk and Pierce), signed certificates for Prince Williams and Frisbee Way. Across the river, a former slave named Peter Dawson, who was living in Schenectady by way of New Jersey, Maryland, and four different towns in the Hudson Valley, missed the deadline for the April election but obtained his certificate in time to vote in the June election for convention delegates. He made the cutoff by two days.[44]

Black voters knew that these were unsettling times, locally and nationally, for black citizenship. Some of these voters were older members of the children of gradual abolition. Born into servitude in the 1790s and very early 1800s, they were just coming of age. Other members of this generation—women who were not allowed to vote and men who had not yet reached the age of majority or did not meet property requirements—may not have cast ballots, but they were old enough to understand what was at stake. Formal political belonging had given black New Yorkers access to concrete benefits of citizenship: incorporation laws for their associations and churches, education requirements and tax-supported schools, property ownership, the ability to enter local and state courts as plaintiffs and witnesses, kidnapping protections, freedom of movement, and the vote. If some of these civic prerogatives were already under attack, was there even worse to come as the state considered a new constitution?

Of the 126 delegates elected to the convention, 98 were Bucktails or Bucktail-aligned.[45] Martin Van Buren, the newly chosen U.S. senator and Bucktail leader, was in the 98. Peter Sharpe, sponsor of the 1815 certificate law, arrived from New York. Aside from the Bucktails, the convention comprised a smattering of Clintonians and Federalists. Among the latter were James Kent, Jonas Platt, Peter A. Jay, Peter Jay Munro, Rufus King, William W. Van Ness, Stephen Van Rensselaer—all men with experience supporting black suffrage. The Federalists were in the minority, but they were respected elder statesmen. Also present were James Tallmadge Jr., who had strained ties with the Clintonians, and Peter Livingston, the Bucktail who beat him in the 1819 state senate election. Daniel D. Tompkins, the former governor and Manumission Society lawyer, was elected president of the convention. In his Bucktail hands lay the power to appoint members to ten different committees, each charged with addressing an area of reform.

Over the course of the convention, it became clear that the question of black suffrage was personal for many of the delegates. Most of those men who debated the issue most loudly were men who had previously interacted with black voters or engaged intensely with legislative regulation of black suffrage; some had won or lost elections due to black voters' balance of power. It also became clear that discussions of the black vote forced delegates to consider the history of slavery on their own soil. The convention took place after the 1817 general abolition act had passed but before its main clause went into effect in 1827. The children of gradual abolition were every day reaching the age of majority. The delegates were thus in the position of knowing that more and more free black men would join the electorate.[46]

In their initial proposal, the suffrage committee wrote an amendment declaring that "every white male citizen" who paid taxes, worked on public roads, or served in the militia would be allowed to vote—no more property requirements, no more dual suffrage system. A Bucktail from Genesee County explained that black voters were excluded because they lacked "discretion" and did not serve in the militia. (The militia was regulated by federal legislation that applied only to free able-bodied white male citizens.) Stephen Van Rensselaer—who as the Federalist candidate for governor in 1800 had been popular among black voters—proposed, instead, that the clause read "every male citizen." Here the fight began. What would be done with the word "white"?[47]

Black voters, via Peter A. Jay, joined the debate. Jay introduced a petition signed by fifty black men requesting a constitutional provision to prevent the legislature from passing "laws interfering with their rights, by requiring them to be registered, &c previous to being allowed to exercise the right of suffrage." Jay spoke in favor of safeguarding not only the rights of the petitioners, but also those of the maturing children of gradual abolition. "You made [their parents] slaves," he noted, but will "you punish the children for your own crimes; for the injuries you inflicted upon their parents?" Referencing the students of the African Free School, Jay noted their "progress in learning, seldom to be seen in other schools." Jay also appealed to the sectional pride stoked by the Missouri Crisis: denying black men their rights would elicit "a shout of triumph" from the South. Citing the privileges and immunities clause of the U.S. Constitution, Jay argued it was unconstitutional to deny a citizen the privilege of voting because of race.[48]

Root replied with arguments echoing articles in the Republican press. There was cause for alarm "when a few hundred free negroes of the city of New-York" could "change the political condition of the whole state." Robert Clarke, a fellow Bucktail, disagreed. He could not deprive "a large and respectable number of the people of the state of the privileges and rights which they have enjoyed in common with us." Clarke cited the upcoming 1827 general abolition. It was foolish to deprive "any of your citizens" every "inducement to become respectable members of society." Samuel Young accused Clarke of confusing natural rights with political rights. Yes, black New Yorkers should be free, but the "minds of the blacks are not competent to vote."[49]

The next morning, Federalist Abraham Van Vechten, who had helped Benjamin Lattimore Sr. and his fellow black petitioners incorporate their Albany school in 1816, rose to speak. He did not want to "deprive electors of colour a right which they have enjoyed since the adoption of the constitution"; they had been "citizens of the state nearly half a century." Indeed, "some of them were citizens when this state came into political existence—partook in our struggle for freedom and independence, and were incorporated into the body politic at its creation." (John Peterson, the black Revolutionary War soldier who had foiled Benedict Arnold's plan to hand West Point over to the British, would have certainly agreed.) Kent, meanwhile, made a similar point to Van Vechten: "We did not come to this Convention to *disfranchise* any portion of the community." Tallmadge, taking a different tack, found it absurd to disfranchise black men given how few had been voting recently in his district—why were they perceived as a threat?—and mentioned the election two years previous in which he had lost to Peter Livingston.[50]

On the second day of debate, Jay made a final speech. He implored the delegates not to violate the principles concerning "the natural equality of all men." The convention decided 63 to 59 to strike out the qualification "white." Jay, Platt, Tallmadge, Kent, Munro, Van Rensselaer, Clarke, Van Vechten, Van Ness, and, interestingly, Van Buren were among those who voted against racial disfranchisement. Tompkins, as president of the convention, did not vote, but a contemporary reported that he disagreed with the disfranchising contingent, despite their being fellow Bucktails. Perhaps Tompkins could not bring himself to forget the vocal minority of black voters who had supported him in the 1810s.[51]

But the victory on behalf of equal male suffrage was short-lived. A new suffrage committee was formed. It proposed a generous extension of the franchise for white men but added a proviso that black men could vote only if they possessed a freehold estate of $250. This requirement was far more onerous than the 1777 constitution's requirements to vote for assembly, Congress, and local office. Platt moved to expunge the proviso. "All men are born equal, in civil and political rights," he admonished. The convention owed black men "more than mere emancipation." His efforts came to naught. The revised clause won by 71 to 33.[52]

In January 1822, the new constitution was submitted to the electorate for ratification. The choice was either yes or no to the entire document. The convention's final draft encompassed many of the suggestions that been promoted in Bucktail political circles. The councils of appointment and revision were abolished; the judicial system was reorganized; the governor's term was shortened and his right to prorogue the legislature ended. It was, in fact, a more democratic constitution—with the major exception that it damaged the rights of black citizens. The state's electorate approved the convention's work by a vote of 74,732 to 41,402.[53]

Although they lost equal access to the vote in 1822, the defenders of black citizenship put on record a series of lasting arguments in favor of constitutional equality. These dissenting arguments remained in circulation, especially among the children of gradual abolition. The fact that this generation had experienced the dismantling of their voting rights meant, perhaps ironically, that they became particularly well-versed in arguments about equality before the law and about the fundamental tie between full citizenship and the right to vote.[54]

* * *

Black voters across New York State had made clear for years that their right to vote was as much a tool for the collective security and advancement of black Americans as it was a mechanism for individual interest. A priority among black voters was the education and protection of black children. Voting fathers and elders, who comprised both the parents of the children of gradual abolition as well as the oldest members of the generation, passed on a tradition of engaging with good laws and protesting bad ones. When the rising generation spoke so persistently in the 1830s, '40, and '50s about the content of citizenship and the right the vote, it is in part because of the activities they saw and the words they had heard as they were growing up.

The Jinnings family of New York City were among the most visible black New Yorkers to shape and witness the lived realities of black voting and citizenship during the first half of the nineteenth century. But they were not alone in their experiences; there were others like the Jinningses across the state. The family's intergenerational story helps illuminate the broad impact black voting had in long-term efforts in political organizing and conceptualizations of citizens' rights among men and women alike.[55]

Born in 1791, Thomas L. Jinnings, the paterfamilias, was a native New Yorker who was either born free or freed as a young child. Apprenticed to a tailor as a boy, by 1810 he had opened his own tailor shop in lower Manhattan and married Elizabeth Cartwright, the daughter of a politically active Revolutionary War veteran named Jacob Cartwright. Over the course of his career, Jinnings not only became one of the first black Americans to acquire a U.S. patent—in 1821, for a form of dry cleaning he invented—but seems to have participated in nearly every key development in New York's black political history between the 1810s and the 1850s.[56]

Jinnings's civic work began at least as early as 1812, when he was twenty-one years old and helped men in the Fifth Ward acquire certificates of freedom in order to vote. In 1812, he assisted Henry Parsons of Virginia by swearing to a local official that Parsons was free. In 1814, he did the same for George White of New Jersey and John Johnson of New York City. It is likely that Jinnings aided even more men; not all of the city's certificates survive. (Jinnings, in his own handwriting, signed his name with an *i*; in later decades, some in the family used "Jennings" with an *e*.) In 1813, as black Federalists met in taverns to express their opposition to the War of 1812, they organized ward-level efforts to encourage black voting and formed committees to promote "habits of industry, honesty, and sobriety." Jinnings represented the Fifth Ward.[57]

During this same time, Thomas and Elizabeth began having children. Although we cannot transport ourselves directly to the conversations at the family's shop or breakfast table in the 1810s and '20s, we know that Thomas and Elizabeth prioritized their children's formal educations and emphasized the family's community responsibilities. The Jinningses supported both the African Free School and black-run independent schools. There is no question that the five Jinnings children knew their father had once voted on equal terms with white men and that he subsequently faced greater barriers at the polls. The children watched their father and his male peers—parents of their own schoolmates—organize to regain equal access to the ballot.[58]

Thomas Jinnings later recalled how in 1821, when delegates met at the state constitutional convention, his fellow voter and education advocate Henry Sipkins had been one of the men to sign the black petitioners' memorial, introduced by Jay, highlighting "the injustice of depriving citizens of color of the elective franchise." He noted that the petition caused

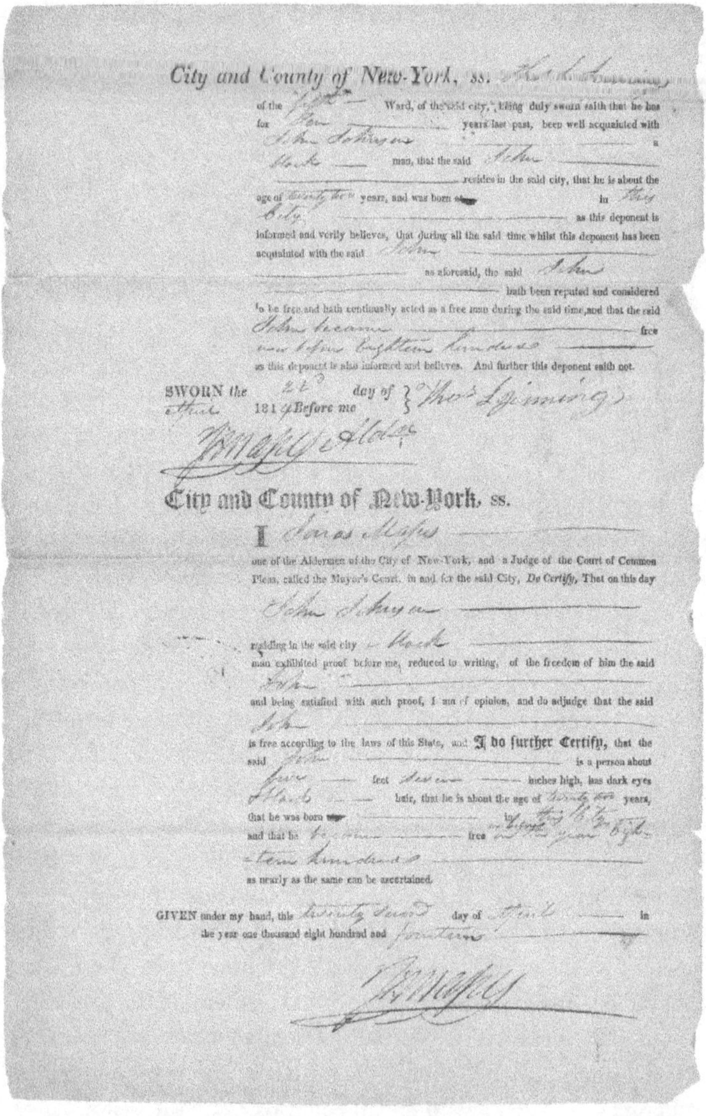

City and County of New-York, ss. Thos L Jinnings

of the fifth Ward, of the said city, being duly sworn saith that he has for ten years last past, been well acquainted with John Johnson a black man, that the said John resides in the said city, that he is about the age of twenty two years, and was born in this City as this deponent is informed and verily believes, that during all the said time whilst this deponent has been acquainted with the said John as aforesaid, the said John hath been reputed and considered to be free and hath continually acted as a free man during the said time, and that the said John became free in or before eighteen hundred as this deponent is also informed and believes. And further this deponent saith not.

SWORN the 22d day of April 1814 Before me } Thos L Jinnings

City and County of New-York, ss.

I Jonas Mapes one of the Aldermen of the City of New-York, and a Judge of the Court of Common Pleas, called the Mayor's Court, in and for the said City, *Do Certify*, That on this day John Johnson residing in the said city a black man exhibited proof before me, reduced to writing, of the freedom of him the said John and being satisfied with such proof, I am of opinion, and do adjudge that the said John is free according to the laws of this State, and I do further Certify, that the said John is a person about five feet seven inches high, has dark eyes black hair, that he is about the age of twenty two years, that he was born in this City and that he became free in the year eighteen hundred as nearly as the same can be ascertained.

GIVEN under my hand, this twenty second day of April in the year one thousand eight hundred and fourteen

Figure 9. John Johnson's 1814 certificate of freedom, signed by Thomas L. Jinnings, who swore that Johnson became free "in or before eighteen hundred." Johnson would have taken a copy of this certificate to the polls in order to vote. Jinnings was an active abolitionist and political leader in New York State for fifty years. His children, who also appear in this book, participated in midcentury civil rights campaigns. New-York Historical Society, New York City Indentures Collection, 1718–1727, 1792–1915.

the delegates to "deliberate for the space of twelve days, and thereby secured to use the right of suffrage with certain restrictions."[59] In this framing, black men had stopped an even worse outcome—complete disfranchisement—from occurring. The story stood as proof of the insidiousness of racist lawmaking and, at the same time, the importance of employing formal legal tools and cultivating advantageous relationships with white partners through a politics of access.

Sipkins and Jinnings had voted in the same ward in the early 1800s and were nearly the same age. They appeared at countless political meetings together. It seems reasonable to imagine that the Jinnings children knew Sipkins personally, that he was the sort of family friend who stopped by to visit after work—the Jinnings home and the Sipkins family granary business were in walking distance. When Sipkins died, Jinnings remembered that Sipkins had been a founding member of the Mutual Relief Society in 1808, which was "the first incorporated benevolent society in this state." Since its founding, "society after society" had formed, both "male and female." In this wide view of civic participation, voting was important, but so too were state-recognized associations and female intellectual efforts. It was precisely these sorts of activities that had "prepared" black New Yorkers to challenge the "hydra-headed monster" called "the colonization society." Jinnings and Sipkins may not have advocated for female suffrage, but they nonetheless placed political value on girls' educations, associationlism, and civil rights.[60]

In various ways, all five Jinnings children carried on their parents' legacies: William was a businessman who supported the black press; Thomas Jr. was a dentist who developed new techniques for teeth preservation and resisted segregation on the Massachusetts railroad; Matilda was a dressmaker; Sarah moved to San Francisco with her Pennsylvania-born husband and safeguarded her family's history; and Elizabeth, a teacher, became the most famous of the Jinnings children after she successfully sued a New York City streetcar company, forcing desegregation on some common carriers. Thomas Sr. also mentored, in addition to his own impressive children, Samuel Ringgold Ward, the African Free School graduate who, born enslaved in Maryland in 1817, became an influential abolitionist, minister, and politician.[61]

Elizabeth's celebrated streetcar protest was the product of decades of accumulated knowledge and experience. She was her father's daughter in more ways than one. When, in 1854, she boarded a streetcar in downtown Manhattan and was refused service, she protested that she "was a respectable person, born and raised in New York" and on her "way to church." After the conductor violently removed her from the car, the family's church hosted a public meeting whose participants resolved to "bring the whole affair before the legal authorities" and demand, as "citizens," the "equal right to accommodation of transit."[62]

Several months later, the Brooklyn Circuit Court heard the case of *Elizabeth Jennings v. the Third Ave. Railroad Company*. Jennings's lawyers included Chester Arthur, future president of the United States, and Erastus D. Culver, an abolitionist politician with connections to the Jay family. The judge instructed the jury that common carriers were bound to carry all respectable persons, including people of color. The jury found the company liable and awarded Elizabeth $225. Horace Greeley's *New York Tribune*, by then one of the nation's largest papers, urged railroads, steamboats, omnibuses, and ferries to heed "the rights of this class of citizens." James McCune Smith and Jinnings Sr. advertised that public conveyances were now open on "equal terms." Should a conductor discriminate, "have him arrested, or call upon Dr. Smith" and "we will enter your complaint at the Mayor's office." The "law is right," they concluded.[63]

Jinnings Sr. also published an "Appeal to the Citizens of Color, Male and Female, of the City and State of New York" describing the case. It was certainly not lost on Jinnings, the father of three daughters, that females were citizens, too, and that they were part of the struggle for equal rights in New York. His emphasis on citizenship "male and female" underscored his generation's success in making local black citizenship a legal and social fact.[64]

Although much had changed between the 1820s and the 1850s, there were revealing continuities in black legal and political practice. Elizabeth and her supporters knew how to navigate local courts, find good lawyers, appeal to their educations and religiosity, and publicize when the "law is right." Elizabeth had grown up in a home, a school, a neighborhood, a city, and a state where black men, women, and children had employed such strategies for years. Voting mattered to women like Elizabeth. She knew that men like her father and brothers could elect lawmakers whose acts mattered to her daily life. Perhaps she thought she deserved the franchise, too. But enjoying the rights of citizenship was not just about voting. It was also the right to use public transport and to access courts. Women and girls, like men, needed to get to church, school, work, and home. Over multiple generations, the men and women of the Jinnings family helped define more expansive visions of what it meant to be an American citizen.[65]

* * *

In April 1821, as the Missouri Crisis came to a close and New York prepared for its constitutional convention, black men such as Thomas L. Jinnings cast ballots in a congressional election under the same constitutional rules as white men for the last time until 1870. In New York City, black voters helped elect Cadwallader D. Colden, former president of the Manumission Society, as a United States representative for New York's first district. Once in Congress, Colden led the charge against a new fugitive slave law. Neither Colden's single term in Washington nor the failed bill are much discussed among scholars, but both illustrate how local black antislavery efforts influenced national politics. Black children's and families' years of resistance to kidnapping, along with their citizenship claims as students, taxpayers, associators, and voters, informed Colden's stance against a proslavery bill that would have further harmed black people throughout the United States.

Born in 1769, Cadwallader D. Colden was the grandson of Cadwallader Colden, one of the colonial province's most well-known imperial officials. Cadwallader D.'s father, a wealthy landowner in Orange County with Loyalist sympathies, sent his son to London for his education. Cadwallader D. returned to New York in 1785 and studied law. After practicing for several years in Poughkeepsie, he opened an office in New York City in 1796, served as an assistant district attorney from 1798 to 1801, and was elected to the Manumission Society in 1802.[66]

When Colden first joined the Manumission Society, kidnapping was on the rise. He was a member of the legal committee that successfully drafted model legislation for the state legislature to better address the crime in 1807 and 1808 laws.[67] In 1816, he became the Society's president and began arguing publicly for general abolition. In 1817, he won election to the state assembly. The following year, he was appointed mayor of New York, a position that included presiding over the municipal court. In all of these capacities, Colden encountered incidents of human trafficking. The prevalence of the crime forced Colden and men of his ilk to consider the state's role in protecting its most vulnerable. In this sense, kidnapping—just like voting—informed conversations about who could claim the prerogatives of citizenship. One of the roles of government, after all, was to protect citizens. Indeed, this was a point New York's antislavery advocates had made explicitly during the Missouri Crisis.[68]

That "protection" is a right of citizenship is all the more important to emphasize because it allows us to see the full range of people who forged practices and ideas around what citizenship meant in the early republic. In 1823, in one of the few descriptions of the "privileges and immunities of citizenship" articulated in a contemporary federal court, Justice Bushrod Washington noted that "citizens of all free governments" could claim "protection by the government." He also listed the right to "safety."[69] This understanding of citizenship's multiple features helps us appreciate how an otherwise rather powerless and disfranchised woman named Mary Underhill influenced how a man of high political stature like Colden learned firsthand how precious these aspects of citizenship could be. Colden encountered Underhill roughly a year before he was elected to Congress, when her kidnapping case came before his mayor's court.

Underhill was a domestic working in lower Manhattan. According to her December 1819 grand jury testimony, she had moved to the city from Greene County upstate. Under New York law, Underhill, as a free black woman, could testify against white people in court.[70] She explained she had recently met a nefarious man named Joseph Pulford, who promised "her a place where she could get a Hundred dollars a month." Pulford's real intention was to kidnap her. After enticing Underhill onto the ship of one Captain Glasshouse, Pulford told Glasshouse that he was looking for someone to buy her. Glasshouse, pretending to collaborate, got word to a longtime Federalist constable in the Second Ward who agreed to pretend to be a merchant who had come to New York to smuggle a slave. When the "merchant" met Pulford, he insisted on seeing Underhill in person, on dry land, before paying. As soon as Pulford accepted money, the "merchant" revealed himself as the constable and dragged Pulford to the police office.[71]

Underhill testified again on her own behalf during Pulford's trial. In his directions to the petit jury, Colden told the men that under New York law, "to constitute kidnapping or inveigling, no force is necessary." Underhill's testimony, he noted, was "unimpeached." When the jury found Pulford guilty, Colden sentenced Pulford to the maximum term: fourteen years at hard labor.[72]

A little over a year later, when Colden, a longtime Federalist, ran on the Federalist-cum-Independent ticket for Congress, he already had a career's worth of antislavery experience. His supporters emphasized his philanthropic credentials. The *Post* urged voters to support one who "will oppose the slave holders of the south, and prove the protector and advocate of a helpless race."[73] It could not have been lost on these pro-Colden editors that the First Congressional District included a sizable number of black voters. Suffolk and Queens Counties included 223 and 273 black male heads of household, respectively. Manhattan's First and Second Wards, long home to the sort of merchant and professional elite who formed the backbone of the Manumission Society, were also in the district. Underhill herself lived a few blocks away from the edge of Colden's congressional district, in the Sixth Ward.[74]

Colden's main rival in the election was Bucktail Peter Sharpe. Sharpe, the longtime proponent of black disfranchisement, was painted as an unprincipled proslavery coward by his opponents. The *Columbian* tied him directly to Missouri Crisis doughface turncoat Henry Meigs.[75] After the ballots were counted, Colden bested Sharpe by roughly 580 votes. Although it is impossible to know how many black voters chose Colden, it is reasonable to assume that the majority of the 641 black male heads of household in Colden's district favored him.[76] It is also reasonable to suspect that some of these voters knew of Underhill's case, or even knew her personally. Did Underhill tell her black neighbors that the judge who had sent her kidnapper to prison was now running for Congress? It is certainly possible. Whether black voters provided the precise margin of Colden's victory or not, it is clear that he won his seat in part because of the way his candidacy was framed in relation to local and national antislavery politics.

Colden took his seat in the Seventeenth Congress on December 12, 1821. Five days later, Maryland congressman Robert Wright began efforts to pass a new fugitive slave law. Wright submitted a resolution by Maryland's General Assembly complaining that the state's slaves were successfully escaping north. He "deprecated the interference of Quakers and others to prevent the reclamation of slaves in some of the states."[77] Colden likely blanched at the hostile reference to the "interference" of men like himself and his Manumission Society colleagues.

When Wright's bill was released to the Committee of the Whole several weeks later, Colden attacked. The New Yorker argued that the proposed law made it so preposterously easy for a master to claim an alleged fugitive that the law would essentially license kidnapping. There would be no need to prove anything before a free state judge, no trial by jury, no right to habeas corpus, no interference from state anti-kidnapping or liberty laws, no serious penalties for surreptitiously claiming a free person as a slave. "Is this to be endured?" he challenged.[78]

In Colden's view, the 1793 Fugitive Slave Act was bad enough already: "The [1793] law had been made the means of supplying the market with slaves. This was not a mere fiction. In the city which he, in part, represented, from a public street, a man with a family, a respectable man, differing in nothing from other citizens, except that his colour was a little dark, has been seized under colour of this law and sold to a distinct part of the Union as a slave."[79] Colden referred to black New Yorkers as "citizens," which, given the debate over the Missouri constitution that had recently occurred in the same room, was not an insignificant choice of language. Throughout his speech, Colden drew on his knowledge of people like Underhill. Colden had heard from dozens, if not hundreds, of black New Yorkers about the family separations, physical violence, and routine fear that characterized kidnapping.

Hugh Nelson of Virginia was dismayed by Colden's obstruction. He raised both the specter of the Missouri Crisis and the threat of "civil war" were southerners' constitutional rights ignored. Tensions rising, Bucktail David Woodcock did what Bucktails were learning to do best: find a northern way to compromise with southern interests. Woodcock convinced the House, by a vote of 61 to 40, to give the "friends of the bill" time to revise it in order to meet Colden's objections. The bill was referred to a new committee, which included Colden and Wright.[80] It is unclear exactly what the new version contained, but the bill eventually died, despite Wright's ongoing efforts. The session ended in May, with no new fugitive slave law.[81]

In his successful efforts to defeat the 1822 fugitive slave bill, Colden won a small battle in Congress on behalf of antislavery New Yorkers and black people vulnerable to kidnapping across the nation. But it is telling that he did so as a dying breed of Federalist, and that he arrived in Congress during the last election in his lifetime in which black men in his state had equal access to the polls. In the wake of Colden's single term in Congress, Americans witnessed continued partisan political fracturing as the First Party System fully disintegrated. During both the Missouri Crisis and the Seventeenth Congress, New York's Bucktails foreshadowed what was to come: perhaps a refashioned national Jeffersonian party could find a way to keep sectional issues at bay by uniting northerners and southerners under series of mutually advantageous policies that did not include support for black citizenship rights or the use of the federal government to promote free soil out west.

Scholars have rightly noted that, in the 1820s, something qualitatively shifted in antislavery politics in the United States. There was a "transformation," a shift from a "first wave" to a "second wave" of abolitionism. This narrative makes sense. But in cleaving the two moments, we at the same time should be cautious not to forget that an influential generation of black and white northerners lived through and participated in antislavery efforts across both waves. There was change *and* continuity. People living in the 1820s did not know what was coming down the pike. Remembering this fact makes events during this decade in New York all the more interesting and worth pondering on their own terms. Politically minded New Yorkers, black and white, were charting various paths for what might come next.[82]

One path was laid out by New York's most well-known Bucktail, Martin Van Buren. In January 1827, Van Buren wrote a famous public letter to Virginia editor Thomas Ritchie explaining the need to form a new national party in order to suppress hostilities between "free and slaveholding states." The most "beneficial" thing for the country would be a "political combination" between "the planters of the South and the plain Republicans of the north." The new party would soon be called the Democrats, with Andrew Jackson at the helm.[83]

This was one vision. But black and white antislavery New Yorkers, a few months later, expressed another way forward during the state's general abolition of 1827. Proponents of these alternate visions would battle for the next three decades within the framework of what became the Second Party System.

* * *

In July 1827, black New Yorkers used the occasion of the state's July 4 general abolition to talk about past, present, and future. When Austin Steward celebrated statewide abolition during the festivities in Rochester, he was not the only black New Yorker to stress the importance of legislative politics, the travesty of state disfranchisement, the fact of black citizenship, the responsibility to promote abolition elsewhere, and the role of the rising generation of children. Black New Yorkers in 1827 were by no means a homogenous population—they were born in different places, possessed different educations, inhabited different class and gender roles, attended different churches, expressed different political preferences, and recalled different experiences of slavery and freedom. But there were commonalities that bound them together. Living within New York's borders, they were subject to the same laws and state political forces. On July 4 and 5 of 1827, black New Yorkers heard and celebrated similar messages.

In Albany, Benjamin Lattimore Jr. and Sr. were part of a meeting of black men who began making plans for a July celebration months before the day. Lewis Topp, a musician and the father of future wealthy abolitionist William H. Topp, expressed a preference to celebrate on July 5 rather than July 4 since the latter marked "the National Independence of this country."

According to the minutes of the Albany common council, two of the black men, "Messrs Butler and Blake," applied for "permission to assemble in the Capitol," which was granted. When July 5 arrived, "the coloured population of this and the adjoining counties" marched in the streets and gathered in the Second Baptist Church to hear Nathaniel Paul preach. "We do well to remember," he said, "that every act of ours is more or less connected with the general cause of the people of colour, and with the general cause of emancipation" in "every part of the world." The "rising generation," he noted, "is advancing under more favorable auspices than we were permitted to enjoy, soon to fill the place we now occupy." Paul's audience carried banners bearing the names of Daniel Tompkins and his Manumission Society colleagues, including John Jay. One banner read simply, "The Legislature of 1817."[84]

In New York City, meanwhile, Thomas L. Jinnings and William Hamilton presided over a meeting at the Mutual Relief Hall, where they signed resolutions proposing that the various black denominations offer thanksgivings on July 4. Hamilton prepared a speech to give at the African Zion Church. When the day arrived, he addressed his "fellow citizens," calling on the "YOUTH OF MY PEOPLE" to uphold "the character of" the race and exhorting the girls in particular to "*improve your own minds*." The audience surveyed portraits of Tompkins, Jay, and President Jean-Pierre Boyer of Haiti. It seems reasonable to suppose that Hamilton's young sons, the future abolitionist editors Robert and Thomas Hamilton, as well as the Jinnings children, sat in the pews. Satisfied with the speech, the Mutual Relief officers arranged for its publication and sold copies at Jinnings's tailor shop and in others businesses throughout lower Manhattan.[85]

To the chagrin of the *Freedom's Journal* editors and the Mutual Relief officers, who preferred restrained celebrations in churches rather than more raucous processions in the streets, New York City's festivities continued into the following day as thousands of black New Yorkers paraded through Manhattan. They followed a horse-mounted Grand Marshal, who saluted the mayor, watching from the City Hall steps. James McCune Smith later recalled what an exhilarating occasion it had been for his group of school-aged friends: "It was a proud day, never to be forgotten by young lads" who "felt themselves impelled along that grand procession of liberty, which . . . is still *marching on*." Like the 1827 orators, Smith understood the day as one important landmark on a much longer road to global emancipation.[86]

While the celebrations in cities like Rochester, Albany, and New York City drew in celebrants from the surrounding areas, there is evidence that black citizens of some of the smaller towns and more rural areas of the state also marked the day in their local communities. In Cooperstown, for example, sixty black citizens paraded on July 4 to the Presbyterian Meeting House, where a respected elder named Hayden Waters dispensed advice on the "necessity of sobriety, honesty, industry, together with a proper regard to the education of their children." In Deerfield, a small agricultural town in Oneida County, the Scottish emigrant doctor Alexander Coventry noted in his diary on July 5 that "the blacks are celebrating their freedom today." Though the comment is brief, Coventry's note is evidence that black New Yorkers in the less urban and cosmopolitan regions of the state knew the significance of legislative abolition.[87]

As the July festivities wound down, *Freedom's Journal* editor Samuel Cornish called for the formation of uplift societies throughout the state and highlighted the responsibilities of the next generation. The efforts of New Yorkers, he argued, were of national import: "The total annihilation of slavery in the Union, depends much, very much on the conduct of the coloured people of New-York."[88] Cornish, like Steward, Paul, Hamilton, and Waters, emphasized the role the "rising coloured generation" would play in the next chapters of a more nationalized, more black-led antislavery movement.[89] These boys and girls were the sons, daughters, and protégés of leaders like himself. They were the black servant children in white households and the students graduating from the African Free School. They were important not simply because they would step into the shoes of their forebears, as all younger generations do; they were important because they were the first black generation in New York to enter adulthood in a free state. Their forebears had survived centuries of slavery. They entered adulthood under a different set of political, legal, and social rules. Unlike previous generations, they did not have to focus on ending slavery for themselves. They could focus on ending the enslavement of others.

The editors of *Freedom's Journal* advocated a genre of respectable, self-help, uplift abolitionism, with class politics typical of the emerging, reform-minded northern middle class. They recommended that owners of newly freed slaves "retain them for their service, or, in the cultivation of their lands; the arrangement might be mutually beneficial." Masters should give former slaves "advice, as may influence their future conduct." The paper also reprinted a *New York Times* article that praised the 1827 general abolition, which had "been effected without any disturbance to the public tranquility, without complaint on the part of slave owners, and without expense to the state." The black editors were liberal in their support for general abolition, but conservative—from a class and culture standpoint—in supporting a version of emancipation in which newly free people would behave according to bourgeois values, masters would have a benevolent role to play, and city vices (drinking, dancing, brothels) would be avoided.[90]

There were generational components to these dynamics, as well. Sometimes those who came from impoverished, laboring backgrounds saw their children make a leap in class status, especially when the parents in question were born enslaved and their children born free. In other words, some formerly enslaved parents understood uplift as an opportunity.[91] James McCune Smith, for example, described the memories of "the Boot Black" in a series he published on black laborers. The Boot Black had been enslaved on Livingston Manor in Sullivan County until "Governor Tompkins caused the New York Legislature" to enact general abolition. Like many freed slaves, the Boot Black, "in possession of himself on Emancipation day, 1827," moved to New York City, where he joined a church, worked for wages, and married. At first, when his business shining shoes was slow, the couple depended on the wife's income as a laundress. They sent their children to school. The Boot Black was inspired by exhibitions at Charles Andrews's African Free School—Smith's alma mater—where he saw boys "stand upon a platform, before a multitude of white people, and read out loud in books . . . 'speak pieces' about liberty, and never seem afraid." The Boot Black's own children were girls: "his first born, well skilled in English, French, Drawing and Music" eventually opened a school with her sister. In retirement, the Boot Black owned "property in sight of the Manor on which he was 'raised,' and on which, but for Gov. Tompkins, he and his children might have remained in brutal ignorance."[92]

Whether the Boot Black was one real person or a composite is hard to say. The specific details Smith provides suggest he was drawing on a real person's biography. The erudite Smith certainly had his own agenda in this tale of uplift. But it is also true that Smith went to school with hundreds of children like the Boot Black's daughters and saw himself as sharing mutual interests. Indeed, he may have known the Boot Black precisely because he was the father of Smith's real-life female classmates. The Boot Black's life had changed on July 4, 1827, and his daughters, born after that date, lived lives that his own parents would have had a hard time imagining for their son. The children of gradual abolition were, in many ways, a generation born in optimism. That optimism was, in itself, a political weapon.[93]

* * *

While the 1827 general abolition was most significant for the black New Yorkers whose lives were immediately affected, the moment also served as a lesson and even a moment of pride for a host of other Americans. New York's singular emancipation day showcased a legislative model for ending slavery, an instance in which a relatively democratic interracial political process in the 1810s had worked in favor of abolishing slavery on one set date. July 4, 1827, was a moment—well past the enactment of gradual abolition laws in the 1780s and '90s—in which regional differences were publicly defined and national black confraternity was openly affirmed.[94]

New York's white newspapers from across party lines marked the day. A month before July 4, the *Times* explained that soon "slavery will not be known to the laws of New York." "Would to God," the editors continued, "that our southern brethren could do likewise." On July 6, the *Daily Advertiser* announced that "one of the greatest moral and political evils that ever stained the character of a Christian community" had ceased to exist. Delaware and Maryland should "without unnecessary delay follow the example of their eastern associates."[95]

The children of gradual abolition received special attention in this public discussion. The *Troy Sentinel* published a letter from a "man of high legal attainment" who explained the legal status of black children born under New York's laws. He noted that, per the 1817 general abolition act, all adult slaves were now free but children born to slaves since 1817 remained servants until age 21 as if "bound to service by the overseers of the poor." All other black children, including those born to servants, were "absolutely free," their "condition by law is the same as that of white children, except as to the qualifications for voting at elections." Papers inside and outside of New York republished this letter. The *Schenectady Cabinet,* citing the *Catskill Record,* explained that the children who remained servants were "domestics for a stated period (pretty nearly in the same light as apprentices bound out by the overseers of the poor) and not as slaves to be sold as pleasure."[96]

Like black citizens, white citizens used July 4 to celebrate both the nation's birthday and the general abolition. In Albany, a recent graduate of Union College named Salem Dutcher Jr. spoke in the State Capitol before "state officials, the judiciary, senate, members of congress, members of the Cincinnati [and] revolutionary worthies." Dutcher linked New York's emancipation to the possibility of abolition nationwide. "In future ages," he predicted, "this day will be no less celebrated in the history of this state than it now is memorable in the annals of the nation. It is an event of no ordinary moment; its effects will be great, and will continue to be felt" until all "sons of Africa" were free. He anticipated the day when "slavery in this *country* is extinct forever."[97]

Dutcher offered an inclusive vision of what the slavery-purged nation would look like. This was no apologia for colonization. He cited the newly established *Freedom's Journal.* He praised the African Free Schools. He observed that Albany, his hometown, likewise supported black schools and churches. "African scholars," he argued, would be "no less brilliant" than Newton, Bacon, Franklin, or Fulton. He was sure that one of the black men who "inhales his first breath of freedom on this day" would soon become a historian and write of the moment he became "a freeman entitled to all the privileges which the constitution vouchsafes to the freeborn citizen."[98]

To be sure, Dutcher was on one end of antislavery politics in the state, but he was not an outlier, nor speaking before a fringe audience. Even the *Albany Argus,* mouthpiece of the Albany Regency—an emerging Bucktail/Democratic political machine—praised Dutcher's message. The *Argus* did have one complaint, however: he had given too much credit to the Federalist-dominated Manumission Society and to John Adams (father of the Bucktails' current enemy, President John Quincy Adams) and not enough to the Democrats and their First Party System Republican forebears. Northern Democrats, very willing to protect slavery on a national level, were also willing, at least in 1827, to cite their role in state-based antislavery politics.[99]

Historians have often made the point that dyed-in-the-wool abolitionists were a tiny portion of the North's population. This is true. Scholars have similarly emphasized the virulent racism of white northerners and the multiple legal and economic barriers black northerners regularly faced.[100] But these vital observations should not obscure the moderate antislavery outlook that persisted among some of the citizenry and especially the political elite. Dutcher's speech evokes the mainstream acceptability of antislavery politics at a moment well after the Revolution but before David Walker's or William Lloyd Garrison's famous "second wave" writings began to circulate in the late 1820s and early '30s. Many of the New Yorkers who voted for the Liberty Party, the Free Soil Party, and the (second) Republican Party in comparatively high numbers in the 1840s and '50s had experienced the antislavery discourse of 1827.

New Yorkers' willingness to trumpet their antislavery traditions occasioned a wider awareness of the state's 1827 abolition throughout the region.

Northern newspapers reported widely on New York's actions and, in the process, helped to create a "free North" identity. (Coverage was far thinner in the southern press.[101]) As early as June 14, the *Scioto Gazette* in Chillicothe, Ohio, reported that black people in Albany were meeting to prepare celebrations. The *New-Hampshire Patriot* expressed "hope that at no very distant period," slavery "will be unknown in every part our happy Republic." In nearby Portsmouth, the *Journal* reported:

> [There are now] *six* states in which there are no slaves, viz: *Maine, New Hampshire, Vermont, Massachusetts, New-York and Ohio.* In 1820, there were in Rhode Island, 48 slaves, in Connecticut, 98; in Pennsylvania, 211; in Indiana, 190; in Illinois, 917. In some of these states there may be no slaves *now* . . . in all of them and in several others, provisions have been made by law for the termination of slavery. In 1820, New-York had 10,088 slaves. New Jersey, at the same time, had 7,557, and Delaware, 4,509.

In Massachusetts, the Newburyport *Herald* republished *Freedom's Journal*'s coverage—a white paper reprinting a black newspaper's version of events. Multiple articles noted that the founding fathers—like "venerable John Jay"—supported the "liberal and free principles" of antislavery.[102]

Free black Americans throughout the nation were equally attuned. In Baltimore, members of the Friendship Society held a July 4 dinner during which they toasted abolition in New York and urged "the example be followed by every state in the Union." They praised John Jay as a "friend of our colour" and hoped that *Freedom's Journal*'s fame would "spread throughout this great Continent." Their final toast called for "*Emancipation* without *emigration,* but equal rights on the *spot.*" In Fredricksburg, Virginia, a "respectable number of Coloured Inhabitants" gathered to praise the legislature of New York and prayed that "the Anchor now cast for Freedom, by the State of New-York, sink deeply in the breasts of our Southern States." In Washington, D.C., the "coloured people" believed that New York's emancipation was of "great importance in relation to themselves." For black Americans—whose occasions to celebrate good national news in the 1820s were rare—New York's abolition day offered a moment of relief and hope.[103]

In retrospect, the optimism expressed by antislavery Americans in July 1827 seems idealistic, naïve, merely rhetorical. And yet few misunderstood how hard it would be to achieve total emancipation in the United States.

Most acknowledged how entrenched slavery was in the South, especially in the lower and cotton South. Except for the most radical commentators, most agreed that slavery was, constitutionally, a matter of state concern—protected from federal interference by the federal consensus. As the *Boston Commercial Gazette* phrased it, slavery was a matter "the people of every State must judge for themselves." No one, at least in the context of the July 4 celebrations, mentioned the idea of a war that would achieve emancipation. But it is nevertheless clear that politicians and ordinary citizens thought that it was important that the most populous state in the country had legislatively rid itself of slavery. As the Boston-based Unitarian minister Noah Worcester wrote, "Never before in our country had there been such a number of slaves emancipated at one time. . . . This experiment may prepare the way for the emancipation of many thousands of their brethren in other states."[104]

Indeed, Americans remained familiar with the idea that state laws were potential tools for a state-by-state project of national abolition. Judge William Jay, the son of John and brother of Peter, argued that previous emancipations could inspire southerners to adopt their own measures. Northerners had a "right to exhort slaveholders to liberate their slaves" and "give advice" based on their own "history of emancipation." In one of his many publications, Jay asked sardonically, "What necessity prevented Kentucky from liberating her twelve thousand slaves in 1790, when New-York could liberate ten thousand in one day in 1827? What necessity will render [the territories of] Florida and Arkansas slave States?" If slavery could end in New York—with "*not one* case of insurrection or bloodshed"—was it so impossible to do elsewhere?[105]

Tellingly, Jay insisted on labeling New York's 1827 abolition an "immediate emancipation." No "conscientious man," he wrote, "after considering the results" in New York, Haiti, Latin America, and the West Indies, could "clamour against" this method. "Gradual emancipation" was desirable only "if no other can be obtained." In some respects, referring to the 1827 general abolition as immediate emancipation was a stretch. The date had been announced a decade in advance—not exactly "immediate." But Jay had a point: on one day in 1827, thousands of enslaved New Yorkers were freed at once. Jay and his allies could now claim that legislatively enacted immediate emancipation had occurred on American soil. Put another way, New York's general abolition represented in its very construction an important transformation in antislavery culture. The spirit and intent of the 1817 law was indeed different, and more immediate, than the child-based gradualist laws of the 1780s and '90s.[106]

Jay's trumpeting of New York's general abolition stood alongside antislavery northerners' general awareness of what had happened in antislavery history during their lifetimes. They could look to the Northwest Ordinance of 1787 and the Missouri Compromise of 1820 as models of congressional action forbidding slavery in federal territories. They did not forget that between 1777 and 1818, Vermont, Massachusetts, Pennsylvania, New Hampshire, Connecticut, Rhode Island, New York, Ohio, New Jersey, Indiana, and Illinois had banned slavery in their state constitutions, passed gradual abolition acts, or dismantled slavery in courts. New York's 1827 general abolition seemed like a high point of possibility within this larger context of antislavery progress. The Empire State now had the largest population of free black people in the North. It linked together a geographical region of free and nearly free states. One of the reasons the politics of slavery and antislavery shifted in the late 1820s and the 1830s is precisely because, at this very juncture, the North truly began to look like a part of the country where slavery was dying or dead.[107]

* * *

The New Yorkers who celebrated July 4, 1827 as a moment of potential had good reason to hold onto it as an example of hope, especially given the turbulent years that followed. In the ensuing decade, the nation experienced a series of events that provoked ever-increasing anxiety and violence over slavery, antislavery, and black citizenship. In 1828, slave-owning Tennessee Democrat Andrew Jackson, the standard-bearer of the "white man's democracy," won the presidency. Martin Van Buren served as his loyal secretary of state and vice president. In 1829, *Freedom's Journal* agent David Walker published *An Appeal to the Coloured Citizens of the World*, a widely circulated pamphlet that prompted white backlash. In 1831 and 1832, William Lloyd Garrison founded the immediatist *Liberator* and formed the New England Anti-Slavery Society. The American Anti-Slavery Society followed on its heels. Meanwhile, Nat Turner's slave rebellion in Virginia resulted in a slew of southern laws to restrict free black people's rights and prevent northern antislavery meddling. In 1832, the Virginia legislature rejected a plan to gradually emancipate and colonize the state's slaves. In 1833, Britain's parliament passed an act ending slavery in the West Indies, launching an Atlantic emancipation that would figure large in American political discourse. In 1836, Congress passed a controversial "gag rule" declaring that antislavery petitions would be automatically tabled. Meanwhile, racial violence intensified in the North as rioters terrorized black businesses and neighborhoods. White immigrants competed with black laborers for jobs. Tennessee, North Carolina, Arkansas, Michigan, and Pennsylvania approved new constitutions between 1834 and 1838 that disfranchised black men, leaving New England (excluding Connecticut) and New York (with its race-based property requirements) as the only places where black men could vote.

In the years following 1827, black and white antislavery New Yorkers did not always agree with one another in their abolitionist philosophies or in the precise manner in which laws, politics, and parties could be harnessed to their aims. But as they faced forward from 1827, with a rash of nationally cataclysmic events lying in wait—events that were crucial conflicts in the lead-up to the Civil War—they had a certain set of transformative experiences to draw from. Though New York's legal landscape was a far cry from perfect, the gains black citizens made for themselves served as footholds as they clung to their existing rights and sought to climb higher.

CHAPTER 5

Male and Female "Citizens of the State"

Rights, Politics, Petitions, and Parties

In the winter of 1846, a black laundress named Phebe Ray appeared before the Rochester Board of Education to petition its Committee on Grievances. She explained that she wished to send her grandchildren to School Number 11 on Chestnut Street, a short walk from the Rays' home. The city's single "colored school," by contrast, stood on the far side of the river.[1]

Phebe was the fifty-six-year-old widow of a New Jersey–born man named Isaac Ray and the matriarch of a politically active family. Born in Pennsylvania in 1790—ten years after the state passed the nation's first gradual abolition act—she lived in unpredictable emancipation environments her whole life. She gave birth to her first child, the future abolitionist barber David H. Ray, in New Jersey in 1810. A daughter, Mary, followed in 1817. When the children were young, the Rays moved to western New York. Phebe, David, and Mary were all born in gradual abolition states where they and their generational peers inhabited a range of liminal statuses along a spectrum of free and unfree. By the time Phebe approached the Rochester school board in 1846, she was settled with David, Mary, their spouses, and her grandchildren in the Fifth Ward, a few blocks from the Chestnut Street school.[2]

The Rays lived in an especially civic-minded black community. Phebe's efforts to secure equitable school access for her grandchildren formed part of a long and spirited campaign by ordinary black Rochesterians to educate their children. Although the school board denied Phebe's request in the winter of 1846, it allocated funds to move the colored school to a better building, "centrally located."[3] Unsatisfied with half measures, black Rochesterians continued to fight for full school privileges. It took several more years, but they eventually succeeded in opening the city's common schools to black children.

230 DAILY AMERICAN CITY DIRECTORY.

Pope, Arthur, Barber, 193 State, h. S. W. cor. Frank and Jay
Prince, George, Shoe-maker, h. Division, near N. St. Paul.

R.

Ransom, Elijah, Grocery, 139 Buffalo, h. 39 S. Ford.
Ray, David H., Barber, 39 Exchange, h. 6 Mechanic Alley.
Ray, Phebe, Cook, b. 6 Mechanic Alley.
Reid, Sarah, Mrs., Dress-maker, h. cor. Jay and Brown's Alley.
Robinson, John, Barber, shop 14½ Exchange, b. Mrs. Stanley's.

S.

Sampson, George, Hostler, Farmers' Hotel, Main.
Schuyler, James, Boatman, h. 103 Clay. [Spring.
Scott, Henry, Barber, shop next 93 State, h. S. Washington, near
Sharp, James, Carman, h. 35 Magne.
Shorters, William, Cook, b. Dr. Jenkins', Brown.
Simmons, James H., Laborer, b. 44 Grand.

Figure 10. In the late 1840s, Phebe Ray appeared in the Rochester city directories as a cook and a laundress. She ran her businesses out of the family home, where she lived with her son, David H. Ray, her daughter, Mary, and various grandchildren. Phebe petitioned the Board of Education to send her grandchildren to the local white school. David, a barber, was politically active like his mother. *Daily American Directory of the City of Rochester, for 1847-48* (Rochester, 1847), p. 230, courtesy of Rochester Public Library.

In many respects, Phebe Ray's petitioning fell in line with a tradition of black political and legal action that reached back to the earliest days of gradual abolition. Black New Yorkers were familiar with engaging local officials, appealing to useful laws, and lodging formal complaints. There were, nonetheless, important differences between black politics in the first and the second quarter of the nineteenth century. In 1821, the new state constitution stripped most black men of voting rights, revoking a vital tool of political influence and a marker of equal citizenship; in 1827, the state abolished slavery, which gave black New Yorkers more space to focus on challenges beyond their own bondage; in the 1830s, the Whig Party—a counterweight to the Democrats (formerly called Bucktails)—and antislavery third parties began to emerge, reshaping mainstream party politics in ways that reoriented and refueled local, state, and national conflicts over slavery and citizenship. This was the era of the Second Party System.

Phebe's efforts tell us a great deal about what it meant, and what it took, for ordinary black northerners to advocate for rights during the Second Party System. Black New Yorkers did not cease to be politically and legally influential simply because black men voted in smaller numbers. The everyday struggles inherent to the region's slow and patchwork abolition process taught families like the Rays how to seek redress in courts, councils, boards, and legislatures. Voting, they knew, was not the *only* way to practice politics—a fact black women grasped particularly well, never having had the right to begin with. In campaigns small, large, individual, coordinated, short-lived, and long-sustained, black New Yorkers engaged with government institutions to protect and expand the privileges and rights attached to their status as free citizens. Moreover, black women, despite the disadvantages imposed by their race and gender, entered public antislavery conversations with greater visibility. In this regard, northern black women created and encountered a sea change similar to what their white counterparts experienced in the materializing women's rights movement—the famous 1848 Seneca Falls convention occurred fifty miles from the Rays' home—and yet black women faced distinct transformations, challenges, and threats. Understanding the day-in and day-out of political practice in postabolition New York reveals underexplored aspects of women's history.[4]

At the same time that black New Yorkers worked to persuade officials to respect their rights and privileges as citizens and taxpayers, they also urged the state to combat the Slave Power. In the 1830s, black men and women petitioned the legislature for three critical measures: a law repealing the "nine months law," which allowed visiting masters to keep slaves in the state for up to nine months; a law guaranteeing accused runaways the right to a jury trial; and a law promoting the return of equal male suffrage. Allying with white abolitionists, black New Yorkers injected these concerns into political campaigns, applying pressure on Whigs and Democrats to adopt antislavery policies. In so doing, they not only urged legislative change, but created an atmosphere that encouraged amenable partisan leaders to adopt antislavery policies in unpredictable moments. In a noted example, from 1839 to 1841, Whig Governor William Seward defended black citizenship in a clash with Virginia over fugitive slaves and state sovereignty. Seward, now settled in Cayuga County, was responding to the growing energy of political abolitionism, especially in the western counties that formed his base.

As the rise of antislavery Whigs and the Rays' activities in Rochester suggest, the story of black politics in postabolition New York requires a statewide perspective. Although cities and towns on the Hudson River and Long Island remained politically vital, the center of gravity for reform politics shifted westward. In the 1820s and '30s, thousands of households, many from New England, settled along the Erie Canal, a man-made waterway stretching west from Albany to Lake Erie. The region's economy, geography, and demography created fertile ground for social and religious movements, including abolitionism, women's rights, temperance, anti-Masonry, utopianism, and evangelical perfectionism. Both the Liberty Party, founded in 1840, and the Free Soil Party, founded in 1848, held their first conventions in this energetic slice of New York. Eminent black leaders—including Austin Steward and Thomas James, as well as African Free School graduates Samuel Ringgold Ward, Henry Highland Garnet, and Charles Reason—worked along the canal. In 1847, Frederick Douglass moved to Rochester. Harriet Jacobs, future author of *Incidents in the Life of a Slave Girl,* soon followed. Harriet Tubman, the "Moses" of the Underground Railroad, lived on land she bought from Governor Seward in Auburn. This "Burned-Over District" became a model and a cautionary tale, an example of what was either most promising or most horrifying in predicting where the nation was headed. As proslavery polemicist George Fitzhugh of Virginia taunted: "Why have you Bloomer's and Women's Right's men, and strong-minded women, and Mormons, and anti-renters [and] a thousand other superstitious and infidel isms at the North? . . . Why all this, except that free society is a failure?" Black New Yorkers thought differently; they defended "free society" and fought to make it freer.[5]

The rising generation created a postabolition society in which the language and substance of citizenship, constitutional rights, school access, and legislative politics were in constant discussion. Ultimately, their record of success was mixed. They lost important objectives, like equal suffrage. They achieved others, including the repeal of the nine months law, a jury trial law, and goals within education campaigns. Far more than contemporary observers or modern scholars have recognized, ordinary black New Yorkers shaped the careers, ideas, and policies of some of the nation's most influential white antislavery figures, including Seward, Gerrit Smith, Myron Holley, Luther Bradish, John A. Dix, Thurlow Weed, and Horace Greeley. By creating situations in which officials, editors, and politicians were compelled to stake a position, black New Yorkers pushed myriad arms of the state—from local school boards to southern legislatures—to confront questions about racial equality and the future of slavery in the nation.

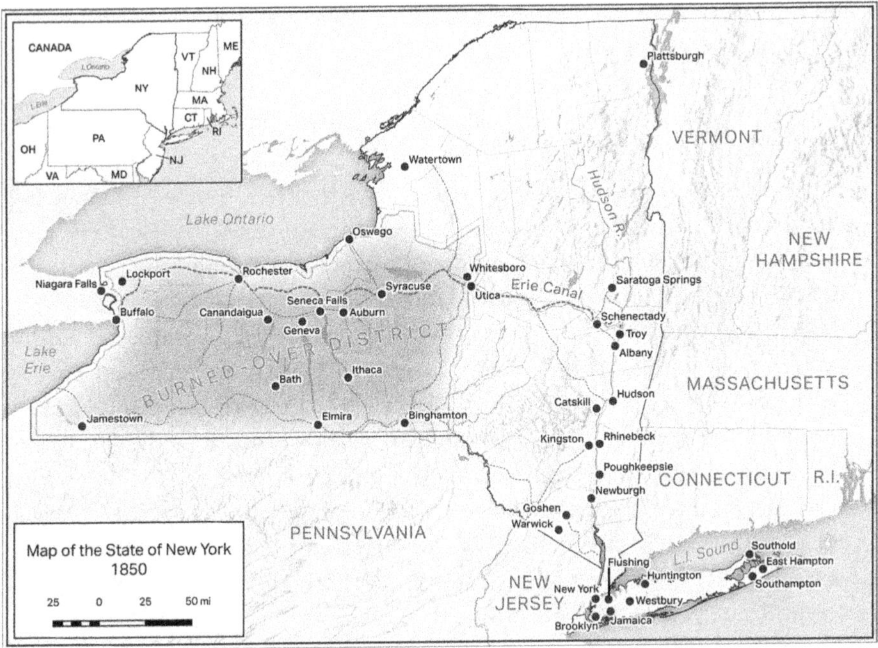

Figure 11. Map of New York State, 1850. In the 1830s and '40s, the area of western New York along the Erie Canal and around the Finger Lakes was a hotbed of reform politics, including antislavery. This "Burned-Over District" was home to famous black abolitionists, like Frederick Douglass and Harriet Tubman, and prominent antislavery politicians, like William H. Seward and Roscoe Conkling. Many ordinary black families likewise called the region home, including the Rays of Rochester. Map by Dan Miller.

By the 1830s and '40s, most of the children of gradual abolition were adults. Like their parents, they worked with white partners. But their practices also reflected generational change. Phebe Ray did not ask a local white abolitionist to confront the Rochester school board; she went herself. Black New Yorkers began appearing at the state capitol with their own mass petitions and providing their own testimony. They scheduled their own meetings with lawmakers. They ran their own newspapers. They became administrators of their own schools. This was what James McCune Smith had meant when he said that the "children" of his generation "took up the burden of their fathers, and their dreams and their plays were of freedom." They were conscious of their opportunities and their responsibilities, and they were equipped to do things the enslaved generations before them could not have done.[6]

* * *

Like Phebe Ray, black parents and guardians across New York advocated for "educational rights" and "school privileges" in the 1830s and '40s. Their investment in education, as well as their occasional success in compelling officials to address their claims, was informed by the prominent role that schools and literacy laws had played during the most intensive decades of gradual abolition. Between the 1780s and the 1820s, New York City's African Free School had enrolled thousands of black children—many now parents themselves. Outside the city, a fair number of children had also received formal instruction. The state's 1810 antislavery law required masters to teach black servant children to read; the 1817 addendum encouraged masters to employ local common schools for this purpose. By the 1830s, black New Yorkers could draw on legal and social traditions of using local resources to educate black children.

In Brooklyn, for example, where the Croger brothers and the Woolman Society had done so much in the early 1800s to foster black schools in the absence of robust government support, a new wave of parents and teachers maintained momentum. The persistence with which black adults advocated for schoolchildren did not go unnoticed. The Whig editor of the *Long-Island Star,* Alden Spooner, regularly printed black citizens' letters and notices while editorializing on behalf of black education. Over time, black Brooklynites managed to persuade officials to meet some of their demands. In 1839, five years after the legislature chartered Brooklyn as a city and granted the common council the power to appoint school trustees, the council placed three black men—George Hogarth, Sylvanus Smith, and Henry Brown—in charge of the city's African School. Hogarth, a grocer, A.M.E. minister, and *Liberator* agent, was also a teacher. Smith was a prosperous pig farmer with particularly bright daughters (one, Susan, became the state's first black female M.D.). Brown was a cab driver active in a variety of uplift societies.[7] In 1841, after the city council reappointed the three men, Spooner informed his readers that the colored school was directed by "three intelligent colored citizens" who employed a "very competent" instructor to teach the school. The institution received better public funding than in the past, but remained housed in the Woolman Society's private school building.[8]

The "very competent" teacher was Augustus Washington, a child of gradual abolition from New Jersey. His father and stepmother, both formerly enslaved, ran an oyster refectory in Trenton. By no means wealthy, the family had nonetheless been comfortable enough to send Washington to "private white schools" as a boy. At twelve, he began reading abolitionist newspapers and aspiring to college. At sixteen, he opened a school for black children, which he ran briefly before matriculating at the Oneida Institute, where Jermain W. Loguen and Thomas James, among others, also studied. When his father ran into business trouble, Washington left Oneida, worked as a clerk for an abolitionist pharmacist in Manhattan, and then "took charge of the Public School of Brooklyn" in 1838. Like other black teachers, Washington was involved in political and moral uplift campaigns. It would not have been uncommon for students to see Washington in school during the day and then again on weekends as he solicited subscriptions for black newspapers and gave speeches in church in favor of the equal franchise.[9]

For a brief time, Washington had a female counterpart in Brooklyn, a young woman named Rosetta Morrison, who opened an independent primary school for black children on the edge of Brooklyn Heights near the East River, a few blocks away from Washington's school. Like Washington, Morrison had received an exceptionally strong education in the Burned-Over District. She was a graduate of the Young Ladies Domestic Seminary, an institution in Oneida County run by a white abolitionist.

Originally from Connecticut, Morrison was a "stranger" to Brooklyn when she arrived, but she had ties through the seminary with local black leaders. In the spring of 1841, with references from *Colored American* editor Charles B. Ray and Presbyterian minister Theodore S. Wright, she announced her school. For most of the year, she conducted her classes on the same Chapel Street property where she lived with a black family named the Hamptons. She almost certainly taught children who worshipped at the nearby African Methodist Episcopal Church on High Street, the oldest black church in the city and a four-minute walk from her lodgings. When enrollment grew to seventy students, she enlisted her seminary classmate Ursula James to help her teach the "usual" subjects, as well as "morals and manners." In the fall, Morrison and James held an exhibition in the church basement where the "dear little interesting children" showed off their spelling, arithmetic, and geography. Reverend Hogarth, one of the aforementioned Brooklyn common school commissioners, congratulated the "ladies on the success of their enterprize," especially since they operated "without public patronage." Morrison married soon thereafter and closed her school.[10]

Although Morrison's institution was short-lived, the fact that it existed—and flourished—tells us about the milieu in which she operated and how ordinary free black people sustained local political and community life. Morrison's project succeeded because black Brooklynites were civic-minded, densely situated, and generous. Morrison's landlords, Benjamin and Maria Hampton, for example, provided Morrison an ideal headquarters. The middle-aged couple were originally from New Jersey and new to Brooklyn themselves. Benjamin, who worked as a waiter at a nearby restaurant by the ferry dock to Manhattan, owned the significant property on Chapel Street where Morrison lived and taught school. The Hamptons' household included Benjamin's mother, Lucy, a daughter named Mary, and, over the years, various boarders (including, after Morrison left, the pioneering Baptist minister Sampson White from Virginia). Maria Hampton could read and write, and it is possible that Mary attended Morrison's school. Benjamin could not write, but was active in formal politics. A member of the African Tompkins Association, whose purpose was raising funds "to assist the widows and orphans of deceased members, and the improvement of the members in morals and literature," Benjamin was among the members who successfully petitioned the state legislature for articles of incorporation. He was also listed on the state census as a voter, which makes sense given his sizable property holdings.[11]

In many respects, the Hamptons were similar to Phebe Ray and her family. These were northern free black families whose adult members came of age during gradual abolition. The parents acted as civic pillars within their neighborhoods, engaged in local politics, and committed themselves to black education. They created autonomous institutions while also engaging with the legal mechanisms of the state in order to support their projects. The men were more public facing than the women, but the women were claiming space, roles, and respectability in ways that would have been near impossible a generation or two earlier. Together, these ordinary and striving free black northerners formed a foundational layer of action and strength that undergirded the more recognized social, legal, and political transformations characterizing this period in the history of northern reform.

The Rays and the Hamptons had their equivalents in New York City. Like their peers in Brooklyn, and less like their peers in Rochester, black parents in the city cared more about the quality of their own schools than access to white schools. Predictably, their educational politics were deeply informed by their experiences with the Manumission Society's African Free School, which had expanded into six buildings by the 1820s. Black leaders had quarreled with the school's paternalistic white trustees over the years, but they had also forged productive relationships. When the Manumission Society handed its schools over to the Public School Society in 1834, the 1,600 children in the African Free School lost their longtime benefactors.[12]

The Public School Society handled the transfer poorly. Black parents started withdrawing their children and sending them to private school. When the School Society investigated the matter, a group of "leading coloured citizens" explained the black flight: parents did not know or trust the society, the society had reduced "all the schools except one to rank of primaries," and the society had fired beloved African Free School teachers.[13] Receptive to the complaints, the society ordered that both black and white schools be "conducted strictly" according to the same regulations, that an additional black schoolhouse be built, that a new black female monitorial school be opened, and that a black agent be hired to communicate with black families.[14]

As the School Society implemented the reforms, black mothers forged relationships with the school trustees. In August 1836, when the society called a meeting to report the improvements, "mostly females" appeared in the "new African School House" to discuss the developments. The society noted that the "interview was on the whole pretty satisfactory."[15] Although unnamed, these women were no doubt a group that included graduates of the African Free School, members of the African Dorcas Society, and former servant children who had tussled with masters over literacy laws. In other words, some of the women would have had previous experience advocating for school rights, and they would have been able to help strangers to the city's political scene manage relationships with local officials and reformers.[16]

The women's encounter with the school officials, briefly recorded on paper, is one of those archival moments that tells us both so little and so much. Why were there more black women than men? Assuming the meeting was during the day, were women more able to break from their household labor in order to attend? Were some of the fathers at sea, which would have been common within the city's port economy? To be sure, men remained interested in children's educations—black newspapers, conventions, and teachers are proof—but was the female engagement with the Public School Society part of a wider cultural moment in which women were stepping into public life as specialized advocates of causes related to children and families? Whatever the case may be, what we do know is that in August 1836, black women met with school officials who ran public schools—schools authorized by the state, funded by taxpayer money. These women were citizens whose children were recipients of a government service. Their involvement in the school meeting, like Phebe Ray's related activity in Rochester, was a form of formal politics that has too often been hidden from view.[17]

As the stories of school politics in Brooklyn and New York City suggest, when black New Yorkers pressed for school rights, they raised larger questions about black citizenship and civic belonging. These conversations mattered on the local level—when negotiations went well, black children received better education. Sometimes, these conversations also burst beyond their local settings. In these cases, school politics in even the smallest of places made an impact on state policy and wider understandings of black citizenship.

In 1833, for example, white citizens in the rural town of Hunter, on the west side of the Hudson River, filed a complaint with state superintendent John A. Dix after the district's trustees appointed "a colored man to teach the district school, which was attended almost exclusively by white children." Dix, a moderately antislavery Democrat (and future Free Soil Party candidate), noted that the law was "silent as to the description of persons to be employed as teachers." His personal view was that the trustees had neglected to cultivate "a spirit of harmony and good feeling" in their district. Dix hoped the trustees would reverse course, but legally, he could not compel them to fire the black teacher. The trustees should "pay the teacher the public money for his wages," and the rest "must be collected from those who send to school."[18]

The Hunter story is intriguing. On the one hand, certain details are not surprising. Integrated schooling occurred in rural areas. Small towns did not always have the funds or the populations to support separate schools. On the other hand, it was rare to find a black teacher instructing white children. For whatever reason, Hunter's trustees had hired a black man, a choice that upset some white parents. Ultimately, Dix's response reflected a consensus among the state's centrist white politicians about the nature of black citizenship: black New Yorkers were indeed state citizens, they had access to many rights under the law, but social separation was salutary, especially in cases where black people held positions of authority.

In 1836, Dix received another question from a rural area about black participation in the school system. Residents of Schodack, in Rensselaer County, asked Dix for an opinion "with regard to the right of colored persons, who had been assessed to pay highway taxes, to vote at school district meetings." Dix was unequivocal: "Colored persons have the right to vote at meetings in the school districts in which they reside. . . . Indeed, colored persons are permitted to vote at popular elections under certain circumstances."[19] It is unclear, from Dix's report, whether black taxpayers had asked him to grant or affirm their right to vote, or if white residents had appealed in an attempt to stop black residents who had already been voting. Whatever the query's origins, Dix ruled in favor of black political rights in local school governance.

School districts across the state were supposed to abide by Dix's rules. In 1837, the legislature ordered his most important rulings printed to render them "serviceable as precedents." Dix, who made the selections himself, included the Hunter and Schodack cases. Every town in New York received a copy.[20]

All the same, local officials retained a great deal of control over black education. In Schenectady, for example, black parents had a particularly hard time acquiring their fair share from city officials. In 1833, the African School Society petitioned the common council for a lot to build a school building, to no avail. Despite the fact that their families paid taxes, they received no portion of the school fund, nor were they permitted to enroll in the local Lancaster school. Instead, they relied for years on their own resources to sustain a Sabbath school and a day school. The Female Benevolent Society was especially instrumental; in 1837, the women donated fifty dollars "for a lot purchased by the people of colour, as a site for a school room." The "Colored Ladies" also organized fundraising fairs. Simultaneously, black citizens petitioned the common council repeatedly for funds. In 1843, the council deigned to grant the "African School" twenty-five dollars; it raised the sum to seventy-five dollars a few years later.[21]

Meanwhile, two hundred miles west, black Rochesterians were facing their own difficulties. In 1832, when Rochester was still relatively small, black citizens successfully petitioned the state legislature to open a colored school with money from the local fund. As Rochester expanded, black adults were increasingly upset that their children had to cross the city to receive an education, especially since their school was habitually neglected. In 1841, a black "clothes renovator" named John H. Bishop spearheaded a petition to the common council asking to be "exempted from taxation for building school houses for white children because their children are not permitted to attend the schools thus taxed." After the council conceded that black children had the "right to attend the common schools in the districts where they live," the trustees of School Number 3 obtained an ambiguous letter from the new state superintendent, responding to white parents, counteracting the council's decision.[22] In other words, even after local officials had ruled in favor of school equality, white parents managed to prevent any changes. This was the school campaign that Phebe Ray joined when she went before the school board in 1846 to protest that fact that her grandchildren had to travel all the way across town to receive an education when a perfectly good school stood a few blocks away.[23]

Phebe's visit to the school board is worth highlighting not only for what it reveals about how black northerners, including women, practiced politics, but also because her example helps restore ordinary local people to the center of an important story. The Rochester school campaign was one of the most sustained and successful in the mid-nineteenth-century United States, and remains well-known because of Frederick Douglass's role in its later stages. But Douglass's involvement has also served to draw focus away from "everyday" people like Ray and John H. Bishop, and from the fact that black Rochesterians' efforts had a history that long predated Douglass's arrival. Douglass did not start a school campaign; he joined one.[24]

When Douglass moved to Rochester in late 1847, he entered a city with a tight-knit and politically engaged black community. At some point, he grew acquainted with the Ray family. Phebe's son, David, owned a barbershop, working alongside his sister Mary's husband, Elza, and an apprentice named Henry W. Johnson. In 1848, Douglass joined David, Elza, and Henry to commemorate West Indian emancipation. Elza led the parade, David read the British and French Emancipation Acts, Henry gave a speech, and Douglass delivered an address. One can only imagine the discussions of black rights that took place at work as David, Elza, and Henry cut their customers' hair, or what was said at the table in the Ray–Johnson house on Mechanic Alley, where Phebe also brought home wages, and likely political news, from her cooking and laundry businesses. This was a three-generation household, with a matriarch at the helm, whose members cared deeply about community uplift and educating the next generation of children.[25]

In the fall of 1849, with Douglass's support, black Rochesterians boycotted the separate schools. They made this tactical choice after the Democrat-leaning school board decided to open a new black school rather than to adopt a proposal to drop the color restrictions. At a meeting led by James Sharp, a cartman, and Z. D. Patterson, a barber, on the subject of "Equal School Privileges," black parents resolved they would not send their children to black schools. They also crafted a petition to the school board, signed by "colored citizens of Rochester," praying for their "legal right to equal participation in the common schools." At another school meeting a few weeks later, a group of black and white Rochesterians signed resolutions noting that "every unjust act towards the free colored citizens of the North is an additional prop to slavery everywhere." Shortly thereafter, Douglass noted "the colored schools are almost deserted."[26]

The Rays almost certainly joined the boycott. It is also likely that Phebe and David attended the "meetings against colored schools" and signed the ongoing petitions to the school board. David had run political meetings with James Sharp in the past.[27] David's wife, Betsey, may also have participated, along with Elza, Mary, and Henry. With children out of school, added care-taking responsibilities would have fallen on black families, and it is easy to imagine that it was mostly women who stepped in to tend to the young children now at home. In this sense, women's private labor supported a public political campaign.

One of the reasons the Rochester campaign was ultimately successful was because black parents had committed allies on the school board. Just before the boycott, the Committee on Colored Schools—a four-man body including the white abolitionist Samuel D. Porter—released a report agreeing that the current situation was unjust, observing that black Rochesterians had been asking for full access to public schools for almost a decade and that they paid taxes "equally with other citizens." It made no financial sense, they said, to maintain boycotted schools. Moreover, equal school access would relieve "the mortification [black families] must feel in being forced from the districts in which many of them were born and have ever lived, and where the property of their parents has been taxed to build commodious school buildings which they are not permitted to enter."[28] In March 1850, four months after the boycott started, the Special Committee on the Colored School System noted that twenty-four black students were now enrolled in five different white neighborhood schools. Referencing the black parents' fall 1849 petition, the officials acknowledged black families' clear preference for integration. Soon thereafter, the school board closed the colored schools entirely.[29]

In September 1854, Douglass reported in his newspaper that he led "four of our little ones" to their neighborhood school on the first day of term. "Our liberal city," he explained, "does not compel a colored child to walk by the door of the school house in his own District." The school's senior teacher invited him to say a few words.[30] Phebe Ray, meanwhile, was still living in Rochester with two granddaughters, Mary and Emma. Perhaps Phebe, like Douglass, had the satisfaction of walking her own little ones to a school whose doors she had helped open.[31]

School campaigns like Rochester's were important in their own right, but they also spurred families and leaders to develop skills and relationships that applied to their work on behalf of other objectives. The same black New Yorkers who petitioned local school boards, appealing to their equal rights under the law, also petitioned the state legislature using similar language. School politics helped forge ties and promote leaders within local communities in a manner that helped these same communities mobilize across New York to advocate for changes in state policy.

* * *

Black New Yorkers' intensifying interest in mass petitioning and legislative lobbying at the state level coincided with a broader movement of antislavery campaigns across the nation. In 1833, a group of white and black abolitionists from ten states, under the leadership of William Lloyd Garrison, founded the American Anti-Slavery Society (AASS) in Philadelphia. Its executive committee included prominent white New Yorkers (William Jay, Arthur Tappan, and Lewis Tappan) as well as notable black New Yorkers (Theodore S. Wright and Samuel Cornish).[32] Soon thereafter, the AASS launched a mass petition campaign to Congress, which drew hundreds of people across the northern states, including women, into political agitation. In 1836, during the Twenty-Fourth Congress, southern congressmen succeeded in instituting a "gag rule" that forbade consideration of antislavery petitions in the House of Representatives. Viewing the gag as a violation of their First Amendment rights, many northerners, nonabolitionists among them, found the rule offensive and dangerous.[33] Amid this national controversy, black New Yorkers increasingly took advantage of the right to petition for antislavery remedies in their home state.

Black New Yorkers had sent petitions to the state legislature since well before the 1830s, but the tenor and context was now different. In earlier cases, black citizens from a given town or city had prayed for locally targeted legislation; they had raised concerns about schools and asked for articles of incorporation for mutual aid societies and religious organizations. These were important interactions because they gave local citizens practice engaging with state government. But the work black petitioners undertook in the mid-1830s to promote three state laws—laws that challenged southern masters and affirmed black civil rights—raised the profile and stakes of black political engagement. The three-pronged campaign required black strangers living miles away to work together to push for legislation that, to be sure, affected their daily lives but, even more grandly, affected people they had never met before. This was petitioning in the name of mass antislavery politics during the competitive and fractious Second Party System.

Thousands of black men and women took part in the campaign for the repeal of the nine months rule, a jury trial law, and equal suffrage. Scholars of antislavery and political abolitionism have written about white abolitionists' embrace of these three state law goals as part of their state-based agitation in the late 1830s, but ordinary black citizens' foundational role in prioritizing these policies has been underexplored and undertheorized. The first petitions during the 1830s to reach the legislature with hundreds of names attached were from black New Yorkers. Many of the petition movement's leaders had been children at the height of gradual abolition: former students of the African Free School, young abolitionists in western New York like Austin Steward and David H. Ray, and countless if nameless black women.[34]

In early 1837, in the second issue of the *Colored American*, Samuel Cornish and Philip A. Bell reported on the progress of three petitions submitted by "the colored People" of New York City to the legislature. The first, signed by 607 men and 271 women, asked for the repeal of state laws protecting slavery (the nine months law allowing visiting masters into the state was most offensive). The second, signed by 489 men and 272 women, asked for a jury trial for any person accused of fleeing slavery. The third, signed by 620 men, asked for a constitutional amendment to remove the "distinction of color" from the right to vote. Although some of the petitioners were part of the educated middle class, many were common laborers. Thomas L. Jinnings and Henry Sipkins—who had signed certificates of freedom back in the 1810s—were among the more elite participants. Yet nearly half of the signatories could not write their names.[35]

The language of the petitions underscored the participants' vernacular, sophisticated conceptions of citizenship. The jury trial petition, signed by "fathers and mothers, and men and women of color" explained that the government's duty was to throw the "shield of your protection" over the "colored people of this City and State." Echoing core Anglo-American republican rhetoric going back decades, they noted that "trial by jury is an invaluable privilege. Liberty is not safe without it." As "citizens," they needed safeguards, including taxpayer-funded legal representation in court, in order to resist the "kidnappers" who "prowl about the country." The equal franchise petition, for its part, went back to the original promise of the 1777 state constitution, which gave "colored citizens" the same rights as "white male inhabitants."

It was against "just and republican equality" to deny the vote to "we, *native* born Americans, the children of the soil." They paid taxes and served in the military; they were "included in the number of the population which regulates the representation of this State in Congress."[36]

As they began this petition campaign, black New Yorkers knew they were not alone. Cornish and Bell's newspaper reported that, in Ohio, "colored citizens of the city of Cleveland" held a meeting to discuss "petitioning the Legislature" to "repeal those laws which oppress us" and to facilitate communication with fellow citizens in Cincinnati and Chillicothe. The Ohioans' goal was to change state laws that said free black people could not move there without posting expensive bonds, could not attend public schools, could not vote, and could not testify against white people in court. In Pennsylvania, meanwhile, there were "favorable indications" that a "trial by jury" law for "fugitive slaves" might pass. And in Massachusetts, the legislature defended northern petitioners' right to ask the Congress for "the removal of" slavery, which was a "great social, moral and political evil." All "the free States," wrote Bell and Cornish, should do the same. In this late 1830s moment, black New Yorkers combined an awareness of strategies and tactics occurring across state lines with a focus on state-based politicking.[37]

In the spring of 1837, the New York legislature received various antislavery petitions signed by "colored citizens" from four cities: New York City, Brooklyn, Troy, and Albany.[38] A dozen similar antislavery petitions arrived from the state's western counties, as well, signed by "sundry citizens." White petitioners likely provided the majority of signatures on these western petitions, which is not to say that no black citizens signed. Black men and women did sometimes sign petitions organized by white recruiters, especially in areas like western New York, where radical abolitionism had taken root.[39] In instances of interracial petitioning, petitioners often presented themselves as "sundry citizens" or used a similar non-racially-specific designation. Black-only petitions, however, often cited "colored citizens" or "men and women of color."[40]

The *Journal of the Assembly* rarely printed petitions in full, but the clerk did record that two of the petitions from New York City and Brooklyn were submitted by "fathers and mothers, and men and women of color."[41] The clerk's choice to adopt the self-identifying language of the petitioners hints at a wider acknowledgment of the transforming nature of black women's political engagement. Black women had long interacted with officials, judges, and lawyers in their neighborhoods to protect their own and their families' interests, but the 1830s petitions marked a shift in the visibility of female engagement in the public sphere, especially at the state level. Black women—like white women—were entering formal politics in new ways, often seizing on the personal and ideological politics of motherhood to explain their involvement.[42]

Some black men were explicit in urging women to sign petitions. David Ruggles, the Connecticut-born secretary of the New York Committee of Vigilance, welcomed citizens both "male and female" to sign petitions to overturn the nine months law in New York, to abolish slavery in Washington, D.C., and to oppose the annexation of the slavery-friendly republic of Texas. The Ladies Literary Society—which included one of the Jinnings daughters as well as African Free School teachers Eliza Richards and Sarah Ennalls—raised money for Ruggles's committee and no doubt signed petitions. When "A Friend" in Poughkeepsie wrote to the *Colored American* asking if women should sign petitions for equal male suffrage, the reply was yes, for "with their husbands and sons, they are aggrieved by this arrangement in our State Constitution, and why may they not petition for this, as well as upon any other subject with which law may be concerned."[43]

After the legislature declined to grant black citizens' requests during the 1837 session, a number of commentators in the *Colored American* discussed how to improve their campaign.[44] One contributor observed that even though black citizens in different parts of the state had been sending petitions since 1834, they needed to collaborate more methodically and to recruit even more signatories: "We must have simultaneous petitions come in from every quarter and district of the state. Let every member of the next Legislature see the names of as large a portion as possible of his own constituents, on the petitions." Changes in state law required statewide coordination. Leaders in the cities should communicate with "brethren in the country."[45]

The rising generation in New York City agreed. That summer, Bell announced that he would tour the state to excite interest "among our colored brethren" in "their political rights." He made an explicit plea to the men of his generation. His fellow classmates Henry Highland Garnet, Thomas Sidney, Elver Reason, Charles Reason, Peter Guignon, and George Downing joined him in forming an organization devoted to black suffrage rights. Their plan was to "DELUGE the Legislative Hall, at the next sitting of the Legislature, with PETITIONS, praying the Legislature to grant the colored citizens, in common with other citizens of the State, that RIGHT." They asked all "the colored young men of the State, to be up and doing." The elder generation agreed: "The young men of New-York must talk *less*, and DO MORE."[46]

Bell and his partners set up a committee of correspondence to write to their peers in "the cities and towns of the Hudson border, as well as the many in the Inland counties."[47] Bell and Charles B. Ray, the paper's new general agent, began their tours in the fall of 1837. Bell canvassed towns up and down the Hudson while Ray traveled west to the Burned-Over District. The *Colored American* printed a model petition so that groups across the state could compose matching documents. The model asked the legislature to abolish "the odious distinction, which, while it acknowledges them as citizens, denies them the rights which all others possess as attached to that honorable appellation."[48]

In 1838, white New Yorkers, petitioning in higher numbers than ever before, joined black New Yorkers, also petitioning in higher numbers than ever before, in a statewide push to convince the newly Whig-majority assembly to grant their antislavery requests. According to the *Journal of the Assembly*, 518 "colored young men" from New York City prayed for "an extension of the right of suffrage"; "colored citizens of Troy and Lansingburgh" prayed for "equal political rights and privileges with other citizens"; "inhabitants of the county of Albany" prayed for the repeal "of the [nine months] law authorizing the holding of persons coming into this State, as slaves" and a law "securing a jury trial to all persons claimed as fugitive slaves"; 650 "ladies of the city of Rochester" prayed "an act to immediately repeal all laws which make any distinction on account of color"; 3,737 ladies of New York City did the same.[49]

Similar petitions also streamed in from rural areas, especially from Burned-Over District counties. They arrived from places like Jasper in Steuben County, Mexico in Oswego, Homer in Cortland, Ogden in Monroe, Whitestown and Paris in Oneida, Butternuts in Otsego, Vernon in Oneida, Collins in Erie, Williamson in Wayne, Auburn and Sennett in Cayuga, Russia in Herkimer, Shelby in Orleans, Granville in Washington, Moriah and Jay in Essex, Champlain in Clinton, and Lowville in Lewis—and this is an incomplete list. On February 5 alone, lawmakers received *thirty* petitions from the towns of Cazenovia, De Ruyter, Eaton, Nelson, Lenox, and Sullivan in Madison County. Two weeks later, another batch came in from "numerous inhabitants, male and female, of the counties of Livingston, Ontario, New-York, Oswego, Ulster, Monroe and Westchester."[50] What had been a trickle of petitions in 1837 was a flood in 1838. The number of petitions the assembly received in 1838 compared to 1837 is staggering.

The 1838 legislature did not respond to the petitioners' appeals that session, but reformers, politicians, and ordinary citizens grasped that antislavery political fervor was building. In June, after the legislature adjourned, black men in New York City created the permanent Political Association, which we first learned about in Chapter 3, and urged "our people throughout the state" to do the same. Several of the association's officers were African Free School graduates, who reemphasized that the "rising generations" and "colored young men" of the state had a particular responsibility to be active. Among those who answered their call was David H. Ray, Phebe Ray's son, who became an agent for the *Colored American* in Ontario County a few weeks after the Political Association printed its plea in the paper. David was eighteen years old.[51]

Significantly, the Political Association welcomed women to its meetings. Given the number of African Free School alumni involved in the organization, this invitation meant that male graduates were inviting their former female classmates to participate. On the one hand, the increasing willingness to include women in formal political action was not unique to black New Yorkers; in general, the antislavery societies of the 1830s, especially Garrisonian ones, were more far more inclined to include female members or to support women's auxiliaries than their Revolutionary-era counterparts. But the young men in the Political Association may have been especially amenable to welcoming female peers because they had known these women since the days when the Manumission Society routinely reported that the girls in their coeducational schools were outperforming the boys. While the Political Association did not morph into an egalitarian women's rights society, it is not surprising that some of its men believed that women, including those who could read and write as well as they, should take part in the "effective distribution of petitions." Their constitution made clear that any person could become a member "who shall pledge himself or *herself* to advance its object."[52]

The founding of the Political Association coincided with a heightened interest among the state's white abolitionists in "political action" and electoral politics. In September 1838, the New York Antislavery Society (NYASS), the state affiliate of the AASS, met in Utica to discuss its goals for the upcoming year. White reformers William Goodell, Beriah Green, Henry Stanton, Gerrit Smith, and Myron Holley (the former Ontario County clerk who had signed certificates of freedom) were in attendance, as were black leaders Nathaniel Paul, Theodore S. Wright, and Charles B. Ray. Aware that the gubernatorial election was in November, the abolitionists debated whether it was prudent to support only those candidates who backed immediate emancipation, regardless of party, or create a third party devoted to antislavery. The men decided to hold off on a third party, but planned to make their voices heard in the upcoming election.[53]

To wit, the NYASS decided to seize on the election as an opportunity to press state politicians to recognize that the nine months law repeal, the right to a jury trial, and equal suffrage were vitally important to a small but committed group of voters. They would publicly request that the candidates answer their "interrogations" on these policies, prompting antislavery voters to choose candidates accordingly. In a tight election, which 1838 promised to be, antislavery voters had the potential to swing the outcome. The society appointed two of their most eminent members, Gerrit Smith and William Jay, to send queries to the candidates asking where they stood on the three stated policies.[54]

The rising generation had laid the groundwork for the 1838 interrogation. Ray had crisscrossed the state in 1837 recruiting petitioners. Wright, who was a member of the NYASS business committee that developed the interrogation plan, brought blank equal suffrage petitions printed by the Political Association with him to the meeting.[55] Indeed, black New Yorkers persistently urged the broader antislavery movement to focus on both the end of slavery and the cause of equal citizenship. Ultimately, the NYASS adopted black New Yorkers' three main state legislative goals and then executed a novel strategy for putting pressure on politicians.

The moment was ripe for the NYASS to intervene in electoral politics. Rising star William Seward had just won the Whig nomination and was trying for the second time to unseat the Democratic incumbent, William Marcy. Seward and his running mate, Luther Bradish, held moderate antislavery views, but it was unclear to abolitionists and other voters how far they would take their antislavery predilections if elected. Marcy and his lieutenant, John Tracy, like many politicians in Martin Van Buren's Albany Regency—the state's Bucktail-turned-Democrat political machine—had demonstrated little interest in the rights of slaves or black citizens.

The NYASS interrogations produced some unpredictable results. Bradish, apparently without consulting with Seward, responded quickly, stating his support for all three antislavery goals. The *Colored American* printed Bradish's answers in full.[56] Seward, who agreed with Bradish in principle, feared alienating conservative swing voters, including business-oriented Whigs who worried about angering southerners with financial interests in New York's ports and banks. Acting cautiously, Seward declared support for a jury trial law, but refused to endorse equal suffrage or the nine months repeal. Marcy and Tracy, less surprisingly, replied the same as Seward. On hearing the news, black men in New York City who met the $250 property requirement vowed "to use all lawful means in our power to elect Bradish" and recommended that similar black freeholders throughout the state do the same.[57]

But black voters in the state were a tiny minority, and Seward's inner circle fretted that Bradish had hurt Whig chances by trumpeting his bold positions. Powerful editor Thurlow Weed, Seward's rainmaker and political advisor, told Seward that he would have preferred that neither Whig candidate respond to the queries, but Bradish "having answered, there was no escape." Weed had warned Seward that were he to give abolitionist-friendly answers, it would "expose" him "hard" to the Democrats.[58]

White abolitionists and black citizens were dismayed by Seward. At an abolitionist meeting in New York City, Arthur Tappan issued a statement that "Mr. Seward and Governor Marcy show that the course of human rights has nothing to expect from the election of either of them" and offered support to Bradish alone. Weed wrote privately to Seward that he worried that the abolitionists had gone as far as to "have tickets printed for Bradish leaving a Blank for Governor." With the race so tight, it was conceivable that Seward might lose.[59]

Meanwhile, Bradish was receiving correspondence that suggested that he may, on balance, have helped his candidacy. Gerrit Smith wrote Bradish that he had initially been worried that the candidates would ignore the interrogations. But then, "This hour your answer comes—and it is of such a character as to fill my whole heart with joy. The friends of equal rights and of universal and impartial liberty, throughout the state, will thank you for it" and "evince their gratitude significantly and effectively at the polls." Even Weed, clearly irritated at Bradish, acknowledged that one of their political informants "thinks *your* election safe."[60] A Whig congressional candidate in upstate New York wrote Bradish that "your letter to Wm Jay and Gerrit Smith entitles you to the gratitude of every American, for spreading before the world, such adamant and imperishable truths."[61] A supporter in New York City explained, "I highly approved your manly answer."[62] Of course, some conservative Whigs were still displeased, and no one knew for sure if Bradish's antislavery support could outweigh antiabolitionist defections. Bradish, Weed, and Seward were learning in real time—without yet knowing how the election would turn—that abolitionists could wield balance-of-power strength at the ballot box.[63]

Days before the election, Weed wrote Seward that were "it not for the abolition question I should say all is well. But now I am full of apprehension." The two men also worried, and rightly so, about the possibility of a future antislavery third party that could siphon votes from the Whigs. Weed wrote that "Smith, Tappan, Birney, Stanton, etc." hoped "to build an Abolition party on the ruins of the Whig Party." Seward replied that he was certain "that the abolition question defeats us."[64]

The anxious Whigs were jubilant when both Seward and Bradish won. Statewide, Seward earned 192,864 votes, and Bradish took in 192,992. The *Colored American* declared the result an "Abolition Victory": "We assert that there were 1,500 abolition votes given in the city for Seward, and more than 1,800 for Bradish. In the State, Bradish received more than 20,000 votes from abolitionists, and Seward more than 15,000. Their election has been effected by *abolition suffrage*."[65] Although it was impossible to know for sure exactly how many votes were won or lost because of Seward's tepid antislavery responses and Bradish's full-throated ones, both abolitionists and politicians concluded that antislavery voting had mattered.

The 1838 gubernatorial campaign demonstrated how black citizens' political priorities could, in the right circumstances, shape the political discourse of an election and determine legislative priorities for the winning side. Bradish's support of the abolitionists' three legislative goals gave them the stamp of mainstream-party legitimacy. Seward's private letters show that both he and his advisors realized that black citizens' demands were popular among a small but significant number of voters. Even though Seward won the election without promising his support to two of the three demands, he had been forced to contemplate what he might do as governor if confronted with questions about black citizenship, the purity of New York's free soil, and fugitive slaves' rights. Once in office, he routinely cast his lot with the antislavery side.

During Seward's tenure as governor, black citizens achieved two of their three legislative goals. In early 1840, blessed a Whig majority in the legislature, Seward called for "informal conferences" with lawmakers to craft new acts. One result was "An Act to extend the right of trial by jury," which incorporated black petitioners' request that alleged fugitives be provided "professional services" by a district attorney or other counsellor "in good standing," who would be paid by the "expenses of the county." He also signed a related new anti-kidnapping law "to protect the free citizens of this state," which authorized the governor to employ agents to restore a victim to liberty at the expense of the state.[66] Seward's son later wrote that his father had acted because he "felt a ground-swell of popular opinion." The *Colored American* agreed that it had been the "intelligent citizens" of the "grand Empire State" who deserved credit for the "progress." It is also likely Seward knew that

Massachusetts had passed a strong anti-kidnapping law at the behest of abolitionists a year earlier. Politicians across northern states kept eyes on each other and their electorates.[67]

National Democrats were wary of this northern antislavery Whiggery. The *Globe,* an influential Jacksonian paper in Washington, D.C., printed one of the New York equal suffrage petitions in full, negatively highlighting that black men and influential New York Whigs were working together. "Our friends at the SOUTH," the paper wrote, should know that Thurlow Weed's and Horace Greeley's names appeared alongside "people of color" such as "W. M. Topp, Michael Douge, and Benjamin Paul," names familiar to us—though likely not to the *Globe*—from Albany school politics. The petition itself noted that "colored people are among the oldest inhabitants of the State, and have contributed by their labors [and taxes] to its support." It was "unjust that this portion of the citizens of this free State should be disfranchised."[68]

Unhappily for the Democrats, the Whigs maintained control of both houses of the legislature the following year and black citizens maintained pressure. After another onslaught of petitions, lawmakers addressed the nine months rule. To encourage the repeal, black men and women flocked to the galleries of the capitol building to watch the deliberations.[69] Their very presence rankled doughface legislators. Democrat Jacob Skillman proposed "a portion of the gentlemen's gallery" be "set apart exclusively for the use of persons of colour." At a moment when many members were absent, the resolution passed.[70] Five days later, antislavery Whig Erastus Culver made a successful attempt to remove "the negro pew." One of his supporters, Whig Enoch Strong of Monroe County, "thought that a separate gallery for these people would be too much like the way in which they were treated at the South." William Duer, a Whig from Oswego, remarked that, "We might as well have a separate place for men with red hair. These people have never intruded, but had behaved at all times with proper decorum, and were entitled to be protected by this House in all proper privileges." Culver's motion won 57 to 42. Of the 42 who wanted to keep the segregated section, 39 were Democrats.[71]

The 1841 assembly gallery story raises intriguing questions. Why did these men and women even have the *time* to be at these legislative sessions? Some of their children must have been at school, in classrooms that black families built and supported, where female teachers taught. And who was caring for the children *not* in school, who were too young? Who was minding the small businesses that still had to operate while men met with Whig allies? Who was doing the laundry that allowed these public-facing men, with some women, to enter a formal political space in presentable dress? Here was another instance of women's myriad forms of domestic and educational labor bolstering black men's more obvious public politicking. Assemblyman Duer's defense of the black presence in the gallery in part hinged on his interpretation of the constituents' respectability, a sense that the black participants treated the place with, in his words, "proper decorum." The very class snobbery that Whigs were (and are) often accused of played to black New Yorkers' advantage in this case, when Duer saw, through his own class lens, black citizens who deserved both "protection" and "privileges." The little-known 1841 "negro pew" controversy is a fascinating moment both because of Whigs' assertiveness against Democratic segregationalism and because it can make more visible women's specific, multifaceted roles in black politics. It is visible, that is, if we know how to think about it.[72]

In April 1841, those black citizens in the galleries witnessed a victory. The Assembly Judiciary Committee issued a report arguing that when slaves entered New York, they became "members of the State" under "the protection of our institutions." Since the state constitution declared, "no person shall be deprived of life, liberty, and property without due process of law," the nine months law was "unconstitutional and void." (The report also assured "free persons of color" that they were "citizens," even if visiting slaves were only "members.") The *Colored American,* keeping track of every development, cheered when Seward signed the repeal, thereby removing the last legal means of holding slaves, excepting runaways, in the state.[73]

That summer, black New Yorkers celebrated their victory. Beyond the social pleasure of expressing joy in achievement, the celebrations served as a means of spreading the news about the new law—making it more likely to be enforced—and to affirm that legislative change was possible. In June 1841, for example, Ruggles arranged a gathering at Manhattan's Asbury Methodist Church so that "every colored person" could learn the "facts growing out of the repeal." Two months later, in Williamsburg on Long Island, black citizens celebrated both West Indian emancipation and the nine months repeal. Boys and girls from the "Sabbath and day schools" were front and center of the festivities.[74]

* * *

When Seward took office in January 1839, he knew that antislavery was a political force. What he did not know was that in his first summer as governor, he would have to determine how far he was willing to go to anger a powerful slave state's government over fugitive slaves and northern black citizens who helped them. Seward's decision to take an antislavery stand during the so-called Virginia Controversy was national news. The northern Whig governor learned that there could be advantages to standing up to the Slave Power.

The conflict began in July 1839, when three free black New York sailors on the *Robert Center* met a slave named Isaac in Norfolk, Virginia. Isaac was a local ship's carpenter who was performing repairs on the *Robert Center* in Norfolk's port. The sailors—Isaac Gansey, Peter Johnson, and Edward Smith—encouraged Isaac to escape, informing him that he "was foolish to remain in Virginia, as he could get good wages north."[75] Isaac hid onboard, landed in New York, and was promptly recaptured by agents of his owner who had chased after him. The incident likely would have ended there, with Isaac returning to slavery in Virginia, as federal law required, had Virginia not then insisted that the three black New York sailors be arrested on charges of theft. According to Virginia law, "stealing" a slave was a felony. Virginia's lieutenant governor, Henry Hopkins, sent Seward an extradition request.

Seward refused to extradite the black sailors. He told Hopkins, "there is no law of this state which recognizes slavery, no statute which admits that one man can be the property of another, or that one man can be stolen from another. On the other hand, our constitution and laws interdict slavery in every form." He would not betray three black "citizens of this state" for a charge that "imports no crime" in New York.[76] Virginia's politicians found this ludicrous. Governor David Campbell told his legislature that Seward's "interpretation of the Constitution is incompatible with the rights, and destructive of the safety of all the states holding slaves. None of the fanatic doctrines or disorganizing practices of the abolitionists are so well calculated to endanger the security of our property or to jeopardize and hazard the dissolution of the Union."[77]

Following Seward's lead, the Whig-majority New York legislature stood fast. The Assembly Judiciary Committee issued a report expressing its belief that Seward's position was "sound and judicious," consistent with the "sovereignty of the state and the rights of the citizens." The Virginia legislature, for its part, resolved that New York's actions had broken the "compact between the states." On behalf of "the slave-holding states," Virginia's lawmakers asked Governor Campbell to "open a correspondence with the executive of each of these states, informing them the importance which Virginia attaches to this subject" and "asking their co-operation." By 1841, Mississippi, Alabama, Maryland, South Carolina had all expressed their solidary with Virginia.

South Carolina went as far as to pass an act that required the inspection of any New York ship departing its ports for any port in New York State; the cost of the inspection was $10, and were a runaway slave to be found onboard, the penalty was $500.[78]

Seward may have sincerely believed in his position, but he also used the Virginia Controversy as a means to keep the Whig coalition together, and even draw in new supporters. As the controversy was unfolding, his advisors remained in a panic over the political abolitionists' capacity to muddy state elections.[79] Making matters even more complicated, some abolitionists were in the process of launching the previously proposed antislavery third party, the Liberty Party, with the extraordinarily wealthy Gerrit Smith at its helm. One Whig friend asked Seward to send copies of the Virginia Controversy documents to several influential antislavery Democrats who "will come out bright for the Whig cause." The friend also recommended Seward reach out to abolitionists, "who would take it a great favor to be noticed by the Governor." A few days later, NYASS officer Henry Stanton (husband of Elizabeth Cady) wrote Seward to express his "high gratification." Stanton predicted that the time would come when "every Northern state would be compelled to go to the utmost verge of its constitutional rights to resist" the "assaults of the slave power." Stanton, who at this point had only cautiously embraced the idea of a third party, thought Seward could hold on to antislavery votes.[80]

Black New Yorkers, for their part, looked to Seward and their legislature with pride during the Virginia Controversy. But they also declined to let Seward off the hook for his earlier tepidness. In 1841, the editors of *Colored American* recalled that his 1838 answers to the abolitionists' election interrogations had not given them much confidence. At the same time, they surmised—correctly, it turns out—that Seward had been told by some of his advisors in 1838 to tread carefully. Now, in his dealings with Virginia, Seward had proved that he could be "manly" and "intrepid." He was "number one on the gubernatorial list"; the "Virginians find the slave power lame and insufficient to make Governor Seward crouch to its bidding."[81]

In one of most personal acts of appreciation from a black New Yorker who approved Seward's stance toward Virginia, the longtime black voter, abolitionist, and restaurateur Thomas Downing sent the governor a batch of oysters. Downing's son, former African Free School pupil George, delivered his father's note along with the culinary delicacy. "Allow me," Thomas wrote, "the distinguished honour of presenting to you (through my son) some oysters of a superior quality from my own beds."[82]

The state's black editors and antislavery leaders also understood that sectional quarreling with Virginia was politically and legislatively connected to the jury trial law and the nine months law. In spring 1841, as Virginia proposed various punishments for New York in response to its failure to extradite the free black citizen sailors, the *Colored American* professed faith in Seward. The governor would not "deliver up the men," nor would "the honest, free citizens of New York repeal any law existing among the statutes of the State, as just in itself, as the jury trial law." In fact, New York was preparing to "repeal the nine months law." The Virginians would find that antislavery New Yorkers were made of "sterner stuff," opposing "the slaveocracy." This was not the first or last time that antislavery New Yorkers would stress the fact of black citizenship in their state. The status was more than merely symbolic; it came with the expectation that the state would protect its citizens—including the three sailors—in their most vulnerable moments. This had been an expectation articulated and realized by black New Yorkers, including the rescued kidnapping victim Mary Underhill (from Chapter 4), for a generation.[83]

If one had asked a black New Yorker in 1841 which of the state's major politicians he or she would like to see advocating for black citizens on the national stage—say, in the United States Senate or the White House—it is likely that Seward would have been near the top of the list. By the same token, if one had asked a member of the Virginia legislature what he thought of Seward assuming a prominent national career in the future, most would have rued the thought. Neither black New Yorkers nor Virginia lawmakers knew, in 1841, that Seward would go on to be one of the most important antislavery politicians of the century, that he would be considered a radical northern senator in the 1850s, that he would help build the Republican Party in the late 1850s, and that he would become one of Abraham Lincoln's closest advisors, as secretary of state, during the Civil War. Seward may not have had a perfect antislavery record, but there is no question that, time and again, he took visible antislavery positions during the 1830s, '40s, and '50s. Black New Yorkers were key to showing Seward that he could take strong positions in favor of antislavery and black citizenship and win elections.

* * *

Although black citizens achieved several legal and political wins in postabolition New York, they also suffered profound disappointments. Among their most bitterly unmet goals was the reinstatement of equal male suffrage. Some of the men who fought for the restoration of voting rights had in fact voted earlier in their lives, before the adoption of the 1821 constitution. Others had witnessed their fathers vote and hoped to claim the right for themselves. There is no sugar coating the sense of betrayal black citizens felt at their state's failure to erase this inequality, or the reality that restricted poll access meant less political power for black individuals and communities. That said, black New Yorkers' persistence in fighting for the vote meant that there was a sustained discussion in New York about the meaning of suffrage and citizenship. Their long campaign promoted the principle that voting was a fundamental part of what it meant to be free in a democracy, regardless of one's race or former status. Voting was not meant to be a remote privilege that only special citizens could exercise.

Restoring equal suffrage in New York was a particularly challenging object because it required changing the state constitution. There were two ways this could be done: the state could hold another constitutional convention, which was a massive undertaking, or the legislature could vote for two years in a row for a specific amendment to the constitution, and then present the amendment to the state's electorate for ratification. In the 1830s, black New Yorkers concentrated on the second method. For the most part, it was men who mobilized for equal suffrage and they framed their right to vote in gendered terms. At the same time, equal suffrage advocates stressed the collective import of their efforts: "a political disadvantage to one portion of our people," said one male suffrage campaigner, "is a disadvantage to the whole." Black people's interests were "so closely allied" that each individual man who voted had the opportunity to "enhance" the position of all black citizens, including "our children."[84]

Black men's interest in equal suffrage encouraged everyday conversations about legislative change, constitutionalism, and democracy. In 1838, for example, after petitions to the legislature failed to yield results, Peter Vogelsang Sr.—a local elder statesman—addressed the Political Association in New York City: "It is not only necessary to obtain Legislative approval, but also the sanction of a majority of the people through the ballot box, before the Constitution can be amended. . . . We must petition session after session. . . . Our Legislature, though they may refuse to grant our prayer, they cannot avoid receiving our memorial. The Right of Petition is secured to us, by the United States and State Constitutions. . . . The basis of anti-slavery principles is to carry into practice what the declaration of American Independence proclaims in theory."[85] Vogelsang shared not only a strategic awareness of constitutional change, but also an argument for the connection between state suffrage rights and the wider principles at stake in the national fight against slavery. Who had access to the federal Bill of Rights? Who fell under the umbrella of "all men"? These were not flash-in-the-pan questions. They were fundamental to the abolition movement and to party politics. Ordinary black citizens' campaigns for rights in the northern states nurtured a much broader ideology of freedom and democracy, one that was fundamentally at odds with proslavery interpretations of the nation and its Constitution.

Conversations about equal voting occurred across the state. In 1839, for example, Austin Steward, the Rochester abolitionist, organized a suffrage petition to the state legislature. The assembly reported that Steward and "twenty three other colored citizens" prayed for "an alteration of the [state] Constitution as will allow colored men to vote without the possession of real estate." Unlike antislavery petitions to the United States Congress in this decade, the Rochester petition was at least read and referred to the appropriate committee. Several days later, a similar petition arrived from "twenty five colored citizens in the county of Niagara."[86]

The Niagara County petition deserves special attention. The county's black population was much smaller than Rochester's and New York City's, but it was well-organized. In Lockport, the county's main town, black citizens had started lobbying for school rights back in 1835. In 1837, Charles B. Ray found a welcome audience when he visited to enroll subscribers to the *Colored American*. In 1838, Ray returned and crowned his hosts the "true friends of universal liberty." In 1839, when the *Colored American* encountered financial trouble, black Lockportians, including three men named James Morgan, Wolford Mills, and William Bromley, raised funds so the paper might survive. During these same years, black Lockportians also established their own Methodist church. Living on the opposite side of the state from New York City, in a newly developing county, these northwestern citizens formed yet one more link in the chain of politically organized black communities dotted and connected across New York.[87]

Indeed, it was the very widespread interest in black political rights in diverse areas of New York that inspired Charles B. Ray to propose the first New York black political convention. In the summer of 1839, he suggested via the *Colored American* that black men come together to "devise measures whereby we could all act in concert" on behalf of their political rights.[88]

The response was enthusiastic. A number of familiar names joined the printed call inviting black men to Albany with the purpose of discussing "our deprivation of the free exercise, in common with other men, of the elective franchise." David H. Ray, Phebe Ray's son, joined the committee of correspondence from Canandaigua. Steward signed on from Rochester, as did J. H. Bishop, the "clothes renovator" from the local school campaign. Morgan, Mills, and Bromley, who had helped save the *Colored American* the year before, represented Lockport. Garnet, now living in Troy, relayed that a "large and spirited meeting," agreed to the convention. Michael Douge, Benjamin Lattimore Jr., and Benjamin Paul joined the effort from Albany. In New York City, Wright and a host of African Free School graduates hoped that "every portion of our great and growing State" would take part. The invitation itself cited additional participants in Williamsburg, Brooklyn, Jamaica, Flushing, Newburgh, Poughkeepsie, Catskill, Hudson, West Troy, Utica, Schenectady, Whitborough, Little Falls, New Hartford, Syracuse, Oswego, Volney, Geneva, Canandaigua, Palmyra, Ithaca, Bath, Buffalo, Sacketts Harbor, and Fishkill.[89]

The very process of organizing and holding a state convention was an exercise in democracy and electoral politics. In late July, black men met in their respective locations to choose delegates to send to Albany.[90] In these local meetings, black citizens discussed the invitation, which explained, "A free suffrage is the basis of a free government, the safe-guard of a free people, the strength of the strong, the defence of the weak" and a "man cannot be considered in a democratic sense, a *freeman*" without the vote. The "invidious requisition to the exercise of a birth-right privilege," it added, "weakens our standing as citizens of the State." These were important ideas: in a free government, all male citizens should vote; the right was a right by birth; the right was attached to the status of being free. Not every black man in New York, of course, attended the Albany convention, but hundreds of men, and likely some women, took part in the local meetings where they elected delegates to the state convention.[91]

The Albany convention in the summer of 1840 was the first state convention in New York. Steward was elected president. Charles Reason and Garnet were secretaries. Alexander Crummell and Patrick Reason joined the petition committee and printing committee, respectively. (James McCune Smith, another school friend, would join the convention movement the following year.[92]) Spectators included black men and women from Albany, Troy, and other nearby towns. White New Yorkers participated as well, including leading Whigs. At the close of the three-day meeting, the convention announced a renewed petition campaign.[93]

The delegates went home and began organizing county committees to petition the legislature. Once local canvassers acquired enough signatures, their task was to forward the petitions to a "central committee" that would deliver the collected documents in person to the 1841 session of the legislature. Garnet, who lived across the river from Albany in Troy, was appointed chairman of the central committee. A number of towns' active citizens wrote to the *Colored American* to report their enthusiasm for the effort.[94]

Men who had experience organizing, preaching, and teaching in local areas took charge of gathering names for the 1841 suffrage petitions. For example, in Brooklyn, George Hogarth and Benjamin Croger, two of the city's most active black school leaders, held a meeting whose purpose was to organize a petition to repeal the unjust rules affecting the "colored voter." These "colored citizens of Brooklyn" canvased the city for black and white signatures.[95] As the volunteers went door to door, they no doubt encountered the familiar faces of the parents and grandparents of school children, and of school children themselves, who had already been thinking about their rights and citizenship well before the suffrage petition campaign of 1841.

At the start of the 1841 session, as this flurry of equal male suffrage activity was taking place, Governor Seward delivered his annual message to the legislature. Seward cited the black men who were "excluded from the franchise by an arbitrary property qualification incongruous with our institutions." Several Whig assemblymen created a committee to consider black voting rights.[96] To an observer looking at state-printed political sources, it would seem that the liberal wing of the Whig Party had started to embrace equal suffrage more overtly—and this would be true. But only by simultaneously observing the groundswell of grassroots black campaigning on the ground does it become clear how and why Sewardite Whigs felt encouraged to place the subject on their agenda. Neither white politics nor black politics occurred in a vacuum.

A few weeks after Seward's message, Garnet reported that he had received 107 signatures from Rochester, 101 from Poughkeepsie, 84 from Utica, 55 from Newburgh, 21 from Windsor, 80 from Troy, 12 from Lansingburgh, 26 from Schenectady, 70 from Syracuse, 82 from Hudson, 100 from Flushing, 1,300 from New York City, and 20 from Saint Andrews. More would keep coming. As this list suggests, the 1841 campaign was a genuinely statewide movement; black elites may have orchestrated it, but ordinary citizens literally signed on. Garnet began lobbying the legislators: "The petitions . . . have all been presented to some member by [me] in person. Previous to my presenting the petitions, on every occasion, I have taken the opportunity of conversing with some influential member, and have not failed to receive his word, promising his favor in regard to the measure. . . . Those gentleman have informed [me] that they believed the time had come, when the mind of the House was prepared to act."[97] On February 18, Garnet addressed the Judiciary Committee, highlighting several facts: "1st. Our citizenship, the right of which we claimed as our birth-right. . . . 2ndly. Our conduct, when we enjoyed the elective franchise, which was purely republican and loyal. 3dly. The fallacy of the reasons . . . that disfranchised us. 4thly. The deleterious effect that the arrangement has had."[98]

On March 10, Alvah Worden—a Whig from Canandaigua who was also Seward's brother-in-law—delivered a report on behalf of the Judiciary Committee. Worden rehearsed the constitutional history of black voting in New York and reminded the assembly that New York had once embraced slavery. Arguing that freedom meant more than the right not to be human property, he observed that black citizens were not yet "all together emancipated" if they did not have the equal vote. He then turned to the petitions, signed by "many thousand." These citizens, Worden reported, should be trusted: "All matters of this kind are safe in their hands, and the committee are of opinion that the Legislature should take the necessary measures to bring the question, in the mode provided in the Constitution, before the electors of this State." The report concluded with the text of a proposed constitutional amendment that would remove the word "white" from the franchise clause. On receiving Worden's report, Thurlow Weed's *Albany Journal* declared the proposed amendment "in accordance with the spirit of the age and the genius of our Institutions." The *Colored American* commented that Weed put his paper on "the right side of this question."[99]

Despite this promising energy, the assembly failed to pass an act recommending an equal franchise amendment. When Erastus Culver called for a vote on the question, he lost 46 to 29. Most of the "nays" came from Democrats, but 12 Whigs voted with them. Another Whig tried again to pass the measure a few days later, losing 50 to 37. On May 2, Worden himself tried. The pro-suffrage camp came closer this time, but lost 59 to 50. The Democrats, along with a few Whig defectors, doomed the effort (the Whig majority in the assembly was very slim).[100]

In many respects, failure is simply failure. The 1841 Whig assembly could not harness the votes to pass a measure supporting equal voting rights for men, which would have been the first important step in creating constitutional change. On the other hand, if we paint what happened in black political history between the mid-1830s and 1841 solely as failure, we neglect to see how successful ordinary black citizens were in making equal suffrage a serious political issue. The Whigs in 1841 came close. Seward, who in the 1838 election had declined to support equal suffrage, was now in favor. Weed, also skeptical in 1838, now endorsed the policy.[101]

Between 1841 and 1845, black New Yorkers held three state conventions similar in purpose to the first and continued to petition the legislature for equal suffrage. The larger partisan picture, however, had shifted. In 1842, Seward declined to run for reelection, and Democrat William C. Bouck took the seat. Successive Democratic majorities in the legislature meant little movement on black voting rights. Meanwhile, the Liberty Party had managed to make itself consequential in a painfully controversial way: in the 1844 presidential election, Liberty voters in New York managed to peel off enough votes from Whig Henry Clay, who was somewhat antislavery, to tip the entire contest in favor of Democrat James Polk, who was decidedly proslavery. Whether the Liberty Party was entirely to blame for the outcome or not, there was a sense on the ground that third-party voters made the mess. Among New York's antislavery politicos, accusations and counteraccusations abounded.

In this moment of inter- and intraparty factionalism in 1845, a new opportunity for equal suffrage emerged when various political constituencies began clamoring for a new state constitution. The Whigs hoped to find a way to decrease the number of officials appointed directly by the governor and reorganize voting districts so that they might perform better in elections. The Seward branch of the Whig party believed that the return of equal suffrage, were such a clause to make it into a new constitution, would benefit them, both because an enlarged black electorate would support antislavery Whigs and because a Whig effort to enfranchise black men would appeal to white Liberty Party men who could be brought back into the fold. An emergent radical wing of the Democratic party, the Barnburners, wanted measures to limit state funding on internal improvements and to aid tenant farmers. The conservative Democrats, called Hunkers, were less enthusiastic. The Hunkers lost the debate when, during the 1845 legislative session, Whigs and Barnburners passed a bill for a constitutional convention referendum. The state's electorate then voted overwhelmingly in favor of holding a convention.[102]

During the same legislative session that passed the referendum bill, antislavery Whigs made clear where they stood on equal suffrage. Legislators sympathetic to the cause invited James McCune Smith to the assembly chambers, after hours, to address a friendly audience. The chair of the meeting was Assemblyman William C. Bloss, an abolitionist Whig from Monroe County—a classic Burned-Over District reformer. Smith explained the four ways that the 1821 constitution's suffrage rules violated political freedom:

one, "there shall be no *taxation* without *representation*"; two, "*manhood* and not *property*, should be represented" in republican government; three, there should be "no *caste*" among "free people"; four, no one should be "disenfranchised except by the law of the land, or a jury of his peers." These principles melded republican ideals going back to the Revolutionary era with the nineteenth-century notion that manhood, not wealth, was enough to grant a person the vote. Unlike many Jacksonian Democrats, Smith did not think that only white men possessed full "manhood."

Smith then challenged the various rationales used to deny black men the vote, including the fear that equal suffrage would anger the "Southern portion" of the nation. It was within New York's "State's rights," Smith countered, to do as it pleased within its own borders. Furthermore, the North should be a moral role model: "Having safely and advantageously emancipated their slaves, it is the next duty of the North to *affranchise* those freedmen, in order that the example may be complete, and the South may follow." Freedom was not "complete" unless it was attached to equal citizenship. Smith projected a vision of a nation purged of slavery once the North decided to live up to its founding ideals. In some ways, it was a quixotic argument. But Smith was not entirely wrong: it would take an antislavery North to compel the South to give up slavery—slavery, along with its badges and incidents, was not going to dissolve on its own. Within two decades, Smith's idea would be mainstream among many Republicans in the Third Party System.[103]

In a reflection of antislavery Whigs' optimism that equal suffrage was possible, William Seward himself released a public letter to black voters echoing many of the points that Smith made in his assembly address. The popular former governor told the New York State Free Suffrage Convention, a meeting led by Austin Steward in the Burned-Over District, that he looked "impatiently for the restoration of your right of suffrage" and saw "in its consequences not merely the elevation of a large portion of my fellow men, to highest social virtues and enjoyments, in our own State, but also an influence which will strengthen public opinion, and direct it to the banishment of human Slavery from the face of the earth." Like Smith, Seward linked equal citizenship rights in the state to the wider cause of national emancipation.[104]

The question for the black men reading Seward's letter, and for all interested in equal suffrage, was how to execute an electoral strategy that would result in a majority of constitutional convention delegates friendly to their objective. The members of Free Suffrage Convention resolved that it was the "duty of every friend of equal suffrage to vote for those delegates, in the Whig and Democratic parties, that are in favor of extending to the colored people of this State, equal suffrage."[105] In other words, vote the issue, not the party.

Differences over this strategy, however, bitterly split the state's abolitionists, black and white. Garrisonians, who disavowed joining the party system and engaging in such electoral gambles, quarreled with men like Henry Highland Garnet, who was a strong Liberty Party supporter. James McCune Smith and Stephen Myers (an Albany abolitionist), who had cultivated fruitful relationships with white Whigs, found the Liberty Party men's unwillingness to support the antislavery elements of the major parties to be unproductive. Making matters even more complicated, black Liberty men realized they could not necessarily rely on white Liberty leaders. When a group of "colored citizens of the city and County of New York," including Alexander Crummell, wrote to Gerrit Smith asking if he would direct the Liberty Party to support equal suffrage delegates, regardless of party affiliation, Smith proved a disappointment. As Smith explained in a March 1846 letter to black Albanians, including William H. Topp, he did not believe that black suffrage was the only or most important issue for the convention, and he would not countenance voting for anyone in the two major parties, since those parties included men "who think slaveholders fit to administer Civil Government." A few weeks later, in Rochester, David H. Ray and the white Quaker abolitionist Lindley Murray Moore presided over a "meeting of the colored citizens" in which they came to the opposite conclusion. The Rochester group encouraged the "friends of equal suffrage to vote for those candidates" favorable to their cause, "irrespective of party."[106] Needless to say, antislavery New Yorkers in this instance were far from united in terms of how to make the party system work for them or even what to prioritize within that system.

The results of the April 1846 election were devastating for black New Yorkers. Seventy-eight Democrats and 53 Whigs were elected delegates to the convention. Among antislavery ranks, recriminations over the results flew fast and sharp. Gerrit Smith carped about lack of discipline within his party. Thurlow Weed accused Smith's Liberty Party of incompetence "first by helping Texas into the Union [by unintentionally helping to elect President Polk in 1844], and now by defeating Free Suffrage.... Mr. Smith and his 'editors and orators' strangely refused to act with opponents of Texas and the friends of free suffrage."[107] Regardless of whose fault it was, it was clear that prospects for a return to racially equal voting were bleak.

That summer, the convention held four major votes on black suffrage. In the first, the delegates voted not to strike the word "white" from the constitution's suffrage clause. In the second, the delegates narrowly defeated a measure to lower the $250 freehold property requirement to $100. In the third, the $250 qualification was reapproved. In the fourth, a motion for equal suffrage was lost. For the most part, Democrats favored either keeping property restrictions or disfranchising black voters entirely, while the Whigs favored some sort of liberalization. In the end, the delegates decided to put the question of equal black suffrage to the electorate in a separate ballot question.[108]

Between the end of the convention and the November election, newspapers tried to convince voters to say yes or no to equal black voting. Weed's *Albany Journal* and Horace Greeley's *New York Tribune,* a new and increasingly influential Whig newspaper, both argued in favor of equality. Most Democratic newspapers and conservative Whig papers did not.[109] When election day came, the state's voters were given two ballots, one asking whether they approved of the new constitution, which included most of the hoped-for reforms, and a second asking whether to maintain the $250 freehold property requirement for black voters. The electorate said yes to the constitution and, in response to "Equal Suffrage to Colored Persons?", voted no. The tally on suffrage was 224,336 to 85,406.[110]

Rarely in American history has an electorate, by means of a majority vote, chosen to widen access to rights or to resources for a minority.[111] Most black New Yorkers probably knew this—they certainly had day-to-day experiences that confirmed the notion—but the electorate's choice still stung. In December 1846, a dispirited James McCune Smith wrote Gerrit Smith, "Each succeeding day, that terrible majority feels sadder, heavier, more crushingly on my soul. . . . There is in that majority a hate deeper than I had imagined. Caste, the creature of condition, I supposed to be feebler than any strong *necessity.* Yet, here came a necessity—a political necessity—and lo! it is weaker than caste! Money is weaker than caste; political necessity is weaker than caste—to what else will this stiff-necked people yield?"[112] Smith's lament was hardly melodramatic. Over 70 percent of the electorate—white men of voting age who made up black New Yorkers' neighbors, employers, and fellow laborers—had killed black equality at the ballot box. "The hearts of whites must," Smith concluded, "be changed thoroughly, entirely, permanently changed."[113]

The years immediately following the 1846 constitutional convention marked what was, in retrospect, the beginning of the breakdown of the

Second Party system. On the national stage, the debate over the 1846 Wilmot proviso—a failed congressional proposal to prohibit slavery in the territory acquired by the United States in the ongoing Mexican-American War—fueled sectional tensions anew. New York was the site of the most obvious party shifts and ruptures. The Barnburner Democrats, with their antislavery proclivities, broke with the Hunkers, eventually forming the Free Soil Party, led by, of all people, Martin Van Buren. Free Soilers wanted to prevent slavery's extension in the west, but many in their fold did not care much about black equality. Meanwhile, the Sewardite Whigs won a series of victories in state elections. Seward himself won election to the U. S. Senate in 1849, where he became nationally prominent as an opponent of the Slave Power and an expounder of antislavery constitutionalism.

Black New Yorkers followed these developments, at times engaging in robust debates about which party or faction to support, or whether to involve themselves in politics at all. Although the $250 property requirement remained in place, more and more black men met the bar and thus went to the polls. In New York City, Thomas and George Downing led a decisive bloc of voters who remained partial to antislavery Whigs; in 1849, their power at the ballot box resulted in a series of Whig victories. James McCune Smith, however, moved away from the Whigs and formed ties with Gerrit Smith and Henry Highland Garnet's Liberty Party, whose numbers had dwindled with the rise of the Free Soilers. Samuel Ringgold Ward also remained a Liberty Party advocate, so skeptical of the Free Soilers that he went so far as to publicly advise the "Four Thousand Colored Voters of the State of New York" to steer clear of Van Buren's new outfit. Douglass, who in the late 1840s remained wary of "political action," nonetheless defended black New Yorkers who cast their lot with the Free Soilers, arguing that Ward's strategy amounted to throwing away votes. Douglass explained, presciently, that Free Soil men, as time went on, might move antislavery politics in a better direction and that white politicians were capable of positive evolution. In 1851, Douglass himself evolved: casting aside the Garrisonian view that the U.S. Constitution was proslavery, he explained that he had "arrived at the firm conviction that the Constitution, construed in the light of well established rules of legal interpretation, might be made consistent in its details with the noble purposes avowed in its preamble" and demanded "that it be wielded on behalf of emancipation."[114]

Black New Yorkers thus entered the decade of 1850s without the equal right to vote but with considerable experience thinking about the relationship among antislavery policies, partisan politics, and constitutional change. Many of those who could vote, did vote. And their voting mattered in part because the tensions stirred by the Wilmot proviso proved to be no flash in the pan. On the contrary, sectional political events continued to sow instability in the existing party system. Black New Yorkers were poised, in this context, to ensure that the issues of equal male suffrage in their state and of slavery in the existing United States did not get lost amid the wider seismic shifts of national party change that characterized the 1850s.

* * *

1850 marked a year of high political and legislative drama over the meaning and future of slavery in the expanding United States at the conclusion of the Mexican-American War. Prompted by California's desire to enter the Union as a free state, Senator Henry Clay—echoing his role in the Missouri Crisis—brokered a series of compromises. California joined the nation with an antislavery constitution, becoming the thirty-first state. At the same time, Utah became a formally recognized territory and was left to enact its own slave code should white voters there see fit, which they did. Southerners also received a much-desired stronger federal Fugitive Slave Act that made it impossible for northern states to give accused runaways due process rights and also financially incentivized officials to declare people slaves. Antislavery northerners, in return, achieved the abolition of the slave trade in Washington, D.C. In a fifth measure, Texas relinquished a portion of land to the United States, leading to the creation of New Mexico territory, where slavery would be decided by popular sovereignty, as in Utah.

Moderates and unionists—including the long-serving Massachusetts Whig Senator Daniel Webster, who made a famous speech in support of the Compromise of 1850—hoped that Clay's legislative bargains would calm tensions. But many in the North, including Webster's own constituents, were in no mood to brook compromise with slaveholders. It was New York's new senator, William Seward, who met the moment, at least from the perspective of antislavery Americans. In his maiden speech in the Senate, Seward did not hold back. Appealing to a "higher law," Seward argued that Americans were God's "stewards" on earth, which meant that, given the choice, they should not establish human bondage where it did not exist. He noted that the Revolutionary founders had, via the 1787 Northwest Ordinance, excluded slavery from the states of Ohio, Indiana, Michigan, Illinois, and Wisconsin. He expressed dismay that his country had reached such a state of "degeneracy" that her politicians could even contemplate allowing slavery in any new territory. Seward's speech, 100,000 copies of which were promptly printed and distributed, was labeled a triumph by Horace Greeley as well as ordinary constituents.[115]

All of this congressional history—what we now call the Compromise of 1850—is familiar to historians. But national epics are often experienced through the lens of state and local affairs for citizens on the ground. This was especially true for black New Yorkers. In Albany, for example, black parents reported to the *North Star* that their children, who had been attending regular district schools alongside white students, were "expelled." The black Albanians wondered if the school commissioners had been poisoned by "Webster's nefarious speech" or frightened by "Seward's most glorious vindication of the rights of the colored race." They were nevertheless convinced that a denial of equal school access was against the state's laws. Inspired by the school desegregation campaign in Rochester—the one in which Phebe Ray played a prominent role—the black parents in Albany met to petition the commissioners to repeal their decision. At the conclusion of this gathering, "one pleasing feature" was "the acknowledgment of Woman's Rights."[116]

Here were black citizens of Albany, writing to a newspaper in the Burned-Over District, inspired by a campaign of black mothers, fathers, and children in Rochester, framing their local school problem as a violation of state law and as a component part of the fractious debate in the United States Senate over the future of slavery in the country. In their meeting to decide how to respond, these citizens embraced the increasingly popular notion in reform circles that women deserved a protected and valued place in formal law and politics. In their minds, and in their day-to-day experiences, all of these issues intertwined.[117]

This Albany meeting was not well-known, no one printed the speeches made there, and the organizers were hardly household names. But gatherings like these—with their discussion of local, state, and national laws, with their production of petitions, with their inclusion of women—formed an everyday antislavery politics that helped define constituencies, policies, and goals that trickled upward to history's more well-known settings, platforms, and people. Black New Yorkers were not equal citizens—black was not equal to white, female was not equal to male—but they nonetheless influenced formal political developments and wielded privileges and rights as citizens of their state to the extent that they could.

As both their state and their nation entered the second half of the nineteenth century, these children of gradual abolition continued to participate in electoral and legislative politics. Simultaneously, as the next chapter explores, these same New Yorkers turned to the courts in old and new ways to combat the Slave Power.

CHAPTER 6

Antislavery Legal Culture

The *Lemmon* Slave Case and the Coming of the Civil War

In 1853, Governor Howell Cobb of Georgia warned that an unfavorable ruling in the *Lemmon* slave case by New York's appellate court would be a "just cause of war." The following year, New York abolitionist Gerrit Smith, now a member of Congress, argued that "slavery lacks but two things to make sure of her victory": the success of the Kansas-Nebraska Bill and a "final decision in the Lemmon case sustain[ing] the claim to carry slaves through the free States." In 1859, after the case was appealed for the second time, Republican stalwart Salmon Chase told an Ohio crowd that if the United States Supreme Court ever got hold of *Lemmon*, "It will be decided" just "as the Dred Scott case was decided . . . by the slave power." In late 1860, mere weeks before southern states began to secede, the Washington *Constitution* explained that the crisis stemmed from "the States of the North, their personal liberty bills, their violation of the Constitution" and "their underground railroads, their judicial decisions, etc., as in the Lemmon (N. Y.) case."[1]

Politicians, editors, and their audiences understood that *Lemmon* was a significant case. What they did not know, or what some did not want to acknowledge, was that the generation of black New Yorkers born during gradual abolition were crucial to *Lemmon*'s existence. This famous case framing debates about the future of the Union, and slavery's place within it, was the product of years of black citizens' engagement with the formal legal and political mechanisms of their state.

The standard narrative of the *Lemmon* case begins in 1852, when Jonathan and Juliet Lemmon, a white couple from Virginia, embarked on a journey to Texas, where they planned to settle with their seven children and eight slaves. The most efficient route was through New York City, where the household would board a steamship bound for New Orleans. The Lemmons hoped to spend only a few hours in port, but when they arrived, plans went awry. Forced to stay in the city overnight, the couple woke the next morning to find that Justice Elijah Paine of the local superior court had issued a writ of habeas corpus requiring the eight enslaved people appear before him. The writ's petitioner was Louis Napoleon, a seemingly obscure black laborer. When the eight anxious black Virginians arrived in court, they found themselves represented by two prominent abolitionists: Erastus Culver, the Whig politician who had successfully desegregated the Albany Capitol galleries during William Seward's governorship, and John Jay, grandson of the antislavery founding father and son of William Jay.

A week later, Justice Paine, citing the 1772 English *Somerset* case and the Seward-era 1841 state law known as the nine months repeal, emancipated the slaves. "States have the power," Paine said, to pass laws like the 1841 repeal, "entirely abolishing slavery, or forbidding the bringing of slaves into a State." Since the Lemmon slaves were not runaways, New York was not bound by federal law to uphold the property rights of the Lemmons within the state's borders. Southerners and doughface northerners were outraged by the ruling. The "Lemmon freemen," as abolitionists called them, fled to Canada. The governments of Virginia and New York subsequently funded two appeals in New York's higher courts, one in 1857 and one in 1860. Both benches ruled against the Lemmons. Many assumed the federal Supreme Court was next. By the end of the decade, *Lemmon* was regularly mentioned in the same sentence as *Dred Scott* (1857); both cases suggested that the country was headed for a reckoning.[2] In December 1860, when South Carolina seceded from the Union, its successionists claimed, among their reasons: "increasing hostility on the part of the non-slaveholding States to the institution of slavery. . . . In the State of New York even the right of transit for a slave has been denied."[3]

It was no secret to Americans that sectional tensions were intensifying in the 1850s due to the struggle over slavery in the territories and correlated debates over where masters could travel and reside with the people they called their property. The nation's westward expansion had provoked political and legal conflicts for decades. New Yorkers, in particular, remembered their state's outsized role in the Missouri Crisis of 1819–1821. In the 1850s, hostilities and mistrust between proslavery and antislavery advocates over the fate of slavery on the continent were again at fever pitch. The annexation of Texas, the Mexican-American War, the birth of the Free Soil Party, the Compromise of 1850, the Kansas-Nebraska Act (which negated the antislavery features of the Missouri Compromise), and *Dred Scott* were all, in retrospect, signposts on the road to civil war. When the Republican Party released its first national platform in 1856, the document was explicit about its desire to stymie the spread of slavery into federal territory.[4]

The *Lemmon* case, which has not traditionally received lengthy attention in the scholarship on the coming of the war or black abolitionism, was an important signpost on this same road. Between 1852 and 1860, the case fed escalating anxieties about where slaves could be transported, whether northern states had the right to regulate the status of people on their soil, and which politicians and judges at various jurisdictional levels would have authority to decide these questions. Indeed, *Lemmon* demonstrates how the alarm Americans expressed over the expansion of slavery into the western territories and conflicting visions of federalism intertwined with their alarm over fugitive slaves, sojourner slaves, and in-transit slaves moving among the existing states.[5]

Lemmon becomes even more revealing of significant historical dynamics if we the widen the temporal scope and expand the roster of participants. A close examination of *Lemmon* and its precursors shows that black northerners were instrumental to the case's success and thus key figures in provoking sectional tensions in the lead-up to secession. Who "the Lemmon slaves" were themselves is also important. The group was led by two mothers—Emmeline, age 23, and Nancy, age 20—who were, in the midst of all this turmoil, caring for their four small children and Emmeline's two younger brothers. The mothers made the choice to let the case go forward. Indeed, they accepted great risk by putting their fates into the hands of northern strangers and courts. Had things gone wrong, their bodies, minds, and families might have been destroyed in numerous ways. Without legally conscious black New Yorkers protecting the rights of traveling black Americans in their borders, and without Emmeline's and Nancy's fortitude, there would have been no Governor Cobb of Georgia threatening that *Lemmon* would bring civil war.[6]

The black New Yorkers involved in *Lemmon*, including Louis Napoleon, were of the generation born during the height of gradual abolition. They had seen the effects of antislavery and proslavery laws on their daily lives from childhood. They knew that crossing borders, triggering conflict of law cases, appealing to common law writs and precedents, and employing prominent counsel could be effective methods of resisting slavery. They and their parents had protected freedom in these ways since the late 1700s, albeit not always successfully, and they employed this experience as they encountered increasing numbers of enslaved southerners who wanted freedom, too. It was black petitioners, after all, who had been crucial to securing the 1841 nine months repeal, the most important state law Justice Paine cited when he freed Emmeline, Nancy, and their families. This earlier history helps explain why Napoleon—a laboring child of gradual abolition who was now middle-aged—petitioned for habeas corpus on the slaves' behalf, how he might have known to do so, and what he hoped the outcome would be. Napoleon was at once an extraordinary and a merely representative member of his generation.

It was clear that formal law was important to the rising generation, but there were nonetheless circumstances in which breaking the law was a corresponding or preferred option. Men and women who during the day appealed to the courts often turned to the Underground Railroad at night. Napoleon himself was an indispensable member of a regional Underground Railroad coalition—a truth undiscovered by most of the public at the time, but well-known to white associates and myriad black New Yorkers.[7] This coalition included black seamen and dockworkers and hard-laboring housewives, white abolitionists like Sydney Howard Gay and Lewis Tappan, sympathetic police officers, elite black leaders, and even Horace Greeley, one of the most persuasive editors in the nation and emerging messenger of the Republican Party. The lawyers associated with the group, including but not limited to Culver and Jay, practiced antislavery law in court but were also willing to exploit or avoid courts in order to assist in unlawful solutions to slavery.

Incendiary cases like *Lemmon,* which often concluded with a surreptitious relocation of the (freed or not) enslaved people in question, relied for their success on the exertions of this diverse set of participants, all of whom—not just the lawyers—used the law both purposefully and selectively. These collaborators were aided by what newspapers commonly called, in various phrasings, "great masses of colored people." An expansive narrative of *Lemmon* is therefore also about the ways in which black crowds and specific but often nameless people within them served as crucial links in the antislavery chain. The everyday and local uses of law among a wide range of friends and strangers, many of whom had their first brush with antislavery laws as children during gradual abolition, ultimately provoked watershed legal events with national implications.

* * *

Among the lessons that black New Yorkers internalized during the era of gradual abolition was that crossing state borders could generate opportunities for freedom and that the state was at times willing to alter a person's status against a master's wishes. In 1785 and 1788, New York approved statutes forbidding the import and export of slaves across state lines; the penalty for violators was the enslaved person's liberty. The 1799 gradual abolition act prompted questions about the nuanced rules under which a person might claim freedom or prevent a master from carrying a servant or slave into or out of the state. The 1817 general abolition act declared that all resident New York slaves would be free in 1827, but it did not overturn an existing law that allowed visitors to bring slaves into the state for up to nine months. An additional series of statutes guaranteed black petitioners' access to the writs of habeas corpus and de homine replegiando, two forms of English common law action traditionally used to resist unjust imprisonment. In 1841, Governor Seward, in response to petitioning and politicking by the black and white New Yorkers we met in Chapter 5, signed the repeal of the nine months rule. It was this change that made it technically illegal for visiting masters—like the Lemmons—to bring slaves into the state.[8]

All told, this prolonged emancipation era prompted antislavery New Yorkers to develop traditions that defined liberty through the language of positive legal rights and the notion that the state owed its citizens—as well as enslaved people who entered its borders—specific protections. By the 1840s and '50s, black New Yorkers certainly talked about freedom using the stirring but not always operational language of, say, the Declaration of Independence or the biblical Golden Rule, but they also referred to the words of state laws and court decisions, words that judges and lawyers could then use to ensure real people became legally free based on those precious phrases. The adult children of gradual abolition wielded the rights of citizenship—however second-class it was—to enter courtrooms and make claims on state actors.

As black New Yorkers consolidated the gains they made during gradual abolition, black editors, teachers, reformers, ministers, and association leaders shaped a conversation that stressed the importance of law. The men who published *Freedom's Journal* and the *Colored American*, for example, reported on legal precedent and practice. English common law, which the individual American states had adopted by various means into their own bodies of law when they became independent from Britain, was of particular interest.[9]

In November 1827, in one of their very first issues, Samuel Cornish and John Russwurm printed a series of articles in *Freedom's Journal* covering the history of antislavery law in the Anglo-Atlantic world. In "Case of

Somerset," they explained how, in 1772, Lord Mansfield of the King's Bench in London had freed James Somerset, an enslaved American brought to England by his master, after London abolitionists petitioned for a writ of habeas corpus on his behalf. "The ever memorable result of this trial," they taught, "established the following axiom, that, as soon as any slave sets his foot on English ground, he becomes free." Lord Mansfield had written that slavery was "so odious, that nothing can be suffered to support it, but positive law." The timing of *Freedom's Journal*'s coverage was fortuitous, because within days, Americans would learn of *The Slave, Grace,* a British Court of Admiralty case that called into question the fullest antislavery implications of *Somerset.* Reviewing *The Slave, Grace* in January 1828, the editors objected to the idea that a slave freed in England could then be reenslaved were she brought back to a jurisdiction where slavery was legal: "We conceive, the woman Grace, became to all intents a subject of the empire, as soon as she touched the soil of Britain, by the express decision of Lord Mansfield, as delivered in the case of Somerset."[10]

The editors were right to pay attention to these two English cases. In the 1830s and '40s, American jurists would increasingly refer to *Somerset* and *The Slave, Grace* in decisions and treatises about enslaved people in the United States. In other words, American judges, lawyers, and legal writers cited English common law—including English cases decided after the American Revolution—to uphold their various opinions about what should happen when people enslaved in one jurisdiction crossed boundaries into another within the federal union.[11]

For black New Yorkers, the principle that a slave became free on touching free soil became a persistent refrain. Theirs was the most proliberty reading of *Somerset.*[12] As sectional tensions rose over the movement of slaves across state borders and into the western territories, abolitionist editors explained the stakes. The *Colored American* insisted repeatedly that *Somerset* applied as a common law precedent in analogous American cases. The paper also cited Justice Lemuel Shaw's arguments in *Commonwealth v. Aves,* an 1836 case in Massachusetts concerning an enslaved girl brought to Boston from Louisiana who was freed because, as *Somerset* suggested, slavery could exist only by positive law.[13] In 1840, the paper reported the decision of New York City's recorder Robert Morris, who freed an enslaved maid from Puerto Rico named Calacita, visiting with her mistress, because, according to the New York constitution, English "common law" was also "the law of the State." Citing Justice Joseph Story in his authoritative *Conflict of Laws* (1834), who himself cited *Somerset,* Morris explained that "by the common law, as soon as a slave lands on her shores, he becomes ipso facto a freeman."[14]

In addition to reporting cases, the *Colored American* publicized procedural methods for escaping slavery by legal means. The editors explained what common law writs, state statutes, and precedents were available for use.[15] In 1837, a white abolitionist lawyer living in the upper Hudson Valley (in Troy and soon in Albany) named William Yates told the editors that he was at work "inquiring into the disabilities of the free people of color in other States, for which the copious supply of the statutes and laws of other States, contained in the State Library here affords a good opportunity."[16] Yates ultimately wrote a legal treatise, *The Rights of Colored Men to Suffrage, Citizenship, and Trial by Jury* (1838), which the *Colored American* excerpted. Thomas L. Jinnings and Charles Reason presided over a meeting of the Political Association in New York City where Yates discussed his research. Yates explained the rights of freedmen, slaves, and runaways, beginning his section on "trial by jury" with a summary of William Blackstone's analysis of this ancient right. The English common law, Yates observed, "is the common inheritance of the people of these states." This sentiment—a reverence for the common law—was echoed by the black newspaper: "The common law, the birthright of every American, without distinction of color, gives the right of trial by jury, which law is moreover expressly recognized by the constitution of this country. Nay, the common law existed long anterior to the formation of the constitution." Trial by jury remained an "inherent and invaluable right, emphatically the palladium of our security."[17]

The interest in the practical uses of common law was not confined to the formally educated. Indeed, black New Yorkers did not need to know how to read to learn about precedents and ancient English writs. They flocked to trials where they could watch the law at work. The 1829 freedom suit of an accused fugitive slave named Elizabeth Cunningham is a case in point. The suit began after Cunningham was imprisoned in New York City by a man from Alabama claiming to be her master. She protested that she was a free woman from North Carolina who had been kidnapped there, taken to Alabama, and then sold to the West Indies, from where she escaped to New York. Someone (the case report does not say who) petitioned for a writ of habeas corpus on her behalf, and she was brought before a supreme court judge, who remanded her. The Manumission Society then intervened with a writ de homine replegiando, prompting the sheriff of New York City to bring her to a session of the supreme court in Albany. By the rules of the writ,

Cunningham needed to provide a security for the new trial to proceed. "Four colored people," including Nathaniel Paul, volunteered the entire amount. (Michael Douge and Benjamin Lattimore Jr. may also have contributed; they otherwise supported Cunningham's efforts.) Six black friends who had known Cunningham in North Carolina signed affidavits claiming her free status. The national press reported that, while the judges administered "the peculiar rules" of de homine replegiando, "a great number of very respectable colored people" looked on.[18]

The rules of the writ were peculiar, as were other intricacies of law. This reality was precisely why black leaders like David Ruggles planned meetings so that diverse New Yorkers could keep abreast of legal developments. In 1837, Ruggles's Committee of Vigilance supported an alleged runaway named William Dixon, whose case became a contest over the right of a jury trial for accused fugitives. According to the *New York Express,* two or three thousand black spectators appeared in court to hear Dixon's case. That same year, Ruggles reported his committee's involvement in fifty-two cases of local kidnapping. He made his address public so that those who needed help knew where to apply. Over one thousand black New Yorkers supported Ruggles's efforts with either their organizational skills or small but meaningful financial contributions. All together, these were the sorts of cases, meetings, publicity efforts, and charitable offerings that informed black and white petitioners' simultaneous campaign for the jury trial act that, as we learned in Chapter 5, Governor Seward signed into law in 1840.[19]

The following year, after Seward signed the nine months repeal—the 1841 act forbidding owners from bringing slaves into the state for any period of time—Ruggles held one of his routine public meetings at Manhattan's Asbury Methodist Church. Within weeks, local black citizens' knowledge was put to use when a visiting slave girl, informed of the law, "took the liberty to assert her freedom, by leaving the residence of her oppressor." After she was recaptured by "human bloodhounds," "a band of heroic, noble-hearted women" wrested her free again. In a similar case, black residents in Albany protected a visiting slave who was dragged to court after leaving her masters. As the purportedly free woman spent the night in jail waiting for a county judge's opinion, the white press reported that a "large number of colored citizens" kept watch lest "some trick would be played." This "host of citizens" was relieved when the judge declared the woman free by virtue of the 1841 act. As these incidents make clear, laws were useful only when their content was disseminated and when their rules were enforced, whether on the street or in a court.[20]

Louis Napoleon came of age in this environment of gradual emancipation and legal protest. Born in 1800 in New York, one year after the state's "Act for the gradual abolition of slavery" declared that future children born to enslaved mothers would be "born free," Napoleon was reportedly the son of a white father and an enslaved mother. At the age of 14, he was apprenticed to "Mrs. Miller's tobacco manufactory," one of the largest such operations in the city. He seems to have received little to no formal schooling.[21] Census reports note that he could not read or write, a fact that squares with his signing *X* on various legal documents. In the 1840 federal census, Napoleon was listed as a "free colored person," living unmarried in the city's Fifth Ward. In the 1840s and 1850s, Napoleon moved frequently around Manhattan, listing his occupation at various times as "polisher," "varnisher," "whitewasher," "porter," and "seaman." In 1859, he listed his occupation in *Trow's New York City Directory* as an "agent" at 138 Nassau Street, the offices of the American Anti-Slavery Society. In 1850, Napoleon was married to a woman named Catherine and listed as "mulatto" on the census. By 1860, he was married to Elizabeth Seaman from Virginia, with whom he was raising two children from her previous marriage, and their newborn son, Louis A. Napoleon.[22]

Napoleon did not have the education of men like the *Freedom's Journal* editors or David Ruggles, and his name never appeared on the lists of officers of the city's abolitionist, mutual aid, political, and educational societies. He left no writing of his own. But we do know about the generational world in which he lived. The boys and girls we encountered in Chapters 2 and 3 were his childhood peers. They were the black laborers who had developed a specific culture of resistance that drew, in some instances, on legal knowledge. This now-adult generation comprised people who, like the servant girl Charlotte, had told local courts in the 1810s that she knew she would be free when she "was a big woman." And people like William and Jeffrey Jarvis, who knew that the education clause in the 1810 gradual abolition act could free Jeffrey early from service. They were the graduates of the black schools, common and private, that an older generation of parents, teachers, and civic leaders had worked so hard to open in places such as Brooklyn, Albany, Troy, Schenectady, and Rochester. They were the children who labored in rural households like William Seward's boyhood home in Orange County. They were now adults with considerable freedom to decide where to live and whom to work with or for.

To be sure, this generation had eminent leaders—men and women who wrote their own memoirs or have since had books written about them—but it also consisted of thousands and thousands of political effective ordinary people. We know almost nothing about Napoleon's enslaved mother, but we know that she had a son who made a tremendous if underappreciated mark on nineteenth-century antislavery history. Perhaps she had been one of his earliest teachers and protectors. What we do know for certain is that Napoleon, due to his legal knowledge and relationships, was precisely the sort of black northerner whom southern masters would not want their slaves to meet.

* * *

Louis Napoleon was also a member of a transforming antislavery organizational world. In the mid-1830s, as the New York Manumission Society began to slow its operations, the new crop of abolitionist groups emerged. In 1833, the American Anti-Slavery Society located its headquarters in New York City. In 1834, John Jay, a student at Columbia University, became president of the Young Men's branch of the AASS. In 1840, the AASS established the *National Anti-Slavery Standard,* which Sydney Howard Gay edited for fourteen years. (He later joined Greeley's *Tribune.*)[23] That same year, a faction of the AASS left to form the American and Foreign Anti-Slavery Society, an organization spearheaded by Lewis and Arthur Tappan, James G. Birney, Edward Beecher (brother of Harriet), and, among black abolitionists, Samuel Cornish, Theodore S. Wright, and Henry Highland Garnet, who all believed in leveraging the formal political system to fight slavery. Although these various associations tussled over strategy and objectives, they together represented a generational shift. Their members, black and white, collaborated frequently across organizational lines. This new generation of abolitionists, unlike their parents, began their antislavery careers with experiences and memories of a state-sponsored, legally structured transition from slavery to freedom.

One of the most significant national cases about slavery to absorb the attention of this generation was *Prigg v. Pennsylvania,* decided by the United States Supreme Court in 1842. *Prigg* arose out of legal dispute involving the devastating separation of the Morgan family. Margaret Morgan, a mother born into slavery in Maryland, was by the 1830s living as a free woman in Pennsylvania with her husband, Jerry, and their children. In 1837, her former owner's heir sent agents, including one Edward Prigg, to recapture her. In the middle of the night, Prigg and his associates kidnapped Margaret and her children and forced them into Maryland. A Pennsylvania jury subsequently indicted the men for violating an 1826 Pennsylvania personal liberty law that required a local official to issue a warrant for the removal of any person held in labor or servitude. When the case eventually reached the federal Supreme Court, Justice Story held that Pennsylvania's 1826 law was unconstitutional because it conflicted with the fugitive slave clause of the U.S. Constitution and the 1793 federal Fugitive Slave Act. Although some read antislavery implications into *Prigg*—Story also said that state officials were not under obligation to help in federally mandated slave recaptures—many abolitionists were furious at the evisceration of Pennsylvania's personal liberty law. In 1843, for example, the Liberty Party, with its strong base in western New York, included in its plank resolutions declaring (1) that "the provisions of the Constitution of the United States which confer extraordinary political powers on the owners of slaves [i.e., the three-fifths clause]" and the "provision for the reclamation of fugitive slaves" are "anti-republican" and "ought to be abrogated," and (2) that the 1793 Fugitive Slave Act, if "Prigg v Pennsylvania be correct," ought to be "immediately repealed," for it "nullifies the *habeas corpus* acts of all the states" and "takes away the whole legal security of personal freedom."[24]

Napoleon's first obvious antislavery activity appeared in the wake of *Prigg*, although it is likely he had been active even earlier. In the fall of 1846, the middle-aged Napoleon encountered an adolescent from Georgia named George Kirk who was in danger of being reenslaved under the rules of *Prigg* and the 1793 Fugitive Slave Act. Napoleon's ability to get Kirk into court precipitated a series of events that would not only result in Kirk's freedom, but prompt a group of black and white New Yorkers to collaborate in ways that would prove critical to the success of the ongoing antislavery movement and, eventually, to the fate of Emmeline, Nancy, and their families during the *Lemmon* trial. The Kirk case was either the first or an early collaboration among Napoleon, Jay, and Gay. This trio, and their wider circle of colleagues, spent twenty years working to free slaves through court cases, the establishment of free soil/*Somerset* precedents, the Underground Railroad, and the propagation of antislavery legal principles.

The publicized version of the Kirk case can be culled from the heavy press attention it received. In early October 1846, Kirk snuck aboard a brig in Savannah that he knew was bound for New York. He "hid behind some cotton, covered with some sail cloth." Two days into the journey, the crew discovered Kirk and the captain imprisoned him onboard, vowing to return him to his master.[25] When the brig arrived in New York, Kirk tried to escape, but the mate beat him. Unbowed, Kirk issued cries loud enough to "attract the attention of several persons in the neighborhood." Alerted to the boy's captivity, "a colored man by the name of Lewis [Louis Napoleon]" hurried to the offices of the AASS, where Gay published the *Standard*. From there, an AASS lawyer named Elias Smith helped Napoleon apply for a writ of habeas corpus from Justice John Edmonds, then presiding over the city's court of oyer and terminer, the local felony court. Armed with the writ, a city sheriff demanded Kirk from the captain and brought him before Edmonds and two aldermen the next morning.[26]

Jay, with his law partner Joseph White, represented Kirk. As the trial began, the courtroom filled with black observers, who spilled through the passageways of City Hall and into the park outside.[27] The audience watched as counsel sparred. Did Georgia's recapture laws apply in New York? Did New York's free soil confer automatic liberty to slaves in its borders? How did this *Somerset* principle conflict with federal laws about fugitives? How did *Prigg* apply? The lawyers debated these questions of comity, conflict of laws, state versus federal sovereignty, police power, and reception of British common law. On October 27, a majority led by Edmonds decided in Kirk's favor. They ruled, first, that federal laws regulating fugitives allowed only the master, his attorney, or his agent (and not a random ship captain) to pursue a runaway and, second, that New York's own statute on such matters required the mayor or recorder to issue a certificate permitting the slave's recapture (which the captain did not have).[28]

After the verdict, the *Tribune* reported, Kirk was hurried away toward Gay's office. Worried that the mayor would issue the captain his necessary certificate, sympathetic crowds surrounded the area. Police officers arrived searching for Kirk, who remained hidden indoors and protected by the mass of New Yorkers outside. Around 4:30 p.m., two officers spotted a box being delivered from a nearby building. Suspicious, they saw that it was addressed to Reverend Ira Manly in Essex County, near the Canadian border. Kirk was found tucked inside. (Manly was an abolitionist, although it is unclear whether the officers knew this.) Kirk was transported to the city jail, where the mayor and Jay were already preparing for round two. Jay summoned Justice Edmonds and asked for another writ of habeas corpus, this one directed to the circuit judge of the state's supreme court.[29] As Jay well knew, the circuit judge in the city at that time was none other than . . . Edmonds, who would rule on the case by himself. Jay also successfully appealed to the state jury trial law that Governor Seward signed in 1840 that required the local district attorney to assist in cases of "alleged fugitives," at a cost to be reimbursed by the state.

In the second Kirk case, Edmonds acknowledged the captain to be in possession of the requisite certificate allowing him to repossess Kirk. But, Edmonds questioned, was the state certificate law itself constitutional? No, he decided. In a clever bit of legal reasoning, Edmonds argued that New York's certificate law overstepped the appropriate boundaries of state police power and violated the principle in *Prigg* that federal law must hold supreme to state law with regard to fugitive recapture. When Edmonds gave Kirk his freedom once more, the courtroom, "thronged with spectators," erupted with "much applause." Outside, a white abolitionist named L. P. Noble, borrowing a line from *Somerset*, told the crowd, "Slaves cannot breathe in New York. They touch our City, and their shackles fall."[30] The next day, the *Tribune* reported that Kirk made "an immediate departure from the City."[31] This account of the Kirk case, told in law reports and newspapers, highlights the public events of the case. It is clear, even from nonabolitionist sources, how invested black New Yorkers were in the legal affairs of the city.

It is within reason to suppose that *In re Kirk* introduced Napoleon to the 32-year-old Gay and the 29-year-old Jay for the first time. Gay had only recently (in June 1844) moved to New York City from Massachusetts to edit the *Standard.* And *In re Kirk* was Jay's first "slave case," as contemporaries often referred to cases involving the freedom of enslaved people. "Slave case" was a catch-all term that applied to litigation over "fugitives" as well as over "in transit" slaves and "sojourning" slaves traveling alongside their masters. Napoleon, Gay, and Jay worked together on all of these sorts of freedom suits.

In the public records of the *Kirk* case, both the *Standard* and the habeas corpus petition recorded Napoleon's first name as "Lewis," a mistake that would *not* be made in the later sources, both private and public, associated with Gay and his office. When Jay and Gay wrote privately about Kirk in the aftermath of the 1846 case, Napoleon was not mentioned—a marked contrast from later correspondence in which Napoleon was written about as familiar figure.[32] By the mid-1850s, Napoleon was on salary at the offices of the Anti-Slavery Society, where Gay was in charge of keeping accounts.[33] Whether or not the *Kirk* case was the first time Napoleon contacted the office for legal assistance is unclear, but Napoleon's subsequent actions demonstrate that he continued to trust the AASS men in the years following.

The *Kirk* case set a useful legal precedent—it was cited in favor of freeing the slaves in the *Lemmon* case, for one[34]—but it also affected the participants in significant personal ways. Figures like Kirk and Napoleon were important not only because they prompted controversial cases, but because they pushed white abolitionists to demonstrate—to themselves, their peers, the city's black population—the nature and depth of their convictions. Cases like Kirk's underscored the importance of ensuring that slaves freed by the state's courts had ways to leave the area immediately, before their masters or masters' sympathizers could reenslave them. Gay, Napoleon, Jay, and their friends became adept at sneaking people out of harm's way.[35] Southerners, angered enough by the trials, were further incensed by these extralegal activities. *In re Kirk* was one of several well-publicized cases in northern courts during this decade that both resulted in an antislavery opinion and exposed adjacent evidence of an increasingly well-organized, bold, and multibranched Underground Railroad.[36]

Jay's and Gay's personal papers reveal just how important Kirk's adventure was to their own sense of selves as protagonists in the antislavery movement. Jay was emotionally invested in the fate of Kirk. When Kirk was discovered packed away in the box after the first trial, Jay scribbled a frantic note from the "Office of Chief of Police" to his partner, Joseph White: "The poor fellow has been nabbed—and the investigation to commence at once. . . . Pray come down at once." In reply, White wrote that he had "just come home and have had no dinner and am worn out." White was also annoyed that he had worked the first case for free, and he would not participate again unless Kirk's "abolition friends" paid his fee.[37] Jay, by contrast, worked spiritedly and without pay. In the aftermath of the case, he wrote lengthy letters to the unsympathetic New York *Globe* defending the authenticity of both his and other newspapers' accounts of the case.[38] When a report of the *Kirk* case was published in the *New York Legal Observer*, Jay sent a copy to James Tallmadge Jr., the former congressman famous for trying to abolish slavery in Missouri in 1819. Tallmadge replied to Jay that *Kirk* was "of great individual and national interest" and that Jay's arguments "show talent of a high order."[39] Gay, too, was swept up by the thrill. The day after Kirk was freed the second time, Gay wrote his friend Edmund Quincy: "For a fortnight I hardly took time to eat or sleep—in fact for ten days. I actually had not a regular dinner—for the slave-case. It was altogether the most exciting and worrisome time I ever had."[40] Kirk and Napoleon had handed Jay and Gay their most stimulating brush with antislavery to date, a chance to put their abolitionist beliefs into practice. Doing the right thing, apparently, felt good.

The published accounts of the Kirk case did not give details as to his subsequent fate, but both Gay and Jay stayed apprised of what happened next. Gay arranged for Kirk to be sent to the Boston-based editor of the *Standard*,

Francis Jackson. Jay paid for a New York police chief, John Bowyer, to escort Kirk as far as New Haven, in a party that also included white abolitionist lawyers Elias Smith, who had helped obtain the initial writ, and John Hopper.[41] Smith and Hopper would remain important colleagues of Napoleon, Jay, and Gay.

A week after Kirk left New York, Jackson wrote Gay that, "George Kirk is here and is well pleased with Boston. Harriet gives him one or two lessons a day and is preparing him for a Northern freeman. He is anxious to learn and gains very fast." In a postscript, Jackson continued: "I rec'd a letter from John Jay of your city a few days since in which he entertains fears that efforts may be made to recover him." Jackson told Kirk of the possible danger, offering to send him to Canada, but Kirk preferred to stay nearby. In December, Jackson wrote to Gay with further details about Kirk's escape from Georgia. Kirk had run away after his master, who had hired him out at a livery stable in Savannah, tried to take him back to the rural plantation where he was born. Kirk escaped north from Savannah's docks with the assistance of a black stranger. (He may in fact have known the man, but did not want to implicate him in the escape.) Jackson told Gay that George "was never known by any other name than George—I asked him why he added the name of *Kirk*—he replied because his father's name was 'Kirk.'"[42]

After Kirk's escape, Jay, Gay, Napoleon, and the other central participants in the case—including various anonymous black dockworkers and sympathetic crowds—continued to collaborate. Less than a year later, Jay and Hopper represented three Brazilian slaves who had arrived on a ship from Rio de Janeiro with their owners.[43] The circumstances of their journey from the ship into a local courtroom were familiar, despite the fact that they were not runaways, as Kirk had been. As the *Tribune* described it, after the Brazilian vessel docked in port, "rumor becoming rife that several slaves were confined in hold . . . a crowd of colored persons gathered upon the wharf . . . a writ of habeas corpus was issued." Another paper explained that "a cluster of our native, ill-clad negroes . . . surrounded them, seeking, by all sort of signs, as they do not speak each other's language, to impress them with the beauties of freedom." These laboring New Yorkers may not have had fancy clothes, but they certainly cared about their own freedom, wanted others coming into their state to have it, and knew courts might help.[44]

In the so-called Brazilian slave case, a black grocer named John Inviness petitioned for the writ. On the first day of the trial, in a courtroom packed with a black audience, Hopper was accompanied by "two or three colored men, who seemed to take an active part in the proceedings." In his argument, Hopper cited *In re Kirk* and the *Somerset* principle that a slave "brought voluntarily into this State" is "free and may go where he likes."[45] Disappointingly, the judge remanded the slaves to the captain. As Jay stewarded the case through more hearings, the captain lodged the slaves in a city jail. As a third trial loomed, Jay and Hopper's colleagues smuggled the Brazilians out of jail and onto the Underground Railroad. When newspapers implicated Smith and Gay in the escape, Jay insisted that neither he nor they had anything to do with it.[46]

Despite Jay's disavowals, it is clear that Jay, Gay, and Smith were in fact absolutely involved in the escape. Only days after the prison break, Smith wrote Jay that "a certain coachman has been examined" about "the escape of the B slaves." It is possible the coachman was Napoleon; there is evidence from only a few years later that Napoleon was the Anti-Slavery Office's most trusted Underground Railroad conductor. But in a sense the argument remains the same whether it was Napoleon or not; by the late 1840s, a group of black and white collaborators had formed among a cross section of New Yorkers. Allied with this group was a reinstated Vigilance Committee, a reincarnation of what David Ruggles had started in 1835. Jay made his own commitment to this revamped organization clear, writing to Gay that, as for the "Brazilian case," he "never regarded you or Smith as responsible for the money [for his legal fees] . . . I have relinquished all my claims in favor of the new Vigilance Committee." Members of the new committee included Hopper and a black runaway from Maryland named Jacob Gibbs. Gibbs would later prove an integral but unseen figure in the *Lemmon* case.[47]

Between the conclusion of the Brazilian case in 1847 and the first of the three *Lemmon* trials in 1852, various members of this antislavery collective worked together on several slave cases. These included the 1848 Joseph Belt case, the 1850 James Hamlet case, the 1851 Henry Long case, the 1851 John Bolding case, and the 1852 Nicholas Dudley case.[48] A few months after the first *Lemmon* case concluded, Culver, Gibbs, and Lewis Tappan collaborated on the 1853 Jane Trainer case.[49] All of these cases concerned the freedom of alleged slaves in New York, and they all involved legal arguments, expressed both inside and outside the courtroom, that anticipated *Lemmon*. This is not to say that every case was precisely the same in terms of the question before the court. For example, alleged runaways were subject to different laws than slaves who, like the Brazilians and Lemmon slaves, were brought into New York by masters. And the Brazilian slaves were in a distinct category because they were the property of foreign nationals, a fact that required attention during the trial. Nevertheless, the abolitionists in all of these cases appealed to similar precedents and principles, tailoring them to the situation at hand.

The James Hamlet affair, arguably the most famous slave case in New York before *Lemmon*, offers a window into how ordinary New Yorkers approached the uses and meaning of law and provides hints about Napoleon's place within black abolitionist circles. At once a recognized and a silent presence, Napoleon's role in the Hamlet proceedings reveals the ambiguous position of a laboring, formally uneducated black leader.

In September 1850, Hamlet captured headlines as the first victim of the nation's stringent new Fugitive Slave Act, passed by Congress as part of the Compromise of 1850. The act made the procedure for returning alleged runaways significantly easier for owners, and trampled on northern laws that were designed to give accused runaways access to due process. Mere days after the legislation was finalized, Hamlet, a young father of two, was seized by police near the merchant firm where he worked as a porter in downtown Manhattan. That same afternoon, he was summarily tried and convicted by the clerk for the Circuit Court of the Southern District of New York and returned to his former owner in Maryland. The city's black population was incensed. Whether Napoleon knew Hamlet personally is uncertain—they both worked as porters downtown—but there is little doubt that Napoleon wanted him returned to his wife and children.

After Hamlet was taken from the city, a committee of New York's black elite printed a handbill calling for a "GREAT MASS MEETING" at the African Methodist Episcopal Zion Chapel on Church Street to devote a night to the question of "YOUR DUTY in the CRISIS." This was the very church founded by James Varick, Thomas Sipkins, Peter Williams Sr., John Teasman, and Francis Jacobs in the 1790s, now serving as a meeting place for the rising generation. Thousands attended the meeting, two thirds of whom were women and a handful of whom were white.[50]

Over the course of the evening, these concerned citizens engaged in a lengthy, sophisticated, and highly specific discussion about law. They denounced the Fugitive Slave Act. They listened to a five-hour-long series of lectures on the U.S. Constitution, New York's constitution, New York's statutes, British common law, the law of nations, and *Magna Carta*. The meeting's leaders explained they had written letters to Horace Greeley, Caleb Woodhull (the mayor), and Pennsylvania Representative Thaddeus Stevens (the staunchest antislavery representative in Congress) and would petition the state legislature for new laws to "protect its free colored citizens from slavery." Gibbs told the crowd that he would "give assistance and shelter to every fugitive that wants it, and the bloodhounds of the law are welcome to take his life." William P. Powell, a well-known abolitionist writer and sailors' advocate, presided over the meeting, taking names of volunteers "who may be willing to act on the secret committee" to assist fugitives. Napoleon might have been on this list. At the end, Charles B. Ray announced that $800 had been raised to purchase Hamlet from his owner and return him to New York.[51]

It seems likely that Napoleon was there. At the very least, he was present at a meeting five days later, where his name appeared on a list of six men elected to preside over a celebration of Hamlet's return home. John Raymond, a black Baptist minister, gave the keynote address. Standing with Hamlet on the steps of City Hall, Raymond thanked the mayor—who had just issued an order forbidding any police officer from assisting slaveholders looking for fugitives—and praised newly elected Senator William Seward for repudiating that "hell-concocted scheme, the fugitive slave bill."[52] James McCune Smith, William Powell, Robert Hamilton, and Ray also spoke. Napoleon did not. Only a few papers recorded the names of the meeting's leadership; Napoleon was one of two men on the list whose name did not regularly appear in print.[53]

Napoleon's silent but supportive presence at this moment seems characteristic. He was clearly well-known *within* New York's black population. There were two thousand New Yorkers, mostly black, at Hamlet's homecoming, and only six men elected to oversee the meeting. That Napoleon was one suggests his activities were in fact broadly recognized, despite an otherwise lack of public or printed attention to much of his work. Perhaps he was quiet at the homecoming because he was not an orator. Perhaps the city's well-educated leaders disliked the idea of a common laborer's overt participation at such a public event. Perhaps, less cynically, there was good reason to keep Napoleon's identity secret when the press was watching.

Ultimately, Hamlet's freedom did not depend on a court case. On the contrary, a federal court official had worked directly against him. Black New Yorkers' collective response to the Hamlet case nonetheless involved mass discussions about legal methods of resisting slavery and the correct interpretations of common, state, and national law. Non-elite New Yorkers like Napoleon were a part of this conversation. In fact, it was absolutely necessary that they were involved. Due to their numbers and their occupations, black workers were often the first to encounter runaways and sojourner slaves, and the first to discover when a fellow worker like Hamlet was arrested. It was these ordinary laborers who guarded and guided the pathways to legal remedy.

It was these ordinary laborers who instigated *Lemmon.*

* * *

When the *Lemmon* case first broke, the *Journal of Commerce,* a newspaper sympathetic to the Lemmons and eager for the city to maintain strong commercial ties with slave states, published a statement by Jonathan Lemmon himself. It was reprinted widely.[54] Lemmon explained that his household had left Norfolk on the *City of Richmond* a few days earlier. During the journey, a clerk on the ship, Mr. Ashmead, promised that "immediately after the City of Richmond got into the harbor," he would "procure a passage for myself, family, and slaves, in some ship going at once." When the ship arrived, however, Ashmead had difficulty making the arrangements, and sent Lemmon to see a man who could book them on the *Memphis,* a ship leaving New York the next day. This man organized for two hacks to transfer the household from the *City of Richmond* to the *Memphis*. But what actually occurred next was unexpected: after picking up the Lemmons and the slaves, the two hacks proceeded to a house at 3 Carlisle Street, where they were told to stay overnight. As the *Journal of Commerce* asked, but never seemed to find out, "Who sent those carriages professedly to take Mr. Lemmon and his family to the steamer Memphis, but in reality to drop them down in Carlisle Street?"[55]

In 1874, a black man named Nathan "Nate" Lobam, who appeared nowhere in contemporary accounts of the case, gave the *Troy Times* an interesting report. "At one time," Lobam explained, "he was steward of the steamer City of Richmond." One day in 1852, he learned that on board were a family named the Lemmons and eight enslaved people. As the ship left Norfolk for New York, Lobam "went to steerage and asked the slaves secretly concerning their condition, and whether they would like their freedom." There were two women, two adolescents, and four children: Emmeline, 23; her brothers Lewis and Edward, 16 and 13; her daughter Amanda, 2; Nancy, 20; Nancy's twins, Lewis and Edward, 7; and her daughter Ann, 5. The two women were the first to say yes, but all eventually agreed they would try their luck. They wanted freedom. When the ship arrived in New York, Lobam "sent out three of the boys of the boat." One went to see Napoleon, "one of prominent conductors of the celebrated 'underground railroad,'" another went to David Curry, a black restaurateur, and the third went to a "lawyer named Culver."[56]

Lobam's story fills in some blanks. It certainly explains how Napoleon, Culver, and Jay were able to put a trial in motion only hours after the *City of Richmond* arrived in port. These details, however, were kept out of the press in the 1850s. For employment and safety reasons, Lobam would have had little reason to broadcast his or the cabin boys' roles. But this need for silence at the time has had the longer effect of shadowing the legal knowledge of black laborers and obscuring their roles in consequential cases.

In 1852, Napoleon received more recognition than Lobam and his cabin boys, for his name did appear in print—but that was about it. As newspapers reported on *Lemmon*, quite a few noted that a man named Napoleon had petitioned for the writ of habeas corpus.[57] Other papers simply credited (or blamed) "the abolitionists."[58] The *Philadelphia Tribune* wrote that, "Louis Napoleon, though but a black man, and most probably acting at the instance of our antislavery friends in New York, had covered himself in glory." Similarly, the *Washington Union* decided that Napoleon was "instigated to the act by the Abolitionists."[59] Napoleon's race, illiteracy, and lack of public profile apparently precluded some journalists from allowing him a protagonist's role. The antislavery press said very little, as well, although perhaps for different reasons. Gay's extensive coverage of *Lemmon* in the *National Anti-Slavery Standard* mentioned Napoleon just once, and only to say he was "a respectable coloured man of this city." *Frederick Douglass' Paper* noted that the petitioner's name, "strange to say is Louis Napoleon." Lewis Tappan, in a letter published in the *British and Foreign Antislavery Reporter,* explained that, "the free colored people obtained a writ of *Habeas Corpus.*"[60] Was their silence about Napoleon's identity purposeful, given the dangerous nature of his work? There is no question that Gay and Tappan, and maybe Douglass, knew who Napoleon was.

When the trial began, black scrutiny of the proceedings was, as usual, intense. The *Evening Post* reported that "the greatest interest has been manifested by the colored population of New York, a large portion of whom had assembled in front of the City Hall an hour before the court opened." When the eight enslaved people entered, Mrs. Lemmon appealed to them, hoping they would repudiate their lawyers' agenda: "Have I ever ill-treated you?. . . Did you ever refuse to come along with me, until you were prompted to do so?" One of the young mothers started to speak, but a "white and black abolitionist, in the same breath, told her to make no answer." (Was the "black abolitionist" Napoleon? Greeley's *Tribune* noted that Napoleon attended the trial.) The slaves were asked again that week if they would prefer to remain with the Lemmons, and they replied "that they preferred freedom to Texas."[61]

During the trial, Culver and Jay used arguments familiar to the black New Yorkers present, arguing that the 1841 nine months repeal meant that even slave owners passing briefly through New York could not hold people as property because New York law did not sanction that right. Culver maintained that "the introduction of slaves into a free state" was "a legal emancipation of them," referring to "the statutes of N. York" and "the famous Somerset case." [62] Jay noted that the common law "belongs to us as it did to our ancestors" and that Mr. Lemmon would not find a "*positive statute, binding upon this court,* authorizing him to hold" slaves as he traveled through New York.[63] Henry Lapaugh, the Lemmons' lawyer, countered that the law of nations, congressional law, and the "full faith and credit" (comity) clause of the Constitution required New York to respect "the property of a citizen of Virginia."[64]

Although New York's press thoroughly covered the legal details of the case, there was almost no journalistic curiosity about what Emmeline, Nancy, and their kin were experiencing. Nonetheless, we might pause and imagine what the young mothers traveling with their dependent family members would have endured, defying their masters in an unfamiliar place, all of sudden thrust into a sensational public trial. Did Nancy and Emmeline spend every night of the week comforting frightened little ones? Was anyone sleeping? Eating? Did they lie in bed wondering if their families would be separated as punishment if the judge ruled against them? Where would they go if they were freed? How would they support themselves, released but destitute? Were these antislavery New Yorkers trustworthy? There are aspects of the *Lemmon* case that we will never know, and it was quickest for everyone to refer to the "Lemmon slaves" as an abstract group—even the abolitionists called them some version of that—but Emmeline, Nancy, the two Lewises, the two Edwards, Amanda, and Ann were women and children starring in a terrifying public event that must have affected their private selves deeply. They were extremely visible and utterly invisible at the same time.

Despite the lack of outward attention to the specifics of who the eight enslaved people were, the presence of the young mothers and children in the packed courtroom would have played directly into an increasingly powerful antislavery northern narrative, fueled by the recent massive success of Harriet Beecher Stowe's *Uncle Tom's Cabin.* Stowe's novel focused heavily on slavery's assaults on enslaved women and children. Published serially in the *National Era* in 1851 and in novel form in early 1852, *Uncle Tom's Cabin* was a cultural juggernaut, praised by the likes of Frederick Douglass and reviled by proslavery Americans. As white northerners learned about the *Lemmon* case, there is no question that thousands of them would have had a newspaper account of *Lemmon* set down in the same room where they had read *Uncle Tom's Cabin* earlier that year, or near tickets stubs from seeing one of the multiple play versions that sold out across the region. They would have seen the two mothers in *Lemmon* as versions of Eliza, the female protagonist of Stowe's narrative, who risks her life by fleeing north to protect herself and her little boy, George, from losing each other through the domestic slave trade. When Culver, during the *Lemmon* trial, remarked in one of the few hints about the slaves' personal lives that "one of them" had "her husband sold away from her for the last three years," some observers no doubt thought about Eliza's separation from her beloved husband, the intellectually and physically impressive George Harris. In short, *Lemmon* would have helped make *Uncle Tom's Cabin* feel even more real to white northern audiences, and *Uncle Tom's Cabin* would have helped some of this same audience begin to imagine the interior lives of the two enslaved families and the varieties of pain they experienced. The legal sensation and the cultural sensation went hand in hand, stoking white northerners' mistrust of the Slave Power.[65]

The final moments of the *Lemmon* trial, in fact, felt novelistic—or at the least, narratively familiar to the primed audience. When Justice Paine delivered his decision aloud, he reaffirmed legal principles that the antislavery audience held dear. The law of nations did say, Paine conceded, that strangers "have a right to pass with their property through the territories of a nation," but "a man cannot have that full and absolute property in a person." In considering federal law, Paine observed that the Constitution was explicit on the matter of fugitives and the slave trade, but that the absence of additional rules meant that state laws "entirely abolishing slavery, or forbidding the bringing of slaves into a State" were "not affected by the Constitution." Last, Paine noted that New York's own laws—such as the 1841 nine months repeal—rendered it "impossible that such property should exist within [its] limits, except in the single issue of fugitives." The judge finished by ordering that the "eight colored persons mentioned in the writ be discharged."[66]

According to the *Herald,* when Paine read these last words, there was "a wild burst of 'ya, yes,' cheers, knocking of sticks against the floor, and clapping of hands from the colored ladies and gentlemen present."[67] After this moment of jubilation, Lapaugh asked the judge to oversee an agreement by which Culver and Jay would promise that the eight freedpeople would not leave the city. He preferred they "remain as they are until your Honor's decision can be reviewed in another court." Jay replied that even if he had the power to keep them in the city "he would decline doing so."[68] The Lemmons had tipped their hand; they would fight to keep the "slaves."

According to the *Tribune*, after Lapaugh's request was denied, "the eight persons were placed in coaches by Louis Napoleon, who accompanied them, and some other friends, and driven off amid great cheering and waving of handkerchiefs from the colored persons (females as well as males being present)." A Philadelphia paper reported that a "stout-built mulatto old woman, having a child with her, and holding up his hands as the parties passed her on their way out through the Hall—[cried] thank God! Thank God!"[69] Napoleon must have taken them somewhere secret, where they could avoid the sort of difficulties that had plagued George Kirk when efforts were made in 1846 to rearrest him right after he had been declared free.[70]

THE SLAVES FREE—IMPORTANT DECISION.—A large number of colored persons, from an early hour, assembled Saturday forenoon in and around the City Hall. The Judge took his seat in one of the main Court rooms, between 11 and 12 o'clock, when as many persons as the room would hold, were admitted, and large numbers, of course, had to remain in the corridors without being able to obtain admission.—Previous to the entry of the Judge, Mr. and Mrs. Lemmon, the claimants, Mr Lepaugh, their counsel, and a number of other persons had been admitted to the Court-room. The eight persons (slaves) were brought in by Mr. Thompson, the officer having them in charge, accompanied by Louis Napoleon, (the colored man who presented the petition on which the habeas corpus to bring the parties up was founded.) Mr. Culver, the counsel, and a number of others. Mr. John Jay, the other counsel on their behalf, came in a few minutes after the Judge commenced reading his opinion. The deepest attention was paid while the Judge was pronouncing his decision, and at points, such as that the law says persons are not goods, much feeling was evinced, and many of the colored people exhibited tears. On the announcement of the decision, that the persons must be discharged, much applause was exhibited (which the officers suppressed,) and the cheers were loudly reëchoed outside. We give the decision as follows:

the matter into consideration. No one would feel more desirous than himself, to see some means provided for their temporary maintenance. I must confess, I felt much distress, the Judge said, in regard to the decision, that these persons may not be very happily situated hereafter. Some other little conversation occurred, and the Court adjourned.

The eight persons were placed in coaches by Louis Napoleon, who accompanied them, and some other friends, and driven off, amid great cheering and waving of handkerchiefs from the colored persons, (females as well as males being present.) Oh, thank God and good men! was the ejaculation of a stout built mulatto old woman, having a child with her, and holding up her hands as the parties passed her, on their way out through the hall—thank God! thank God!

Mr. and Mrs. Lemmon appeared to be much dejected. The value of the slaves (they being, except the two women and the lad of 17, all children, including the infants of the women) is not, probably, however, very great, and it is said they did not intend to sell them after their arrival in Texas.

Figure 12. Horace Greeley's *New-York Tribune* covered the *Lemmon* case very closely. These paragraphs reveal that the courtroom was filled with black men, women, and children concerned for the eight enslaved people's fate. When Judge Paine freed the slaves, Louis Napoleon escorted them outside amidst the celebrating of the black audience. "The Slaves Free – Important Decision," *New-York Daily Tribune*, November 15, 1852.

Wherever he drove them, Napoleon delivered his charges safely. Jay and a number of his and Napoleon's Underground Railroad associates made immediate plans to transport the two families to Canada. Lewis Tappan, Greeley, and Culver orchestrated logistical and financial support. Working closely with them were several black abolitionists in the region, including Jacob Gibbs and the minister J. W. C. Pennington and his wife, Almira, of New Haven, Connecticut. A police officer named Thompson, who had been responsible for taking the families to and from court each day, was now employed as their ongoing protector.[71]

Shortly after Paine released the slaves, Jay had written a letter to an unknown person from 20 Nassau Street, down the block from the Antislavery Office. "I think," Jay began, "that it be safest for our eight sable friends to leave New York . . . this is such a wicked world and the spot where we live so desperately corrupt and mean that I think we had best avoid even the remote possibility of danger." Jay was "confident that a large subscription can be raised" to assist the freedpeople.[72] Culver, meanwhile, asked Officer Thompson to take them to Connecticut. Thompson delivered the freedpeople to the Penningtons in New Haven. Almira accompanied them further north to Hartford. She then traveled to New York with a letter from her husband addressed to Greeley, which was forwarded to Jay. Pennington's letter explained that "the 8 Lemmon slaves" were now in Hartford "under the legal care of Hooker and Hawley" (two abolitionist lawyers) and "in the social care of Brown, Gardner, and Crass colored men." The black hosts were "poor laboring men" and needed more funds to support their guests.[73]

Jay, Tappan, and Greeley worked to address the need. Jay penned a leaflet for well-heeled white New Yorkers asking readers "to contribute towards a fund for [the freedpeople's] education and support." Among those who contributed was his father, William. Greeley's *Tribune* issued a notice observing that although the "kinsmen" of "the late slaves" produce "nearly all the Cotton, Rice, Tobacco and Sugar made in this country, they have little or none of it to sell"; therefore, it was up to the *Tribune*'s readers to provide "relief and sustenance." Tappan, a few days later, wrote Jay that he had reimbursed the black hosts in Connecticut and that he assumed "Mr. Greely sent you all the moneys" from the *Tribune*.[74]

The freedpeople's friends were not the only New Yorkers raising funds. Anticipating Southern outrage, dozens of New York merchants, men whose businesses profited from their dealings with the Cotton South, raised a collection to compensate the Lemmons for their lost property. The *Times* wrote approvingly that "Such action cannot fail greatly to strengthen the attachment of Southern slaveholders to our commercial metropolis." The Lemmons accepted the merchants' $5,000. In return, they signed an affidavit declaring that "any time after the final decision and termination of this matter in the last court to which it can be taken" were "pronounced, we shall manumit and discharge from labour or services the eight slaves."[75] The *Journal of Commerce* explained that the Lemmons could not manumit their "slaves" at that moment since to do so would contravene their grounds for appeal.[76] Although news of the Lemmon indemnity was printed throughout the South, not all were mollified. As the *Richmond Whig* opined, "New York has miscalculated the feelings of the South if she thinks they will rest satisfied with the indemnity to Mr. Lemmon." New York should "*repeal the* [1841 nine months repeal]. . . . Should it not be done . . . *let Virginia look to Virginia.* Let her sustain her own trade—support her own commerce—stand upon her own bottom."[77]

The 1841 nine months repeal that so enraged proslavery Richmonders in 1852 was the law that black petitioners in New York had made one of their legislative priorities in the 1830s. Ordinary male and female black northerners, wielding a political tool separate from the vote and appealing to their status as citizens of their state, helped pass a law that then led to a watershed court case in 1852 that freed eight human beings and provoked massive sectional debate.

As news of *Lemmon* made its way through the country—with little attention to black New Yorkers' role in the case—citizens across the nation reacted in a variety of ways. The *Alexandria Gazette* reported that a group of Virginians held a meeting in which they resolved, "the decision of Judge Paine" is "a palpable violation" of "the constitution" and "is detrimental to the rights and insulting to the citizens of the South." Virginia's legislature should "take this matter into their serious consideration." Fellow southerners rallied to the Lemmons' side. A Louisiana citizen offered Jonathan Lemmon "a permanent home in Texas, in the fee simple, of as much land as he may require for farming and stock raising, or the culture of cotton."[78] (The Lemmons did not take up the offer; they moved back to Virginia.)

Northern citizens found the case troubling, as well, for opposite reasons. From Pontiac, Michigan, a man writing to the *National Era* in Washington, D.C., explained that he was not an abolitionist, but that the proslavery reaction to *Lemmon* served only "to render slavery more hated, and our laws more loved." The Michigander noted that "these questions are not unwatched in this part of the country" and that prosouthern forces were "doing more against their aims than all the Abolitionists can do." Of course, not all southerners disagreed with the "states rights" reasoning of Judge Paine's decision, and not all northerners approved of Paine's disregard for "private property" and sectional harmony. Commentators approached *Lemmon* from a variety of perspectives, but few misunderstood the controversial nature of the case.[79]

Black readers took note of *Lemmon*, as well—in one instance with a particularly remarkable outcome. Shortly after Paine rendered his verdict, a black waiter named Richard Johnson in Cleveland, Ohio, listened to one of his fellow workers read aloud from an article on the case. Hearing the details, he realized that several of the freedpeople were his relatives. Nancy was his sister and her children were his nephews and niece. He had been separated from them years earlier in a series of estate sales. More recently, he had fled to Ohio.[80] Johnson made plans to reunite with his family on the east coast, arriving in New York just around the time that his relatives were being shepherded *back* to New York in secret. From there, all nine of them would head to Canada.

Gibbs and his wife took care of the reunited family as they prepared to leave the country. He collected $127.50 from Tappan and Gay, $40 of which he placed in the hands of Richard Johnson, now serving as the head of his family. The rest of the money was set aside for the journey to Canada, including sums for two trunks, bread, cheese, and shoes.[81] In the middle of December, "the Lemmon freemen," as they were now called, made their way to Buxton, Ontario, where they were received by William King, a white Presbyterian minister who had connections to Lewis Tappan. King had founded a refuge for free black families called the Elgin Settlement; this would be the Lemmon freemen's new home. Over the next several years, King wrote Jay to report on the freedpeople's progress, and Jay continued to send King money for their support.[82]

During that same time, Napoleon and Gay worked incessantly to help dozens of escaping slaves reach freedom both in and beyond New York City. Gay had been assisting runaways since the mid-1840s, but the most detailed accounts of his collaboration with Napoleon emerge from two journals he kept between 1855 and 1857.[83] In the pages of these books, titled "Records of Fugitives," Gay recorded information about the runaways. He noted brief biographies, the circumstances of escape, and expenses paid. Napoleon's responsibilities included discovering and aiding slaves on their arrival in New York and, on occasion, accompanying and protecting them during their onward journeys.

In July 1855, for example, Gay got word that a fugitive named Sarah Moore, who was living in New Haven with her baby, was "in danger of capture." Napoleon "was sent in the next train" to find her and "take her immediately to Albany." Although Napoleon found Moore in New Haven quickly, they ran into difficulty at the train station. Napoleon "saw a NY marshal well-known to him" who "about a year since arrested and returned to slavery the brother and nephews of Dr. Pennington" and "a man who answered to Sarah's description of her master." Napoleon altered their itinerary, hiding with Moore and her infant for "a day and a night" before accompanying them to Albany. From there, the mother and child traveled to Syracuse, a popular destination for runaways. (Gay and Napoleon arranged for most of their charges to be welcomed there by Jermain W. Loguen, whom we met in Chapter 3, and a white abolitionist named Samuel May.) Back in New York City, Gay made efforts to find Moore's older children, who were living nearby. Once he located them, "a colored woman" took care of them until Napoleon could take them safely to their mother in Syracuse. After Napoleon did so, he told Gay that he "never saw such a time" as when the family was reunited. These were the moments—the human moments—that must have sustained Gay and Napoleon though their years of dangerous and expensive work.[84]

Accounts of Napoleon's clandestine activities also help illustrate what made the success of the *Lemmon* case possible. When the eight enslaved Virginians arrived in New York's port, a practiced coalition of male and female black laborers was already in place to help. Were these laborers not versed in the art of spiriting slaves away in secret, they would not have been able to get the slaves so quickly into court. Antislavery New Yorkers had crafted an entire ecosystem of aboveground and underground routes to freedom, alternately using both very public laws and very covert resources to achieve their objectives. There was a sophistication to the execution of the *Lemmon* case and the freedpeople's subsequent flight to Canada that few outsiders fully understood at the time. But the momentous consequences of the case were not secret at all.

* * *

In March 1857, the press began reporting on Chief Justice Roger Taney's contentious, divisive, and confusing opinion in the *Dred Scott* case. Scott was an enslaved man in Missouri who argued that his long stints working for a master in the free state of Illinois and in the federal territory of Wisconsin, which was free soil due to the Missouri Compromise, made him free. Put another way, Scott thought that the *Somerset* principle, which Missouri state courts in the 1820s and '30s had recognized, should apply to him. But Missouri courts in the 1850s subsequently changed course, and the case eventually reached the U.S. Supreme Court. Chief Justice Taney, after controversially ruling that Scott had no standing in federal court because black people were not citizens of the United States, went on to state (arguably in obiter dicta) that the Missouri Compromise had been unconstitutional because Congress could not deprive white American citizens of their slave property in the territories created after 1787. *Dred Scott* had the potential to affect cases like *Lemmon.* If Taney said it was unconstitutional to deny a master the right to bring slaves into federal territory, would he next say that masters had a fundamental right to bring slaves into the individual sovereign states, like New York? In vigorous dissents, Justice McLean of Ohio and Justice Curtis of Massachusetts refuted Taney's conclusions. New York's Justice Nelson concurred with Taney on narrow grounds, mostly avoiding the topics of black citizenship and the Missouri Compromise, but upholding the Missouri judges' view that Scott was a slave.[85]

The Republican-dominated New York state legislature reacted swiftly. In the assembly, former state judge Samuel Foot, representing Ontario County in the Burned-Over District, introduced resolutions protesting *Dred Scott* and suggesting the legislature take action. A fellow Republican, Elias W. Leavenworth, noted that "when the Lemmon case comes up, the same [U.S. Supreme] Court will say Slavery has a right here." A Joint Committee of the Assembly and Senate released a report declaring that the Taney Court's pronouncements on black citizenship were a "violation" of the Declaration of Independence, a "departure" from common law, and "opposed to the weight of judicial authority in this country." The notion that black people did not have "rights which white men were bound to respect" was "atrocious." The legislature, by substantial majorities, passed resolutions concluding that the Supreme Court majority had made itself "sectional and aggressive" and had "impaired" the confidence of the people of New York.[86]

A few weeks later, in the spring of 1857, the first of the *Lemmon* appeals came before the First District of the New York Supreme Court. At this stage, the case—retitled *Jonathan Lemmon, a Citizen of the State of Virginia, vs. the People of the State of New York, ex rel. Louis Napoleon*—no longer involved a band of black and white New Yorkers trying to emancipate eight enslaved people from their Virginian masters. Emmeline, Nancy, and their children were safe in Canada, and both sides acknowledged as much. The contest was now between the government of Virginia and the government of New York over the principle of state versus federal capacity to regulate slavery on state soil. As if this North versus South component were not enough to heighten the controversy, *Dred Scott* was now implicated. Everyone understood that New York's bench would be asked to consider how the Taney court's reading of slave property affected New York's right to free people arriving within her borders.

In December 1857—after Virginia's counsel succeeded in a motion to postpone the case because he wanted more time to study *Dred Scott*—the First District ruled against Virginia. Despite the fact that lawyers on both sides cited *Dred Scott,* the state judges ignored it in their majority opinion, instead relying on New York's 1841 nine months repeal, a reading of the privileges and immunities clause of the U.S. Constitution that did not require New York to grant Virginia citizens rights that New York's own citizens did not have, and an interpretation of Congress's powers over interstate commerce that did not preclude individual states from regulating the status of people on their soil.[87] Virginia vowed to appeal. John King, New York's antislavery Republican governor, responded by requesting his legislature for additional funds "for the maintenance of the rights of the State as the importance of the question requires." New York's Court of Appeals, the state's highest court, would hear the case next, followed, it was assumed, by the United States Supreme Court. Observers on all sides expected that the Taney Court might find a way to ensure that masters could take slaves wherever they wished, rendering northern states incapable of keeping slavery out of their borders.[88]

Lemmon, more than ever before, became a rallying cry for proslavery and antislavery forces alike. A few months after the 1857 decision, New Hampshire Republican Mason Tappan warned Congress that when *Lemmon* "shall find its way to the same tribunal which decided Dred Scott, slavery, by virtue of it, will be planted in every free State of the Union." This linking of *Dred Scott, Lemmon,* and the Slave Power became commonplace in Republican rhetoric. Abraham Lincoln, in his 1858 "House Divided" speech, remarked that *Dred Scott* declared that the Constitution neither "permits Congress nor a Territorial legislature to exclude slavery from any United States Territory." He warned that "we may ere long see" a "decision declaring that the Constitution" does not permit "*a State* to exclude slavery from its limits."[89] Southerners, of course, saw the danger of *Lemmon* in a different light. A writer in the *Charleston Mercury,* after suggesting that southern legislatures respond to

Lemmon by passing laws thwarting northern creditors' ability to recoup debts via slave property, quoted Senator Alfred Iverson of Georgia approvingly: "he would vote for no measure, the benefits of which, upon a dissolution of the Union, would accrue to the North alone; and that one southern State, swinging from the Union, would carry the rest with her."[90] No matter who was using *Lemmon* as evidence, these were all fighting words.

In early 1860, the third iteration of *Lemmon* appeared before the New York Court of Appeals. The *Herald* described the case as creating "an excitement almost equal to the Harper's Ferry foray."[91] Virginia's lawyers relied for their main arguments on the privileges and immunities and commerce clauses of the U.S. Constitution. As federal citizens, the Lemmons were allowed to travel from state to state without their property being harmed. Furthermore, it was Congress, not the states, who could regulate "intercourse between our citizens of different States." They also appealed to *Dred Scott,* warning that the nation's highest court might hear *Lemmon* and decide in favor of American citizens' right to move across state borders holding slaves as property. In April, the Lemmons and Virginia lost again. In a 5-3 decision, the Court of Appeals disagreed that the Lemmons were engaging in commerce by moving their slaves from one place to another. In wording similar to Paine's, Justice Hiram Denio observed for the majority that individual states had "the power" to "deal with the status of all persons within their territory." Justice William B. Wright, in a concurring opinion, put an antislavery gloss on *Dred Scott*: if Missouri had the right to declare Scott a slave, then New York had an equal right to declare anyone in its borders free; anything else Taney had said "beyond this was *obiter.*"[92]

By the summer, Greeley's *Tribune* was suggesting a reading list for the "friends of the Republican cause" that included a biography of Lincoln, a report of the *Dred Scott* case, and a report of the *Lemmon* case. Put another way, a case instigated in New York in 1852 through the cooperation of eight enslaved women and children, Louis Napoleon, black seamen and dockworkers, and white antislavery lawyers had morphed into Republican campaign literature during one of the most consequential elections in United States history.[93]

As Virginia made plans to appeal to the federal Supreme Court and the country prepared for the national election in the fall of 1860, *Lemmon* continued to shape regional and political identity. In October, Governor Herschel Johnson of Georgia, placed on the Democratic presidential ticket with Illinois' Stephen Douglas in a bid to maintain the party's commitment to union, traveled to New York to make the case for sectional reconciliation. In a speech at the Cooper Institute, Johnson noted that the "celebrated Lemmon slave case" had abolished the principle of comity "in this sisterhood of States." Because of such northern aggression, the "South will not submit" to a Lincoln presidency. "The only way of averting the peril," he continued, "is for New York to do her duty" by rejecting Lincoln and the Republican party.[94] An editorial in the proslavery *DeBow's Review,* the most widely circulated periodical in the South, noted that "the court of appeals of the largest State in the Union has, at last, decided in the Lemmon case, against the right of a slaveholder with his property even to touch *in transitu,* from one slaveholding State to another. . . . The Democratic party has opposed all these things."[95]

Debow's also publicized features of the Republican Party platform that would ultimately choke slavery out of existence, explaining that the party's "immediate purpose" was to "seize upon all the territories of the United States, and in due time, to bring them into the Union as free States." It was not lost on opponents of the *Lemmon* decisions that the Lemmons had been heading west. *Lemmon* thus fed into southern fears that northern states wanted to meddle with their human property and that slaveholding states would eventually lose the contest to colonize the West. When this happened, free states and their politicians would surround and overwhelm proslavery jurisdictions and drown out proslavery representatives in the national government. For doughface and proslavery voters, these were reasons to vote against Lincoln's party.

But Lincoln and the Republicans, with the help of New York's decisive 35 electoral college votes, won the election. Soon thereafter, on the same day in December that South Carolina cited the *Lemmon* case in its Declaration of Secession, the *Tribune,* where Gay now worked, worried that the case would soon appear in Taney's court: "Virginia now cites us before the Federal Supreme Court. . . . A more momentous question has not in our day be submitted to any legal tribunal. Shall New-York make her own laws? Or shall they be made by Virginia and other states? . . . And why should New-York stand alone in defense of rights vital to every Free State? . . . Why then, should not New-England and Ohio, Pennsylvania and the North-West, be invited to participate in the defense of their common rights?"[96] In closing, the *Tribune* warned that it would be a mistake to respond to the "cry of 'The Union in danger!'" by submitting to a "grand compromise or Northern *slump,* wherein Justice and Liberty are to be bartered for ease."[97] *Lemmon* was a reason not to compromise.

But on *Lemmon*'s seemingly inevitable route to the Supreme Court, the appeal hit a roadblock. Despite various powerful Virginians' previous claims that the state would see the case all the way into Taney's courtroom, Virginia's recently elected governor, John Letcher, was unenthusiastic about pursuing a new round of appeals. Letcher was a Douglas Democrat and conditional Unionist. Given *Lemmon*'s history of inflaming sectional tensions, Letcher apparently felt wary of making things worse. Whatever his motivation, the new governor declined, unlike his predecessors, to make *Lemmon* a cause célèbre. Letcher made no obvious efforts to appeal the case to the Supreme Court, nor, by the fall of 1860, had he made any public declarations about his intentions.[98]

Whether or not *Lemmon* was en route to the Taney Court, the timing of the New York Court of Appeals ruling—the spring preceding the election of 1860—ensured that the case would act as a bugbear for secessionists. And so when secession finally occurred, the Confederate states' foundational political and legal documents blamed, in part, the determination of northern legislatures and courts to deny southerners their right to go where they wanted with slave property. South Carolina, the first state to secede, made a direct reference to *Lemmon* in the *Declaration of the Immediate Causes which Induce and Justify the Secession of South Carolina*: "In the State of New York even the right of transit for a slave has been denied by her tribunals."[99] A month later, Georgia complained in her own declaration: "In several of our confederate States a citizen cannot travel the highway with his servant who may voluntarily accompany him." Three days later, Texas accused the "non-slave-holding States" of "encourage[ing] and sustain[ing] lawless organizations to steal our slaves and prevent their recapture." In April 1861, Virginia's convention agreed to adopt the recently ratified Constitution of the Confederate States. This constitution included a clause stating, "The citizens of each State shall be entitled to all the privileges and immunities of citizens in the several States; and shall have the right of transit and sojourn in any State of this Confederacy, with their slaves and other property." Virginia's objectives in the *Lemmon* case were explicitly written into the Confederacy's ruling compact. In May, the vast majority of Virginia's eligible men voted to ratify the secession convention's actions, thereby approving the Confederate constitution.[100]

Lemmon and other similar northern cases did not, of course, by themselves cause the Civil War. They did, however, give northerners and southerners, proslavery forces and antislavery forces, a striking example of increasingly tense relationships among the states and the difficulties of protecting or abolishing slavery within a federal union. For nearly a decade, *Lemmon* provided politicians, abolitionists, secessionists, voters, and everyday black and white Americans a lens through which to articulate their fears about slavery and to explain the reasons the country could or should go to war.

* * *

As a long and multicharactered history of the *Lemmon* case suggests, the children of gradual abolition and their white partners contributed to the nation's sectional reckoning through their particular commitment to legal proficiency, state legislative power, and on-the-ground protection and transportation of vulnerable freedom seekers. When black men and women crossed state borders or helped others cross state borders, they triggered conflict of law disputes that resulted in problems much bigger than those related to the particular master and slave at hand. These cases pitted state against state, and states against the federal government. By disseminating knowledge of the law, pushing their claims in court, and using their expertise to help strangers, law-oriented New Yorkers hastened the unraveling of slavery in the North and the stoking of "abolitionist conspiracy" anxieties in the South.

As these northern slave cases progressed through the courts, a corresponding extralegal otherworld operated behind the scenes. This covert antislavery movement operated simultaneously and in conjunction with the legal and public-facing antislavery movement. This is hardly a new observation. But it is worth recognizing the degree to which ordinary black northerners were as willing to spend their days in courtrooms as they were willing to house, feed, and protect those slaves and free people who needed help in the shadows of the law. Without recognition of the nurtured vernacular legal culture among ordinary black northerners of the rising generation, we can never fully understand the most provocative legal cases of the 1840s and '50s, the reasons for the cases' success, and the safety of the freedom seekers involved.

Louis Napoleon was still alive when the South Carolina Declaration of Secession cited the slave case that he had started in 1852 as a reason to leave the Union. He lived on through the war that followed. He survived well past the dates when three quarters of the United States ratified constitutional amendments abolishing slavery, establishing birthright citizenship, and extending the vote to black men. When he died, in 1881, several city papers ran obituaries, giving Napoleon a recognition in death that he little received in life. These tributes focused on his role in the Underground Railroad and his association with famous white New Yorkers. The *Sun*, for example, reported that "the old man never wearied of relating his experiences with runaway slaves. Often, he said, he and his colleagues packed fugitives in barrels or boxes . . . he delighted to recall his acquaintance with such men as Gerrit Smith, Arthur and Lewis Tappan, and Horace Greeley."[101]

These eulogies praised Napoleon's courage on the Underground Railroad and memorialized white abolitionists in the process. The rest of Napoleon's antislavery story was left out. There was no mention of George Kirk, James Hamlet, or Nancy, Emmeline, and the children. In fact, there was no mention of law or legal cases at all. There was likewise no indication that Napoleon was part of a much broader cohort of black New Yorkers who worked alongside men like Smith, the Tappans, Greeley, Jay, Culver, and Gay. But Napoleon and seemingly ordinary black New Yorkers were critical to the common law traditions, state laws, and famous cases that forced the nation to reckon with the human and constitutional facets of slavery.

For decades before the Civil War, black New Yorkers fought to make the legal system work for them. They did not always win. But they won enough to transform the legal landscape and alter the terms of debate. The origins of the Civil War lie, in part, among a unique generation of black men and women in New York who understood law and politics as imperfect—but powerful—tools of freedom.

CHAPTER 7

The Great Question of Equality Before the Law

The Civil War and Reconstruction

In May 1863, four months after President Lincoln issued the Emancipation Proclamation, a black woman in San Francisco named Mrs. Samuel A. Smith published a history of Elizabeth Jennings's successful discrimination suit against the New York Third Avenue streetcar company. Taking up three columns in the *Pacific Appeal,* Smith's account explained how Jennings had employed lawyers after she was violently dragged off the car in 1854. "Colored citizens" and the local Republican press had supported Jennings's claims to her "rights." There was no law in New York "in relation to persons of color, except the elective franchise." The state judge had instructed the jury that, under the common law, "common carriers" must "carry all respectable persons." The subtext in 1863 was not subtle: for free black westerners and northerners like the Smiths and the Jennings, it was vital that the present war to end slavery also result in "equality before the law."[1]

Mrs. Samuel A. Smith was Elizabeth Jennings's older sister, Sarah. The *Appeal,* a "Weekly Journal devoted to the Interests of the People of Color," had been cofounded by Philip A. Bell, a graduate of the New York African Free School who had organized political meetings with the sisters' father, Thomas L. Jinnings, before he moved to California. The Smiths owned a local resort whose amenities they advertised in Bell's paper. To read Smith's account of her sister's civil rights case is to read the story of a grown child of gradual abolition, in a newspaper founded by a male counterpart on the other side of the country, in the midst of a Civil War that became a struggle over the fate and content of black freedom, black citizenship, and American federalism.[2]

Smith's rendering of her sister's case, which included the legal musings of their sixty-three-year-old father, suggests how uniquely prepared many free black northerners were to shape the course of national emancipation. They saw this as a moment to reemphasize longstanding claims about their own state-based rights as well as an opportunity to ensure that national abolition avoided the pitfalls so obvious from their own history. As the *Pacific Appeal* explained, northern "freemen" were "well versed in the Federal system and the workings of the Government." They had taken advantage of common schools and deserved the vote. They deplored "Free State people" who imitated "Southern-bred men" by impeding citizens' rights to "ride in a railway car, sit in a church, enter a bar-room, or visit a theater." Americans should abandon these "relics" of slavery and treat "all persons according to their qualities."[3]

The right to attend school, use public transport, buy lunch, stay at an inn, go to a play, and be welcome in church were activities of everyday life. How could a child, man, or woman be meaningfully free if these basic civil rights lay unenforced? And what about the right to sue and testify in court—maybe these were not rights people used every day, but they were fundamental to protecting property and personal liberty. Why did Elizabeth have those judicial rights in New York, but Sarah did not in California? How was it that their father had voted equally with white men in the 1810s, but in later life had to meet racially specific property requirements to vote? Sarah's husband, Samuel, had come from Pennsylvania, where black men could not vote at all after 1838, then moved to New York, where he could vote on unequal terms, and then to California, where the state's 1849 constitution disfranchised nonwhite men. This unjust morass of laws was the result of the United States' particular constitutional order and hazy definitions of citizenship. It is no wonder that both ordinary and prominent free black Americans saw the upheaval of the Civil War as a potential revolution in the federal balance of power. Their desire and rationale for adequate answers became all the more salient as regiments of black men fought for the Union after the Lincoln administration finally permitted their enlistment in 1862–1863.[4]

As this account of Sarah Smith's 1863 article suggests, there is something new to explore in tracing how the children of gradual abolition connected their experiences of northern emancipation to the cataclysmic national events of the 1860s and '70s. In their home state and elsewhere—out west, on southern battlefields, in Washington, D.C.—this generation of New Yorkers raised their voices and exposed their bodies to harm as purposefully as ever. Small in number compared to the national population, their activities and work nonetheless shaped the war and its aftermath. They comprised an especially visible and effective portion of the thousands of active black northerners whose legal, political, and military efforts resulted in victories on behalf of civic equality that would not have occurred otherwise.[5]

One oft-forgotten reason this generation of New Yorkers was so determined and precise in their politics was the fact that so many had already lived through an emancipation. New York's general abolition had occurred in 1827. Some of the state's black servant children had been held in bondage into the 1840s. As the forty-eight-year-old editor Robert Hamilton noted in his own paper in 1863, black northerners had "for years" struggled "for the rights and privileges of free citizens" and survived "the oscillating process of gradual emancipation." The war was an opportunity both to end southern slavery the right way—that is, immediately—and to fix the inadequacies of the North's patchwork regimes of unequal citizenship.[6]

Some of these New Yorkers, like the Jenningses and Hamiltons, had been prominent before the war. But the story involves a wider cast of characters. Ordinary, laboring citizens boarded streetcars, enlisted in regiments, signed petitions, demanded better schools, and filled churches and streets to celebrate good days and mourn dreadful ones. One year after Smith recounted her sister's case, an otherwise obscure war widow in New York City named Ellen Anderson made news after she successfully sued a streetcar company for racial discrimination. As Anderson's litigation suggests, at the very local level—riding a railcar, stopping a street fight, buying refreshments—unfamous women were regularly out front. In the formal rooms of state and national politics, however, men were the mouthpiece of the race. These loci of activity were intimately connected. It takes moving back and forth among them to see the whole.[7]

What is especially striking about New York in this period is how the state was at once a national model for what was possible and a place, at least at moments, just as in need of federal intervention as the slave states. On the one hand, black New Yorkers highlighted the education, associationalism, civic knowledge, property ownership, religiosity, and patriotism of their communities as arguments for a nationally enforced emancipation that would bring enslaved southerners into the polity. On the other hand, New York was a jurisdiction where unfair laws, racial violence, and corrupt elections muffling black political will sometimes looked as horrific as in the South. As had been the case for a century, New York was a swing state where antislavery citizens inspiringly pushed the envelope of what was possible at the same time that doughface politics and the flaws of an incomplete emancipation remained stark.

By virtue of their multifaceted efforts, the children of gradual abolition were among the founders of the Thirteenth, Fourteenth, and Fifteenths Amendments (1865–1870), the Civil Rights Acts of 1866 and 1875, and federal election legislation. For decades, they were instrumental in promoting the idea that citizenship and political equality were fundamental corollaries of emancipation and that rights had to be written into permanent law. Their past had taught them that states could be mercurial in their commitment to black safety and belonging. National citizenship—uniform, race-neutral, defensive against discriminatory state action—could solve problems they had faced during and after their own emancipation. As people across the United States clashed over the war's settlement, the rising generation did not get everything they wanted. But they took part in achieving a number of critical changes. As they died in the late nineteenth century, they left a world that was substantially different from the one they had entered.[8]

* * *

In the years leading to the Civil War, no one knew exactly how, when, or if slavery would end. Even among Americans favoring emancipation, there was debate about how the process might unfold. Black New Yorkers, despite not holding office, shaped this discourse. The children of gradual abolition's literacy, press acumen, and ties to influential white men proved critical as the nation faced increasingly bitter conflicts over slavery and citizenship. Male spokesmen appealed to their status as "respectable men of color," but their efforts included the men, women, and children who filled public meetings and pews. There was a collective ethos, honed over decades, even amidst elite politics and class differentiation.

New York's black abolitionists were routinely in the position of fighting three ideological battles at once: one over the wisdom of emancipation in the past, one over emancipation's contemporary results, and one over what should be done in the future. When they faced proslavery critics who claimed black people were better off under owners' control or colonizationists who said they were unsuited to live in the United States, they pointed to ordinary black citizens' accomplishments in the context of northern gradual abolition. At the same time, when they encountered new proposals for gradualism in the slave states, they balked.[9]

James McCune Smith's thirty years' worth of letters, speeches, and editorials illustrate this balancing act. In 1844, for example, Smith challenged the white Unitarian minister Orville Dewey after the latter made an ostensibly antislavery speech at an evangelical church in Manhattan. Dewey emphasized that "slavery was wrong," but then besmirched the local results of abolition: "Free Blacks are worse off than the Slaves of the South—not being so well clothed, fed, or so happy." The remedy "was to assign them a State somewhere in the West."[10] Dewey was not the first to make these claims. What made the situation notable was Smith's front-page rejoinder in Horace Greeley's widely read *Tribune,* the future trumpet of the Republican Party. Smith wrote from experience: "Being the son of a slave, owing my liberty to the Emancipation Act of the State of New York . . . I feel called upon by gratitude to this my native State, and by a deep solicitude for my brethren at the South, thus publicly to deny the proposition which you have announced as above. And I hold myself prepared to prove [that] emancipation in the free States, proves the safety and expediency of emancipation."[11] Smith added that even though black northerners were "yet partially enslaved—denied a large share of the rights of citizenship," they showed "steady improvement." Sympathetic readers concurred. "Dr. Smith," opined the *Boston Courier,* "is treated rather cavalierly by Mr. Dewey, but he is his equal as a man, a gentleman, and a scholar."[12]

Several months after the Dewey dispute, Smith and his peers, alongside ordinary citizens, made similar arguments in response to the controversy created by the annexation of Texas. When President Tyler's secretary of state, the rabidly proslavery John Calhoun of South Carolina, signed a treaty of annexation, he justified his actions in part on the need to keep the antislavery British government out of Texas. In the so-called Pakenham Letter, Calhoun spouted Dewey-like arguments, listing dubious statistics and census data about black northerners who were "in jails or houses of correction," or "dumb, blind, idiot, insane." The letter, which exploded in the press and rallied anti-expansionists, made the annexation treaty even more controversial.[13]

Black leaders in New York City responded with several audiences in mind: the U.S. Senate, white newspaper readers, and the ordinary black northerners whom Calhoun insulted. At a "Mass Meeting" of black locals, a cohort of luminaries—including African Free School classmates Smith, Bell, Henry Highland Garnet, Charles and Patrick Reason—agreed to write a rebuttal. The masses met again a few days later at the A.M.E. Zion Church along with "citizens from Brooklyn and Williamsburg." Robert Hamilton, whose father William had written to John Jay advocating abolition back in the 1790s, presided. Smith noted that "in the free States," where 170,000 black people lived, 40,000 children "go to school . . . in addition to a large number of children attending white school," while "the children of slaves are forbidden to read." Necessary census reforms would show that Calhoun's claims were bogus. Charles B. Ray, former editor of the *Colored American*, and Junius C. Morel, a colored conventions regular who had recently moved to Brooklyn to teach, also addressed the crowd.[14]

In a practice that would continue into the Civil War and Reconstruction, sympathetic national lawmakers took black words into the Capitol. New York Whig Senator Nathaniel P. Tallmadge, who had studied law with his famous antislavery first cousin, James Tallmadge Jr., presented the black citizens' anti-Calhoun memorial to his colleagues. Joshua Giddings, an antislavery Congressmen from Ohio, used the New Yorkers' evidence in an anti-annexation speech he later published. He was "mortified" at Calhoun's "loosely penned lecture in favor of slaveholding" and credited Dr. Smith for pointing out "palpable errors." Giddings added feistily that "friends will not hesitate to place [Smith's] publication beside the honorable Secretary's letter, and let the world judge from the two productions which exhibits the greatest evidence of insanity."[15]

The challenge to Calhoun did not cause slavery's apologists to see the error of their ways or prevent Texas's entry into the Union—the Lemmons of Virginia would try to move there in 1852, after all. But the claims in defense of free black life were significant. Black northerners' intellectual work was integral to the volatile politics of slavery and expansion that led to the breakdown of the Second Party System and the rise of the Republican Party. Just as important, these antislavery messages reached the families who packed political meetings and churches. It was Smith's words that were published, but he existed in a wider world. His career and soul were fed by his work with hundreds of black patients, voters, and students. He and his wife, the well-educated abolitionist Malvina Barnett, treasured being parents. The 40,000 school children he cited in his rebuttal to Calhoun were critical to the black antislavery argument and a source of political weaponry. It was, moreover, ordinary people's choice to travel across or into Manhattan on a Friday night to hear refutations of Calhoun's slanders. When the meeting's proceedings appeared in the *Tribune* and the *Liberator*—with directions urging "our people in every town and city throughout the free states" to spread the message—subscribers read and disseminated the information to others, including those without formal schooling. Phebe Ray in Rochester and Elizabeth Wicks in Troy and Catherine Mary Douge in Albany made what Smith was showing and asking for possible. Free black communities were represented by male elites but not cut off from them. Nor could these men have done their work without the laboring and middling folks who comprised the vindicative data read by Giddings in Congress. Those numbers represented countless moments of sacrifice, labor, bravery, and community pride.[16]

On some policy issues—such as slavery's expansion into the West—black New Yorkers found common ground with the vast majority of white antislavery northerners. But on other questions, such as immediate emancipation or equal rights in existing states, they encountered a wide spectrum of belief and had to perform the perpetual labor of holding white political leaders to account. Debates with such figures foreshadowed debates that would soon occur during the Civil War. White New Yorkers such as Greeley, William Seward, Thurlow Weed, and Roscoe Conkling (influential Republicans) and Horatio Seymour, Fernando Wood, and Samuel Tilden (influential Democrats) faced questions in the 1860s that were hardly new to them. The children of gradual abolition were at times appreciative of the work of the white politicians they knew, and at other times furious, but they did not have the luxury of ignoring these men, for the Sewards and the Seymours of the world wielded tremendous public power and backroom sway.

In 1853, for example, Weed, the North's most famous political kingmaker and editor, proposed national gradual abolition combined with colonization. With the sale of public lands, Congress could provide funds to any "slave State whose Legislature should accept it upon such terms as follows: Every slave born after that year—to be free at the age of twenty-five years, the Owner receiving just equivalent." Weed imagined that border states would be amenable to such policies. The major difference between Weed's midcentury proposals and New York's earlier emancipation scheme was the inclusion of compensation for owners.[17]

Black New Yorkers and their most steadfast white connections, meanwhile, stressed the more immediatist examples in the state's history. A few weeks after Weed published his proposal, "coloured citizens" in Binghamton celebrated the general abolition of 1827. It is telling that this was the moment black citizens feted in the 1850s, not the passage of the 1799 gradual abolition act. The following winter, William Lloyd Garrison addressed a crowd in New York City, noting that he should hardly be considered a fanatic when he was simply proposing what "the Empire State" did in 1827 when it proclaimed "liberty to all in bondage on your soil."[18]

The gradualist notions of men like Weed, however, remained popular. Lincoln, in an 1854 speech in Peoria that he later excerpted during his career-accelerating debates with Senator Stephen Douglas in 1858, argued that the principles of the Revolution had "led to emancipation" in the North. He concluded that "gradual emancipation might be adopted" by "our brethren in the South." Once the war began, he routinely urged Delaware, Maryland, Kentucky, and Missouri to adopt gradual, compensated emancipation paired with colonization. When Lincoln made these suggestions, he spoke to a public familiar with these ideas precisely because editors like Weed had been discussing them for a generation. The architects and expositors of northern emancipation constructed much of the policy terrain on which Lincoln later operated.[19]

In the mid-1850s, as the Republican Party gained ground precisely because a critical mass of northern voters could no longer brook certain compromises over slavery, black New Yorkers remained on the radical end of abolitionist politics. In 1855, at an interracial meeting honoring Frederick Douglass at Reverend Levin Tilmon's Colored Methodist Congregational Church in the Bowery, a "crowded audience" resolved that "while others talk, it is the duty of the free colored People to work, to complete their Emancipation in the free States in order that the contagion of perfect equality in civil and social life may spread" to the South. A few months later, hundreds of politicians met in Syracuse at the state's inaugural Republican Party convention. Douglass was optimistic. The Republican platform was not as radical as he wanted—it affirmed the federal consensus, for example— but at least the party's birth indicated that voters were ready to "relinquish those old and disgraceful political affinities."[20]

Seward, a New Yorker with intimate knowledge of slavery, emancipation, and political abolitionism, was one of the new party's most visible leaders. As an antislavery Whig and then Republican stalwart, he portrayed himself as a politician from both the Slave North and the Free North, rarely shying away from his family's and New York's slaveholding past.[21] He regularly referred to New York in order to explain his prescriptions for the national future, approaching southerners not as a holier-than-thou northern saint, but as a messenger from a state that had once condoned slavery, too. In an 1855 Senate speech, Seward claimed that were he a member of a slaveholding state, he would urge "Emancipation" through "the action of the State legislature." He promised federal support: "while I retain a place in the National Councils, *any slaveholding State willing to adopt the humane policy which had already been adopted by my own State and by other States*, shall have my vote for any aid, either in lands or money, from the Federal Government." If New York could abolish slavery without payment to owners, surely it was reasonable to ask southern states to do so with the added incentive of compensation.[22]

In the summer of 1860, after Seward lost the presidential nomination to Lincoln (to Seward's, Weed's, and many Americans' surprise), the senator nursed his wounds and then campaigned widely across nine states on behalf of the nominee. In Kansas, Seward confessed he "was born a slaveholder" and knew what it meant to ask owners to give up their slaves. He reminded the westerners that forty years earlier, three New Yorkers—John Taylor, James Tallmadge Jr., and Rufus King—fought to keep slavery out of Missouri.[23] Seward insisted that there were ways the federal government could extinguish slavery without violating property rights. Throughout the campaign, Republicans were keen to emphasize that they were both antislavery and respectful of the federal government's limited powers.

Although Seward was on a national mission that fall, New York remained at the forefront of his mind. Lincoln desperately needed the state's 35 electoral votes and New York had a long history of doughface tendencies. Complicating Republican chances was the fact that the majority-Republican legislature had, after several years of partisan effort and lobbying from black citizens, succeeded in placing equal male suffrage on the ballot. Voters would be asked whether to remove the $250 color bar from the 1821 constitution.

Local Democrats were quick to tie the struggle for equal rights to the policies of the Republican party, hoping to paint Lincoln supporters as dangerously radical and beholden to abolitionists. Hershel Johnson of Georgia, the (northern) Democrats' vice-presidential nominee, warned a New York crowd that the idea of "equality between the white and black races" was growing "stronger every day in our midst." Unlike the Republicans, for whom it was "all 'negro negro negro,'" the Democrats cared about peace in the Union. Seward and other prominent Republicans, cognizant of this Democratic strategy, emerged only cautiously in favor of equal suffrage, wary of alienating swing voters in such a heated and unpredictable election.[24]

Black New Yorkers tried to place suffrage above the partisan fray, basing their claims on the rights and obligations of citizenship. In a historical essay, Smith noted that in Rome, private rights included the right to personal liberty, family, marriage, and paternal control over the household. Public rights comprised inclusion in the census, military service, taxation, voting, office holding, and religious worship. This collection of fundamental rights, which constituted "citizenship as expressed in the Constitution of the United States," had nothing to do with race or party. A suffrage committee in New York City printed statistics about black achievement and insisted that suffrage was not a question "of party." In a few years, these same men would make similar arguments in support of equal suffrage guarantees in the United States Constitution.[25]

On November 6, 1860, when New York's white men went to the polls, the majority voted *for* Lincoln and *against* black suffrage. They rejected voting rights by a larger margin than they elected Lincoln: Lincoln won 362,646 to 312,510; equal suffrage lost 345,791 to 197,889.[26] Could there be any clearer indication that an electorate could be opposed to slavery and to equal black citizenship at the same time? This lesson was fresh in the minds of the rising generation when the Civil War began.

* * *

In early 1861, as a string of states in the Deep South followed South Carolina into secession, Lincoln prepared his inaugural address. He worked closely with Seward on the speech. The New Yorker, belying his prewar reputation as a radical (as he would throughout the war), urged Lincoln to soften his tone.[27] The speech repeated core Republican unionist bromides, promising not to attack "slavery in the States where it exists." At the same time, Lincoln insisted the federal government could regulate slavery in the territories. He promised to uphold the Fugitive Slave Act, but also insisted that all Americans should be able to protect themselves with Article IV guarantees of citizenship. He still disagreed with the majority in *Dred Scott* that free black people were not United States citizens.[28]

Black New Yorkers were disappointed. Thomas Hamilton expressed feeling "no comfort from the Inaugural" in the *Weekly Anglo-African.* His assessment was informed by historical knowledge. Born in 1823, Hamilton was the younger son of William Hamilton. When he was 14, he had worked as a newsboy for the *Colored American.* In the 1840s and '50s, Thomas and his brother Robert promoted equal male suffrage alongside other leading lights of their generation. In 1861, he was irked by Lincoln's claim that slavery's extension was the only "substantial" dispute: "It is the *existence,* not the *extension of slavery* that is at issue," he insisted.[29]

Employing their literacy and well-honed politics of access, black abolitionists pushed white counterparts to move more boldly. After the embarrassing Union loss at the Battle of Bull Run, James McCune Smith wrote Gerrit Smith expressing dismay that Gerrit had written an open letter to the compromise-seeking State Democratic Committee downplaying the problem of slavery.[30] The letter did not express "the only terms in which peace be made—emancipation." Knowing Gerrit's opinion held sway "with the masses," James criticized his friend for missing a chance to rally northerners around emancipation. Gerrit had lent his "great name to the support of an Administration" that "endeavored to pacify the South by returning fugitive slaves!"[31]

James was not naïve. He was aware that the Lincoln administration had to please many factions at once, on the one hand maintaining enough conservative and border state support to hold the Union together while on the other acknowledging that slavery was evil and the cause of the war. James had seen this sort of political needle threading and coalition building over policy issues since he was a boy in New York. But, the doctor argued, saving the Union and ending slavery were necessarily intertwined. He told Gerrit, "The only salvation of this nation is *Immediate Emancipation.*" Once people were convinced of this fact, they would "cause the Administration and Congress to move." A few days later, Gerrit wrote a public letter to Lincoln. Gerrit highlighted slavery as the war's cause and urged Lincoln not to obsess over a strict adherence to the Constitution in his treatment of the South. But Gerrit failed to ask unequivocally for immediate emancipation. No doubt James had hoped for more.[32]

Other longtime white partners rose more satisfactorily to the occasion. John Jay, for example, entered a particularly energetic phase of his career. Like his namesake, Jay saw in the crisis of war a moment that might disassemble slavery. In the tumultuous summer of 1861, after a former congressman accused "fanatic" Jay of alienating "Southern citizens who have remained devoted to the Union," Jay replied on the front page of the *Tribune*: "I have never forgotten the lessons I learned in childhood under the roof of my grandfather, and which were impressed on me by the pure precept and example of my father." Jay refused to give the Constitution "the Pro-Slavery gloss attempted to be given it by the men who are now trampling it in the dust."[33]

At the same time that doughfaces called Jay a fanatic, black New Yorkers urged Jay to be bolder. "It is true that Mr. Jay does not," Douglass wrote, "tell us that he is opposed to the abolition of slavery in the present impending crisis. But the course of his argument implies the possibility to return to peace without any disturbance of the relation of master and slave."[34] Jay was treading carefully, but wartime abolition was nonetheless his goal. In September 1861, after he was attacked by James Gordon Bennett's *Herald*, a powerful

Democratic paper that frequently spouted antiblack rhetoric, Jay wrote a response explaining ways to end slavery constitutionally. The *Herald* refused to print it. The paper's readers, Bennett explained, saw "nigger worshippers and nigger drivers equally odious to true patriots."[35]

The *Herald*'s response evinced the lack of uniform northern opinion about the war. New York City, in particular, was a hotbed of both antislavery Unionism and outright Copperheadism. The mayor, Democrat Fernando Wood, went so far in 1861 as to suggest to the city council that New York peacefully secede from the state and form itself into an independent "Free City" that retained friendly commercial ties with the Confederacy. The variety of opinion in New York—from black editors' radical antislavery positions to Wood's embrace of the Confederacy—mirrored the range of views in the Union writ large.[36]

Black New Yorkers were largely united in their belief that the administration was not doing enough to abolish slavery. This unanimity of opinion, however, did not extend to all subjects. Most notably, there was little agreement, particularly early in the war, about military service. Some New Yorkers, including Reverend Tilmon, wanted black men in the fight. "If your Honor wishes colored volunteers," the Maryland slave turned New York clergyman wrote to Lincoln in 1861, "you have only to signify by answering the above note at 70 E. 13th St, N.Y.C., with instructions, and the above will meet with prompt attention." Douglass was another early proponent of enlistment. When one of his readers urged that black men "take a prominent part in a war which will eventually lead to a general emancipation of the race," Douglass agreed.[37]

Others were less convinced. One group in New York City, for example, gathered to consider whether to "tender our services." William J. Wilson, a leader in state suffrage movement, opposed the measure, stating that the government's lack of interest in recruiting black men and refusal to grant equal citizenship made him unenthusiastic about offering "ourselves to be kicked and insulted." The meeting "refused to volunteer." Another local abolitionist, Robert Vandyne, agreed that blind loyalty to an indifferent government was a mistake: "Have not two centuries of cruel and unrequited servitude in this country, alone entitled the children of this generation to the rights of men and citizens?" A reader of these events from Troy agreed: "We of the North must have all the rights which white men enjoy; until then we are in no condition to fight."[38]

Black citizens in favor of enlistment had an ally in Jay. And Jay had an ally in Charles Sumner of Massachusetts, who was both his old friend and the fiercest Radical Republican senator in Congress. As early as spring 1861, Jay wrote Sumner requesting a change in national policy: "at present no blacks are admitted to the army or navy except in menial capacity . . . will you not look to the correction of this." In 1862, Jay published a rousing "To Arms" editorial in the *Anglo-African*. He believed that black enrollment would not only boost the war effort, but help black Americans gain the vote. They would "be treated with a wholesome respect," Jay wrote to Sumner, "for the power to punish will in some extent be placed in their hands."[39]

As the months went by, those on the pro-enlistment side were forced to admit that anti-enlisters were right to highlight the administration's cold response to black volunteerism. Douglass grew so irritated with the White House that he called for Congress to act over the president's head. His call included arguments that overlapped with the claims of enlistment skeptics. Black New Yorkers on both sides of the question believed that citizenship should not *depend* on black enrollment. Douglass explained:

> That colored free men are citizens, was never questioned in the earlier days of the Republic. . . . MARTIN VAN BUREN admitted our citizenship in the Convention which framed the Constitution of this State. Judge KENT has strongly asserted our rights as citizens. . . . Mr. SEWARD, consistently with all his well-known principles, and in the face of Judge TANEY, has granted a passport to a free black man of this State [Henry Highland Garnet] to travel about the world as a citizen of the United States. It now remains for the National Congress [to] affirm our complete citizenship . . . by immediately authorizing the enrollment of colored men.[40]

Douglass's language echoed the conversations black New Yorkers had been having about citizenship since the early 1800s, but the insistence on national citizenship was a change in emphasis. The newer claims were a response both to *Dred Scott* and to the realization that the war might reshape the constitutional terrain of federalism. It was the Union that needed men to fight on behalf of a national idea. If Congress acted wisely, then the states could not deny universal black citizenship. After all, black New Yorkers reasoned, the Constitution's Supremacy Clause meant federal law trumped state law when the two conflicted.[41]

At this stage in the war, most elected Republicans were more concerned with respecting the conventional prerogatives of state sovereignty than black

New Yorkers were. Since the founding, the states had exercised great power in determining questions of citizenship, suffrage, and enlistment. Most Republicans were not ready to upend this balance. Some of this caution stemmed from basic political concerns. Issuing federal emancipation decrees or raising colored regiments seemed—at least to moderate Republicans, at least at this juncture—to be foolhardy.

Republican dithering was increasingly frustrating to northern abolitionists. In May 1862, when Lincoln overturned General David Hunter's order freeing all the slaves in the Department of the South (South Carolina, Georgia, and Florida), black editors pounced. Bell lambasted Lincoln in the *Pacific Appeal.* The editor said he understood that Lincoln may have wanted to overturn Hunter's order so that he, Lincoln, "could order that action" from "the highest source." But Lincoln had taken too long to act, and Bell accused the administration of perpetuating slavery. Bell's old friend Robert Hamilton agreed, asserting in the *Anglo-African* that it was time to urge "IMMEDIATE EMANCIPATION" on Congress. The president was "stubborn as a mule."[42]

In September of 1862, better news emerged. Lincoln had issued the Preliminary Emancipation Proclamation. On January 1, 1863, all of the slaves residing in any jurisdiction acting in rebellion against the United States would be "forever free."[43] Although neither the preliminary nor the final proclamation freed that many slaves in practice—since the president's orders applied only to areas outside of Union control—these proclamations nonetheless formed a crucial ideological turning point in the war.

The final proclamation also authorized black men "to garrison forts, positions, stations" and "to man vessels of all sorts." This was not a full sanctioning of black men in combat roles, but the administration was moving in the right direction. Black New Yorkers were energized. At a series of meetings in the spring of 1863, they gathered to rouse enthusiasm for black enrollment. At one "of the largest meetings ever held in this city," Garnet welcomed men, women, and children into Shiloh Church to encourage enlistment. Douglass, J. W. C. Pennington, Robert Hamilton, and Garnet's childhood classmate, George Downing, joined the effort. Garnet said he now supported military service on behalf of the Union with "his whole heart."[44]

Compounding black New Yorkers' satisfaction with the proclamation was Attorney General Edward Bates's affirmation of black Americans' national citizenship. The occasion for Bates's ruling was a small one: a black ship captain was cited for coastal trading without authorization. Was he to be penalized as a citizen of the United States? Bates wrote an opinion repudiating

Dred Scott. Black New Yorkers saw promise in Bates's conclusions. An A.M.E. congregation in Brooklyn resolved "that no person born and residing in the country can, in the nature of things, be exempt from [citizenship]: That as this allegiance is to the general government as the supreme power, [that] government is bound to protect the citizen in his rights." Bates's ruling gave black New Yorkers a chance to articulate their view that "supreme" national citizenship would armor them against state discrimination.[45]

A revolution in the administration's legal and military policies, however, was not the same as a revolution embodied in everyday life. Bates's judgment shaped the administration's approach, but it was not a detailed law or a constitutional amendment. The Emancipation Proclamation, which welcomed black soldiers into the Union forces, said nothing about their citizenship and pay, nor the role of states in raising regiments. Neither document spelled out what emancipation would look like for former slaves in the Confederacy.

The rising generation was distraught, for example, when the administration endorsed a plan that looked remarkably like a gradual abolition program. In January 1863, General Nathaniel Banks, stationed in New Orleans, outlined one of the most closely watched experiments of the war. His General Orders 12 proposed the establishment of "a yearly system of negro labor, which shall provide for the food, clothing, proper treatment, and just compensation for the negroes, at fixed rates of an equitable proportion of the yearly crop." The orders also declared that "those who leave their employers will be compelled to support themselves and families by labor upon the public works." Lincoln did not intervene. The president had only days earlier written to a different general suggesting that states "adopt systems of apprenticeship for the colored people, conforming substantially to the most approved plans of gradual emancipation." Junius C. Morel, the black abolitionist and teacher in Brooklyn, expressed a common view among his peers when he wrote that "General Banks' system of serfdom must be lifted and held up to the gaze and scorn of the nobler portion of mankind." Many black New Yorkers had seen or survived an emancipation process involving years-long terms of service and heavy borrowing from poor law. They did not want to see that again.[46]

Although black New Yorkers found themselves in a complicated relationship with the Lincoln Administration—a feeling they knew well from their long-complicated relationship with their own state government—many embraced the chance to join the war effort on the front lines. Indeed, New Yorkers played an outsized role in organizing and manning the first and most famous black northern regiment of the war, the 54th Massachusetts

Volunteer Infantry. In January 1863, Governor John Andrew of Massachusetts received permission from Secretary of War Edwin Stanton to recruit black troops. Twenty-five-year-old Robert Gould Shaw, a battle-tested son of wealthy white Boston abolitionists, agreed to command the volunteers.

The regiments' organizers turned to influential black men to find recruits. In Albany, the barber William H. Johnson, who had married into a prominent free black family, the Stewarts, enlisted dozens. His wife Sarah's father, John G. Stewart, and William H. Topp, from another long-active political family, served as his "principal assistants." Jermain W. Loguen, the Underground Railroad king of the Burned-Over District, found recruits in Binghamton and Elmira. Garnet did his part from New York City. The oldest man to enroll was Peter Vogelsang of Brooklyn, whose father had been among the most optimistic voices, alongside Garnet, in the 1830s state petition campaign that resulted in jury trials for fugitive slaves and the end of the nine months rule. A literate young man named James Henry Gooding, originally from Troy, signed up in New Bedford, Massachusetts, and agreed to write for the local paper about his exploits. Sojourner Truth's grandson, James Caldwell, enlisted from Michigan.[47]

Douglass was a strong voice on behalf of the 54th. He issued a rousing broadside, crisscrossed western New York in search of recruits, and addressed meetings in New York City and Philadelphia. His sons, Charles and Lewis, enrolled from Rochester and Syracuse. Ultimately, far more men from outside than inside Massachusetts arrived at the training camp near Boston in the spring of 1863. The regiment included 294 men from Pennsylvania, 183 from New York, 155 from Ohio, 133 from Massachusetts, and dozens from other states. In May, in an emotional parade, Shaw and his soldiers marched through Boston on their way to South Carolina. Douglass was there to witness as both statesman and father.[48]

A month later, in their first major battle, the 54th lead the attack on Fort Wagner at the entrance of Charleston Harbor. It was a deadly and unsuccessful assault—over 250 of the regiment's men were captured, wounded, or killed—but news of the men's bravery proved electrifying on the northern home front. Shaw died a martyr. A war correspondent for the New York *Evening Post* informed readers that the black troops had earned "fresh honors" by marching into battle on little sleep. Wounded men expressed "their desire for a speedy recovery" so that they may "try it over again" to "help this war of freedom for all the oppressed."[49]

The soldiers themselves reported similar feelings and scenes to their loved ones. Lewis Douglass wrote to his fiancée, Amelia Loguen (daughter of Jermain), that although exhausted, the men were eager to fight. He was pleased on arriving in South Carolina to have come across fellow upstate New Yorker Harriet Tubman, who had come south to nurse Union soldiers and was captaining "a gang of men who pilot the Union forces *into* the enemy's country." As for the Battle of Fort Wagner, Lewis recounted, "our men fought well" but "it was terrible." He reported on their mutual friends: "DeForrest of your city is wounded, George Washington is missing, Jacob Carter is missing, Chas Reason wounded, Chas Whiting, Chas Creamer all wounded." In closing, he told her to "remember if I die I die in a good cause." Lewis survived the war.[50]

Charles Reason, cited in Lewis's letter, did not. Reason, not to be confused with the African Free School graduate of the same name, was a twenty-year-old farm laborer who had enlisted in Syracuse. In the hospital, before he died, Reason confessed to Dr. Esther Hill Hawks, a New Hampshire physician tending Union troops, that he had been enslaved in Maryland and run away to New York several years earlier. He was fighting "*not* for my country, I never had any, but to gain one." Reason, it seems, had found a toehold in New York. Whoever had employed him no doubt knew or suspected he was a runaway, but gave him work. If Lewis and Amelia both knew Charles, we can infer he made friends with local citizens. "I know what I am fighting for," Reason told Hawks: there was "a man in Maryland who said he owned me" but now he "worked on a farm in Syracuse." New York was an improvement on Maryland, and a country rid of slavery was why he "came to fight." Struggling to survive an amputation, Reason died with the hope of meeting his mother in heaven.[51]

In one of those painful symmetries of historical timing, during the same week that the men of the 54th sacrificed their lives and limbs, antislavery New Yorkers fell victim to one of the worst mobs in American history. For six days in mid-July, rioters in New York City attacked the homes and bodies of black residents and their political friends. The catalyst for this northern violence was Congress's controversial March 1863 Enrollment Act, which included a provision that a rich man could hire a substitute or pay a fee to avoid service. The draft law provoked fury among some white northerners. Immigrants, many of whom were Irish, and the poor in general felt particularly slighted. These were white New Yorkers who competed with black laborers for jobs and tended to vote Democrat. When officials began to implement the draft, the city exploded.

Over the course of a week, the mob targeted representatives of the federal government, white abolitionists, wealthy Republicans, and black New Yorkers. Associating the war with freeing slaves and elevating black citizens, the rioters reserved particular venom for black city dwellers. On the first afternoon, they attacked the Colored Orphan Asylum, an institution founded by two Quaker women, Anna Shotwell and Mary Murray, whose ancestors were members of the New York Manumission Society. The asylum's doctor was James McCune Smith. In the following hours, a black coachman was tortured, hanged, and then dragged down the street by his genitals; a black sailor was attacked by a gang of rioters who took turns assaulting him until he bled to death; a seven-year-old black boy was killed after being separated from his mother in the chaos. Black homes, schools, and businesses were demolished. The riot was quelled after a frantic War Department dispatched Union regiments from Gettysburg to subdue the looting, arson, and murder. All told, 105 people died during the riots, including 11 black New Yorkers.[52]

In the days after the nightmare, black New Yorkers who remained in the city as well as those who fled the terror cataloged their losses and began to put their lives back together. Black newspapers published lists of the people who had lost property. Some—like William Powell and Albro Lyons Sr.—were well-known abolitionist business owners. Most were ordinary people, laborers and cooks and cartmen and seamstresses, who listed $10 or $50 or $80 of ruined belongings. One woman, Maria Barnes, was a teacher at the Colored Orphan Asylum who lost "$251.95 of personal property." To help the victims, a group of white merchants formed a Committee for the Relief of the Colored People, raising $40,000. The committee noted that 5,000 black citizens had taken refuge in local police stations and on the outskirts of the city. Hundreds resettled permanently in Brooklyn and nearby enclaves, including Weeksville, home to a tight community of black landowners and institutions, including the school where Morel taught.[53]

In the short term, New York City after the riots was not the same. Manhattan's black population had been roughly 12,000 at the start of the war and was down to 10,000 by 1865. Yet, as the numbers suggest, the majority remained. In September 1863, the *Pacific Appeal* pointedly reprinted an article from the *Tribune* highlighting black perseverance. "Policemen, soldiers, and citizens," reported Greeley's paper, "speak in the highest terms of the remarkable fortitude" exhibited by black New Yorkers during and after the days when "brutal, bloodthirsty rioters were yelling for their prey." Many black residents must have been traumatized, but events in the year after the riot also demonstrated their resolve to stay where their roots were.[54]

The draft riots provided further evidence to black New Yorkers that they needed robust federal protection, enforceable federal laws, and the opportunity to enlist. The antislavery Republican mayor, George Opdyke, had proved essentially helpless in the face of the mob. The doughface Democratic governor, Horatio Seymour, had allied himself with the rioters.[55] With renewed urgency and justification, antislavery New Yorkers appealed to the federal government to authorize black regiments in their state. Spearheading the effort among white men was the Union League Club. Composed of "five hundred of the wealthiest and most influential gentlemen of the city," including Jay, the club was in some respects a descendent of the New York Manumission Society. Like the Society, the League's preferred method of working on behalf of black New Yorkers was exerting elite influence on politicians, raising funds for white-supervised black institutions, and collaborating with educated black men.[56]

In December 1863, after correspondence between the League and the War Department, Secretary Stanton agreed the club could raise a regiment. "Eminent colored clergymen and leaders" signed handbills calling for soldiers and explaining the "bounties and wages paid to colored men, and the right of their families to the Relief Fund." Statewide, churches handed these materials to their congregants. Garnet, army officers, and League members attended public meetings. By the end the month, black men had signed up for the 20th Colored Regiment in such high numbers that the League asked to raise a second regiment, the 26th. In January, a third regiment, the 31st, was formed. All told, 2,300 black New Yorkers enlisted in the space of weeks. Among them were men who had grown up in the Colored Orphan Asylum.[57]

To provide the new soldiers with resources and morale, the children of gradual abolition relied on their longstanding associational capabilities and friendships. As the troops trained on Rikers Island, east of Manhattan, Garnet served as chaplain and organized an "association of colored women" to visit the men and care for those who fell sick. Garnet had been a student at the African Free School in the 1820s when the female African Dorcas Association provided clothes for the children; it is reasonable to assume that some of the women tending the troops were former classmates of Garnet's and daughters of the women in the Dorcas Association. In February, the *Evening Post* reported that two women crossed the icy river every day to cook for the soldiers. This was yet another instance in which unnamed black women put their time and labor toward a cause that was overtly political.[58]

Sympathetic observers perceived this enlistment enthusiasm to be both a response to the riots and support for the national government. On March 6, 1864, the Republican *New York Times* described the 20th Regiment's parade through the city as the soldiers embarked for Louisiana: "A thousand men, with black skins, and clad and equipped with the uniforms and arms of the United States Government" marched through the streets, receiving "a grand ovation." It was "noble vengeance" for the riots. The black journalist Thomas H. C. Hinton hoped that the rioters "shed tears of repentance." Two weeks later, Jay addressed the 26th as the soldiers departed for South Carolina. Jay's speech to his "fellow-citizens" underscored that the Union owed something to these men. They were now, he said, a "permanent part" of the national polity.[59]

Black enrollment signaled newfound inclusion in the Union, but it also created a fresh reminder of inequality. In a policy that was at once unsurprising and ridiculous, the administration paid black troops less than white troops. The men of the 54th refused wages until the policy changed (which finally occurred in mid-1864). The New Yorker James Henry Gooding wrote a letter to Lincoln that wended its way to the White House through the hands of white sympathizers in New York and Boston. When the war started, Gooding recalled, "the black man begged" to aid "his Country" and was rebuffed. Once allowed to enlist, black men "dyed the ground with blood, in defense of the Union, and Democracy." In some aspects, they were treated equally: Lincoln had insisted black soldiers "be treated according to the usage of war." But "uniformity of treatment" should extend to pay: "We have done a Soldier's Duty. Why Can't we have a Soldier's pay."[60]

This "uniformity of treatment"—the great question of equality before the nation's laws— was a battle black northerners kept fighting.

* * *

In the winter of 1863–1864, it was becoming increasingly clear that the Union would likely win the war. What remained unclear were the terms on which the nation would be reunited. In December, Lincoln offered possible answers in his annual message to Congress. The president's Proclamation of Amnesty and Reconstruction proposed that a state could rejoin the Union once 10 percent of its 1860 vote count pledged an oath of allegiance and promised to uphold wartime emancipation measures. Lincoln's plan suggested, but did not require, that newly reconstructed governments adopt provisions to abolish slavery. The plan did not apply to the border states. Lincoln acknowledged that wartime legislation "with reference to slaves" might be "repealed, modified or held void by Congress, or by a decision of the Supreme Court."[61] None of this was heartening to those who favored immediate nationwide emancipation, federal guarantees of equal citizenship, and a permanent alteration to the federal balance of power.

In the weeks following Lincoln's proposal, more ardent antislavery politicians tried to expand the potential terms of reconstruction. James Ashley, a radical from Ohio, introduced two bills in the House: one for a constitutional amendment banning slavery and one for a stronger reconstruction plan.[62] In suggesting the amendment, Ashley was acknowledging the truth behind Lincoln's comment that wartime legislation was vulnerable to modification or revocation. There was nothing preventing a reunited national legislature from taking action to affirm the prewar federal consensus. The Supreme Court, for its part, faced few legal barriers should its justices choose to rule that Lincoln's wartime actions were unconstitutional.

Committed antislavery New Yorkers were united in pursuing two broad goals in 1864: to make slavery obsolete and to make freedom robust. Jay, for instance, approved of Ashley's efforts but wanted more explicit language in the reconstruction bill. "The 5th section," Jay wrote Ashley, "gives [the vote] to all male citizens of the United States of the age of 21." Jay told Ashley to add language affirming that black men were included in "the designation of citizen" so that no one "should be able to say that he was misled by the phraseology."[63] Here Jay took a lesson from gradual abolition. Black New Yorkers had often been forced to make claims based on their implied citizenship rights because some laws and constitutional provisions used imprecise language. Now Jay urged national legislators to avoid New York's mistakes.

Jay also wrote to Sumner constantly, pestering him to act against potential reversals. "I would like to see [the slaves'] freedom secured beyond all question," Jay wrote, for "Northern Democrats" might succeed in prompting the Supreme Court to "set aside your anti-slavery legislation." Jay also suggested that Republicans increase the number of justices on the court—he wanted to stack the bench with abolitionist judges. Jay's proposal was not entirely outlandish. There had not been a constitutional amendment in fifty years, and Jay had no reason to believe, at least prior to 1864, that three-quarters of the states would ratify an abolition or equal rights amendment. But as the

Union kept winning battles and the public's eagerness for immediate abolition increased, Jay became more optimistic. In February 1864, the rather staid *New York Times* observed "how completely the idea of *gradual* emancipation has been dissipated from the public mind. . . . There seems to be an almost unanimous agreement that immediate emancipation is the wisest." In this changed context, Jay wrote Sumner that the matter of chief importance was the "Amendment abolishing slavery forever." He traveled to Washington to share his ideas with anyone who would listen.[64]

The wider embrace of immediatism and snowballing Republican support for an abolition amendment in 1864 stemmed from a variety of factors: shifting public opinion in the midst of a bitter war, evidence that emancipation was a military necessity, partisan maneuvering in advance of the 1864 presidential election, and signs of the Confederacy's weakness. Black New Yorkers and their white supporters did not single-handedly defeat gradualism. Calls for bolder action came from across the Union and not always for the same reasons. But the children of gradual abolition and their loyal partners had firmly marked out where they stood on the political territory and, in preparing the ground, helped make Lincoln's and his party's growing acceptance of immediatism seem like a reasonable evolution.

This is where the long view of northern emancipation becomes especially revealing: since the late 1700s, black New Yorkers had used a range of strategies, including employing law and politics, to speed up gradual abolition. In the process, they raised the cry of immediatism and made immediate emancipations happen in reality. When New York became "free soil" with the repeal of the nine months law in 1841, a change that black men and women petitioned for, it became even easier for the state's citizens to imagine a government taking slaves out of southern owners' hands; in 1852, in the *Lemmon* case, New York's courts did just that, drawing national fascination and, in proslavery quarters, outrage. In the 1850s and '60s, when black New Yorkers and their white allies spoke in the press and to politicians about immediatism, it was not coming out of blue. In this sense, black children born in the early 1800s influenced how citizens and officials in the 1860s understood what government action with respect to abolition could be. This generation also argued for what should happen alongside abolition—i.e., equal citizenship—since this was also a subject they understood intimately. In the context of wartime "emergencies," they knew there could be changes for "permanent good of the country."[65]

The question of the civic status of former slaves arose in Congress from the moment the new immediatist amendment was introduced. When Senator

Lyman Trumbull's Judiciary Committee proposed a thirteenth amendment modeled on the 1787 Northwest Ordinance—"neither slavery nor involuntary servitude ... shall exist within the United States"—Sumner countered with a version addressing individual rights. Sumner's version did what Jay insisted emancipation laws ought to do: "All persons are equal before the law, so that no person can hold another as a slave; and the Congress shall have power to make all laws necessary and proper to carry this declaration into effect everywhere within the United States." But Sumner failed to convert his colleagues. The Judiciary Committee's final draft kept the free soil rather than the equal rights approach. But for the moment it did not matter. Even the more moderate proposal was too much for Democrats. The House rejected the amendment almost entirely along party lines. The *Albany Evening Journal* conveyed its disgust at Democratic reluctance: "The fact that the Democracy had gone back to slavery like the dog to his vomit has been painfully illustrated!"[66]

On the same day the *Journal* compared Democrats to disgusting dogs, a woman in New York City made plain the need for "equality of all persons before the law." The story of twenty-seven-year-old Ellen Anderson's suit against the Eighth Avenue Streetcar Company is not especially well-known, which may be reason enough to retell it. A cursory read of newspapers from the summer of 1864 indicates that the main drama happened in a streetcar and a courtroom in a matter of days. But a reperiodized account of Anderson and her "laborer" husband's experiences highlights how a deep history of northern emancipation reorients and reinforms wartime stories of citizenship claims. When Anderson insisted that she knew her rights, she echoed the hundreds of black women who had, half a century earlier, told their masters, their children's masters, abolitionist lawyers, and local officials that state or common law was on their side. Like many of them, Anderson was arguably correct in her view about the existing law, but she also, like her foremothers, played a part in making and reforming the law. She appealed to promising but uncertain features of the law and widened possibilities for others. This dynamic was old, and Anderson was consciously playing her own part in it. What made her actions especially potent, however, was the changed context. She claimed a civil right, as a war widow, at the precise moment the nation was entering a ferocious debate over Congress's power to enumerate and guarantee the rights of long-free and newly free black Americans.[67]

In June 1864, the *Tribune* reported, a "ladylike" woman named Ellen Anderson was ordered to leave a streetcar because of her "complexion." She refused. She explained she was "the widow of a soldier, sick, and in sorrow." The conductor, failing to remove her, called for a policeman to assist, "thrusting the woman onto the street." Some passengers, including "several merchants," were alarmed. These witnesses, along with the Union League, helped Anderson take her case to the city's police court, where "eminent counsel" argued that "the charter of the railroad company requires them to afford accommodation to travelers." This was not so different from how women in the 1790s went to John Jay's Manumission Society for legal aid, except that now it was the Union League, helmed in part by Jay's eponymous grandson.[68]

Anderson's lawyers chose the Board of Commissioners of the city police as the forum for a reason. It was a strategic choice: Commissioner Thomas C. Acton was an abolitionist and a member of the Union League himself.[69] Anderson explained what had happened: "I am the widow of Sergeant Anderson, of Co. F, 26th regiment, who died in discharge of his duty at Beaufort, S.C.; I was going up home . . . the conductor came up and said I could not ride in it; I told him I was sick . . . I told him not to touch me; then he went out and brought in a policeman . . . I said [I] had a right to ride there as well as anyone. . . . They pulled me and dragged me. . . . The conductor said he did not care for me or my husband."[70] A merchant witness corroborated Anderson's account. The director of the railroad company—from either conviction or a desire to lay blame on the conductor, or both— testified that "there was no order of the Board excluding colored citizens from the use of the Eighth Avenue Railroad cars."[71]

Commissioner Acton ruled in Anderson's favor. If anyone had broken the peace, it was the police officer and the conductor. There was no law against black people riding in cars. Under the common law, public inns and conveyances chartered to serve the public were duty bound to serve any customer whose conduct did not disrupt the functioning of the business. New York had no statutes to the contrary. Shortly after Acton's verdict, the railroad company issued a public notice: "colored people are allowed to ride in all the cars (both large and small) of this Company." The *Tribune* reported that now only one company in the city discriminated against black passengers, the Sixth Avenue line. But even it caught up with the times. In July, the Sixth Avenue Company removed "Colored People" signs from its cars.[72]

Many white readers would have read about Anderson's case and seen its connections both to the sacrifices black families made for the Union and to the civil rights legislation making its way through Congress as Republicans responded to similar streetcar scrapes in the national capital. In Boston, the *Commonwealth* stressed that Ellen had received a letter from William's captain about his death, speaking "in high terms of her husband's soldierly qualities." The editors were glad that Senator Sumner's efforts to end "similar disgraceful outrages of which Washington, like New York, has often been the scene, have been crowned with success." These sorts of stories framed voters' and lawmakers' increasing attention to civil rights—and Congress's newfound willingness to flex federal muscle—in the 1860s.[73]

But black readers and supporters also saw something less understood by white editors and readers. The Andersons were deeply enmeshed in the web of religious, educational, legal, and benevolent organizations and social circles that, strand by strand, black citizens had woven together since the days when John Teasman, William Hamilton, and Peter Williams Jr. hatched plans to incorporate the African Society for Mutual Relief in 1807. The couple were members of Henry Highland Garnet Tabernacle No. 1 of the Brothers and Sisters of Love and Charity, a mutual aid association. Even the order's name was telling: Garnet was one of the most prominent members of the children of gradual abolition and had received his early education in the African Free School that Teasman had helped build. Among the members of the Garnet Tabernacle was fifty-four-year-old waiter Peter S. Porter, a leader in the Legal Rights Association, which had been cofounded by Thomas L. Jinnings after his daughter Elizabeth's earlier skirmish with the Third Avenue Streetcar Company. When William Anderson died in South Carolina, it was Porter who delivered his eulogy, and, along with two women named Margaret A. Jackson and Harriet Ensley, composed resolutions in the couple's honor to be printed in the *Weekly Anglo-African,* a paper founded and run by the sons of William Hamilton. When Ellen successfully applied for a widow's pension from the U.S. government, Porter and the Reverend Richard Wilson, who had married Ellen and William in the 15th Street African Union Methodist Episcopal Church in 1856, corroborated her marriage and identity. Ellen, moreover, could write.[74]

Put another way, Anderson's legal resistance emerged within the organizational world that Teasman, Hamilton, Williams, and their ilk had built for the children of gradual abolition. Some of the now-adult children were prominent, like Garnet and the Hamiltons; some were locally recognized if not nationally famous, like Porter and Wilson; and some were ordinary folks who were crucial to maintaining the civic fabric, like the Andersons, Jackson, and Ensley. In August 1864, a "grand union of colored citizens of Brooklyn and New York, New Jersey" and "Schools and Churches in the vicinity" gathered to celebrate "the bravery of colored soldiers," the "Progress of Freedom," and "last but not least, the recent great victory of equal rights to coloured people in all the New York city cars." Children sang a song called "'The Golden Rule.'"[75]

In the fall of 1864, the result of these sorts of local organizational efforts in sites across the county manifested in the first national colored convention to occur in nine years. As Lincoln ran for reelection on a platform endorsing the Thirteenth Amendment, black men from seventeen states and Washington, D.C., gathered in Syracuse, New York. Of 129 delegates, 53 were New Yorkers. (George Downing arrived from Rhode Island, where he spent considerable time in the 1860s.) In the convention's "Address to the People of the United States," the delegates insisted upon "complete emancipation, *enfranchisement* and elevation of our race." Although they wanted laws guaranteeing "the right to testify in courts of law; the right to buy, own, and sell real estate; the right to sue and be sued," they placed special emphasis on male suffrage. More basic privileges, they argued, would be weakened without recourse to "a voice in making the laws of the country." The delegates launched a new organization, the National Equal Rights League.[76] For the New Yorkers— Garnet, Downing, Loguen, Robert Hamilton, Stephen Myers, William Rich, among others—the stress on voting had particular historical resonance. They had been raised and encouraged by fathers, teachers, and neighbors who shaped, through their votes, the course of their state's emancipation in the early 1800s. The children of gradual abolition now found their own generation in a similar moment, only nationalized.

It may be partly for this reason that black New Yorkers seemed to pause only briefly for celebration when Congress approved the Thirteenth Amendment in early 1865. The prospect of constitutional, immediate abolition was momentous, but there was no time to lose in ensuring the full measure of freedom was achieved. The sooner the war ended and Confederates reentered federal courts and legislatures, the sooner doors to equal suffrage and to other rights would close. As one editorial, "Action! Action! Action!," explained, "we should not let a little sunshine lull us asleep. . . . We have feasted on celebrations enough to go on and do a little more work."[77]

It was with these thoughts in mind that Garnet delivered a sermon in the National Capitol in February 1865. The long-active child of gradual abolition, who on this occasion became the first black man to speak in the House Chamber, began his address with a warning. The problem was white lawmakers who "knew their duty, but did it not." Channeling the eighteenth-century Quakers who petitioned the New York legislature for antislavery laws, he urged members of Congress to "take up the golden rule." Complete and equal freedom would be achieved when "all invidious and proscriptive distinctions shall be blotted from our laws, whether they be constitutional, statute, or municipal laws. When emancipation shall be followed by enfranchisement, and all men holding allegiance to the government shall enjoy every right of American citizenship.... When, in every respect, he shall be equal before the law."[78] The federal government should step in where the states had failed, promoting and enforcing a new construction of national citizenship.

Garnet's wary concern about the status of black freedom in 1865, as well as his prescriptions for a robust alternative, derived from experience. Garnet had started his life enslaved in Maryland, developed his politics as a schoolboy in gradual abolition New York, received aid from Quakers when his former masters tried to reenslave his family, spent years as a Presbyterian minister fighting for equality in the legislature and courts of his adopted state, joined antislavery political parties, and relocated to the nation's capital during the Civil War. He was cognizant of the complicated relationship between federalism and black liberty. Individual states, left to their own devices, had the power to undo or prevent progress. He knew that Black Codes—state acts restricting black rights—existed and would only worsen, especially in the South. An amendment abolishing slavery that did not specify the rights, privileges, and status of formerly enslaved people would lead to disappointment. The Thirteenth Amendment in this regard was worryingly similar to New York's 1799 abolition law. Black Americans in the age of national emancipation would have to insist on specific legal correctives to slavery and quasi freedom, and officials would have to make these remedies reliable and permanent in practice.

Black Americans young and old, northern and southern, educated and poor, received Garnet's advice with enthusiasm in 1865. His address in the Capitol was published by local black leaders. Garnet's childhood friend and sometime antagonist, James McCune Smith, wrote an introduction that was part glowing biography, part history of gradual abolition. Garnet himself went on the road. In Philadelphia, he lectured at the Banneker Institute on the "progress of freedom"; in New York, he argued at the Cooper Institute that "the rights and privileges so dear to every American citizen" should "be equally secured to all" and that black men were "as fitted to vote as the foreigner who came to our shores ignorant of our language, our customs, or our Government"; in Norfolk, he told fifteen hundred black schoolchildren about "his boyhood" and promoted a tract titled *Equal Suffrage*; in Alexandria, he addressed a crowd about "the right of suffrage"; in Cincinnati, Garnet "preached" on "political equality"; in Louisville, he "spoke to the little ones with regard to their future usefulness" and delivered "spicy remarks" to their parents; and in Chicago, he told black Illinoisans that the time would come when "they *would* vote, when they would send their black brothers to halls of Congress."[79]

Black northerners' demands for federal intervention proved all the more justified as northern states rejected equal suffrage measures in the months after the war ended. In the fall of 1865, white voters in Connecticut, Wisconsin, and Minnesota rejected proposals to give black men the vote. William W. Grimes, an itinerant A.M.E. minister who had recruited for the Massachusetts 54th regiment, observed from Albany that Republicans in the various states were shaky in their commitment to voting rights. As for the Democrats, well, Grimes knew his local history: "colored men [in New York] did vote until the Democrats disfranchised them in 1821; and in 1846 the Democrats defeated the equal suffrage bill,—and in 1860, after the Republican Legislature had passed the equal suffrage bill, the Democrats defeated it."[80]

Drawing on practices going back to the very early republic, but with the venue shifting from state to national, a group of prominent black northerners decided to plant a delegation in Washington to advocate for their interests. In December 1865, the *New York Times* reported that Douglass, George and Thomas Downing, Charles Reason, and J. Sella Martin would join with regional peers to "labor with those Senators and members of the House of Representatives who may be willing to give the black man his rights as a freeman." At a meeting at Garnet's Shiloh church in New York, the group announced plans to raise $10,000 to fund the Washington mission. The *Tribune* approvingly dubbed the men an "Outside Congress," and considered "their election" more "dignified and creditable than those of average Members."[81]

The Outside Congress arrived in Washington just as the U.S. Congress was considering a number of critical measures. In January 1866, Senator Trumbull introduced a civil rights bill in order to define the freedom secured by the Thirteenth Amendment. The bill affirmed the citizenship of black people and guaranteed equal access to some rights. Trumbull was clear, however, that such rights did not include the vote, which was a so-called political right. The bill was "intended to carry out a constitutional provision, and guarantee to every person of every color the same civil rights," which included the right to the fruits of one's labor, to contract, to buy and sell, and to enjoy liberty and happiness.[82] As Trumbull promoted his bill, Representative John Bingham of

Ohio simultaneously urged that a similar set of protections be incorporated into the Constitution via a fourteenth amendment. This would both ensure the constitutionality of Trumbull's bill as well as stymie any future efforts by Congress or the Supreme Court to dismantle civil rights legislation.[83]

Radical Republicans wanted to go farther. The House, for example, managed to pass a bill granting black men in D.C. the right to vote. In the Senate, Sumner gave a two-day speech objecting to the clause in the proposed fourteenth amendment that would allow states to disfranchise black men (and lose related proportional representation as a result). This was not, Sumner thought, the time for carrots. He proposed instead a constitutional stick: "there shall be no denial of rights, civil or political, on account of color or race . . . all persons [in the U.S.] shall be equal before the law, whether in the court-room or at the ballot box." Echoing Garnet's recent speech, Sumner noted that "Emancipation itself will fail without Enfranchisement."[84]

The Outside Congress wrote to Sumner praising his work "in favor of justice and equal suffrage." As representatives of the northern free black polity, they reassured him that he had affirmed "the first and complete wish of the colored man." Garnet, who attended the speech in person, expressed the "gratitude of my entire race" and urged Sumner to publish the address, which he did. Knowing Sumner was busy, Garnet "refrained from calling in person." Downing, who developed an especially close relationship with Sumner, wrote to him about the D.C. suffrage bill. On behalf of "colored persons," Downing inquired whether Sumner thought the "bill granting the elective franchise to the col'd people of the District of Columbia" could pass the Senate and survive a veto by President Johnson. Garnet and Downing were not in elected office, but as they employed the same strategies that their forefathers and they themselves had used in the New York legislature, they influenced the lawmaking process in Washington.[85]

In the latter half of the year, the Outside Congress and their constituents saw movement. By summer, Congress had passed the 1866 Civil Rights Act (over President Johnson's veto) and sent the Fourteenth Amendment (which included language similar to Trumbull's bill and not Sumner's more suffrage-friendly ideas) to the states for ratification. In January 1867, in part due to the lobbying of local black citizens, Congress enacted universal manhood suffrage in Washington. To some, it was a heartening example of federal power on behalf of black rights. To Democratic naysayers, it proved reason to amplify cries of congressional overreach, the deterioration of local control, and the dangers of race mixing. In the turbulent period of presidential

Reconstruction, the local, state, and national politics of racial equality clashed and reverberated as Congress wrestled over how much the contours of federalism would change.[86]

Indeed, much was still happening at the state level. At the same moment Congress was acting on suffrage in D.C., black New Yorkers watched their state replay the 1821, 1846, and 1860 debates over equal suffrage yet again. In late 1866, after the state electorate voted in favor of a constitutional convention, the question of voting rights rose immediately as legislators considered whether black men would vote for delegates on equal terms. Despite Republican efforts, the legislature voted the measure down. According to the *Tribune*, the problem was not that Republicans disliked equal suffrage, but that Democrats would use the legislature's preemptive granting of equal suffrage to rally their base in advance of the delegate election.[87]

In New York City, Charles Reason, Garnet, and Downing, along with Erastus D. Culver—the former Whig state legislator and lawyer in the *Lemmon* case—gathered to prepare petitions to the state convention. William H. Johnson, the Albany barber who had recruited for the 54th, oversaw similar efforts on behalf of the Colored Citizens' State Central Committee. The black signatories, appealing to their patriotism during the war, asked the convention to "vote for impartial manhood suffrage for the State of New York."[88]

The state constitutional convention, which began in June 1867 and ended in February 1868, proved a disaster for proponents of equal suffrage and for Republicans trying to control the larger narrative of national reconstruction. At first, prospects had looked bright. The Republicans won 97 of 160 seats. Convention president William A. Wheeler opened the proceedings by announcing that "every man" of "whatever race" was "entitled to the full employment of every right appertaining to the most exalted citizenship." Greeley, who had supported equal suffrage for thirty years in the *Tribune*, was head of the Committee on the Right of Suffrage, which quickly proposed to "strike out all discriminations based on color." To stymie momentum, the Democrats issued a minority report arguing for a separate ballot measure on suffrage.[89] They warned that if New York adopted equal suffrage, the "example" would encourage Congress to guarantee formerly enslaved men in the South the vote as well, a menacing extension of federal power. Aided by the partisan press, the Democratic campaign for "separate submission" gathered more steam after the Republicans lost badly in the 1867 state election. Democrats boasted they won because they had the true interest of white voters and American federalism at heart.[90]

Wary national Republicans watched these events unfold from their perch in Congress. The same summer of New York's constitutional convention, Sumner introduced a bill "securing the elective franchise to colored citizens." He noted that the March 1867 Military Reconstruction Act had, for the moment, granted suffrage to black men in the former Confederacy. Anticipating objections from moderates that such regulation was warranted in the "rebel states" but not the "loyal" ones, Sumner relied on the Constitution's republican guarantee clause, the Article IV privileges and immunities clause (which had been similarly wielded by New York restrictionists during the Missouri Crisis), and the Thirteenth Amendment's stipulation that Congress could abolish slavery with appropriate legislation. Arguably—and Garnet had recently made the very argument in the very building—abolishing slavery included enfranchising black men. Congress, in the Sumner and Garnet view, could both fix the problematic legacies of northern emancipation and ensure a just Confederate reconstruction at the same time. In addition to constitutional arguments, there were practical ones. Enfranchised black men in Connecticut, Pennsylvania, and New York, noted Sumner, would mean tens of thousands of new voters in favor of the Union.[91]

Sumner's gambit failed in 1867. But events north, south, and west slowly convinced enough white Republicans that the traditional deference to states on suffrage was undermining the democratic potential of Reconstruction, suppressing votes they needed, and inflaming violence against former slaves, free black northerners, and white Republicans in hostile areas.

For good reason, histories of Reconstruction focus on the vicious riots, bloody rampages, and sexual violence against black southerners. Incidents of cruelty against formerly enslaved people occurred regularly, in daily negotiations over labor arrangements and in the routine exercise of rights. Elections were especially fraught. White northerners, even the more complacent ones, were jolted by the accounts of brutality and havoc. The rise of the Ku Klux Klan prompted members of Congress, even the initially reluctant ones, to support more federal intervention in the South on behalf of black safety and general law and order.[92]

Events in the North, however, also captured the attention of national Republicans. Election chaos in New York City proved most alarming. In December 1868, after General Ulysses S. Grant won the presidency without New York's electoral votes, a group of Union League members, including Greeley and Jay, petitioned Congress for help. They argued that a majority of the state's legal voters had cast ballots for Grant but their electoral will had been "subverted by wholesale fraud." New York's Democratic governor, Horatio Seymour, had won the state's popular vote for president by 1 percent. The state's Republicans had evidence proving that the margin of victory stemmed from nonexistent and illegal voters. The petitioners provided data showing how "irregular and illegal naturalization" and "fraudulent papers" had resulted in ward-level vote totals that could not possibly be accurate. They accused various Democrats, including William "Boss" Tweed and Samuel Tilden, of enabling "terrorism and violence" toward the honest men who had challenged the disorder. The petitioners asked that these "evils" be "remedied by national legislation in pursuance of the national Constitution."[93]

Republicans in Congress took the Union League's request seriously, creating a Select Committee on Alleged New York Election Frauds. The chairman of the committee, William Lawrence of Ohio, oversaw hours of witness testimony in New York City and Washington in the early weeks of 1869. The committee appointed John I. Davenport, a young lawyer active in the Union League, as clerk of the commission.

The resulting Lawrence Report, released in February 1869, opened by drawing connections between the "outrages, robberies, and murders" committed on "loyal people" in the South and the "appalling" problems in New York.[94] Although there were differences between dynamics in the former Confederacy and in the Empire State—New York was on the winning side of the war, the majority of its black population had been free for years, an especially high percentage of white voters were recent immigrants—the report made a convincing case that parts of the North were as badly in need of federal oversight as parts of the South.

The testimony of John J. Mullen, for example, exposed the methods of fraud, the prevalence of violence, and the racial dynamics of election politics in New York City. An Irish immigrant, Mullen had lived in city for twenty-eight years but never naturalized. He described how a Democratic grocer he knew enticed him to register to vote ten different times in various districts, where he encountered little resistance from corrupt clerks. Aldermen handed out naturalization papers like free candy. Newly registered voters would receive "$2 . . . every time they voted." Mullen explained that his plan the whole time was "to find out what kind of swindle was going on, in order that I might expose them." He reported his intel to the superintendent of police a few days before the November election. On reading about the Lawrence committee in early 1869 in the *Herald*, Mullen again came forward. (Given the number of addresses and names that Mullen provided, as well as evidence in the Lawrence report and local press, it seems likely that Mullen was describing real events. Less clear are his motives. Was he really risking his life in the name of election integrity? Maybe! Or maybe there was a personal neighborhood beef?)[95]

Mullen's testimony also provided insight into black New Yorkers' grasp of election culture. When asked if he had suffered repercussions for reporting the fraud, Mullen replied that, recently, when walking with his wife, "I got a blow that knocked me senseless. I heard a voice singing out: 'That is the son of a bitch who sold us! Kill him!'" After his wife screamed for help, "two colored women threw themselves on top of me, and two colored boys shouted 'murder!'" When Mullen regained consciousness, he and his wife were at the police office. "These colored women," he concluded, "were the only persons to save me." Local Democratic officials, whom Mullen named, refused to prosecute his attackers, even though he knew who they were.[96]

The black women's physical intervention recalled earlier forms of protective politics. Black women had thrown their bodies between runaway slaves and their predators for decades. This was part of how ordinary women expressed their own political commitments. In Mullen's case, two unnamed women had saved a man exposing election fraud. Everyone involved in the melee understood that Mullen had challenged a party whose policies and rhetoric disavowed black equality. The black women and children who came to his aid could not vote, but they knew which side they were on. Their physical courage played a small but direct role in conversations in Congress about the need to ensure fair and peaceful elections.

Stories of partisan violence and voter suppression aimed at black men also appeared in the report. A man named Joseph Johnson from Orange County testified that he had voted for the Republican ticket in the recent election. In this rural part of the state, the resulting controversy stemmed from the nature of his property ownership. Black men in New York still had to own $250 of property to vote in 1868. The white man who had sold Johnson and his father-in-law their land, which they paid for in installments under an informal agreement, told a local Democratic lawyer that "they had no right to vote" (presumably because the black men did not own the property outright). Johnson's account was evidence that his vote was under threat by local Democrats insinuating he did not meet franchise requirements.[97] How could Republican lawmakers hear stories like Mullen's and Johnson's and not act? Whether for moral or practical reasons, they needed safer, fairer elections. The report recommended a new law to prevent frauds at elections.

As the Lawrence committee gathered its evidence, a delegation of black leaders from New York joined counterparts from across the country at a convention in Washington. The purpose was to address the "exclusion of colored citizens from the exercise of the elective franchise and other citizen rights." Promoting the new balance of federal power, the men argued that the Fourteenth Amendment should be interpreted to guarantee male suffrage in the states. Downing, who chaired the business committee, led a group to visit the House Judiciary Committee. The lobbyists reported giving a "speech on the subject of State rights and suffrage." Congressman Bingham, author of the Fourteenth Amendment, "assured them that Congress was fully alive to the question of equal rights, and would not fail to take action."[98]

Bingham's reassurance was real. Republicans were pushing for a fifteenth amendment that would forbid states from abridging voting rights on the basis of color. The amendment was certainly about the freedom of former slaves in the South, but it was also about black northerners. As Republican senator Oliver Morton of Indiana noted, "the great body of men upon whom the right of suffrage is to be conferred by this amendment are men who have long been free, who live in the northern States—not men just emerged from slavery, but a comparatively educated class living throughout the entire North." The *Tribune* put it less delicately: "the United States should have the power to protect all the People of this country from local tyranny, degradation and vassalage." In February, Congress approved the amendment and sent it to the states. New York's legislature, now in Republican hands, ratified quickly, along party lines, in April. Fifteen more states had to ratify before the amendment became operative.[99]

That summer, a young black woman in western New York named Maud Molson reminded audiences that their state had an antislavery past worth celebrating and that "impartial suffrage" was the goal of the season. In June, she gave a "strong and eloquent" speech at the state convention of colored men in Binghamton, where the delegates resolved that the war had been fought both for the overthrow of slavery and for "the recognition of our own claims to citizenship in these United States." Black New Yorkers' ongoing work included not only advocating for the Republican Party and the not-yet-ratified fifteenth amendment, but sparking political conversations in "social circles around the fireside" among every "man, woman, and child." In July, in Mohawk, Molson spoke at an anniversary celebration of the 1827 general abolition, where her remarks were "enthusiastically received." Several weeks later, she traveled to Pennsylvania for a meeting of the National

Equal Rights League, where she spoke "for nearly an hour" in an "appeal for 'impartial suffrage,' in which she included *female* as well as *negro* suffrage." Next, she lectured at the Wesleyan Union Church in Harrisburg, where she explained that females had "as great a claim to vote as the men." Molson seems to have thread the needle between advocating for the ratification of the fifteenth amendment as it was and prodding listeners not to leave women out of the larger moment. The men who repeatedly gave her platforms to speak that summer, including her future husband, did not always agree with her on female suffrage, but they did not silence her, either. Many of those men would have been hard-pressed, given the long history of black women's legal and political work in New York, to deny that their wives, sisters, daughters, and female friends had been vital to the progress of emancipation and the day-to-day exercising of black citizenship. Molson's embrace by the "hundreds" who heard her and by myriad editors across the Burned-Over District are a reminder of women's civic influence at a critical moment in the history of American rights. The history of gradual abolition helps explain why Molson's public presence and arguments were welcomed that summer.[100]

For Molson and for all black New Yorkers, the ensuing fall election of 1869 was fraught not only because of the unresolved issues of voter fraud outlined in the Lawrence report, but because the state electorate would now cast ballots for or against the new state constitution and the "separately submitted" question of whether to end racialized property requirements. New Yorkers had a chance to constitutionalize equal male suffrage while the Fifteenth Amendment's fate hung in the balance. In the days leading up to the election, a group of black clergymen, including Charles B. Ray, alongside longtime civic leaders William Powell, John Zuille, and Peter Downing (George's brother), issued an appeal. Calling themselves "citizens of the State" whom "it had pleased God to make black," they asked "to vote as men." They paid taxes as men and died in war as men. The property requirement had been imposed in 1821, when "New York was still a slaveholding state." Denying equal suffrage perpetuated the "*spirit*" of slavery.[101]

One of the appeal's signers, the Methodist minister William F. Butler, had just encountered precisely the sort of terrorizing street violence that threatened to upend the November 1869 election. Butler, born in Nova Scotia and new to the city, was fast becoming a crucial figure in the two-pronged movement for equal rights legislation in the state and in the nation. According to the *New York Times*, Butler and a clergyman friend had been "attacked by stones by a band of Irish laborers" from the Hudson River Depot for no discernable reason other than their race. Citing ongoing patterns of "negro hate" by the Irish, the *Times* was pleased when the accused laborers were fired from their job. But this sort of punishment was not exactly helpful in dampening the ethnic, racial, class, and partisan tensions that roiled the city's politics, especially around election day.[102]

On November 2, 1869, New York's largely white electorate rejected the new constitution and, by a vote of 282,403 to 249,802, refused to remove the $250 race-based property requirement from the state constitution. This margin of defeat was far smaller than it had been in 1860 (when equal suffrage lost 345,791 to 197,889), but some white voters' distaste for black political equality was clearly alive and well.[103]

In short, New York's legislature approved an equal suffrage amendment to the federal constitution during the same year that the state's voters rejected a similar amendment to the state constitution. In a sense, this outcome confirmed the usefulness of strategies that the children of gradual abolition had long employed: direct appeals to legislatures. It mattered, of course, what voters did; after all, they were the ones who elected lawmakers in the first place, and, on occasion, the electorate voted in the interest of black Americans. But the rising generation, as a racialized minority, had long realized that when it came to questions about their rights, they tended to fare better when legislators, executives, and judges with antislavery proclivities made the decisions. This is one reason why they remained so attuned to what national politicians and jurists were doing during the war, why they cultivated relationships with influential white citizens, and why they tracked the composition of legislative and judicial bodies. Secession had resulted in the presence of a unique majority of antislavery politicians in Washington. These lawmakers had the potential to enact reforms that even the voters who had put them there might not have enacted were the choice submitted to them directly.[104]

In the political whiplash so characteristic of the era, better news appeared in early 1870. In February, the twenty-eighth state ratified the Fifteenth Amendment. That same month, Representative Bingham introduced a bill to address atrocities in the South and election fraud in the North. Drawing in part on the Lawrence report, the proposed legislation became the "Act to Enforce the Right of Citizens of the United States to vote in Several States of this Union," which President Grant signed into law in May. Later referred to as the First Force Act or the Ku Klux Klan Act, the statute's opening clauses explained the need to protect voters' poll access regardless of "race, color, or previous condition of servitude." The latter clauses, as the New York press was quick to note, addressed the sorts of fraudulent activities that Mullen, Johnson, and countless other New Yorkers had reported in 1869. Federal courts and officials were empowered to enforce the new regulations. The Democratic *Herald* griped that the Force Act was like an overbearing "nurse" charged with taking care of the new "child" known as "the fifteenth amendment."[105]

That spring, celebrations of the Fifteenth Amendment in New York reflected how, within neighborhoods and families, the vote had never been simply about the individual rights of black men. There remained a collective, cross-gender, intergenerational understanding of the vote's import. This culture was at once hierarchical and inclusive. Families remembered when male relatives voted on equal terms in the early 1800s and shaped the passage of critical state antislavery legislation. To be sure, there were black women who wanted the vote, but for the moment, more black voters, even if only male ones, augured potential changes in daily life.[106]

When news of ratification reached New York City, one black woman wrote a letter to the *Tribune* expressing her gratitude that "we are to-day a free people, and know that henceforth and forever we shall enjoy all rights and privileges equally with other true citizens of the United States." The boys and girls at the Mulberry Street Colored Grammar School—the same location where Garnet, Smith, Reason, Downing and their friends had studied together—honored the day with singing and recitations. Their teacher, Rebecca Samuels, read President Grant's special message to Congress, in which he explained that, "the fifteenth amendment to the Constitution completes the greatest civil change and constitutes the most important event that has occurred since the nation came into life." Later that day, black citizens poured into the A.M.E. Zion Church. Charlotte Harper, also a teacher, "read the official proclamation announcing the ratification." The gathering prayed, sang, listened to a sermon, and cheered a Quaker abolitionist.[107]

William F. Butler likewise celebrated, but in a sermon he delivered at his Methodist church, he stressed that the Fifteenth Amendment was not the end of the struggle, but rather a tool in the ongoing campaign for full civil rights. This was not the time to "fold arms, sit down, and all would go smoothly on." As "American citizens," they "must have education and equal rights."[108]

As the new amendment came to life, both Butler and William H. Johnson of Albany fashioned themselves as spokesmen on civil rights and welcomed their wives, Elizabeth and Sarah, into the work. Strategically, this made sense: protective husbands with respectable wives made black men appear even more sympathetic within an American bourgeois culture that worshipped the family. Both men were adept at placing sympathetic stories in the press. In a conversation with a *Times* journalist, Butler explained how he and his wife had entered an "ice-cream saloon" and were told "that they were not in the habit of accommodating colored people." In a different instance, he found that he could order dinner at a particular restaurant on Sixth Avenue when it was empty, but not when "full of white people." Butler also stressed problems related to work; laboring men and women were denied equal access to employment. In Albany, Johnson reported a story about buying tickets to see a play in the dress circle at the Opera House. His assumption was that as "an orderly, respectable colored citizen, with his family," he would face no problem. However, his "wife, child, and self were forcibly ejected." After Johnson sued, a compromise was reached: the defendant "agreed to do business in the future upon equal rights principles." Thereafter, at least for a time, all Albany theaters desegregated. Like Ellen Anderson, the Johnsons had appealed to the common law—licensed theaters were supposed to serve respectable members of the public—to effect changes on the ground in advance of legislation. Playing crucial roles, Mrs. Anderson, Mrs. Butler, and Mrs. Johnson all appeared in the press as proper wives deserving of the same protection from men and from laws as respectable white women were afforded.[109]

Radical Republicans in Washington were aware of the problems that black Americans like the Butlers, the Johnsons, and Ellen Anderson faced. As the Fifteenth Amendment celebrations died down, Sumner introduced a bill "supplementary" to the 1866 Civil Rights Act. It proposed "to secure equal rights in railroads, steamboats, public conveyances, hotels, licensed theaters, houses of public entertainment, common schools," as well as on juries, in churches, and in cemeteries. Although the bill went nowhere that session, Congress did move to further protect elections in cities like New York. Two Radical Republican New Yorkers, Noah Davis in the House and Roscoe Conkling in the Senate, shepherded the 1870 Naturalization Act—at the time also called the Election Act—into law at lightning speed. With the intent of further dampening fraudulent voting in New York City, especially by Democratic Irish immigrants, Davis, Conkling, and their allies pieced together a bill that extended federal control over naturalization and empowered U.S. circuit judges and marshals to appoint supervisors and deputies. The final clause of the act, which Grant signed into law in July, overturned part of the Naturalization Act of 1790 by extending to "aliens of African nativity" the right to become U.S. citizens.[110]

Three months later, white and black reformers met in New York City to strategize on achieving the sort of stronger civil rights legislation that Sumner had recently proposed in his "supplement." In a sign that congressional enfranchisement measures were working, black lawmakers, including Texas State Senator George Thomas Ruby and Mississippi State Senator J. J. Spelman, joined the meeting. George Downing meditated on the connections between slavery and civil rights. Slavery "still has an existence," he argued, if his color meant that he could not enter railcars, steamboats, hotels, or schools on equal terms. He noted that "from boyhood days," he had been active against this "caste" system. He urged men to use their vote in support of "Senator Sumner's bill supplementary to the civil rights bill." Butler agreed that, "armed with the ballot," they should insist on their "just rights."[111]

In November 1870, black men went to the polls with the Fifteenth Amendment and the two new national election laws on their side for the first time. In New York City, where elections had been so dysfunctional, the federal government swarmed the city with supervisors and marshals. The *Tribune* listed the places where men could register to vote under the new rules, reminded readers that "no property requirement is now required of colored men," and explained that the July 1870 Naturalization/Election Act authorized Judge Lewis B. Woodruff of the U.S. Circuit Court to name election supervisors. John I. Davenport, clerk of the Lawrence committee, was appointed U.S. Commissioner to oversee registration and voting. He swore in inspectors, one from each party in each ward, as well as dozens of deputy marshals, including black men. The *World* noted that fifty black men in the Seventh District registered safely under the eyes of black deputy marshals who stood at the door. When election day came, the Democrats edged the Republicans statewide, but even Republicans acknowledged that the election had been cleaner. In retrospect, black Americans were entering a period of robust participation in the nation's democracy, including at the polls, that would not last in many places outside the North.[112]

Black New Yorkers made up only a tiny portion of the state electorate—15,000 male voters in a state where almost 800,000 men cast ballots. They were aware of this fact. They planned to use a combination of petitioning, lobbying, balance-of-power voting, relationship building, and public appeals to achieve their aims. Just as they had been persistent in campaigns for school access, jury trials, and free soil legislation in the 1830s and '40s, they now began a multiyear effort to secure new civil rights acts in New York and the United States.[113]

In 1871, Garnet began to wield the same skills he had used in Albany in the 1840s in Washington. In December, from Bleecker Street in Manhattan, Garnet wrote Sumner on behalf of "your colored fellow citizens of New York," who were "with you to a man in your efforts to obtain the passage of your 'Civil Rights Bill.'" Garnet was preparing petitions and asked Sumner to help him draft language "best adapted to the purpose." This was the same Garnet who, three decades earlier, had explained to the *Colored American* that during state lawmaking sessions, "previous to my presenting the petitions, on every occasion, I have taken the opportunity of conversing with some influential member, and have not failed to receive his word, promising his favor." The same month Sumner heard from Garnet, he introduced to the Senate a "petition from a large number of colored citizens of Brooklyn." A few weeks later, black citizens from Albany sent another: "without [Sumner's bill] the thirteenth, fourteenth, and fifteenth amendments to the Constitution fall short of their full effects." As the language of the Albany petition suggests, the signatories saw Sumner's bill as part of a larger national redefinition of freedom, which included protecting the rights of former slaves in the South.[114]

As they had since the late 1700s, black New Yorkers also looked to their state legislature. On the upper Hudson, Johnson replaced Garnet as the leading state-based lobbyist and petition organizer. In the spring of 1872, he helped organize a Republican state convention in Troy, across the river from his Albany home. "Colored citizens" of Brooklyn, including 54th Massachusetts veteran Peter Vogelsang, elected delegates in advance of the wider meeting. Vowing to support Grant and his wing of the Republican Party in the upcoming election, the Brooklynites committed to backing lawmakers who supported both "civil rights" and "justice to the people in the Southern States." Indeed, black New Yorkers were in an unusual partisan position that year, since Horace Greeley had broken off to lead the "Liberal" wing of Republicans, the result of an intraparty revolt aimed at fixing corruption in the Grant administration and promoting conciliation toward former Confederates in hopes of attracting southern white voters. Although black New Yorkers acknowledged that Greeley had long been their ally, the vast majority preferred Grant, even when Sumner joined the Greeley wing.[115]

At the Troy convention, the delegates affirmed the majority's preference for Grant. Butler, representing New York City, proposed a permanent state organization, the Colored State Committee, to advocate for black Republican interests. Johnson was elected president of the committee. The junior officers included men from the farther-flung counties of Erie, Steuben, and

Tompkins. William Rich, the longtime school supporter from Troy, was named treasurer. A few weeks later, Johnson and Butler—the latter as a formal delegate—attended the Republican National Convention in Philadelphia, where Grant was renominated. The party included a reassuring plank on its platform: "Complete liberty and exact equality in the enjoyment of all civil, political, and public rights should be established throughout the Union, by efficient and appropriate state and federal legislation." On his way back home to Albany, Johnson stopped off in Brooklyn to assure a political meeting that black southerners would swing for Grant.[116]

Less than a year later, after Grant romped his way to a second term in the White House and New York Republicans swept all state offices and the legislature, a Westchester assemblyman named James Husted introduced a civil rights bill drafted by Johnson on behalf of the Colored State Committee. Johnson's model legislation proposed that "no citizen of this state" would be denied, on account of race or previous condition of servitude, equal access to inns, common carriers, theaters, cemeteries, or common schools. Any reference to "white" in state law would be "repealed." The supportive *Troy Daily Times* noted in a refrain typical of Republicans trying to stave of Democratic race-baiting that the "proposed measure has nothing to do with social distinctions" or what people did in private. In New York City, black Republicans including Butler, Zuille, and Charles Reason gathered to discuss how best to support the bill and to coordinate with the state committee. Peter S. Porter, who had championed Ellen Anderson in her streetcar suit in 1864, advised "measuring their strength in numbers." Over the following weeks, petitions arrived in the legislature from across the state. Johnson remained in close connection with the "officers, reporters, and attachés of both Houses." The press noted how similar the New York bill was to Sumner's unpassed supplemental civil rights bill.[117]

In April 1873, the New York civil rights bill, backed by large Republican majorities, passed the legislature. Governor John A. Dix, the same man who as school commissioner in the 1830s had ruled that black teachers could work in white common schools and that black citizens could vote in school elections, signed the bill.[118]

On the other side of the continent, Bell published an account of the resulting celebrations in New York City in the San Francisco *Elevator*, the successor of the *Pacific Appeal*. The event's headliners made up a who's who of state leaders. Many had been advocating for civil rights since their childhoods alongside Bell and the Jenningses at the African Free School. Garnet, Butler,

Powell, Charles Reason, and Alexander Crummell were there. Johnson came down from Albany and Husted traveled in from Westchester. Professor John Mercer Langston of the brand-new Howard University came up from Washington. Governor Dix, Senator Conkling, Gerrit Smith, Frederick Douglass, and William Lloyd Garrison sent letters to be read aloud. Sumner, whom the organizers invited, was ill, but cheered in absentia. Johnson's speech acknowledged a fact that was often submerged in the male-centered political meetings of the postwar period: the civil rights law mattered to women and children as much as to men. Relatedly, the *Tribune* noted that the festivities included an "unusually large proportion" of "ladies." Was Sarah Johnson, who had helped her husband desegregate the Albany theaters, there? Was Elizabeth Jennings? Or Ellen Anderson? What about the women and children who had saved election whistleblower John Mullen from his attackers? It is entirely possible. These women and children did not have the same public voices as the men making speeches, but they had been part of the interactive politics in streets and businesses that amplified the need for the law that everyone was applauding.[119]

Women and children were especially invested in the 1873 Civil Rights Act because of its effects on schools, which had been sites of female and youth politics and legal organizing for at least two generations. Black schools across the state were almost uniformly coeducational, and many employed female teachers. Mothers and grandmothers, like Phebe Ray in Rochester, had taken energetic roles in school campaigns and knew their own place in the longer story. The polls may have been a mostly adult male reserve, but schools were not.

In the wake of the 1873 law's passage, some colored schools stayed open, including in Brooklyn and Manhattan, where local black communities had put decades of work into building their own institutions and where white school boards were content to keep institutions segregated. But school boards in Newburgh, Albany, Geneva, Schenectady, Troy, Hudson, and Poughkeepsie closed their black schools, either allowing or continuing to allow black children into white schools. In Poughkeepsie, it was two sisters, Marietta Rhodes, age 9, and Josephine Rhodes, age 15, who integrated the white schools. Their new principal, Lydia Vail, set the tone for the experiment by meeting Marietta and Josephine on the sidewalk on their first day. Vail took the girls' hands and led them together into a school room. At the midday break, according to the *Poughkeepsie Eagle*, "no one had left because of the presence of the Civil Rights representatives." During afternoon recess, "two little white girls approached the youngest colored girl and asked her to go out

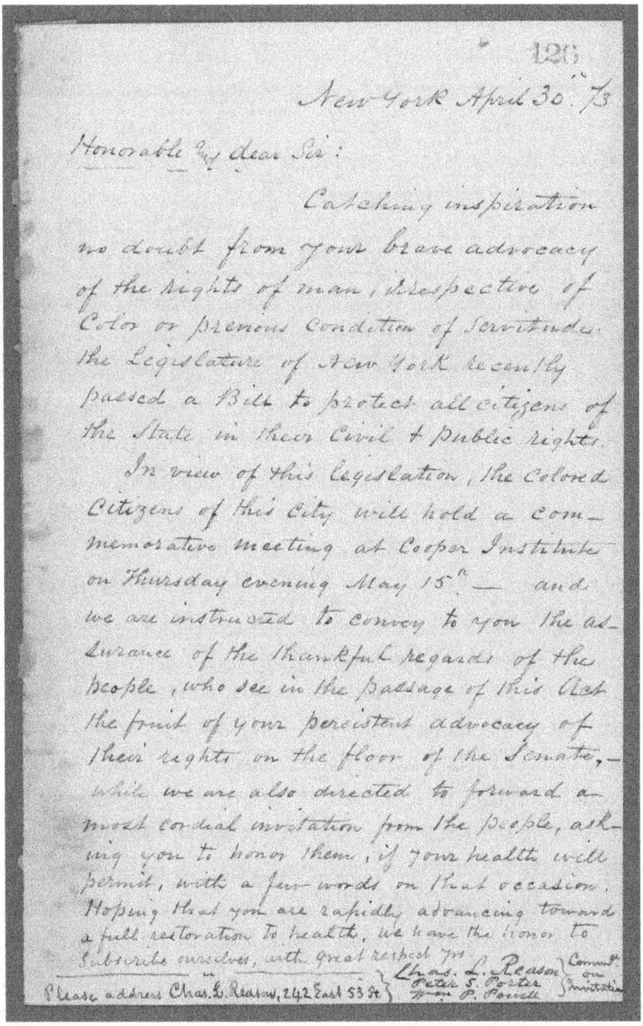

126

New York April 30th 73

Honorable & dear Sir:

Catching inspiration no doubt from your brave advocacy of the rights of man, irrespective of Color or previous Condition of Servitude, the Legislature of New York recently passed a Bill to protect all citizens of the State in their Civil & public rights.

In view of this legislation, the Colored Citizens of this City will hold a commemorative meeting at Cooper Institute on Thursday evening May 15th — and we are instructed to convey to you the assurance of the thankful regards of the people, who see in the passage of this Act the fruit of your persistent advocacy of their rights on the floor of the Senate, — while we are also directed to forward a most cordial invitation from the people, asking you to honor them, if your health will permit, with a few words on that occasion. Hoping that you are rapidly advancing toward a full restoration to health, we have the honor to subscribe ourselves, with great respect yrs

Chas. L. Reason
Peter S. Porter
Wm P. Powell
Commt. on Invitation

Please address Chas. L. Reason, 242 East 53 St.

Figure 13. In the early 1870s, black New Yorkers campaigned for civil rights legislation in both their home state and in Washington, D.C. In 1873, as Senator Charles Sumner's "civil rights supplement" was pending in Congress, New York's legislature passed a civil rights act that had been drafted by the black barber and lobbyist William H. Johnson. In this letter, Charles Reason, who had attended the African Free School in the 1820s, writes to Sumner to invite him to a New York City celebration commemorating the passage of the state act. Charles Reason, Peter S. Porter, and William P. Powell to Charles Sumner, April 30, 1873, Charles Sumner Correspondence, 1829–1874, Houghton Library, Harvard University.

and play with them." Miss Vail and two other white teachers reported pride in their students, including "their new pupils." The *Eagle* was likely aiming for a bit of cheek by calling the sisters "Civil Rights representatives," but in truth Marietta and Josephine were. Their day had gone well, all things considered, but that did not take away from the fact that they were children undertaking a public, political, and frightening task.[120]

Both inside and outside New York, reformers highlighted the connection between New York's new civil rights law and Sumner's bill in Congress. Echoing language going back to the Missouri Crisis and the 1827 general abolition, Assemblyman Husted suggested that others would follow the Empire State's model: "The example of New York will prevail, and all the sister States will follow her." In August, in a speech published in Douglass's new Washington-based newspaper, the *New National Era and Citizen*, Langston hoped that New Yorkers, "having achieved equality before the law in your own State," would not forget the "cooperation which may be justly claimed of you" to "secure the passage of that national civil rights bill."[121]

The New Yorkers did not forget. During the 42nd Congress (1871–1873), they joined black Americans from across the country to champion Sumner's supplement. Sumner made their efforts part of his pitch to colleagues. In explaining why his bill was justified by Anglo-American common law and the revolutionized U.S. Constitution, he interspersed arguments from black citizens. In a typical instance, he placed "George T. Downing face to face" with a reluctant Republican colleague by employing Downing's legal views verbatim. Downing denied the bill was an overreach of federal power or that it would "invade the domiciliary rights of a citizen in any State." He maintained, however, that "when the supreme law says" that legal equality was a right, as the Fourteenth Amendment did, then "Congress, which has that supreme law as its guide" had "the power to enforce the same." "As a lawyer," Sumner concluded, Downing won the argument. As the exchange among Sumner, Downing, and the reluctant senator suggests, the supplement faced headwinds even in a Republican-majority Congress. Many thought it went too far in challenging the boundaries of federalism and in seeking to regulate objects of law—like schools—that traditionally fell under local control.[122]

One of Sumner's and black Americans' strongest allies in the push for a bolder civil rights law was the energetic and pompous Senator Conkling. Conkling, as Frederick Douglass later eulogized, was a lot like Sumner, but was never fully recognized for his advocacy because he "stood in the shadow of Thaddeus Stevens, Benjamin F. Wade, and Charles Sumner," who were older "though not abler servants." Like William Seward, Conkling had a New York judge with antislavery proclivities for a father and had developed his career in the Burned-Over District. During the same 1872 session that Sumner quoted Downing, Conkling backed Sumner's attempt to attach a civil rights amendment to a general amnesty bill. When a coalition of Democrats and Liberal Republicans sank the amendment but approved the amnesty bill, Conkling wrote to Gerrit Smith expressing both anger and determination. "The juggles and tricks of this session exceed all of the kind I have seen," he fumed. "This remark in no way includes Mr. Sumner of course, + I hope we shall not fail in obtaining final action on Civil Rights. We shall try."[123]

That fall, from across the country, black New Yorkers reignited a petition campaign to help Sumner, Conkling, and their partners maintain pressure on civil rights. From Washington, Lewis Douglass, now editor-in-chief of the *New National Era,* argued that black Americans would "rise or fall as a race" and that civil rights legislation would help the whole. Noting that the 43rd Congress included black members, Douglass reasoned that these men were representative "of the colored race throughout the country" in addition to their specific districts. The young editor invited "men, women, and children" to labor for "our civil rights." For weeks in advance of the winter 1873–1874 congressional session, he included a model petition on the corner of one the paper's pages, with directions to "every man, woman, and child" to "cut out the petition" and "get signers to it." The petition itself emphasized that, "as citizens of the United States," the signers were not asking for "special legislation," but rather the removal of "whatever legislation there is" against colored "citizens, tax-payers, and members of the human family." Bell ran a copy of the same petition in the *Elevator*, providing information about locations throughout San Francisco, including bars, where citizens could sign. In December, when the session began, Sumner began submitting the resulting petitions for consideration.[124]

That same month, hundreds of black men traveled to Washington for a national convention. The meeting had been called by the Pennsylvania Equal Rights League to impress on Congress "the absolute necessity of passing a Civil Rights Bill." New York sent Butler, Garnet, Reason, and fifteen others. They arrived with a petition carrying, incredibly, the names of over 6,000 black citizens. "Senator Conkling," they understood, would "present the memorial" and "engineer the bill through the Senate." A few days into the convention, Downing and Frederick Douglass led a group to meet with

Grant in the White House to reiterate their claims. Grant replied that he had "always believed that enfranchisement and equal rights should accompany emancipation. . . . I hope the present Congress will give the relief you seek." It helped that the president was on record indicating he would sign legislation. Before the convention ended, the men formed a permanent National Civil Rights Council with Downing at its head.[125]

Despite the fact that all the parts seemed to be in place, it was a torturous path from December 1873 to the passage of the supplement. Sumner remained steadfast, but died of a heart attack in March 1874. Downing, who was with the senator in his final hours, reported that he "continually referred to the Civil Rights bill." The press reported widely on Sumner's last words: "Take care of my civil rights bill." A group of Radical Republicans, including Conkling, picked up where Sumner had left off. Over the next two months, they debated, strategized, amended, and regrouped. They ultimately and painfully took out the language guaranteeing school access, one of the most controversial parts of the bill. In late May, Republicans determined that they would sit out Democratic filibustering until there was no choice left but to vote. Conkling stayed on the Senate floor for a day and a half straight, waiting for the dissenting Democrats to tire out. When the bill passed, 28 to 16, "colored men in the gallery, where they had been all night, applauded." Conkling moved that the senate adjourn. Now the bill had to pass the House.[126]

Complicating passage of the bill, but in ways that should not be read with overreactive hindsight, the Supreme Court had recently issued its opinion in the *Slaughterhouse Cases*. The controversy involved a law passed by the biracial Republican legislature of Louisiana regulating slaughterhouses in New Orleans in the name of public health, under the auspices of state police power. White butchers sued, citing violations of the Thirteenth and Fourteenth Amendments. (Wasn't the right to pursue one's calling an essential right of freedom? Wasn't Louisiana now making that difficult?) In a 5–4 decision, the former doctor and moderate Republican Justice Samuel Miller ruled against the white butchers, upholding states' capacity to regulate aspects of citizens' lives and cautioning against too broad a reading of the Reconstruction Amendments. Yes, there was a new national citizenship, but certain rights remained within the purview of the states and state citizenship.[127] During House debate on the civil rights bill, Democrats seized on the "two citizenships" element of *Slaughterhouse* and argued that the rights the Sumner supplement sought to guarantee fell under the umbrella of state citizenship and state sovereignty.

Downing objected to this reading of *Slaughterhouse* in ways that recapture the uncertainty and the potential of antidiscrimination constitutionalism in the early 1870s. "Those who would leave us to the mercy of the states," he wrote in an editorial, "seem to gloat over some fancied aid given them in the Louisiana slaughterhouse case." But their reading of the case was cherry-picked. The court also said, and Downing quoted, that the "general purposes" of the Reconstruction Amendments were "the freedom of the slave race, the security and firm establishment of that freedom, and the protection of the newly-made freeman and citizen." The court's view of the amendments did not make the Sumner supplement unconstitutional, but on the contrary affirmed a reading that allowed robust congressional action. Members of the House made similar arguments. As the black congressman from South Carolina, Robert Elliot, noted, it was ridiculous to conflate state regulation of "noxious slaughter-houses" with "State laws which deny us the common rights and privileges of other citizens." The former was a sound use of police power, the latter had nothing to do with keeping people safe.[128]

Benjamin Butler of Massachusetts, who as a Union officer had been a crucial supporter of military emancipation early in the war, now played the role of Sumner and Conkling in the House. He had seen slavery and southern racism up close. He had seen the tremendous, tear-invoking bravery of black soldiers. He mocked the hypocrisy of southerners who seemed content to mingle intimately with slaves when they were in bondage but now refused to sit in an integrated inn or railcar. When the House finally prepared to vote in early 1875, during the lame duck session, Butler made the final speech on the bill. "The foundation of all democracy was equality of right, equality of burden, equality of power in all men under the law. . . . [This] bill is the very essence of constitutional liberty. What does it do? It simply provides that there shall be an equality of law all over the Union." In February 1875, the bill passed the House 162 to 99, twenty-eight not voting. There was a news story printed across the country that, a few days later, a basket of flowers arrived on Butler's desk with a card: "Justice to all is equality before the law. The country owes you its gratitude. From a friend in New York."[129]

In truth, the 1875 Civil Rights Act was confusing from the start and mixed in its effects. Mere weeks after it passed, Butler explained which sorts of businesses he thought were affected. A barber shop, he said, was a "private business" and the act did not reach it. But, as common law rules suggested, "public" places and services, like conveyances, licensed taverns and inns, and licensed theaters could not discriminate on account of race. Meanwhile, ordinary citizens began to test the act's boundaries. In Troy, Margaret E. Wicks and Caroline Kelly tried to buy ice cream at a restaurant and, when rebuffed, successfully entered a complaint with a U.S. commissioner for the owner's arrest; a few weeks later, the commissioner ruled that "the new law contemplated inns only, Sinsabaugh's restaurant not coming within the range." In New York City, a theater employee was arrested on a warrant issued by none other than U.S. Commissioner Davenport after the employee refused to sell a ticket to a black man named William R. Davis. Two months later, a grand jury "couldn't be persuaded that there had been any infraction of the civil rights law." By contrast, that same week, a U.S. District Court judge in Minnesota "read an opinion very pointedly sustaining the constitutionality of the Supplementary Civil Rights bill." In April, the Pullman Car Company "issued orders to allow respectable and cleanly colored people" to "take berths in the sleepers running on Southern railroads." It would be inaccurate to say that the 1875 law did not do anything. Black people sued and sometimes won. And of course, there were business owners who simply complied, making litigation unnecessary. Moreover, as Downing argued, part of what made the law important was that Congress had declared that something wrong was wrong: "the negation of a principle is the first step in its final overthrow." Black citizens' rights had been "asserted affirmatively by national legislation."[130]

The story of civil rights in New York during the final years of the lives of the children of gradual abolition thus does not end neatly. The 1873 state law and the 1875 national law were not panaceas. Judicial review of both laws resulted in setbacks, although more devastatingly at the national level. In 1883, New York's Court of Appeals, in *King v. Gallagher,* interpreted the state civil rights law as mandating equal access to schools but not necessarily integrated schools. As a result, some districts remained integrated and some kept separate schools. In 1888, in *People v. King,* the same court upheld the act's regulation of public accommodations and places of amusement, forbidding the owners of a skating rink from turning away black customers. In 1900, after a black businesswoman in Queens County named Elizabeth Cisco sued her local school district on behalf of her child, the legislature passed a law rejecting the state court's earlier "separate but equal" interpretation of the 1873 law. When this new school bill passed, William H. Johnson, still active at the age of 67, held a reception in Cisco's honor. Nationally, things were worse. In 1883, within days of New York's ruling in *King v. Gallagher,* the U.S. Supreme Court, in the *Civil Rights Cases,* struck down the entire 1875 federal Civil Rights Act. Sumner's supplement, which black Americans had worked so hard to see passed, was gone. In 1896, the majority in *Plessy v. Ferguson*, a case about Louisiana's separate railcar act, inscribed the "separate but equal" doctrine in federal constitutional law. In short, by the end of the century and at the start of the new one, New York's courts, legislature, and citizens managed, fitfully and imperfectly, to hold on to the promises of civil rights legislation and beat back some of Jim Crow. In the nation, however, much of the promise of "equality before the law" had been lost.[131]

* * *

The children of gradual abolition, born in the early republic, grew up in a time when most of the legal questions that affected daily life were regulated at the state level. Rules about slavery and freedom, judicial rights, voting, schools, citizenship, and associations were decided by their state legislature. Their parents, teachers, and mentors taught them how to operate within this system of American federalism. Even ordinary black New Yorkers who did not have law treatises sitting on their shelves knew about important aspects of state law and which local officials and lawmakers were useful. As this generation reached adulthood in the 1840s and '50s, they employed the laws and the political dynamics of their state to protect and enlarge local visions of freedom as well as to shape their state's response to national conflicts over slavery and racial belonging. When the Civil War started, they were ready to use their local experiences to shape national outcomes. Their voices were crucial during Reconstruction, as well.

By the time this generation took their last breaths in the closing decades of the nineteenth century, they had witnessed a revolution in federal constitutional law and then stark reversals on the contemporary possibilities of that revolution. New York State, while no egalitarian paradise, nonetheless proved better at protecting black citizens' rights than the federal government in the aftermath of Reconstruction. This was American federalism, altered by the war but still there.

And so a new generation picked up where their elders left off. Chattel slavery was gone in the United States. Black men in New York voted. Good state civil rights laws had been put on the books. New York was moving, slowly but perceptively, to desegregate its schools. There, at the dawn of the twentieth century, the new work began. As James McCune Smith had predicted, "There is a great work for the colored people to do in this land: a work not of today only but of centuries. A generation must be raised up who can recognize the work, and who under God will have the mental & moral discipline to assay and to do it. . . . I must have had a coral insect for a millio-millio-grandfather, loving to work beneath the tide in a superstructure, that some day, when the labourer is long dead & forgotten, may rear itself above the waves & afford rest & habitation for the Creatures of his Good, Good Father of All."[132] Smith was right that the work was slow, that achieving complete freedom and equality would be tasks ongoing, and that new generations would rise to confront old challenges and new obstacles. But Smith was wrong, at least I hope he was wrong, that his labors would be forgotten. The efforts of Smith and his generation changed the legal and social realities of freedom and equality in the United States. The results of their efforts continue to rear themselves "above the waves."

EPILOGUE

The Two Charlottes

In the summer of 1870, Charles B. Ray sat down at his desk at 311 East 62nd Street in New York City to write a letter about his daughter, Charlotte. Now sixty-two years old, Ray had spent a lifetime working on behalf of black Americans as editor of the *Colored American,* supporter of the Liberty and Republican parties, promotor of black education, minister in the Congregational Church, and advocate for political and civil rights in both New York and the United States. "You are aware," he wrote the white abolitionist Gerrit Smith, "that my Daughter Charlotte is a Law Student of the Howard University Washington DC and is doing well as such. Prof. Langston writes to me that, she will make a lawyer. She decided upon this profession of her own choice." To help pay her tuition, Charlotte was "teaching in the University."[1]

Charlotte Rays' matriculation at Howard, a university founded in 1867 with the mission to provide black Americans professional and graduate education, made national news. From New Hampshire to Georgia to Iowa to California, papers reported that Miss Charlotte E. Ray was "the first colored woman to enter upon the study of law in the United States." Two years later, her acceptance to the bar of the Supreme Court of the District of Columbia also fetched headlines. In San Francisco, Philip A. Bell, the African Free School graduate who had published the *Colored American* with Charlotte's father in New York in the 1830s, explained that, "In Washington, where a few years ago colored women were bought and sold under sanction of law," Ray made "her appearance in the clerk's office" and requested "a certificate which would entitle her to practice." The court had to amend its rules for admission by striking out the word "male." She had "the honor of being the first lady lawyer in Washington."[2]

A lifetime earlier, in 1811, the black servant girl named Charlotte who opened this book appeared before the New York City grand jury to explain

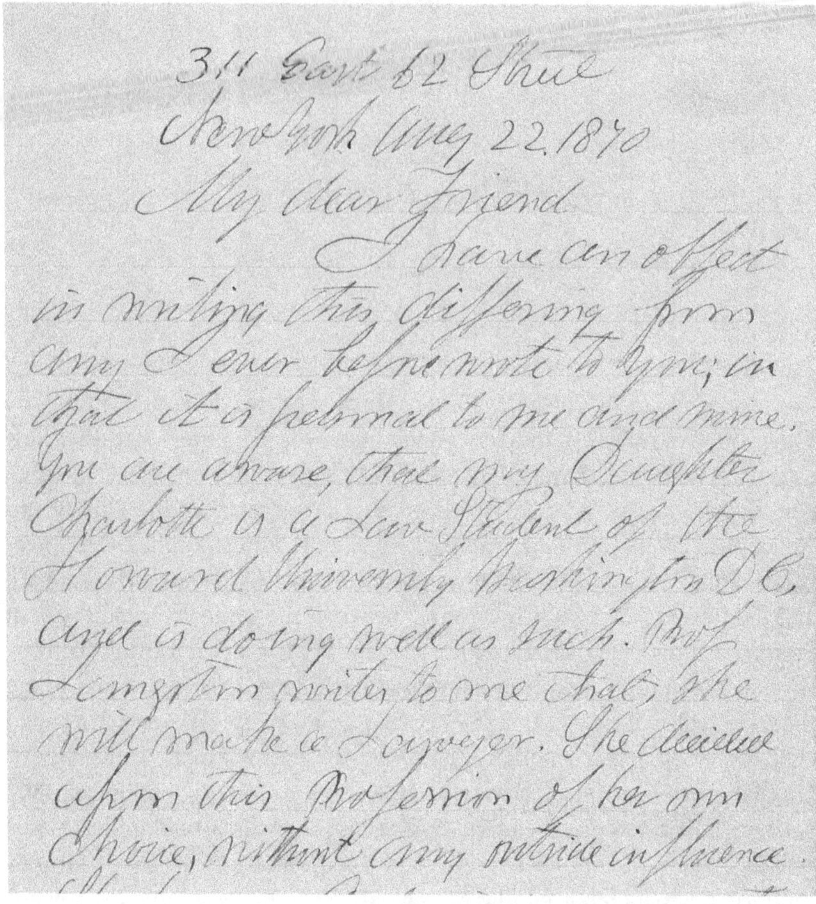
311 East 62 Street
New York Aug 22. 1870
My dear Friend
I have an object in writing this differing from any I ever before wrote to you; in that it is personal to me and mine. You are aware, that my Daughter Charlotte is a Law Student of the Howard University Washington D.C. and is doing well as such. Prof Langston writes to me that, she will make a Lawyer. She decided upon this Profession of her own choice, without any outside influence.

Figure 14. In 1870, Charlotte E. Ray, daughter of Charles B. Ray, entered law school at Howard University. Here, the proud father writes to Gerrit Smith to share news about his daughter. Charles B. Ray to Gerrit Smith, August 22, 1870, Gerrit Smith Papers, Special Collections Research Center, Syracuse University.

how her master's whipping her had prompted her desire to burn his house down. She had told the district attorney that she was free, "bound for a certain number of years only." This Charlotte, like Charlotte E. Ray in 1872, knew that the law mattered. Like Charlotte the lawyer, the Charlotte of 1811 lived in a world where black people routinely dealt with clerks and certificates and courts. Those realities of daily life had not changed in six decades. But the two Charlottes nonetheless operated on different terrain. In 1811, enslaved mothers in New York hoped that town clerks were recording their free-yet-bound children's status on birth certificates. In 1811, black men in New York had to register certificates of freedom with county clerks in order to vote. In 1811, black New Yorkers often found themselves in court because someone was trying to kidnap them or steal a family member. No one, in 1811, would have expected that a black woman would be passing the bar anywhere in the United States any time soon.

Charlotte E. Ray's world was different. During the same years she was in law school, black New Yorkers were also in Washington as part of the "Outside Congress," lobbying for Senator Sumner's supplemental civil rights bill in the wake of nationwide abolition. Some black men were officially inside Congress, representatives elected to formal political office. Back in her home state, the black barber William H. Johnson was about to write the bill that became New York's 1873 Civil Rights Law. The Fifteenth Amendment and national election acts had granted black men widespread access to polls across the country in ways never seen. Charlotte E. Ray, unlike fifteen years earlier, was unquestionably a citizen of the United States.

Charlotte E. Ray could have also told us about all the things still going wrong. She would have liked the vote herself. In one of her first trial experiences, she represented a woman suing for divorce on the grounds of "cruelty and neglect," a case which suggested the ways that certain forms of

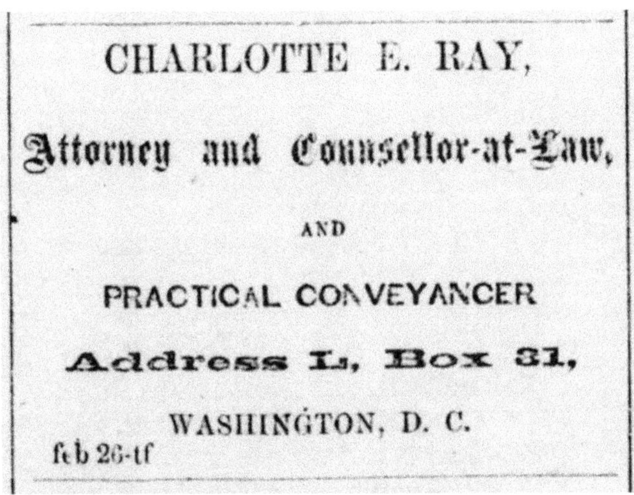
CHARLOTTE E. RAY,

Attorney and Counsellor-at-Law,

AND

PRACTICAL CONVEYANCER

Address L, Box 31,

WASHINGTON, D. C.

feb 26-tf

Figure 15. Charlotte E. Ray, Attorney and Counsellor-at-Law. *New National Era,* March 26, 1874.

patriarchal household governance had not fully changed. And Ray appears to have struggled in her career as a lawyer. She eventually left the profession, moved back to New York, and became a teacher and school superintendent. She lived to see her home state's courts and lawmakers preserve the 1873 New York Civil Rights Act but also witnessed the United States Supreme Court crush Sumner's similar national legislation.[3]

The story of the two Charlottes is as complicated as the story of nineteenth-century freedom and citizenship itself. These are all stories full of bravery and achievement and disappointment and things we cannot know. They are stories that, pieced together, show meaningful changes in law, in politics, in citizenship, in education, and in day-to-day experience over time. From one Charlotte to another, they are stories to share.

ABBREVIATIONS

ACR	"Albany County Register of Manumitted Slaves 1800-1828," in Local Records on Microfilm (Reel #74-40-5), New York State Archives
AEJ	*Albany Evening Journal*
AFS	New-York African Free-School Records, 1817–1832, New-York Historical Society
BAP	C. Peter Ripley et al., eds., *The Black Abolitionist Papers,* 5 vols. (1985–1992)
CA	*Colored American* (New York)
ComAd	*Commercial Advertiser* (New York)
COF	Certificate of Freedom (voting document required of black men per the New York State 1811 law)
CSC	Charles Sumner Correspondence, Houghton Library, Harvard University
CWAL	Roy Basler, ed., *The Collected Works of Abraham Lincoln,* 9 vols. (1953–1955)
DAIP	District Attorney Indictment Papers, 1790–1895, New York Municipal Archives
DM	*Douglass' Monthly* (Rochester)
EP	*New-York Evening Post*
FDP	*Frederick Douglass' Paper* (Rochester)
FJ	*Freedom's Journal* (New York)
FHL	Friends Historical Library, Swarthmore College
GSM	New York County Court of General Sessions, Minutes of the Sessions, 1684–1920, New York Municipal Archives
GSP	Gerrit Smith Papers, Special Collections Research Center, Syracuse University
JER	*Journal of the Early Republic*

JFP	Jay Family Papers, 1828–1943, Rare Book & Manuscript Library, Columbia University
JJH	John Jay Homestead State Historic Site, Katonah, New York
JANY	*Journal of the Assembly of the State of New York*
JCWE	*Journal of the Civil War Era*
JSNY	*Journal of the Senate of the State of New York*
MC	May Anti-Slavery Manuscript Collection, Division of Rare and Manuscript Collections, Cornell University
NA	*National Advocate* (New York)
NASS	*National Anti-Slavery Standard* (New York)
NS	*North Star* (Rochester)
NYH	*New York Herald*
NYTrib	*New-York Daily Tribune*
NYT	*New-York Daily Times* (1851–1857), *New-York Times* (1857–1896)
NY Laws	*Laws of the State of New York* (sessions laws of the New York State Legislature)
NYHS	New-York Historical Society
NYMA	New York Municipal Archives
NYMS	Records of the New York Manumission Society, New-York Historical Society
NYYMM	Records of New York Yearly Meeting of Friends [microform], Milstein Division, New York Public Library
NYYMP	New York Yearly Meeting Records, Periodicals and Microfilm Reference Room, New York Public Library
NYSA	New York State Archives
NYSL	New York State Library
OCR	Ontario County Archives and Records Center, Canandaigua, New York
PA	*Pacific Appeal* (San Francisco)
PAS	Papers of the Pennsylvania Abolition Society (microfilm), Columbia University
SHG	Sydney Howard Gay Papers, 1748–1931, Rare Book & Manuscript Library, Columbia University
TWP	Thurlow Weed Papers, Manuscripts and Special Collections, University of Rochester

WAA *Weekly Anglo-African* (1859–1861), *Anglo-African* (1861–1865) (New York)
WHS Papers of William H. Seward (microfilm), Firestone Library, Princeton University
WMQ *William and Mary Quarterly*

NOTES

Introduction

1. Statement of Charlotte, *The People v. Charlotte, a black girl*, filed June 7, 1811, DAIP. On longstanding white fears that black people were plotting arson, see Jill Lepore, *New York Burning: Liberty, Slavery, and Conspiracy in Eighteenth Century Manhattan* (New York, 2005). For a note on language, see the section titled "A Note on Language" in this Introduction.

2. Like many scholars of American slavery, I'm indebted to Ira Berlin's work on "generations of captivity." The people he calls the "Revolutionary Generation" are the parents of the children of gradual abolition. *Many Thousands Gone: The First Two Centuries of Slavery in North America* (Cambridge, MA, 1998); *Generations of Captivity: A History of African-American Slaves* (Cambridge, MA, 2004). For readers interested in theory, the study in this book provides a potential illustration of the sociologist Karl Manheim's concept of generations and their relationship to social change. *Essays on the Sociology of Knowledge* (New York, 1952), ch. 7.

3. There have been recent efforts to connect antislavery movements to the coming of the Civil War, but the history and effects of gradual abolition remain underemphasized or absent. For overviews, see W. Caleb McDaniel, "The Bonds and Boundaries of Antislavery," *JCWE* (Mar. 2014): 84–105; Corey M. Brooks, "Reconsidering Politics in the Study of American Abolitionists," *JCWE* (June 2018): 291–317. Scholars of northern emancipation have done tremendous research, but their work rarely discusses the implications of this earlier history for the national politics of sectionalism, the Civil War, and Reconstruction. See James J. Gigantino, *The Ragged Road to Abolition: Slavery and Freedom in New Jersey, 1775-1865* (Philadelphia, 2015); Leslie M. Harris, *In the Shadow of Slavery: African Americans in New York City, 1626-1863* (Chicago, 2003); Graham Russell Hodges, *Root and Branch: African Americans in New York and East Jersey, 1613-1863* (Chapel Hill, 1999); David Gellman, *Emancipating New York: The Politics of Slavery and Freedom, 1777-1827* (Baton Rouge, 2006); Michael E. Groth, *Slavery and Freedom in the Mid-Hudson Valley* (Albany, 2017); Joanne Pope Melish, *Disowning Slavery: Gradual Emancipation and "Race" in New England, 1780-1860* (Ithaca, 1998); Gary Nash and Jean Soderlund, *Freedom by Degrees: Emancipation in Pennsylvania and its Aftermath* (Oxford, 1991); Richard Newman, *The Transformation of American Abolitionism: Fighting Slavery in the Early Republic* (Chapel Hill, 2002); Shane White, *Somewhat More Independent: The End of Slavery in New York City, 1770-1810* (Athens, GA,

1991); John Wood Sweet, *Bodies Politic: Negotiating Race in the American North, 1730-1830* (Philadelphia, 2003). By the same token, scholars who study midcentury black abolitionism tend not to examine how day-to-day experiences in northern emancipation shaped black politics and legal knowledge. See Benjamin Quarles, *Black Abolitionists* (New York, 1969); Patrick Rael, *Black Identity and Black Protest in the Antebellum North* (Chapel Hill, 2002); James Horton and Lois Horton, *In Hope of Liberty: Culture, Community and Protest Among Northern Free Blacks, 1700-1860* (New York, 1997); John Stauffer, *Black Hearts of Men: Radical Abolitionists and the Transformation of Race* (Cambridge, MA, 2001); Timothy Patrick McCarthy and John Stauffer, eds., *Prophets of Protest: Reconsidering the History of American Abolitionism* (New York, 2006); James Brewer Stewart, *Abolitionist Politics and the Coming of the Civil War* (Amherst, 2008); Stanley Harrold, *Border War: Fighting Over Slavery Before the Civil War* (Chapel Hill, 2010); Andrew DelBanco, ed., *The Abolitionist Imagination* (Cambridge, MA, 2012); R. J. M. Blackett, *The Captive's Quest for Freedom: Fugitive Slaves, the 1850 Fugitive Slave Law, and the Politics of Slavery* (New York, 2018); P. Gabrielle Foreman et al., *The Colored Conventions Movement: Black Organizing in the Nineteenth Century* (Chapel Hill, 2021). A burst of new work links black antislavery/rights campaigns and the remaking of citizenship in the Civil War era. I join this scholarship with an interest in the effects of gradual abolition and how early modern legalities both persisted and changed in the post-Revolutionary period. By following an especially influential cohort of black northerners from birth to death, we can see even more clearly why subsequent black political and legal goals looked the way they did. See Christopher James Bonner, *Remaking the Republic: Black Politics and the Creation of American Citizenship* (Philadelphia, 2020); Andrew Diemer, *The Politics of Black Citizenship: Free African Americans in the Mid-Atlantic Borderland, 1817–1863* (Athens, GA, 2019); Steven Hahn, *The Political Worlds of Slavery and Freedom* (Cambridge, MA, 2009); Eric Foner, *The Second Founding: How the Civil War and Reconstruction Remade the Constitution* (New York, 2019); Martha S. Jones, *Birthright Citizens: A History of Race and Rights in Antebellum America* (New York, 2018); Stephen Kantrowitz, *More Than Freedom: Fighting for Black Citizenship in a White Republic, 1829-1889* (New York, 2012); Kate Masur, *Until Justice Be Done: America's First Civil Rights Movement, from the Revolution to Reconstruction* (New York, 2021); Manisha Sinha, *The Slave's Cause: A History of Abolition* (New Haven, 2016). Two books that argue for placing early U.S. emancipation and Civil War emancipation in the same narrative are Ira Berlin, *The Long Emancipation: The Demise of Slavery in the United States* (Cambridge, MA, 2015) and Patrick Rael, *Eighty-Eight Years: The Long Death of Slavery in the United States, 1777-1865* (Athens, GA, 2015). I agree with the usefulness of a long chronological sweep and aim to show more of the granular "how" and "why" of those books' conclusions. The literature on the causes of the Civil War, the emancipation politics of the war, and the constitutional history of Reconstruction—some of which is cited here—is voluminous. Readers will find more detailed historiographical discussions in Chapters 6 and 7.

4. *NY Laws,* 22nd sess. (1799), ch. 62; *NY Laws,* 33rd sess. (1810), ch. 115; *NY Laws,* 40th Sess. (1817), ch. 137; *NY Laws,* 64th sess. (1841), ch. 247; "Abolition of Slavery," *Mercantile Advertiser* (New York), May 30, 1800.

5. NYMS, vol. 6., Feb. 21, 1798, pp. 96–97; Samuel Cornish, "Dear Sir," *FJ,* July 13, 1827; Elizabeth Wicks, *Address Delivered Before the African Female Benevolent Society of Troy* (Troy, 1834), 6. Philip A. Bell, a child of gradual abolition, founded the *Pacific Appeal* with the slogan, "A Weekly Journal Devoted to the Interests of the People of Color." *PA,* Apr. 5, 1862. For black children during southern emancipation, see Mary Niall Mitchell, *Raising Freedom's Child: Black Children and Visions of the Future After Slavery* (New York, 2010).

6. Henry Highland Garnet, *A Memorial Discourse by Henry Highland Garnet . . . February 12, 1865; with an introduction by James McCune Smith* (Philadelphia, 1865), 85–86, 89.

7. Although there is a wealth of fine scholarship on black abolitionism in New York, it underemphasizes ordinary black people's engagement with law and their involvement in formal politics. Much of it also misses the *state*wide scope of black politics, and the dynamics by which local campaigns for rights bled into state campaigns. Judith Wellman, for example, argues that black New Yorkers were "less tied to the formal political system" than white abolitionists. *Grassroots Reform in the Burned-Over District of Upstate New York: Religion, Abolitionism and Democracy* (New York, 2011), ix. Leslie Alexander, in emphasizing black men's failure to regain equal suffrage, misses black men and women's success in achieving two other statewide goals (the 1840 jury trial law and the 1841 nine month repeal). *African or American? Black Identity and Political Activism in New York City, 1784-1861* (Urbana, 2018), 94–96, 110, 118. There has been a fruitful recent turn toward integrating black politics with major party politics: Kantrowitz, *More Than Freedom*; Masur, *Until Justice Be Done*; Van Gosse, *The First Reconstruction: Black Politics in America from the Revolution to the Civil War* (Chapel Hill, 2021). I use "ordinary," "everyday," "common," and "regular" to describe people who were not elite or famous. These were often people who made their livings primarily with their hands and/or lived modest material existences. For a treatment of ordinary actors during the Revolutionary era, and the difficulties of terminology, see Alfred F. Young, Gary Nash, and Ray Raphael, *Revolutionary Founders: Rebels, Radicals, and Reformers in the Making of the Nation* (New York, 2011); Pauline Maier, "Not Your Usual 'Founders,'" *Reviews in American History* (Dec. 2012): 557–565.

8. Erica Armstrong Dunbar's *A Fragile Freedom: African American Women and Emancipation in the Antebellum City* (New Haven, 2008), which focuses on black women in Philadelphia during gradual abolition, is crucial for revealing the ways that women negotiated emancipation in distinct ways in an urban environment. For promising new work on New England, see Jerrad P. Paccate, "The Work of Freedom: Black Women and the Process of Emancipation in New England, 1740-1840" (PhD diss., Rutgers, in progress). Martha S. Jones's *All Bound Up Together: The Woman Question in African*

American Public Culture, 1830-1900 (Chapel Hill, 2007) shows that black women, far from being relegated to a separate female sphere, entered black public culture directly, shaping both intra- and interracial conversations about female autonomy and authority. Kabria Baumgartner's *In Pursuit of Knowledge: Black Women and Educational Activism in Antebellum America* (New York, 2019) demonstrates how girls and women, especially among the elite, advocated for equal school rights—a story I take inspiration from and expand on by including school children in rural areas and school politics in a famously contentious state legislature. In a much-needed study, Crystal Lynn Webster explores the histories of black children and conceptions of childhood in early national Philadelphia, New York City, and Boston, with a particular interest in "the social history" of their "play, labor, and schooling." I agree with Webster that black children's activities were "political" and part of "freedom-making," and that it can be difficult to find them in some archives, but black children also abound in nineteenth-century legal and political sources, including those related to town governance, black and white philanthropic associations, and statewide school infrastructure. *Beyond the Boundaries of Childhood: African American Children in the Antebellum North* (Chapel Hill, 2022), 1–2, 4. As historiographical conversations throughout the notes will indicate, my hope is to link a growing field of northern black women's and children's history with legal, political, and constitutional narratives of nineteenth-century antislavery.

9. US Const. (1787); art. IV, § 2, cl. 3; amend. X. The literature on early constitutionalism/citizenship is vast, but for a start, see Gordon S. Wood, *The Creation of the American Republic, 1776-1787* (Chapel Hill, 1969); James H. Kettner, *The Development of American Citizenship, 1608-1870* (Chapel Hill, 1978); David Hendrickson, *Peace Pact: The Lost World of the American Founding* (Lawrence, KS, 2003); Mary Sarah Bilder, *The Transatlantic Constitution: Colonial Legal Culture and the Empire* (Cambridge, MA, 2004); Douglas Bradburn, *The Citizenship Revolution: Politics and the Creation of the American Union* (Charlottesville, 2009); Allison L. LaCroix, *The Ideological Origins of American Federalism* (Cambridge, MA, 2010); Emily Blanck, *Tyrannicide: Forging an American Law of Slavery in South Carolina and Massachusetts* (Athens, GA, 2014); Jonathan Gienapp, *The Second Creation: Fixing the Constitution in the Founding Era* (Cambridge, MA, 2018); Van Gosse, "Patchwork Nation: Racial Orders and Disorder in the United States, 1790–1860," *JER* (Spring 2020): 45–81. My thinking on these subjects developed substantially under the guidance of Annette Gordon-Reed and Peter S. Onuf in a seminar titled "Union, Race, and the Nation: Creating the Federal Republic, 1776-1801" (Institute for Constitutional History, New-York Historical Society, Fall 2012).

10. Many studies of northern abolition and black politics focus on major cities—Philadelphia, New York, Boston. By contrast, this book emphasizes the value of employing a statewide scope and exploring rural areas in conjunction with urban ones. Some revealing county census data: in 1800, 2,257 slaves lived in Ulster, 1,609 lived in Dutchess,1,528 lived in Queens, and 1,145 lived in Orange, compared to 2,868 in New York County (coterminus with New York City/Manhattan Island). *Census of the State of New York, for 1855* (Albany, 1857), xiii, xi; Susan B. Carter et al., eds., *Historical Statistics*

of the United States (New York, 2006), Tables Aa4941–5041, Bb1–98. For a statewide study of antislavery in Massachusetts, see Bruce Laurie, *Beyond Garrison: Antislavery and Social Reform* (New York, 2005).

11. Here I disagree with Stephen Kantrowitz, who writes that nineteenth-century black Bostonians "spearheaded the first substantial alliances with antislavery whites." There is a tendency to distinguish early national abolitionism and post-1829/Garrisonian abolitionism by underplaying the interracial relationships undergirding earlier efforts. Kantrowitz, *More than Freedom*, 7. For scholars highlighting earlier collaborations, see Paul J. Polgar, *Standard-Bearers of Equality: America's First Abolition Movement* (Chapel Hill, 2019); Nicholas P. Wood, "A 'class of Citizens': The Earliest Black Petitioners to Congress and Their Quaker Allies," *WMQ*, (Jan. 2017): 109–144.

12. I thank Christopher Bonner for noting my interest in the "politics of access." The phrase is his.

13. NYMS, vol. 9, Nov. 25, 1811, p. 280, Jan. 18, 1814, p. 359. In explaining the turn to immediatism in the late 1820s and 1830s, historians point to a range of causal factors: religious revivalism and new Protestant theologies, the spread of market capitalism and its attendant ideologies, the rise of the middle class and its family norms, backlash against the colonization movement, political confrontations between slave and free states, and the spread of print culture. These were important factors, but I aim to show earlier reasons, roots, and inspirations. For an overview, see James B. Stewart, "Humanitarian Reform and Antislavery," in *A Companion to the Civil War and Reconstruction*, ed. Lacy Ford (Malden, MA, 2005). On the Garrisonian version of immediatism, see W. Caleb McDaniel, *The Problem of Democracy in the Age of Slavery: Garrisonian Abolitionists and Transatlantic Reform* (Baton Rouge, 2013).

14. Paul Finkelman's *An Imperfect Union: Slavery, Federalism, and Comity* (Chapel Hill, 1981) and Edlie L. Wong's *Neither Fugitive nor Free: Atlantic Slavery, Freedom Suits, and the Legal Culture of Travel* (New York, 2009) are vital works on the legal consequences of black people's movements across state borders. I'm interested in the black northerners who instigated some of the cases in addition to influencing the politics around them.

15. James McCune Smith to Gerrit Smith, July 14, 1848, GSP; William Henry Johnson, *Autobiography of Dr. William Henry Johnson, Respectfully Dedicated to his Adopted Home, the Capital City of the Empire State* (Albany, 1900), 18; Sydney Howard Gay, Record of Fugitives, May 14, 1856, SHG; "Harriet Tubman, or 'Moses,'" *NASS*, Aug. 1, 1868.

16. There has been an outpouring of innovative legal histories of nineteenth-century African Americans. Scholars doing this work have stressed the importance of understanding local context and of probing grassroots uses of law. On legal cultures among free black and enslaved people in Baltimore, St. Louis, Annapolis, New Orleans, and the Natchez District, see, variously, Jones, *Birthright Citizens*; Kelly M. Kennington, *In the Shadow of Dred Scott: St. Louis Freedom Suits and the Legal Culture of Slavery in Antebellum America* (Athens, GA, 2017); Loren Schweninger, "Freedom Suits, African American Women, and the Genealogy of Slavery," *WMQ* (Jan. 2014): 35–62; Rebecca J.

Scott, "Public Rights, Social Equality, and the Conceptual Roots of the Plessy Challenge," *Michigan Law Review* (Mar. 2008): 777–804; Anne Twitty, *Before Dred Scott: Slavery and Legal Culture in the American Confluence, 1787-1837* (Cambridge, UK, 2016); Lea VanderVelde *Redemption Songs: Suing for Freedom before Dred Scott* (New York, 2014); Kimberly Welch, *Black Litigants in the Antebellum American South* (Chapel Hill, 2018). Hendrik Hartog's *The Trouble with Minna: A Case of Slavery and Emancipation in the Antebellum North* (Chapel Hill, 2018) focuses on New Jersey, a state where black people faced an especially bleak, disenfranchising version of gradualism. Dylan Penningroth's *Claims of Kinfolk: African American Property and Community in the Nineteenth-Century South* (Chapel Hill, 2003) demonstrates how slaves and freedpeople protected property in formal and informal legal contexts. His newest book examines the wide uses of law among African Americans between the last decades of slavery and the late twentieth century: *Before the Movement: The Hidden History of Black Civil Rights* (New York, 2023). Ariela J. Gross's *Double Character: Slavery and Mastery in the Antebellum Courtroom* (Princeton, 2000) explores slave agency in warranty trials. Aaron Hall's book-in-progress, *The Founding Rules: Slavery and the Creation of American Constitutionalism, 1789-1889* reveals sophisticated methods of constitutional interpretation developed by leading black northerners. Laura Edwards's *The People and Their Peace* depicts black southerners' engagement with the law and provides an illuminating point of comparison to my account of northern black legal practices. Edwards traces the participation of black southerners in the legal system in the early 1800s, arguing that the basis for their inclusion was an emphasis on maintaining "the peace" and a reliance on informal and local legal traditions. The forces that Edwards describes as slowly pushing black southerners (and others) out of the legal system worked to the opposite effect, at times, in New York. Black New Yorkers gained access to some formal legal and political rights over the course of the early 1800s, often through the decisions of the state legislature and courts; they also found reasons to insist on the legitimacy of common law precedents originating in both state and foreign jurisdictions. Edwards, *The People and Their Peace: Legal Culture and the Transformation of Inequality in the Post-Revolutionary South* (Chapel Hill, 2009).

17. For an account that highlights the importance of African legacies, see Craig Steven Wilder, *In the Company of Black Men: The African Influence on African American Culture in New York City* (New York, 2001); for the development of class divisions in New York City's black population, see Harris, *In the Shadow of Slavery*; for an examination of autonomous black cultural life, see Shane White, *Stories of Freedom in Black New York* (Cambridge, MA, 2002); for the ongoing tension between strategies of moral uplift versus nationalist calls for emigration, see Alexander, *African or American?*; for anti-imperialism as central to black political thought, see Justin Leroy, "Empire and the Afterlife of Slavery: Black Anti-Imperialisms of the Long Nineteenth Century" (PhD diss., NYU, 2014); for the political uses of violence, see Kellie Carter Jackson, *Force and Freedom: Black Abolitionists and the Politics of Violence* (Philadelphia, 2019); and for the centrality of the body in abolitionists' campaigns to end slavery and provide restorative

physical care, see Kathleen M. Brown, *Undoing Slavery: Bodies, Race, and Rights in the Age of Abolition* (Philadelphia, 2023). When referencing "formal" law and politics, I aim to highlight how black New Yorkers engaged with official manifestations and channels of the state.

18. In 1780, on the cusp of the first gradual abolition laws, there were 21,054 black residents in New York, 10,460 in New Jersey, 7,855 in Pennsylvania, 5,885 in Connecticut, and 2,671 in Rhode Island. The vast majority were enslaved. Slaves made up roughly 2.5 percent to 10 percent of each state's population, with New Jersey and New York on the higher end. There were about 4,800 black people in Massachusetts, 1.7 percent of the population. There were several dozen slaves in Vermont. New Hampshire's enslaved population was roughly 500 at the time of its 1783 constitution. For the 1780 statistics, see Carter et al., *Historical Statistics,* Series Eg1–59. For an overview of northern emancipation, see Arthur Zilversmit, *The First Emancipation: The Abolition of Slavery in the North* (Chicago, 1967). For recent reassessments of emancipation in Massachusetts and Vermont, see Gloria McCahon Whiting, "Emancipation Without Courts or Constitution: The Case of Revolutionary Massachusetts," *Slavery and Abolition* (Apr. 2020): 458–478; Harvey Amani Whitfield, *The Problem of Slavery in Early Vermont, 1777-1810* (Barre, VT, 2014). See note 3 for state studies of gradual abolition. There were unsuccessful efforts for gradual abolition in Delaware, Maryland, and Virginia during these years.

19. "An Ordinance for the Government of the Territory of the United States, North West of the River Ohio," July 13, 1787, *Journals of the Continental Congress,* 32:334–343. On the Midwest: Christy Clark-Pujara, "Contested: Black Suffrage in Early Wisconsin," *Wisconsin Magazine of History* (Summer 2017): 21–27; Allison Mileo Gorsuch, "Midwestern Territorial Courts and the Development of American Citizenship" (PhD diss., Yale, 2013); M. Scott Heerman, *The Alchemy of Slavery: Human Bondage and Emancipation in the Illinois Country, 1730-1865* (Philadelphia, 2018); Anna-Lisa Cox, *The Bone and Sinew of the Land: America's Forgotten Black Pioneers and the Struggle for Equality* (New York, 2018); Kate Masur, *Until Justice Be Done*; Matthew Salafia, *Slavery's Borderland: Freedom and Bondage Along the Ohio River* (Philadelphia, 2013); Nikki M. Taylor, *Frontiers of Freedom: Cincinnati's Black Community, 1802-1868* (Athens, OH, 2005). On "free states" and the "Free North," see Kellen Heniford, "Slavery Is Slavery: Early American Mythmaking and the Invention of the Free State" (PhD diss., Columbia, 2021); John L. Brooke, *"There is a North": Fugitive Slaves, Political Crisis, and Cultural Transformation in the Coming of the Civil War* (Amherst, 2019).

20. E. B. O'Callaghan, *The Documentary History of the State of New-York,* vol. 1 (Albany, 1850), 470–473; Carter et al., *Historical Statistics,* Series Eg1–59; White, *Somewhat More Independent,* 16–17. The colonial census counted "white" or "black"; there were some free black people. For this reason, I have rounded down the proportions.

21. New York State had the largest population of free black people in the North between 1810 and 1840, at which point Pennsylvania's black population grew larger. In 1860, New York was home to 49,005 free black people and Pennsylvania to 56,949. Carter et al., *Historical Statistics,* Series Bb1–98. This book is not a comparative study, but

it does suggest that the priorities and strategies of black northerners varied in revealing ways from state to state. For example, achieving equal suffrage was particularly important to black New Yorkers after 1821; by contrast, black Massachusettsans, who could vote on equal terms, concentrated on desegregating schools and the state militia. Scholars seldom tie such differences to the particular nature and timing of emancipation in each place.

22. *Autobiography of Andrew D. White*, vol. 1 (New York, 1905), 57; Samuel Ringgold Ward, "To the Four Thousand Colored Voters," *NS*, Sept. 1, 1848; Jabez D. Hammond, *The History of Political Parties in the State of New-York*, 2 vols. (Albany, 1842); Homer Adolph Stebbins, *A Political History of the State of New York, 1865-1869* (New York, 1913); Lee Benson, *The Concept of Jacksonian Democracy: New York as a Test Case* (Princeton, 1961); John L. Brooke, *Columbia Rising: Civic Life on the Upper Hudson from the Revolution to the Age of Jackson* (Chapel Hill, 2010). On New York as "the one true prize of nineteenth-century electoral politics," see Daniel Carpenter and Benjamin Schneer, "Party Formation through Petitions: The Whigs and the Bank War of 1832-1834," *Studies in American Political Development* (Oct. 2015), 217. On Congress's view that New York's political economy was crucial to the nation as a whole, see Jane Caroline Manner's "Congress and the Problem of Legislative Discretion, 1790-1870" (PhD diss., Princeton, 2018), ch. 4. For the state's "enormous socioeconomic, political, cultural, and legal influence in the antebellum period," see Amalia D. Kessler, *Inventing American Exceptionalism: The Origins of American Adversarial Legal Culture, 1800–1877* (New Haven, 2017), 17.

23. For a foundational work on archival records, the telling of history, and who and what get silenced, see Michel-Rolph Trouillot's *Silencing the Past: Power and the Production of History* (Boston, 1995). On creative uses of unpublished archives in the history of northern slavery, see Gloria McCahon Whiting, "Race, Slavery, and the Problem of Numbers in Early New England: A View from Probate Court," *WMQ* (July 2020): 405–440. Whiting argues that in mining underutlitized sources, scholars can make the invisible more visible and provide insight into "the particularity of the experiences of the people we study" (p. 440). See also the beginning of Chapter 1 in this book, where both the body text and accompanying secondary-source citations demonstrate a way to read the story of a specific unnamed black woman in the census records of Ulster County.

24. "Report of the Board of Accounts on New Netherland, 1644," in E. B. O'Callaghan, ed., *Documents Relative to the Colonial History of the State of New York* (Albany, 1856), 1:154.

25. Thelma Wills Foote, *Black and White Manhattan: The History of Racial Formation in Colonial New York City* (Oxford, 2004), 40.

26. Joyce D. Goodfriend, *Before the Melting Pot: Society and Culture in Colonial New York* (Princeton, 1992), 113; Berlin, *Many Thousands Gone*, 181, ch. 7; O'Callaghan, *Documentary History*, 3:503; Foote, *Black and White Manhattan*, 213, 217; White, *Somewhat More Independent*, 5, 16, 49–50.

27. P[hilip] A. Bell, "Our People and Our Paper," *Weekly Advocate* (New York), Feb. 25, 1837. See also the resolutions of "Messrs. Mabury, Binks and [Austin] Steward"

on a "school house for black children" in "School for Colored Children," *Ontario County Times,* May [?] 1851, clipping in OCR; Bob Markle, "The Constitution - Colonization," *FDP,* Sept. 4, 1851; James McCune Smith, "Citizenship," *Anglo-African Magazine,* May 1859; "Abolish the Property Qualification," *NASS,* Oct. 23, 1869. In 1850, Samuel Ringgold Ward and George T. Downing argued about black voters' partisan preferences. Ward, here and elsewhere in his newspaper, *The Impartial Citizen,* used "black." Downing preferred "colored." Both men used a lowercase for the adjective. "The Dirty Deed of Meanness," *Impartial Citizen* (Syracuse), June 12, 1850. As this one example suggests, language preferences were never universal. *N.B.* As historians of the early modern era (c. 1500–1800) know, writers used capital letters in the middle of sentences in ways that would become far less common in the nineteenth century. The rising generation's grammar and style, in the mid-1800s, looks more familiar to our contemporary eyes in this regard.

28. I'm indebted to the following scholars for shaping my consideration of language. I would posit that their choices, even when they differ, all have the capacity to do useful work when tailored to specific places, time periods, and methodological approaches. Vincent Brown, "BAR Book Forum: Vincent Brown's 'Tacky's Revolt,'" https://www.blackagendareport.com/bar-book-forum-vincent-browns-tackys-revolt, May 27, 2020; Leslie M. Harris, "Names, Terms, and Politics," *JER* (Spring 2023): 149–154; Jones, *Birthright Citizens,* 164; Elise A. Mitchell, Twitter, Jan. 18, 2022, 5:41 p.m., https://twitter.com/byeliseam; Tiya Miles, *All That She Carried: The Journey of Ashley's Sack, A Black Family Keepsake* (New York, 2021), 277–289; Jennifer Morgan, "Q & A with Jennifer Morgan, Author of *Reckoning with Slavery,*" https://dukeupress.wordpress.com/2021/06/11/qa-with-jennifer-morgan-author-of-reckoning-with-slavery/, June 11, 2021; Stephanie McCurry, *Masters of Small Worlds: Yeoman Households, Gender Relations, and the Political Culture of the Antebellum South Carolina Low Country* (New York, 1995); Kathleen M. Brown, *Good Wives, Nasty Wenches, and Anxious Patriarchs: Gender, Race and Power in Colonial Virginia* (Chapel Hill, 1996); Nicholas Rinehart, "Reparative Semantics: On Slavery and the Language of History," http://commonplace.online/article/reparative-semantics/, Jan. 4, 2022; David Waldstreicher, "Author's Note" in *The Odyssey of Phillis Wheatley: A Poet's Journey Through American Slavery and Independence* (New York, 2023); Penningroth, *Before the Movement,* xxvii–xxviii. I refer in the body text to ideological terrain. I have been influenced by Barbara Jeanne Fields's "analogy of terrain" in thinking about how people with authority shape landscapes of governance and power, and how those with little to no authority still have to move within this space. It may be hard to create the world anew, but generations of struggle do alter the terrain. "Slavery, Race and Ideology in the United States of America," *New Left Review* (May–June 1990): 113–114.

29. Miles agrees with the current preference for "enslaved person" and employs this language throughout her work, but also finds "slave" useful when "referring to categories defined and imposed by southern owners of people, to societal as well as legal dictates, and to racial systems of capture." Harris is "somewhat skeptical of the thinking that *slave* is a more dehumanizing or offensive word than *enslaved*" and looks for "the work

of humanity [in] the body of the whole" article or book. Miles, *All That She Carried,* 288; Harris, "Names," 150–151.

30. David Brion Davis, *The Problem of Slavery in the Age of Revolution, 1770-1823* (Ithaca, 1975), 21–22.

Chapter 1

1. Society for Apprehending Slaves, Call No. 11155, NYSL. Fourteen years later, Ulster County's masters continued to have the same problems. See Society of Negroes Unsettled (Sept. 5, 1810), Roelof J. and Ezekiel Elting Family Papers, Historic Huguenot Street Library, New Paltz, NY.

2. John Addison, Speech of John Addison . . . against the Bill for the gradual Abolition of Slavery, Senate House State Historic Site, Kingston, NY; Addison to Peter Van Gaasbeck, Mar. 10, 1796, ibid.; *JANY* (New York, 1796), 50–51, 61, 64–65; John Addison [and 6 slaves], 1790 US Census, Kingston, Ulster County, NY, accessed on Ancestry.com. On the circulation of news and rumor as political practice among slaves and the "masterless," see Julius S. Scott, *The Common Wind: Afro-American Currents in the Age of the Haitian Revolution* (Brooklyn, 2018); Steven Hahn, *A Nation Under Our Feet: Black Political Struggles in the Rural South from Slavery to the Great Migration* (Cambridge, MA, 2010). On insights gleaned from "expansive interpretation of the records while retaining the historical integrity of the documents," see Marisa J. Fuentes, *Dispossessed Lives: Enslaved Women, Violence, and the Archive* (Philadelphia, 2016), 78. I've long been influenced by Tiya Miles's *Ties that Bind: The Story of an Afro-Cherokee Family in Slavery and Freedom* (Berkeley, 2005), in which Miles pieces together the story of an enslaved woman named Doll from scraps of evidence and warns of the things we'll never know.

When Addison died in early 1800, he was a widower with one child, a daughter named Catherine, who had recently married Zachariah Hoffman, a descendent of a Dutch emigrant who settled in Ulster County in the 1650s. Hoffman, who administered Addison's estate, listed six slaves in his household on the 1800 census, which was tabulated in late 1800. Catherine and Zachariah likely inherited enslaved people from Addison (and possibly from Hoffman's own father, also a Zachariah). In 1820, the first time the U.S. census noted ages and sexes of enslaved people, Hoffman owned a woman over 45 and another between 26 and 44. One of these women may have labored for Addison in the 1790s. In any case, it is highly likely, given the number of people Addison owned and the common patterns of Hudson Valley slaveholding, that an enslaved woman was in Addison's household when he wrote his 1796 proslavery speech. "Died," *Rising Sun* (Kingston), Jan. 9, 1795; Roswell Randall Hoes, ed., *Baptismal and Marriage Records of the Old Dutch Church of Kingston, Ulster County* (Baltimore, 1980), 386, 671; "Died," *American Citizen* (New York), Mar. 25, 1800; Letters of Administration, vol. B (1796–1807), Surrogate's Court, Ulster County, p. 84; Arthur C. M. Kelly, *Baptism and Marriage Records of the Reformed Churches of Upper Red Hook . . . 1776-1899*, vol. 1 (Rhinebeck, 1973), 46; Zachariah Hoffman, 1800 US Census, North East, Dutchess County, NY; Zachariah Hoffman, 1820 US Census, Red Hook, Dutchess County, NY.

3. "For the Argus," *Argus* (New York), Jan. 23, 1796; "To the Person Whose Signature Is Justice," *Argus,* Jan. 28, 1796; "When the bill for a gradual abolition . . . ," *American Minerva* (New York), Feb. 11, 1796.

4. *NY Laws,* 22nd sess. (1799), ch. 62.

5. Douglas Egerton, *Rebels, Reformers, & Revolutionaries: Collected Essays and Second Thoughts* (New York, 2002), 3–20; Gordon Wood, *Empire of Liberty: A History of the Early Republic* (New York, 2009), 517.

6. The classic essay is Robert Fogel and Stanley Engerman, "Philanthropy at Bargain Prices: Notes on the Economics of Gradual Emancipation," *Journal of Legal Studies* (June 1974): 377–401. The authors don't address the "political, economic, and social issues related to the struggle over emancipation" because "little is known about the motivation of particular groups with respect to particular legislative proposals." I aim to provide that account.

7. Important books on gradual abolition have yet to devote much attention to early modern abolitionism and relevant labor practices: Melish, *Disowning Slavery,* 50; Gellman, *Emancipating New York,* 27–29; Harris, *In the Shadow,* 51; Polgar, *Standard-Bearers of Equality,* ch. 1. The Age of Revolution likewise plays an explanatory role in hemispheric histories: Robin Blackburn, *The Overthrow of Colonial Slavery, 1776-1848* (London, 1988); David Brion Davis, *Inhuman Bondage: The Rise and Fall of Slavery in the New World* (New York, 2006). Davis's *The Problem of Slavery in Western Culture* (Ithaca, 1966), however, explores early modern antislavery. For work deemphasizing the Revolution as a turning point, see Phillipe Rosenberg, "Thomas Tryon and the Seventeenth-Century Dimensions of Antislavery," *WMQ* (Oct. 2004): 609–642; Kristen Sword, "Remembering Dinah Nevil: Strategic Deceptions in Eighteenth-Century Antislavery," *Journal of American History* (Sept. 2010): 315–343. On connecting colonial to national legal history, see *The Many Legalities of Early America,* ed. Christopher Tomlins and Bruce Mann (Chapel Hill, 2001). On the difference between antislavery ideas being in existence versus operational, see Christopher Leslie Brown, *Moral Capital: Foundations of British Abolitionism* (Chapel Hill, 2006), 40–41. On the British metropole's lack of support of colonial antislavery measures in the 1770s: Bruce A. Ragsdale, *A Planter's Republic: The Search for Economic Independence in Revolutionary Virginia* (Madison, 1996), 134; Christian McBurney, "The First Efforts to Limit the African Slave Trade Arise in the American Revolution, Part 1 of 3, the New England Colonies," *Journal of the American Revolution,* Sept. 14, 2020.

8. Quakers have been underemphasized in the New York policy story, in part because New York was not a "Quaker colony" like Pennsylvania. Jean Soderlund rightly calls for "further study of the growth of abolitionism among New England and New York Friends." *Quakers and Slavery: A Divided Spirit* (Princeton, 1988), 22.

9. In worrying about dependency, early abolitionists were similar to later counterparts. That said, assumptions about political economy, labor markets, and the nature of childhood shifted over time. Compare William Lloyd Garrison's 1833 definition of freedom—"parents shall have the control and government of their own children, and

that the children shall belong to their parents"—with abolitionists' ideas in this chapter. "Annual Report of the New England Slavery Society," *Abolitionist* (Boston, 1833). For the U.S. Civil War era, see Mitchell, *Raising Freedom's Child*, ch. 4; Barbara Jeanne Fields, *Slavery and Freedom on the Middle Ground: Maryland During the Nineteenth Century* (New Haven, 1985), 139–156. On these dynamics across the Americas, see Yesenia Barragan, *Freedom's Captives: Slavery and Gradual Emancipation on the Columbian Black Pacific* (Cambridge, UK, 2021); Frederick Cooper, Thomas C. Holt, and Rebecca Scott, *Beyond Slavery: Explorations of Race, Labor, and Citizenship in Postemancipation Societies* (Chapel Hill, 2000); Camillia Cowling, *Conceiving Freedom: Women of Color, Gender, and the Abolition of Slavery in Havana and Rio de Janeiro* (Chapel Hill, 2013); Alejandro de la Fuente and Ariela J. Gross, *Becoming Free, Becoming Black: Race, Freedom and Law in Cuba, Virginia, and Louisiana* (Cambridge, UK, 2020). On older patterns persisting, see Laura F. Edwards, "The Problem of Dependency: African Americans, Labor Relations, and the Law in the Nineteenth-Century South," *Agricultural History* (Spring 1998): 313–340.

10. On poor, labor, and slave law, see Edmund Morgan, *American Slavery, American Freedom: The Ordeal of Colonial Virginia* (New York, 1975), chs. 16–17; Thomas D. Morris, *Southern Slavery and the Law, 1619-1860* (Chapel Hill, 1996), ch. 2; Michal Rozbicki, "To Save Them from Themselves: Proposals to Enslave the British Poor, 1698-1755," *Slavery and Abolition* 22 (2001): 19–50; Christopher Tomlins, *Freedom Bound: Law, Labor and Civic Identity in Colonizing America, 1580-1865* (Cambridge, UK, 2010), ch. 6. Allison Madar emphasizes the persistence of nonheritable servitude: "Servitude in the 18th-Century British Atlantic World: Old Paradigms and New Directions," *History Compass* (Sept. 2017): 1–10. On poverty, mobility, race, and local police power, see Masur, *Until Justice Be Done*, ch. 1; Kristin O'Brassil-Kulfan, *Vagrants and Vagabonds: Poverty and Mobility in the Early American Republic* (New York, 2019); Samantha Seeley, *Race, Removal, and the Right to Remain: Migration and the Making of the United States* (Chapel Hill, 2021).

11. Philip Morgan, "Slaves and Poverty," in *Down and Out in Early America*, ed. Billy G. Smith (University Park, PA, 2004), 93. For a concise overview of labor coercion in the English Atlantic that will further contextualize the colonial laws and examples I'm about to discuss, see David Eltis, "Labour and Coercion in the English Atlantic World from the Seventeenth to the Early Twentieth Century," *Slavery & Abolition* (April 1993), 207–226.

12. *The Colonial Laws of New York from the Year 1664 to the Revolution* (Albany, 1894), 1:18, 26, 36–37, 48–49, 147–148, 157–159, 519–521, 631, 761–767; ibid., 2:655–656; ibid., 3:194–195; ibid., 4:924–925. Law was crucial to processes of racialization. This chapter is not a study of that process, but it bears mentioning that to be black and/or a slave meant being grouped in a "problematic" underclass as well as being made distinct within it. On racial formation, see Foote, *Black and White Manhattan*.

13. *Colonial Laws of New York*, 1:131–133, 237–238, 328–331, 348–351, 539–542.

14. *Colonial Laws of New York,* 1:761–767. The twenty-pound yearly stipend for freedpeople was revoked in 1717, but the two-hundred-pound bond remained in effect. *Colonial Laws of New York,* 1:761–767, 922–923.

15. Richard Morris, ed., *Select Cases of the Mayor's Court of New York City, 1674-1784* (Washington, DC, 1935), 69; Kenneth Scott, "The Church Wardens and the Poor in New York City, 1732-1735," *New York Genealogical and Biographical Record* (July 1970): 172; *Colonial Laws of New York,* 3:1017–1018; Edward Durand, *The Finances of New York City* (New York, 1898), 30–31.

16. William Blackstone, *Commentaries on the Laws of England* (Oxford, 1765), 1:441; Holly Brewer, *By Birth or Consent: Children, Law, and the Anglo-American Revolution in Authority* (Chapel Hill, 2005), ch. 7; Michael Grossberg, *Governing the Hearth: Law and the Family in Nineteenth Century America* (Chapel Hill, 1985), 259–268.

17. Colonial Indentures (1718–1721), 340–341, New York City-Indentures, NYHS.

18. Town of Huntington, *Records of the Overseers of the Poor: Part 1, 1752-1804* (Huntington, 1986), 8, 9, 17.

19. Town Meeting and Election Records (1712–1824), Box 1, Folder 3 (1797–1816), Historic Huguenot Street Library; Martha Branscombe, *The Courts and the Poor Laws of New York State, 1784-1829* (Chicago, 1943), 20. For an eighteenth-century view, see A Jersey Man, *The Countryman's Lamentation, on the Neglect of a Proper Education of Children* (Philadelphia, 1762). Holly Brewer's analysis is instructive: "Apprenticeship Policy in Virginia: From Patriarchal to Republican Policies of Social Welfare," in Ruth Wallis Herndon and John E. Murray, eds., *Children Bound to Labor: The Pauper Apprentice System in Early America* (Ithaca, 2009).

20. Morris, *Select Cases of the Mayor's Court,* 368–369.

21. Sarah L. H. Gronningsater, "Born Free in the Master's House: Children and Gradual Emancipation in the Early American North," in *Child Slavery Before and After Emancipation: An Argument for Child-Centered Slavery Studies,* ed. Anna Mae Duane (New York, 2017), 129–131; Wendy Warren, "'Thrown upon the world': Valuing Infants in the Eighteenth-Century North American Slave Market," *Slavery and Abolition* (May 2018): 623–641.

22. "To be sold," *New-York Gazette,* Dec. 19, 1748; "To be sold," *New-York Gazette,* May 13, 1751; "A Negro Wench," *Royal Gazette* (New York), Feb. 26, 1780. *Colonial Laws of New York,* 2:876–884; [David Cooper], *A Mite caste into the Treasury: Or, Observations on Slave-Keeping* (Philadelphia, 1772), 14.

23. George Fox, *Gospel-Family Order* (Philadelphia, 1701), 17, 19. The Biblical references are Exodus 21:2–6, Deuteronomy 15:12, Leviticus 19:18 and 19:34, Matthew 7:12, Luke 6:31. For citations of Fox in the 1700s, see John Hepburn, *The American Defense of the Christian Golden Rule* (New York, 1715), preface; Ralph Sandiford, *A Brief Examination of the Practice of the Times* (Philadelphia, 1729), preface, 14, 36; Elihu Coleman, *A Testimony Against that Antichristian Practice of Making Slaves of Men* (Boston, 1733). Pennsylvanian Robert Pyle's 1698 epistle urged masters to free their slaves after

a term of years: "An Early Antislavery Statement," *Journal of Negro History* (Oct. 1937): 488–493. On Fox's antislavery, see Bryccan Carey, "'The Power that Giveth Liberty and Freedom': The Barbadian Origins of Quaker Antislavery Rhetoric, 1657-76," *Ariel* (Jan. 2007): 27–48; Katharine Gerbner, "Antislavery in Print: The Germantown Protest, the "Exhortation," and the Seventeenth-Century Quaker Debate on Slavery," *Early American Studies* (Fall 2011): 552–574.

24. *Oyster Bay Town Records, 1653–1878* (New York, 1924), 2: 335, 388, 453. The 1708 date is a best guess.

25. In Quaker organizational structure, a yearly meeting is the highest level of institutional authority. A yearly meeting comprises local monthly and regional quarterly meetings in the surrounding area. Yearly meetings were in close contact with one another, writing each other for guidance. In the colonies, the Philadelphia Yearly Meeting held sway. The American meetings looked to the London Yearly Meeting for leadership. In the late 1700s, there were about 40,000 Quakers in the American colonies and 50,000 in Britain. In 1750, there were 70 Quaker meetings in Pennsylvania, 41 in New Jersey, and 20 in New York. Barry Levy, *Quakers and the American Family: British Settlement in the Delaware Valley* (New York, 1988), 278; Soderlund, *Quakers and Slavery*, Appendix A; Frederick Tolles, *Quakers and the Atlantic Culture* (New York, 1960), 24.

26. Early American Quaker antislavery tracts were printed without the permission of the Quaker overseers of the press. This did not mean the tracts were "illegal," but rather that they did not bear the official sanction of the yearly meeting. There were a few early non-Quaker protests against slavery, but these were not voices that sustained a coherent antislavery movement within a religious group. See Samuel Sewell, *The Selling of Joseph, a Memorial* (Boston, 1700); Cotton Mather, *The Negro Christianized . . . the Instruction of Negro Servants in Christianity* (Boston, 1706); Rosenberg, "Thomas Tryon." In 1652, Rhode Island adopted a law ordering slaves brought to the colony be freed after ten years, "as the manner is with English servants," but it was not enforced. Elizabeth Donnan, ed., *Documents Illustrative of the History of the Slave Trade to America* (Washington, DC, 1932), 3:108.

27. On Quakers regulating private households, see Levy, *Quakers and the American Family*, esp. ch. 3.

28. George Keith [and others], *An Exhortation & Caution to Friends Concerning buying or keeping of Negroes* (New York, 1693), 2–3.

29. Sarah Lelia Crabtree, "A Holy Nation: The Quaker Itinerant Ministry" (PhD diss., University of Minnesota, 2007).

30. Lay, *All Slave-Keepers*, 6; "Flushing, Queens, NY, Monthly Meeting, Men's Minutes 1703-1784," NYYMM, Dec. 23, 1716, Mar. 25, 1717, Mar. 24, 1718 (Mullinex's name appears as "Mulloneaux"); New York Yearly Meeting, "Long Island to the Yearly Meeting in London" (1718), Epistles Received Vol. 2. 1705–1738, pp. 235–237, Library of the Society of Friends, London; John Cox Jr., *Quakerism in the City of New York, 1657-1930* (New York, 1930), 56; New York Yearly Meeting of the Religious Society of Friends,

Discipline (Philadelphia Yearly Meeting), 1719 [Matinecock copy] and New York Yearly Meeting of the Religious Society of Friends, Book of Discipline (Philadelphia Yearly Meeting), 1719 [Purchase Monthly Meeting Copy], FHL.

31. Coleman, *A Testimony*, 15; J. William Frost, "Quaker Antislavery: From Dissidence to Sense of the Meeting," *Quaker History* (Spring 2012): 32.

32. Jack Marietta, *The Reformation of American Quakerism, 1748-1783* (Philadelphia, 1984), preface, ch. 5.

33. John Woolman, *Some Considerations on the Keeping of Negroes* (Philadelphia, 1754), 11; John Woolman, *Considerations on Keeping Negroes . . . Part Second* (Philadelphia, 1762), 47; John Woolman, *The Journal and Essays of John Woolman*, ed. Amelia Mott Gummere (New York, 1922), 58, 62, 170, 242–244; "Register of the Names of Ministering Friends," Seaman Family Papers, 1752–1838, Brooklyn Historical Society.

34. Anthony Benezet, *A Short Account of that Part of Africa Inhabited by Negroes* (Philadelphia, 1762), 70–71.

35. Harold D. Wax, "Negro Import Duties in Colonial Pennsylvania," *Pennsylvania Magazine of History and Biography* (Jan. 1973): 42–44.

36. Gary B. Nash, "Urban Wealth and Poverty in Pre-Revolutionary America," *Journal of Interdisciplinary History* (Spring 1976): 556–560; Edward Countryman, *A People in Revolution: The American Revolution and Political Society in New York* (Baltimore, 1981), 10–11.

37. *Colonial Laws of New York*, 4:924; 5:513, 533, 583.

38. NY Const. (1777), art. 35.

39. Oblong Monthly Meeting, Men's Minutes 1757–1788, NYYMM. On Quaker internal discipline, see Marietta, *Reformation of American Quakerism*, ch. 1. In the late 1700s, Quakers freed slaves whom they could have sold for profit. For the subtle ways Quaker antislavery may have been related to economic interests in later decades, see David Brion Davis's argument in Thomas Bender, ed., *The Antislavery Debate: Capitalism and Abolitionism as a Problem in Historical Interpretation* (Berkeley, 1992). Nash and Soderlund dispute Davis's thesis for the case of Pennsylvania. *Freedom by Degrees*, 47–48. For an explanation focusing on sectarian reform, see Marietta, ch. 5.

40. See Oblong Monthly Meeting, Men's Minutes 1757-1788, meeting records between 1764 and 1766.

41. New York Yearly Meeting, Minutes, 1746–1800 (microfilm), pp. 55, 57–58, FHL.

42. Flushing Monthly Meeting, Women's Minutes, 1771-1806, NYMMM, Dec. 6, 1775; Drake, *Quakers and Slavery*, ch. 4.

43. Flushing Monthly Meeting, Men's Minutes 1703-1784, NYYMM, 1779–1781, passim. As a meeting ritual, Quakers answered a prescribed set of questions—queries—in order to assess the spiritual well-being and discipline of the group. Quakers throughout a yearly meeting would use the same queries.

44. Westbury Women's Minutes 1774-1776, Aug. 28, 1776, NYYMP.

45. Westbury Monthly Meeting, Manumissions (Original Certificates), NYYMP; Flushing Monthly Meeting, Men's Minutes 1703-1784, NYYMM, Summer (?) 1782.

46. Cooper, *A Mite Cast into the Treasury*, 13–14.

47. Cooper, *A Mite Cast into the Treasury*, 17. For another Quaker paying attention to the age of release, see William Dillwyn, *Brief Considerations on Slavery, and the Expediency of its Abolition* (Burlington, NJ, 1773).

48. Catherine Adams and Elizabeth H. Pleck's *Black Women in Colonial and Revolutionary New England* (New York, 2010) explores both obscure black women and more well-known figures in Massachusetts such as Elizabeth Freeman. Kristin Sword's *Wives Not Slaves: Patriarchy and Modernity in the Age of Revolutions* (Chicago, 2021) examines debates over marriage, slavery, and imperial power more broadly. On Phillis Wheatley, the most famous black woman of the age, see Waldstreicher, *Odyssey of Phillis Wheatley.* My chapter here only scratches the surface of what could be written specifically about black women in Revolutionary-era New York.

49. Gary Nash, *Forging Freedom: The Formation of Philadelphia's Black Community, 1720-1840* (Cambridge, MA, 1988), 40; Benjamin Rush, *An Address to the Inhabitants of the British Settlements in America, upon Slave-Keeping* (Philadelphia, 1773), 22–23. Rush published the pamphlet anonymously, but as the newspaper article cited in note 52 suggests, it was no secret that Rush was the author.

50. Maurice Jackson, *Let This Voice Be Heard: Anthony Benezet, Father of Atlantic Abolitionism* (Philadelphia, 2009), 109–117; Humanus [Thomas Paine], "A Serious Thought," *Pennsylvania Journal*, Oct. 18, 1775.

51. Formation of the Pennsylvania Abolition Society, 1775–1788, Cox-Parish-Wharton Papers (Collection 0154), Historical Society of Pennsylvania; Sword, "Remembering Dinah Nevil," 316.

52. "Mr. Holt," *New York Journal,* Feb. 18, 1773. Eleutheros is Greek for "free, one who is not a slave."

53. On New Light Calvinism, see Davis, *Slavery in the Age of Revolution,* ch. 7; John Saillant, "Slavery and Divine Providence in New England Calvinism: The New Divinity and a Black Protest, 1775-1805," *WMQ* (Dec. 1995): 584–608; Jonathan Sassi, "The Whole Country Have Their Hands Full of Blood on This Day," *Proceedings of the American Antiquarian Society* (June 2004): 29–92,

54. Sword, "Remembering Dinah Nevil," 327; Samuel Hopkins, *The Works of Samuel Hopkins, D.D.*, ed. Edwards Park (Boston, 1854) 1:121, 123, 137, 160; Hopkins, *A Dialogue Concerning the Slavery of the Africans* (Norwich, 1776), 62.

55. Hopkins, *A Dialogue*, 35–36, 45. Hopkins had read Benezet. See Jonathan Sassi's "The Whole Country," 55–56.

56. Hopkins, *The Works,* 2:551, 747. For other Protestant antislavery sermons, see John Allen, *An Oration on the Beauties of Liberty, Or the Essential Rights of the American* (Boston, 1773); Levi Hart, "Some Thoughts on the Subject of Freeing the Negro Slaves in the Colony of Connecticut" (1774), ed. John Saillant, *New England Quarterly* (Mar 2002): 107–128; Jacob Green, *Sermon Delivered at Hanover (in New-Jersey) April 22, 1778* (Chatham, 1779). Hart and Green proposed abolition plans focused on children.

57. Petition for freedom to Massachusetts Governor Thomas Gage, His Majesty's Council, and the House of Representatives, May 25, 1774, Jeremy Belknap Papers, Massachusetts Historical Society; Petition for freedom to the Massachusetts Council and the House of Representatives, Jan. [13,] 1777, ibid; Chernoh Momodu Sesay Jr., "Freemasons of Color: Prince Hall, Revolutionary Black Boston, and the Origins of Black Freemasonry, 1770–1807" (PhD diss., Northwestern, 2006).

58. Jupiter Hammon, *An Address to the Negroes in the State of New-York* (New York, 1787), 12–13. One biographer surmises Hammon heard John Woolman preach in the mid-1700s. Sondra Ann O'Neale, *Jupiter Hammon and the Biblical Beginnings of African-American Literature* (Metuchen, 1993), 28–30. Cedrick May and Julie McCown argue for Hammon's strong antislavery convictions in "'An Essay on Slavery: An Unpublished Poem by Jupiter Hammon," *Early American Literature* (Spring 2013): 457–471.

59. Hammon, *An Address to the Negroes*, 12. In 1809, Joseph Sidney, a black abolitionist in New York City, expressed doubt about "immediate emancipation" for slaves on southern plantations, but saw no "argument against their *gradual* emancipation." *An Oration, Commemorative of the Abolition of the Slave Trade* (New York, 1809), 5.

60. "A Proclamation," *Virginia Gazette*, Nov. 23, 1775; "Williamsburgh, December 2," *Constitutional Gazette* (New York), Dec. 16, 1775; Cassandra Pybus, "Jefferson's Faulty Math: The Question of Slave Defections in the American Revolution," *WMQ* (Apr. 2005): 243–264; "Three Pounds Reward," *New York Journal*, Mar. 14, 1776.

61. Judith Van Buskirk, "Crossing the Lines: African-Americans in the New York City Region During the British Occupation, 1776-1783," *Pennsylvania History* 65 (1998): 74–100; "Run-away, from Samuel Sackett," *New-York Gazette*, Nov. 25, 1776.

62. "Committee Chamber," *New-York Journal*, Apr. 11, 1776; "Five Dollars Reward," *Constitutional Gazette* (New York), Aug. 21, 1776; "By His Excellency," *Royal Gazette*, July 3, 1779; Evert Bancker to Abraham Bancker, Sept. 23, 1780; Abraham B. Bancker to Evert Bancker, Oct. 7, 1780, Bancker papers, NYHS.

63. "Forty Shillings Reward," *Constitutional Gazette*, July 10, 1776; *NY Laws*, 4th sess. (1781), ch. 32; William Heath to Gov. George Clinton, June 24, 1782, Sol Feinstone Collection, Item 2369, American Philosophical Society.

64. *New York in the Revolution as Colony and State* (Albany, 1904) 29, 36; John Peterson, 1810 US Census, Cortlandt, NY; "Recollections of the Revolution," *Albany Argus*, Mar. 15, 1833; "Fourth of July," *Hudson River Chronicle*, July 10, 1838; "Jack Peterson, A Volunteer of the Revolution," *Westchester Herald*, Dec. 24, 1850; William Cooper Nell, *Property Qualification or No Property Qualification: A Few Facts From the Records of Patriotic Services of the Colored Men of New York* (New York, 1860), 7–9.

65. Ira Berlin, foreword to Cassandra Pybus, *Epic Journeys of Freedom: Runaway Slaves of the American Revolution and Their Global Quest for Liberty* (Boston, 2006); Christopher Leslie Brown and Philip D. Morgan, eds., *Arming Slaves: From Classical Times to the Modern Age* (New Haven, 2006).

66. William Jay, *The Life of John Jay, with Selections from His Correspondence and Miscellaneous Papers* (New York, 1833), 1:69; *Journals of the Provincial Congress,*

Provincial Convention, Committee of Safety and Council of Safety of the State of New York: 1775-1776-1777 (Albany, 1842), 1:887, 889–890; John Jay to Robert R. Livingston and Gouverneur Morris, Apr. 29, 1777, in *The Correspondence and Public Papers of John Jay*, ed. Henry P. Johnston (New York, 1890), 1:127–128; VT Const. (1777), ch. 1, § 1.

67. Nash and Soderlund, *Freedom by Degrees*, 101; Horace Binney, *Leaders of the Old Philadelphia Bar* (Philadelphia, 1859), 25; "William Lewis," *Poulson's American Daily Advertiser* (Philadelphia), Aug. 19, 1819; Robert Vaux, *Memoirs of the Life of Anthony Benezet* (Philadelphia, 1817), 103.

68. "An Act for the Gradual Abolition of Slavery" (Mar. 1, 1780) in *Laws Enacted in the Second Sitting of the Fourth General Assembly, of the Commonwealth of Pennsylvania . . .* (Philadelphia, 1780), 296–299.

69. "An Act concerning Indian, Molatto, and Negro Servants and Slaves" (1784) in *Acts and Laws of the State of Connecticut, in America* (New London, 1784), 233–235; "An Act authorizing the Manumission of Negroes, Mulattoes and others, and for the gradual Abolition of Slavery" (Feb. 1784) in *Records of the State of Rhode Island and Providence Plantations in New England*, vol. 10, 1784 to 1792 (Providence, 1865), 7–8; "An Act Repealing part . . . 'An Act Authorizing the Manumission of Negroes . . .'" (1785) in ibid., 132–133.

70. Melish offers a cogent analysis of these laws, but I disagree that offering owners the uncompensated service of children "in exchange for the expense of raising them" constituted "an entirely new form of servitude." Melish, *Disowning Slavery*, 69.

71. John Jay to Egbert Benson, Sept. 17, 1780, *Public Papers of John Jay*, 1:406–407.

72. John Jay to J. C. Dongan, Feb. 27, 1792, *Public Papers of John Jay*, 3:413–415. The origins of Jay's antislavery beliefs are hazy. His father owned over ten slaves and Jay owned slaves himself. Egbert Benson wrote that Jay "almost from his infancy" was "principled against negro slavery." Benson to Peter Van Schaack, Mar. 1792, Van Schaack Family papers, 1686–1887, Rare Book and Manuscript Library, Columbia University. As a legal apprentice in the 1760s, Jay was mentored by an antislavery Quaker named Lindley Murray. Herbert Johnson, *John Jay: Colonial Lawyer* (New York, 1989), 17–19; NYMS, vol. 6, Aug. 10, 1786, p. 48. For a new and deeply researched study of the Jay family and their relationship to antislavery policy and the black people in their lives, see David N. Gellman, *Liberty's Chain: Slavery, Abolition, and the Jay Family of New York* (Ithaca, 2022).

73. Manumission Document for Benoit (Mar. 21, 1784), John Jay Papers, 1688–[ca. 1862], Rare Book & Manuscript Library, Columbia University; Jay, *The Life of John Jay*, 1:230; New York Manumission Society, Register of Slaves Manumitted, pp. 3–4, Museum of the City of New York; Frederick Jay to John Jay, Nov 18, 1781, in *John Jay: The Winning of the Peace: Unpublished Papers, 1780-1784*, ed. Richard B. Morris (New York, 1975), 201.

74. John Jay to Peter Jay Munro, Sept. 14, 1794, John Jay Family Papers, Museum of the City of New York.

75. For examples of towns supporting old or sick slaves, see Town of Huntington, *Records of the Overseers of the Poor: part 1*; Records of the Town of Eastchester, Overseers of the Poor, 1778–1824, NYSA.

76. John Jay to Benjamin Rush, Mar. 24, 1785, John Jay Papers; *Secret Journals of the Acts and Proceedings of Congress* (Boston, 1821), 4:277. For similar ideas expressed by Quakers, see George Brown to John Pemberton, Feb. 18, 1786, Pemberton Family Papers, 1641–1880, Historical Society of Pennsylvania.

77. For evidence of antislavery slave owners in Jay's circle debating what to do with their own slaves, see NYMS, vol. 6, Feb. 4, 1785, p. 16, Nov. 10, 1785, pp. 28–31, Feb. 8, 1786, p. 36, May 11, 1786, p. 40, Aug. 10, 1786, p. 49, Nov. 9, 1786, p. 56; vol. 9, Apr. 11, 1809, p. 214. On legal technicalities of freeing those yet born: "When the bill for a gradual abolition . . . ," *American Minerva*, Feb. 11, 1796.

78. François Furstenberg, "Beyond Freedom and Slavery: Autonomy, Virtue, and Resistance in Early American Political Discourse," *Journal of American History* (Mar. 2003): 1295–1330; Michal Rozbicki, *Culture and Liberty in the Age of the American Revolution* (Charlottesville, 2011), esp. ch. 1.

79. White, *Somewhat More Independent*, 16, 23, 27.

80. Brooke, *Columbia Rising*, ch. 6; Gellman, *Emancipating New York*, 177–179. In 1785, Aaron Burr (yes, that Aaron Burr) proposed an act that "declared absolutely free" any slave in the state. The motion was quickly defeated. Burr, like other antislavery lawmakers described in this chapter, owned slaves himself. *JANY* (New York, 1785), 53; Nancy Isenberg, *Fallen Founder: The Life of Aaron Burr* (New York, 2007), 90–91. The Federalists and Republicans competed in what historians later named the First Party System.

81. *NY Laws*, 4th sess. (1781), ch. 32; Jackson *ex dem.* the People v. Lervey, 5 Cowen 397 (1826); Ira Berlin and Leslie Harris, eds., *Slavery in New York* (New York, 2005); Groth, *Slavery and Freedom*, ch. 3; Vivienne Kruger, "Born to Run: The Slavery Family in Early New York, 1626 to 1827" (PhD diss., Columbia, 1985), chs. 11, 12; White, *Somewhat More Independent*, ch. 2; Sherill D. Wilson, *New York City's African Slaveowners: A Social and Material Culture History* (New York, 1994); Harry B. Yoshpe, "Record of Slave Manumissions in New York During the Colonial and Early National Periods," *Journal of Negro History* (Jan. 1941): 78–107; New-York Manumission Society, vols. 2 and 3, Register of Slaves Manumitted, Slavery Collection, Museum of the City of New York; ACR, 132; Town of Beekman records, 1772–1925, Division of Rare and Manuscript Collections, Cornell University, n.p.; Records of Poughkeepsie Precinct: 1769–1831, Local History Room, Adriance Memorial Library, Poughkeepsie; Manumission of Hester's child, Susanna, 1800, Documents Related to Slavery in Westchester County, New York, 1799–1809, Manuscripts and Special Collections, NYSL; Catherine Bleeker's Contract with Daniel Paris of Canajoharie, New York for slave Tom, 1796 Feb. 25, MS AM 899.478 (1), Houghton Library, Harvard University.

82. *JSNY* (New York, 1784), 38, 45, 54; Henry D. Paine, ed. *Paine Family Records* (New York, 1883), 2:206; Edmund Prior to James Pemberton, Feb. 26, 1784, Mar. 3, 1784, Mar. 10, 1784, Pemberton Family Papers; *JSNY* (New York, 1785), 8, 15; *JANY* (New York, 1785), 14.

83. New York Yearly Meeting, Meeting for Sufferings Minutes, 1758–1796, Friends Historical Library, pp. 129–130; *JSNY* (New York, 1785), 18; Petition of the Subscribers, Freeholders and Inhabitants . . . in the County of Ulster, Mar. 31, 1785, Senate House.

84. *JANY* (1785), 14, 48, 55.

85. *JANY* (1785), 53, 55, 56. See also Changes to Bill, Mar. 2, 1785, Manuscripts and Special Collections, NYSL.

86. *JANY* (1785), 56, 62, 63, 77; Comfort Sands, 1790 US Census, East Ward, New York, NY; Stephen Bielinksi, "Peter W. Yates," accessed July 30, 2014, http://www.nysm.nysed.gov/albany/bios/y/pwyates.html; Changes to Bill, Mar. 2, 1785; *JSNY* (1785), 42, 45.

87. Alfred Street, ed., *The Council of Revision of the State of New York* (Albany, 1859), 268. Livingston wrote the report. The record does not say whether the council was unanimous. This is one of the few instances in which Clinton *may* have made a clear antislavery political decision.

88. *NY Laws*, 8th sess. (1785), ch. 67.

89. Drake, *Quakers and Slavery,* 98; NYMS, vol. 6, Feb. 4, 1785, pp. 3–4, Feb. 4, 1785, pp. 8–13, Feb. 10, 1785, p. 16. For a membership list, see NYMS, vol. 6, Feb. 4, 1785, pp. 8–13. Barbour et al., *Quaker Crosscurrents*, 70.

90. See, for example: Hodges, *Root and Branch,* 166; Edgar McManus, *A History of Negro Slavery in New York* (Syracuse, 1966), ch. 9. For the quote, see William Hamilton, *An Oration Delivered in the African Zion Church on the Fourth of July, 1827* (New York, 1827), 7.

91. Brooke, *Columbia Rising,* 6, William J. Novak, "The American Law of Association: The Legal-Political Construction of Civil Society," *Studies in American Political Development* (Fall 2001): 163–188; Susan J. Pearson, "A New Birth of Regulation: The State of the State After the Civil War," *JCWE* (Sept. 2015): 422–439.

92. NYMS, vol. 6, Feb. 10, 1785, p. 17, May 12, 1785, p. 19. Paul Polgar is right that the Manumission Society promoted abolition from the start, despite using the word "manumission" in its name, which some historians have used to claim that the organization was not "abolitionist" but rather only a supporter of voluntary private manumissions. They were gradualists at this stage, but also explicitly abolitionist. Polgar, *Standard-Bearers,* 54.

93. NYMS, vol. 6, Nov. 10, 1785, pp. 26–28, Feb. 8, 1786, pp. 35, 37, May 11, 1786, p. 40; Samuel Hopkins, *A Dialogue Concerning the Slavery of the Africans* (New York, 1785).

94. NYMS, vol. 6, Nov. 15, 1787, pp. 81–83, Feb. 19, 1789, p. 127. See also Chapter 3 in this book.

95. On slavery and the U.S. Constitution, see Blanck, *Tyrannicide*; Don E. Fehrenbacher, *The Slaveholding Republic: An Account of the United States Government's Relations to Slavery* (Oxford, 2001); George Van Cleve, *A Slaveholders' Union: Slavery, Politics and the Constitution in the Early American Republic* (Chicago, 2010); David Waldstreicher, *Slavery's Constitution: From Revolution to Ratification* (New York, 2009); William Wiecek, *The Sources of Anti-Slavery Constitutionalism in America, 1760-1848* (Ithaca, 1977); Sean Wilentz, *No Property in Man: Slavery and Antislavery at the Nation's*

Founding (Cambridge, MA, 2018). These scholars do not always agree on matters of interpretation and emphasis; it's worth reading all of them.

96. NYMS, vol. 6, Aug. 16, 1787, p. 72, Aug. 17, 1787, p 74.

97. On the powers reserved to the states, see discussion of the "federal consensus" in Fehrenbacher, *The Slaveholding Republic;* Wiecek, *Sources of Antislavery Constitutionalism*. For examples of early abolitionists trying to influence national politics, see William C. diGiacomantonio, "'For the Gratification of a Volunteering Society': Antislavery and Pressure Group Politics in the First Federal Congress," *JER* (Summer 1995): 169–197; Wood, "A class of Citizens"; NYMS, vol. 6, Feb. 18, 1790, p. 72, Dec. 14, 1790, pp. 148–150.

98. NYMS, vol. 6, Nov. 9, 1786, p. 55, Feb. 15, 1787, pp. 60, 62; *NY Laws,* 11th sess. (1788), ch. 40.

99. *JANY* (New York, 1790), 13–15.

100. John Kaminski, *George Clinton: Yeoman Politician of the New Republic* (Madison, 1993), 206–207; George Clinton, Esq., 1790 US Census, New York City East Ward, NY; Peter Tappen, 1790 US Census, Kingston, Ulster County. Historians often write that Clinton was a member of the Manumission Society. I have found no evidence in any primary source, nor do any of the secondary sources I have read cite primary sources showing his membership. See, for example, John Kaminski, *George Clinton,* 193, which cites Alfred Young's *Democratic Republicans of New York* (Chapel Hill, 1967), 253, which cites Sidney Pomerantz, *New York: An American City, 1783-1803* (New York, 1938), 221. These are all great books, but the chase through the footnotes doesn't lead to evidence of Clinton in the NYMS. The Society was filled with his political enemies. Paul Finkelman is right that Clinton had little to no interest in antislavery. *Slavery and the Founders: Race and Liberty in the Age of Jefferson* (Armonk, NY, 2001), 119. Thomas Mosely doesn't mention Clinton once in "A History of the New-York Manumission Society, 1785-1849" (PhD diss., NYU, 1963). Interestingly, some Federalists tried to argue Clinton was antislavery, too, as a way of mitigating the negative effects (among some swing voters) of Jay's obvious abolitionism. But this was political messaging more than it was a comment on Clinton's (utter lack of) active antislavery efforts. See John C. Wynkoop to Peter Van Schaack, Apr. 17, 1792, in John P. Kaminski, ed., *A Necessary Evil?: Slavery and Debate over the Constitution* (Madison, 1995), 236–237.

101. *Public Papers of John Jay,* 3:413.

102. *JANY* (New York, 1796), 27, 51; Charles Adams to Vice President John Adams in *The Adams Papers, Adams Family Correspondence, Volume 11: July 1795–February 1797,* ed. Margaret A. Hogan et al. (Cambridge, MA, 2013) pp. 164–166. See also *JSNY* (Albany, 1797), 32.

103. William Hamilton to John Jay, Mar. 8, 1796, John Jay Papers; *Longworth's . . . New-York Register and City Directory* (New York, 1797), 195.

104. Brooke, *Columbia Rising,* 264 (the new counties were Oneida, Rockland, and Chenango); *JANY* (Albany, 1798), 112, 262. It remained common to hear complaints

of the "expensiveness" of young servants. In 1788, the legislature reasoned that since "apprentices and servants, when they are very young, are rather a burthen, than otherwise," those who ran away would have their terms of service extended by double the time they were absent. *NY Laws,* 11th sess. (1788), ch. 15. See also *Griffin v. Potter*, 14 Wendell 209 (1835), 212. Well into the early republic, poor white children were bound out until 18 and 21 by overseers of the poor. See, for example, Indenture of Benjamin Evans, Pauper apprentice of Shawangunk, NY, 1797, Robert E. Brooker III Collection of American Legal and Land Use Documents, No. 2019, Boston College Libraries; Indenture of Elizabeth Morison, poor child of the Town, 1804, New Windsor, New York Precinct Records, 1763–1779, p. 203.

105. "Common law," which New York State received in its 1777 constitution, was the part of English law deriving from custom and judicial precedent rather than statutes or positive law.

106. *JANY* (Albany, 1798), 267–268; *NY Laws,* 11th sess. (1788), ch. 62.

107. Kunal Parker, "Making Blacks Foreigners: The Legal Construction of Former Slaves in Post-Revolutionary Massachusetts," *Utah Law Review* 75 (2001): 75–124; Cornelia H. Dayton and Sharon V. Salinger, *Robert Love's Warnings: Searching for Strangers in Colonial Boston* (Philadelphia, 2014).

108. Samuel Ten Broeck, 1790 US Census, Clermont, Columbia County, NY.

109. Samuel Ten Broeck to William Wilson, Mar. 24, 1798, Wilson Family Papers, 1704–1884, Clements Library, University of Michigan.

110. "Legislature of New York," *Daily Advertiser* (New York), Feb. 6, 1799; "Gradual Abolition," *Gazette of the United States* (New York), Mar. 20, 1799; "Legislature of New York," *Gazette of the United States,* Mar. 29, 1799. Van Cleve emphasizes the connections among poor law, abolition, and taxpayer concerns, as well. *Slaveholders' Union,* 80, 90–93. New Jersey taxpayers were similarly concerned. See Bergen County petition to the Legislature requesting repeal of the NJ Abolition Act of 1804, Jan. 4, 1806, State Library MSS Collection, Box 5-3, Folder 419, New Jersey State Archives. I thank Jim Gigantino for sharing this source.

111. *JANY* (Albany, 1799), 47, 77, 81, 102, 107–108.

112. *NY Laws,* 22nd sess. (1799), ch. 62. Some historians have read the state payments for freed children's support as a form of compensated emancipation, and indeed, some sneaky masters initially bound back the very children they abandoned. But there was a long tradition of using poor relief funds to pay assigned masters for housing young paupers. When lawmakers saw the ruse, they ceased funding. It may be that masters and their political allies always intended to cheat in this way, but a good-faith reading of the wider evidence suggests that antislavery reformers had no intention of letting masters abandon and then rebind children for a profit. *NY Laws,* 27th sess. (1804), ch. 50.

113. Record of Children Born of Slaves after the Fourth Day of July One Thousand Seven Hundred and Ninety Nine, p. 1, Rhinebeck Historical Society, Starr Library, Rhinebeck, New York; Register of Slaves, p. 1, Historic Huguenot Street; A Record of Children Born of Slaves in Hempstead after the 4th of July 1799, p. 1, NYSA; Birth

certificate of a certain female child named Betty, and Birth certificate of a certain male child named Thomas, Slavery Collection, 1709–1899, MS 569, Box 5, NYHS.

114. Birth certificate of a certain female child named Susan and Birth certificate of a certain female child named Harriet, Manuscript Collections Relating to Slavery.

Chapter 2

1. NYMS, vol. 11, Mar. 7, 1825, pp. 139–148.

2. *NY Laws,* 22nd sess. (1799), ch. 62; *NY Laws,* 33rd sess. (1810), ch. 115.

3. The following laws addressed the status, treatment, and rights of children born to enslaved mothers: *NY Laws,* 24th sess. (1801), ch. 188; *NY Laws,* 25th sess. (1802), ch. 52; *NY Laws,* 27th sess. (1804), ch. 40; *NY Laws,* 30th sess. (1807), ch. 77; *NY Laws,* 32nd sess. (1809), ch. 44; *NY Laws,* 33rd sess. (1810), ch. 115; *NY Laws,* 36th sess. (1813), ch. 88; *NY Laws,* 40th sess. (1817), ch. 137. For a broader, if incomplete, survey of New York's slave and abolition laws, see A. J. Northrup, "Slavery in New York," *New York State Library Bulletin* (May, 1900).

4. See Horton and Horton, *In Hope of Liberty,* 83–84 ("New York's black children [were] born into slavery after July 4th, 1799"); Melish, *Disowning Slavery,* 88 ("statutory slaves"); Robert Steinfeld, Review of *Disowning Slavery, Law and History Review* (Summer 2000): 470–474 (challenging some of Melish's conclusions); Gigantino, *Ragged Road,* ch. 4 ("slaves for a term"); Groth, *Slavery and Freedom in the Mid-Hudson,* 49 (assuming New York's experience was the same as New Jersey's). Two recent dissertations that elucidate differences among states are Kellen Heniford, "Slavery Is Slavery" and Cory James Young, "For Life or Otherwise: Abolition and Slavery in South Central Pennsylvania, 1780-1847" (PhD diss., Georgetown, 2021). On the complexities and continuums of "free" and "unfree" labor, see Stanley Engerman and Robert Steinfeld, "Labor—Free or Coerced? A Historical Reassessment of Differences and Similarities," in Tom Brass and Marcel van der Linden, eds., *Free and Unfree Labour: The Debate Continues* (New York, 1997); Robert J. Steinfeld, *The Invention of Free Labor: The Employment Relation in English and American Law and Culture, 1350-1870* (Chapel Hill, 2002); Tomlins, *Freedom Bound;* Eltis, *"Labour and Coercion."*

5. I am indebted to Shane White's superb work, but I urge more attention to the political and legal aspects of abolition. White argues that by the early 1800s, "slavery was shifting from the center of New York City's economic life to its periphery" for reasons other than the 1799 law. He cites the trend toward a more flexible, wage-based labor market that Nash and Soderlund also describe in Pennsylvania. White, *Somewhat More Independent,* 46; Nash and Soderlund, *Freedom by Degrees,* ch. 2. Even if there is weight to White's point with respect New York *City,* there is ample evidence that owners in rural areas remained content to own slaves. It took political effort to abolish slavery in New York, and the 1799 law was crucial for some slaves' progress toward freedom. Black people understood this, too. Without the 1799 law, New York could have become a state like Delaware or Maryland, where many masters did free slaves and/or increasingly hire wage workers within a growing free labor economy, while other masters held on

to slaves to the bitter end. By the Civil War, both states demonstrated that slavery and free labor could coexist, as long as lawmakers didn't interfere. Patience Essah, *A House Divided: Slavery and Emancipation in Delaware, 1638-1865* (Charlottesville, 1996); Heniford, "Slavery Is Slavery"; Seth Rockman, *Scraping By: Wage Labor, Slavery, and Survival in Early Baltimore* (Baltimore, 2009).

6. See, for example, Edmund Prior to James Pemberton, Mar. 13, 1786, Pemberton Family Papers. In 1788, Pennsylvania's act to "explain and amend" its 1780 gradual abolition law added a birth certificate requirement. *PA Laws*, 12th sess. (1788), ch. 149.

7. Across records from over fifty towns, I have found only a couple of officials using the word "slave" to describe children affected by the 1799 law, and even in these cases, the language suggests the distinctive nature of their status. In Coxsackie, the clerk created a "Record of Free Born Slaves in the Town of Coxsackie Agreeable to an Act . . . 1799" (FDR Presidential Library, Hyde Park). In Flatbush, the clerk kept a record titled "Abandoned Slaves"; each abandonment itself recorded a master abandoning "my right to the service of a female [or male] child." Those children were bound out on the same terms and conditions as white paupers (until ages 18 and 21, taught to read or write). Notifications of Abandoned Slaves, Indentures of Poor Black Children, Old Town Kings County Records, Microfilm 17, NYMA. Almost all other records in New York State describing the children born after July 4, 1799, refer to their mothers as "slaves" but use different language to describe the children. By no means do I minimize the coercive and violent realities these children faced, but I do emphasize the on-paper legal distinctions, because black New Yorkers and abolitionists used these distinctions to push for better outcomes.

8. Town book for Castleton for the entry of black children, 1799–1827, NYHS, p. 2; Documents Related to Slavery in Westchester; Slavery Collection, NYHS; ACR, p. 10; Town of Beekman records, n.p.; Slave Births and Manumissions (Flatbush), p. 272, Old Town Kings County Records, Microfilm 2, NYMA. It has always struck me that Frederick Douglass began his famous narrative with the comment that, "I have no accurate knowledge of my age. . . . By far the larger part of the slaves know as little of their ages as horses know of theirs. . . . I do not remember to have ever met a slave who could tell of his birthday." I don't wish to romanticize the certificates recording the children of gradual abolition's births, but it nonetheless seems noteworthy, in this context, that many of the children of gradual abolition, unlike Douglass, had evidence of their birthdays. *Narrative of the Life of Frederick Douglass, an American Slave* (Boston, 1845), 1.

9. *NY Laws*, 25th sess. (1802), ch. 52; "Albany, Jan. 28," *New-York Gazette*, Feb. 2, 1802; *NY Laws*, 27th sess. (1804), ch. 40. In Albany, before 1804, thirty-five children were abandoned and fifteen were registered regularly as household servants. ACR. After the state ceased funding in 1804, abandonments dropped to a handful. In Palatine, Montgomery County (later Oppenheim, Fulton County), nine children were abandoned before 1804, and none thereafter. Record of Birth of Slaves, Town of Palatine

1802–1808, Town of Oppenheim 1808–1825 [transcript], Department of History and Archives, Fonda, NY. A New York Supreme Court case noted that a black child's "service was not worth more than her living" expenses. *Cook v. Husted* (1815), 12 Johns. 188.

10. ACR, 1½.

11. Birth certificate of a female child named Jude, Slavery Collection, NYHS.

12. Yoshpe, "Record of Slave Manumissions in New York," 106.

13. Audited accounts of payments made by overseers of the poor for support of children born to slaves, 1799–1820, NYSA.

14. On Anglo-American legal practices concerning apprenticeship and pauper children, see Tapping Reeve, "Master and Servant," *The Law of Baron and Femme* (1816; 3rd ed., Albany, 1862), 482–492.

15. Branscombe, *The Courts and the Poor Laws*, 20. In 1821, the New York term of the supreme court heard a case in which the plaintiff sought to recover money owed after assigning a white pauper child to the defendant. Judge Jonas Platt expressed uncertainty as to whether assigning pauper children was legal. *Nickerson v. Howard* (1821), 19 Johns. 113. See also Ruth Wallis Herndon, "Children of Misfortune: Growing Up Poor in Early New England," paper presented at the Boston Early American History Seminar (Dec. 2011), cited with permission.

16. Articles of Apprenticeship of a Negro girl named Bet, Box 2, Folder 26, Henry R. Wendell Papers, ca. 1709–1834, NYSL. In Flatbush, abandoned black children were bound out until 18 and 21, which fits with a reasonable reading of the law (be bound "in the same manner as if such children had been bound by the overseers of the poor"). See also Indenture of Tom (June 26, 1804), Historical Society of Rockland County; Indenture of Cynthia Haycorn by Brooklyn Overseers of the Poor, 1829 July 27, MS Am 889.478 (3), Houghton Library, Harvard University; Town of Florida Record of the Births of Slaves, p. 11, Department of History and Archives, Fonda, NY. Since the 1799 law wasn't explicit on this point, it's not surprising to find local variation.

17. *Minutes of the Common Council of the City of New York, 1784-1831* (New York, 1917), July 18, 1803; July 25, 1803.

18. Reeve, "Master and Servant," William Blackstone, "Chapter XIX: Of Master and Servant," *Commentaries on the Laws of England: in four books* (1765; 1884 edition) 1:421–432; James Kent "Of Master and Servant," *Commentaries on American Law* (1827; New York, 1836 edition), 2:248–266.

19. There were other rights and protections servants could claim that slaves could not. For example, slaves could not testify in court as witnesses against white people; convicted of felonies, slaves could be transported out of state as punishment; masters could permanently leave New York with their slaves, but not with their black servants. *NY Laws*, 11th sess. (1788), ch. 62; *NY Laws*, 13th sess. (1790), ch. 28; *NY Laws*, 30th sess. (1788), ch. 77. On free black people as permissible witnesses against white people, see *Rogers v. Berry* (1813), 10 Johns. 132. In contrast to other legal records throughout the

state, federal census returns from 1800 and 1810 often listed children born to enslaved mothers after 1799 under the "slave" category rather than "all other [free] persons" category. There was no "servant" category to choose. That said, there was clearly local variation, and perhaps even variation from household to household within a census district. My preliminary exploration of the census records also suggests that more and more children were listed in the "free" category as time went on; in other words, census workers marked down (and/or masters reported) such children as free more often in the 1820 and 1830 census forms (which added "free colored persons" as a category, as well as age brackets) than they had in earlier decades. For example, Phillis Jackson and John Francis, black servant children whose stories appear later in this chapter, seem to emerge in the 1820 census as "free." Samuel S. Seward's black servant children, born in the 1810s and discussed in this chapter, appear as "slaves" in the 1820 census. In 1830, however, they are listed as "free colored persons." John Brooke and Michael Groth provide helpful tabulations of census records for Columbia and Dutchess counties, respectively, which conform with the general picture I paint here. Groth's tables also show how much faster the free black population grew in New York City as opposed to in agricultural areas of the state, a trend I explore in this chapter. Overall, it is clear that the federal census forms were not created with the intent of capturing the on-the-ground demographic and legal realities of household status during localized northern abolition. The census forms both reflected and helped create a nineteenth-century world in which the early modern "spectrum" of slave-to-free, which included substantial numbers of bound white laborers in the middle, gave way to a modern world with hardened and even more deeply racialized lines between "slave" (black) and "free" (white), with a specific second-class "free colored person" alternate category that was defined and experienced in a range of localized ways across the growing United States. Sylvanus Miller [Jackson's master], 1820 US Census, Ward 4, New York, NY; William F. Seaman [Francis's master], 1820 US Census, Ward 2, New York, NY; Samuel S. Seward, 1820 US Census, Warwick, Orange, NY; Samuel S. Seward, 1830 US Census, Warwick, Orange, NY; Brooke, *Columbia Rising,* 266–278, Groth, *Slavery and Freedom,* 50–52, 72–73, 90.

20. "Law of New York," *Suffolk Gazette,* Mar. 17, 1806; Book of Records of the Black Children Born within the Town of Warwick [inside volume Book of Strays], Warwick Town Clerk Office; Marks and Strays [and slavery material], Newburgh Municipal Records; Record of Birth, Town of Oppenheim

21. NYMS, vol. 9, July 19, 1808, pp. 188–189.

22. NYMS, vol. 9, July 19, 1808, pp. 188–189. Chapter 3 of this book explores black civic associationalism in depth.

23. NYMS, vol. 9, Nov. 8, 1808, p. 193, Jan. 10, 1809, p. 201.

24. Olive Gilbert and Sojourner Truth, *Narrative of Sojourner Truth: a northern slave, emancipated from bodily servitude by the state of New York, in 1828* (Boston, 1850), 23.

25. NYMS, vol. 7, July 10, 1804, pp. 147–148, 261; vol. 10, Mar. 7, 1809, pp. 60–61; vol. 9, Mar. 13, 1800, p. 36; vol. 7, July 27, 1795, pp. 52–54.

26. NYMS, vol. 7, July 20, 1801, Aug. 28, 1801, Dec. 22, 1801, pp. 194–195, 201, 205.

27. NYMS, vol. 7, Mar. 4, 1800, p. 141. The NYMS's involvement in the case of a mother named Effy Sable and her child is a telling example. See NYMS, vol. 7, Mar. 4, 1800, p. 141; *Sable v. Hitchcock,* 2 Johns. (1800), 79; *Hitchcock v. Sable,* 2 Johns. (1802), 487. On similar dynamics in Philadelphia, see Dunbar, *Fragile Freedom.* For comparative contexts, see Michelle McKinley, *Fractional Freedoms: Slavery, Intimacy, and Legal Mobilization in Colonial Lima, 1600-1700* (New York, 2016); Max Mishler, "'Improper and Almost Rebellious Conduct': Enslaved People's Legal Politics and Abolition in the British Empire," *American Historical Review* (June 2023): 649–684.

28. Statement of Charlotte, *The People v. Charlotte, a black girl,* filed June 7, 1811, DAIP.

29. *The People v. Charlotte, a black girl,* June 1811, GSM.

30. *The People v. Rose, a black girl,* filed Dec. 4, 1811, DAIP.

31. Charlotte's and Rose's testimony recalls Shane White's arguments about cultural shifts in the black population in this era. "Black Life in Freedom: Creating a Popular Culture," in Berlin and Harris, eds., *Slavery in New York,* 155. Incidentally, Rose, unlike Charlotte, was acquitted. *The People v. Rose, a black girl,* Jan. 1812, GSM. For another example, see *The People v. Eleanor Rankin,* filed Dec. 8, 1806, DAIP.

32. NYMS, vol. 10, Apr. 4, 1807, pp. 3–4.

33. NYMS, vol. 9, Jan. 15, 1811, p. 269.

34. NYMS, vol. 7, Apr. 25, 1800, pp. 158–162, Aug. 22, 1800, p. 169, Mar. 15, 1802, pp. 215–228, July 13, 1802, p. 234. See also "James H. Thompson and Royal A. Bowen's Cases," *New York City Hall Recorder* (1817), 120.

35. NYMS, vol. 7, July 28, 1802, p. 231.

36. *Fish v. Fisher* (1800), 2 Johns. Cas 89; NYMS, vol. 6, Aug. 18, 1795, p. 210; *Link v. Beuner* (1805), 3 Cai. R 325. Munro's cocounsel was Richard Harrison. Compare New York's outlawing of these practices with what was legal in Illinois. Gorsuch, "Midwestern Territorial Courts."

37. NYMS, vol. 9, Jan. 13, 1807, p. 167.

38. *NY Laws,* 30th sess. (1807), ch. 77.

39. NYMS, vol. 9, Apr. 14, 1807, p. 170, Nov. 17, 1807, p. 176.

40. NYMS, vol. 9, Jan. 12, 1808, p. 177, Dec. 21, 1808, pp. 200–201, Jan. 17, 1809, p. 205, Jan. 9, 1810, p. 231.

41. New York Yearly Meeting, Meeting for Sufferings Minutes, 1796–1821, FHL, pp. 157–162

42. *NY Laws,* 33rd sess. (1810), ch. 115.

43. In this chapter, I aim to show how important black voting was to the passage of state legislation. In Chapter 4, I return to black voting as a marker and exercise of citizenship as a civic and legal category.

44. For an extended exploration black voting in early republican New York, see Sarah L. H. Gronningsater, "'Expressly Recognized by Our Election Laws': Certificates of Freedom and the Multiple Fates of Black Citizenship in the Early Republic," *William*

and Mary Quarterly (July 2018): 465–506. For black voting more broadly, see Gosse, *The First Reconstruction*.

45. Carter et al., *Historical Statistics*, Series Bb–98; Freeman, *Free Negro*, 439; Stefan Bielinksi, "The Jacksons, Lattimores, and Schuylers: First African-American Families of Early Albany," *New York History* (Oct. 1996), 381; Brooke, *Columbia Rising*, 386; *Minutes of the Common Council* (1805–1808), 4:649–651; *NY Laws*, 24th sess. (1801), ch. 61.

46. "Columbia County," *Albany Register*, May 11, 1810.

47. "Editor's Closet: The New Election Law," *Balance, and State Journal* (Albany), Apr. 16, 1811; "Black Representation," *Albany Argus*, May 18, 1813 (quotations); "Black Representation," *Columbian Gazette* (Utica), May 25, 1813; "Black Representation," *Otsego Herald* (Cooperstown), May 29, 1813.

48. Gronningsater, "Expressly Recognized by Our Election Laws." For evidence of extremely tight elections in a rural area, see Town Minutes, Town of Carmel, Putnam County, New York, 1795–1839, p. 14, Carmel Town Hall.

49. Sidney, *An Oration*; John Teasman, *An Address Delivered in the American Episcopal Church* (New York, 1811), 7–8; Gronningsater, "Expressly Recognized by Our Election Laws"; Christopher Rush, *A Short Account of the Rise and Progress of the African Methodist Episcopal Church in America* (New York, 1843), 10–11; *Longworth's . . . City Directory* (New York, 1813), 285; Thomas Sipkins' Will (1830), Record of Wills, vol. 67, Surrogate Court, New York County, p. 23, accessed on Ancestry.com; Henry Sipkins' COF (Apr. 28, 1813), New York City-Indentures, NYHS.

50. "Reuben," *Suffolk Gazette* (Sag Harbor), Jan. 12, 1807; Ruben [sic], 1810 US Census, Southold, NY; Charles E. Craven, *A History of Mattituck, Long Island, N.Y.* (n.p., 1906), 206–209; Reuben Reeve's COF, Apr. 26, 1813, in Magdaline Goodrich, ed., *Southold Town Records, 1683–1856* (Southold, NY, 1971), 88; Elymas Reeve, 1850 US Census, Southold, NY; Clarence Ashton Wood, "'Lymas Reeve, Southold Slave," *Long Island Forum* (Spring 1988): 27–28; William J. Simmons, *Men of Mark: Eminent, Progressive and Rising* (Cleveland, 1887), ch. 16; M. A. Majors, *Noted Negro Women: Their Triumphs and Activities* (Chicago, 1893), 44–50.

51. NYMS, vol. 10, Mar. 20, 1811, p. 121, Apr. 4, 1811, p. 122. See also pp. 136, 156, 164. *JANY* (Albany, 1810), 288–289, 295. Suffolk County members Abraham Rose, John Rose, and Tredwell Scudder all voted in favor of the 1810 antislavery law. Both Roses also voted for a failed amendment that would have freed slaves who were physically abused by their masters. All three were Republicans.

52. NYMS, vol. 9, Jan. 13, 1807, p. 167, July 19, 1808, p. 188, Nov. 8, 1808, p. 193.

53. NYMS, vol. 9, Apr.11, 1809, p. 212.

54. NYMS, vol. 9, Apr.11, 1809, p. 212; *The People v. Amos Broad* and *The People v. Demis Broad*, filed Feb. 25, 1809, DAIP.

55. Statements of Margaret Taupell, Maria Tillick, and Lavinia Van Wyck, *The People v. Amos Broad* and *The People v Demis Broad*, filed Feb. 25, 1809, DAIP.

56. *The Trial of Amos Broad and His Wife . . .* (New York, 1809); "Horrid Barbarity!", *American Citizen*, Mar. 7, 1809; "Amos Broad," *American Citizen*, Mar. 13, 1809. The manumissions are in NYMS, vol. 3, Apr. 4, 1809, pp. 6–7.

57. NYMS, vol. 9, Jan. 9, 1810, p. 230. On "correction," see Reeve in note 14. New York's slave code didn't allow slaves to testify against a white person. Free black people and servants *could* testify. See the 1801 and 1817 acts cited in note 3.

58. NYMS, vol. 10, Feb. 3, 1812, pp. 162–163, May 11, 1812, pp. 173–174; vol. 10, July 16, 1811, p. 136, Aug. 27, 1811, p. 143.

59. NYMS, vol. 9, Jan. 15, 1811, p. 268, Nov. 25, 1811, p. 280.

60. Elias Hicks, *Observations on the Slavery of the Africans* (New York, 1811), 11–12

61. NYMS, vol. 9, Jan. 10, 1804, p. 113, Dec. 16, 1811, p. 282, Jan. 3, 1812, p. 290.

62. *JANY* (Albany, 1812), 150.

63. *JANY* (Albany, 1812), 150–151; *NY Laws,* 36th sess. (1813), ch. 88.

64. NYMS, vol. 9, Jan. 3, 1812, p. 289; NYMS, vol. 9, Jan. 18, 1814, p. 359; NYMS, vol. 9, Apr. 12, 1814, p. 363. For a useful discussion of "immediate emancipation" and "immediatism," see David Brion Davis, *The Problem of Slavery in the Age of Emancipation* (New York, 2014), 187–188.

65. "Black Votes," *Columbian* (New York), Jan. 6, 1813; "Attention! People of Colour," *NYH,* Apr. 28, 1813.

66. "Black Representation," *Albany Argus,* May 18, 1813; "Black Representation," *Columbian Gazette* (Utica), May 25, 1813. There were 8,137 free blacks in New York City in 1810 (out of a total population of 96,373) and 946 were listed as heads of households in the federal census. Presumably, many of these 946 could vote at the very least in local and assembly elections. Freeman, *Free Negro in New York City,* 439; Alice Einholtz and James M. Rose, *Free Black Heads of Households in the New York State Federal Census, 1790-1830* (Detroit, 1981).

67. *JANY,* 38th sess., 2nd mtg. (1815), 359, 420–421, 469–478; *JSNY* (Albany, 1815), 327–328; *NY Laws,* 38th sess. (1815), ch. 145.

68. *Public Papers of Daniel D. Tompkins, Governor of New York, 1807-1817* (Albany, 1902), 2:446–447; *NY Laws,* 38th sess. (1814), ch. 18. Tompkins wrote Secretary of State James Monroe to ask that the United States "agree to take them in to service, & to pay clothe and enlist them." Black volunteers informally took action to guard the state during the war, but the evidence is hazy as to whether black regiments ever formed. The war ended shortly after the act passed. *Papers of Daniel D. Tompkins,* 3:616; Anthony Gero, *Black Soldiers of New York State: A Proud Legacy* (Albany, 2009), 9–12); [No title], *Columbian,* Apr. 29, 1816.

69. *JANY* (Albany, 1816), 163, 241. Jay's draft also sought to omit two longstanding clauses in the state's slave code. One was the ability of masters to transport a slave out of state if the slave committed a crime. The other was a rule that denied slaves a trial by jury for striking a white person. See Jay's draft of the 1816 law, as well as an unnamed colleague's "Observations on the draft of a law concerning Slaves and Servants" and "In Assembly, Feb. 26, 1816: An Act Relative to Slaves and Servants," in the Elizabeth Clarkson Jay Papers, NYSL. For an example of a white apprentice being released from his master due to abuse in 1805, see Records of Poughkeepsie Precinct, 63.

70. *JANY* (Albany, 1816), 370–371, 382; *JSNY* (Albany, 1816), 229.

71. Charles C. Andrews, *The History of the New-York African Free Schools* (New York, 1830), 32–33.

72. Cadwallader D. Colden, "To the Citizens of the State of New York," *Albany Advertiser,* Jan. 8, 1817.

73. New York Yearly Meeting, Meeting for Sufferings Minutes, 1796–1821, FHL, pp. 218–220, 223.

74. *Messages from the governors . . . 1683 to and including the year 1906* (Albany, 1909), 2:880–881; *NY Laws,* 40th sess. (1817), ch. 137.

75. On partisan motivations and disfranchisement, see Polgar, "Whenever They Judge in Expedient," 2; Strum, 360–361; Wilentz, *Rise of American Democracy,* 193–196. Wood, "A Sacrifice on the Altar of Slavery," 76–80.

76. Olive Gilbert and Sojourner Truth, *Narrative of Sojourner Truth: A Northern Slave, Emancipated from Bodily Servitude by the State of New York, in 1828* (Boston, 1850), 23–25.

77. Carter et al., *Historical Statistics,* Series Bb1–98. For an example of a "black girl" in Albany asserting some choice, even while bound to a master, see John Kirkland to William Swetland, June 11, 1812, Call #11015, NYSL.

78. NYMS, vol. 11, Nov. 8, 1821, p. 107, Jan. 18, 1822, p. 110; vol. 11, June 11, 1823, p. 123, June 8, 1824, p. 132; vol. 11, June 11, 1823, p. 124, Nov. 10, 1823, p. 128.

79. NYMS, vol. 11, Oct. 7, 1826, pp. 154–155, Apr. 10, 1827, p. 161, Nov. 13, 1827, p. 166.

80. Darby's Discharge, Feb. 3. 1819, photocopy of original, Office of the Historian, Town of Southold.

81. Brooke, *Columbia Rising;* Sarah L. H. Gronningsater, "James Tallmadge, Jr. and the Personal Politics of Antislavery," in *A Fire Bell in the Past: The Missouri Crisis at 200, Volume 1: Western Slavery, National Impasse,* ed. Jeffrey L. Pasley and John Craig Hammond (Columbia, MO, 2021); Groth, *Slavery and Freedom;* Kathryn Grover, *Make a Way Somehow: African-American Life in a Northern Community* (Syracuse, 1994); Moss, *Slavery on Long Island: A Study in Local Institutional and Early African-American Communal Life* (New York, 1993); Margaret Washington, *Sojourner Truth's America* (Urbana, 2011).

82. Black Children Born Within the Town of Warwick. Seward freed Dina, one of the mothers, in 1820.

83. Frederick W. Seward, *William H. Seward: An Autobiography from 1801 to 1834* (New York, 1891, orig. 1877), 27–28; Park Dixon Goist, "William Henry Seward and His Father," *New York History* (Apr. 1963): 128–138.

84. Robert W Brennan, *Genealogical History of Black Families in Orange County, New York* (Goshen, NY, 2001–2006).

85. Kathryn Grover, *Make a Way Somehow,* ch. 1.

86. Austin Steward, *Twenty-Two Years a Slave, and Forty Years a Freeman* (Rochester, 1857), 106.

87. Steward, *Twenty-Two Years a Slave,* chs. 1, 4, 6, 10, 11, 13; *NY Laws,* 35th sess. (1812), ch. 228. Darius Comstock, a Quaker, was the Society's president. James Moore

was a wealthy farmer. There is question as to whether Steward really had recourse to the 1810 act. The legislature passed another law in 1810 that allowed slave owners from Maryland and Virginia who had moved to the Genesee Country "within ten years last past" to hire out their slaves. In other words, Helm may have been hiring out Steward legally. In 1821, Steward received a certificate of freedom from a local judge asserting that he had been free since January 1, 1811 (the date he had first been hired out). There are a few possibilities as to the legal reasoning here. One, Helm may have emigrated with his slaves outside of the "ten years past" time frame; it is unclear when in 1800 he moved to New York. Two, Steward and his allies may have willfully ignored the exemption law and followed the wording of the March 30, 1810, act forbidding emigrants from hiring out their slaves. In any case, Helm wasn't happy, and for a time, he tried to reenslave Steward. *NY Laws,* 33rd sess. (1810), chs. 115, 193; Austin Steward COF, Apr. 10, 1821, Miscellaneous Records, Liber # 1 Year 1821, Monroe County Clerk, Rochester.

88. *In re Tom,* 5 Johns. (New York) 365 (1810); *Ketletas v. Fleet* (1811), 7 Johns. 324; *Livingston v. Ackeston* (1826), 5 Cowen 531; *Livingston v. Bain* (1833), 10 Wendell 384.

89. NYMS, vol. 11, June 22, 1825, p. 142. For more detail on New York City's police offices, as well as incredible details about a black lawyer named Moses Simons who practiced in the city in the 1810s and '20s, see Shane White's forthcoming *Moment in the Sun: Freedom in Black Manhattan* (under contract, Liveright).

90. *NY Laws,* 32nd sess. (1809). For an example of this law working to a black family's advantage in an inheritance case, see *Jackson v. Lervey,* 5 Cowen 397.

91. ACR, 165.

92. ACR, 193.

93. Manuscripts and Special Collections, NYSL, Call #15598. For a similar example, see Call #18079. For other examples of children being released early, either because their terms were sold to their parents or because they were released voluntarily, see ACR, 35, 70, 82, 109, 115, 147, 164.

94. On evolving notions of fathers' right to children's labor in the early republic, see Holly Brewer, "The Transformation of Domestic Law," in *The Cambridge History of Law in America,* vol. 2, *The Long Nineteenth Century,* ed. Michael Grossberg and Christopher Tomlins (Cambridge, UK, 2008). New York lawmakers' decisions to legalize the slave family in 1809 and to force masters to provide black children with schooling in 1810 are all the more fascinating in light of the overall trends Brewer describes. Antislavery lawmakers in New York made attempts to include black families in the broader changes taking place in domestic and education law. For the juridical impact of the 1809 law, see Lauren Feldman, "Creating Law Through Regulating Intimacy: The Case of Slave Marriage in Nineteenth Century New York and the United States," *Law and History Review* (Feb. 2023): 119–143.

95. For examples of slave prices, see Zilversmit, *The First Emancipation*, appendix; Carter et al., *Historical Statistics,* Series Bb209–214; Fogel and Engerman, "Philanthropy at Bargain Prices." For an older enslaved boy worth $250, see *Ketletas v. Fleet* (1811), 7 Johns.

324. In 1817, Hendrek Turnure of Clarkstown valued two (noninfant) servant boys at $30 and $50. Record of Wills, B, Rockland County, p. 27, accessed on Ancestry.com.

96. Technically, the children born to servant children were wholly free—neither slaves nor forcibly bound to their mothers' masters until adulthood. A lawyer commented to a newspaper in 1827 that "The children of servants are absolutely free, and their condition by law, is the same as that of white children." "Termination of Slavery in New York," *Newburyport Herald* (reprinted from the *Troy Sentinel*), July 17, 1827. New Jersey citizens likewise understood the children of servant children born under gradual emancipation to be free, with no labor obligations to a white master. See Bergen County petition to the Legislature requesting repeal of the NJ Abolition Act of 1804, Jan. 4, 1806, New Jersey State Archives, State Library MSS Collection, Box 5-3, Folder 419. Thanks to Jim Gigantino for sharing this document. Cory Young explores masters in the interior of Pennsylvania who forced the children of children of gradual abolition to serve as bound servants as well, thereby making the status heritable. The Pennsylvania supreme court declared the practice illegal in 1826. Young, "For Life or Otherwise," introduction.

97. NYMS, vol. 7, Mar. 11, 1796, p. 57.

98. NYMS, vol. 10, Apr. 12, 1814, p. 232.

99. *NY Laws,* 11th sess. (1788), ch. 62.

100. Town of Huntington, *Records of the Overseers of the Poor: part 1*, 106, 111.

101. The Manumission Society worried about the extent of their reach outside of the metropolitan area and crafted an agenda to address the problem. NYMS, vol. 7, May 10, 1792, p. 8.

102. NYMS, vol. 11, Nov. 9, 1827, p. 165, Nov. 8, 1828, p. 167; Washington, *Sojourner Truth's America,* ch. 4. See also Nell Irvin Painter, "Soul Murder and Slavery: Toward a Fully Loaded Cost Accounting," in *Southern History Across the Color Line*, ed. Nell Irvin Painter (Chapel Hill, 2021): 15-39.

103. *Oatfield v. Waring* (1817), 14 Johns. 188. For a similar case, see *Wells v. Lane* (1812), 9 Johns. 144. It is likely that Oatfield was Henry Oatfield, a black man listed as a laborer in the 1819 Albany directory and as head of a free household of five people on the 1820 census. *The Albany Directory for the Year 1819* (Albany, 1819), 47.

104. *Overseers of the Poor of Marbletown v. Overseers of the Poor of the Town of Kingston* (1822), 20 Johns. 1.

105. Wills, vol. A, pp. 60, 192, Rockland County Surrogate Office; vol. B, pp. 140, 190; accessed via Ancestry.com. See also Wills, vol. A (1787–1797), Orange County Surrogate's Office. Rockland split off from Orange in 1798.

106. Black Children Born Within the Town of Warwick.

107. Wills, vol. I, Orange County Surrogate's Office, p. 43.

108. Edward P. Livingston to William Wilson, Feb. 17, 1819, Wilson Family Papers. Wilson was a doctor in the eastern Hudson Valley who served as an agent for the powerful Livingston family. There are numerous letters, indentures, and bills of sales in Wilson's papers that give texture and detail to the history of slavery and gradual abolition in the area. Chancellor Livingston was not, as far as I can tell, a member of the New-York

Manumission Society, but he had once been on good terms with John Jay. Jay and Livingston were the first two signatories, as the most prominent politicians, on a Manumission Society-backed petition to the state legislature in 1786 asking for a law to forbid slave exports because the practice tore families apart. NYMS, vol. 6, May 11, 1786, p. 43. Among other endeavors, Livingston helped draft the Declaration of Independence and purchase Louisiana from France.

109. Carter et al., *Historical Statistics*, Series Bb1–98; Gellman, *Emancipating New York*, 195; David Gellman and David Quigley, eds., *Jim Crow New York: A Documentary History of Race and Citizenship, 1777-1877* (New York, 2003), 77.

Chapter 3

1. Julia A. J. Foote, *A Brand Plucked from the Fire* (Cleveland, 1879), 9–11.

2. Foote, *A Brand Plucked from the Fire*, 18–19. Foote calls the white couple the "Primes," but it is likely they were part of the "Pruyn" (rhymes with "Prime") family, who were indeed an old and influential family in the Hudson Valley.

3. Church Patents No. 1 from 1784 to 1842, p. 181, Albany County Hall of Records; Foote, *A Brand*, 35–36, 39, 76. Foote calls Prudence Crandell "Mrs. Phileos," her married name. For more on Foote's adult career, see Jones, *All Bound Up Together*, ch. 1.

4. For examples of integrated schools, see Attendance Records for Schools in Clermont (1797–1799), Wilson Family Papers; Frederick W. Seward, *Autobiography of William H. Seward, from 1801 to 1834* (New York, 1877), 28; Marjory Allen Perez, "The Bradington Family" (unpublished paper on Wayne County slaves, in my possession); Wayne E. Morrison Sr., *History of Monroe County, New York* (Philadelphia, 1877), 235; Kettleborough School District Minutes and Records, 1827–1927, Historic Huguenot Street, New Paltz; Samuel Sidwell Randall, *The Common School System of the State of New York* (Troy, 1851), 70; *JANY* (Albany, 1835), 326 (implying Newburgh schools had been integrated up until that date); "For the Colored American," *CA*, Nov. 4, 1837; "From Our New York Correspondent," *FDP*, Feb. 16, 1855. In 1845, James McCune Smith noted that "there are 22 colored schools supported by the State, independently of the colored children who attend white schools." "Extending the Right of Suffrage," *Albany Argus*, Apr. 25, 1845; *Autobiography of Andrew D. White*, 7.

5. Alexander Crummell, *The Eulogy on Henry Highland Garnet* (Washington, DC, 1882), 25. See also "The Late Peter Guignon," *New York Freeman*, Jan. 31, 1885.

6. Scholars have written extensively about the African Free School, its pupils, and its public meanings. They have explored the trustees' paternalistic approach to education and respectability-focused cultural goals. They have scrutinized how some of the white benefactors espoused African colonization in the 1820s and '30s, during the school's final years. Biographers have traced the careers, triumphs, and disappointments of prominent graduates. Female students and teachers, once rather neglected in scholarship, have moved to the center. John Rury, "Philanthropy, Self Help, and Social Control: The New York Manumission Society and Free Blacks, 1785-1810," *Phylon* (Sept. 1985): 231–241; Webster, *Beyond the Boundaries of Childhood*, ch. 4; Harris, *In the Shadow of*

Slavery, 64–65, 103, 130–132; R. J. M. Blackett, *Samuel Ringgold Ward: A Life of Struggle* (New Haven, 2023); Carla L. Peterson, *Black Gotham: A Family History of African-Americans in Nineteenth-Century New York City* (New Haven, 2011); Anna Mae Duane, *Educated for Freedom: The Incredible Story of Two Fugitive Schoolboys Who Grew Up to Change a Nation* (New York, 2020); Wilson Jeremiah Moses, *Alexander Crummell: A Study of Civilization and Discontent* (New York, 1989); John Stauffer, ed., *The Works of James McCune Smith: Black Intellectual and Abolitionist* (Oxford, 2006); Shane White, *Stories of Freedom*. On black women's education, see Baumgartner, *In Pursuit of Knowledge*. For black education and common schools in Boston, New Haven, and Baltimore in the 1830s to 1850s—the decades after the focus of this chapter—see Hilary J. Moss, *Schooling Citizens: The Struggle for African American Education in Antebellum America* (Chicago, 2009). Moss argues that "by advancing an argument for universal education that privileged citizenship rather than equality, [antebellum] school reformers inadvertently reinforced efforts to deny black people access to public schooling" (4). New York State's chronologically earlier histories of public, public/private, and common school education for black children don't necessarily dispute Moss's findings, but they do reveal some alternate roads taken in New York.

7. On (mostly white) childhood, youth culture, and generational consciousness in the early republic, see Mary Ryan, *Cradle of the Middle Class: The Family in Oneida County, New York, 1790-1865* (Cambridge, UK, 1981); Karen Halttunen, *Confidence Men and Painted Women: A Study of Middle-Class Culture in America, 1830-1870* (New Haven, 1982); Steven Mintz, *Huck's Raft: A History of American Childhood* (Cambridge, MA, 2004); Joyce Appleby, *Inheriting the Revolution: The First Generation of Americans* (Cambridge, MA, 2001). For a social history of urban black school children, including a detailed look at school exercises and writing, see Webster, *Beyond the Boundaries*, ch. 4. Webster makes the particularly well-taken point that black children at once saw school attendance as politically meaningful and did not always want to go to school for a host of reasons (p. 91). Like Webster, I aim to place black school children at the center of a history of early republican childhood. My particular focus in this chapter is tracing how schools created relationships among children, parents, civil society, and the state in urban and *rural* areas. There is a political/associational literature of the early republic that mostly ignores black schools and also a literature of black schools and school children that does not fully explore the implications of schools as literal and practical sites of democracy building and state building.

8. Novak, "The American Law of Association," 183.

9. Brooke, *Columbia Rising*; Kevin Butterfield, *The Making of Tocqueville's America: Law and Association in the Early United States* (Chicago, 2015); Johann N. Neem, *Creating a Nation of Joiners: Democracy and Civil Society in Early National Massachusetts* (Cambridge, MA, 2008); Mark Boonshoft, *Aristocratic Education and the Making of the American Republic* (Chapel Hill, 2020); Johann Neem, *Democracy's Schools: The Rise of Public Education in America* (Baltimore, 2017). Work on black "counterpublics" and internally focused associationalism includes Joanna Brooks, "The Early American

Public Sphere and the Emergence of a Black Counterpublic," *WMQ* (Jan. 2005): 67–92; Richard Newman, "Faith in the Ballot: Black Shadow Politics in the Antebellum North," *Commonplace* (Oct. 2008); Wilder, *In the Company of Black Men*; *Colored Conventions*, esp. Foreman's introduction on "parallel politics." My goal here is to think about how black citizens were at once a part of and also distinct within the civil life of an early republican state. I don't disagree with Brooks', Newman's, Wilder's, or Forman's analysis but rather call attention to the flip side of the story—focusing on the "noncounter" and the "nonshadowed," so to speak—and argue for why this flip side mattered in the development of American democracy and black political culture. Sarah Barringer Gordon provides a rare exploration of black associationalism in the formal legal sphere. "The African Supplement: Religion, Race, and Corporate Law in Early National America," *WMQ* (July 2015): 423–460.

10. Black leaders saw direct links among state-recognized black associationalism, citizenship, and anticolonization. Thomas L. Jinnings, "Eulogy: On the Life and Character of Henry Sipkins," *CA*, Nov. 17, 1838.

11. NYMS, vol. 6, May 11, 1786, pp. 39–40; Novak, "The American Law of Association," 182–183. Despite what many secondary sources report, the school did *not* obtain an act of incorporation by the legislature in 1794, although the legislature did begin funding the school in 1796. In 1808, the NYMS, including the school, was finally granted a charter of incorporation. *NY Laws*, 31st sess. (1808), ch. 19.

12. NYMS, vol. 6., Aug. 10, 1786, p. 49; Elihu Smith, "To . . . General Convention of Delegates from the Abolition Societies . . . at Philadelphia in January 1795," PAS, Reel #2; NYMS, vol. 6., Feb. 21, 1798, p. 97.

13. Carleton Mabee, *Black Education in New York State: From Colonial to Modern Times* (Syracuse, 1979), 1–16; Carl F. Kaestle, *The Evolution of an Urban School System: New York City, 1750-1850* (Cambridge, MA, 1973); [No title], *Loudon's New-York Packet*, Nov. 17, 1786; [No title], *New-York Journal*, Nov. 30, 1786. In 1800, New York City's Common Council listed seven "public Free Schools" in the city. The AFS was the only non-church affiliated school as well as the school with the highest enrollment (110 scholars). The AFS received $517. *Minutes of the Common Council of the City of New York*, vol. 3, *1801-1805* (New York, 1917), 628.

14. NYMS, vol. 6, Aug. 10, 1786, p. 49, Nov. 15, 1787, p. 85, Feb. 21, 1788, p. 96; [No title], *Daily Advertiser*, Aug. 16, 1788. John McCusker, *How Much Is That in Real Money?* (Worcester, 2001), 34.

15. NYMS, vol. 6, Nov. 15, 1787, pp. 83–84, Feb. 21, 1788, pp. 96, 99. See also New-York African Free-School Records, 1817–1832, vol. 1, "Regulations, By-laws and Reports, 1817-1832," 1–2, AFS.

16. NYMS, vol. 6, Feb. 21, 1788, pp. 94–97; Nov. 20, 1788, p. 123. See also "The Trustees of the African School," *American Minerva*, Aug. 22, 1794; James Brewer Stewart, *"The Emergence of Racial Modernity and the Rise of the White North, 1790-1840," JER* (Summer 1998): 181–217; Lois Horton, "From Class to Race in Early America: Northern Post-Emancipation Racial Reconstruction," *JER* (Winter 1999): 629–649.

17. The justices of the peace presided over what was commonly called the Police Court. This was a city court charged with hearing petty offenses on a daily basis.

18. Special Justices for Preserving the Peace (New York Police Court Minutes), July 16–Aug. 13, 1799, NYMA. These are the earliest extant records of the Police Court, although the court was in operation before this date.

19. For more on these themes, see Stephanie M. H. Camp, *Closer to Freedom: Enslaved Women and Everyday Resistance in the Plantation South* (Chapel Hill, 2004); Tamika Nunley, *At the Threshold of Liberty: Women, Slavery, and Shifting Identities in Washington, D.C.* (Chapel Hill, 2021); Jessica Marie Johnson, *Wicked Flesh: Black Women, Intimacy, and Freedom in the Atlantic World* (Philadelphia, 2020).

20. NYMS, vol. 6, Feb. 21, 1788, pp. 99–101; Smith, "To . . . the General Convention . . . 1795"; Smith, *Memorial Discourse,* 22.

21. NYMS, vol. 6, Feb. 15, 1791, p. 152; Andrews, *History of the New York African Free Schools,* 35, 38, 50; "African School," *Greenleaf's New Daily Advertiser* (New York), Nov. 16, 1796; "African School," *Herald: A Gazette for the Country* (New York), Nov. 16, 1796.

22. NYMS, vol. 6, Jan. 17, 1797, pp. 245–246; *Minutes of the Proceedings of the Fourth Convention of Delegates from the Abolition Societies . . . at Philadelphia* (Philadelphia, 1797), 30–31; "Communication," *ComAd,* Nov. 25, 1797; NYMS, vol. 6, Jan. 17, 1797, pp. 245–246.

23. *Fourth Convention of Delegates from the Abolition Societies,* 39; Craig Steven Wilder, "Black Life in Freedom" in Harris and Berlin, eds., *Slavery in New York.*

24. William Oland Bourne, *History of the Public School Society of the City of New York* (New York, 1870), 670; *New-York Gazette,* Dec. 7, 1807; *American Citizen,* Dec. 16, 1807; *Daily Advertiser,* Dec. 19, 1807; *Minutes of the Common Council of the city of New York,* vol. 4, 1805–1808, 663, 682.

25. Peter Williams Jr., *An Oration on the Abolition of the Slave Trade* (New York, 1808), 22, 24.

26. Robert J. Swan, "John Teasman: African American Educator and the Emergence of Community in Early Black New York City, 1787-1815," *JER* (Fall 1992): 331–356; Daniel Perlman, "Organizations of the Free Negro in New York City, 1800-1860," *Journal of Negro History* (July 1971): 183; Hamilton, "Address to the New York African Society for Mutual Relief," 37.

27. NYMS, vol. 9, July 14, 1807, p. 172. The Lancaster method dominated the expanding public school system of the early 1800s. Kaestle, *Evolution of an Urban School System,* 83.

28. AFS, vol. 2, 101–105.

29. See, for example, Chapter 7 of this book, where Smith incessantly and effectively pushes white interlocutors to see and do better in the realm of midcentury antislavery politics.

30. NYMS, vol. 9, Jan. 12 (?), 1808, p. 176, Nov. 8, 1808, p. 194, Jan. 10, 1809, p. 202, Apr. 11, 1809, p. 214; NYMS, vol. 9, Nov. 14, 1809, p. 223, Jan. 9, 1810, p. 231; Smith,

"Sketch of the Life," 21. For the importance of black parades in the early republic, see David Waldstreicher, *In the Midst of Perpetual Fetes: The Making of American Nationalism, 1776–1820* (Chapel Hill, 1997) 323–328.

31. John Teasman, *An Address Delivered in the American Episcopal Church*, 7–8.

32. *NY Laws,* 33rd sess. (1810), ch. 192; NYMS, vol. 9, Jan. 9, 1810, p. 229; *NY Laws,* 33rd sess. (1810), ch. 115; *NY Laws,* 36th sess. (1813), ch. 52. See also "Common School Fund," *ComAd,* Sept. 4, 1817.

33. White, *Somewhat More Independent,* 26; Carter et al., *Historical Statistics,* Tables Aa4941–5041. New York City comprised the island of Manhattan. The other four boroughs now inside the city joined starting in the late 1800s.

34. See the 1812, 1814, 1819, 1821, 1822 common school laws in *Laws of the State of New York*; "Of Public Instruction," *Revised Statutes of the State of New-York, Passed During the Years 1827 and 1828,* vol 1. (Albany, 1829), ch. 15; *Revised Statutes of the State of New York . . . for the Use of Schools and Families* (New York, 1844); Walter John Gifford, *Historical Development of New York State High School System* (Albany, 1922), 29–33. For school laws in practice, see "Communication: District School Meeting," *Long-Island Star* (Brooklyn), May 8, 1816. For an overview of school funding up until the passage of state 1867 Free School Law, see James C. Mohr, *The Radical Republicans and Reform in New York During Reconstruction* (Ithaca, 1973), 175–197.

35. George E. Haynes, *Negro at Work in New York City* (New York, 1912), 47; "African School," *Long-Island Star,* Jan. 18, 1815; "Communication," *Long-Island Star,* Apr. 22, 1824; "White Washing," *Long-Island Star,* Apr. 10, 1834. See also "African Celebration" *Long-Island Star*, July 19, 1827. In 1831, the Crogers and Joseph Smith received articles of incorporation for the Woolman Society by the state legislature. *NY Laws,* 54th Sess. (1831), ch. 17. On black Brooklyn's long traditions of mutualism, see Wilder, *In the Company of Black Men* and *A Covenant with Color: Race and Social Power in Brooklyn* (New York, 2000).

36. "District School," *Long-Island Star* (Brooklyn), Apr. 22, 1818; "Communication," *Long-Island Star,* Apr. 22, 1824; "Exhibition in the African Church," *Long-Island Star,* May 19, 1825. See also "African Schools," *Long-Island Star,* Oct. 30, 1830; "For the Long Island Star," *Long-Island Star,* Apr. 3, 1833; William J. Wilson to Henry Reed Stiles, "Public Schools for Colored Children," late 1862 (?), Henry Reed Stiles Papers, Brooklyn Historical Society; "To the Public," *Long-Island Star,* Oct. 4, 1827; "For the Long Island Star," *Long-Island Star*, Apr. 3, 1833.

37. "Licensed Sweep-Office," *Albany Gazette,* Jan. 29, 1810; Francis Jacobs pension files, National Archives and Records Administration, accessed on Ancestry.com; New York City Register's Office, Microfilm NC0015, Liber Conveyances 52, 229; *Longworth's American Almanac* (New York, 1800), 239; *Albany Directory* (Albany, 1813), 28, 81; Benjamin Lattimore pension files, National Archives and Records Administration; Benjamin Lattimore [Jr.], 1850 US Census, Moreau, NY; Hughes, *Refusing Ignorance: The Struggle to Educate Black Children in Albany, New York 1816-1873* (Albany, 1998), 16; Register of Marriages, Baptisms, and Deaths in the Presbyterian Church, Albany, From November 1785, accessed on Ancestry.com; Benjamin Lattimore's COF, Apr. 30, 1820, ACR.

38. Indenture between Elizabeth Hamilton and Benjamin Lattimore, Albany Deed Books (vols. 24, 25, 1815–1819, 1819–1822), Albany County Hall of Records, pp. 33–34; "African Society in the City of Albany," *Albany Gazette,* Dec. 14, 1812; "Wanted Immediately," *Albany Register,* Dec. 24, 1813; *JSNY* (Albany, 1816), 113; *NY Laws,* 39th sess. (1816), ch. 87; "Notice," *Albany Daily Advertiser,* July 26, 1816.

39. Register of Marriages, Baptisms, and Deaths in the Presbyterian Church, Albany; *Klinck's Albany Directory for the Year 1822* (Albany, 1822), 45; Lancaster School Society Minutes, 1811–1834, vol. 1, p. 195, NYSL. Albany didn't set up common schools until 1830. Hughes, *Refusing Ignorance,* 35.

40. "Albany Lancaster School," *Albany Gazette,* Feb. 16, 1821; Lancaster School Society Minutes, 171, 181. The Society received money from the city and state to fund its operations. *JANY* (Albany, 1824), Appendix A.

41. *JANY* (Albany, 1824), 27–28; Hughes, *Refusing Ignorance,* 24, 27.

42. "Married," *FJ,* Apr. 6, 1827; "The State Committee-Man," *New York Freeman,* Oct. 8, 1887; Maria Coe Lattimore gravestone, Greenridge Cemetery, Saratoga Springs, Findagrave.com (Memorial 120559083); Jonas Coe's Will, Rensselaer County Probate Records, vol. 007, 1822–1827, County Courthouse (it's likely that Maria was the indented servant girl cited in Jonas Coe's will, but I cannot be certain); "The Colored Females . . . ," *AEJ,* Feb. 27, 1838; "School for Colored Children," *Albany Journal,* Aug. 14, 1840; "Union Meeting of the Colored People of Albany, Troy, and Vicinity," *CA,* Apr. 15, 1837; "Meeting of the Colored Citizens of Albany," *CA,* May 23, 1840; "A Call for a Convention of the Colored Inhabitants of the State of New York," *CA,* July 18, 1840; Hughes, *Refusing Ignorance,* chs. 1–3; "Saratoga Springs" [Lattimores' children in AME Zion Church in Saratoga], *New York Age,* Jan. 3, 1891; "Convention of the Colored Inhabitants," *CA,* Sept. 12, 1840; "Federalism and Abolition United," *Globe* (Washington), Sept. 25, 1840; "Albany, April 1, 1850," *NS,* Apr. 5, 1850.

43. Minutes of the Meetings of the Jericho Charitable Society, 1794–1987, Friends Historical Library, Swarthmore College; Flushing Monthly Meeting, "Women's Minutes, 1771-1806," Dec. 6, 1775, NYMMM.

44. *Christian Herald* (New York, 1817), 3:305–306, 311; K. Elise Leal, "'All Our Children May Be Taught of God': Sunday Schools and the Roles of Childhood and Youth in Creating Evangelical Benevolence," *Church History* (Dec. 2018): 1056–1090.

45. "African School," *Troy Budget,* June 3, 1823; "Notice," *Farmers' Register* (Troy), Dec. 25, 1820. Apparently one of the white common schools in Troy in the 1820s accepted black students, but most did not. "William Rich School," *Troy Daily Times,* Nov. 13, 1866.

46. "William Rich School," *Troy Daily Times,* Nov. 13, 1866.

47. Jermain Wesley Loguen, *The Rev. J. W. Loguen, as A Slave and as A Freeman* (Syracuse, 1859), 346–347, 351, 356.

48. Thomas James, *Life of Rev. Thomas James, by Himself* (Rochester, 1866), 5. In the 1820 US Census, James is listed in the column for "free coloured person" between 14 and 26. Asa Kimball, 1820 US Census, Canajoharie, Montgomery County, NY.

49. James, *Life*, 6–7; William Farley Peck, *Semi-Centennial History of the City of Rochester* (Syracuse, 1884), 276, 302; "African Church and School" and "African School and Church in Rochester," *Rochester Telegraph*, July 24, 1827; Steward, *Twenty-Two Years a Slave*, 114; *Report of the Trustees of the African Church in the Village of Rochester* (Rochester, 1828).

50. James, *Life*, 7–9; Blake McKelvey, "Lights and Shadows in Local Negro History," *Rochester History* (Oct. 1959): 3–4; William S. McFeely, *Frederick Douglass* (New York, 1991), 82–83, 149–155; Howard Coles, *The Cradle of Freedom: A History of the Negro in Rochester, Western New York, and Canada* (Rochester, 1943), 129; David Henry Bradley, *A History of the A. M. E. Zion Church, Part 1: 1796-1872* (Nashville, 1956), 122.

51. There were five buildings and six schools. Schools #2 and #4 were in the same building on Mulberry Street. In January 1833, there were 1,429 students enrolled: 144 in #1, 272 in #2, 385 in #3, 298 in #4, 179 in # 5, and 160 in #6. Full attendance was rare. Numbers dipped due to weather, truancy, students' labor obligations, illness, etc. NYMS, vol. 8, p. 85. In 1830, there were 14,083 black inhabitants in New York City. In Charles Andrews's 1830 history of the school, he cited an enrollment of 620 students and estimated the number of school-aged children in the city to be 1,800. Rhoda Freeman, "The Free Negro in New York City in the Era Before the Civil War" (PhD diss., Columbia, 1966), appendix (Table 1); Andrews, *History of the New-York African Free-Schools*, 113.

52. On white man's democracy, see Michael Morrison and James Brewer Stewart, eds., *Race and the Early Republic: Racial Consciousness and Nation-Building in the Early Republic* (Lanham, MD, 2002); Phyllis Field, *The Politics of Race in New York: The Struggle for Black Suffrage in the Civil War Era* (Ithaca, 1982); Polgar, *Standard Bearers*, chs. 5–6.

53. NYMS, vol. 9, Nov. 8, 1808, p. 194, Jan. 10, 1809, p. 202, Apr. 11, 1809, p. 214, July 11, 1809, p. 218, Apr. 10, 1810, p. 245, July 10, 1810, p. 256; Samuel Ringgold Ward, *Autobiography of a Fugitive Negro: His Anti-slavery Labours in the United States, Canada and England* (London, 1855), 28.

54. AFS, vol. 3, 7–8. (*N.B.* Vol. 3 has repetitive pagination.) For laws against black education, see "Observations on the Education of Slaves (1841)" in Junius Rodriguez, ed., *Slavery in the United States: A Social, Political, and Historical Encyclopedia* (Santa Barbara, 2007), 2:616–617.

55. AFS, vol. 1, Oct. 1817, 1818 [p. 6]; Andrews, *History of the African Free Schools*, 22.

56. AFS, vol. 1, Oct. 1817, 1818; B. F. Wheeler, *The Varick Family* (Mobile, 1906), 26; "To the Friends of Freedom and the Press," *NS*, Apr. 12, 1850; "The Fifteenth Pennsylvania Antislavery Fair," *Pennsylvania Freeman*, Nov. 28, 1850; "Fugitive Slave Fair," *NS*, Jan. 23, 1851.

57. "The African Free School," *National Gazette and Literary Register* (Philadelphia), May 15, 1824; "From the New York Daily Advertiser of Saturday: African Free School," *National Gazette and Literary Register*, May 11, 1824; Andrews, *History*, 36; "Report," *Statesman* (New York), May 21, 1824.

58. AFS, vol. 3. For students' original work, see vol. 4.

59. "An Address," AFS, vol. 4; "Lafayette in New York," *New Hampshire Observer*, Sept. 20, 1824; "The Nation's Guest: Compiled from *Niles' Register* and Other Papers," *Supporter and Scioto Gazette* (Ohio), Sept. 30, 1824; "Letter from Communipaw," *FDP*, Jan. 21, 1859. Reviewing the 768-page *History of the Public School Society*, it seems that the society organized public exhibitions very rarely. See also Kaestle, *The Evolution of an Urban School System*, 80–88.

60. Harris, *In the Shadow of Slavery*, 96–97; Stewart, "The Emergence of Racial Modernity," 191–193; White, *Stories of Freedom*, 33–34. A British traveler observed that "even in the state of New York, where negro slavery has been abolished by law," a "negro be ever so industrious or well-informed" has "little or no fair chance." Basil Hall, *Travels in North, in the Years 1827 and 1828* (Edinburgh, 1830), 1:30. A Swedish visitor concurred: Carl David Arfwedson, *The United States and Canada, in 1832, 1833, and 1834* (London, 1834) 1:238–239.

61. "Emigration to Hayti," *New York Observer*, Sept. 11, 1824; New York County Jury Census, 1819, Ward 6, p. 62, NYMA.

62. "Emigration to Hayti," *New York Spectator*, Nov. 9, 1824; A. Mott, *Biographical Sketches and Interesting Anecdotes of Person of Color* (New York, 1837), 215–216.

63. William Baldwin, S Baldwin, William Baldwin [son], Mrs. Baldwin, on Brig Lark, June 11,1828, *New York, US, Arriving Passenger and Immigration Lists, 1820-1850*, Ancestry.com. More generally, see Sara Fanning, *Caribbean Crossing: African Americans and the Haitian Emigration Movement* (New York, 2015). After the 1820s Haiti experiment, there were other waves of emigrationism in the nineteenth century. Floyd J. Miller, *The Search for a Black Nationality: Black Emigration and Colonization, 1787-1863* (Urbana, 1975). And a strong black countermovement to white colonizationism: Ousmane K. Power-Greene, *Against Wind and Tide: The African American Struggle Against the Colonization Movement* (New York, 2014).

64. "To Our Patrons," *FJ*, Mar. 16, 1827.

65. "African Free Schools in the United States," *FJ*, May 18, 1827; "African Free Schools in the United States," *FJ*, June 1, 1827; "English Grammar," "School Notice," "Evening School," and "Notice," *FJ*, Dec. 14, 1827.

66. "New York African Free School," *FJ*, Nov. 9, 1827.

67. "City African Free Schools," *FJ*, Dec. 14, 1827; "City Free Schools," *FJ*, Jan. 11, 1828; "School Meeting," *FJ*, Jan. 11, 1828; "African Free School," *FJ*, Jan. 11, 1828.

68. "African Dorcas Association," *FJ*, Feb. 15, 1828; "Notice," *FJ*, Feb. 1, 1828. I have no proof that Serena DeGrasse attended the African Free School, but it's likely that she (and other siblings) did. Her brother was a student. At sixteen, she enrolled in the integrated Young Ladies' Domestic Seminary in Clinton, New York, where she wouldn't have been admitted without previous schooling. Serena later married George T. Downing, an African Free School graduate who became a forceful advocate for civil rights (see Chapter 7 of this book). For a stunningly researched account of the Young Ladies' Domestic Seminary, see Baumgartner, *In Pursuit of Knowledge*, ch. 2.

69. "Our Dorcas Society," *FJ*, Jan. 9. 1829; American Convention of Abolition Societies, *Minutes, Constitutions, Addresses, Memorials, Resolutions, Reports, Committees, and Antislavery Tracts, 1794-1829* (New York, 1969), 3:1051.

70. "Coloured Free Schools," *FJ*, Sept. 12, 1828; "Dorcas Association," *FJ*, Nov. 21, 1828; "African Schools," *FJ*, July 18, 1828.

71. American Convention, *Minutes, Constitutions, Addresses*, 3:1049, 1080; "George W. Moore's Essay," *FJ*, Mar. 14, 1829; "Elver Reason's Essay," *FJ*, Mar. 14, 1829.

72. "George Allen's Essay," *FJ*, Mar. 14, 1829.

73. "The Late Peter Guignon," *New York Freeman*, Jan. 1, 1885; Smith, "Sketch of the Life," 20.

74. Smith, "Sketch of the Life," 22; Andrews, *History*, 7, 16, 35, 121.

75. "Outrage," *ComAd*, Feb. 27, 1830. The article does not mention Andrews by name, but he was the instructor at the Mulberry Street School (cited in the article) at the time.

76. Smith, *Memorial Discourse*, 25. The City Recorder was an appointed city judge who frequently presided over the Mayor's Court.

77. Alexander Crummell, *Africa and America: Addresses and Discourses* (Springfield, MA, 1891), 276–277; Smith, *Memorial Discourse*, 26.

78. Henry Highland Garnet, "Pioneers of the A.M.E. Church No. III," *Christian Recorder* (Philadelphia), Mar. 13, 1869; NYMS, vol. 11, Jan. 13, 1829, p. 179. Jonathan Daniel Wells's depiction of the kidnapping of seven-year-old Henry Scott from his desk at the African Free School in 1834 also shows how slavery reached right into schoolchildren's lives. Wells notes that Riker, who had a reputation as being helpful to slave owners, occasionally (as the Garnet story suggests) demonstrated antislavery sympathies. *The Kidnapping Club: Wall Street, Slavery, and Resistance on the Eve of the Civil War* (New York, 2020), 33–37, 307.

79. On these themes, see Jackson, *Force and Freedom*.

80. Andrews, *History of the New York African Free-Schools*, 119. For a discussion of why colonization was so contentious in the black community, see C. Peter Ripley et al., *BAP*, vol. 3 (Chapel Hill, 1991), 3–12.

81. NYMS, vol. 8, Sept. 11, 1830, p. 53; NYMS, vol. 8, Jan. 10, 1832, p. 69; Elizabeth J. Graham, "New York's Lack of Public Spirit," *New York Age*, Sept. 20, 1890. For more on NYMS members with colonizationist views, see Anna Mae Duane, "'Can You Be Surprised at My Discouragement?' Global Emulation and the Logic of Colonization at the African Free School," in *Warring for America: Cultural Contests in the Era of 1812*, ed. Nicole Eustace and Fredrika J. Teute (Chapel Hill, 2017). *N.B.* William Jinnings spelled his own name with an *i*, but in print the name often appears as *Jennings* and some of his children later used Jennings.

82. NYMS, vol. 8, Jan. 10, 1832, p. 69, Apr. 10, 1832, p. 78, July 10, 1832, p. 81, Nov. 11, 1832, p. 84.

83. NYMS, vol. 8, July 10, 1832, p. 80; "Report of the Committee of Education presented to the Convention of Citizens of Color," *NS*, Apr. 17, 1851; NYMS, vol. 8, Nov. 13, 1832, p. 82.

84. Smith, "Sketch of the Life," 23.

85. *NY Laws*, 49th sess, (1826), ch. 25; Public School Society of New-York Records, Minutes of the Trustees, Aug. 1, 1834, NYHS; Smith, *Memorial Discourse,* 21. For the next phase of black education in New York City, see ch. 5.

86. Smith, *Memorial Discourse,* 21.

87. "The Following are the . . . ," *CA,* June 23, 1838; "Public Meeting on the 4th of July," *CA,* July 14, 1838; "For the Colored American," *CA,* Aug. 25, 1838.

88. "A Call for a Convention of the Colored Inhabitants of the State of York," *CA,* July 18, 1840.

89. "For the Liberator," *Liberator* (Boston), June 29, 1833; "For the Colored American," *CA,* July 11, 1840; Henry Highland Garnet, *The Past and the Present Condition, and the Destiny, of the Colored Race, a Discourse Delivered at the Fifteenth Anniversary of the Female Benevolent Society of Troy* (Troy, 1848), 2; Elizabeth Wicks, *Address Delivered Before the African Female Benevolent Society of Troy* (Troy, 1834), 6.

90. "To the Friends of Freedom and the Press," *NS,* Apr. 12, 1850; "North Star Fair," *NS,* Apr. 3, 1851.

Chapter 4

The chapter title—"Citizenship National"—is a riff on "Freedom National; Slavery Sectional," Massachusetts senator Charles Sumner's famous speech, which drew on decades of antislavery constitutional thought to protest the 1850 Fugitive Slave Act. His argument was that even if slavery were permitted in the states, the national government had the power and responsibility to promote freedom everywhere else (in the territories, on the seas, in Washington, D.C.). In this chapter, I show how antislavery New Yorkers in the 1820s took their conceptions of black citizenship into the national arena—i.e., took citizenship national—arguing that the federal constitution's ill-defined guarantees of national citizenship applied to free black people. I thank Daniel Hulsebosch for suggesting this title. Sumner, *Freedom National; Slavery Sectional* (Boston, 1852); James Oakes, *Freedom National: The Destruction of Slavery in the United States, 1861–1865* (New York, 2013).

1. For more on Steward, see Chapter 2.

2. Steward, *Twenty-Two Years,* 113–115, 128–131; Austin Steward's COF, Apr. 10, 1821, Miscellaneous Records, Liber 1, Year 1821, Monroe County Clerk, Rochester; NY Const. (1821), art. 2, § 1; "On the Rights of Colored People to Vote," *CA,* Mar. 4, 1837. *N.B.*: The constitution refers to citizens "of colour," the *Colored American* uses "of color."

3. The precise number of slaves freed in 1827 is unknown. William Jay estimated 10,000, but he was likely relying on the 1820 federal census, which means that 10,000 is too high. Many slaves negotiated manumissions, purchased themselves, ran away, or died between 1820 and 1827. The 1825 New York State census, which counted roughly 40,000 "persons of color," did not record slave status; this may have been an indication of the growing reluctance to catalog people as property. Some current secondary sources report 3,000 people freed in 1827, but I believe that is a misreading

of sources citing 3,000 black people who paraded in New York City to celebrate general abolition. William Jay, *Slavery in America: or, An Inquiry into the Character and Tendency of the American Colonization and the American Anti-Slavery Societies* (London, 1835), 94; "Recapitulation," *Census of the State of New York, 1825*, OCLC/NY ID 1083547477, NYSL; "Commemoration of the Africans," *ComAd*, July 6, 1827. The *New-York Observer* also estimated 10,000 freed in 1827: "General Slave Emancipation," June 16, 1827.

4. Steward, *Twenty-Two Years*, 150–152; "Fifth of July," *Rochester Telegraph*, July 6, 1827.

5. Steward, *Twenty-Two Years*, 153–162; "Mr. A Steward's Address," *FJ*, July 27, 1827.

6. *A Century of Population Growth . . . 1790-1900* (Washington, DC, 1909), ch. 14.

7. For works that skillfully integrate local, state, and national political histories of this time period, see Matthew Mason, "The Maine and Missouri Crisis: Competing Priorities and Northern Slavery Politics in the Early Republic," *JER* (Winter 2013): 675–700; Nicholas Wood, "A Sacrifice on the Altar of Slavery: Doughface Politics and Black Disfranchisement in Pennsylvania, 1837-1838," *JER* (Spring 2011): 75–106; Gosse, *First Reconstruction*; Jones, *Birthright Citizens*; Masur, *Until Justice be Done*. On black disfranchisement in various states, see Alexander Keyssar, *The Right to Vote: The Contested History of Democracy in the United States* (New York, 2000), 320.

8. For a contemporary study of citizenship, see the New Yorker William Yates's, *Rights of Colored Men to Suffrage, Citizenship, and Trial by Jury* (Philadelphia, 1838). See also the Introduction to this book, note 9.

9. In exploring early U.S. citizenship in all its legal and constitutional messiness, this chapter joins a robust field. I'm particularly influenced by Masur, *Until Justice Be Done*; William J. Novak, "The Legal Transformation of Citizenship in Nineteenth Century America," in *The Democratic Experiment: New Directions in American Political History*, ed. Meg Jacobs et al. (Princeton, 2003), 85–119; Jones, *Birthright Citizens*; Nathan Perl-Rosenthal, *Citizen Sailors: Becoming American in the Age of Revolution* (Cambridge, MA, 2015); Rebecca Scott, "Paper Thin: Freedom and Re-enslavement in the Diaspora of the Haitian Revolution," *Law and History Review* (Nov. 2011): 1061–1087; Wood, "A Class of Citizens." My contribution is both substantive and methodological. While there were similarities in experience and formal definitions of citizenship for free black people across the U.S., each state had histories and dynamics that weren't always universalizable. Close attention to social, rural, and women's history sources helps make important but abstract legal and political conversations more legible. By integrating local, state, and national history, and showing precisely how ordinary people interacted with government officials, we achieve a ground-up view of how conceptions of citizenship were formulated and also how they mattered in daily life.

10. This particular language comes from the pre-printed and executed manumission documents in the New York City Common Council Papers, 1670-1831, Box 54, Microfilm 54, NYMA. For similar language elsewhere, see, for example: Liber of Conveyances, L98 P117 to L101 P19, Microfilm NC0032, New York City Register's Office, 66

John St.; ACR; Marie Hall Cormack Transcripts, Schenectady County Historical Society; Records of Poughkeepsie Precinct.

11. NY Const. (1821).

12. Franklin B. Hough, ed., *Census of the State of New York, for 1855* (Albany, 1857), ix–x; John L. Brooke, "'King George has Issued Too Many Pattents for Us': Property and Democracy in Jeffersonian New York," *JER* (Summer 2013): 187–217.

13. "Shameful Violation of the Right of Suffrage," *ComAd*, Apr. 26, 1809; "Charter Election," *Northern Whig* (Hudson), Apr. 12, 1811; "More Lamentations," *Bee*, Apr. 19, 1811; [No title], *Northern Whig*, Apr. 26, 1811.

14. Sidney, *An Oration*, 9, 14.

15. *JANY* (1811), 231, 243, 251–252, 310–311, 315–316, 338, 351, 359–360, 394–395, 401, 404–407, 412; *JSNY* (Albany, 1811), 142–145, 150, 164, 173, 197; "Communication: Legislative Anecdote," *Albany Register*, Mar. 29, 1811.

16. Minutes of the Council of Revision (Series A0027-78), vol. 3, pp. 206–208, Apr. 5, 1811, NYSA. The Republican chancellor, John Lansing Jr., reviewed the bill and "reported certain objections to the same." Although a majority of the council agreed to veto the bill, there is no roll call.

17. *NY Laws*, 34th sess. (1811), ch. 201.

18. "The New Election Law," *Balance* (Albany), Apr. 16, 1811; "Freedom of Election," *EP*, Apr. 16, 1811.

19. ACR, 92–94; Nathaniel H. Carter and William L. Stone, *Reports of the Proceedings and Debates of the Convention of 1821 . . .* (Albany, 1821), 201–202.

20. Philip Smedes's COF 17, Apr. 1811, 101 Box Collection, Ulster County Hall of Records, Kingston, New York; Thomas Miller's COF, June 3, 1811, Coxsackie Town Record of Freeborn Slaves, 1800–1827; Cato Sherli's COF, Apr. 29, 1813, Marie Hall Cormack Transcripts of Books #118 and #119 from the Schenectady County Clerk's Office, Schenectady County Historical Society; Isaac Plato's COF, Apr. 26, 1811, East Hampton Town Records, "Volume G," 1698–1874, p. 220, East Hampton Library, Long Island Collection; Archelaus and James Fletcher's COFs, Misc. Records, B (Mar. 1804 to Jan. 1814), pp. 217–218, 252–253, OCR.

21. [No title], *EP*, Apr. 18, 1815.

22. *A View of Exertions Lately Made for the Purpose of Colonizing the Free People of Colour* (Washington, DC, 1817); Harris, *In the Shadow*, 131–135; *American Convention for Promoting the Abolition of Slavery* (Philadelphia, 1818), 49, 65, 69. For a nuanced exploration of black New Yorkers' initial response to colonization, see Polgar, *Standard-Bearers of Equality*, ch. 2.

23. For a lengthier treatment of Tallmadge, see Gronningsater, "James Tallmadge Jr. and the Personal Politics of Antislavery."

24. James Tallmadge Jr., "An oration upon the infringement of the rights of man, to be delivered at the commencement of Rhode Island College, Sept. 5, 1798," Student essays and orations, 1786–1983, MS-1N-C1, John Hay Library, Brown University.

25. J .Talmadge, Jr. [*sic*], 1810 Federal Census, Poughkeepsie, Dutchess County, NY.

26. Records of Poughkeepsie Precinct, p. 99. Tallmadge was elected during a special election in June; his term began in December 1817. There is no evidence that I have found, despite reports in secondary sources, that Tallmadge was involved in crafting the 1817 general abolition act (or any other state emancipation law).

27. *Annals of Congress*, 15th Congress, 2nd sess., Feb. 13, 1819, p. 1166, Feb. 15, 1819, p. 1170.

28. *Annals of Congress*, 15th Congress, 2nd sess., Feb. 15, 1819, pp. 1172–1175, Feb. 16, 1819, pp. 1203–1204.

29. *Speech of the Honorable James Tallmadge* . . . (New York, 1819), 20, 24; [No title], *New-York Daily Advertiser*, Mar. 6, 1819.

30. "People of Colour," *Columbian*, Apr. 23, 1819.

31. "People of Colour," *NA*, Apr. 23, 1819.

32. Theodorus Bailey to Matthias B. Tallmadge, Apr. 27, 1819, Tallmadge Family Papers, NYHS; [No title], *NA*, May 4, 1819; [No title], *Columbian*, May 4, 1819.

33. Forbes, *Missouri Compromise*, 71–73, 100; "The Voice of Freedom," *Albany Register*, Apr. 21, 1820.

34. US Const., art. IV, § 2.

35. "Constitution of Missouri," *American* (New York), Nov. 29, 1820. James Kent, New York's foremost jurist, later explained in his influential *Commentaries on American Law*: "If a slave born in the United States be manumitted, or otherwise lawfully discharged from bondage, or if a black man be born within the United States, and born free, he becomes thenceforward a citizen, but under such disabilities as the laws of the states respectively may deem it expedient to prescribe to free persons of colour." Kent thus confirmed black state citizenship and national citizenship as facts, while also describing how a black person and a white person did not exercise equal "civil and political rights" in "any part of the country." Black citizenship was legally real, but so were the racialized disabilities various states attached to it. *Commentaries on American Law* (New York, 1836), 2:258–259.

36. "Monday, November 13," *Albany Gazette*, Nov. 14, 1820; "Legislature of New-York," *Albany Gazette*, Nov. 17, 1820.

37. *JANY* (Albany, 1820), 45; *Journal of the Senate of the United States of America* (Washington, 1820), 26–27.

38. *Annals of Congress*, 16th Congress, 2nd sess., Feb. 10, 1821, pp. 1078–1080, Feb. 13, 1821, p. 1124.

39. *Acts of the First General Assembly of the State of Missouri* (St. Charles, 1821), 9–11 (ch. 11); "Admission of Missouri," *Niles' Weekly Register* (Baltimore), Aug. 16, 1821. The best treatment of the second Missouri Compromise is Kate Masur, "The Second Missouri Compromise, State Citizenship, and African Americans' Rights in the Antebellum United States," in *A Fire Bell in the Past*, vol. 2.

40. [No title], *Spectator*, Mar. 2, 1821.

41. On the prominent place of New York and Massachusetts in national debates, see Masur, *Until Justice Be Done,* chs. 2, 4. Masur's treatment of black New Yorker Gilbert Horton's 1826 imprisonment and rescue in Washington, D.C. is superb on this theme. *N.B.* In his *Dred Scott* dissent, Justice Curtis wrote that Congress's acknowledgment in 1821 (during the second Missouri Crisis) that black citizens were citizens of their states led him to conclude that "as free colored persons born within some of the States are citizens of those States, such persons are also citizens of the United States" (thus refuting Chief Justice Taney's conclusions about black citizenship and Taney's overall reading of the history of the subject). *Dred Scott v. Sandford,* 60 US (19 How.), 588 (Curtis, J. dissenting).

42. *NY Laws,* 44th sess (1821), ch. 90.

43. "From the New York Statesman," *EP,* Apr. 19, 1821, and *Columbian,* Apr. 18, 1821.

44. Austin Steward COF; Sam Harris's COF, Apr. 25, 1821, Record of Roads, 1756–1788, film 285, Dutchess County Clerk's Office, Poughkeepsie; Miscellaneous Records, C (Oct. 1813 to July 1828), pp. 275, 376–377; Town of Canandaigua Records, 1791–1846, pp. 313–315, 318–320, OCR. A man named Joseph Adams obtained his certificate of freedom on Apr. 23, 1820, but filed the certificate on Apr. 26, 1821 (Miscellaneous Records, C, p. 376); Prince Williams's COF, Apr. 25, 1821, Frisbee Way COF, Apr. 25, 1821, Albany Institute of History and Art; Peter Dawson COF, June 19, 1821, Marie Hall Cormack Transcripts, Schenectady.

45. Wilentz, *Rise of American Democracy,* 191. The delegates did not attend the convention under the official partisan banners, but for a list of many considered Bucktails, see "Republican Nominations for Delegates to the Convention of Albany," *Albany Argus,* June 19, 1821.

46. Existing scholarship, while otherwise illuminating, does not investigate delegates' personal experiences with black voters. Wilentz, *Rise of American Democracy,* 189–196; Polgar, "Whenever They Judge it Expedient," 13–17; Peterson, *Democracy, Liberty, Property,* 115–241.

47. Carter and Stone, *Report of the Convention,* 134, 180, 183. On Van Rensselaer, see Gronningsater, "Expressly Recognized by Our Election Laws," 475–476.

48. Carter and Stone, *Report of the Convention,* 134, 184.

49. Carter and Stone, *Report of the Convention,* 185–186, 189–191. These arguments sound similar to those made by politicians discussing black citizenship during the Civil War era. See Eric Foner, "The Strange Career of the Reconstruction Amendments," *Yale Law Journal* 108 (1999): 2003–2009; Kate Masur, "Civil, Political, and Social Equality After Lincoln: A Paradigm and a Problematic," *Marquette Law Review* 93 (2010): 1399–1406.

50. Carter and Stone, *Report of the Convention,* 193, 190, 197–199. For Peterson's story, see Chapter 1.

51. Carter and Stone, *Report of the Convention,* 201–202; Hammond, *The History of Political Parties,* 2:19.

52. Carter and Stone, *Report of the Convention,* 288–291, 374–376, 377.

53. "State of New York," *Albany Argus,* Feb. 19, 1822.

54. Black editors and convention delegates repeatedly referred to their supporters at the 1821 constitutional convention in later decades as they asserted their citizenship rights. See, for example, "Question of Slavery in the State of N.Y.," *CA*, Mar. 11, 1837; "On the Rights of Colored People to Vote," *CA*, Mar. 4, 1837.

55. I delve more deeply into black women's politics, and related historiography, in Chapter 5.

56. "Letters Patent," *New York Gazette,* Mar. 13, 1821; "Legal Rights Vindicated," *FDP,* Mar. 2, 1855; "Thomas L. Jennings," *Anglo-African Magazine* (New York), Apr. 1859.

57. "At a General Meeting of the Electors of Colour," *ComAd,* Nov. 9, 1813; "At a numerous and respectable meeting of the Electors of Colour," *EP,* Nov. 11, 1813; Henry Parson's COF, Dec. 16, 1812, New-York City Indentures, ser. 3, Free Papers (1803–1814), NYHS; John Johnson's COF, Apr. 22, 1814, ibid.; George White's COF, Apr. 22, 1814; George A. Plimpton Papers, Box 52, Rare Book & Manuscript Library, Columbia University.

58. See Chapter 3 on the Jinnings family and schools.

59. "Eulogy," *CA,* Nov. 17, 1838; Smith and Garnet, *Memorial Discourse*, 23.

60. "Eulogy," *CA,* Nov. 17, 1838; *Longworth's . . . and City Directory* (New York, 1823), 258, 400.

61. *Longworth's . . . City Directory* (New York, 1810), 252; "Worthy of Imitation," *Weekly Advocate,* Feb. 18, 1837; "Married," *CA,* Mar. 16, 1839; "Another Disgraceful Rail Road Outrage," *Liberator,* Nov. 12, 1841; "Improvements on a Valuable and Important Discovery," *Emancipator* (New York), Feb. 4, 1842; "Legal Rights Vindicated," *FDP,* Mar. 2, 1855; "Thomas L. Jennings," *FDP,* Feb. 18, 1859; Sarah C. Smith, 1860 US Census, San Francisco, District 2, CA; "The Right of Colored Persons to Ride in the Railway Cars," *PA*, May 16, 1863. On Ward, see Ward, *Autobiography of a Fugitive Negro,* 30. On Thomas Jr. and New England's railroads, see Mia Bay, *Traveling Black: A Story of Race and Resistance* (Cambridge, MA, 2021), 26–28. For black travelers and radical abolitionism, see Elizabeth Stordeur Pryor, *Colored Travelers: Mobility and the Fight for Citizenship before the Civil War* (Chapel Hill, 2016), ch. 3.

62. "Outrage upon Colored Persons," *FDP,* July 28, 1854. The most thorough exploration of black experiences on streetcars in New York City and Brooklyn is Darryl Heller's "The Poor Man's Carriage: Street Railways and their Publics in Brooklyn and New York, 1850-1899 (PhD diss., University of Chicago, 2012). Heller shows there was no uniform practice regarding segregation on common carriers in the mid-1800s, and that black people often didn't know what to expect when they boarded a given carrier. He argues that passengers' legal *and* street-level struggles desegrated streetcars in practice in the 1860s. As Chapter 7 of this book explains, in 1873, black New Yorkers' lobbying resulted in a civil rights law forbidding discrimination on common carriers. *NY Laws,* 96th sess. (1873), ch. 186.

63. "A Wholesome Verdict," *New York Semi-Weekly Tribune,* Feb. 23, 1855; "Notice," *FDP,* May 11, 1855.

64. "Appeal to the Citizens of Color, Male and Female, of the City and State of New York," *PA*, May 16, 1863.

65. "Legal Rights Association," *FDP*, Sept. 7, 1855; "Another Outrage upon the Eighth Avenue Railroad," *Liberator*, Dec. 26, 1856; "A New York Scene," *Provincial Freeman* (Toronto), Mar. 10, 1855.

66. Russel Headley, ed., *The History of Orange County New York* (Middletown, NY, 1908), 388–389; [No title], *Poughkeepsie Journal*, Mar. 23, 1796; "Cadwallader D. Colden," *Argus*, May 25, 1796; Isaac Hopper, A List of the Members of the New York Manumission Society, Friends Historical Library, Swarthmore College.

67. NYMS, vol. 9, Jan. 13, 1807, p. 167; NYMS, vol. 9, Nov. 17, 1807, pp. 175–176; *NY Laws*, 30th sess. (1807), ch. 77; *NY Laws*, 31st sess. (1808), ch. 96.

68. Cadwallader D. Colden, "To the Citizens of the State of New York," *Albany Advertiser*, Jan. 8, 1817.

69. *Corfield v. Coryell*, 6 F. Cas, 546, 551–552.

70. *Rogers v. Berry* (1813), 10 Johns. 132.

71. "The People vs. Joseph Pulford," filed Dec. 8, 1819, DAIP; "Facts are Stubborn Things," *ComAd*, June 12, 1807; *Longworth's American Almanac* (New York, 1816), 233; "To the Electors of the Second Ward," *Mercantile Advertiser* (New York), Apr. 23, 1819; "Died," *EP*, Mar. 19, 1821. "Joseph Pulford's Case," *New-York City-Hall Recorder for the Year 1819* (New York, 1819), 172–174.

72. "The People v. Joseph Pulford," CGSM, "Joseph Pulford's Case," 174.

73. "To the Electors of the First District," *EP*, Apr. 24, 1821; "Mssrs. Editors," *New-York Spectator*, Apr. 24, 1821.

74. Kruger, *Born to Run*, 911; Congressional Nomination," *EP*, Apr. 10, 1821; "The People vs. Joseph Pulford," filed Dec. 8, 1819, DAIP.

75. "To the Electors of the First Congressional District," *Columbian*, Apr. 10, 1821.

76. Kruger, *Born to Run*, appendix. "To the Electors of the First District," *EP*, Apr. 24, 1821; "The Election," *EP*, May 2, 1821; [Official Canvas], *EP*, May 28, 1821; "The Late Election," *Spectator*, May 30, 1821.

77. "Congress," *EP*, Dec. 20, 1821; *Annals of Congress*, 17th Congress, 1st sess., Dec. 17, 1821, p. 553.

78. "House of Representatives," *Boston Daily Advertiser*, Apr. 3, 1822.

79. "Seventeenth Congress," *Boston Weekly Messenger*, Apr. 11, 1822.

80. "Seventeenth Congress," *Boston Daily Advertiser*, Apr. 3, 1822.

81. *Annals of Congress*, 17th Congress, 1st sess., Apr. 18, 1822, p. 1618, May 2, 1822, p. 1778.

82. On "transformations" and "waves," see Newman, *Transformation of American Abolitionism*; Sinha, *The Slave's Cause*; Stewart, "*The Emergence of Racial Modernity*."

83. Martin Van Buren to Thomas Ritchie, Jan. 13, 1827, Series 5, Martin Van Buren Papers, Library of Congress. For a thoughtful essay on *national* antislavery politics during the transition between party systems, see Donald Ratcliffe, "The Decline of Antislavery Politics, 1815-1840," in *Contesting Slavery: The Politics of Bondage and*

Freedom in the New American Nation, ed. John Craig Hammond and Matthew Mason (Charlottesville, 2011), 267–290.

84. "Abolition of Slavery," *FJ,* Apr. 20, 1827; Lewis Topp, 1820 US Census, Albany, NY; *Hoffman's Annual Advertiser and Albany Directory 1838* (Albany, 1838), 239; William H. Topp's Will, Book of Wills, vol. 16, 1856–1859, p. 223, Ancestry.com; Minutes of the Albany Common Council 1826–1827, vol. 29, p. 356, Albany County Hall of Records (the petitioners were likely Adam Blake and John Y. Butler); Nathaniel Paul, "An Address delivered on the Celebration," in Gellman and Quigley, ed., *Jim Crow New York* (New York, 2003), 226–234; "Celebration of the Abolition of Slavery," *Albany Argus,* July 10, 1827.

85. "Cooperstown," *FJ,* July 13, 1827; "July 4th 1827—Jubilee from Domestic Slavery," *EP,* July 3, 1827; "Commemoration by the Africans," *Albany Argus,* July 10, 1827; William Hamilton, *Oration Delivered in the African Zion Church on the Fourth of July, 1827* (New York, 1827) 14–16; "With pleasure . . . ," *FJ,* Oct. 12, 1827.

86. Smith, *A Memorial Discourse,* 24–25. On the tensions between those who wanted to celebrate July 4 versus July 5, see "For the Information of our friends," *FJ,* June 22, 1827; "Messrs. Editors," *FJ,* June 29, 1827. Alexander provides an extended discussion of the division in *African or American,* ch. 3.

87. "Memoirs of an Emigrant, The Journal of Alexander Coventry, M.D.," typescript, vol. 2, p. 2242, NYSL.

88. Samuel Cornish, "Dear Sir," *FJ,* July 13, 1827.

89. Samuel Cornish, "Dear Sir," *FJ,* July 13, 1827.

90. "As the period of emancipation . . . ," *FJ,* June 22, 1827; "Abolition of Slavery," *FJ,* June 22, 1827. The secondary literature on uplift/respectability politics is vast. My aim is to add useful information about the ways that black northerners who embraced respectability language in educational, journalistic, and convention contexts were cocreators of changing legal norms concerning black citizenship in partisan politics, lower courts, state legislatures, and Congress. I have learned from Erica L. Ball, "Performing Politics, Creating Community: Antebellum Black Conventions as Political Rituals," in Foreman et al., *Colored Conventions*; Chernoh M. Sesay, Jr., "Respectability and Representation: Black Freemasonry, Race, and Early Free Black Leadership," in *Black Knowledges/Black Struggles: Essays in Critical Epistemology,* ed. Jason R. Ambroise and Sabine Broeck (Liverpool, 2015); Harris, *In the Shadow of Slavery,* chs. 6–8; Kantrowitz, *More Than Freedom,* ch. 4; Pryor, *Colored Travelers*; Rael, *Black Identity and Black Protest*; Peter Wirzbicki, "Black Transcendentalism: William Cooper Nell, the Adelphic Union, and the Black Abolitionist Intellectual Tradition," *JCWE,* (June 2018): 269–290; David Brion Davis, *The Problem of Slavery in the Age of Emancipation* (New York, 2014), 130; Gosse, *The First Reconstruction,* 451, 461, 463, 469–470, 688.

91. See Chapter 3.

92. "Heads of the Colored People - No. 2," *FDP,* Apr. 15, 1852.

93. For Smith's class solidarity, see Stauffer, *Works of James McCune Smith,* Part 4. For analysis of how women's household labor and educational work sustained public black politics, see Chapter 5 of this book.

94. Few secondary sources address *white* antislavery responses to July 4, 1827, or place the day's significance within a wider national context. Newman's *Transformation of American Abolitionism* does not mention the 1827 abolition at all. Susan-Mary Grant discusses northerners' conceptions of southern slavery as fundamental to their comparative identity, but does not treat northern states' relationship to their own emancipation processes. *North Over South: Northern Nationalism and American Identity in the Antebellum Era* (Lawrence, 2000), esp. ch. 2.

95. "Abolition of Slavery," *Baltimore Gazette*, June 22, 1827; "Fourth of July, and Final Extinction of Slavery in New York," *ComAd*, June 25, 1827; "Friday Morning, July 6," *New York Daily Advertiser*, July 10, 1827.

96. "From the Troy Sentinel," *Connecticut Herald* (New Haven), July 10, 1827; *American Mercury* (Hartford), July 17, 1827; *Newburyport Herald*, July 17, 1827; *Poughkeepsie Journal*, July 18, 1827; "Termination of Slavery in N. York," *Portsmouth Journal of Literature & Politics*, July 21, 1827; "Abolition of Slavery," *Schenectady Cabinet*, June 27, 1827. See also "Emancipation," *Ohio Monitor* (Columbus), July 6, 1827.

97. [No title], *Albany Argus*, July 10, 1827; "Extract from an ORATION delivered in Albany, before the Municipal Authorities. July 4, 1827. By SALEM DUTCHER, Jr. ESQ," *FJ*, July 20, 1827. For antislavery addresses on July 4 in the 1820s, see Forbes, *Missouri Compromise*, 219–222.

98. "Extract from an ORATION," *FJ*, July 20, 1827.

99. [No title], *Albany Argus*, July 10, 1827. On the Regency, Jacksonian views of slavery, and Van Buren, see Brooke, *Columbia Rising*, 438–439; William Shade, "'The Most Delicate and Exciting Topics': Martin Van Buren, Slavery, and the Election of 1836," *JER* (Autumn 1998): 459–484; Wilentz, *Rise of American Democracy*, 234, 295–297, 566–568. For a contemporary assessment, see William Jay, *A View of the Action of the Federal Government, in Behalf of Slavery* (New York, 1839), 22, 90, 178–179, 199–217.

100. Melish, *Disowning Slavery*; James Brewer Stewart, "Humanitarian Reform and Antislavery," in *A Companion to the Civil War and Reconstruction*, ed. Lacy Ford (Malden, 2005), 94–111; Elizabeth Varon, *Disunion! The Coming of the American Civil War 1789-1859* (Chapel Hill, 2008), ch. 3.

101. "Abolition of Slavery," *Baltimore Gazette and Daily Advertiser*, June 12, 1827; [No title], *Alexandria Gazette*, June 26, 1827. *Niles' Weekly Register*, the era's national news magazine, emphasized that the end of slavery in New York bore positive effects for the white population. [No title], *Niles' Weekly Register*, June 23, 1827, 274. None of these papers discussed in any detail the black celebrations or the fine print of the emancipation laws.

102. [No title], *Scioto Gazette*, June 14, 1827; [No title], *New-Hampshire Patriot and State Gazette*, July 2, 1827; "Termination of Slavery in N. York," *Portsmouth Journal of Literature and Politics*, July 21, 1827; [No title], *Newburyport Herald*, July 10, 1827; "Termination of Slavery in the State of New York," *New Hampshire Republican*, July 3, 1827; [No title], *New-Hampshire Republican*, July 17, 1827.

103. "Domestic News," *FJ*, July 13, 1827; "For the Freedom's Journal," *FJ*, July 13, 1827; "For the Freedom's Journal," *FJ*, July 30, 1827; [No Headline], *Ohio Monitor*, Aug. 18, 1827.

104. Wiecek, *Sources of Antislavery Constitutionalism*, 15–19, and Oakes, *Freedom National*, 2–8, on the "federal consenus" that slavery was a state concern; [No title], *Boston Commercial Gazette*, June 18, 1827. "Emancipation in New York," *Friend of Peace* (1827), 4:415.

105. "Letter from the Hon. William Jay," *Emancipator*, June 25, 1833; Jay, *Slavery in America*, 94, 162. This latter tract was republished in its sixth edition in 1838. In 1830, there were 15,501 slaves in Florida Territory and 4,576 slaves in Arkansas Territory. In the 1790s, Kentucky Territory had 12,430 slaves. Even in 1830, Kentucky had far fewer slaves than some of its southern neighbors, and it remained a border state that inspired abolitionists' hopes. In 1835, James Birney, future presidential candidate for the Liberty Party and friend of Jay's, organized the Kentucky Anti-Slavery Society. William Birney, *James G. Birney and his times: The genesis of the Republican Party with Some Account of Abolition Movements in the South before 1828* (New York, 1890), 176, passim.

106. Jay, *An Inquiry*, 190.

107. The waning of gradual abolition coincided with the intensification of U.S. industrialization and related shifts in political economy. For connections between changing labor dynamics and the politics of slavery, see John Ashworth, *Slavery, Capitalism, and Politics in the Antebellum Republic*, vol. 1 (New York, 1996); Eric Foner, *Free Soil, Free Labor, Free Men: The Ideology of the Republican Party Before the Civil War* (New York, 1970).

Chapter 5

1. "Board of Education," *Rochester Daily Democrat*, Feb. 21, 1846; "Board of Education," *Rochester Daily Democrat*, Mar. 5, 1846; *Second Annual Report of the Superintendent of Common Schools of the City of Rochester* (Rochester, 1844), 6, 31; *Fourth Annual Report of the Superintendent of Common Schools of the City of Rochester* (Rochester, 1845), 3, 6; *Canfield and Warren's Directory of the City of Rochester, for 1845-46* (Rochester, 1845), 14; *Daily American Directory of the City of Rochester, for 1847-48* (Rochester, 1847), 230 [Phebe Ray as cook]; *Daily American Directory of the City of Rochester, for 1849-50* (Rochester, 1849), 256 [Phebe Ray as laundress].

2. Issac Ray, 1820 US Census, Fayette, Seneca County, NY; *Rochester Directory for 1847*, 230; David Ray, 1850 US Census, Rochester, Ward 6, Monroe County, NY; Phebe Ray, 1850 US Census, Rochester, Ward 5, Monroe County, NY; Phebe Ray, 1855 NY State Census, Rochester City, Ward 10; Phebe Ray, 1880 US Census, Rochester, Monroe County, NY; David Ray, 1880 US Census, Palmyra, Wayne County, NY; *Rochester Directory for the Year Beginning July 1, 1880* (Rochester, 1880), 310; David H. Ray Death Certificate, Register #172, Aug. 19, 1884, Town Clerk, Palmyra, NY. In the late 1830s, both Phebe and David were living in Canandaigua, Ontario County, thirty miles south

of Rochester. "Pastry, Fruits" and "Ontario Hair Dressing Room," *Ontario Repository and Freeman*, May 10, 1837. The Rays likely moved to Rochester around 1843 or 1844. Isaac Ray appears to have died in the late 1830s. In 1847, Phebe and David were listed separately—she as a cook, he as a barber—in the Rochester directory, but they lived at the same address on Mechanic Alley. The birth years for David Ray and Mary Johnson (née Ray) are estimates; census data conflicts. Samantha Seeley's work sheds light on the Rays' relocations; freedom of movement was a meaningful, and hardly universal, right. Seeley, *Race, Removal, and the Right to Remain.*

3. "Board of Education," *Rochester Daily Democrat*, Apr. 20, 1846; *Fourth Annual Report of the Superintendent*, 3; *Sixth Annual Report of the Superintendent of Public Schools of the City of Rochester* (Rochester, 1847), 4.

4. Historians of women have written persuasively about ordinary and disfranchised people's political practices. We could do more, however, to apply their insights to the history of black northerners' interactions with the state and to synthetic accounts of the First and Second Party Systems. What if we pieced together black women's stories from local evidence—moments when they wielded their rights and privileges as citizens (albeit second-class)—and integrated their political work with the familiar narratives of mainstream party politics? I aim to build on Kabria Baumgartner, "Building the Future: White Women, Black Education, and Civic Inclusion in Antebellum Ohio," *JER* (Spring 2017): 117–145; Mia Bay, Farah J. Griffin, Martha S. Jones, and Barbara D. Savage, *Toward an Intellectual History of Black Women* (Chapel Hill, 2015); Julie Roy Jeffrey, *The Great Silent Army of Abolitionism: Ordinary Women in the Antislavery Movement* (Chapel Hill, 1998); Laura F. Edwards, "Sarah Allingham's Sheet and Other Lessons from Legal History," *JER* (Spring 2018): 121–147; Psyche Williams-Forson, "Where Did They Eat? Where Did They Stay? Interpreting the Material Culture of Black Women's Domesticity in the Context of the Colored Convention," in Foreman et al., *Colored Conventions*; Lori D. Ginzberg, *Untidy Origins: A Story of Woman's Rights in Antebellum New York* (Chapel Hill, 2005); Jones, *All Bound Up Together*; Sinha, *The Slave's Cause*, ch. 9; Barbara Clark Smith, *The Freedoms We Lost: Consent and Resistance in Revolutionary America* (New York, 2010); Susan Zaeske, *Signatures of Citizenship: Petitioning, Antislavery, and Women's Political Identity* (Chapel Hill, 2003); Shirley J. Yee, *Black Women Abolitionists: A Study in Activism, 1828-1860* (Knoxville, 1992); Rosemarie Zagarri, *Revolutionary Backlash: Women and Politics in the Early American Republic* (Philadelphia, 2007). For a call to learn more about "the overwhelming mass of black inhabitants who were laborers and domestics, often on the move, and prone to distinctive forms of militancy and public politics," see Hahn, *Political Worlds of Slavery and Freedom*, 44.

5. George Fitzhugh, *Cannibals All! Or, Slaves without Masters* (Richmond, 1857), 152. The literature on the Burned-Over District is vast. For a start, see Paul E. Johnson, *A Shopkeeper's Millennium: Society and Revivals in Rochester, New York, 1815-1837*, rev. ed. (New York, 2004); Spencer W. McBride and Jennifer Hull Dorsey, eds., *New York's Burned-Over District: A Documentary History* (Ithaca, 2023). On black reformers, see Milton C. Sernett's *North Star Country: Upstate New York and the Crusade for African*

American Freedom (Syracuse, 2002); Stauffer, *Black Hearts of Men*. The diary of Lemuel Strong Pomeroy, a white antislavery businessman in the district, would have fed directly into George Fitzhugh's disdain for and arguments against northern reform sensibilities had Fitzhugh read it. Strong wrote happily about watching Samuel Ringgold Ward and Henry Highland Garnet preach. Lemuel Strong Pomeroy Diary, 1849–1867, Strong Family Papers, Onondaga Historical Association, Syracuse. I regret not having the space to explore here one of the Burned-Over District's most fascinating and bold institutions, New York Central College in McGrawville (Cortland County). Founded in 1849, the school was co-educational and interracial from the start, and employed black professors such as Charles Reason, a graduate of the African Free School. I thank Mary Kimberly and Carl Kimberly (now deceased), longtime stewards of the college's history, for a meaningful day in McGraw in August 2015, and point readers to John Frederick Bell's 2017 Harvard dissertation: "Equality by Degrees: Abolitionist Colleges and the Throes of Integration, 1833–1895."

6. Smith, *Memorial Discourse*, 21.

7. "The Liberator," *Long-Island Star*, Nov. 9, 1831; "Exhibition," *Long-Island Star*, Dec. 19, 1839; *Brooklyn Alphabetical and Street Directory for 1843 & 4* (Brooklyn, 1843), 33, 164; "A Competent Colored Male Teacher," *CA*, Aug. 7, 1841; *NY Laws*, 68th sess. (1845), ch. 221.

8. "The Committee on Common Schools," *Brooklyn Evening Star*, Feb. 4, 1841. In 1843, the legislature placed Brooklyn common schools under the control of the common council, abolishing the district trustees. Hogarth, Smith, and Brown lost their positions. Two years later, black Brooklynites sent petitions to the legislature praying that their schools would "receive the same support as other Public Schools." After the legislature agreed, William J. Wilson, new principal of the colored school, "was sent to Albany to obtain a copy of the Act, that steps might be immediately taken to purchase a site and erect a suitable building." Wilson, "Public Schools for Colored Children"; *JANY* (Albany, 1845), 621; *NY Laws*, 66th sess. (1845), ch. 306.

9. "Letters to Rev. T. S. Wright, of New-York, No. II," *Chartered Oak* (Hartford), Feb. 12, 1846; "Garden," *Emporium and True American* (Trenton), July 9, 1831; "Enterprise of a Trentonian in Africa," *Daily True American* (Trenton), Nov. 12, 1856; "Colored School," *Brooklyn Evening Star*, Aug. 13, 1841; "Mr. Augustus Washington," *CA*, Oct. 13, 1838; "Great anti-Colonization Meeting," *CA*, Jan. 12, 1839; "Brooklyn Mass Meeting," *CA*, Jan. 2, 1841; "Colored School," *Brooklyn Evening Star*, Aug. 13, 1841; "Williamsburgh Celebration," *CA*, Aug. 14, 1841. Washington left Brooklyn for higher education, attending Kimball Academy and Dartmouth College in New Hampshire in the 1840s. In 1853, he emigrated with his wife, Cordelia, and children, Alonzo and Helena, to Liberia. He prospered there, running a daguerreotype business, teaching, and serving in the Liberian legislature. A revealing minority of the children of gradual abolition were ultimately unsure that the United States was the place they wanted to call home. "Letters to Rev. T. S. Wright, No. II," "List of Emigrants," *African Repository* (Washinton), Mar. 1, 1854; "Letter from Augustus Washington," *African Repository*, June 1, 1854; "Enterprise

of a Trentonian in Africa," *Daily True American* (Trenton), Nov. 12, 1856; "Late from Liberia," *African Repository*, Oct. 1, 1875.

10. "Notice," *CA*, Apr. 24, 1841; "School Exhibition," *CA*, Nov. 13, 1841; *Brooklyn Alphabetical and Street Directory . . . for 1841-42* (Brooklyn, 1841), 67, 103, 188, 307, 319; Benjamin Hampton's Will, Wills, vol. 42–43, 1870–1871, pp. 479–480, New York Surrogate's Court (Kings County), Ancestry.com.

11. Benjamin Hampton, 1840 US Census, New York, Ward 8, NY; Benjamin Hampton and Sampson White, 1850 US Census, Brooklyn, Ward 4, NY; Benjamin Hampton and Sampson White, 1855 NY State Census, Brooklyn, Ward 4; *Brooklyn City Directory and Annual Advertiser. . . 1848-49* (Brooklyn, 1848), 98, 214; *NY Laws*, 68th sess. (1845), ch. 221. Henry Brown, one of the Brooklyn school commissioners, petitioned for the incorporation of the African Tompkins Association alongside Hampton. "Another Old Brooklynite Gone," *Brooklyn Daily Eagle*, Oct. 31, 1870. In the 1841 *Brooklyn Directory*, the address at 11 Chapel Street is listed as "Mrs. Benjamin Hampton's" residence. There are clues here. Benjamin may have been earning money elsewhere that year. No matter where he was, Maria Hampton was a respectable "Mrs." representing her household.

12. *NY Laws*, 49th Sess. (1826), ch. 25; Public School Society Records, Aug. 1, 1834.

13. Public School Society Records, May 6, 1836, May 13, 1836.

14. Public School Society Records, May 13, 1836, Aug. 5, 1836.

15. Public School Society Records, Aug. 5, 1836.

16. American Convention of Abolition Societies, *Minutes of the Adjourned Session of the Twentieth Biennial American Convention for Promoting the Abolition of Slavery* (Philadelphia, 1828), 39; "African Dorcas Association," *FJ*, Feb. 15, 1828; "Dorcas Association," *FJ*, Nov. 21, 1828.

17. See Baumgartner's exploration of black women and girls in Salem's and Nantucket's public high schools in Massachusetts during this same decade. I heartily endorse her point about paying attention to the "hyperlocal"; school experiences could differ even among different schools in the same town. *In Pursuit of Knowledge*, ch. 4.

18. In 1829, Dix was a founding member of an Otsego County auxiliary of the national Society for Colonizing the Free People of Color. Morgan Dix, comp., *Memoirs of John Adams Dix* (New York, 1883), 1:115–119. John A. Dix, *Decisions of the Superintendent of Common Schools of the State of New York* (Albany, 1837), 139.

19. Dix, *Decisions of the Superintendent of Common Schools*, 318.

20. Dix, *Decisions of the Superintendent of Common Schools*, iii–v. For black citizens' voting in school district meetings and a controversy over teachers' religious affiliations, see "The Public School" and "Our School Trustees," *Williamsburgh Gazette*, Mar. 9, 1842; "The Public School," *Williamsburgh Gazette*, Mar. 16, 1842.

21. "Notice is Hereby Given," *Schenectady Cabinet*, Feb. 13, 1833; "Corporation Proceedings," ibid., June 12, 1833; "The First Quarterly Examination," ibid., Sept. 2, 1835; "Facts Touching the Condition of the People of Colour, in this City," ibid., Mar. 8, 1837; "Colored Fair," ibid., Nov. 23, 1841; "Annual Report of the City Treasurer," ibid., Mar. 12, 1844; "Fair," ibid., Apr. 8, 1845; "Proceedings of the Common Council," ibid.,

Mar. 18, 1845; "Annual Report of the City Treasurer," ibid., Apr. 7, 1846; "Proceedings of the Common Council," ibid., Aug. 4, 1846; "Proceedings of the Common Council," ibid., June 13, 1848; "Proceedings of the Common Council," ibid., June 27, 1848; "Proceedings of the Common Council," ibid., Jan. 8, 1850." Black citizens also campaigned for local school rights in Auburn, Poughkeepsie, Utica, Geneva, Jamaica, Flushing, Troy, Lockport, and Bath in the 1830s and '40s.

22. *NY Laws,* 55th sess. (1832), ch. 136; *Documents of the Assembly of the State of New-York, Fifty-Fifth Session, 1832* (Albany, 1832), 2: No. 77. (Rochester was incorporated as a village in 1817); Records of the Proceedings of the Common Council of the City of Rochester, Dec. 3, 1839, to June 28, 1842, p. 248 (Jan. 13, 1841); p. 257 (Jan. 26, 1841); p. 412 (June 29, 1841), Municipal Archives, 414 Andrews Street, Rochester; "Office of the Superintendent of Common Schools," *Rochester Daily Democrat,* Feb. 20, 1841. The clothes renovator was John H. Bishop, who lived with his wife and son in Rochester's First Ward. John H. Bishop, 1840 US Census, Rochester Ward 1, Monroe County, NY; *King's Rochester City Directory and Register, 1841* (Rochester, 1840), 165.

23. It is tantalizing to wonder whether Phebe Ray or her family knew any of the black Schenectadians who agitated for school rights. David Ray's wife, Betsey, was from Schenectady, and David spent time in the city in the mid-1830s. Whether the personal connections existed or not, Phebe would have sympathized with the ordinary black women who organized on behalf of schools there. "List of Letters," *Schenectady Cabinet,* July 30, 1836; David H. Ray, 1855 NY State Census, Watertown, Jefferson County.

24. Mabee, for example, writes that the "campaign in Rochester began in 1847 after two leading black abolitionists," Frederick Douglass and William C. Nell, "arrived from Massachusetts." Mabee, *Black Education,* 183. For an article crediting the longer school campaign, see Judith Polgar Ruchkin, "The Abolition of 'Colored Schools' in Rochester, New York: 1832-1856," *New York History* (July 1970): 376–393.

25. *Rochester Directory for 1847,* 229; *Rochester City Directory, 1845,* 182; *Rochester Directory,* July 1, 1885 (Rochester, 1885), 256. "Example of a Colored Boy," *Troy Daily Times,* Jan. 10, 1866; "Celebration at Rochester," *NS,* July 14, 1848; "First of August Celebration," *NS,* Aug. 8, 1848; "First of August Celebration," *NS,* Aug. 11, 1848. (It is possible that Elza Johnson and Henry Johnson were related.)

26. "Equal School Privileges," *NS,* Nov. 2, 1849; "Colored School Meeting," *Rochester Daily Democrat,* Dec. 14, 1849; "Meeting Against Colored Schools," *NS,* Dec. 21, 1849; *Rochester City Directory, 1849,* 256 (for Sharp's and Patterson's occupations). *Note:* The *North Star* listed "B. D. Pattison" as the meeting secretary, but I am nearly certain this is "Z. D. Patterson," a black hairdresser who was also an eventual subscriber to the *North Star.* "Receipts," *NS,* Mar. 20, 1851.

27. "Meeting of the Colored Citizens," *CA,* July 27, 1849.

28. "Board of Education," *Rochester Daily Democrat,* Aug. 11, 1849.

29. "Board of Education," *Rochester Daily American,* Mar. 28, 1850; "Board of Education," *Rochester Daily Democrat,* Mar. 29, 1850.

30. "The Re-Opening of Our City Schools," *FDP,* Sept. 8, 1854.

31. *Dewey's Rochester City Directory, for 1855-56* (Rochester, 1855), 256; Phebe Ray, 1855 NY State Census, Rochester City, Ward 10, Monroe County.

32. *The Constitution of the American Anti-Slavery Society* . . . (New York, 1838), 12.

33. "Report of the Minority of the Committee on the Judiciary, on Various Petitions Relating to Slavery and the Slave Trade," *Documents of the Assembly of the State of New York* (Albany, 1838), 6:No. 359. This report is also useful for elucidating how lawmakers spoke about the purpose of petitioning more generally.

34. Recent scholarship had brought welcome attention to the role of petitioning in the early U.S. I admire this work and seek to add to the cast of characters whom we see as important petitioners. Maggie Blackhawk, Daniel Carpenter, et al., "Congressional Representation by Petition: Assessing the Voteless in a Comprehensive New Database, 1789-1949," *Legislative Studies Quarterly* (Sept. 2020); Carpenter, *Democracy by Petition: Popular Politics in Transformation, 1790-1870* (Cambridge, MA, 2021); Maggie McKinley, "Petitioning and the Making of the Administrative State," *Yale Law Journal* (Apr. 2018): 1448–1741. For a more extensive discussion of the historiography, see Sarah L. H. Gronningsater, "Practicing Formal Politics Without the Vote: Black New Yorkers in the Aftermath of 1821," in *Revolutions and Reconstructions: Black Politics in the Long Nineteenth Century,* ed. Van Gosse and David Waldstreicher (Philadelphia, 2020).

35. "Public Meeting," *Weekly Advocate,* Feb. 25, 1837; "New York Petitions to the Legislature," *CA*, Mar. 11, 1837. As I outline in Chapter 2, initially the "nine months rule" was an antislavery accomplishment, for it limited how long slaveholders could stay in the state and provided slaves a route to freedom if masters stayed too long. By the 1830s, however, "nine months" was no longer palatable. For the original law: *NY Laws,* 33rd sess. (1810), ch. 115.

36. "Important Meeting," *Weekly Advocate,* Feb. 22, 1837.

37. "Important Movement among the Colored Population of Ohio," *Weekly Advocate,* Feb. 25, 1837 (see also Masur, *Until Justice be Done,* chs. 1, 3); "The Interests of the People of Color," *Weekly Advocate,* Feb. 22, 1837; "Massachusetts and the Constitution," *CA,* Apr. 1, 1837.

38. *JANY* (Albany, 1837), 210, 414, 416.

39. Judith Wellman, et al., *Discovering the Underground Railroad, Abolitionism and African American Life in Seneca County, New York, 1820-1880* (Fulton, New York, 2006), esp. pp. 18–19; "To the Editor of the Colored American," *CA,* Aug. 19, 1837.

40. There may have been instances when black citizens just presented themselves as "citizens" (with no racial designation), in part to make the point that their citizenship should not be qualified by race. Many of the state legislature's documents burned in the Albany Capitol Building fire of 1911, so I haven't been able to locate the original petitions that are cited in the assembly's journals and cross-reference names in census records.

41. *JANY* (Albany, 1837), 414.

42. Gerda Lerner, *The Majority Finds Its Past: Placing Women in History* (New York, 1979), ch. 8; Zaeske, *Signatures of Citizenship.* In 1840, the New York Convention of

Colored [Male] Citizens called upon "that portion of the people whose influence is tender, gentle, and benign - . . . the women" to help them. "Address of the New York State Convention," *CA*, Nov. 21, 1840.

43. "For the Colored American," *CA*, July 29, 1837; "Third Anniversary of the Ladies Literary Society," *CA*, Sept. 23, 1837 [the article does not indicate which "Miss Jennings" it is]; "A Fair," *CA*, Dec. 23, 1837; "Shall Women Sign Our Petitions?" *CA*, Nov. 13, 1841. The *Colored American*'s framing of the male right to vote as relevant to women recalls *some* of what Elsa Barkley Brown describes in early postemancipation Virginia, where "black Richmonders enacted their understandings of democratic political discourse through mass meetings attended and participated in (including voting) by men, women and children." She finds a collective investment in "the transition from slavery to freedom," which allowed space for women and children as political actors. Brown, "Negotiating the Public Sphere: African American Political Life in the Transition from Slavery to Freedom," *Public Culture* (Fall 1994), 108–109. Not everyone appreciated female petitioning, by women of any race. See "Petitions, &c," *Hudson River Chronicle*, Feb. 26, 1839, arguing that "if there be one thing in this country" throwing "shade over the female character," it was women "thrusting their names before the public [as] petitioners."

44. *JANY* (Albany, 1837), 312, 355, 414, 416, 573.

45. "To the Editor of the Colored American," *CA*, Aug. 19, 1837. See also "Reception of Our Petition," *CA*, Mar. 11, 1837; "Petition for a Jury Trial from Brooklyn," *CA*, Mar. 11, 1837; "Adjourned Meeting," *CA*, Mar. 11, 1837; "From the Friend of Man," *CA*, Mar. 18, 1837.

46. "Important Meeting," *CA*, Aug. 19, 1837; "Important Meeting," *CA*, Sept. 2, 1837; "Right of Suffrage," *CA*, Dec. 16, 1837.

47. "Important Meeting," *CA*, Sept. 2, 1837.

48. "Notice," *CA*, Aug. 26, 1837; "Right of Suffrage," *CA*, Sept. 23, 1837; "Dear Brother Cornish," *CA*, Sept. 30, 1837; "Right of Suffrage," *CA*, Nov. 25, 1837; "Important Meeting," *CA*, Dec. 2, 1837; "Petitions," *CA*, Dec. 9, 1837; "To the Hon. The Legislature . . . ," *CA*, Dec. 16, 1837; "Right of Suffrage," *CA*, Dec. 30, 1837.

49. *JANY* (Albany, 1838), 228, 317, 443, 672, 699.

50. *JANY* (Albany, 1838), 140, 143–144, 171, 208, 248, 250, 252, 280, 288, 292, 298, 305, 312–313, 326, 342, 348, 370, 382, 387, 392–393, 399–400, 405, 414, 430, 443–444, 469, 490, 503, 516–517, 647, 759–760, 1101.

51. "Public Meeting," *CA*, June 16, 1838; "The Following are the Preamble . . . ," *CA*, June 23, 1838; "For the Colored American," *CA*, Aug. 25, 1838; "New Agents," *CA*, Nov. 3, 1838.

52. "Public Call - Important Meeting," *CA*, Sept. 29, 1838; "The following are the Preamble . . . ," *CA*, June 23, 1838 (my italics). For the NYMS on the impressive girls, see AFS, 1817–1832, vol. 1, pp. 11–20.

53. "The Annual Meeting," *Friend of Man* (Utica), Sept. 26, 1838; "Resolutions: On Political Action," *Union Herald* (Cazenovia), Oct. 12, 1838. On this era in the history of the NYASS, see Alice Hatcher Henderson, "History of the New York State Anti-Slavery

Society" (PhD diss., University of Michigan, 1963), chs. 4–5; Ripley et al., *BAP*, vol. 3, 188; "For the Colored American," *CA*, Oct. 6, 1838.

54. Smith and Jay to Seward, Oct. 1, 1838, WHS.

55. "Our Heart Was with Them," *CA*, Oct. 6, 1838; "The Annual Meeting," *Friend of Man*, Sept. 26, 1838.

56. "Mr. Bradish's Answer," *CA*, Nov. 3, 1838; Thurlow Weed to Luther Bradish, Oct. 28, 1838, Luther Bradish Papers, NYHS.

57. "Answer of Mr. Seward," *ComAd*, Oct. 25, 1838. Seward initially told Weed he wanted to respond in favor to the first two queries and "no" to black voting. Seward to Weed, Oct. 7, 1838, TWP; "Gov. Marcy's Reply," *EP*, Oct. 10, 1838, "Lieut. Gov. Tracy's Letter," *Union Herald*, Nov. 3, 1838; "Public Meeting of Freedholders," *CA*, Nov. 3, 1838.

58. Weed to Seward, Oct. 23, 1838, WHS. During the campaign, the Democrats accused the Whigs of being beholden to the abolitionists. See Stephen Tompkins to Seward, Nov. 12, 1838, WHS; James Watson Webb to Bradish, Oct. 10, 1838, Luther Bradish Papers.

59. Lewis Tappan, *The Life of Arthur Tappan* (Cambridge, MA, 1870), 301; Weed to Seward, Nov. 4, 1838, WHS; "Abolition in 1838," *New York Morning Herald*, Nov. 5, 1838; "Frauds," *ComAd*, Nov. 6, 1838.

60. Smith to Bradish, Oct. 19, 1838, LBP; Weed to Bradish, Oct. 28, 1838, LBP.

61. Henry Van Rensselaer to Bradish, Nov. 21, 1838, Luther Bradish Papers. Henry was Stephen Van Rensselaer's son; the father argued on behalf of equal black suffrage rights at the 1821 constitutional convention. Henry was also the great-great-grandfather of David Crosby, of Crosby, Stills, & Nash.

62. Jacob Harvey to Bradish, Feb. 8, 1839, LBP.

63. In this conclusion, I differ somewhat from Richard Sewell's assessment of "the interrogation system." Sewell, *Ballots for Freedom*, 18–20.

64. Weed to Seward, Nov. 4, 1838, WHS; Seward to Weed, Oct. 7, 1838, TWP; Weed to Seward, Nov. 4, 1838, WHS; Seward to Weed, Nov. 4, 1838, TWP. The election was held November 5 to 7.

65. Stephen B. Tompkins to Seward, Nov. 12, 1838, WHS; "Abolition Victory," *CA*, Nov. 17, 1838; "Official Return of Votes," *EP*, Nov. 30, 1838.

66. *NY Laws*, 63rd sess. (1840), ch. 375; *NY Laws*, 63rd sess. (1840), ch. 225. The most well-known black New Yorker to make use of the kidnapping law was Solomon Northup, author of *Twelve Years a Slave* (Auburn, NY, 1853).

67. Frederick William Seward, *William H. Seward: An Autobiography* (New York, 1877), 464–465; "New York," *CA*, May 30, 1840; "The Legislature of Massachusetts," *Emancipator*, Apr. 4, 1839; "The Worcester Kidnappers," ibid., Oct. 10, 1839.

68. "Federalism and Abolition United," *Globe* (Washington), Sept. 25, 1840.

69. "Movement at Albany," *CA*, Mar. 13, 1841. See also "From the Friend of Man. New York Legislature," *Emancipator*, May 2, 1839.

70. *JANY* (1841), 400–401.

71. *JANY* (1841), 440–441; "Movement at Albany," *CA*, Mar. 13, 1841; "In Assembly—March 2," *ComAd*, Mar. 2, 1841.

72. In thinking about black women's political roles, I'm influenced by Brown, "Negotiating and Transforming the Public Sphere"; Glenda Elizabeth Gilmore, *Gender and Jim Crow: Women and the Politics of White Supremacy in North Carolina, 1896-1920* (Chapel Hill, 1996); Evelyn Brooks Higginbotham, *Righteous Discontent: The Women's Movement in the Black Baptist Church, 1880-1920* (Cambridge, 1993); Jones, *All Bound Up Together*. There's more to be done to connect northern black women's household labor with all it enabled men to do materially, politically, and publicly. I'm inspired here by Jeanne Boydston's study of white women's work in *Home and Work: Housework, Wages and the Ideology of Labor in the Early Republic* (New York, 1990) and by Melish, *Disowning Slavery*, ch. 1., which argues for the importance of enslaved household labor in the development of New England's economy.

73. *Documents of the Assembly of the State of New-York, Sixty-Fourth Session, 1841* (Albany, 1841) 6:No. 239, pp. 6–8; *NY Laws*, 64th sess. (1841), ch. 247.

74. "Nine Months Law," *CA*, Apr. 10, 1841; "Vigilance Committee," *CA*, June 12, 1841; "First of August Celebration at Williamsburg," *CA*, July 24, 1841.

75. *Documents of the Assembly of the State of New York* (Albany, 1842) 1:No. 2, p. 3.

76. George Baker, *The Works of William H. Seward* (Boston, 1884) 2:453, 467. Seward was bluffing here; there *was* a law in the state that recognized slavery: the nine months law.

77. *Journal of the Senate of Virginia* (Richmond, 1839), 17.

78. *Documents of Assembly of the State of New-York, Sixty-Fourth Session, 1841* (Albany, 1841), 1:78; Baker, *The Works of William H. Seward* (Boston, 1884), 2:470; *Acts of the General Assembly of Virginia, 1839-1840* (Richmond, 1840), 167–168; Paul Finkelman, "The Protection of Black Rights in Seward's New York," *Civil War History* 34 (1998): 223; "An Act to Prevent the Citizens of New York from Carrying Slaves . . . ," *Acts of the General Assembly of the State of South Carolina Passed in December 1841* (Columbia, 1842), 149.

79. W. C. Beardsley to Samuel Blackford, Nov. 7, 1839, WHS; Christopher Morgan to Seward, Nov. 11, 1839, WHS; Henderson, "New-York State Anti-Slavery Society," 303.

80. Ephraim Goss to Seward, Jan. 29, 1840, WHS; Henry B. Stanton to Seward, Feb. 4, 1840, WHS; Reinhard O. Johnson, *The Liberty Party, 1840–1848: Antislavery Third-Party Politics in the United States* (Baton Rouge, 2009), 11, 15; Henderson, "New-York State Anti-Slavery Society," ch. 5.

81. "Governor Seward's Special Message," *CA*, Apr. 10, 1841.

82. Thomas Downing to William Seward, Mar. 29, 1841, William Henry Seward Papers, Box 2, Folder 3, University of Rochester.

83. "Virginia and New York," *CA*, Mar. 10, 1841.

84. "Address of Mr. P Vogelsang, Sr," *CA*, July 14, 1838.

85. Ibid.

86. *JANY* (Albany, 1839), 408, 503.

87. Arthur O. White, "The Black Movement Against Jim Crow Education in Lockport, New York 1835–1876," *New York History* (July 1969): 269–270; "For the Colored American," *CA,* Nov. 4, 1837; "New Agencies," *CA,* Nov. 11, 1837; "For the Colored American," *CA,* Nov. 10, 1838.

88. "Political Action," *CA,* July 27, 1839

89. "Great Meeting at Troy, N.Y.," *CA,* June 6, 1840; "For the Colored American," *CA,* June 13, 1840; "Meeting of the Colored Citizens of Albany," *CA,* May 23, 1840; "A Call for a Convention," *CA,* June 6, 1840; "A Call for A Convention of the Colored Inhabitants of the State of New York," *CA,* July 18, 1840.

90. "Public Meeting," *CA,* July 25, 1840; "Poughkeepsie," *CA,* July 25, 1840; "For the Colored American," *CA,* Aug. 1, 1840; "Conventional Meeting at Lansingburg," *CA,* Aug. 8, 1840; "Public Meeting at Williamsburgh, L. I.," *CA,* Aug. 22, 1840.

91. Richard Newman's notion of "shadow politics" is useful here. As he notes, "In community organizations, educational institutions, and autonomous churches, free blacks practiced politics in ways that both shaped their daily lives and echoed the practice of democracy in the broader civic culture." Newman, "Faith in the Ballot," *Common-Place* (Oct. 2008), www.common-place.org.

92. Smith opposed the convention that year for several reasons: he thought it was too expensive, he worried that an all-black meeting would "excite . . . prejudice to our detriment," he wanted an interracial effort to regain the franchise, and he believed that excluding white delegates "violates the principle of equal rights in the attempt to attain equal rights." "Public Meeting," *CA,* Aug. 8, 1840; "Public Meeting," *CA,* Aug. 15, 1840; "Position Defined," *CA,* Aug. 15, 1840. By the following summer, Smith offered strong support for the black convention movement. "Public Meeting in New-York," *CA,* Aug, 7, 1841.

93. "New York State Convention," *CA,* Aug. 29, 1840; Foner and Walker, *Proceedings,* 17, 22; "Petition," *CA,* Dec. 5, 1840.

94. "To the County Committees on Petitions," *CA,* Oct. 17, 1840; "Public Meeting," *CA,* Nov. 21, 1840; "Circulate the Petitions," *CA,* Nov. 28, 1840; "Brethren Awake," *CA,* Jan. 16, 1841; "First Great Mass Meeting of the Colored Citizens of Flushing," *CA,* Dec. 19, 1840; "Public Meeting in Schenectady," *CA,* Dec. 26, 1840; "Meeting of the Colored Citizens in Albany," *CA,* Dec. 26, 1840; "Public Meeting in Troy," *CA,* Dec. 26, 1840.

95. "Brooklyn Mass Meeting," *CA,* Jan. 23, 1841.

96. *JANY* (Albany, 1841), 30, 118.

97. "Reception of Petitions," *CA,* Feb. 13, 1841.

98. "To Messrs. John J. Zuille and P. H. Reason," *CA,* Mar. 13, 1841.

99. *Documents of the Assembly . . . 1841,* vol. 5, no. 183, p. 4; "Amendment of the Constitution," *CA,* Mar. 11, 1841; "Very Ominous," *CA,* Mar. 27, 1841.

100. *JANY* (1841), 877, 1501–1502, 1304. The *Argus,* a Democratic paper, accused the Whigs of delaying the vote on the bill on purpose in order to garner abolitionist sympathy without actually acting on the issue. "The Federal Game of Abolition," *Albany Argus,* June 4, 1841.

101. For this argument at the time, see "New York," *Emancipator*, June 3, 1841.

102. Field, *Politics of Race*, 44; Gosse, *First Reconstruction*, 422–424; Michael F. Holt, *The Rise and Fall of the Whig Party: Jacksonian Politics and the Onset of the Civil War* (New York, 1999), 239–240.

103. "Extending the Right of Suffrage," *Albany Argus*, Apr. 25, 1845.

104. "New York State Free Suffrage Convention," *NASS*, Oct. 30, 1845.

105. "New York State Free Suffrage Convention," *NASS*, Oct. 30, 1845.

106. *BAP*, 5:468; *Gerrit Smith's Reply to the Colored Citizens of Albany* (s.n., 1846); "Suffrage Meeting," *Rochester Daily Democrat*, Mar. 28, 1846.

107. Gosse, *First Reconstruction*, 431; "The Liberty Party," *AEJ*, June 4, 1846.

108. See Field's helpful analysis of the voting results. *Politics of Race*, 52–56.

109. "Amended Constitution - YES Equal Suffrage to Colored People YES," *AEJ*, Oct. 30, 1846; "The Atlas is oblivious," *AEJ*, Oct. 27, 1846; "Lieut. Governor Gardiner's Opinions on the 'Negro Suffrage' Question," *Auburn Journal and Advertiser*, Oct. 28, 1846; "Locofoco Impudence," *Auburn Journal and Advertiser*, Nov. 4, 1846; "Equal Suffrage," *Jamestown Journal*, Dec. 4, 1846; "Constitutional Reform," *AEJ*, Apr. 11, 1846; Field, 58–61; John L. Stanley, "Majority Tyranny in Tocqueville's America: The Failure of Negro Suffrage in 1846," *Political Science Quarterly* (Sept. 1969): 416.

110. William Bishop and William Attree, *Report of the Debates and Proceedings of the Convention for the Revision of the Constitution of the State of New-York* (Albany, 1846), 15–16.

111. The extension of rights to a minority by the vote of a majority does on occasion occur. In 2012, for example, Maine, Maryland, and Washington legalized gay marriage by popular vote. It is questionable, however, whether marriage equality would have become legal throughout the nation soon thereafter, absent a ruling of the United States Supreme Court. The Supreme Court legalized gay marriage nationally in 2015 in *Obergefell v Hodges*.

112. James McCune Smith to Gerrit Smith, Dec. 28, 1846, GSP.

113. James McCune Smith to Gerrit Smith, Dec. 28, 1846, GSP.

114. Gosse, *First Reconstruction*, ch. 10; Samuel Ringgold Ward to Gerrit Smith, Aug. 14, 1848, Box 38, GSP; Samuel Ringgold Ward, "To the Four Thousand Colored Voters of the State of New York," *NS*, Sept. 1, 1848; "Mr. S. R. Ward," *NS*, Sept. 1, 1848; "Change of Opinion Announced," *Liberator*, May 23, 1851; Henry Highland Garnet to Gerrit Smith, Sept. 16, 1858, Box 20, GSP.

115. "Speech of the Hon. W. H. Seward," *ComAd*, Mar. 14, 1850; Stahr, *Seward*, 125.

116. "Albany, April 1, 1850," *NS*, Apr. 5, 1850. Stephen Myers eventually sued the school commissioners for damages arising from their unwillingness to admit his children to their local district school. The state supreme court ruled in Myers's favor, but it is clear nonetheless that Albany's schools remained largely segregated. See Hughes, *Refusing Ignorance*, ch 3; "Circuit Court—June 11," *AEJ*, June 14, 1852.

117. See also "the National Convention of Colored People," *National Era* (Washington), Aug. 7, 1851.

Chapter 6

1. "Governor Cobb of Georgia," *NYT,* Nov. 14, 1853; Gerrit Smith, *No Slavery in Nebraska, No Slavery in the Nation, Slavery an Outlaw* (Washington, 1854), 4; "Ohio Politics: Speech of Governor Chase," *National Era,* Sept. 15, 1859; "From the N.Y. Express," *Constitution* (Washington), Nov. 10, 1860.

2. This synopsis of *Lemmon* draws from the newspapers cited throughout this chapter, as well as case reports of the three trials. *The People ex rel. Napoleon v. Lemmon,* 5 Sandford 681 (NY Super. Ct. 1852); *Lemmon v. The People ex rel. Louis Napoleon,* 26 Barb. 270 (NY Gen. Term 1857); *Report of the Lemmon Slave Case, Containing Points and Arguments of Counsel on both Sides, and Opinions of all the Judges* (New York, 1860). For Justice Paine's quotes, see *Report of the Lemmon Slave Case,* 9–10. Southern attention to *Lemmon* was immediate. See *Alexandria Gazette* on Nov. 12, 16, 20, 22, 23, 24, 29, and Dec. 8, 16, 23, 25 in 1852. For surveys of proslavery responses, see "Pro-Slavery: The Slave Case" and "The Lemmon Slave Case," *NASS,* Nov. 25, 1852; "Lemmon Indemnity Fund," *NASS,* Dec. 2, 1852; "The Lemmon Case," *National Era,* Dec. 16, 1852. *N.B.* John Jay (1817–1894), the founding father's grandson and William Jay's son, is often referred to as John Jay II by researchers. His name appears as such in the Index.

3. "Declaration of the Immediate Causes Which Induce and Justify the Secession of South Carolina from the Federal Union," *Charleston Mercury,* Dec. 27, 1860.

4. Thomas Hudson McKee, *The National Conventions and Platforms of All Political Parties 1789 to 1905* (Baltimore, 1906), 114.

5. Legal historians have taken *Lemmon* seriously, examining the case as a critical moment in antislavery jurisprudence. See Paul Finkelman, *An Imperfect Union,* chs. 4, 6, 9; Albert M. Rosenblatt, *The Eight: The Lemmon Slave Case and the Fight for Freedom* (Albany, 2023); William Wiecek, "*Somerset:* Lord Mansfield and the Legitimacy of Slavery in the Anglo-American World," *Chicago Law Review* (Fall 1974): 86–146; Wong, *Neither Fugitive nor Free*, introduction, ch. 2. Historians of sectional crisis often give *Lemmon* a nod, although with nowhere near the attention given to *Dred Scott.* See William Link, *Roots of Secession: Slavery and Politics in Antebellum Virginia* (Chapel Hill, 2003), 108–109; James M. McPherson, *Battle Cry of Freedom: The Civil War* (New York, 1988), 180–181; Eric Foner, *The Fiery Trial: Abraham Lincoln and American Slavery* (New York, 2010), 101–102. The *Lemmon* case has received little attention from scholars of northern black history. A notable exception is Thomas J. Davis, "Napoleon v. Lemmon: Antebellum Black New Yorkers, Antislavery and Law," *Afro-Americans in New York Life and History* (Jan. 2009): 27–96. Marie Tyler-McGraw and Dwight T. Pitcaithley have written a rich narrative on *Lemmon* focusing on the perspectives of the Lemmons and the enslaved families (the Douglas/Wright/Johnson families). I thank McGraw for sharing her knowledge with me and Paul Finkelman for putting us in touch. McGraw and Pitcaithley, "The Lemmon Slave Case: Courtroom Drama, Constitutional Crisis and the Southern Quest to Nationalize Slavery," *Common-Place* (Fall 2013).

6. Recent literature on the coming of and progress of the Civil War has stressed the importance of slave resistance. The northern free black component to this story,

however, is less emphasized. In Michael E. Woods's overview of the scholarship, for example, neither black abolitionists nor the lasting consequences of northern gradual emancipation appear. Woods, "What Twenty-First-Century Historians Have Said About the Causes of Disunion: A Civil War Sesquicentennial Review of Recent Literature," *Journal of American History* (Sept. 2012): 415–439. See also Frank Towers, "Partisans, New History, and Modernization: The Historiography of the Civil War's Causes, 1861–2011," *JCWE* (June 2011): 237–264. There is excellent work both on the origins of the Civil War and on black abolitionism, but to paraphrase James Brewer Stewart, the fields often treat the same time periods and events without integrating their more distinctive subjects and insights. Stewart, "Reconsidering the Abolitionists in an Age of Fundamentalist Politics," *JER* (Spring 2006): 4–5. Efforts to bridge this gap are appearing. See Blackett, *Captive's Quest for Freedom*; Corey M. Brooks, "Reconsidering Politics in the Study of American Abolitionists," *JCWE*, (June 2018): 291–317; Eric Foner, *Gateway to Freedom: The Hidden History of the Underground Railroad* (New York, 2015); Jackson, *Force and Freedom*, Kantrowitz, *More Than Freedom*; Elizabeth Varon, *Disunion!*. William H. Freehling, emphasizing runaways, has long argued that the problem of slaves moving across borders was a crucial factor in provoking sectional conflict. Freehling, *The South vs. The South: How Anti-Confederate Southerners Shaped the Course of the Civil War* (Oxford, 2001), 29. See also James Oakes, "The Political Significance of Slave Resistance," *History Workshop* (Fall 1986): 89–107.

7. Virtually unknown for decades, Louis Napoleon is now recognized as a protagonist of the Underground Railroad. See Foner, *Gateway to Freedom*; Don Papson and Tom Calarco, *Secret Lives of the Underground Railroad in New York City: Sydney Howard Gay, Louis Napoleon, and the Record of Fugitives* (Jefferson, NC, 2015). Napoleon makes only one appearance in William Still's famous firsthand account of the Underground Railroad, *Still's Underground Rail Road Records: With a Life of the Author* (2nd ed., Philadelphia, 1886), 40–41. For an exploration of Napoleon and an 1857 petition he signed, showcasing his "above ground" rather than underground activities, see Sarah L. H. Gronningsater, "'On Behalf of his Race and the Lemmon Slaves': Louis Napoleon, Northern Black Legal Culture, and the Politics of Sectional Crisis," *JCWE* (June 2017): 206–241.

8. See Chapter 5 for black petitioners' campaign for the nine-month repeal and jury trials.

9. NY Const. (1821), art. 7, § 8; "Calacita Case, *CA*, Apr. 4, 1840.

10. "Case of Somerset," *FJ*, Nov. 30, 1827; *Somerset v. Stewart*, 1 Lofft. 1, 19 (King's Bench, 1772); "Lord Stowell's decision concerning the Slave Grace," *CA*, Jan. 11, 1828; *The Slave, Grace*, 166 Eng. Rep. 179 (High Court of Admiralty, 1827). West Indian newspapers covered *The Slave, Grace* as Lord Stowell heard arguments in the summer of 1827, but there was little to no coverage in the American press.

11. Patti Hagler Minter, "'The State of Slavery': *Somerset, The Slave, Grace*, and the Rise of Pro-Slavery and Anti-Slavery Constitutionalism in the Nineteenth-Century Atlantic World," *Slavery & Abolition* (Oct. 2015): 603–617. For *Somerset's* applications

in court cases in the 1830s–1850s, see Finkelman, *Imperfect Union,* chs. 4–6; Wiecek, *Sources of Antislavery Constitutionalism*, ch. 8.

12. Indeed, northern abolitionists did make *Somerset* theirs. As scholars of the case well know, the original decision freed James Somerset on a rather narrow legal basis. Slaves and abolitionists in the United States, however, took the antislavery implications of the case and ran with them. For a discussion of the original decision, see George Van Cleve et al., "Forum: Somerset's Case Revisited," *Law and History Review* (Fall, 2006). The place of *Somerset* in the politics of the American Revolution has garnered much attention of late. I have found scant evidence that antislavery lawyers or politicians used it or talked about it much in the period during or right after the Revolution, even though they made use of other English legal tools, such as the writ de homine replegiando and the common law maxim *in favorem libertatis.* One reason for the absence, I suggest, is that northern states (and other British colonies that didn't leave the empire, including Canada and the West Indies) still had positive laws protecting slavery. Matt Mason's article is instructive: "North American Calm, West Indian Storm: The Politics of the Somerset Decision in the British Atlantic," *Slavery & Abolition* 41, no. 4 (2020): 723–747.

13. "Speech of Solomon P. Chase," *CA,* July 22, 1837; "Connecticut Coming Around," *CA,* June 16, 1838; "Power of the Free States," *CA,* May 18, 1839. For the case, see *Commonwealth v. Aves,* 18 Pick. 193 (Mass., 1836).

14. "Calacita Case," *CA,* Apr. 4, 1840; Joseph Story, *Commentaries on the Conflict of Laws* (Boston, 1834), 92–95.

15. "Public Meeting of the Political Association," *CA,* Oct. 30, 1838; "New York," *CA,* May 30, 1840; "The Africans of the Amistad No. 1," *CA,* June 6, 1840; "Another Important Judicial Decision," *CA,* June 12, 1841.

16. "To the Friends of Immediate Emancipation in New York," *Evening Star* (New York), Sept. 29, 1835; "Disabilities of Colored People," *CA,* Sept. 30, 1837; "New-York Legislation," *NASS,* June 18, 1840; *Troy Directory for the Year 1836-7* (Troy, 1836), 104; *Hoffman's Albany Directory for the Years 1840-41* (Albany, 1840), 302; William Yates, 1855 NY State Census, Ward 5, Albany.

17. William Yates, *Rights of Colored Men to Suffrage, Citizenship, and Trial by Jury* (Philadelphia, 1838), 76–78; "Very Important Subject," *CA,* Aug. 12, 1837. For more on Yates, see Jones, *Birthright Citizens,* introduction.

18. "Writ de homine replegiando," *Niles' Weekly Register* (Sept. 1829–Mar. 1830), 208; "At a meeting of the [Albany] Clarkson Society," *New-York Spectator,* Nov. 17, 1829. Nathanial Paul was part of a similar de homine replegiando case in Albany a few months later, in which four black people, including two young children (Lawrence Gibbs and Charlotte Handy), were freed. "Slave Cases," *ComAd,* Jan. 16, 1830.

19. "Important Decision of Judge Betts," *CA,* Dec. 9, 1837; "Slave Case-Riot-Rescue and Recapture," *Gloucester Democrat,* Apr. 18, 1837; Hodges, *David Ruggles,* 88–89, 109. See Chapter 5 of this book for the petition campaign. Leslie Harris's treatment of Ruggles emphasizes the class politics in the antislavery community. Ruggles "attempted but failed to find a middle ground between the tactics of middle-class radical abolitionists and those

of black workers in order to create a more inclusive movement against slavery and for racial equality." I appreciate Harris's point. *In the Shadow of Slavery,* 173. The rest of this chapter also shows that laboring black New Yorkers could be quite comfortable in formal court rooms and discussing formal law, and that elite white abolitionists and mainstream antislavery editors were key backers of the completely illegal Underground Railroad.

20. "Vigilance Committee," *CA,* June 12, 1841; "The Great Anti-Colonization Meeting," *CA,* July 3, 1841; "A Slave Case," *AEJ,* Sept. 8, 1843; "The Slave Case," ibid., Sept. 9, 1843; "Slave Case at Albany," ibid., Sept. 9, 1843.

21. "Louis Napoleon's Funeral: Not the French Emperor, but an Old Friend of the Fugitive Slaves," *Sun* (New York), Mar. 31, 1881. The several obituaries that ran in New York papers contained conflicting information about Napoleon's life. For example, the *Tribune* wrote that Napoleon was born a slave in Virginia; this contrasts with Napoleon's own reports on various census records that he was born in New York City. His death certificate likewise states New York City as his birthplace. (His wife Elizabeth, however, was born in Virginia.) In 1875, the *Commercial Advertiser* ran a note that "Louis Napoleon, the old negro, formerly a slave in this state, who claims to have run 3,000 slaves out of Maryland, is around again picking up his monthly collection." "News Notice," Oct. 12, 1875. For the *Tribune* obituary, see "Louis Napoleon," *NYTrib,* Mar. 30, 1881. A copy of Louis Napoleon's death certificate is on file at the Sandy Ground Historical Society, Staten Island, New York.

22. Louis Napoleon, 1840 US Census, New York Ward 5, NY; Louis Napoleon, 1850 US Census, New York Ward 5, NY; Elizabeth Seaman, 1850 US Census, New York Ward 15 western half, NY; Louis Napoleon, 1860 US Census, New York Ward 20, District 5, NY; Elizabeth Napoleon, 1860 US Census, New York Ward 20, District 5, NY; Louis Napoleon, 1870 US Census, Westfield, Richmond County, NY; Eliza Napoleon, 1870 US Census, Westfield, Richmond County, NY; Louis Napoleon, 1880 US Census, Staten Island, Richmond County, NY; "Elizabeth Napoleon," 1900 US Census, Richmond Ward 5, Richmond County, NY. Louis Napoleon appears in the following city directories: *Doggett's New-York City Directory* for 1842–1843, 1843–1844, 1844–1845, 1850–1851; *Trow's New York City Directory* for 1853–1854, 1857, 1859, 1860; *Brooklyn City and Business Directory* for 1869 and 1878.

23. For useful biographies of Gay and Jay, see Raimund Erhard Goerler, *Family, Self, and Anti-Slavery: Sydney Howard Gay and the Abolitionist* (PhD diss., Case Western Reserve, 1975); "John Jay" in Augustus Rogers, *Sketches of Representative Men, North and South* (New York, 1874).

24. McKee, *National Conventions and Platforms,* 53–54; *Prigg v. Commonwealth of Pennsylvania,* 41 US 539 (1842); Patricia A. Reid, "Margaret Morgan's Story: A Threshold between Slavery and Freedom, 1820-1842," *Slavery & Abolition* 33, no. 3 (2012): 359–380.

25. "Law Courts . . . Deferred," *NYTrib,* Oct. 24, 1846.

26. "An Interesting and Important Fugitive Slave Case," *Liberator,* Nov. 6, 1846; "Case of a Runaway Slave" and "The Slave Case," *NYTrib,* Oct. 23, 1846.

27. "An Interesting and Important Slave Case"; "The Slave Case," *Spectator,* Oct. 28, 1846; "The Case of the Slave George," *NYTrib,* Oct. 26, 1846. "Another Negro Riot" (reprinted from the *Globe*), *NASS,* Nov. 5, 1846.

28. The *Spectator* reported on many of these legal details immediately. "The Slave Case," *Spectator,* Oct. 28, 1846. There were several case reports, including *In re George Kirk,* 9 Monthly Law Reporter 355 (NY Ct. Oyer and Term. 1846); 1 Parker Cr. R. 67 (NY Cir. Ct. 1846); 4 New-York Legal Observer 456 (NY Cir. Ct. 1846); 5 New-York Legal Observer 52 (NY Ct. Oyer and Term. 1846). James Kent also discussed the case in *Commentaries on American Law* (New York, 1851), 1: 640.

29. "Case of the Fugitive Slave," *NYTrib,* Oct. 26, 1846. For a similar account, see "An Interesting and Important Fugitive Slave Case," *Liberator,* Nov. 6, 1846; "Letters from New York," *Pennsylvania Freeman,* Nov. 19, 1846.

30. "The Slave Case, Saturday October 31," *NYTrib,* Nov. 2, 1846; "Release of the Slave Boy George," *NYDT,* Nov. 3, 1846. The oft-repeated line was, "England was too pure an Air for slaves to breathe in." During the *Somerset* trial, this phrase was repeated several times by Sergeant Davy in his arguments on behalf of Somerset.

31. "Monday, Nov. 2: Release of the Slave Boy George," *NYTrib,* Nov. 3, 1846.

32. For references to Napoleon by Jay and Gay in later correspondence, see Sydney Howard Gay to William Still, Aug. 15, 1855, in Still, *Still's Underground Railroad Records,* 40–41; John Jay to William Still, Oct. 8, 1858, JFP; Sydney Howard Gay to James Miller McKim, Sept. 18, 1858, MC; Sydney Howard Gay to John Jay, Oct. 14, 1858, JFP.

33. Sydney Howard Gay, Account Book (1854–1860), Account Book (1860–1862), passim, Sydney Howard Gay Papers, ca. 1837–1886, Manuscripts and Archives Division, New York Public Library. Napoleon began receiving payments on a regular basis from the Anti-Slavery Society in 1857. He usually received between $1.60 and $3.00.

34. *Report of the Lemmon Slave Case* (1860), 23–24.

35. In fact, the court system itself could be useful in helping the group buy time to sneak slaves out of the city. During the John Bolding case (1851), a colleague of Jay's wrote, "I am sorry that you are not in town to conduct the Boldin [*sic*] case, for I am now certainly convinced that the only way to fight slave hunters is with writs and delays and not to go to the merits until forced to do so." John Sedgwick to John Jay, Sept. 2, 1851, JFP. After the Nicholas Dudley case (1850) concluded in 1852, Jay recalled how he had assisted in Dudley's escape. Dudley, a runaway, had been indicted for larceny in 1850. Jay advised Dudley to plead guilty, so he would remain in prison rather than risk being returned to his owner. Two days before his sentence was up, Dudley was pardoned and escaped from New York before his owner could reenslave him. Bright, *Happy Country This America: The Travel Diary of Henry Arthur Bright* [1852] (Columbus, 1978), 81–84.

36. Finkelman, *Imperfect Union,* chs. 4–5; Harrold, *Border War,* chs. 4–5.

37. John Jay to Joseph L. White, undated, JFP.

38. "Pro-Slavery," *NASS,* Nov. 26, 1846; "The Recent Slave Case," *NYDT,* Nov. 18, 1846.

39. James Tallmadge to John Jay, Jan. 22 (?), 1847, JFP. Jay sent Tallmadge the *Supplement to the New-York Legal Observer, containing the report of the case in the matter of George Kirk, a fugitive slave, heard before the Hon. J.W. Edmonds, circuit judge: also the argument of John Jay of counsel for the slave* (New York, 1847).

40. Gay to Edmund Quincy, Nov. 1, 1846, SHG.

41. John Jay II, Notes of slave cases (typescript), Slavery Research Folder, JJH; "The Slave Case - The Fugitive Freed!" *Liberator,* Nov. 20, 1846.

42. Francis Jackson to Gay, Nov. 8 and Dec. 3, 1846, Apr. 11, 1847, SHG. Kirk seems to have done well in his first years in the North. Jackson found him a place in Holliston, Massachusetts, where he was going to school and learning how to make shoes. But in 1850, Kirk, working as a "seaman," died of smallpox in Boston. *Massachusetts, Town and Vital Records, 1620-1899,* s.v. "George Kirk," Ancestry.com.

43. For a law report of what was commonly called "the Brazilian Slave Case," see "In the matter of Jose Da Costa and Jose Da Rocha," 5 New-York Legal Observer 294 (NY Supreme Court First Judicial District, 1847). There were three slaves involved, two men and one woman. The woman chose to stay with her mistress, so the case ultimately revolved around the freedom suit (and escape) of the men. The case went through three trials; the men escaped from prison during the third.

44. "Brazilian Slaves," *Boston Daily Atlas,* July 14, 1847; "Law Intelligence," *NYH,* July 12, 1847.

45. "The Brazilian Slave Case," *New-Bedford Mercury,* Jan. 30, 1847; *Longworth's American Almanac, New-York Register, and City Directory* (New York, 1835), 384; "Law Intelligence," *NYH,* July 13, 1847; "The Brazilian Slave Case," *Richmond Enquirer,* July 20, 1847.

46. [No Title], *Times-Picayune* (New Orleans), Aug. 8, 1847; "The Brazilian Slaves at New York," *New-Bedford Mercury,* Aug. 13, 1847; "The Brazilian Slave Case," *Emancipator,* Aug. 18, 1847; *Sixteenth Annual Report . . . Massachusetts Anti-Slavery Society* (Boston, 1848), 55. For drafts Jay wrote "to the Editor of the Herald" disavowing the involvement of Gay and Smith in the rescue, see "The Escape of the Brazilian Slaves," JFP.

47. Elias Smith to Jay, Aug. 24, 1847, JFP; Jay to Gay, Apr. 22, 1848, JFP; "Anniversary of the Vigilance Committee," *NS,* May 18, 1849. According to a letter published in Still's *Underground Railroad* (p. 40), Gibbs was another New Yorker who worked with Napoleon and Gay on a regular basis. William Harned, a white member of the Vigilance Committee, also played a role behind the scenes in the *Lemmon* case. Donations for the Vigilance Committee were directed to Gay's Anti-Slavery Office on Nassau Street. William Harned, Charles B. Ray, Andrew Lester, "Anti-Slavery circular of William Harned et al.," Quaker and Special Collections, Haverford College.

48. *In re Belt,* 1 Parker Cr. R 169 (1848), 136; Lewis Tappan, *The Fugitive Slave Bill: Its History and Unconstitutionality, with an account of the Seizure and Enslavement of James Hamlet* (New York, 1850); "The Case of Henry Long," *National Era,* Jan. 9, 1851; "The Case of John Bolding," *FDP,* Sept. 4, 1851; "Governor Hunt and the Fugitive Slave Nicholas Dudley," *Richmond Enquirer,* May 25, 1852. Synopses of most of these cases,

including the Jane Trainer case, are in Samuel May, *The Fugitive Slave Law and Its Victims* (New York, 1861). A *select* list of the men involved in these cases includes John Jay, Asa Child, William Harned, James McCune Smith, Louis Napoleon, Horace Greeley, Lewis Tappan, Joseph White, J. W. C. Pennington, and Erastus Culver. Although much has been written about the Hamlet case, Napoleon's role in the large public gathering organized to welcome Hamlet home is not well-known. For Napoleon's presence, see "City Intelligence: Meeting of the Colored People," *EP*, Oct. 5, 1850. John Jay's participation in the John Bolding case is likewise little known. Jay gave advice from afar (the case took place in Poughkeepsie) after James McCune Smith came to his offices for help. See letters from John Sedgwick to John Jay, Aug. 26, 29, and Sept. 2, JFP.

49. "The Jane Trainer Case," *FDP*, June 4, 1853; "Jane Trainer Once More," *FDP*, Aug. 5, 1853. J. W. C. Pennington was also involved in this case; Pennington, as we shall see, was an important figure in the *Lemmon* case.

50. "Meetings of Colored Citizens of New York," *NS*, Oct. 24, 1850.

51. "Meetings of Colored Citizens of New York," *NS*, Oct. 24, 1850; "Denunciation of the Fugitive Slave Bill," *EP*, Oct. 2, 1850; Rush, *African Methodist Episcopal Church*, 9–11. The 1850 meeting was called by the Committee of Thirteen, a group of prominent black abolitionists: John Zuille, T. Joiner White, Philip A. Bell, Robert Hamilton, George T. Downing, Jeremiah Powers, John T. Raymond, William Burnett, James McCune Smith, Ezekial Dias, Junius C. Morel, Thomas Downing, and William Wilson. Decades later, Zuille recalled Napoleon in a manner that confirms that he was known among black leaders. "Helped to Freedom," *Daily News* (Denver), Nov. 17, 1889.

52. "Rev. Mr. Raymond," *NASS*, Oct. 10, 1850.

53. The other unknown figure was Wm. C. Inners. As far as I can tell, Inners left even less of a trail than Napoleon.

54. "The Slave Case - Mr. Lemmon's Statement," *Albany Journal*, Nov. 18, 1852; "Shall New York be a Slave-Mart?" *National Era*, Nov. 18, 1852; "The Slave Case Decision of Judge Paine," *Sun* (New York), Nov. 19, 1852; "New York Slave Case," *Fayetteville Observer*, Dec. 2, 1852.

55. "The Slave Case - Proposed Subscription - Interesting Statement of Mr. Lemmon" (reprinted from *New York Journal of Commerce*), *Richmond Whig*, Nov. 23, 1852.

56. "Adventures and Bananas: The Strange Story of a Colored Man's Life" (reprinted from the *Troy Times*), *Daily Courant* (Hartford), May 8, 1874. Interestingly, Lobam called Napoleon "Napoleon Gibbs." Either Lobam or the writer was confused. Both Louis Napoleon and Jacob Gibbs were involved in the *Lemmon* case, but it is almost certain that Lobam sent the boy to Napoleon, for Napoleon petitioned the writ almost immediately. In his 1855 letter (see note 7) to William Still, Gay noted of Napoleon, "He has friends on board the boat who are on the lookout for fugitives, and send them, when found, to his house." Napoleon clearly had many friends on many boats. For the names and ages of the Lemmon slaves, see *Report of the Lemmon Slave Case* (1860), 4. The *Weekly Herald* (New York) called one of the Edwardses "Robert." "Important Slave Case," *Weekly Herald*, Nov. 20, 1852.

57. "City Intelligence," *EP,* Nov. 8, 1852; "Alleged Slave Case," *Albany Journal,* Nov. 8, 1852; "The Slave Case," *Farmer's Cabinet,* Nov. 18, 1852.

58. "The Slave Case - Manumission of Eight Slaves," *Weekly Herald,* Nov. 20, 1852; "Degraded into Liberty. By Henry Ward Beecher," *FDP,* Nov. 26, 1852.

59. "The New York Slave Case" (reprinted from *Philadelphia Tribune of the People*), *Liberator,* Dec. 3, 1849; "The Recent Slave Case - Decision of Judge Paine (reprinted from *Washington Union*), *NASS,* Dec. 2, 1852.

60. Lewis Tappan, "To the Editor of the Reporter," Nov. 20, 1852, in "Correspondence of Lewis Tappan and Others with the British and Foreign Anti-Slavery Society" (Part 11), *Journal of Negro History* (July 1927): 490.

61. "The New York Slave Case (citing *EP*)" *AEJ,* Nov. 11, 1852; "From the N. Y. Journal of Commerce: Slave Case," *Liberator,* Nov. 19, 1852; "The Slaves Free - Important Decision," *NYTrib,* Nov. 15, 1852; "Important Slave Case," *Weekly Herald,* Nov. 20, 1852.

62. "The Slave Case," *EP,* Nov. 10, 1852.

63. *The People ex rel. Napoleon v. Lemmon,* 700, 702.

64. "The Slave Case," *EP,* Nov. 10, 1852.

65. Harriet Beecher Stowe, *Uncle Tom's Cabin* (Boston, 1852); "Important Slave Case" *Weekly Herald,* Nov. 20, 1852; "A Card from Mr. Lemmon," *NASS,* Nov. 25, 1852. For an account that weaves the cultural history of *Uncle Tom's Cabin* with the political history of sectional crisis, see Brooke, *There Is a North.* On slavery's violation of the home as key to the midcentury abolitionist critiques, see Amy Dru Stanley, *From Bondage to Contract: Wage Labor, Marriage, and the Market in the Age of Slave Emancipation* (Cambridge, UK, 1998).

66. "Judge Paine's Decision - Comments on the Pro-Slavery Press," *National Era,* Nov. 25, 1852.

67. "Important Slave Case" *Weekly Herald,* Nov. 20, 1852.

68. "From the N. Y. Journal of Commerce: Slave Case," *Liberator,* Nov. 19, 1852.

69. "The Slaves Free - Important Decision," *NYTrib,* Nov. 15, 1852; "The New York Slave Case - Freedom Triumphant," *Philadelphia Freeman,* Nov. 18, 1852.

70. On the request of the Lemmons's lawyers, Henry Clinton and Henry LaPaugh, Justice Edwards of the New York Supreme Court granted the Lemmons a *writ of certiorari* on November 19, 1852. The Supreme Court was New York's midlevel appellate court. This grant of appeal occurred six days after Paine gave his original opinion. For the Lemmons's petition and the writ, see "The Lemmon Slave Case," *NASS,* Nov. 25, 1852.

71. "Slave Case in this City," *NASS,* Nov. 11, 1852.

72. John Jay to My Dear Sir, Nov. 23, 1852, John Jay II Letterbook, JJH.

73. J. W. C. Pennington to Horace Greeley (and William Harned), Nov. 27, 1852, JFP. Abolitionist and lawyer John Hooker was married to Isabella Beecher, of the famous abolitionist family. Joseph Roswell Hawley was a Hartford lawyer, the son of abolitionist Baptist minister Francis Hawley. Charles Gardner was a black minister who previously

presided over the church where Pennington preached. I do not know who Brown and Crass were.

74. "The Late Slaves," *NYTrib,* Nov. 23, 1852; "Documents relative to the Lemmon Slave Case," JFP.

75. "The Slave Case," *New York Daily Times,* Nov. 22, 1852; "Supreme Court - The People of the State of New York *ex. rel.* of Louis Napoleon v. Jonathan Lemmon," *NASS,* Dec. 9, 1852. The *Tribune* reprinted the document in their coverage of the 1857 appeal. [No Headline], *NYTrib,* Oct. 3, 1857.

76. "The Slave Case Appealed," *Richmond Whig,* Nov. 23, 1852.

77. "A Chance for the Benevolent," *Richmond Whig,* Nov. 23, 1852.

78. "The Recent Slave Case," *Alexandria Gazette,* Nov. 24, 1852; "News of the Day," *Alexandria Gazette,* Dec. 14, 1852.

79. "Extracts from Our Correspondence," *National Era,* Dec. 16, 1852; "The Lemmon Case," *National Era,* Dec. 16, 1852.

80. "My Dear Sir," Dec. 10, 1852, "Correspondence of Lewis Tappan," 493; "The Lemmon Slaves: A Family Sketch," *NYTrib,* Jan. 25, 1853; Erastus Culver to John Jay, Dec. 4, 1852, JFP; Pennington to Jay, Mar. 2, 1853, JFP.

81. Lewis Tappan to Jay, JFP; Jacob Gibbs to Jay, Dec. 11, 1852, "Documents relative to the Lemmon Slave Case," JFP.

82. In spring 1853, King wrote that he used $160 of Jay's funds to buy land for the families and that "Nancy and Richard Johnson are hired out, Lewis Wright and the rest are on the Farm. All appear industrious, in good health, and happy." The children were in school, "learning by will." By the fall, King wrote that some were supporting themselves. By the end of 1854, Emmeline was married "to a person in the settlement," and Nancy Johnson and Edward Wright were "out at service and supporting themselves." Richard Johnson had also married. Because of these changes, the freedpeople expressed a desire to have their land divided up among them (the acres were held in trust by King and Tappan). The following month, King told Jay that the land would soon be divided. William King to Jay, Feb. 4, May 3, June 21, Oct. 4, 1853, Feb. 16, Sept. 1, Oct. 13, 1853, JFP. Jay told the New York Supreme Court in 1857 that the "slaves, after being declared free by Judge Paine, were sent to Canada," where "they were there permanently settled on lands bought for the purpose." "Law Intelligence," *NYT,* Oct. 2, 1857.

83. For earlier evidence of Gay assisting fugitive slaves, see Gay to John W. Browne, Dec. 15, 1846, and Jan. 3, 1847; Gay to Caroline Weston, Jan. 4, 1847; Francis Jackson to Gay, Dec. 23, 1848, and May 1, 1851, SHG.

84. Gay, "Record of Fugitives, 1855," SHG. Many decades later, John Zuille recalled Napoleon in a manner that confirms that he was known for the work he did in secret. Speaking of the Underground Railroad, Zuille reported that Napoleon "was as great genius in his way as the emperor of his name. In place of killing people, he saved their lives." "Helped to Freedom" (reprinted from the *New York Sun*), The *Daily News* (Denver), Nov. 17, 1889.

85. Don E. Fehrenbacher, *The Dred Scott Case: Its Significance in American Law and Politics* (New York, 1978), chs. 13–17; "Mr. Justice Nelson," *NYTrib,* Mar. 12, 1857.

86. *JANY* (Albany, 1857), 622; "The Dred Scott Decision," *New-York Semi-Weekly Tribune*, Mar. 20, 1857; *The Case of Dred Scott . . . and Some Concluding Observations* (New York, 1857); *JSNY* (Albany, 1857), 672–673; "State Sovereignty in the New York Legislature" and "The Personal Liberty Bill," *NASS*, April 25, 1857.

87. "Law Intelligence," *NYDT,* May 6, 1857; *Lemmon v. The People ex rel. Louis Napoleon,* 26 Barb. 270 (NY Gen. Term, 1857).

88. John King, "Annual Message of the Governor," *JSNY* (Albany, 1858), 24; "The Lemmon Slave Case," *National Era,* May 28, 1857; "The Lemmon Slave Case," *Mobile Register,* Feb. 9, 1860. "The Lemmon Case," *New Hampshire Patriot*, Apr. 25, 1860. Napoleon actually reemerged as a figure in the case after the second appellate trial, although this was unknown to the public. Jay was desperate to avoid the appeals, for he feared *Lemmon* would reach the Taney Supreme Court, with disastrous consequences. Jay wanted Governor King and the legislature to remove New York State as a party in the case, and then allow Napoleon, the original relator, to apply for a dismissal. See Gronningsater, "On Behalf of His Race and the Lemmon Slaves."

89. "Slavery Agitation," *National Era,* Apr. 22, 1858; Abraham Lincoln, *Selected Speeches and Writings,* ed. Don Fehrenbacher (New York, 1989), 432. For other examples, see Charles Francis Adams to William Lloyd Garrison, *Liberator,* Aug. 10, 1860; "Speech of Hon. Lyman Trumbull of Illinois at Mass Meeting in Chicago," *National Era,* Sept. 2, 1858; "The Late Debate," *Charleston Mercury*, Mar. 23, 1859; "The Republican Party: Its History and Policy: A Speech by the Hon. John Sherman of Ohio," *NYTrib,* Apr. 14, 1860.

90. "The Lemmon Case - Proposed Remedy," *Charleston Mercury,* Mar. 26, 1859.

91. "The Lemmon Slave Case," *NYH,* Jan. 24, 1860.

92. *Report of the Lemmon Slave Case* (1860), 24, 115, 130, 135; "Campaign Documents," *NYTrib,* Aug. 25, 1860.

93. "Campaign Documents," *NYTrib,* Aug. 25, 1860.

94. "Another Union Mass Meeting," *NYH,* Oct. 25, 1860.

95. "Art. V - The South, in the Union or Out of It," *DeBow's Review,* Oct. 1860.

96. "New-York at Bar," *NYTrib,* Dec. 24, 1860.

97. "New-York at Bar," *NYTrib,* Dec. 24, 1860.

98. Nonetheless, several newspapers mistakenly reported that the case was en route to the Supreme Court. "The Lemmon Case," *New-Hampshire Patriot,* Apr. 25, 1860; "New York At Bar," *NYTrib,* Dec. 24, 1860. For Letcher's actions, see McGraw and Pitcaithley, "The Lemmon Slave Case."

99. *Declaration of the Immediate Causes Which Induce and Justify the Secession of South Carolina* (Charleston, 1860), 8.

100. Constitution of the Confederate States, art. IV, § 2. Although Virginia did join the Confederacy, the decision to secede was a divisive and contested issue among the

state's citizens. Stephanie McCurry, *Confederate Reckoning: Power and Politics in the Civil War South* (Cambridge, MA, 2010), 63–75.

101. "Louis Napoleon's Funeral," *Sun,* Mar. 31, 1881.

Chapter 7

Gentle Reader: I know this is a long chapter. My hope is that the full implications of the history told earlier in this book will become most clear when interwoven with a narrative of black New Yorkers' multiple roles in the Civil War and Reconstruction told within a single chapter frame.

1. "The Right of Colored Persons to Ride in the Railway Cars," *PA,* May 16, 1863. In 1865, the Appeal's successor, the *Elevator,* adopted "equality before the law" as its slogan. This chapter's title comes from Frederick Douglass's *New National Era* (Washington), Oct. 23, 1873.

2. "Important Public Meeting," *CA,* Aug. 5, 1837; "Married," *CA,* Mar. 16, 1839; "Sam'l A. Smith" and "Sarah C. Smith," 1860 U.S. Census, 2nd District, San Francisco, CA; "Death of Henry Smith [Samuel's brother]," *PA,* May 9, 1863, "Lodge House," *PA,* June 6, 1863; "Lodge House," *WAA,* Aug. 19, 1863. When she married, Sarah spelled her name *Jinnings* with an *i*. Others in the family adopted *Jennings*. As late as 1861, Thomas L. Jinnings's widow, Elizabeth, still used *i*. "Masonic Head Quarters," *WAA,* Feb. 23, 1861.

3. "Freemen, Freedmen, and Slaves," *PA,* May 16, 1863.

4. Black reformers, including Bell, achieved desired changes to California state testimony laws in 1863. "Our Petition" and "The Rights of Testimony," *PA,* Apr. 5, 1862; Kevin Waite, *West of Slavery: The Southern Dream of a Transcontinental Empire* (Chapel Hill, 2021), chs. 4, 8.

5. Some of the most exciting twenty-first-century scholarship on the Civil War and Reconstruction highlights the importance of black men as soldiers, southern women as integral to histories of the Confederacy, enslaved people as crucial to the politics and mechanics of emancipation and citizenship-making, and black northerners' roles as teachers, missionaries, and advocates in the South. What is missing is a full account of how black northerners, many of them ordinary men and women whose lives spanned multiple emancipations, were pivotal actors in shaping the "high" politics and lawmaking of the era. Key to their influence were their prior, personal experiences of abolition and rights campaigns at the state level. Their earlier battles, often considered separately in the literature, should be incorporated into our accounts of national emancipation and enfranchisement. For a representative sample of recent work that foregrounds a wide range of historical actors and/or inspires my views on the war and Reconstruction, see Laura F. Edwards, *A Legal History of the Civil War and Reconstruction: A Nation of Rights* (Cambridge, UK, 2015); Foner, *Second Founding*; Judith Giesberg and Randall M. Miller, eds., *Women and the American Civil War: North-South Counterpoints* (Kent, OH, 2018); Thavolia Glymph, *The Women's Fight: The Civil War Battles for Home, Freedom, and Nation* (Chapel Hill, 2020); Hahn, *A Nation Under Our Feet*; Dale Kretz,

Administering Freedom: The State of Emancipation After the Freedmen's Bureau (Chapel Hill, 2022); Chandra Manning, *Troubled Refuge: Struggling for Freedom in the Civil War* (New York, 2016); Kate Masur, *An Example for All the Land: Emancipation and the Struggle over Equality in Washington, D.C.* (Chapel Hill, 2021); Stephanie McCurry, *Women's War: Fighting and Surviving the American Civil War* (Cambridge, MA, 2019); Oakes, *Freedom National*; Hannah Rosen, *Terror in the Heart of Freedom: Citizenship, Sexual Violence, and the Meaning of Race in the Postemancipation South* (Chapel Hill, 2009); David Quigley, *Second Founding: New York City, Reconstruction, and the Making of American Democracy* (New York, 2003); Scott, "Public Rights"; Amy Murrell Taylor, *Embattled Freedom: Journeys Through the Civil War's Slave Refugee Camps* (Chapel Hill, 2018). Masur's *Until Justice Be Done* and Kantrowitz's *Beyond Freedom,* like this book, start well before the Civil War and follow northern antislavery politics into Reconstruction; this particular chronological framing is rare and reaps benefits. For older but crucial studies, see W. E. B. Du Bois, *Black Reconstruction* (New York, 1935); Thomas Holt, *Black over White: Negro Political Leadership in South Carolina During Reconstruction* (Urbana, 1977); Eric Foner, *Reconstruction: America's Unfinished Revolution* (New York, 1988); Joseph Glatthaar, *Forged in Battle: The Civil War Alliance of Black Soldiers and White Officers* (Baton Rouge, 1990); Tera Hunter, *To 'Joy my Freedom: Southern Black Women's Lives and Labors After the Civil War* (Cambridge, MA, 1997); Brown, "Negotiating the Public Sphere"; Willie Lee Rose, *Rehearsal for Reconstruction: The Port Royal Experiment* (Indianapolis, 1964).

6. "The Perils by the Way," *WAA,* Sept. 26, 1863; Robert Hamilton, 1855 NY State Census, Kings County, Brooklyn.

7. *Trow's New York City Directory for the Year Ending 1863* (New York, 1863), 35; "Boarding and Lodging," *Pine and Palm* (Boston), May 18, 1861.

8. The following are important legal histories of the amendments, but they miss the totality of black northerners' roles in the origins. Black northerners, and not just the famous ones, were foundational (a) because of the politics they practiced well before the war as result of gradual abolition, and (b) because of the ways they effectively lobbied for certain outcomes during and after the war. Randy E. Barnett, "Whence Comes Section One? The Abolitionist Origins of the Fourteenth Amendment," *Journal of Legal Analysis* (Spring 2011): 165–263; Kurt T. Lash, *The Fourteenth Amendment and the Privileges and Immunities of American Citizenship* (New York, 2014); Earl Maltz, "The Coming of the Fifteenth Amendment: The Republican Party and the Right to Vote in the Early Reconstruction Era," *Louisiana Law Review* (Winter 2022): 395–451; Gerard N. Magliocca, *American Founding Son: John Bingham and the Invention of the Fourteenth Amendment* (New York, 2013).

9. As this chapter demonstrates, black and white New Yorkers frequently referred to their state's history of slavery and emancipation to make both political arguments and policy suggestions for the present. For a point of comparison, and an illuminating study of this general theme, see Margot Minardi, *Making Slavery History: Abolitionism and the Politics of Memory in Massachusetts* (New York, 2010).

10. "The Rev. Dr. Dewey's Lecture," *NYTrib,* Jan. 11, 1844.

11. "Freedom and Slavery for African Americans," *NYTrib,* Jan. 20, 1844.

12. "Freedom and Slavery for African Americans," *NYTrib,* Jan. 20, 1844; "To the Editor of the Tribune," *NYTrib,* Jan. 22, 1844; "Dr. Dewey and Mr. Smith," *Boston Courier,* Jan. 29, 1844; "Dr. James McCune Smith," *FDP,* June 3, 1853; James Lundberg, "Reading Horace Greeley's America, 1834–1872" (PhD diss., Yale, 2008).

13. "Mr. Calhoun to Mr. Pakenham," *Niles' National Register,* May 11, 1844.

14. "Hon. John C. Calhoun and the Free Colored People," *NYTrib,* May 8, 1844; "Selections," *Liberator,* May 31, 1844. It was widely acknowledged among northern reformers that the census contained errors. Carroll D. Wright, *The History and Growth of the United States Census* (Washington, DC, 1900), 37–48. Although the 1840 census was never formally corrected, the 1850 census *did* satisfy a request of James McCune Smith et al. The 1850 form asked whether a person over the age of 20—regardless of race—could read and write.

15. *Journal of the Senate of the United States of America,* 28th Congress, May 27, 1844, p. 304; Joshua Giddings, *Speech of Mr. J. R. Giddings of Ohio, upon the Annexation of Texas* (Washington, DC, 1844), 15.

16. "Hon. John C. Calhoun and the Free Colored People," *NYTrib,* May 8, 1844; James McCune Smith to Gerrit Smith, Dec. 17, 1846, May 12, 1848, Mar. 22, 1848, Sept. 1, 1860, GSP. "Meeting in New York," *NS,* May 4, 1849; "Mrs. Douglass' Lecture," *WAA,* Nov. 24, 1860.

17. "The Free Blacks—Northern Philanthropy vs. Northern Legislation—The Colonization Question," *AEJ,* May 23, 1853; Thurlow Weed, *Life of Thurlow Weed* (Boston, 1883), 1:428.

18. "Celebration of the Coloured Citizens," *NASS,* July 30, 1853; "No Compromise with Slavery," *NASS,* Feb. 25, 1854.

19. "Speech at Peoria, Illinois," *CWAL,* 2:247–283; *Political Debates between Hon. Abraham Lincoln and Hon. Stephan A. Douglas* (Columbus, 1860), 74; Edward McPherson, *The Political History of the United States During the Great Rebellion* (Washington, DC, 1865), 209–211; Foner, *Fiery Trial,* 197–198. For similar proposals from Greeley and Weed, "A Reasonable Compromise," *NYTrib,* Jan. 16, 1861; "The Only Possible Compromise," *NYTrib,* Jan. 19, 1861; "Slavery Bleeding to Death," *AEJ,* May 10, 1862; Thurlow Weed, *Life of Thurlow Weed* (Boston, 1844), 1:428. On Lincoln's notorious August 1862 colonization meeting with five black Washingtonians, see Kate Masur, "The African American Delegation to Abraham Lincoln: A Reappraisal," *Civil War History* (June 2010): 117–144.

20. "Our Correspondents," *FDP,* Feb. 9, 1855; "Fusion: The Masses Moving," *FDP,* Oct. 5, 1855; "The Convention at Syracuse," *FDP,* Oct. 5, 1855. Tilmon, who like many of his peers was a politico, is understudied and fascinating: Tilmon, *Brief Miscellaneous Narrative . . . of the Life of L. Tilmon, Pastor* (Jersey City, 1853).

21. Seward wrote about sectional differences over slavery as early as his time at Union College from 1817 to 1820. William Seward to Samuel S. Seward, May 1820,

Samuel S. Seward Papers, 1790–1851, NYSL. Biographical accounts of Seward don't emphasize the fact that he lived through two American slave emancipations.

22. Frederick William Seward, *Seward at Washington as Senator and Secretary of State* (New York, 1891), 86; "The Usurpations of Slavery," *FDP,* Mar. 9, 1855. Melish argues that white New Englanders tried to erase their slaveholding past. By contrast, antislavery New Yorkers routinely acknowledged slavery's place in their state history. *Disowning Slavery,* ch. 6.

23. George E. Baker, ed., *Recent Speeches and Writing of William H. Seward, 1854-1861* (New York, 1861), 391.

24. "Another Union Mass Meeting," *NYH,* Oct. 25, 1860; "Negro Suffrage," *NYDT,* Sept. 15, 1860; Thurlow Weed to William Seward, Oct. 25, 1860, WHS; Baker, *Recent Speeches,* 414–417, 680.

25. James M'Cune [*sic*] Smith, "Citizenship," *Anglo-African Magazine* (New York), May 1859; New York City and County Suffrage Committee of Colored Citizens, *The Suffrage Question in Relation to the Colored Voters in the State of New York* (New York (?), 1860).

26. Field, *Politics of Race,* 127.

27. Oakes provides a nuanced view of Seward's conciliatory stance toward the South in early 1861. *Freedom National,* 64–68. Frederick Douglass, at the time, was disappointed in Seward's loss of antislavery backbone. "Wm. G. Seward Modified," *DM,* Feb. 1861. See also Goodwin, *Team of Rivals,* 324–326; Stebbins, *Political History of the State of New York,* 27–28, 62–63, 88.

28. "First Inaugural Address," *CWAL,* 4:262–263.

29. "President Lincoln's Inaugural," *WAA,* Mar. 16, 1861; Ripley et al., *BAP,* 5:27–28; [Obituary of Thomas Hamilton], *Elevator,* July 14, 1865; "New-York Delegation," *CA,* Aug. 14, 1841; "New Publications," *DM,* Sept. 1860; James McCune Smith to Gerrit Smith, June 21, 1860, GSP.

30. "No Terms with Traitors," *DM,* Sept. 1861.

31. James McCune Smith to Gerrit Smith, Aug. 22, 1861, GSP. See also "Important Revelations: Treachery in the Republican Camp. The Radicals Revolting. Lincoln Still in Danger," *NYH,* Oct. 27, 1860.

32. James McCune Smith to Gerrit Smith, Aug. 22, 1861, GSP; "Letter to the President from Gerrit Smith," *DM,* Oct. 1861.

33. "A Letter from Mr. John Jay," *NYTrib,* Sept. 30, 1861. For more on Jay, see Gellman, *Liberty's Chain,* Part 3.

34. "The Great Conspiracy and England's Neutrality," *DM,* Aug. 1861.

35. John Jay to Charles Sumner, Sept. 1861, CSC; "Abolition Incendiaries Conspiring to Overthrow the Union," *NYH,* Sept. 16, 1861; John Jay to the Editor of The Herald, Sept. 16, 1861, JFP; "Abolitionists and Mr. John Jay," *NYH,* Sept. 19, 1861.

36. "City Government for 1861," *NYT,* Jan. 8, 1861. In 1863, Wood was elected to Congress, where he was an opponent of the Thirteenth Amendment. Vorenberg, *Final Freedom,* 115, 137.

37. Levin Tilmon to Abraham Lincoln, Apr. 8, 1861, Abraham Lincoln Papers, Library of Congress; "Black Regiments Proposed," *DM,* May 1861; "The Progress of the War," *DM*, Sept. 1861; "What We are Fighting For," *WAA*, Sept. 14, 1861.

38. "Colored Americans and the War," *Pine and Palm* (Boston), May 25, 1861; "Formation of Colored Regiments," *WAA*, Oct. 26, 1861; "What are We Colored People Doing? Or Likely to Do?" *WAA*, Oct. 19, 1861. For analogous debates in Boston, see Kantrowitz, *More than Freedom,* 198–204, 214–222, ch. 7.

39. John Jay to Charles Sumner, June 19, 1861, CSC; "To Arms," July 10, 1862, JFP; John Jay to Charles Sumner, Jan. 5, 1863, CSC. See also Jay to Sumner, Aug. 22, 1863, CSC.

40. "The Approaching Congress," *DM,* Dec. 1861.

41. "The Manhood of the Negro," *DM,* Nov. 1861; "Brooklyn Correspondence," *Christian Recorder,* Sept. 12, 1863.

42. "We have refrained . . . ," *PA,* June 14, 1862; "The Fatal Step Backward," *WAA,* Sept. 21, 1861.

43. "Preliminary Emancipation Proclamation," *CWAL,* 5:433–436.

44. "Emancipation Proclamation, January 1, 1863," *CWAL,* 6:28–31; "Great Meeting at Shiloh Church," *DM*, June 1863.

45. "Attorney-General Bates on the Dred Scott Decision," *NYT,* Dec. 17, 1862; "Citizenship of Colored Persons," *DM,* Mar. 1863. On antislavery politicians' understanding that the national government would need to restrain the power of the states in order to better protect black citizens, see Masur, *Until Justice Be Done,* ch. 9.

46. *The War of the Rebellion: Formal reports, both Union and Confederate*, series 1 (Washington, DC, 1886), 15:667–668; Abraham Lincoln to John A. McClernand, Jan. 8, 1863, *CWAL,* 6:48–49; "Brooklyn Correspondence," *Christian Recorder,* July 30, 1864. See also James McCune Smith to Gerrit Smith, Feb. 17, 1865, GSP.

47. Johnson, *Autobiography,* 61; "The Movers," *DM,* Apr. 1863; Edwin S. Redkey, "Profile of the Fifty-Fourth Massachusetts Regiment," in Martin H. Blatt et al., *Hope and Glory: Essays on the Legacy of the Massachusetts Fifty-Fourth Regiment* (Boston, 2001), 22; David W. Blight, *Frederick Douglass: Prophet of Freedom* (New York, 2018), 392. Some sources claim James Henry Gooding was originally an orphan from South Carolina who ended up at the New York Colored Orphan Asylum. But that orphan was Henry Gooding (no "James"), who died in a different part of the war than James Henry Gooding of Troy. I'm persuaded by Virginia Matzke Adams's research that Gooding was from Troy: *On the Altar of Freedom: A Black Soldier's Civil War Letters from the Front* (Amherst, 1991). For Henry Gooding of South Carolina, see Association for the Benefit of Colored Orphans Records, 1836–1972, Series III, Admissions Records, 1837–1937, vol. 23, p. 78.

48. Redkey, "Profile of the Fifty-Fourth Massachusetts," 22; Blight, *Frederick Douglass,* 392–393, 397–398.

49. "Colored Troops in Charleston Harbor," *EP,* July 27, 1863.

50. Celeste-Marie Bernier and Andrew Taylor, eds., *If I Survive: Frederick Douglass and Family in the Walter O. Evans Collection* (Edinburgh, 2018), 187–188; Carter G. Woodson, ed., *The Mind of the Negro as Reflected in Letters Written During the Crisis, 1800-1860* (Washington, DC, 1926), 544.

51. Gerald Schwartz, ed., *A Woman Doctor's Civil War Diary* (Columbia, SC, 1984), 51–52.

52. Iver Bernstein, *The New York City Draft Riots: Their Significance for American Society and Politics in the Age of the Civil War* (New York, 1990), 28–29; J. T. Headley, *The Great Riots of New York* (New York, 1873), 275.

53. "List of Colored Sufferers," *PA*, Sept. 19, 1863; "Additional List of Colored Sufferers," ibid., Sept. 26, 1863; *Report of the Committee of Merchants for the Relief of Colored People . . . the Late Riots* (New York, 1863), 3, 7, 30; [Junius C. Morel], "Brooklyn Correspondence," *Christian Recorder* (Philadelphia), July 25, 1863.

54. Bernstein, *Draft Riots*, Appendix C; "Fortitude of the Negros," *PA*, Sept. 5, 1863.

55. J. W. C. Pennington, "The Position and Duties of the Colored People," in Philip S. Foner and Robert James Branham, eds., *Lift Every Voice: African American Oratory, 1787–1900* (Tuscaloosa, 1998), 397–407. See also "Colored Troops No. 5," *Christian Recorder*, Aug. 1, 1863.

56. Henry W. Bellows, *Historical Sketch of the Union League of New York* (New York, 1879), 183.

57. Union League Club, *Report of the Committee on Volunteering* (New York, 1864), 10–12, 17, 37–38. See also William Seraile, *New York's Black Regiments During the Civil War* (New York, 2002), ch. 2.

58. *Report of the Committee on Volunteering*, 17; "Our Colored Troops," *EP*, Feb. 4, 1864; "The Twenty-Sixth Regiment," *NASS*, Jan. 30, 1864.

59. "Ovation to Black Troops," *NYT*, Mar. 6, 1864; Association for the Benefit of Colored Orphans, *Twenty-Eighth Annual Report* (1864), appendix, NYHS; "Our Washington Correspondent in New York City," *Christian Recorder*, Mar. 12, 1864; "Twenty-sixth Regiment, U.S.C.T.," *NYT*, Mar. 28, 1864.

60. Adams, *On the Altar of Freedom*, Appendix A.

61. "Proclamation of Amnesty and Reconstruction," Dec. 8, 1863, *CWAL*, 7:53–56.

62. Herman Belz, *Reconstructing the Union: Theory and Policy During the Civil War* (Ithaca, 1969), ch. 7; Oakes, *Freedom National*, 437–445; Vorenberg, *Final Freedom*, 50.

63. John Jay to Charles Sumner, Jan. 5, 186[4], CSC. See also Belz, ch. 7, on Ashley's bill. (Ashley destroyed his papers, but Jay reported to Sumner the content of Jay's letter to Ashley.)

64. John Jay to Charles Sumner, July 16, 1862, Dec. 10, 1863, Jan. 5 [1864], Mar. 8, 1864, May (?) 1864, CSC; "No Gradual Emancipation," *NYT*, Feb. 25, 1864. Jay also wrote to William Seward and Lyman Trumbull. John Jay to William Seward, June 27, 1862, WSP; John Jay to Lyman Trumbull, July 5, 1862, JFP.

65. "The Radical Wisdom of the Administration," *PA*, Feb. 20, 1864. On the rapidly shifting ground of immediatism, see Vorenberg, *Final Freedom*, 36–46, ch. 4. For a first-hand account by a previously anti-Lincoln white citizen whose views on emancipation, the Confederacy, and the need for the protection of black citizens shifted after the 1863 draft riots, see "From the Tribune," *NASS*, July 25, 1863,

66. *Congressional Globe*, 38th Congress, 1st sess., Apr. 8, 1864, pp. 1482–1483; Vorenberg, *Final Freedom*, 50–60, 138, 252; "A Relapse," *AEJ*, June 21, 1864.

67. *Trow's New York City Directory for the Year Ending 1863* (New York, 1863), 35; "Boarding and Lodging," *Pine and Palm*, May 18, 1861. Kyle Volk is one of the few to give a rich treatment of Ellen Anderson's case. *Moral Minorities and the Making of American Democracy* (Oxford, 2014), ch. 5. I'd like to place the Andersons' politics within a deeper, longer history.

68. "A Question to be Settled," *New York Semi-Weekly Tribune*, June 21, 1864; "Letter from New York," *Sacramento Daily Union*, July 27, 1864; "Railroad Outrage," *WAA*, July 2, 1864.

69. *NY Laws*, 76th sess. (1853), ch. 228; "Thomas C. Acton is Dead," *New York Times*, May 2, 1898.

70. "Justice Restored," *Christian Recorder*, July 9, 1864.

71. "Justice Restored," *Christian Recorder*, July 9, 1864.

72. "Justice Restored," *Christian Recorder*, July 9, 1864; "Trial at Police Headquarters," *NYH*, July 1, 1864; "General News," *NYTrib*, July 9, 1864. On the common law right to ride, see Barbara Welke, *Recasting American Liberty: Gender, Race, Law, and The Railroad Revolution, 1865–1920* (New York, 2001). In 1866, black abolitionist Frances E. W. Harper noted that she was more confident that she could ride a street car in New York than in Philadelphia, where Harriet Tubman had recently been violently ejected from a car. See *Proceedings of the Eleventh National Women's Rights Convention* (New York, 1866), 46–48.

73. "Outrage Upon a Soldier's Widow," *Commonwealth* (Boston), June 24, 1864. On women and streetcars elsewhere, see Judith Giesberg, *Army at Home: Women and the Civil War on the Northern Home Front* (Chapel Hill, 2009), ch. 4; Masur, *An Example for All the Land*, ch. 3; Bay, *Traveling Black*, ch. 1.

74. "Love and Charity," *NYTrib*, May 19, 1859; "Grand Union Entertainment," *WAA*, Feb. 18, 1860; "In Memoriam," *WAA*, July 16, 1864; "A Palace for Colored Men," *Providence Evening Press*, Nov. 20, 1871; Ellen [Walker] Anderson's widow's pension claims, Box 33216, WC 137098, U.S. National Archives and Records Administration. Ellen signed her own name to pension documents, and she may well be the "Ellen Walker" who is listed in the 1850 federal census (New York City, Ward 18, district 2) as a 14-year-old from Maryland who had recently attended school.

75. "Negro Jubilee," *Brooklyn Daily Eagle*, Aug. 2, 1864.

76. *Proceedings of the National Convention of Colored Men, held in the City of Syracuse, NY, October 4, 5, 6, and 7, 1864* (Boston, 1864), 36, 59–60. Emphasis in original.

77. "Action! Action! Action!" *Christian Recorder*, Mar. 25, 1865.

78. Garnet, *A Memorial Discourse*, 69–71, 78, 85.

79. "Celebration of the Emancipation Proclamation," *Liberator*, June 20, 1865; "The Rev. Henry H. Garnet's Lecture," *NYTrib*, June 28, 1865; "Letter from Norfolk," *Christian Recorder*, July 1, 1865; "Garnet in Alexandria," *Massachusetts Spy*, Oct. 4, 1865; "A Colored Political Preacher," *Cincinnati Enquirer*, Sept. 11, 1865; "Editorial Correspondence," *Christian Recorder*, Sept. 23, 1865; "Reverend H. H. Garnet in Louisville, Kentucky," *Christian Recorder*, Sept. 30, 1865; "To Irishmen," *Cincinnati Enquirer*, Oct. 19, 1865.

80. "Albany Correspondence," *Christian Recorder*, Oct. 21, 1865.

81. "Black Men Intend to Help Themselves," *NYT*, Dec. 11, 1865; "An Outside Congress," *NYTrib*, Dec. 13, 1865; "Colored Congressmen," *Weekly Louisianian*, May 2, 1874.

82. *Congressional Globe*, 39th Congress, 1st sess., Feb. 2, 1866, p. 599. On conceptions of different sorts of rights—political, social, civil, public—see Masur, *An Example*, ch. 4, and Scott, "Public Rights."

83. Harold Hyman and William M. Wiecek, *Equal Justice Under Law: Constitutional Development, 1835-1875* (New York, 1982), 405–416.

84. Charles Sumner, *The Equal Rights of All . . . to Maintain a Republican Government* (Washington, 1866), 3, 6.

85. George T. Downing et al. to Charles Sumner, Feb. 13, 1866; Henry Highland Garnet to Charles Sumner, Feb. 7, 1866; Downing to Charles Sumner, May 5, 1866, CSP.

86. Masur, *Example for All the Land*, ch. 4.

87. "Constitutional Convention," *NYTrib*, Feb. 8, 1867.

88. "A Large Meeting," *NASS*, June 15, 1867; "State Constitutional Convention," *NYH*, June 21, 1867.

89. *Journal of the Convention of the State of New York: Begun and Held at the Capitol, in the City of Albany, on the 4th Day of June, 1867* (Albany, 1867), 17; *Documents of the Convention of the State of New York, 1867-1868* (Albany, 1868), vol. 1, issues 1–39, no. 15–16.

90. *Proceedings and Debates of the Constitutional Convention of the State of New York* (Albany, 1868), 1:237; "Our Albany Correspondence," *Brooklyn Daily Eagle*, July 27, 1867; "Separate Submission," *ComAd*, June 29, 1867; "Suffrage—Extension or Restriction," *Albany Argus*, July 2, 1867; "Negro Suffrage—Beating a Retreat," *Albany Argus*, Feb. 18, 1868.

91. *Congressional Globe*, Senate, 40th Congress, 1st sess., July 12, 1867, p. 614.

92. Foner, *Reconstruction*, chs. 6, 9; Kidada E. Williams, *I Saw Death Coming: A History of Terror and Survival in the War Against Reconstruction* (New York, 2023).

93. "Memorial of the Committee of Union League Club, New York," US Congressional Serial Set (1868): 1–18.

94. "Election Fraud Investigation in New York City and State, vol. 1, with Minority Views," US Congressional Serial Set (1868), 3–4.

95. Mullen may have seen "The Election Frauds," *NYH*, both July 10 and July 12, 1869.

96. "Election Fraud Investigation in New York City and State, vol. 1," 42–42; "Election Fraud Investigation in New York City and State, vol. 2, supplement," US Congressional Serial Set (1868), 642–645, 761.

97. "Election Fraud Investigation . . . vol. 2," 782–785, 862; Russel Headley, ed., *History of Orange County* (Middletown, NY, 1908), 537; "Appointments by the Governor," *AEJ,* Apr. 1, 1870.

98. *Proceedings of the National Convention of the Colored Men of America: held in Washington, D. C., on January 13, 14, 15, and 16, 1869* (Washington, DC, 1869), 1, 19, 36, vii–viii (appendix).

99. *Congressional Globe,* 40th Congress, 3rd sess., Feb. 8, 1869, p. 990; "The Suffrage Amendment," *NYTrib,* Feb. 18, 1869; Field, *Politics of Race,* 183.

100. "Colored Voters," *NYDT,* June 4, 1869; "Colored Men's Convention," *Cortland Standard,* June 8, 1869; "A Binghamton correspondent . . ." *NASS,* July 10, 1869; "Anniversary of Freedom," *Utica Morning Herald,* July 3, 1869; "Lecture Last Evening," *Harrisburg Telegraph,* Sept. 15, 1869; "Equal Rights League," *NASS,* Sept. 25, 1869; "In Memoriam," *Addison Advertiser,* Sept. 18, 1881. In 1870, Molson was named as a speaker at the annual meeting of Elizabeth Cady Stanton and Susan B. Anthony's National Woman's Suffrage Association. In the announcement of the meeting, the organizers cited both the promise of state-by-state female enfranchisement and the need for a sixteenth amendment to the federal constitution. As far as I can discern, there is very little written about Molson, but it's intriguing to wonder how her approach to female suffrage was informed by her understanding of the long history of emancipation and black citizenship in the North and changes in U.S. federalism. "Anniversary of the National Woman's Suffrage Association," *Revolution* (New York), April 7, 1870.

101. "Abolish the Property Qualification," *NASS,* Oct. 23, 1869.

102. "Gross Outrage," *NYT,* Oct. 16, 1869; "The Negro Outrage," *NYT,* Oct. 17, 1869.

103. Charles Z. Lincoln, *Constitutional History of New York* (Rochester, 1906) 2:419.

104. Bruce Ackerman explores these themes in *We the People: Transformations* (Cambridge, MA, 1998), chs. 2–8. Foner, reviewing Ackerman, makes the point that despite ratification of the Reconstruction amendments, it's clear that white Americans, as a whole, didn't subscribe to the racially egalitarian principles inscribed therein. The Republicans who inserted these amendments into the Constitution—in part by making it difficult for the Confederate states to reenter the Union without agreeing to ratify—were ahead of the nation's white majority. I'd add that black New Yorkers espoused the principles inscribed in the Reconstruction amendments before the 38th to 40th Congresses themselves got on board. Foner, "The Strange Career of the Reconstruction Amendments." On marginalized groups finding ways to wield legal power separate from their capacities as voters, see Maggie Blackhawk, "Legislative Constitutionalism and Federal Indian Law," *Yale Law Journal* (May 2023): 2205–2303.

105. *U.S. Statutes at Large,* 41st Congress, sess. 2, ch. 114; "Congress—Nursing the Fifteenth Amendment," *NYH,* May 17, 1870; "The Elective Franchise to be Protected by the General Government," *Troy Daily Times,* May 28, 1870.

106. For a similar argument in the southern context, see Brown, "Negotiating and Transforming the Public Sphere." For female suffrage, see Faye Dudden, *Fighting Chance: The Struggle over Female Suffrage and Black Suffrage in Reconstruction America* (New York, 2011).

107. "How a Colored Lady Regards the Fifteenth Amendment," *NYTrib,* Apr. 1, 1870; "Special Message of President Grant on Ratification of the XVth Amendment" in Edward McPherson, *The Political History of the United States;* "The Fifteenth Amendment Thanksgiving Meeting," *NYTrib,* Apr. 1, 1870; [No title], *NYTrib,* Apr. 7, 1870.

108. "The Fifteenth Amendment," *NYT,* Apr. 25, 1870.

109. "The Dusky Race," *NYT,* Mar. 2, 1869; "Cruel Caste," *Christian Recorder,* Apr. 13, 1872. The *Herald,* previously no friend to black New Yorkers, also began printing positive coverage of Butler as the paper shifted its political tone in the '70s. "Zion Colored Church," *NYH,* Feb. 28, 1870; "The Colored Labor Convention," *NYH,* Aug. 27, 1870. On Johnson see "Mr. Editor," *AEJ,* Jan. 24, 1870; Johnson, *Autobiography,* 149–153. On family norms, see Ryan, *Cradle of the Middle Class;* Jones, *All Bound Up.* There was an evolving notion of theaters as "public places." See "The Civil Rights Case," *Argus,* May 6, 1873; "Butler on Civil Rights," *Cincinnati Commercial,* Mar. 22, 1875; Amy Dru Stanley, "Slave Emancipation and the Revolutionizing of Human Rights," in Gregory Downs and Kate Masur, eds., *The World the Civil War Made* (Chapel Hill, 2015), 269–303.

110. *U.S. Statutes at Large,* 41st Congress, sess. 2, ch. 254; "Bill of Abominations," *World* (New York), May 30, 1870; "New Election Law of Congress," *NYH,* June 1, 1870. Debates over the bill also revealed growing anti-Chinese sentiment. See Xi Wang, *The Trial of Democracy: Black Suffrage and Northern Republicans, 1860-1910* (Athens, GA, 1997), 68–78.

111. "Caste: Meeting of the Reform League," *National Standard* (New York), Oct. 15, 1870; "Caste: Meeting of the Reform League," *National Standard,* Oct. 22, 1870.

112. "The States," *NYTrib,* Sept. 23, 1870; "Registration," *NYTrib,* Oct. 17, 1870; "Powers of the United States Supervisors," *NYTrib,* Oct. 22, 1870; "The Election Law," *EP,* Oct. 31, 1870; "Reconstructing New York," *World,* Nov. 1, 1870; "The Elections," *National Standard,* Nov. 12, 1870; Quigley, *Second Founding,* 87–89.

113. "Grant Mass Meeting," *NYH,* May 3, 1872; "Equal Rights League," *National Republican* (Washington), Jan. 21, 1874; William Gillette, *The Right to Vote: Politics and the Passage of the Fifteenth Amendment* (Baltimore, 1965), 180–189. Gillette made a key point: "if Negro suffrage, the fundamental condition of Reconstruction, was short-lived in the South, it became permanent in the North. . . . Northern Negro voters would exert their power in national politics . . . intensify pressures on Presidents, congressmen and judges . . . and the Republicans benefited from a solid Negro vote in the close elections of the 1870's, 1880's, and later" (pp. 163–165).

114. Henry Highland Garnet to Charles Sumner, Dec. 31, 1871, CSP; "Reception of Petitions," *CA,* Feb. 13, 1841; "The Colored People and the Republican Party," *New National Era,* Feb. 23, 1871; *Congressional Globe,* 42nd Congress, 2nd sess., Dec. 4, 1871, p. 2, Dec. 7. 1871, p. 36.

115. "Our Colored Citizens," *Brooklyn Daily Union,* May 3, 1872; "The State Convention of Colored Men," ibid., May 11, 1872. On shifts in northern white politics during Reconstruction, see Heather Cox Richardson, *The Death of Reconstruction: Race, Labor, and Politics in the Post-Civil War North, 1865-1901* (Cambridge, MA, 2001).

116. "Republican State Colored Convention—Not a Break Against Grant," *Troy Daily Times,* May 8, 1872; "Ratification of the Republican Ticket," *NYH,* June 8, 1872; "The New York delegation . . . ," *Elevator,* Aug. 3, 1872; McKee, *National Conventions,* 150.

117. "Civil Rights," *Troy Daily Times,* Feb. 12, 1873; "Civil Rights Movement," *NYH,* Feb. 13, 1873; *JASY* (Albany, 1873), 367, 424, 449; *JSNY* (Albany, 1873), 380; "New York," *New National Era,* May 1, 1873.

118. *NY Laws,* 96th sess. (1873), ch. 186.

119. "Civil Rights in New York," *Elevator,* May 31, 1873, "Mass Meeting of Colored Citizens," *NYTrib,* May 16, 1873.

120. "Now to School Again," *Poughkeepsie Daily Eagle,* Sept. 2, 1873; "The New Idea," ibid., Sept. 4, 1873; "Board of Education," ibid., Sept. 10, 1873; Mabee, *Black Education,* ch. 14.

121. "Civil Rights in New York," *Elevator* (San Fransisco), May 31, 1873; "Equality before the Law," *New National Era and Citizen,* Aug. 7, 1873.

122. *Daily Globe,* Feb. 1, 1872, 5–6.

123. "The Fugitive, Daniel, Discharged," *New-York Observer,* Sept. 4, 1851; Eulogy for Roscoe Conkling, Speeches and Articles by Douglass, 1846-1894, mss 11879, box 25, Frederick Douglass Papers, Library of Congress; "The Supplementary Civil Rights Bill," *New National Era,* Jan. 4, 1872; Roscoe Conkling to Gerrit Smith, May 17, 1872, GSP; (Amnesty Act) ch. 193, 17 Stat. 142.

124. "What Are We Doing," "Petition! Petition!!," "Petition," *New National Era and Citizen,* Oct. 23, 1873; "Petition," *Elevator,* Nov. 8, 1873; *San Francisco Directory for the Year . . . 1873* (San Francisco, 1873), 566. *Journal of the Senate,* 43rd Congress, 1st sess., Dec. 8, 1873, p. 40, Dec. 9, 1873, p. 50, Dec. 10, 1873, p. 55.

125. "Call for a Convention," *New National Era and Citizen,* Oct. 16, 1873; "The Colored National Convention," *NYH,* Dec. 9, 1873; "Colored Convention," *National Republican* (Washington, D.C.), Dec. 13, 1873.

126. "Senator Sumner's Law Hours," *AEJ,* Mar. 12, 1874; "Another Account," *Boston Daily Advertiser,* Mar. 12, 1874; "All Night Debate on Civil Rights Bill, *NYH,* May 23, 1874; "The Civil Rights Bill," *Troy Daily Times,* May 23, 1874; "Our Friends in the U.S. Senate" and "The Civil Rights Bill," May 28, 1874; "An All Night Session in the Senate," *National Aegis* (Worcester), May 30, 1870.

127. *Slaughterhouse Cases,* 83 US (16 Wall.) 36 (1873). I'm influenced by Michael Ross and Pamela Brandwein, who agree that *Slaughterhouse* ended up being a terrible decision in the long run for the ways it was employed to limit federal protection of black Americans' rights and to reinforce states' ability to permit and construct segregation, but who also suggest that the *Slaughterhouse* majority in 1873 didn't intend for their decision to enable the Jim Crow regime in the ways it subsequently did. Pamela Brandwein,

Rethinking the Judicial Settlement of Reconstruction (New York, 2011); Michael A. Ross, *Justice of Shattered Dreams: Samuel Freeman Miller and the Supreme Court During the Civil War Era* (Baton Rouge, 2003). These books help make sense of Downing's reading of the case in this chapter.

128. George T. Downing, "Christianity, Law, and Civil Rights," *Independent,* Feb. 26, 1874; Speech of Robert Elliott, *Congressional Record,* 43rd Congress, 1st sess., Jan. 6, 1874, pp. 407–410.

129. *Congressional Record,* 43rd Congress, 1st sess., Jan. 7, 1874, pp. 455–458; *Congressional Record,* 43rd Congress, 2nd sess., Jan. 29, 1874, p. 1005, Feb. 4, 1875, p. 1011; "Washington News," *Jamestown Journal,* Feb. 12, 1875.

130. "Butler on Civil Rights," *Cincinnati Commercial,* Mar. 22, 1875; "The popular idea . . . ," *NYTrib,* Mar. 26, 1875; "First Suit in Troy Under the Civil Rights Bill," *Troy Daily Times,* Apr. 3, 1875; "An Important Decision Concerning Civil Rights," *Troy Daily Times,* Apr. 17, 1875; "Civil Rights in New York," *Daily Graphic* (New York), Apr. 21, 1875; "Law Reports: Test Case Under the Civil Rights Act," *NYT,* Apr. 27, 1875; "William R. Davis, Jr. . . . ," *Troy Daily Times,* June 18, 1875; "The Law Sustained," *World,* June 8, 1875; "There's a Nigger in the Sleeper," *Buffalo Express,* Apr. 12, 1875; "The Courts," *NYH,* June 12, 1875; George T. Downing, "The Civil Rights Bill," *NYTrib,* Feb. 27, 1875. See also John Hope Franklin, "The Enforcement of the Civil Rights Act of 1875," *Prologue* (Winter 1974): 225–235; Alan Friedlander and Richard Allen Gerbner, *Welcoming Ruin: The Civil Rights Act of 1875* (Leiden, 2019).

131. *King v. Gallagher* (1883), 93 NY 438; *People v. King* (1888), 110 NY 418; *NY Laws,* 123rd sess. (1900), ch. 492; "John Brown's Birthday Celebrated by Colored Citizens in Connection with the Signing of the Elsberg Bill," *Colored American* (Washington, D.C.), May 19, 1900; *Civil Rights Cases* (1883), 109 US 3; *Plessy v. Ferguson* (1896), 163 US 537. For an excellent article on civil rights litigation in New York, see David McBride, "Fourteenth Amendment Idealism: The New York State Civil Rights Law, 1873-1918," *New York History* (Apr. 1990): 207–233.

132. James McCune Smith to Gerrit Smith, May 12, 1848, GSP.

Epilogue

1. Charles B. Ray to Gerrit Smith, Aug. 22, 1870, GSP.

2. "Female Suffrage," *Cincinnati Daily Enquirer,* May 14, 1867 [Charlotte's father promoting female suffrage]; "The First Colored Woman . . . ," *Daily Iowa State Register,* Mar. 12, 1870; "A Colored Female Lawyer," *Elevator,* May 11, 1872.

3. "The Colored Female Bar," *Brooklyn Daily Eagle,* Feb. 21, 1870; "Application for Divorce," *Daily Critic* (Washington), Apr. 12, 1875; "Application for Teacherships," *Evening Star* (Washington), Aug. 7, 1878.

INDEX

abolitionism, 12, 122, 154, 301n11; antislavery slaveowners, 41, 137, 314n72, 315n80; Civil War and, 252; as core feature of Quaker practice, 32; different visions before Civil War, 242–47; Garrisonians versus Liberty Party supporters, 199; goal of total emancipation in the United States, 161, 198; relation to "antislavery" term, 20; three legislative goals of, 178–88; uplift/respectability politics and, 157–58, 345n90; in western New York State, 167, 168. *See also* black abolitionists; Thirteenth Amendment; white abolitionists
access, politics of, 8, 104, 149, 248, 301n12
Addison, John, 22, 26, 50, 306n2
African Dorcas Association, 119, 173, 257
African Free School, 14, 48, 144, 157, 170, 279, 331n13; Andrews's history of, 123; black associationalism and, 119; as black town square, 102; criticized in *Freedom's Journal*, 118; curriculum, 99–100; enrollment figures, 113, 124, 335n51; female faculty, 124; female graduates of, 114–15, 126; graduates' activism, 96, 125–26, 168, 179, 183, 239, 243; historiography of, 329n26; Lancaster method implemented in, 103, 113; New York Manumission Society and, 49, 71; origins of, 98–99, 331n11; parents and, 99–100; public exhibitions and, 115–16, 158; run by Public School Society, 124, 173; state funds for, 105; white philanthropists and, 100. *See also* New York Manumission Society
African Methodist Episcopal (A.M.E.) Church, 109, 171; Civil War and, 253; A.M.E. Zion Church (NYC), 73, 117, 156, 221, 243, 275; A.M.E. Zion Church (Saratoga), 334n42; Julia A. J. Foote and, 96
African Society for Mutual Relief, 73, 102, 103, 104, 149, 156, 263
Albany, city of, 59, 111, 155, 160, 213, 320n9; African schools in, 108, 109; antislavery petitions in, 180; desegregation of theaters, 276; free black population of, 72; general abolition celebrations in, 156; school equality campaign in, 203, 357n116; state legislature in, 5
Albany Regency (Bucktail/Democratic political machine), 142, 160, 184
American and Foreign Anti-Slavery Society, 214
American Anti-Slavery Society (AASS), 163, 178, 213–14, 216, 217
American Convention for Promoting the Abolition of Slavery, vii (epigraph), 78, 102, 136
American Revolution, 3, 4, 17, 39, 40, 116; black Revolutionary War veterans, 36, 39, 44, 107, 145, 147; British appeals to the enslaved, 38–39; contention over slavery and, 24; Convention of the People (NY), 40; northern abolition and, 25, 35
Anderson, Ellen, 4–5, 241, 261–63, 276, 279, 280
Andrews, Charles, 113–14, 117, 118–19, 335n51; colonization movement and, 123; "respectability" promoted by, 100–101
apprentices, child, 19, 26, 27, 28; age of release from masters, 34; restricted to one master, 62; unequal apprentice rights, 82
Articles of Confederation, 48
Ashley, James, 259, 272n63
associationalism, 126–27, 129, 149, 241, 330–31n9

Baldwin, Serena, 117–18
Baptists, 83, 172, 222
"bastard children," 28, 29, 52
Bastien, Emeline Varick, 114, 115, 126
Bates, Edward, 252–53

Bell, Philip A., 125, 239, 243, 279, 289, 299n5; in Committee of Thirteen, 364n51; Lincoln criticized by, 252; petition movement and, 179, 180, 181, 182
Belt, Joseph, case of (1848), 220
Benezet, Anthony, 32–33, 35, 36, 102
Benson, Egbert, 41, 47, 314n72
Bingham, Representative John, 266–67, 272, 274
birth certificates, 7, 53, 63, 291, 320n6; masters' authority undermined by, 58; masters' failure to register, 82, 83
Bishop, John H., 175, 194, 351n22
black abolitionists, 47, 221, 224, 228, 253, 351n24, 358n6; AASS and, 178, 214; in "Burned-Over District," 169; Committee of Thirteen, 364n51; multiple ideological battles fought by, 242; white counterparts pushed to bolder action by, 248
black children, 25, 35, 43, 94; abolition laws of northern states and, 40–41; allowed into white schools, 280; compared to white apprentices, 63; education and protection of, 146; "father's duty" of masters toward, 34; legal status under 1799 law, 62, 159; literacy of, 3; masters' physical cruelty toward, 75–76; as members of new republic, 99; responsibility for bearing costs of raising, 52; terms of service purchased by parents, 88; Vermont's abolition plan and, 40; violent prejudice towards, 121. *See also* children of gradual abolition; rising generation
Black Codes, 265
black men, 35, 46, 74; American Revolution and, 37, 39; associations and political meetings of, 7, 109, 119, 125; black schools spearheaded by, 107; children's education and, 173; enlistment in Union army, 240, 250–55, 257–58, 368n5; laboring activities of, 75, 99; party affiliation of, 73, 78, 79, 132; petition movement and, 181; as proportion of state electorate, 277; voting activity of, 4, 72–73, 131, 287. *See also* suffrage, equal male; voting rights
black New Yorkers, 2, 4, 10, 19; American Revolution and, 39; antislavery reformers assisted by, 24; antislavery whites and, 245; churches founded by, 102; as citizens and taxpayers, 98; citizenship of, 140–41; Civil War and, 251–53; collaboration with antislavery whites, 7; common law precedents and, 302n16; debates on party politics, 201; discourse of emancipation shaped by, 242; efforts to make abolition laws work faster, 57; engagement with local officials, 166; equal male suffrage issue and, 202; federal constitutional convention and, 48–49; formal political system and, 299n7; illegal transport of, 69; immediatism and, 8; legal system and, 64; *Lemmon* Slave Case and, 207; Lincoln administration relationship with, 253; newcomers absorbed into communities of, 8–9; petitioning and lobbying by, 178–82; Republican Party and, 272; in rural areas, 85, 112, 157, 330n7; suffrage placed above partisanship, 247–48; targeted in New York City draft riots, 256; ties to government officials, 105. *See also* citizenship, black
Blackstone, William, 28, 211
black women, 5–6, 35, 299–300n8, 312n48; advocacy for female suffrage, 273, 275; African Free School graduates, 114–15, 126; associations of, 119; mothers advocating for their children, 36, 65–66; mothers' relationships with School Society trustees, 173–74; petition movement and, 180–81, 183; physical intervention in support of Mullen, 271, 280; political activities of, 167; teachers, 110
Board of Trade, British, 25, 33
Bolding, John, case of (1851), 220, 362n35
Boyer, Jean-Pierre, 117, 156
Bradish, Luther, 168, 184, 185
Brazilian slave case (1847), 219–21, 363n42
Brooklyn (Kings County), 43, 45, 82, 213; antislavery petitions in, 180; common schools, 349n8; education for black children in, 106–7, 111; Morrison's school in, 171–72
Bucktails (faction of Jeffersonian Republicans), 136, 154; Missouri Crisis and, 139, 140, 141, 142; New York State constitutional convention (1821) and, 142, 143, 146, 342n45. *See also* Democratic Party
"Burned-Over District," 168, 171, 182, 197, 232, 254; Conkling's career built in, 283; equal suffrage movement in, 198; female suffrage proposals in, 273; map, 169 (fig.)

Butler, Benjamin, 285
Butler, William F., 273, 275–76, 278–80, 377n109

Calhoun, John, 243, 244
California, 202, 240
Canada: as destination of "Lemmon freemen," 206, 228, 230, 231; runaways' flight to, 112
Cassey, Matilda Williams, 114, 115, 115 (fig.)
census records, 247; federal (1800), 300n10, 306n2; federal (1810), 321n19, 325n66; federal (1820), 306n2, 322n19, 334n48; federal (1830), 322n19; NY state (1825), 338n3
"certificate of freedom" law (1811), 73, 78, 128, 291; addendum to (1815), 134; certificates signed by judges, 134, 135 (fig.); Federalist criticism of, 133
Charlotte (black girl accused of arson in 1811), 4, 213; comparison with Charlotte E. Ray, 289–90, 292; grand jury testimony of, 1, 2 (fig.); literacy and, 3; statement of freedom by, 66, 68
Chase, Salmon, 205
children of gradual abolition, 1, 2, 5, 13, 143; black abolitionism facilitated by, 113; Civil War and, 257–58; federalist system and, 287; formal education of, 14; freeborn children's status certified by town clerks, 7, 58; general abolition law (1817) and, 3; as generation born in optimism, 158; *Lemmon* Slave Case and, 205, 237; multiple means of fighting slavery, 122; parent of, 297n2; voting rights gained and lost, 130; white partners working with, 169, 245. *See also* black children; rising generation
churches, 9, 14, 102, 143. *See also* African Methodist Episcopal (A.M.E.) Church
citizenship, black, 1, 2, 4, 13, 42, 81, 239; complete, 9; contested and coalescing notions of, 131, 132, 339n9; eligibility for, 46; fate of slavery and, 129; federalism and, 6; gradual abolition as apprenticeship for, 48; gradual abolition law (1799) and, 53; importance emphasized by Andrews, 121; Missouri Crisis and, 140; national, race-neutral citizenship and, 242; national birthright citizenship, 10; New York Manumission Society and, 123; New York's defense of black citizens, 191; nonelectoral aspects of, 4; politics and voting connected to, 14–15; protection as right of, 151; remaking of, 298n; schools and construction of, 97; shifting definitions of, 3, 101; state and federal citizenship, 130, 140, 341n35, 342n43; Supreme Court on, 342n43; Taney Supreme Court and, 232
civil rights, 4, 10, 139, 178, 240, 283
Civil Rights Act (NY State, 1873), 279, 280, 286, 291, 292Civil Rights Act (US, 1866), 13, 242, 267, 276
Civil Rights Act (US, 1875), 13, 242, 285–86
civil society, 64, 97, 127, 330n7
Civil War, 1, 2, 15, 164, 238, 265, 287; black enlistment in Union army, 240, 250–55, 257–58, 368n5; causes of, 3, 10, 298n; Fort Wagner battle, 254–55; *Lemmon* Slave Case and, 207, 236; as revolution in federal balance of power, 240; Tubman's exploits during, 9, 255
Clay, Henry, 139, 141, 197, 202
Clinton, DeWitt, 57–58, 73, 104, 134; African Society for Mutual Relief and, 104; powers under 1777 constitution, 136
Clinton, George, 46, 50, 316n87, 317n100
Colden, Cadwallader D., 70, 80, 130, 138; black votes and election of, 151, 152–53; fugitive slave laws criticized by, 153–54
colonization movement, 19, 117, 149, 301n13, 329n6, 370n19; American Colonization Society (and Manumission Society opposition), 136; beliefs of white advocates of, 122–23; black opposition to, 118, 123; gradual abolition combined with, 245
Colored American (newspaper), 125, 171, 184, 195, 244, 278, 289; funds raised for, 193, 194; petition movement and, 179, 181, 182; on repeal of the nine months law, 188; reports on legal precedent and practice, 209; on Seward's election as governor, 186; on the *Somerset* case, 210; on Virginia Controversy, 191
colored conventions, 5, 109, 244, 264; Albany Convention (1840), 125, 193–94; New York State Free Suffrage Convention, 198–99
Colored Orphan Asylum, 256, 257
Columbia County, 52, 79, 322n19
Commentaries on American Law (Kent), 341n35

common carriers, equal access to, 150, 241, 343n62, 374n72; *Ellen Anderson v. Eighth Ave. Streetcar Co.*, 241, 261–63; *Jennings v. Third Ave. Streetcar Co.*, 150, 239, 263
common law, 209, 211, 221, 276, 282, 318n105
Commonwealth v. Aves (Massachusetts, 1836), 210
Confederate States of America, 236, 264, 376n104
Conflict of Laws (Story, 1834), 210
Congress, U.S., 133, 137–38, 145; abolitionist members of, 152, 153, 154, 205, 221; abolition of international slave trade and, 49; antislavery petitions and, 163, 178, 180, 193; black enlistment in Union army and, 251; black men in, 291; Civil Rights Acts and, 267, 276, 281–84, 286; colonization movement and, 136; election fraud crisis and, 269–70, 271; equal suffrage and, 265, 266, 267, 268; fugitive slave legislation and, 129, 151, 221; gradual abolition and, 245; immediate abolition and, 237, 249, 252, 259, 260, 261; Lemmon Slave Case and, 233, 234; Missouri Crisis and, 139, 140, 141, 142, 232; Reconstruction Amendments and, 264, 266, 269, 272, 275, 282; Seventeenth, 140, 153, 154
Conkling, Roscoe, 245, 276, 280, 282–83, 284
Connecticut, 41, 161, 303n18; abolition of slavery in, 163; gradual abolition in, 11, 58
Constitution, federal (1787), 6, 48–49, 140, 201, 247; equal suffrage guarantees in, 248; "full faith and credit" (comity) clause, 225; *Lemmon* Slave Case and, 225, 226, 234; Missouri Crisis and, 141, 142; privileges and immunities clause, 144, 234, 269; proslavery interpretations of, 193; supremacy clause, 251; three-fifths clause, 49, 215
constitutional convention (NY State, 1821), 134, 343n54, 354n61; black voters disenfranchised by, 128; Bucktails at, 142, 143, 146, 342n45; issue of black suffrage and, 143–44; race-based property qualification and, 145–46; vote for equal male suffrage, 145
constitutional convention (NY State, 1846), 197–99
constitutional convention (NY State, 1867), 268–69
Continental Congress, 37, 39
Cooper, David, 34–35
Corfield v. Coryell (Bushrod Washington), 152
Cornish, Samuel, 118, 119, 125, 157, 214; on executive committee of AASS, 178; petition movement and, 179, 180; on the *Somerset* case, 209–10
Council of Revision, 46, 48, 53, 316n87
Croger, Benjamin, 170, 195
Croger, Peter, 106, 170, 333n35
Crummell, Alexander, 96, 111, 121, 122, 280; Albany convention (1840) and, 194; equal suffrage movement and, 199
Culver, Erastus D., 150, 187, 196, 206; equal suffrage movement and, 268; *Lemmon* Slave Case and, 224, 225, 226, 228

Darby ("negro servant" in Suffolk County), vii (epigraph), 82–83
Davenport, John I., 270, 277, 286
Declaration of Independence, 39, 120, 128, 137, 209, 232
DeGrasse, Isaiah, 96, 119, 120
DeGrasse, Maria, 119, 126
DeGrasse, Serena, 119, 336n68
Delaware, 159, 161, 246, 303n18
democracy, 5, 8, 131, 193, 194, 277, 285, 330n7; black voters and changing ideas about, 132; voting rights and, 192; "white man's democracy," 113, 163
Democracy in America (Tocqueville, 1835–1840), 97
Democratic Party (Second Party System), 166, 167, 185, 187, 245, 257; antislavery Democrats, 174, 190; Barnburners (radical wing), 197, 201; birth of, 155; Copperheads, 250; election fraud and, 270; election strategy (1860), 247; equal suffrage movement opposed by, 196, 197, 198, 200, 268; Hunkers (conservative wing), 197, 201; reluctance to confront slavery, 259, 261; *Slaughterhouse Cases* and, 284. *See also* Bucktails (faction of Jeffersonian Republicans)
Dix, John A., 168, 174–75, 279, 280, 350n18
Douge, Catherine Mary, 109, 244
Douge, Michael, 109, 187, 194, 212
doughface politics, 143, 187, 235, 241, 247, 257; Bucktails and, 142; Civil War and, 249; *Lemmon* Slave Case and, 206; Missouri Crisis and, 153; NYC draft riots and, 257
Douglas, Stephen, 234, 246

Douglass, Frederick, 9, 112, 113, 126, 225, 320n8; black enlistment in Union army and, 250, 251, 254; eulogy for Conkling, 282–83; evolving political views of, 201; Grant administration and, 283–84; *Lemmon* Slave Case and, 224; Republican Party and, 246; in Rochester, 168; Rochester school campaign and, 176–77, 351n24
Douglass, Lewis, viii (epigraph), 254, 255, 283
Downing, George T., 96, 181, 201, 305n27, 336n68; black enlistment in Union army and, 252; in Committee of Thirteen, 364n51; equal suffrage movement and, 268; Fourteenth Amendment and, 272, 282; Grant administration and, 283–84; lobbying in Congress, 266; National Civil Rights Council led by, 284; on slavery and civil rights, 277; stress on voting, 264; Virginia Controversy and, 190
Downing, Thomas, 190, 201, 266, 364n51
Dred Scott case (1857), 206, 231–32, 234, 248, 342n43; influence of Slave Power on Supreme Court and, 205; national citizenship and, 251, 253
Dudley, Nicholas, case of (1852), 220, 362n35
Dunmore, Lord, 38, 39
Dutch colonial period, 15, 17
Dutchess County, 44, 53, 136–37, 142, 322n19

Edmonds, Justice John, 216, 217
education, 3, 45, 71, 96; black parents and, 99–100, 106, 170; black private schools, 118; church-run, 98–99; corporal punishment in schools, 123; Croger "Day and Evening School," 106; denied under slavery, 114; "equal" treatment and, 106; integrated, 108, 174, 334n45, 336n68; masters' failure to provide, 3, 7, 72, 82–83; masters forced to provide (1810), 170, 327n94. *See also* African Free School; schools
election fraud, 270–71, 273, 276
Emancipation Proclamation, 239, 252, 253
Emmeline (mother in *Lemmon* Slave Case), 207–8, 215, 223, 225, 232–33, 238, 366n82
Erie Canal, 57–58, 73, 167

federalism, 5, 13, 207, 265, 268, 287; black citizenship and, 6, 376n100; boundaries of, 282; Civil War and, 13, 239, 251
Federalist Party (First Party System), 44, 49, 72, 317n100; antislavery leaning of, 44, 152; black members of, 132, 147; black men's preference for, 73, 78, 132; education policy and, 107; majority in state assembly (1813), 79; New York Manumission Society and, 133; New York State constitutional convention (1821) and, 143
Fifteenth Amendment, 10, 13, 242, 272, 273, 274–75, 278
First Party System (Federalists v. Jeffersonian Republicans), 129, 130, 154, 160, 348n4
Fish v. Fisher (1800), 70, 71
Fitzhugh, George, 168
Florida Territory, 162, 347n105
Foote, Julia A. J., 5, 95–96, 109, 329n2
Force Act, First (Ku Klux Klan Act), 274–75
"formal" law and politics, 4, 105, 130, 172, 299n7, 303n17; breaking the law as alternative to, 208; influenced by black voters in New York, 72; laboring black New Yorkers' familiarity with, 361n19; school meetings as form of, 174; women's place in, 181, 203
Fourteenth Amendment, 10, 13, 242, 267, 272; *Slaughterhouse Cases* and, 284; Sumner's civil rights bill and, 278
Fox, George, 30
Francis, Hannah, 114, 115, 126
Franklin, Benjamin, 36, 37
freedom: constricted definitions of, 43; education and, 97; equal citizenship and, 198; in everyday activities, 240; individual and collective definitions of, 94; national redefinition of, 278; outside bounds of respectability, 100–101; personal autonomy and, 26
Freedom's Journal (newspaper), vii (epigraph), 12, 118, 119, 120, 160, 163; general abolition celebrations and, 129, 156, 157; reports on legal precedent and practice, 209; on the *Somerset* case, 209–10; uplift/respectability politics and, 157–58
Freeman, Elizabeth, 312n48
Free Soil Party, 160, 168, 174, 201
Fugitive Slave Act (1793), 153–54, 215
Fugitive Slave Act (1850), 202, 221, 248
fugitive slave bill (1822), 129, 130, 154

Garnet, Eliza, 121, 122
Garnet, Henry Highland, 194, 195, 278; AASS (American Anti-Slavery Society) and, 214; as African Free School graduate,

Garnet, Henry Highland (*continued*) 96, 111, 168, 263; black enlistment in Union army and, 252, 254; citizenship and, 251; equal suffrage movement and, 195–96, 268; on federal emancipation, 4; Liberty Party and, 199, 201; New York civil rights bill and, 279–80; New York State Colored Convention and, 125; Pakenham Letter rebuttal and, 243; speaking tours of, 265–66; stress on voting, 264; suffrage rights movement and, 181; threat of family's reenslavement, 121–22, 265, 337n78
Garrison, William Lloyd, 8, 160, 245, 307–8n9; AASS and, 178; *Liberator* journal and, 163; New York civil rights bill and, 280
Gay, Sydney Howard, 208, 214, 216, 217, 218; Brazilian slave case and, 220; *Lemmon* Slave Case and, 224; runaways assisted by, 230–31
general abolition (1827), 15, 78, 95, 120, 130, 241; anniversary celebrations, 272; celebrations of, 155–57, 245; as first state act to free slaves immediately, 129; number of slaves freed, 338n3; as transition in antislavery culture, 162; white antislavery responses to, 346n94
general abolition law (1817), 3, 8, 56–57, 128, 138, 209; cruel treatment clause from 1813 retained in, 79–80, 86; everyday practices changed by, 81; New York State constitutional convention (1821) and, 144; Tallmadge and, 341n26; unique character of, 57
Genesee Country, 85, 327n87
Georgia, 11, 70, 205, 207, 219; *Kirk* case (1846) and, 215, 219; secession of, 236
Gibbs, Jacob, 220, 222, 228, 230, 363n47, 364n56
Giddings, Joshua, 244, 245
Golden Rule (Quaker biblical principle), 25, 30, 34, 41, 209; black abolitionists and, 51; general abolition and, 77; "The Golden Rule" (song), 264; lawmakers and, 45
Gooding, James Henry, 254, 258, 372n47
gradual abolition, 3, 5, 10, 18, 313n59; Civil War and, 246, 253, 260; everyday mechanics of, 2, 7; fast progress of, 54, 93; at household and local level, 5; legislative debate over, 45; owners' property rights and, 25; Quaker petition (1785), 44–47, 50; Quaker precedent for, 35; state governments and, 5–6; waning of, 347n107
gradual abolition bill (1796), 22, 23, 24
gradual abolition law (1799), 1, 3, 11, 14, 137, 245; amendments to, 55; black children's status as freeborn servants, 56; black New Yorkers' responses to, 54; child labor and, 25–26; on freeborn children as paupers, 59; passage of, 24; Quakers and, 25; records of children born to enslaved mothers, 59, 60 (fig.); Thirteenth Amendment and, 265; transportation of slaves across state borders and, 209; unintended consequences of, 86
gradual abolition law (1810), 56, 69, 72–73, 75, 84; education clause, 170, 213; masters in violation of, 85
Grant, Ulysses S., 269–70, 274, 275, 278, 279, 284
Greeley, Horace, 150, 168, 187, 200, 221, 238, 243; debates on emancipation policy issues and, 245; *Lemmon* Slave Case and, 224, 227, 228; "Liberal" wing of Republican Party and, 278; as messenger of Republican Party, 208. See also *New York Tribune*
Guignon, Peter, 120, 125, 181

Haiti, black Americans in, 117–18, 336n63
Hall, Prince, 37
Hamilton, Alexander, 47, 187
Hamilton, Elizabeth Schuyler, 107
Hamilton, Robert, 156, 222, 241, 243, 248; Lincoln criticized by, 252; stress on voting, 264Hamilton, Thomas, 156, 248
Hamilton, William, 51, 102, 125, 243, 248, 263; general abolition celebrations and, 156; on Quaker antislavery, 47–48
Hamlet, James, case of (1850), 220, 221–22, 238
Hammon, Jupiter, 37–38, 313n58
Hampton, Benjamin and Maria, 172, 350n11
Hannah (formerly enslaved to Tallmadge family), 137
Harris, Sam (formerly enslaved to Tallmadge family), 137, 142
Haudenosaunee (Iroquois, Six Nations), 15, 85
Haynes, Lemuel, 36
Hicks, Elias, 77, 110
Hogarth, George, 170, 171–72, 195, 349n8

Holley, Myron, 134, 168, 183
Hopkins, Samuel, 36, 37, 48
Howard University, 74, 280, 289
Hudson River Valley, 21, 39, 167, 306n2; black schools in, 111; Dutch-descended slaveowners in, 44, 50, 52
Huntington, 28, 89
Husted, James, 279, 280, 282

Illinois, 11, 161, 163, 203, 231, 323n26
immediatism (immediate abolition), 10, 80, 183, 241, 249; during Civil War, 252, 260; eighteenth-century calls for, 44; general abolition (1827) and, 129, 159, 162; legislative, 8, 301n13; Manumission Society and, 76–78
incorporation laws, 71, 95, 97, 98, 104, 107–8, 143, 172, 178, 331n11
Indiana, 11, 161, 163, 203
In re Kirk (1846), 217, 218, 220

Jackson, Andrew, 155, 163
Jacobs, Francis, 107, 108, 221
Jacobs, Harriet, 168
James, Thomas, 112–13, 125, 168, 171, 334n48
Jarvis, William and Jeffrey, 82, 213
Jay, John, 40, 41–42, 44, 156, 243, 314n72; antislavery views in gubernatorial campaign of, 49–50, 101; cited in northern newspapers for antislavery views, 161; gradual abolition law (1799) and, 53; New York Manumission Society and, 49, 262
Jay, John, II (John Jay's grandson, William Jay's son), 218, 219, 262, 358n2; AASS (American Anti-Slavery Society) and, 214; black enlistment in Union army and, 250–51; Brazilian slave case and, 220; *Kirk* case (1846) and, 216–17; *Lemmon* Slave Case and, 206, 224, 225, 226, 228; on securing the slaves' freedom, 259–60; views on abolition during Civil War, 249–50
Jay, Peter A., 79, 80, 136, 143, 144, 162
Jay, William, 162, 178, 184, 338n3
Jennings, Elizabeth, 5, 123, 126, 149, 239, 240, 280
Jinnings, Thomas L., 119, 123, 125, 149, 239, 337n81; certificates of freedom signed by, 147, *148*; general abolition celebrations and, 156; Legal Rights Association cofounded by, 263; New York State constitutional convention (1821) and, 147; petition movement and, 157; Political Association and, 211
Jinnings (Jennings) family, 146–47, 149–50
Johnson, Andrew, 267
Johnson, Henry W., 176, 351n25
Johnson, Herschel (governor of Georgia), 234–35, 247
Johnson, John, certificate of freedom of, 147, 148 (fig.)
Johnson, Richard, 230, 366n82
Johnson, William H., 9, 254, 268, 275–76, 281 (fig.), 286, 291
jury trial law (1840), 168, 186, 191, 212, 216, 299n7; fugitive slaves and, 167, 182; language of petition for, 179; Seward's support for, 184

Kansas-Nebraska Bill and Act, 205, 206
Keith, George, 31
Kent, James, 47, 70, 134, 143, 145, 341n35
Kentucky, 162, 246, 347n105
kidnapping, 8, 69, 70, 82, 114, 151, 179, 337n78; anti-kidnapping laws, 186–87; court cases involving, 152
King, Rufus, 143, 246
King v. Gallagher (NY, 1883), 286
Kirk, George, 215–16, 217, 219, 227, 238, 363n42
Ku Klux Klan, 269

labor coercion, 25–26, 28, 54, 58, 70, 308n11, 319n4
Lancaster method, in schools, 103, 108, 118, 332n27
Langston, John Mercer, 280, 289
Lapaugh, Henry, 225, 226, 227
Lattimore, Benjamin, Jr., 109, 125, 142, 194; Cunningham freedom suit (1829) and, 212; statewide abolition celebrated by, 155
Lattimore, Benjamin, Sr., 107, 145, 155
Lawrence Report, 270, 274
Lay, Benjamin, 31
legal knowledge, 7, 64–65, 89–90, 212–14, 224, 301n16; basic legal literacy, 9; outside of books, 85–86; statewide spread of, 83
Lemmon, Jonathan and Juliet, 205–6, 223, 244
Lemmon Slave Case (1852–1860), 15, 205–8, 217, 220, 260; appeals following, 232–34;

Lemmon Slave Case (*continued*)
Dred Scott case (1857) and, 231–32, 233; press coverage of, 223–24, 225, 226–27, 228; public reactions in North and South, 229–30; as rallying cry for both sides in conflict over slavery, 233–37; slaves released to Canada, 206, 228–29, 230, 231; trial, 225–26; *Uncle Tom's Cabin* and, 225–26
Liberia, 123, 349n9
Liberty Party, 134, 160, 215, 347n105; as antislavery third party, 190; equal suffrage movement and, 197, 199; founding of, 168
Lincoln, Abraham, 83, 191, 235, 247, 250; black abolitionists' criticism of, 252; Emancipation Proclamation, 239, 252; on gradual emancipation, 245–46; "House Divided" speech (1858), 233; Proclamation of Amnesty and Reconstruction, 258–59; reelection campaign (1864), 264; views on slavery at beginning of Civil War, 248
literacy, 3, 31, 97, 109, 170, 173, 242
Livingston, Robert R., 40, 46, 92, 316n87
Lobam, Nathan "Nate," 223–24, 364n56
Lockport, 193, 194, 351n21
Loguen, Amelia, 255
Loguen, Jermain W., 111, 125, 171, 231, 254, 264
Long, Henry, case of (1851), 220
Long Island, 28, 53, 74, 167; in colonial period, 17; Dutch-descended slaveowners in, 44; Quakers in, 31, 34
Louisiana Purchase lands, slavery question and, 139
Lyons, Albro, 125, 256

manumission, 27, 37, 45, 61, 63; black men's negotiations for, 44; liberalization of rules for, 47; by Quakers, 3, 34, 35, 311n39; wording of manumission documents, 131
Marbleton v. Overseers of the Poor (NY, 1822), 90
Maryland, 85, 112, 121, 149, 159, 265, 303n18, 327n87; Civil War and gradual emancipation, 246; escape of slaves from, 153; Virginia Controversy and, 189
Massachusetts, 12, 37, 112, 161, 304n21; abolition of slavery in (1783), 11, 163; anti-kidnapping law in, 187; black citizenship in, 142; black population of, 303n18; petition campaigns in, 180
masters/owners, 17, 157; African Free School and, 99; American Revolution and, 38, 39; antislavery laws ignored by, 7, 63–64; antislavery laws opposed by, 22–23; black children abandoned to overseers of the poor, 53, 58, 59, 61, 320n7; black children abandoned to parents, 87–88; black New Yorkers' negotiations with, 93; bond posted for support of freed slaves, 27, 309n14; child labor as compensation for, 25, 26; enslaved people traveling with, 8; illegal slave trading by, 69; multiple meanings of "master," 19–20; "poor relief" for sick and old slaves, 29; proslavery organizations of, 22; punished for abuses, 75–76; Quaker abolitionist advice to, 32, 34; sexual exploitation of slaves, 95; wills of, 91–92
Methodists, 83, 112, 193, 273, 275
Mexican-American War, 202, 206
Military Reconstruction Act (1867), 269
Missouri Crisis (1819–1821), 15, 129, 144, 151, 154, 202, 282; antislavery part of compromise negated by Kansas-Nebraska Act, 206–7; *Dred Scott* case and, 232; federal constitution and, 269; first compromise, 139–40, 163; second compromise, 140–42; Tallmadge and, 136–39
Molson, Maud, viii (epigraph), 272–73, 376n100
Morel, Junius C., 244, 253, 364n51
Morris, Gouverneur, 40
Morris, Robert, 210, 211
Morrison, Rosetta, 171–72
Mullen, John J., 270–71, 275, 280
Mulligan, Hercules, 47
Munro, Peter Jay, 42, 47, 69, 70, 79, 143, 145
Murray, John, Jr., 47, 80
Myers, Stephen, 264, 357n116

Nancy (mother in *Lemmon* Slave Case), 207–8, 215, 223, 225, 230, 232–33, 238
Napoleon, Louis, 15, 206, 207, 213–14, 218, 234; as AASS member, 214; Hamlet case (1850) and, 221, 222, 364n48; *Kirk* case (1846) and, 215–16, 217; *Lemmon* Slave Case and, 223–24, 227–28, 227 (fig. 12), 367n88; obituaries after death of, 237–38; runaways assisted by, 230–31, 238; Underground Railroad coalition and, 208, 220, 237, 359n7, 366n84

National Equal Rights League, 264, 272–73
Naturalization Act [Election Act] (1870), 276, 277
"negro pew" controversy (1841), 188
Nell, William C., 351n24
Nevil, Dinah, 36
New England, 11, 164, 168, 235; Anti-Slavery Society, 163; erasure of slaveholding past, 371n22; New Divinity movement, 36; Quakers in, 30, 31
New Hampshire, 11, 161, 163, 303n18
New Jersey, 56, 302n16; abolition of slavery in, 163; black population of, 303n18; in colonial period, 17; enslaved population of, 161; free status of children born to servants, 328n96; gradual abolition law (1804), 11; Quakers in, 31, 34; slavery in, 70
New National Era and Citizen (Douglass's newspaper), 282, 283
newspapers, 5, 12, 14, 97, 118, 169; education and, 173; equal suffrage movement and, 200; "free North" identity and, 161; southern, 229, 233–34
New York Association for the Political Elevation and Improvement of the People of Color (the Political Association), 125, 183, 184, 192, 211
New York City, 6, 27, 59, 172, 300n10; antislavery petitions in, 180; British occupation during Revolutionary War, 38; commercial ties to slave states and Confederacy, 223, 250; court records in Municipal Archives, 13; draft riots (1863), 255–57; enslaved population of, 17, 43; free black population of, 74, 93, 325n66; general abolition celebrations in, 156; indenture records, 28; Manhattan island as, 105, 333n33; Manumission Society based in, 57; New Amsterdam in Dutch colonial period, 17
New York Herald (newspaper), 226, 266, 377n109; antiblack position of, 249–50; on election fraud in New York, 270; on the Force Act, 275; on *Lemmon* Slave Case, 234
New York Manumission Society, 8, 14, 55, 71, 120, 151, 257; abolition as goal from start of, 48, 316n92; black associationalism and, 119; black education promoted by, 104; black families under "patronage" of, 101, 102; borders of influence of, 82; connections to state elites, 68; constitutional convention (1787) and, 49; cruelty cases and, 75–77, 78; Cunningham freedom suit (1829) and, 211; end of educational experiment, 125; Federalist dominance in, 160; founding of, 47; general abolition as goal, 77; merchant and professional elites in, 153; Missouri Crisis and, 138; parents' purchase of children's labor terms brokered by, 89; public and private aspects of, 48; registration of births and, 64; "respectable" version of antislavery promoted by, 99, 100, 120; slave trading combated by, 69–71; strengthening of antislavery laws and, 70–71. *See also* African Free School
New York State: black population of, 7, 105; colonial-era slave code of, 27, 325n57, 325n69; colonial history of, 15, 17–18; county map (1796), 51 (fig.); enslaved population of, 6, 11, 81, 161, 300n10, 303n18; former importance of slavery to economy of, 12; free black population of, 11–12, 72, 93, 303n21; history of slavery and antislavery in, 13; lagging status of abolition among northern states, 43; land bought by Upper South slaveowners, 85, 327n87; L-shaped pattern of European settlement in, 16 (fig.), 17; as most politically powerful state in the North, 12; Quakers in, 31, 71; as swing state of incomplete emancipation, 241; tax code, 29
New York State constitution (1777), 33, 128, 131, 132, 136, 179
New York State constitution (1821), 129, 131, 166, 191, 197–98
New York Tribune (newspaper), 150, 200, 224, 272; on Anderson's suit against Eighth Ave. Streetcar Co., 261; on *Lemmon* Slave Case, 227, 277 (fig.), 234; on NYC draft riots, 256; Smith's rejoinder to Dewey in, 243
"nine months law," 3, 74, 209; as antislavery accomplishment, 72, 352n35; petition for repeal of, 167, 179, 182, 184, 187; repeal of (1841), 168, 206, 212, 226, 229, 233, 260, 299n7
North Star (newspaper), 9, 112, 114, 126, 203
Northwest Ordinance (1787), 163, 202–3, 261
NYASS (New York Antislavery Society), 183–84, 190

Oatfield v. Waring (1817), 90, 328n103
Oblong (eastern Hudson Valley), Quakers of, 33–34, 44
office holding, by freed black citizens, 46, 53, 247
Ohio, 11, 12, 161; abolition of slavery in, 163; Northwest Ordinance and, 202–3; petition campaigns in, 180
Oneida Institute, 111, 171
Ontario County, 134, 142, 183
Orange County, 38, 83, 91, 151, 213, 270
overseers of the poor, 28, 33, 41, 44, 61, 89; black children's indentureships managed by, 53; child apprentices and, 27, 159; freed children given by masters to, 45; gradual abolition bill (1798) and, 52; gradual abolition law (1799) and, 3, 24; masters in role of, 29; ordinary people's engagement with, 6

Pacific Appeal (San Francisco newspaper), 239, 240, 252, 256, 279, 299n5
Paine, Justice Elijah, 206, 208, 226, 229, 365n70
Paine, Thomas, 36, 37
Pakenham Letter, 243–44
party politics, 2, 15, 72, 193; antislavery third parties, 166; equal suffrage movement and, 199; first antislavery party, 134
patriarchal household governance, 5, 19, 25, 86, 88, 292; birth certificates and erosion of masters' authority, 58; gradual abolition in John Jay's household, 42; Quaker emancipation schemes and, 29–31. *See also* masters/owners
Paul, Benjamin, 119, 125, 187, 194
Paul, Nathaniel, vii (epigraph), 108, 119, 156, 183, 212
paupers, 3, 19, 20; age of release from masters, 34; children of, 24; colonial laws relating to, 27; as problematic category, 26. *See also* poverty
Penn, William, 30
Pennington, J.W.C., 228, 252, 365–66n73
Pennsylvania, 10–11, 30, 56, 328n96; abolition of slavery in, 163; black population of, 303n18, 303n21; black voters disenfranchised in, 164; enslaved population of, 11, 161; gradual abolition law (1780), 58, 320n6; legislative breakthrough for abolition (1779), 40–41; personal liberty law, 214–15; petition campaigns in, 180
People v. King (NY, 1888), 286
Peterson, John, 39, 124, 125, 145
petitions, 4, 14, 169, 241, 277; civil rights and, 283; in colonial Massachusetts, 37–38; for equal franchise, 179, 192, 195; for jury trial law, 179; by Quakers, 45–47; to repeal nine months law, 167, 179, 182, 184, 187; from rural areas, 182; school equality campaign in Rochester, 175–78, 193
Philadelphia, 35, 36, 49, 78, 300n10
Platt, Judge Jonas, 72–73, 91, 134, 143, 145, 321n15
Polk, James, 197, 199
Porter, Peter S., 263, 279
poverty, 14, 33, 46; poor laws, 27, 32, 52, 89, 253; postemancipation, 37; slavery connected to, 26, 27. *See also* overseers of the poor
Powell, William P., 222, 256, 275, 280
Presbyterians, 84, 107, 110, 136
property inheritance, by manumitted slaves, 86, 87
property rights, 25, 37, 41, 47, 50, 247
Public School Society, 103, 113, 124; African Free School transferred to, 124, 172; black parents and, 173
Pulford, Joseph, trial of (1819), 152

Quakers, 37, 53, 83, 90, 199, 264, 275; African Free School and, 99, 102, 116; black schools and, 110; in Dutchess County, 137; history of opposition to slavery, 29–35, 47–48; immediatism and, 80; leaders (weighty Friends), 32; masters' complaints about, 24; meetings in rural counties, 14; New York abolitionism and, 307n8; New York Manumission Society and, 47, 71; New York Yearly Meeting, 33, 34, 44, 110; as original designers of gradual abolition, 7; persistent activity in gradual abolition era, 56; proslavery complaints against, 153; as slaveholders, 3, 30, 33–34, 311n39; state abolition laws using model of, 40, 41. *See also* Golden Rule
Queens County, 43, 93, 152, 286

racial violence, 163–64, 241, 269, 273–74
Ray, Charles B., 125, 171, 182, 244, 275; Hamlet case (1850) and, 222; letter about

daughter Charlotte, 289, 290 (fig.); NYASS and, 183
Ray, Charlotte E., 289–92, 291 (fig.)
Ray, David H., 165, 176, 348n2, 351n23; petition movement and, 179, 183, 193–94; in Rochester city directory, 166 (fig.); split in abolitionist movement and, 199
Ray, Phebe, 4, 170, 172, 174, 177, 244; in Rochester city directory, 166 (fig.), 348n2; Rochester school desegregation campaign and, 165–67, 169, 176, 203, 280
Reason, Charles (African Free School graduate), 96, 124, 125, 168, 181, 349n5; Albany convention (1840) and, 194; equal suffrage movement and, 268; lobbying in Congress, 266; New York civil rights bill and, 279, 281 (fig.); Pakenham Letter rebuttal and, 243; Political Association and, 211
Reason, Charles (soldier), 255
Reason, Elver, 96, 120, 181
Reason, Patrick, 96, 125, 194, 243
Reconstruction, 2, 3, 7, 15, 244, 287; constitutional history of, 298n; federalism and, 268
Reconstruction Amendments, 284, 285, 376n104. *See also* Thirteenth Amendment; Fourteenth Amendment; Fifteenth Amendment
Reeve, Reuben ("Reuben the Lawyer"), 74–75, 83
Republican Party (Third Party System), 160, 191, 208, 243, 246; antislavery platform of, 235; "Liberal" wing of, 278, 283; Radical Republicans, 267, 276, 284; state sovereignty and, 251–52
Republican Party, Jeffersonian (First Party System), 44, 50, 132; black supporters of, 73, 79, 81; "certificate of freedom" law (1811) and, 73, 78, 133; "Clintonians," 134, 137, 138–39, 140, 143; efforts to thwart black voters, 79, 81. *See also* Bucktails; Democratic Party
Rhode Island, 37, 161; abolition of slavery in, 41, 163; black population of, 303n18; gradual abolition in, 11, 58
Rhodes, Marietta and Josephine, 280, 282
Rich, William, 111, 125, 264, 279
Riker, Richard, 121, 122
rising generation, 3, 82, 126, 274; African Free School and, 98; black-led antislavery movement and, 157; defined, 18–19; education of, 96; formal law and, 208; general abolition and, 156; legislative immediatism embraced by, 8; literacy of, 13; petition movement and, 181, 184; post-abolition society and, 168. *See also* black children; children of gradual abolition
Rochester, city of, 85, 111, 112, 128, 168, 213; general abolition celebrations in, 156; school board, 165, 169; school equality campaign in, 175–78, 193, 203
Rogers, Elymus P., 111
Rose (black girl accused of arson), 66, 68
Ruggles, David, 181, 188, 212, 220, 360n19
runaways, 8, 22, 93, 100, 318n104; assistance for, 230–31; legal cases involving, 220; Revolutionary War and, 38; from southern states, 111
Rush, Benjamin, 35–36, 37, 42, 312n49
Russwurm, John, 118, 119, 209

Sable, Effa (Effy), 67 (fig.), 68, 322n27
Schenectady, city of, 57, 73, 134, 175, 213, 351n23
schools, 9, 14, 96, 143, 170, 171; civil rights acts and equal access, 286; desegregation of, 287; federal regulation of, 282; racial divisions over, 174–76; school politics, 14. *See also* African Free School; education
Second Party System (Democrats v. Whigs v. third parties), 166, 167, 179; black women and, 348n4; breakdown of, 200–201, 244
Seneca Falls convention (1848), 167
servants, 4, 14; free status of children born to, 328n96; relation to masters, 19, 20; white, 26
Seward, Samuel S., 83, 84, 322n19
Seward, William H., 9, 83–85, 167, 168, 206; anti-kidnapping law signed by, 186–87; conflict with Virginia over fugitive slaves, 188–91; debates on emancipation policy issues and, 245; election to US Senate, 201; equal suffrage movement and, 195, 196–97, 198; Fugitive Slave Act (1850) opposed by, 222; jury trial law (1840) signed by, 216; as Lincoln's secretary of state, 191; on Northwest Ordinance (1787), 202–3; repeal of nine months rule signed by, 209, 212; as a Republican Party leader, 246–47; as Whig candidate for governor, 184, 185, 186

Seymour, Horatio, 245, 257, 270
Sharpe, Peter, 79, 134, 143, 153
Shaw, Lemuel, 210
Shaw, Robert Gould, 254
Shields, Cato, 134, 135 (fig.)
Sidney, Joseph, 73, 132–33, 313n59
Sidney, Thomas S., 125, 181
Sipkins, Henry, 73, 74, 147, 149, 157, 221
Sipkins, Thomas, 73–74
The Slave, Grace (British Court of Admiralty case, 1827), 210, 359n10
Slave Power, 167, 201, 204; *Lemmon* Slave Case and, 225, 233; Supreme Court cases and, 205; Virginia Controversy and, 189, 190
slavery: American Revolution and, 3; in cities versus rural areas, 319n5; civil rights and, 277; cruelties of, 1; dismantled by slave-owners, 54; in Dutch and English colonial periods, 17–18; entrenched position in lower South, 162; expansion into western territories, 129, 136, 207, 244, 245; fugitive slave clause in 1787 constitution, 6; legality in thirteen colonies, 39; local statutes regulating, 27; Protestant theology and, 36; "relics" of, 240; rise in sectional tensions and, 206–7; southern defenders of, 178. *See also* kidnapping; Missouri Crisis
slaves/enslaved people, 4, 14, 62, 305n29; bond posted to support freed slaves, 27, 309n14; cruel physical treatment of, 75–76; fugitive slave rights, 186; "immediate relief" of, 8, 78; laws regulating, 33; legalization of slave marriage (1809), 86–89, 327n94; manumission by self-purchase, 44; Nat Turner rebellion, 163; "poor relief" of former slaves, 25; relation to masters, 19, 20; rights of servants not available to, 63, 321–22n19; sojourner slaves, 207, 222; "statutory slaves," 56; tax code and, 29; "three-fifths" clause of Constitution and, 49
slave states, 8, 129, 223, 241, 301n13; Missouri Crisis and, 139; proposals for gradual abolition in, 242; Virginia Controversy (1839), 189–91
slave trade, laws against, 49, 68; act to prevent kidnapping (1808), 71; illegal sales, 69, 82; import and export across state lines (1785, 1788), 49, 65, 70, 208–9
Smith, Elias, 216, 219, 220
Smith, Gerrit, 168, 183, 184, 190, 199, 238, 283; Charles B. Ray letter to, 289, 290 (fig.); compromising attitude during Civil War, 248–49; *Lemmon* Slave Case and, 205; New York civil rights bill and, 280
Smith, James McCune, 96, 104, 120, 121, 169, 265, 364n48; accomplishments of, 103; Albany convention (1840) and, 194, 356n92; colonization opposed by, 124; in Committee of Thirteen, 364n51; criticism of compromise during Civil War, 248–49; dispute with Dewey, 242–43; equal access to common carriers and, 150; equal suffrage movement and, 197–98; on Frederick Douglass, 9; general abolition celebrations and, 156; Hamlet case (1850) and, 222; immediate emancipation supported by, 249; on memories of "the Boot Black," 158; New York City draft riots and, 256; oration at reception in honor of General Lafayette, 116; Pakenham Letter rebuttal and, 243–44; on tasks of the future, 287–88
Smith, Malvina Barnett, 244
Smith, Sarah Jinnings, 239, 240, 368n2
Society for Apprehending Slaves, 22, 23 (fig.), 24, 51
Somerset case (England, 1772), 206, 210–11, 216, 220, 360n12; *Dred Scott* case and, 232; *Lemmon* Slave Case and, 225
South Carolina, 189–90, 236, 237, 248
Special Committee on the Colored School System (Rochester), 177
Spencer, John C., 140, 141, 142–43
Stanton, Elizabeth Cady, 190, 376n100
Stanton, Henry, 183, 190
Staten Island (Richmond County), 43, 56, 65, 73
Stevens, Thaddeus, 221, 282
Steward, Austin, 84–85, 112, 125, 168, 327n87; Albany convention (1840) and, 194; certificate of freedom of, 142; early life in slavery in Virginia, 128; equal suffrage movement and, 198; petition movement and, 179; statewide abolition celebrated by, 155; voting rights and, 131
Story, Joseph, 210–11
Stowe, Harriet Beecher, 214, 225
Suffolk County, 93, 152
suffrage, equal male, 168, 187, 202; campaign for constitutional amendment, 268–74;

failed campaign to reinstate, 191–92; NYASS and, 184; petitions for, 179, 187, 195; referendum on, 4; Republican Party and, 247. *See also* Fifteenth Amendment; voting rights
Sulware, Cloe (slave in Seward home), 84
Sumner, Charles, 250–51, 260, 261, 267, 280; death of, 284; on enfranchisement of black men, 269; New York State civil rights act and, 281 (fig.); "supplement" to Civil Rights Act (1866) and, 276–80, 282, 286–87, 291
Supreme Court, of New York, 46, 90, 133, 134, 211; *Fish v. Fisher* (1800), 70; *Lemmon* Slave Case and, 236, 365n70
Supreme Court, U.S., 205, 259, 292, 357n111; Civil Rights Cases (1883), 286–87; *Plessy v. Ferguson* (1896), 287; *Prigg v. Pennsylvania* (1842), 214–15, 216; *Slaughterhouse Cases* (1873), 284–85, 378n127. See also *Dred Scott* case (1857)

Tallmadge, James, Jr., 129–30, 142, 218, 244, 341n26; as antislavery slaveholder, 137; Missouri Crisis and, 136–39, 246; New York State constitutional convention (1821) and, 145
Tallmadge, Senator Nathaniel P., 244
Taney, Roger, 231, 232, 236, 251, 367n88
Tappan, Arthur, 112, 178, 214, 238
Tappan, Lewis, 178, 208, 214, 224, 228, 238
Taylor, John W., 138, 246
Teasman, John, 73, 78, 113, 221, 263; dismissed from teaching post, 104; as Manumission Society's first black teacher, 102
Ten Broeck, Samuel, 52, 53
terrain (Barbara Fields's concept), 20, 246, 290, 305n28
Texas: annexation of, 181, 199, 206, 243, 244; secession of, 236
Third Party System (Republicans v. Democrats), 198
Thirteenth Amendment, 10, 13, 242, 264, 265; abolition and, 269; *Slaughterhouse Cases* and, 284; Sumner's civil rights bill and, 278
Thuey, Alexander and Phebe, 111, 125–26
Tilden, Samuel, 245, 270
Tilmon, Levin, 246, 250
Tompkins, Daniel D., 77, 78, 79, 325n68; general abolition celebrations and, 156; as New York governor, 104; New York State constitutional convention (1821) and, 143, 145; as vice president of United States, 80
Tompkins, Fanny, 124, 126
Topp, William H., 109, 155, 187, 199, 254
Trainer, Jane, case of (1853), 220
trial by jury, 153, 179, 186, 277; common law and, 211; denied to slaves, 325n69; for fugitive slaves, 180
Troy, city of, 111, 126, 213, 280; antislavery petitions in, 180; Black men's Republican state convention (1872) in, 278–79
Trumbull, Lyman, 260–61, 266–67
Truth, Sojourner, 5, 64, 254; general abolition law (1817) and, 81; struggle to retain kidnapped son, 90
Tubman, Harriet, 5, 9, 112, 113; black enlistment in Union army and, 255; as "Moses" of the Underground Railroad, 168
Turner, Nat, 163
Tweed, William "Boss," 270

Ulster County, 22, 24, 45, 50, 90, 134, 306n2
Uncle Tom's Cabin (Stowe, 1851–1852), 225–26
Underground Railroad, 7, 215, 237, 254, 361n19; Brazilian slave case and, 220; *Kirk* case (1846) and, 218; Napoleon and, 208, 215, 223, 228, 238; southern resentment of, 205; Tubman and, 9, 112, 168
Underhill, Mary, 152, 153, 154
Union League, 257, 262, 269
uplift/respectability politics, 145, 149, 171, 242, 345n90; African Free School and, 99–100, 117; desegregation of Albany theaters and, 176; *Freedom's Journal* editors and, 157–58; resistance to fugitive slave laws and, 153; Steward's advocacy of, 129

Van Buren, Martin, 143, 154, 251; Albany Regency of, 184; formation of Democratic Party and, 155; Free Soil Party led by, 201; as Jackson's vice president, 163
Van Ness, William W., 134, 143, 145
Van Rensselaer, Stephen, 143, 144, 145, 354n61
Van Vechten, Abraham, 107, 145
Varick, James, 114, 221
Vermont, 11, 40, 161, 163, 303n18
Vigilance Committee, 181, 220, 363n47

Virginia: gradual abolition plan (1832), 163; *Lemmon* Slave Case and, 205–6, 225, 233–34; *Lemmon* Slave Case and, 15; secession of, 236, 367n100; slaveowners moving to New York State, 85, 327n87
Virginia Controversy (1839), 189–91
Vogelsang, Peter, Jr., 254, 278
Vogelsang, Peter, Sr., 192, 254
voting rights, 7, 10, 324n45; betterment of future generations and, 74; black suffrage rejected by northern white men, 248; denial of, 46; expansion of black voting after 1799 act, 72; in former Confederacy, 269; franchise extended to white men, 116, 132; full citizenship and, 146; history of black voting, 15; importance of black votes in elections, 79; Republican Party and, 266; at school district meetings, 174–75; state constitution (1821) and, 166; women and, 150. *See also* "certificate of freedom" law; Fifteenth Amendment; suffrage, equal male
voting rights, race-based property qualification for, 72, 128, 164, 200, 247, 271; failed motion to expunge, 145–46; state constitution (1822) and, 4, 116, 247; white voters' refusal to remove (1869), 274

Walker, David, 160, 163
Ward, Samuel Ringgold, viii (epigraph), 12, 96, 149, 305n27; on Charles Andrews, 113–14; as Liberty Party supporter, 201; New York State Colored Convention and, 125
War of 1812, 147
Washington, Augustus, 125, 171, 349n9
Washington, D.C., 5, 161, 187, 202, 240
Washington, George, 107
Webster, Daniel, 202, 203
Weed, Thurlow, 168, 185, 186, 187; equal suffrage movement and, 196; gradualist notions of, 245, 246; Liberty Party criticized by, 199
Weekly Anglo-African, 248, 251, 252, 263
Westchester County, 38, 39, 93
West Indies, end of slavery in (1833), 162, 163, 176, 188
Whig Party, 166, 167, 182, 186, 188, 246; Albany convention (1840) and, 194; equal suffrage and, 195, 356n100; majority in state legislature, 187; Virginia Controversy and, 190
white abolitionists, 7, 9, 55, 101, 118, 217; Kirk case (1846) and, 218; in New York City, 73; property targeted by mobs, 117; Rochester school campaign and, 177; state-based agitation of, 179; targeted in New York City draft riots, 256; Underground Railroad coalition and, 208
white children, 35, 54, 61, 100; in antislavery households, 7; apprenticed, 62; bound out for service, 59, 63; education of, 98, 103; pauper, 52, 53, 59, 62, 321n15
Wicks, Elizabeth, 111, 126, 244
Wilberforce Philanthropic Association, 73, 102, 132–33
Williams, Peter, Jr., 96, 102–3, 114, 117, 221, 263
Wilson, William J., 250, 349n8, 364n51
women's rights movement, 167, 168, 183, 376n100
Woolman, John, 32, 313n58
Woolman Society, 106, 170, 333n35
Wright, Theodore S., 171, 178, 183, 214

Zuille, John, 275, 279, 364n51, 366n84

ACKNOWLEDGMENTS

It is a privilege to thank the many people who helped me write this book. Looking back, I realize its creation has both a short(ish) and a long history. I am grateful for the chance to acknowledge the scores of generous people who have supported me along the way.

In the spring of 2009, I wrote a research paper in a seminar taught by Christine Stansell at the University of Chicago. Initially curious about the children and women of the New York Colored Orphan Asylum during the Civil War draft riots, I soon found myself tracing the life of the institution's doctor, James McCune Smith, who is now a central figure in this book. As my questions about Smith and his wider generation led to my dissertation, I was beyond fortunate to work under the guidance of scholars who put faith in my ideas, pushed me to separate the wheat from the chaff, and urged me to think big. Thomas C. Holt, who chaired my committee, read each chapter as I finished and sat with me for hours asking conceptual and comparative questions about what I put on the page. His advice about both the work and how to understand my own life as a scholar and a human has proved invaluable. To this day, I know he will take my call if I have a complicated decision in front of me. Tom, thank you for your brilliance, empathy, and steady wisdom. Amy Dru Stanley, for reasons she knows, landed me at Chicago in the first place. Graduate courses with her were an intellectual wonderland. Amy, thank you for your razor-sharp mind, your tenacious dedication to your students, and your insistence that my mediocre drafts of writing had the potential to be better. I am even more grateful in hindsight that Hendrick Hartog agreed to join my committee from his perch at Princeton. I came somewhat late to legal history in graduate school. Dirk's oeuvre shaped my entry into the field and influenced my approach to studying historical experiences of law in everyday life (I now teach "Pigs and Positivism" to my undergraduates!). I also learned a tremendous amount in courses and workshops from my fellow graduate students at Chicago, especially Katie Turk, Emily Remus, Chris Dingwall, Darryl Heller, and Katy Schumaker, and from professors

Jane Dailey, Adam Green, Julie Saville, Kathleen Conzen, and Eric Slauter. Matthew Briones, who encouraged my love of history when I was an undergraduate, arrived as an assistant professor at Chicago when I was finishing my doctorate. Thank you, Matt, for your many years of support and for inviting me to be your apprentice in teaching the history of baseball.

In 2014, I arrived in Philadelphia for a two-year postdoctoral fellowship at the McNeil Center for Early American Studies. Dan Richter, thank you for taking a chance on a "long nineteenth century person" who told you how much she wanted to surround herself with the colonial and the early modern. I learned so much from you and from the junior scholars orbiting the center. I'd especially like to thank Max Mishler, Carolyn Roberts, Sonia Hazard, Brendan Gillis, Rachel Walker, Sarah Rodriguez, Alexandra Finley, Kevin Waite, and Tommy Richards for expanding my thinking. Christine Croxall was a model of community-building and care. At the book manuscript workshop Dan organized for me, I received feedback from an exceptional brain trust of senior scholars. Laura Edwards and John Brooke served as primary readers. Both Laura and John are paragons of scholarly engagement who have shaped not only the writing of this book, but how I hope to treat others as I continue to make my own way as an academic. Steve Hahn, Richard Newman, Brian Luskey, Kathy Brown, and David Waldstreicher generously joined the workshop and provided wonderful ideas. David Gellman sent spot-on notes from afar. During my second year at McNeil, the luminous Elizabeth Ellis joined as a fellow postdoc. Liz, thank you for coteaching with me and for strengthening my grasp of Indigenous history. You supported me in deeply practical ways during my first pregnancy and while breastfeeding. All working mothers should be so lucky.

My first faculty job, which now feels like a faraway dream full of sunny Februarys, was at the California Institute of Technology. I thank Caltech for supporting my research during my McNeil postdoc and for a happy year teaching and writing on campus. Cindy Weinstein, Cathy Jurca, Dehn Gilmore, Christopher Hunter, Jennifer Jahner, Morgan Kousser, and Jean-Laurent Rosenthal were especially welcoming and empathetic. I loved my time with you.

When I arrived at Penn's history department, Beth Wenger welcomed me with her characteristic kindness and efficiency. Since then, both Antonio Feros and Sophie Rosenfeld have, as successive chairs, been supportive of junior faculty in ways I truly appreciate. I'm grateful to all of my colleagues in History. I'd especially like to thank my fellow junior faculty members and my official faculty mentors, Kathy Brown and Ann Farnsworth-Alvear. It has been a joy teaching in the Legal Studies and History minor with Karen Tani and Sally Gordon. Emma Hart has kindly shared her office with me while my own is undergoing renovation. Octavia Carr, Yvie Fabella, Joan Plonski, and Angela Faranda routinely brighten my day with their knowledge, warmth, snacks, and competence. Brent Cebul and I joined the Penn faculty around the same time. Cheers, Brent, for the hours of planned and unplanned conversations about American history, teaching, and parenting.

A number of institutions and organizations have supported my research on this book. First and foremost, I would like to acknowledge the New-York Historical Society, where I was an Andrew W. Mellon postdoctoral fellow from 2017 to 2018. Michael Ryan, Ted O'Reilly, Tammy Kitter, and Marian Touba were supportive before, during, and after that year. Fruitful funds also arrived from the University of Chicago's John Hope Franklin Travel Fellowship and Hanna Holborn Gray Advanced Fellowship, the William Nelson Cromwell Foundation, the Law and Society Association, the American Society for Legal History's Kathryn T. Preyer Early Career Scholars program, and the Trustees' Council of Penn Women.

For over a decade, a number of scholars have read and commented on my work at conferences, seminars, workshops, and coffees. Others have given professional advice. There are not enough words to convey how much I appreciate this engagement. I'm as a grateful for the criticisms ("I really think you are discounting *X* and/or need to address *Y* head-on") as for the encouragement. Sometimes even a small comment made in the hallway after a panel talk made an imprint on this book. For all of these moments, I thank, in alphabetical order, Tera Agyepong, Dee Andrews, Yesenia Barragan, Rabia Belt, Maggie Blackhawk, William Blair, John Blanton, Mark Boonshoft, Christopher Bonner, Holly Brewer, Corey Brooks, Kevin Butterfield, Ben Carp, Daniel Carpenter, Gideon Cohn-Postar, Emily Conroy-Krutz, Sam Davis, Anna Mae Duane, Nicole Eustace, Chris Florio, Mary Freeman, Jonathan Gienapp, Jim Gigantino, Annette Gordon-Reed, Allison Gorsuch, Van Gosse, Aaron Hall, Dan Hamilton, Craig Hammond, Leslie Harris, Ruth Wallis Herndon, Craig Hollander, Dan Hulsebosch, David Huyssen, Matt Karp, Kellie Carter Jackson, Thea Johnson, Martha Jones, Hannah Farber, Nancy Isenberg, Sophia Lee and the Penn Legal History Writers Bloc(k) writ large, Alix Lerner, Jonathan Levy, Maeva Marcus, Katherine Marino, Kate Masur, Patti Minter, Caleb McDaniel, Michelle McKinley, Joanne Pope Melish, Tessa Murphy, Natalie Naylor, Mae Ngai, Johann Neem, Dael Norwood, Kristin

O'Brassill-Kulfan, Jim Oakes, Peter Onuf, Jeff Pasley, Dylan Penningroth, Josh Piker, Paul Polgar, Dana Rabin, Sumi Raghavan, Gautham Rao, Paddy Riley, Andy Robertson, Seth Rockman, Jessica Roney, Christopher Schmidt, Michael Schoeppner, Rebecca Scott, Samantha Seeley, Sarah Seo, David Silverman, Manisha Sinha, Derrick Spires, Matthew Spooner, Christopher Tomlins, Anne Twitty, Sonia Tycko, George Van Cleve, Lea VanderVelde, Kevin Vrevich, Kimberly Welch, Jon Wells, William Wiecek, Shane White, Sean Wilentz, and Jon Zimmerman.

As I was finishing the book, several scholars provided invaluable readings of individual chapters. My sincere thanks to Mia Bay, Kathy Brown, Aaron Hall, Jane Manners, and David Waldstreicher for their sharp eyes on the Introduction. Aaron, Scott Heerman, Tommy Richards, Corey Brooks, Michael Woods, Taylor Prescott, and VanJessica Gladney helped me improve an extremely refashioned Chapter 7.

As many scholars cited in (and reading) these acknowledgments well know, writing a first book is a prolonged and sometimes strange and disorienting process. Life intervenes in alternately expected, jarring, hard, and happy ways. Having steadfast colleagues there for those moments is a gift. I thank Nora Slonimsky, Hayley Negrin, Liz Ellis, and Wendy Warren for text messages that transcend the banality implied by "text message." Michelle McKinley took me under her wing when I was a budding legal historian and never fails to buoy my spirits. Serena Mayeri has made commuting scholarly life with a family possible. About once a year, I have a grounding conversation with Jon Baskin that reassures me that I am not crazy. Greg Ablavksy has been a loyal, intelligent, and cheering interlocutor since our neighboring-office days at McNeil. Nic Wood has always been a ready reader, source sharer, and copanelist. Jane Manners is not only a gifted nineteenth-century legal historian but also an incredible please-read-this-last-draft-before-I-turn-it-in-because-I-know-you-get-my-work editor. Scott Heerman picks up the phone day and night, reads my work quickly and generatively, guides me when I get stuck, and makes me laugh. Scott, I owe you at least one very grand night at Marie's Crisis.

It has been my great fortune to publish this book with Penn Press. Bob Lockhart, you are a true gem of an editor. You've been steadfast, responsive, and kind ever since you first read the dissertation. I also owe a debt of gratitude to Kate Masur and to a second generous reader for the press who provided detailed, precise, and productive feedback on the penultimate draft of the manuscript. Thank you, Kate, for ongoing conversations after your report, as well. I am grateful to Alex Gupta and Lily Palladino for helping to shepherd this book through its final stages. I thank the patient, talented Dan Miller for providing the book's maps and Alex Trotter for precise, careful work on the Index. I must additionally thank Penn Press for publishing an early version of Chapter 5 in *Revolutions and Reconstructions: Black Politics in the Long Nineteenth Century*, which was expertly edited by Van Gosse and David Waldstreicher.

Many caretakers of historical material have helped me research and write this book. I thank all of the archivists, librarians, and town and county clerks who assisted me in finding sources. I would like to mention, in particular, Marcia Kirk at the New York City Municipal Archives; Will Tatum, the Dutchess County historian; Kathie Spiers of the Stanford (New York) Historical Society; Andrea Meyer, Librarian/Archivist of the Long Island Collection; Allen Weinreb at the John Jay Homestead; and Brooke Morse of the Ontario County Records and Archives. Several graduate students at Penn have helped me with research tasks, including Francis Russo, Arielle Alterwaite, VanJessica Gladney, Taylor Prescott, and Jenny Reiss. Penn Law student Nikita Ganesh provided a crucial pair of eyes on the final draft. I thank Lydia Biggs for some critical help with the Gerrit Smith Papers. I would also like to thank Penn undergraduate students Angel Ortiz, Anjie Wang, Bo Goergen, Jacob Ross, Katherine Davies, Justin Freeman, Matthew Breier, Isobel Glass, Will Reason, Ethan Knox, and Nancy Mvogo Mbala for checking citations, tracking down sources, and in general cheerleading their stressed-out professor.

A number of friends have taken me in and buoyed my spirits repeatedly. While none is a professional historian, all have made researching and writing this book more possible. My heartfelt thanks go to Matt Noble and Emily Dill (and Izzy!), Scott and Jackie Orleck, Noah and Heidi Askin, Charlie and Gigi Sparling, DJ Jacobs and Angela Arnold, Sophie Brickman and Dave Eisenberg, Heather Thomason, and Julia Butler and Vignesh Rajendran. Ryan and Adrienne Israel provided sunny and stylish book-finishing office space at a crucial late moment in the journey. Since our college days, Alex Cooley, Jen Neundorfer, Chondita Dayton, Deena Chalabi, and Ana Maria Lopez have been constant sources of laughter, friendship, and "just checking in to see. . . ." Erika Bearman is an exemplary ballet mom. I also want to thank all of the sweet souls who have, over the years, at birthdays and reunions and school pickups and barbecues and Thanksgivings, asked how the book was going and lent a kind word.

Before I thank the people who raised me at home, I want to thank the people who raised me in school. From kindergarten until today, I have had teachers who have made learning a joy. Special appreciation to my high school teachers Mr. Barksy, Ms. Eisenberg, Mr. G(alasso), Ms. Colligan, and the late Ms. Smit, to my college advisor Steven Biel, and to my master's degree advisor Stephen Tuck. Everything I do right in the classroom I owe to Melinda Tsapatsaris, who mentored me when I was a very green high school teacher and taught me how to be a better adult. I thank my students—all of you—from Wildwood, Chicago, Caltech, and Penn. Reading, thinking, searching, questioning, laughing, and yes, even crying with you (thanks, *A League of Their Own,* despite what Jimmy Dugan says otherwise) has been one of the great and ongoing privileges of my life. Teaching you helped me improve this book immeasurably.

This paragraph is the hardest and most important to write. I thank my family. My mother, in many ways my earliest teacher, did not live to see this book in print. She raised me in a house full of books. She valued initiative, independence, worldliness, authenticity, friendship, and lifelong curiosity (she picked up Italian in her 60s, having always wanted to learn). She could be infuriating. I miss her every single day. To my sister, Anna, I need too many pages to say it all. Know that I respect and love you and am grateful we're in the foxhole of life together. To my father, thank you for the decades of support, reliability, and endless car rides. Thank you for the childcare as a grandfather when the girls were infants; that generosity made a material difference in my ability to finish this book. Thank you to Terry Kotseas, the Hellmanns, and the McKinleys/Gronningsaters. My husband, Matt, has been an anchor and a life raft and a lighthouse all at once for our family. Your capacity to do many crucial things all in a single day—from getting little shoes tied in the morning, to working to cure cancer, to overseeing bath time—without a hint of complaint but rather dogged devotion, is extraordinary. Our girls, Caroline and Sophie, are the heart of my heart. I love you, a lot, always and forever.

www.ingramcontent.com/pod-product-compliance
Lightning Source LLC
Jackson TN
JSHW020034200225
79383JS00009B/50/J